Programming with
Macintosh
Programmer's
Workshop

Programming with
Macintosh
Programmer's
Workshop

Joel West
Palomar Software, Inc.

BANTAM BOOKS
TORONTO • NEW YORK • LONDON • SYDNEY • AUCKLAND

Programming with Macintosh Programmer's Workshop
A Bantam Book/November 1987

All Rights Reserved
Copyright © by Joel West
Cover design © by Bantam Books, Inc.
Interior design by Nancy Sugihara
Produced by Micro Text Productions, Inc.

ISBN 0-553-34436-6

Published simultaneously in the United States and Canada

Bantam Books are published by Bantam Books, Inc.
Its trademark, consisting of the words "Bantam
Books" and the portrayal of a rooster, is Registered in
U.S. Patent and Trademark Office and in other
countries. Marca Registrada. Bantam Books, Inc.
666 Fifth Avenue, New York, New York 10103

PRINTED IN THE UNITED STATES OF AMERICA

FG   0   9   8   7   6   5   4   3   2   1

Preface

MACINTOSH PROGRAMMER'S WORKSHOP IS A COMPLETE SYSTEM for developing software for the Macintosh, including compilers, an editor, command processor and development utilities. MPW is the official Macintosh development system from Apple Computer, Inc., and is also the basis for important developer products offered by other companies.

The book is a guide to making effective use of MPW in Macintosh programming with C or Pascal. It assumes no prior Macintosh programming experience, offering a step-by-step explanation of MPW's capabilities. At the same time, it is intended to offer tricks and new ideas for the most seasoned MPW veteran.

In addition to the tutorial introduction, the book also collects important material for later reference use. It is not intended to replace the MPW reference manuals supplied by Apple, but to provide an essential supplement for any serious MPW user.

Every effort has been made to make the text intelligible without having a computer at hand—what I call a "bathtub book," although you're more likely to read it at the beach or on a plane. However, certain sections will benefit from having MPW and your Mac at hand, particularly Chapters 4 through 6.

The book covers the latest beta-test versions of MPW 2.0 available at press time of MPW, including the final MacApp 1.1. However, it's possible that the final software that you buy may have a minor difference or two. Also, the book does not attempt to describe every option and every MPW command; for a complete reference list of MPW 2.0 commands, see Appendix A.

Some may ask why the book spends so much time on programming, particularly on details of the Macintosh OS and Toolbox. One reason is that anyone who buys MPW does so for one reason: to program the Macintosh. Even an experienced Mac hacker may not have made it all the way through all the chapters of all the editions of *Inside Macintosh*, while a prospective Macintosh programmer may not have even cracked the first chapter. In the computer business, we often spend so much time staring at a few trees through a microscope that we miss the broad sweep of the forest.

But the most important reason is that the standard reference books have a deliberately narrow focus. *Inside Macintosh* is development-system independent, while the MPW reference manuals do not cover the OS and Toolbox calls. This compartmentalization is necessary for comprehensive reference works about a complex moving target, or the books would weigh twice as much and come out too late to do anyone any good.

My view is that a book that attempts to teach programming the Macintosh with MPW must tie together both topics, so that the reference works make sense in the context in which they are used. The result was twice as long and later than anyone expected, but I'd like to think it was worth the wait.

Joel West
Vista, California
July, 1987

Acknowlegements

Even when flowing from the keyboard of one author, writing a technical book covering such a broad topic requires the consultation and assistance of many selfless individuals.

First on my list of acknowledgements are two guys who would find themselves at the end of any alphabetical list. Paul Zemlin of Apple continuously worked to provide the latest MPW software and documentation, as well as coordinating the assistance of various Apple departments. Eric Zocher of Silicon Beach Software gave me crucial suggestions for the book before I'd even written a word, as well as spending several hours on an Easter Sunday offering helpful suggestions on how the book could be improved.

At Apple, Rick Meyers patiently explained many of the details behind the MPW design. Harvey Alcabes arranged for me to have the latest information about MacApp. I'd also like to thank the many others at Apple who helped out, including Kurt Bianchi, Jim Friedlander, David Goldsmith, Keithen Hayenga, Fred Huxham, Ginger Jernigan, Sherri Morningstar, Louella Parsons, Larry Rosenstein, Martha Steffen, George Towner, and Katie Willey.

Duane Maxwell of Levco Enterprises shared his knowledge of the Motorola 68020 and 68881. Tom Leonard of TML Systems provided an advance look at his firm's Modula-2 compiler for MPW. In addition to many of the above, Frank Boosman, Dennis Cohen, Steve Falco, Neil Rhodes, and Bill Snider reviewed portions of the manuscript.

In the publishing side of the business, editor Steve Guty at Bantam guided me along and provided weekly reassurance and direction, while his later insistence on rewriting greatly improved several sections. Jack and

Cheryl Rienzo toiled till the 'wee hours laying out the pages, long after sane people would have given up. My agent, Bill Gladstone, is due the credit for connecting me with Bantam in the first place.

The description of the MPW 2.0 commands contained in Appendix A is based on copyrighted material of Apple Computer, Inc., and is used with Apple's express permission. Also, some of the discussions of resources were based on my "Resource Roundup" column in *MacTutor*. I would like to thank the magazine's editor, David E. Smith, for generously allowing me to adapt that material, and also for encouraging me to write about the Macintosh.

Finally, as any writer will tell you, the author's spouse is long-suffering and unheralded, despite any token words to the contrary on a page such as this. My thanks go to Lori for putting up with this yet again.

CONTENTS

Chapter 2

Macintosh System Software 23

Chapter 6

Shell Programming 271

Programming with
Macintosh
Programmer's
Workshop

Chapter 1

About MPW

MACINTOSH PROGRAMMER'S WORKSHOP (MPW) is a complete set of programming tools developed by Apple Computer. This Macintosh-based programming environment is the evolutionary outgrowth of earlier software for Macintosh development, notably the Lisa Workshop system. MPW also provides the basis for third-party compilers and programming utilities.

This chapter discusses the origins of MPW and how it relates to other Macintosh development systems and describes some of the conventions to be used in later chapters. It includes installation tips and a simple introduction to the MPW environment.

1.1 Macintosh Development Software

The release of MPW followed the introduction of the Macintosh by several years. Prior to that time, other development systems from Apple and third parties were used to develop Macintosh programs. If you're new to the Macintosh or if you've always wondered why MPW was not available in year 1 A.M. (*Anno Macintosh*), then you may be interested in how MPW came to be.

IN THE BEGINNING

When Steve Jobs introduced Apple's long-rumored new Macintosh computer in January 1984, the assembled shareholders were enthusiastic. The Macintosh project had been underway for five years and had been influenced by

1

decisions made in the parallel Lisa effort which, in turn, built upon even earlier work done at Xerox's Palo Alto Research Center. However, the Lisa had been awkwardly (and unsuccessfully) positioned midway between the personal computer and workstation markets, a full-featured, gold-plated PC with a $10,000 price tag to match. The Macintosh was being introduced at one-fourth that price, within the range of existing computer prices. The Mac, as it soon was called, promised to be a low-cost, mass-market offering of the new technology. Like the Lisa, the Macintosh included a user-friendly interface based on a graphical display screen and pointing device, the mouse.

Included with the Macintosh were two mind-boggling computer programs, which Apple called "applications." MacWrite was the first word processor for a personal computer that provided a true "What you see is what you get" capability: if you selected italics, the letters slanted to the right; if you wanted larger letters, they expanded before your eyes. MacPaint was a wonderful doodling program that even a preschooler could grasp, spawning a whole league of imitators on rival computers. Anyone could learn how to use them after a 15-minute demo, with no prior experience or manual required. Both faithfully recorded that display on paper, albeit very slowly.

Sensing a revolution in the making, many programmers rushed right out to buy one, the author included. However, the initial Macintosh—128K of random access memory (RAM) and a single 400K floppy—was a laughable configuration for any serious software development. Instead, all the software initially developed for the Macintosh required use of a Lisa.

The Lisa Workshop provided a Pascal compiler and a 68000 assembler. This was used by Apple and third-party developers to develop the Macintosh system software Finder, MacWrite, MacPaint, MacTerminal, and most other commercial software released in that first year.

A year later, Apple introduced the Macintosh 68000 Development System (MDS), which was a fancy name for an assembler and associated tools. This was appropriate for desk accessories and other small programs.

However, as noted in Frederick Brook's classic essay on software development, *The Mythical Man-Month,* the number of lines of code produced by a programmer each week is nearly a constant, no matter what language is being used. Since each high-level language statement translates into 2 to 10 machine language instructions, developing a large program entirely in assembly language would be overwhelming for an individual hobbyist or a small company. This task becomes particularly intimidating when one considers that the Macintosh user interface adds considerably to the code necessary to complete a program.

That's not to say that alternatives to MDS were not available for Macintosh programmers. As Apple has discovered, along with other PC manufacturers, capitalism and an unfilled market niche combine as a powerful force to lure third-party software developers to solve many problems. At last count, there were at least seven C compilers, four Basic compilers, three each for Pascal and Modula-2, an assembler, plus one or more interpretive systems for Basic, Forth, Lisp, and Logo.

Many of these systems were based on MDS tools licensed from Apple. This allowed use of the MDS assembler. Others included their own assemblers and linkers, but used Apple's editor or resource compiler.

However, as a practical matter, there was one major disadvantage to third-party software development tools. As with any successful computer system, the Macintosh is continually evolving. The operating system (System) and command shell (Finder) went through several major revisions.

New models and peripherals were introduced including the LaserWriter, the color ImageWriter II, the HD20 hard disk (along with the Hierarchical File System), and the Macintosh Plus. Although some of these introductions overlapped, each of these major hardware changes required significant modifications or enhancements to the original software architecture.

When Apple introduced a new piece of hardware, there would often be a wait for formal documentation on the new software. Then the vendors of third-party compilers would have to modify their libraries and documentation and issue a new release incorporating these and other changes. As a practical matter, a programmer using a third-party systems faced a delay of six months or more awaiting development software compatible with the new hardware.

If Apple were to use a Macintosh-based system for its own development, that system would have to be kept up to date for Apple's own purposes. The completion of such an Apple-sponsored product would clearly speed the process of getting current information to all programmers.

ENTER MPW

The lack of a suitable hardware configuration for a Macintosh-based development system was a serious obstacle in the path of what was to become MPW. Despite several incompatibilities with the Macintosh environment, the Lisa 2/10 (Macintosh XL) was a far more suitable development system, with 1 megabyte (Mb) of main memory and 10 Mb of hard disk space. It wasn't until Apple introduced the 1 Mb Macintosh Plus, with its high-speed SCSI hard disk port, that there was a Macintosh suitable for doing the sort of work that had been done with the Lisa. Although Apple updated the Lisa twice, to the Lisa 2 and the Macintosh XL, the end of the Lisa Workshop system was assured when the computer itself was discontinued.

Apple had always intended to make its own development tools available for the Macintosh. In fact, a Macintosh version of the Lisa Pascal compiler had once been penciled in for the spring of 1984, within a few months of the Mac's introduction.

Instead, the first summer arrived, and the Lisa Pascal compiler had yet to be ported. Some at Apple felt that Lisa Pascal should still be ported in 1984 as an MDS-compatible compiler. Instead, Apple undertook a more ambitious project, one that would include a complete development environment and a suite of programmer's tools. That project was MPW, and work was begun in 1984 on what eventually became MPW.

This project was announced to the world in February 1985 at the first-ever Macintosh trade show. To a packed room of developers and would-be developers, Apple optimistically announced MPW would be available in the fall of 1985. That projected date proved to be more than a year ahead of the actual release date.

Throughout the history of MPW and its predecessors, Apple and the Macintosh software groups weathered several major reorganizations. In 1984, the earlier Lisa team was merged with the Macintosh team headed by founder and chairman Steve Jobs. A year later, the Apple II and Macintosh groups were merged and Jobs left in a dispute with Apple's board of directors, who backed president (and later chairman) John Sculley.

With the many delays in the long-awaited Macintosh development system, an outside observer might conclude that the difficulty of the task had been seriously underestimated or that the effort applied was inadequate or not focused on meeting realistic deadlines. Commensurate with the enormity of the effort, a team of 15 software engineers was applied to the MPW project in the summer of 1985. After a year of hard work, the first prerelease version of MPW was offered to developers for evaluation. With improved documentation and hundreds of corrections, the software was released to Macintosh programmers as MPW, release 1.0.

1.2   What Is MPW?

Key components of MPW are an evolutionary outgrowth of Apple's earlier Lisa Workshop development system. However, the MPW team has also developed a more comprehensive programming environment from scratch, modeled loosely after the UNIX operating system. The result is one of the most powerful development systems ever for *any* computer.

THE MPW ENVIRONMENT

Unlike the Lisa Workshop, MPW includes a complete environment that is comparable in power to many dedicated operating systems. As available from Apple, the complete Macintosh Programmer's Workshop includes:

- Line-oriented command interpreter
- Integrated full-screen windowing editor
- Assembler and disassemblers
- A linker and librarian, with a standard object file format
- Resource tools
- Text analysis tools

Three packages sold separately include:

- Pascal compiler, including support for Object Pascal and Pascal formatting tools
- C compiler
- MacApp library for object-oriented development

Even more than with other programming environments, the MPW editor is inseparably part of the MPW environment. Commands can be entered and executed in the default command window—or even within an ordinary text file! There is no distinction made between command and text windows, and both command and editing capabilities are always available.

MPW provides its suite of utilities, including the compilers, as components of this programming environment. These utilities are executed from within the programming environment and rely on it to perform many basic functions, such as updating windows and outputting to the printer.

Most are midway between stand-alone applications and simple subroutines. Conceptually, these partial programs—or MPW tools—resemble line-oriented programs from more conventional operating systems. They are run by typing the name of the command followed by a list of control options or related files. MPW provides a framework for linking together any number of tools, which can be combined, controlling the input and output of each command, allowing them to be combined into related groups using automated scripts.

These MPW tools are also much simpler to implement than a stand-alone Macintosh application. Such an application requires a significant effort to support the complete Macintosh user interface, as is described in Chapter 3.

COMPILERS

In 1981, Apple licensed a 68000-based Pascal compiler from Silicon Valley Software, which was based on the enhanced dialect of Pascal developed at the University of California, San Diego, otherwise known as UCSD Pascal. This compiler was originally used by Apple for the Lisa project to develop the Lisa Office System (later Lisa 7/7) that was bundled with the machine when it was announced in 1983.

When the Macintosh was announced a year later, Apple offered to sell developers its only complete development system for the Mac: the Lisa 2 and the Lisa Workshop built around this compiler.

During the next three years, the Lisa Pascal compiler received a number of updates and enhancements to keep up with the evolution of the Macintosh software architecture. MPW Pascal is based on release 3.1 of Lisa Pascal, supplemented by later changes made in the final Lisa Pascal release, 3.9.

By the time it was officially released in 1987, the MPW Pascal compiler had six years of corrections and enhancements under Apple's supervision—

an eternity by microcomputer software standards. This means it is a very reliable and well-tested compiler and one which has had a lot of attention paid to the quality of the generated code.

However, it also means a compiler to which features have been added to make it appropriate for large software development. As described in Chapter 7, MPW Pascal includes a number of significant syntactic extensions to the Pascal standard. Significantly, the *unit* concept of UCSD Pascal was adapted to provide modular libraries that in many ways were similar to the modules added by Pascal author Niklaus Wirth in his next language, Modula-2. In fact, MPW Pascal compares quite favorably with Modula-2 as a practical language for large software development projects.

During the development of MPW, Apple recognized an increasing demand for a compiler based on the C programming language. The earliest third-party compilers for the Macintosh were C compilers, since C compilers are generally designed for portability, to support the portable UNIX operating system on a variety of hardware configurations. The portability of C programs originally associated with UNIX, however, was being turned to an advantage in the microcomputer industry by those forced to support software products on a variety of computers.

Apple licensed an efficient 68000 C compiler from Green Hills Software, Inc., and it was included as an optional component for the Lisa Workshop. This compiler later became MPW C. For compatibility with the Macintosh read-only memory (ROM), the compiler was extended to provide direct calls to Pascal routines and the Pascal-style subroutines in the ROM. Differences between the MPW C compiler and other C compilers are described in Chapter 8.

Both the C and Pascal compilers come with the source to small example programs, including the necessary commands to build these programs.

A few of the Lisa tools were ported to MPW. However, the MPW editor and command scripts have little in common with their Lisa predecessors. The resource compiler is brand new, as are many new utilities that have no Lisa predecessors.

DEVELOPMENT ENVIRONMENTS

There is more to productive programming than a compiler and a text editor. However, that's often been the extent of the software tools provided for microcomputer development.

Minicomputers and workstations typically include complete operating systems intended for software development, such as UNIX, VAX/VMS, AOS/VS, Primos, or Aegis. The operating system includes a complete set of tools. The tools start with a full-screen text editor and an interactive command interpreter that allows combining the result of one or more commands.

Because these operating system have a standard object code format, the associated linker can take those object files—perhaps produced by several different compilers—and merge them into an executable program. The system also will include a standard library of routines called by all programs. Some systems include a provision for combining object files into a library of routines. Finally, the system will normally provide for a standard way of performing repetitive tasks, usually through a series of command interpreter scripts.

On the other hand, the Macintosh does not have a built-in editor. It lacks a line-oriented command interpreter and thus a provision for programming repetitive tasks. Mechanisms have been developed on the Mac for repeating a series of mouse-oriented commands, but these still lack the flexibility necessary for software development.

Apple's first Macintosh-targeted development system, the Lisa Workshop, was basically a UCSD P-System compiler with an improved editor. It also included a batch facility for performing repetitive tasks. Its most significant difference from MPW is that it was not user-extendable.

OBJECT-ORIENTED DEVELOPMENT

The MPW Pascal compiler includes extensions to support Object Pascal. The Object Pascal language, developed by Apple, includes a subset of the capabilities provided by Smalltalk-80, Simula, and other object-oriented languages.

Object-oriented languages promise the next major stage in the evolution of programming languages. Such languages provide a more flexible and yet structured approach to programming than do structured languages such as Pascal, much as Algol-68 and Pascal were a major improvement over FORTRAN IV. As with other such languages, Object Pascal can be used for developing programs based on an inheritance of properties.

As object-oriented languages go, Object Pascal is one of the simplest, offering only a few new concepts beyond Pascal. This is a deliberate choice, for while it limits the capabilities of the language, it does not degrade performance and, more importantly, makes it understandable to anyone who has a grasp of Pascal. The basic Object Pascal concepts can be taught in one lesson; unlike most object-oriented languages, no second lesson is required to learn "advanced" concepts.

However, the most significant use of Object Pascal with MPW is MacApp, a separate component of MPW. MacApp is a library of Object Pascal routines that provides the standard Macintosh user interface, including all aspects of a Macintosh application. A programmer using MacApp concentrates on implementing his or her specific objectives rather than reimplementing the standard Macintosh structure. The savings in development time can be considerable.

Although not released as of this writing, Apple also has announced plans to develop MacApp capabilities for C programmers. These are to be based on an enhanced subset of C++, a popular UNIX-oriented extension to C developed at AT&T Bell Labs.

THIRD-PARTY SYSTEMS

Even more than MDS before it, MPW serves as an ideal platform for third-party development tools. MPW provides an editor, the command shell, and the wealth of utilities. For many vendors, all that's necessary is to supply a compiler as a new tool, supplemented by a few subroutine libraries. Apple has documented the rules for building such tools, and, once complete, they become as fully integrated as those supplied with MPW.

For example, the first MPW-compatible compiler to be released is TML Modula-2 from TML Systems, a company previously known for Pascal compilers on the Mac and Apple IIgs. TML Modula-2 comes with two new MPW tools, the compiler and a pretty-print source formatter. It also includes Modula-2 libraries, the definition modules (equivalent to C includes or Pascal units), and example programs.

It's important to note that TML did *not* have to develop an editor, shell, linker, assembler, or other standard development tools; TML Modula-2 can be used with the same MPW components as other MPW-compatible compilers. In fact, it's possible to install MPW, its assembler, Pascal, C, and TML's Modula-2 and freely use all four languages on the same or different projects.

Other compilers offered by third parties will also take advantage of MPW. No matter what the language, MPW will become the standard development platform for many Macintosh developers for two reasons: It is Apple's standard development platform for Macintosh-related software, and it has a number of important advantages over other environments.

STRENGTHS AND WEAKNESSES

MPW has a number of unique advantages for Macintosh development, but it is not necessarily the system for all projects and all individuals.

Macintosh Programmer's Workshop is a powerful development system. It can handle the largest of programming projects, split across dozens of source files. Its compilers produce code sequences that are among the best available for 68000 processors.

MPW is also a complete development system. In addition to compilers, it includes a suite of tools for text manipulation, modifying, resources and file management. Programmers who use the Mac for other purposes will find themselves using MPW for editing documents, converting data from one application to another, or making file backups. All these can be done without actual programming, using the interactive MPW shell.

Despite this built-in power, MPW is unusual among existing Macintosh programs in the degree to which it is user-extensible. Like other line-oriented development systems, it supports automated scripts; but MPW also can be augmented by new dialogs, windows, and menus. Developers can write their own programs to implement new commands, with access to the full range of MPW's capabilities. For projects based on modular libraries, MPW's compilers and linkers make it easy to supply new include files and libraries without modifying Apple's version, thus making it easier to install updates to the MPW release.

Because they are developed by Apple, the MPW libraries offer the official specifications of the Macintosh software architecture. Of course, it will run on Apple's latest configurations, including HFS-based hard disks, the AppleShare fileserver, and the 68020-based Macintosh II.

Since MPW Pascal is a port of the Lisa Pascal compiler, it is particularly appropriate for those who are adapting code from that earlier system. Developers will find that many large commercial applications can be moved from the Lisa to the Mac in several hours, with much of that time associated with the mechanics of file transfer, setting up compilation scripts, etc., rather than tracking down and making source code changes.

In short, MPW is the most powerful and complete development system yet released for the Macintosh. For many purposes, this makes it clearly the best.

However, this power comes at a cost, and MPW does have a number of weaknesses that should be considered when evaluating your various options.

The price of MPW's power is convenience. A powerful system is a complex one, and, as Macintosh programs go, learning MPW's complete capabilities is a lengthy process. Given the Mac's high standards for user-friendliness, this makes it easier than most development systems on other computers, but an understanding of MPW, like Rome, is not built in a day.

Release 2.0 of MPW is even more complex than its predecessor, but it includes new features—particularly in the form of an interactive help dialog—that should make it easier for novices to get started. Much of the inconvenience in using MPW is in the initial out-of-the-box configuration since MPW allows you to define custom commands to perform any operation.

The speed of the compile-link-run cycle within MPW is less than dazzling. From the Lisa Workshop and a Macintosh XL to a Macintosh Plus with MPW, the improvement in compile time is due to the slightly faster hardware. This is certainly better than some compilers, but, as of this writing, third-party systems from Borland (Turbo) and Think Technologies (Lightspeed) are considerably faster.

However, MPW compilation is highly automated and supports development of large programs in many small, separate modules, which can reduce compilation requirements. It is also quite suitable for starting a series of unattended compiles and walking away to take a short break.

MPW is also a large system, and it requires a comparable hardware platform. Although Macintosh configurations are getting larger, the satisfactory use of MPW requires 1 Mb of memory and at least 5 Mb on your hard disk. The author's MPW system (complete with all optional components and source examples) requires about 8 Mb of disk space, excluding, of course, the necessary System Folder.

This rules out using MPW with the least expensive hardware configurations. The cost of the software itself also removes MPW from the "bargain basement" category.

In short, MPW is not designed to supplant all competitors. It cannot be all things to all people; there is still room for third-party Pascal and C compilers in parallel with MPW.

Those who make only occasional use of their Macintosh for programming may want to consider other products. On the other hand, someone who makes his or her living programming the Macintosh would be foolhardy to go without it, even while taking advantage of the complementary strengths of other systems for portions of the same project.

1.3 Getting Started

Using any component of MPW requires installation of the MPW shell in addition to whatever programs—such as the Pascal or C compiler—you plan to use.

Once MPW is installed, up-to-date summary descriptions of MPW commands are available from the MPW Help command, which also allows you to get help on the exact syntax of a particular command. You can also implicitly get help on any command using a standard dialog.

INSTALLATION STRATEGIES

Before installing MPW, you must first decide how much disk space you have and the strategy you will use in installing MPW.

Release 2.0 of MPW requires the following minimum configuration:

- 128K ROM or later (e.g., Macintosh Plus, SE, and Macintosh II)
- 1 Mb of RAM
- HFS hard disk

Release 1.0 was slightly smaller, and it is possible to use it with two 800K floppy drives and 512K of RAM, but even that is stretching things to the limit.

If you have 4 Mb or more of available space on your hard disk, you should have no problem installing MPW, the MPW assembler, C, and Pascal. MacApp requires several megabytes more. Table 1–1 shows the disk space requirements for MPW subdivided by category.

	MPW 2.0	MPW 1.0
MPW		
Shell & standard files	295K	206K
Tools and scripts	1,385K	706K
Libraries and includes	125K	67K
Other files	450K	179K
Subtotal	2,255K	1,158K
MPW Assembler	655K	480K
MPW C	590K	428K
MPW Pascal	785K	609K
MacApp†	1,380K	1,466K
Grand Total	5,665K	4,141K

Notes: 1K = 1024 bytes
            MPW 2.0 figures are preliminary

† MPW 2.0 was released with MacApp 1.1

Table 1-1:   MPW Disk Space Requirements

In addition to the allocations shown, you should also allow for temporary files. MacApp requires at least another megabyte for its object and temporary files. For maximum compilation speed, other Pascal users should set aside 200K or more for symbol table dump files.

If space is a problem, several of the components could be considered optional. The first to go would probably be MPW assembler, which won't be necessary for most programmers, at least at first. You could also take the examples and put them on a separate disk. After that, you could pare down the number of tools. Only the Rez resource compiler, Link linker, and the corresponding C or Pascal compiler are essential, although by abandoning the remaining tools you will abandon much of the power of MPW.

As a practical matter, MPW 2.0 cannot be run from floppy disks alone. If space is a problem, you might consider using MPW 1.0, which allows the MPW shell, a subset of the tools, and a System Folder to just barely fit on one 800K disk. A variety of second disks could be prepared for the assembler, Pascal, and/or C, with about half of each disk available for your source. The remaining tools could also be run using the second drive.

In short, before you buy MPW, buy a hard disk, the bigger the better— since it will tend to fill up with all the programs you're working on. More RAM will also make your compilations go faster; you will want to allocate a 128K RAM cache, with the remaining available to leave MPW tools and their data resident in memory.

A TEST DRIVE

MPW requires a little more effort for installation than a typical application. Installing MPW requires copying both the MPW application and at least some of the files that MPW expects to have available onto one of your disks.

The instructions for installing MPW will vary with the actual distribution release and with your available disk space. If you have enough disk space and are ready to begin, you can just drag the contents of the various folders onto your hard disk and give it a go. This is well described by the *Macintosh Programmer's Workshop Reference* manual that is included with MPW, which we'll call the "reference manual."

However, if you don't have enough disk space yet or just want to try out your copy of MPW, you can copy just a few files onto your hard disk and try it out. These files are contained on the first distribution disk, named MPW1. Create a folder named MPW in your hard disk and drag all the files at the root level (not in folders) into this folder, as shown in Figure 1–1.

Now launch the application MPW Shell from the Finder. It will offer a display similar to that shown in Figure 1–2. MPW always looks for a single document named Worksheet in the same folder as the shell application; if it's not found, it creates one. This window cannot be closed while MPW is running, and you can't change the name (except to move the shell and worksheet to a different folder).

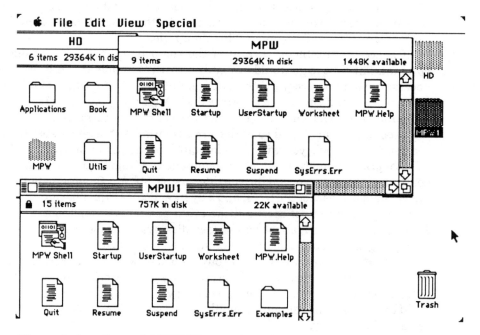

Figure 1–1:   Enough MPW Files to Get Started

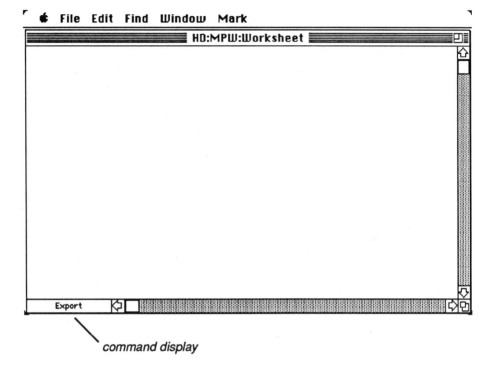

command display

Figure 1-2:   MPW Shell Screen Display

When the MPW shell is executing one or more shell commands, the command being executed at the time is displayed in the lower-left corner of the topmost (active) window, just to the left of the horizontal scroll bar. When you start up the shell, you will normally see a series of commands flash by rapidly as the environment is initialized. When the commands stop flashing, the shell is no longer executing commands, and it indicates this by displaying MPW Shell.

One of the files you copied—Startup—includes the commands to be run when MPW starts up. Go to the File menu and select Open. Look for the Startup document in the MPW folder and open it.

You should see commands that were executed when you launched MPW, the ones that flashed rapidly in the command display. Many of the lines are devoted to defining symbolic names of folders using the Set and Export commands, which requires an understanding of the purpose of each symbolic name. However, it's easy enough to make a simple change to the file to prove a point.

The file has several lines of comments at the top of the document, with each line beginning with the number sign (#). Since you will be changing the document, you should go ahead and put an indication of your changes and the date of the changes as one of the comments. If the file doesn't indicate its version, you might want to include that as well, since that will make it easier later on if you have `Startup` files from several MPW releases. Figure 1–3 shows how the `Startup` file might look after adding some comments.

At the very end of the `Startup` file, we can add a simple command to make an obvious difference in the startup action. Select the end of the file, add a few returns, and then type the following lines:

```
# indicate ready to go
Beep
```

The next time you launch MPW, this additional shell command will cause the `Startup` command file to sound a tone just before completing all the commands. Save the file and quit.

MPW shell commands are part of an interpretive programming language, and files containing those commands are simple programs. If you replace this copy of `Startup` with the original version, the `Beep` command will be absent from the program source and the tone will disappear.

Since most users will want to define custom commands, menus, and so on, Apple supplies an empty file—`UserStartup`—to contain all your initializa-

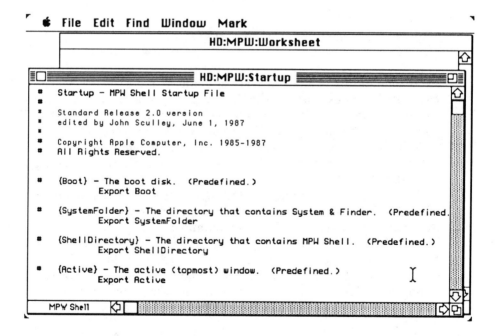

Figure 1–3:   Editing the Startup File

tion commands. That way, when you install a new release of MPW with a new Startup file, your own definitions in UserStartup will be unchanged.

A more detailed set of rules for MPW commands, including modifying the definitions in Startup and UserStartup, is contained in Chapter 4.

TRYING COMMANDS

In Startup, you've already seen examples of textual commands that are automatically used by MPW each time you start it. However, MPW also recognizes textual commands entered interactively, a process you will soon become quite familiar with.

Such commands must be entered in one of the MPW windows. The Worksheet window is always opened by default, and it doesn't have any purpose other than holding commands and their output, so it's the window you'll use most often for interactively entering commands.

To get MPW to recognize a textual command, you must do two things: provide the command with the proper spelling and syntax, and call the command to MPW's attention so that it knows to execute it. For example, you may have a window open to Pascal source, which you don't want MPW to try to interpret, so some form of explicit indication is necessary to signal which text is to be interpreted.

One command that will often be used at first is the Help command, which displays summarized information about MPW commands and their syntax in the active window.

On a blank line in the worksheet, type:

```
Help
```

Now, with the cursor still on the same line, press the Enter key, which is on the keypad on most keyboards.

MPW will interpret this as an indication to run the command called Help. It will display a summary of the available help in the worksheet.

Each of the MPW commands has its own specific syntax. After the name of the command, the remainder of the line contains information that is used by the command to determine what to do. In the case of the Help command, one possibility is to list a command you'd like more information about, as in:

```
Help Files
```

In this case, Help would display information about the Files command, which is used to list the files in a folder or disk volume.

Help also provides information on specific topics related to the syntax of MPW commands. To illustrate a form that will be used throughout the remainder of this book, the syntax of the Help command is summarized as:

Help

Display information about shell commands and syntax

Syntax:

`Help`	Display topics `Help` is available for
`Help commands`	Display all shell commands
`Help command`	Display information about `command`
`Help characters`	Display a summary of special shell characters
`Help patterns`	Explain string patterns (regular expressions)
`Help selections`	Explain selection expressions
`Help shortcuts=`	Explain shortcuts for MPW commands

Input/Output:

`Output`	The `Help` information

Example:

`Help Pascal`	Give information about `Pascal` command

For example, if you type:

```
Help commands
```

and then press Enter, the command will display (output) a list of all the available commands. If you type (and enter) the command at the very top of the `Worksheet` window, you will have a permanent online reference to all the commands to help you as you're learning MPW. If, at any point, you wonder about the name or description of an MPW command, you can scroll to the top of the worksheet and the information will be there.

The `Help` command reads the information from a file called `MPW.Help` in the same folder as the MPW shell. When you install a new release, you must replace this file to get the latest descriptions. You can also print this file out by typing

```
Print "{ShellDirectory}MPW.Help"
```

followed by Enter. This will print the entire file on the default printer selected by the Chooser desk accessory.

INTERACTIVE HELP

Beginning with release 2.0, MPW includes a special dialog box to assist in selecting the options of an MPW command. This assistance, whimsically named Commando, comes in the form of a dialog box with various controls you can use to set the options. If you follow an MPW command with an ellipsis character (..., Option-;), MPW will use the Commando tool to display the dialog box.

For example, if you typed

                    Duplicate...

you would see a dialog similar to Figure 1–4.

When it sees the ellipsis, the shell runs the Commando command to display the help; you don't normally call Commando directly. For those who are familiar with the structure of a Macintosh program, Commando displays the dialog box based on resources of type 'cmdo' in the resource fork of the program you run.

One of the most innovative features in the dialog box is the context-sensitive help, as shown in the figure. When you touch a particular item in

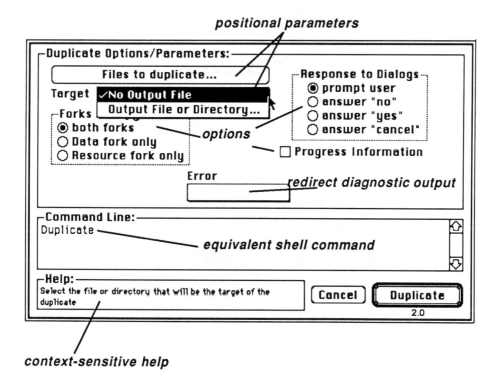

Figure 1–4:   Interactive Help from Commando

the dialog, the help window in the dialog displays information about what changing that item does.

Alternate choices are shown as radio buttons, while on/off toggles are shown as checkbox controls.

One of the areas where Commando provides important assistance is in specifying the name of a file or folder. Instead of typing the name, you select them using Standard File Package dialogs, as shown in Figure 1–5. For many commands, the dialog allows you to select multiple input files or folders.

As you select your command parameters and options, Commando updates the command line equivalent to the selected information and displays it in the dialog, as shown in Figure 1–6. This is the command line that will eventually be passed to the command interpreter if you exit the dialog without cancelling. If you're intimidated by the syntax of the various

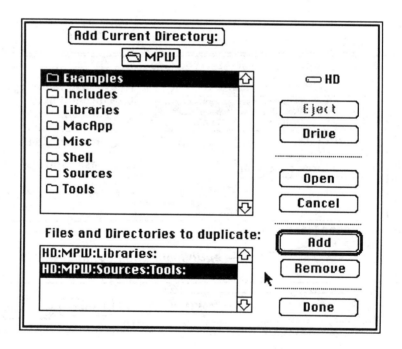

Figure 1–5:   Selecting a File with Commando

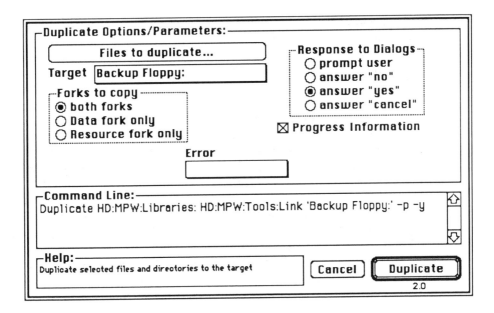

Figure 1–6:   Shell Command Built by Commando

commands, you can use Commando to build the commands for you and then use commands over and over again.

1.4   Where Do You Go From Here?

Although this book is designed to be read front to back, as well as be retained as a reference book, those who already own MPW may wish to skip ahead to a particular topic of interest.

At the other extreme, newcomers to Macintosh programming should be aware of additional references available that will prove extremely helpful.

THE REMAINING CHAPTERS

This book is intended to teach how to use MPW for programming the Macintosh. The key aspects of the MPW design are reviewed and examples are provided to show how to use these components.

The remainder of Part 1 provides an overview of the Macintosh software design. For those without prior Macintosh development experience, a concise overview of the Macintosh OS and Toolbox is provided. Even if you are experienced with developing Macintosh software, you may wish to review Chapter 3, which describes the structure of applications, desk accessories, MPW utilities, and other types of Macintosh code.

On the other hand, some readers may already be experienced Macintosh developers and just want to learn how to use MPW. Part 2 describes the shell, including its command syntax, customizing your configuration, and using shell commands to edit files and perform repetitive tasks.

However, once you've mastered the basics of the MPW shell and editor, you can skip ahead to using the Pascal or C compiler if you have programs you're ready to try (or write) under MPW. Part 3 provides examples of how the two Apple-supplied compilers can be used to compile programs, including compatibility changes with code developed for other Macintosh Pascal and C compilers.

The section also describes the use of Object Pascal with the MacApp library to develop a customizable application. Also included are discussions of MPW's advanced resource tools, the linker and the automated program-building facility.

A NOTE ABOUT STYLE

The examples and program fragments throughout this book are shown in a consistent style that generally conforms to the standard rules. If you're writing in Pascal, formatting programs in your own style is made much easier by MPW's PasMat utility.

Naming decisions for Pascal programs are somewhat arbitrary since the language is utterly case insensitive, to the extent that the same identifier can be spelled two different ways (e.g., environs or eNvIRonS) without making any difference. The examples in this book use all caps for reserved Pascal keywords, which conforms to the style of Apple's early examples and to language-imposed rules of the related Modula-2 language. This rule is also applied to data types built into the MPW Pascal compiler, such as INTEGER or BOOLEAN.

Capitalization of system-defined mixed-case identifiers follows the style put forward by Apple in *Inside Macintosh*. This includes:

- Leading capital for all data types (EventRecord), system global variables (Time), or routines (Line)

- Leading lower case for the field of a record (csCode), other global variables (thePort), enumerated variables (italic), and constants (noErr)

- Embedded capital for a new word (ExitToShell) or letter of an abbreviation (TEInit).

For user-defined identifiers, variables local to a procedure or function do not include capital letters (dmyitem, i).

Unlike Pascal, C is case sensitive, and all reserved keywords must be given in lower case. The examples follow the C convention of capitalizing constants and macros defined using #define. Other capitalizations follow the Pascal conventions of *Inside Macintosh*, which is made easier by an MPW tool (Canon) that will impose standard spellings and capitalizations on a source program.

The indentation of Pascal program includes the BEGIN and END keywords on separate lines, with the blocks within those keywords indented. Although semicolons before the END are redundant, they are included to simplify the coding, as in the fragment:

```
IF something THEN
    BEGIN
        AStatement;
        AnotherStatement;
    END;
```

C programs adopt the author's block indentation style, which is more similar to that of Pascal than the style presented by Kernighan and Ritchie. The opening and closing brackets are grouped at the same level, as in

```
if (something)
{ AStatement;
    AnotherStatement;
}
```

Other aspects of programming style are intended to follow both aesthetic and sound software development practices, although experience has shown that such arbitrary decisions as comments and variable naming tend to be a matter of personal preference.

OTHER REFERENCES

If you're just getting started in Macintosh programming, you should be aware of the other information sources available and necessary to help you out.

Serious development on the Macintosh is not possible without the books of the *Inside Macintosh* series, Apple's official reference for specifications of the Macintosh Toolbox and Operating System, and it is therefore assumed that you have access to a copy. While *Inside Macintosh* alone is not enough to turn you into an experienced developer, it is a valuable reference volume, one that should be kept within reach at all times.

Also important are Apple's *Technical Notes* for the Macintosh, which include tips and additional information to supplement both *Inside Macintosh* and the MPW documentation.

The Apple Programmer's and Developer's Association (ADPA) is Apple's official conduit for providing up-to-date information to the developer, university, and hobbyist community. Apple helped set up APDA so that anyone interested in Macintosh (or Apple II) programming would have a one-stop source of materials.

APDA is the primary source of MPW and its components. Draft copies of *Inside Macintosh,* the Macintosh *Technical Notes,* other technical documentation, and development tools are also distributed by APDA. The specification of all Macintosh system software is contained in *Inside Macintosh.* The first three volumes describe the original 128K Macintosh, the Macintosh 512, and the Macintosh XL (a modified Lisa 2). Volume IV contains a description of the software differences for the Macintosh Plus and Macintosh 512 enhanced, both of which contain a 128K ROM and double-sided 800K internal disk drive. Volume V describes the new software of the Macintosh SE and Macintosh II, which have different versions of a 256K ROM.

As new computers and software are released, additional changes are needed. Draft copies of new *Inside Macintosh* sections are distributed by APDA to make sure that developers have information on the new software in a timely manner. As new systems become available, additional editions of the *Inside Macintosh* family of books will be published, both supplementing and replacing the original three-volume set.

Apple also offers other technical reference books that may be of interest to Macintosh programmers, including a series of books on the Macintosh hardware. See the Bibliography for further information.

The other official conduit for information from Apple is the series the *Macintosh Technical Notes*, which are distributed to Apple developers and also available from APDA. These customarily cover small topics that have been left undiscussed by *Inside Macintosh*, including bugs in the software implementation that fail to match the published standard.

Some of the notes are as important, or even more important, than sections of *Inside Macintosh*. An example of this is *Macintosh Technical Note* No. 2, "Macintosh Compatibility Guidelines," which provides programming tips to make your software compatible across all models of the Macintosh family. It is difficult to emphasize enough the importance of the tech notes as a resource for all Macintosh programmers. Unfortunately, providing pointers here to specific tech notes is not practical since the notes are revised bimonthly and subject to consolidation or elimination.

Other sources of information on Macintosh programming, including books and periodicals, are listed in the Bibliography.

Chapter 2

Macintosh System Software

THIS CHAPTER IS INTENDED TO PROVIDE AN OVERVIEW of Macintosh software development for those who are new to the topic and a reference for all MPW owners. It is not inteded to replace the Apple technical documentation, but is offered as a complement. It is very difficult to program for the Macintosh without grasping both levels—an overview of the entire software architecture and a clear understanding of the details of each section of importance to your program.

2.1 System Overview

As with any other computer system, the Macintosh is defined by a combination of hardware and software. The hardware components include:

- Motorola 68000-family microprocessor
- Read-only memory (ROM) with system software
- Random-access memory (RAM) for system and application software
- 3- 1/2- inch floppy disk drive
- Other disk drives (SCSI drives, external floppy, etc.)
- Serial ports (for printers, modems, and AppleTalk)

- Video display
- Keyboard
- Mouse
- Expansion slots (if any)

The Motorola 68000 is a family of related microprocessors, including the MC68000 used by the Macintosh, Macintosh Plus, and Macintosh SE, and the more advanced MC68020 processor used by the Macintosh II and third-party upgrade boards, such as the Prodigy SE. When a specific model designation is used—such as "MC68000"—the reference is only to that processor and its software-compatible equivalents.

Unless you are designing new hardware, you will rarely deal with these hardware components directly. Instead, access to the hardware is controlled through various software subsystems supplied by Apple, which we will refer to collectively as "managers."

The 68000 uses series of 16-bit words for each machine instruction. Not all of the possible opcodes are defined; the opcodes from $A000 to $AFFF, or "A-line" traps, are used as a compact and rapid mechanism for a Macintosh program to transfer control to Apple-supplied systems software. Each Macintosh contains a trap dispatch table that maps a specific trap word to a corresponding routine address; the table is maintained in RAM so that any trap can be replaced.

There is usually a one-to-one correspondence between each possible trap word and a corresponding routine in one of the managers. Some trap words are shared by multiple routines, while other standard Macintosh routines are not called through traps.

The system software available for your programs can be found in one of the following locations:

- ROM. The most commonly used software components were built into the original Macintosh ROM, which was limited to 64K. Later ROMs have more components, as well as data structures and algorithms optimized for speed rather than size. ROM routines are called through the A-line traps.

- ROM patches. These are corrections to bugs discovered in the ROM routines or new routines not available at the time the ROM was designed. When the Macintosh is turned on, these patches are loaded into RAM, their addresses are installed in the trap dispatch table, and both remain there as long as the machine is turned on.

- "System" file. This file includes all the software that would not fit into the ROM. These disk-based code and data items are loaded by the Macintosh operating system into memory as needed, using the Memory Manager to allocate a block of memory and the Resource Manager to find the particular code or data.

- Linked-in code. Some code is actually included as part of each program that uses it, rather than being made available for all programs. This code is accessed using conventional calling sequences—similar to those used on most computers—rather than invoked using the trap dispatch mechanism. Most of these routines are distinguished in *Inside Macintosh* by the notation: [Not in ROM]. This code is not actually built into the Macintosh system, but is contained in the object libraries included with MPW, normally in file Interface.o.

- "Glue" routines. As noted later, some low-level system routines (normally in ROM) are designed for efficient access from assembly language and can be called directly from assembly language. They cannot, however, be called directly by higher-level languages such as Pascal or C. Instead, small interface routines (commonly known as glue routines) are needed to bind the higher-level language to the system routines. Both assembler and the Pascal/C programs use the same ROM code, but the high-level languages need the glue to set the parameters up before transferring to this common code. This glue is also normally in Interface.o.

TOOLBOX AND OPERATING SYSTEM ROUTINES

The User Interface Toolbox (normally just called the "Toolbox") implements the standardized Macintosh user interface. As the name "user interface" suggests, the Toolbox includes most of the software that determines how the user views and controls the execution of a Macintosh program.

The operating system (OS) includes most of the common functions for any computer system. It would, in fact, be possible to use the OS routines as low-level primitives to implement a computer with a completely different interface. Many of these OS routines are emulated in A/UX, Apple's version of the UNIX operating system.

The OS controls internal functions, including allocating memory, controlling the system clock, trapping system errors, and implementing overlays of code segments in memory. The OS controls all peripheral devices, including the keyboard, video display, and disk I/O. The OS also controls sound output, printing, telecommunications, and AppleTalk and provides extended arithmetic functions beyond those provided by the 68000 hardware.

The Toolbox routines are generally those which do things the user can see, while the OS routines control the unseen lowest-level operations of hardware and software. Generally, Toolbox routines use OS routines but not vice versa.

The OS and Toolbox routines can also be divided into two categories based on their parameter-passing mechanism:

- Stack-based. These routines expect parameters pushed onto the 68000 stack. Because Macintosh software was originally developed using Lisa Pascal, the calling sequence for stack-based routines matches the Lisa Pascal (and MPW Pascal) calling sequence. Most high-level languages, including MPW C, can call routines using the Pascal calling sequence. Of course, any routine can also be called from assembly language.

- Register-based. Certain low-level system routines were designed to take their parameters directly in one, two, or three 68000 registers. As noted above, high-level languages require glue to unload the stack based parameters into registers prior to calling these routines.

Most of the Toolbox routines are stack-based, and most of the OS routines are register-based, although there are exceptions on both sides. All of the packages are stack-based.

The Macintosh traps are implemented as 68000 instructions in a 16-bit word, numbered from $A000 hex to $AFFF. All of the traps from $A000 (hex) to $A7FF are OS traps; nearly all of the traps from $A800 to $AFFF are Toolbox traps.

SUMMARY OF MANAGERS

Table 2–1 divides the Macintosh system software into the Toolbox and OS and subdivides it into the various managers. Except as noted, all of these managers are accessed either directly or indirectly through their own ROM or RAM-based traps.

Figure 2–1 shows a simplified diagram illustrating Macintosh software and hardware dependencies. The complete hierarchy, involving all the managers, packages, and drivers listed in Table 2–1, would require several pages. It also would vary slightly, depending on the ROM and System file version.

COMPATIBILITY

Since the original 128K Macintosh was released, the Macintosh computer family has evolved with the introduction of a series of new models that contain significant improvements over the preceding model. While many aspects remain the same across all models, a programmer may face a dilemma of taking advantage of new features or retaining compatibility across all models.

Very few of the original 128K machines remain unchanged, and the developer can count on having at least 512K of RAM available, with the majority of machines with 1 Mb or more. From a programming standpoint, then, the main difference between the various Macintosh models is in the

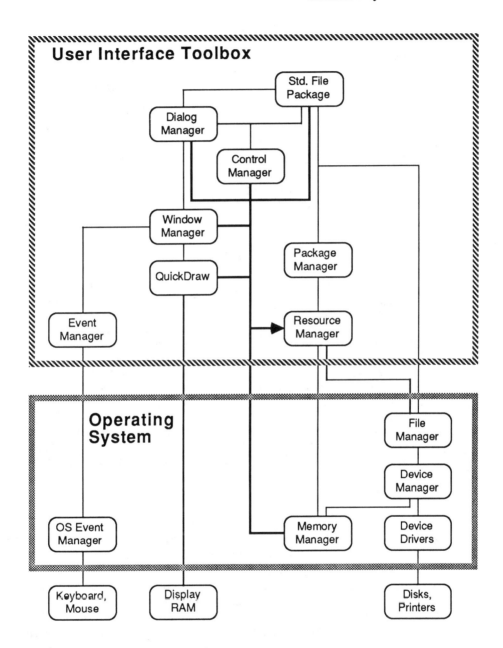

Figure 2-1:   Overall Macintosh System Software Structure

User Interface Toolbox

Color Manager	Palette Manager
Control Manager	QuickDraw
Desk Manager	Resource Manager
Dialog Manager	Scrap Manager
Font Manager	Script Manager
Menu Manager	TextEdit
Package Manager	Toolbox Event Manager
0: List Manager Package	Toolbox Utilities
3: Standard File Package	Window Manager
6: International Utilities Package	
7: Binary-Decimal Conversion Package	
12: Color Picker Package	

Operating System

Apple DeskTop Bus Manager	Printing Manager
AppleTalk Manager	ImageWriter Driver
Deferred Task Manager	LaserWriter Driver
Device Manager	SCSI Manager
Disk Driver	Segment Loader
File Manager	Serial Driver
Memory Manager	Shutdown Manager
Operating System Event Manager	Slot Manager
Operating System Utilities	Sound Driver (Sound Manager)
(Packages)	Start Manager
2: Disk Initialization Package	System Error Handler
4: Floating-Point Arithmetic Package	Time Manager
5: Transcendental Functions Package	Vertical Retrace Manager

Table 2–1:   Macintosh System Software

ROM size and contents. The later machines have revisions to earlier managers and completely new managers.

To make this possible, the size of the trap dispatch table has been expanded in two steps. The original 64K ROM allowed a combined total of 512 OS and Toolbox trap numbers, while the 128K ROM upped this to 256 OS traps and 512 Toolbox traps. With its increased requirements for traps to support color, the Macintosh II supports the maximum number of Toolbox traps possible, 1024. The different Macintosh ROM versions are summarized by Table 2–2.

As new ROMs come out, code that previously was stored on disk—usually in the System file—has moved to the ROM.

One obvious change is that traps that are provided through RAM-based patches to the ROM appear in ROM on the later machines. For example, an

	Macintosh Mac 512	Mac 512Ke Mac Plus	Mac SE	Mac II
ROM size	64K	128K	256K	256K
Configuration limits				
Toolbox traps }	512	256	256	256
OS Traps		512	512	512
Packages	8	16	16	16
RAM Cache		•	•	•
ROM-based AppleTalk Manager		•	•	•
ROM-based resources:				
'DRVR' (drivers)	0†	5	5	5
'FONT' (fonts)	0	1	4	4
'PACK' (packages)	0	3	3	3

† Sound Driver, Disk Driver and subset of Serial Driver are in 64K ROM, but not stored as resources

Table 2-2:   Macintosh ROM Differences

improved File Manager was provided by file "Hard Disk 20" for owners of the original 64K ROM Macintosh because the file system improvements were needed for Apple's first hard disk. These have since been incorporated as standard traps on all subsequent ROMs.

Another change is code and data that were originally stored on disk have moved to the ROM to eliminate the requirement for disk accesses. These include the key packages and drivers, as well as certain resources, such as fonts.

The interface to both types of code and data remained the same, so the change is transparent and automatically available to programs that use the earlier interfaces. If your program references such a routine, it will automatically get the ROM-based version if it is available; otherwise the system will fetch the necessary code from the System file.

However, another type of change requires more programming to provide compatibility. Some code that was originally provided as [Not in ROM] routines is replaced by a dedicated trap. In some cases, only a single routine is changed. In at least one case, the Printing Manager has been moved from being a [Not in ROM] interface to a call by trap.

In this case, the change is not transparent to your program. If you use the trap, your program won't work on the earlier machines unless the trap is provided as a ROM patch. If you don't use the trap, you won't be using the standard version supplied in the ROM, which may have some enhancements made since the initial [Not in ROM] definition.

Fortunately, the MPW libraries take care of this problem. In most cases, if a trap is later provided for a previously [Not in ROM] routine, a new interface routine will be provided with the MPW library. The new routine will call the trap if it's available; if not, it will use the same in-line code as before.

Each ROM also includes entire new managers not provided in previous machines. The managers added since the original Macintosh software design are summarized in Table 2-3.

Some of these new managers are closely tied to hardware changes. For example, the Macintosh Plus was the first machine to include a SCSI peripheral port and the corresponding SCSI Manager. The internal expansion slots of the Macintosh II require a Slot Manager.

	Mac Plus	Mac SE	Mac II
Apple DeskTop Bus Manager		•	•
Color Manager			•
Deferred Task Manager			•
Palette Manager			•
Script Manager	†	†	•
SCSI Manager	•	•	•
Shutdown Manager	†	†	†
Slot Manager			•
Sound Manager			•
Start Manager		§	•
Time Manager	•	•	•

† Available in System file version 4.1 or later
§ Partial implementation

Table 2-3:   Managers not in 64K ROM

Other managers have been enhanced in later machines to provide enhanced functionality. The three most significant enhancements are the hierarchical file system (HFS) changes to the File Manager, RGB color support in QuickDraw, and mixed character formats of the enhanced TextEdit. The enhanced managers are summarized in Table 2-4.

When designing a new piece of Macintosh software, the programmer must choose a functional common denominator—what capabilities will be required to run this program? The lowest common denominator is to use only software provided in the original 64K ROM, plus extensions provided in the current system file (such as packages 0 through 7).

When examining the potential target configurations, the 128K ROM of the Macintosh Plus (and 512Ke) provides additional capabilities beyond the

	Mac Plus	*Mac SE*	*Mac II*
Device Manager (slots)			•
Disk Driver (800K)	•	•	•
File Manager (HFS)	•	•	•
Font Manager ('FOND')	•	•	•
Menu Manager (hierarchical)	†	†	•
Printing Manager (trap-based)	†	•	•
QuickDraw (color)			•
SCSI Manager (blind transfers)			•
TextEdit (formatted)	†	•	•
Vertical Retrace (multiple displays)			•
Window Manager (zoom)	•	•	•

† New traps available in System file version 4.1 or later

Table 2–4:   **Managers Enhanced Since 64K ROM**

original 64K ROM that many developers have chosen to require for their programs. An example of such a program is release 2.0 of MPW.

The 128K ROM provides a hierarchical file system, that is necessary for managing a large number of file on a hard disk. Its Font Manager includes support for font families and fractional spacing for more accurate display of text to be printed on high-resolution laser printers. It has room for more traps and packages than the 64K ROM, allowing for future expansion. The Macintosh Plus (and its upward-compatible successors) also comprise the vast majority of the machines in use today.

The next step up is provided by the 256K ROM of the Macintosh II and, to a lesser degree, the Macintosh SE. However, versions 4.1 and later of the System file provide ROM patches to allow the Macintosh Plus (and SE) to share three important extensions.

In the Toolbox, the extended TextEdit allows mixing different type faces in the same document, providing a ready-built word processor for small documents. It also uses the new Script Manager, allowing for consistent treatment of non-European languages, such as Arabic and Japanese. The Menu Manager has been extended to allow for a hierarchy of submenus. The same system disks also include traps for the Shutdown Manager and Printing Manager.

Thus, if you target your software for the 128K ROM (or later), and require at least System 4.1, your program can take advantage of the capabilities of both the 128K ROM and an important subset of the 256K ROMs.

The final step is to require the full capabilities of the Macintosh II, which has additional managers not provided as ROM patches for earlier machines. The color and slot managers of the Macintosh II ROM are tied to specific hardware features of the II and thus are not appropriate for the earlier machines.

To make it easier to detect what features are available, a standard compatibility routine is provided by the libraries of MPW 2.0 and later. This routine, SysEnvirons, returns a data structure containing the machine type, CPU type and keyboard type, and indications as to whether a floating-point coprocessor and Color QuickDraw are available. Under the proper circumstances it will also return the version of the System file and the AppleTalk drivers.

The library version of SysEnvirons provides Pascal-callable glue for the _SysEnvirons trap, which is provided as a RAM patch in System 4.1 and later—except for 64K ROM machines. If the trap is not available, the "glue" code instead fills whatever fields it can, based on system variables and ROM information. SysEnvirons should be used when it is necessary to target for a particular configuration.

USER INTERFACE GUIDELINES

When introduced, the distinctive characteristic of the original 128K Macintosh was the consistency of the user interface. Whether it was sketching or writing or calculating, each program had a similar use of menus, windows, and the mouse. This idea of a common interface changed the entire direction of the PC industry.

The Macintosh User Interface Toolbox provides a set of software tools that are used by various software developers to implement a standardized user interface. Different programs use the same tools to achieve the same appearance rather than forcing each developer to create his or her own set of tools with a different appearance.

The user's view of the interface was formerly codified into a set of guidelines well in advance of the Macintosh's public unveiling in January 1984. Although originally included as a chapter of *Inside Macintosh*, the guidelines have been revised and extended to the point at which they command their own publication.

The guidelines define all of the aspects that give the Macintosh its distinctive style. As shown in Figure 2–2, the guidelines cover most aspects of what a user sees in a Macintosh program. The Toolbox helps support these guidelines, and most software reviewers castigate any software that does not conform to the standard guidelines—so there's both a carrot and a stick for developers to use the standards wherever possible.

These guidelines are constantly subject to revision and have been extended to cover all Apple microcomputers. Apple has provided a functionally similar Toolbox for the first of a new family of Apple II computers, the Apple IIgs. The IIgs Toolbox includes Control, Desk Accessory, Dialog, Menu, and Window Managers similar to those of the Macintosh, as well as QuickDraw II, an adaptation of the Macintosh graphics framework for the Apple II.

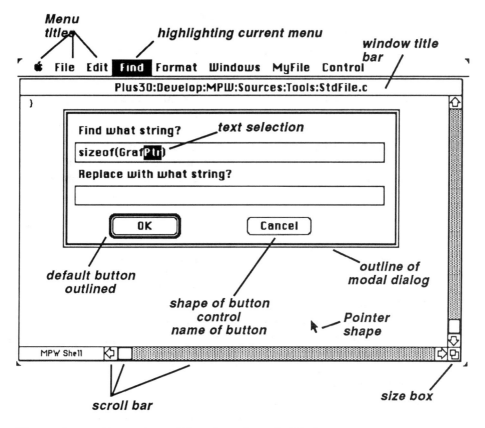

Figure 2–2:   Examples of User Interface Guidelines

Apple's goal is to have a similar look and feel for both the Apple II and Macintosh families. Apple views this interface as providing a distinctive and consistent style for Apple computers. This consistency is primarily an advantage for users, not programmers, since the OS and hardware retain major differences between the two product lines.

The current specification for this common interface is described by the book, *Human Interface Guidelines: The Apple Desktop Interface* by Apple.

2.2 Memory Management

There are three low-level managers that are fundamental to the operation of the OS, Toolbox, and any Macintosh program. Two of these managers pertain to memory management and are the subject of this section. The third, QuickDraw, provides the standard interface for all Toolbox graphics.

The most basic manager in the operating system is the Memory Manager, which provides for dynamic allocation and deallocation of memory blocks. It is used by all managers and programs to consistently manage a scarce commodity, the Macintosh RAM.

Many memory blocks are preinitialized from specific values stored on disk-based resources. The Resource Manager is extensively used by the standard Toolbox routines and most applications.

Figure 2–3 shows a simplified diagram of the relationships between the most basic routines in the OS and Toolbox. These routines are used constantly throughout a Macintosh application, and it is impossible to develop software for the Mac without an intuitive understanding of the principles behind each.

MEMORY MAP

One of the most forgotten and remarkable achievements of the Macintosh development team was that the original Macintosh software—including MacWrite, MacPaint, Microsoft Word, and Microsoft Basic—ran in a 128K RAM configuration, the same amount as an Apple IIc. Once the various RAM-based system software, video, and sound buffers, etc., are deducted, this left slightly more than 70K of memory for both program and data.

To make this work, a sophisticated Memory Manager was required in the Macintosh ROM to eke out every last byte of memory. Effective use of this complex scheme requires more than just an adaptation of existing code and concepts from other machines.

The full Macintosh memory map is as intricate as the memory allocation scheme and is fully described in "The Memory Manager" chapter of *Inside Macintosh*. The map shown in Figure 2–4 provides a simplified view of memory organization. The actual memory map may vary depending on the machine and system software being used; for example, a different memory layout is used during system startup.

The logical address space is divided up into three components. At the low end of memory, memory is allocated for system-wide operations and shared by all programs. This includes a series of system global variables (often called "low-memory globals") that are stored at fixed locations. Many of these locations are documented as containing specific values, but should be used sparingly, as their use (particularly changing system globals) will hinder future compatibility.

The system space also includes a dynamically allocated heap, often used to install code that will remain resident between applications. Prior to System 4.1, the size of this heap was fixed and limited.

The high end of memory has traditionally been used for allocating hardware-related video and sound buffers. The exact location and size of this space—particularly the video display or sound buffers—will vary by machine. For example, the video display buffer for a Macintosh II will be located

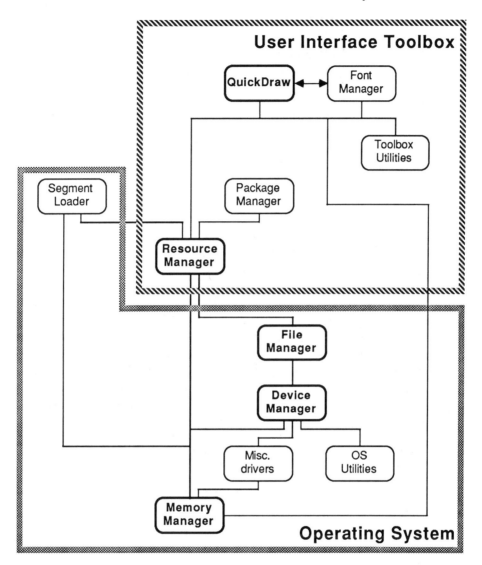

Figure 2–3:   Key Low-Level Managers

in the address space for the corresponding video card. You should consult Apple's hardware technical documentation for more precise information.

Any remaining memory is available for applications to use. This space is bounded by the addresses contained in system globals ApplZone and BufPtr.

Starting at the highest address in the application space, the top part of the application space is reserved for application global variables, including information passed from the Finder to the application.

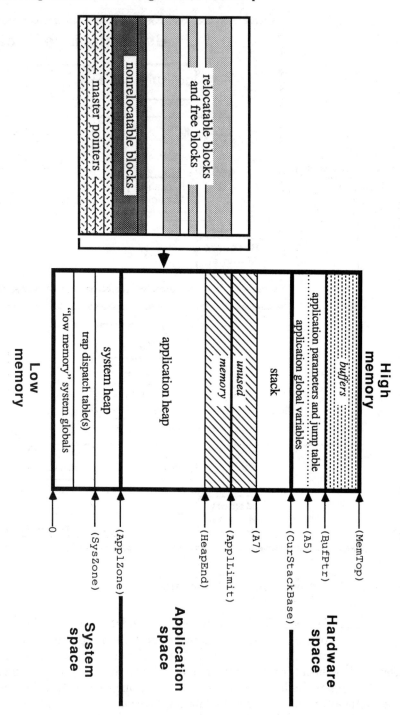

Figure 2–4:   Standard Memory Map

Next comes the stack, which expands towards low memory, as is standard for Motorola 68000 processors. The stack is used for storing local variables by most modern programming languages, including C and Pascal. One of the 68000 address registers is used to point to the current "top" of stack; as with any stack, memory is allocated on a last-in, first-out basis.

The Macintosh uses a conventional approach of placing the heap (dynamic storage) at low memory and expanding it upward toward the stack. The Memory Manager supports multiple heaps, but the same routines are used to access all heaps. There are two types of heap space.

The most often used is the application heap, which is initialized each time an application is run. If more than one application is currently running, each will have its own application heap and stack; an application is also allowed to subdivide its heap space into two or more smaller heaps.

This heap grows toward an imaginary line separating the heap and stack. The Memory Manager will not allocate space above this line, while a "stack sniffer" examines the stack pointer periodically to make sure the stack has not crossed below the line. Since the stack sniffer does not check after every possible instruction, it is still possible to corrupt the heap without being caught.

The single system heap is allocated the same way as the application heap, but it is part of the system space and is used to store code and data shared by all applications. For example, ROM patches loaded at system initialization time are usually stored here, where they remain resident until the machine is shut down. Most programs will not allocate memory in the system heap directly, although they may use memory blocks that have been previously allocated there.

The Motorola MC68000 of the original Macintosh, Macintosh Plus, and Macintosh SE addresses only 24 bits of memory, or 16 million bytes. Of this, 4 million bytes are available for RAM. The remainder of the address space is allocated for the ROM and memory-mapped input/output to specific hardware devices.

The MC68020 of the Macintosh II supports a full 32-bit address. However, by default it uses a compatibility mode that provides 24-bit addressing. When in this mode, the first 8 Mb are available to address RAM. When the operating system is switched to 32-bit mode, up to 1 gigabyte (Gb) of memory can be addressed.

HEAP MANAGEMENT

The Memory Manager allocates two fundamentally different types of memory blocks in either the system or application heap.

Nonrelocatable blocks are allocated and freed using the NewPtr and DisposPtr functions. These functions are similar in result to the standard Pascal NEW, DISPOSE, and C malloc free functions, in that they return or accept a pointer to a block of memory.

To take advantage of the Mac's efficient memory allocation scheme, most of the heap storage used by a Macintosh program should be in relocatable blocks. This allows the memory manager to move the block to maximize the amount of contiguous memory available.

Such relocatable blocks are referenced via a doubly indirect pointer, which is known as a"handle." The double indirection allows the Memory Manager to update references to the block if it is later moved. Most memory allocated by the Toolbox is in the form of relocatable blocks.

When allocating a relocatable block using NewHandle, the Memory Manager allocates a pointer to this block and then returns a pointer to this pointer. When you deallocate a block using DisposHandle, the Memory Manager deallocates both the block and the direct pointer to it.

Using a handle to reference fields of a memory block requires an extra level of indirection beyond that normally used with pointers. For example, printing code in a Pascal program might include the statements:

```
ph: THPrint;(* Handle to TPrint record *)
...
(* NewHandle returns Handle - coerce the type*)
   ph := THPrint (NewHandle (SIZEOF (TPrint)));
PrintDefault (ph);
width := ph^^.rPage.right - ph^^.rPage.left;
height := ph^^.rPage.bottom - ph^^.rPage.top;
```

where rPage is a record embedded within the TPrint record, and top, left, bottom,and right are fields of rPage. The C equivalent would be:

```
THPrint ph;(* Handle to TPrint struct *)
...
   ph = (THPrint) NewHandle (sizeof (TPrint)) ;
PrintDefault (ph);
width = (*ph)->.rPage.right - (*ph)->.rPage.left;
height = (*ph)->.rPage.bottom - (*ph)->.rPage.top;
```

The pointer to the relocatable block (pointed to by the handle) is termed a "master pointer." If more than one handle references the same block, they do so through the same master pointer.

The Memory Manager allocates master pointers as part of a series of special nonrelocatable blocks. Multiple master pointers are allocated in the same master pointer block, which are normally allocated by an application during its initialization.

Each relocatable and nonrelocatable block includes a block header. This header identifies the size and type of the block: relocatable, nonrelocatable, or free. The header for relocatable blocks also includes a reference to the corresponding master pointer, as illustrated by Figure 2–5.

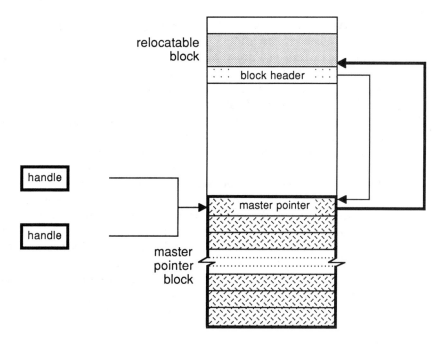

Figure 2–5:   Master Pointers and Handles

To speed and simplify some code, the handle can be temporarily dereferenced to become a singly indirect pointer to the block. That is, your program fetches the value of the master pointer from the address given by the handle and then uses that pointer to directly reference the block. In Pascal, this is often done with the WITH statement, as in:

```
WITH ph^^ DO
   BEGIN
      width := rPage.right - rPage.left;
      height := rPage.bottom - rPage.top;
   END;
```

In C, you might explicitly assign the pointer to a variable, as in the statements:

```
pp = *ph;
width := pp->rPage.right - pp->rPage.left;
height := pp->rPage.bottom - pp->rPage.top;
```

This is known as dereferencing the handle. Such steps, while they may save central processing unit (CPU) cycles, must be chosen with care: Any memory allocation performed while the pointer is being used can cause the pointer to become invalid.

One of the most common mistakes made by programmers new to the Mac is to misuse null (or nil) pointers and handles, as shown in Figure 2–6. Although a few of the OS and Toolbox routines accept a null pointer or handler, most assume that parameters supply a valid memory address.

There are alternatives to using null handles and pointers. If you're passing a string parameter to a system routine, you would normally construct a reference to a string with no characters in it, i.e., one that begins with a 0 byte. An empty handle can also be used with the few routines that dynamically resize the block as needed. For most purposes, null pointers and handles are likely to crash your Mac when a routine attempts to dereference the pointer (or Handle) and instead accesses memory location 0.

Each relocatable block normally has two important state flags. One flag allows your program to lock the block to temporarily prevent it from being relocated during a memory allocation. The second flag indicates that the block is purgeable, allowing it to be changed to a free block if needed by a memory allocation.

Pointers

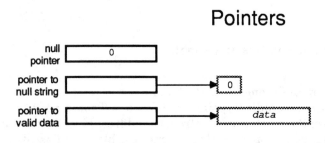

Handles

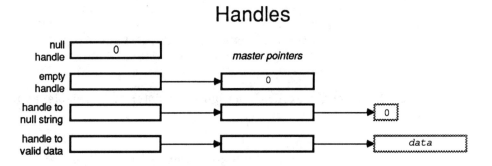

Figure 2–6:   Null Pointers and Handles

The Memory Manager traps HLock, HUnlock, HPurge, and HNoPurge modify the state flags that control what happens to the block during memory allocation. You can also use HGetState to get the current flags all at once and HSetState to assign a new value for these flags.

Although the locked bit will often be used for any relocatable block, the purgeable flag is primarily useful for relocatable blocks that are initialized from values stored on disk. These blocks are allocated through the Resource Manager.

RESOURCES

Among the Macintosh software innovations was the decision to base Macintosh programs on resources. Resources are the equivalent of a simple database for Macintosh software development, providing a standard format for the constant and initialized data used by any program.

The proper use of resources provides a notable benefit over traditional approaches when dealing with the international marketplace. If all the text seen by a user is contained in the application's resources, a program can be translated to run in a foreign country—without making source code available to the translator.

Finally, resources provide an important framework for program design. Resources are normally used in applications to define the user interface, such as windows, menus, and dialogs. Many developers "mock up" the user interface resources of a program before building the code to implement that interface. The use of a resource editor allows someone who doesn't understand technical issues—such as a salesperson—to design or revise the interface to meet user requirements. You should also anticipate that many users may later wish to use a resource editor to change the program's interface, such as the keyboard equivalents of commonly used menu commands.

Despite its many advantages, the resource design has at least one drawback: portability. Each file contains two "forks," or parts: the data fork and the resource fork, which are allocated disk space separately.

Most files you'll find normally have only one component or the other. For example, the Word file that contained this chapter has only a data fork; the Word application, the Finder, and the printer driver all have only resources. Some Macintosh documents have both forks: MPW source files are one example—the text is saved in the data fork, the tab and other settings are saved in the resource fork.

There is no direct analogy to this forked file structure on other computers, which usually have a flag somewhere that indicates whether the file contains program or data. When moved to other operating systems, such as A/UX, the resource and data forks must be stored in separate files.

Every resource has three identifiers that serve to make it unique. The first identifier is a reference to the file that contains the resource, such as the

System file or an individual application. The Resource Manager normally reads resources from one of several files open at the same time and allows your program to specify or identify which file the resource was found in.

The second identifier used in finding a resource is a 32-bit resource type. Normally, this consists of four letters, as in 'MENU', 'WIND', and 'CNTL' for menus, windows, and control information, respectively. However, a few resource names end in a space or number sign, such as 'STR ' and 'STR#', which refer to strings and a list of strings.

Third, each resource within a given type and file should have a unique 16-bit integer, referred to as the resource ID. In most cases, resources that you assign should be numbered between 128 and 32,767. Resources in the range 0 to 127 are reserved for system (Apple-defined) usages; negative IDs are generally used by resources that are grouped with specific code, such as an I/O driver. Instead of the resource ID, a specific resource can also be found using the resource name, a string of 0 to 255 characters. Every resource has a number, but for most resources, the name is unused.

The overall structure of the resource fork of a file is shown in Figure 2-7. Each resource fork contains both the actual resource data and the resource map, which provides an index to where each resource is located. The resource map contains a list of resource types, individual resources, and

resource fork

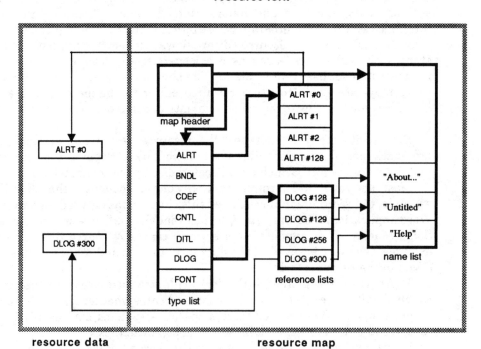

Figure 2-7:   A File's Resource Fork

their resource names. If no resources are included in a file, the resource map is normally omitted and no disk space is occupied by the resource fork.

As suggested by the illustration, each resource of a given type and ID (or name) can be found by tracing the links from the beginning of the resource map. Each link is represented as an offset within the resource map or the resource data, as appropriate.

Normally, a particular resource will be referenced through the appropriate manager routine, e.g., the Menu Manager, Window Manager, or Control Manager. Most such routines only require the resource ID, since they already know the resource type to look for when searching the open resource files of your application.

You can also explicitly find a handle referencing a particular resource given its type and ID using the GetResource trap or given its type and name, using GetNamedResource. The Resource Manager keeps track of the resources currently loaded into memory and will either allocate a new relocatable block or return a handle to an existing block containing the data stored in the corresponding resource.

Each resource also has a 16-bit word that holds resource attributes. One that's often used for menus, for example, is the preload bit, which indicates the resource should be read into memory when the program begins. The attributes also include purgeable and locked bits, which are used by the Memory Manager.

Most resources are stored in the resource file as purgeable. Each time you do a GetResource call for that resource, the resource manager checks to see if it had previously been loaded into memory and has not been purged. If it has been purged (or never loaded), the Resource Manager automatically reads it in again. The use of purgeable resources provides a simple form of virtual memory data storage that is adequate for many applications. When you are done with a resource, you should purge it (if it wasn't stored as purgeable) using HPurge—*never* dispose of it using DisposHandle.

The original copy of the resource in the resource file is distinct from the copy that is currently in memory. Changing resource contents or attributes will have an effect only if the changed resource is later written to disk.

Also, certain resources are not used directly by the Toolbox, but instead are used as a template for filling in the appropriate field of a data structure allocated on the heap. Such templates are defined for menus, windows, controls, dialogs, and alerts, as well as the list of items in a dialog or alert. These templates use resource types 'MENU', 'WIND', 'CNTL', 'DLOG', 'ALRT' and 'DITL', respectively.

MEMORY ALLOCATION

Either directly or indirectly, many of the OS and Toolbox calls used by your program can change the state of the heap. In particular, the Memory Manager may either move or free relocatable blocks used by your program.

If more memory is requested by your program and not enough contiguous space is available, the Memory Manager moves relocatable blocks to obtain more contiguous memory. This process is referred to as "heap compaction."

The master pointers are clustered together to make it easy for the Memory Manager to update the pointer referencing the block after it is moved. However, if your program has its own pointer to the block—created by dereferencing the handle—the Memory Manager will not update that pointer. Such a pointer will still reference the former location of the block, which now contains some other data. If you continue to use the pointer, you can either read meaningless (and possibly invalid) data or write over memory that is being used elsewhere.

Such wild pointers created through heap compaction are a potential source of crashes during program development. Wild pointers will sometimes crash your program immediately, but often the result is a gradual corruption of the program's data until the crash is well removed from the point of inception.

If you need to use a pointer to a relocatable block in a series of statements that may allocate memory, you must lock the block to prevent it from moving during a possible heap compaction. While locked and nonrelocatable blocks are safer for certain types of operations (they won't move during a memory allocation), they also limit the efficiency of the memory relocation scheme. These immovable blocks prevent the consolidation of smaller free blocks into a larger free block during heap compaction.

If compacting the heap does not provide enough contiguous memory, the Memory Manager will next attempt to purge any unused relocatable blocks. Only blocks marked as unlocked and purgeable will be purged.

Marking a block as purgeable using HPurge does not remove it from memory. Instead, the data in the block remains valid until the next time the heap is purged, at which time it is reclaimed by the Memory Manager and any previous references to the block become empty handles. Purgeable blocks are primarily useful for resources, as described earlier. For other types of memory blocks, your program is responsible for regenerating the data in the block if it is needed again.

Although not every memory allocation will compact or purge the heap, any memory allocation can potentially do so. Your program should allow for moving or purging relocatable blocks for either of two types of requests to the Memory Manager:

- When a new block of memory is allocated on the heap

- When an existing block of memory is made larger

These are the direct memory allocation requests. However, many other Macintosh traps used by your program may also allocate or expand memory blocks, thus indirectly causing a heap compaction or purge. The most common ways of implicitly allocating memory are:

- A Resource Manager request to find a particular resource
- Drawing on the screen, since dynamic memory is used to keep track of the changes that have been made
- Calls to routines that may be currently stored on disk

Most Toolbox routines that do anything useful can cause a memory allocation. Simple Toolbox functions that do not have side effects—such as FixMul, GetCtlValue, or AddPt—are safe, as are most of the OS routines that do not explicitly involve memory allocation. Apple provides a list of all the routines that can move or purge memory as an appendix to each edition of *Inside Macintosh*.

Table 2–5 lists when references to relocatable blocks can be used by your program after the heap is compacted or purged. By default, the Memory Manager creates relocatable blocks are created as neither locked nor purgeable. The Resource Manager sets the initial state using the corresponding resource attributes.

Note that a locked block will not be purged by the Memory Manager, even if it is marked as purgeable. Either a locked or purgeable block can always be freed by a DisposHandle.

	Status bits	*Valid*
After heap compaction		
Nonrelocatable		yes
Handle to relocatable	(any)	yes
Pointer to relocatable	Locked	yes
	Unlocked	no
After purging the heap		
Nonrelocatable block	yes	
Relocatable block	Locked	yes
	Nonpurgeable	yes
	Unlocked, purgeable	no

By default, relocatable blocks are allocated as unlocked and nonpurgeable.

Table 2–5:   **Accessing Blocks After Memory Allocation**

CODE RESOURCES

The executable code of a Macintosh program is stored as binary data in the resource fork of an application or other file.

A resource fork is used by all applications of type 'CODE', which contains the machine code for the application. All applications contain multiple code resources, known as segments. When a routine is called in a segment that is not currently in memory, the calling code automatically invokes the Segment Loader, which brings the needed code segment into memory using the Resource Manager and Memory Manager. About the only time you will use the Segment Loader directly is when your program no longer needs a particular segment and marks it as purgeable using the UnloadSeg trap. Strategies for managing code segments and maximizing contiguous available memory in the heap are discussed further in Chapter 3.

Another manager that depends on the Resource Manager is the Package Manager, which handles calls to the Macintosh subroutine libraries that have been grouped as packages. Each package is stored as a resource of type 'PACK', where the resource number is used to select the desired package. Although separate traps are provided for each of the available packages, these all must go through the Package Manager before transferring control to the appropriate package. Although the Package Manager is described as part of the Toolbox, three packages of mathematic functions are considered part of the OS.

Note that calls to other program segments or a package will require a resource to be loaded into memory if it's not already present. As with any such memory request, this can cause a heap compaction. Therefore, although a particular routine may contain no Memory Manager calls, if it's called through the Segment Loader or the Package Manager, it can result in block relocation unless you can guarantee that the resource is already in memory from a previous call.

Finally, the System file includes resources of type 'PTCH' to provide patches to the ROM traps. When the Macintosh is booted from disk, the ROM version determines the ID of the 'PTCH' resource that is loaded into RAM.

2.3 QuickDraw

The basis for all Macintosh graphics is QuickDraw, the standard drawing manager. QuickDraw is optimized for fast two-dimensional drawing using integer coordinates.

All Macintoshes include this classic QuickDraw design, which provides for monochrome display and limited color printing. Beginning with the Macintosh II, some machines include a version of QuickDraw that supports color output. To allow upward compatibility for existing programs, color operations are provided using as a superset of the classic QuickDraw framework.

BASIC CONCEPTS

The more than 100 routines of QuickDraw provide the foundation for the Macintosh user interface Toolbox. These routines provide a complete and fast set of bit-mapped graphics primitives.

The basis of QuickDraw is the coordinate plane, with two coordinates as 16-bit integers in the range [-32767, +32767], inclusive. The QuickDraw plane does not include the coordinate value -32768.

Each drawing space has its own coordinate space and contents. Such a drawing space—or graphics port—is referenced through QuickDraw GrafPort data structure. Each program will typically use multiple GrafPorts simultaneously.

Within a GrafPort, a Point is used to represent an arbitrary location. A Point is stored as a Pascal record (C struct) with two consecutive coordinates of the form (vertical, horizontal). Normally, the upper left corner of any GrafPort is the point (0,0), while the horizontal and vertical coordinates always increase toward the lower-right corner.

A Rect (rectangle) consists of two points, or four coordinates, in the order of top, left, bottom, right. Except for the QuickDraw traps `Move`, `MoveTo`, `Line`, and `LineTo*` , Toolbox operations use either a `Point` or `Rect` to express a position in the QuickDraw plane.

The actual coordinate lines that intersect in a QuickDraw point are infinitesimally small and do not correspond to anything you can see on the screen. Instead, four points form the corners of a displayed dot (pixel) on the Macintosh screen. Any visible drawing operation changes pixels, although the drawing location is typically expressed in terms of points, rectangles, and other GrafPort coordinates.

Most QuickDraw operations involve the pen, which draws a specified width and height below and to the right (toward increasing coordinates) from the specified point or coordinate line. Lines are drawn in the pen size, as shown by Figure 2–8. Polygons are drawn as a series of lines, with the pen always below and to the right of the line. Other closed shapes are drawn within the boundaries of the coordinate lines so that a wider pen does not make the outer dimensions of the shape larger.

Macintosh graphics operations typically require bitmaps to hold the actual bits or display pixels. A bitmap is the memory image of the display

---

* These traps require the horizontal and vertical coordinates as explicit parameters in the opposite order as specified for a Point. The coordinate order is also reversed for parameters to the SetRect trap, which expects left, top, right, and bottom.

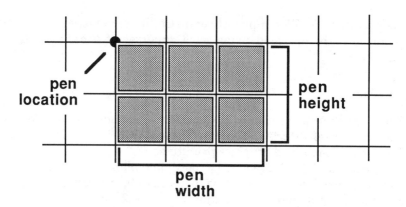

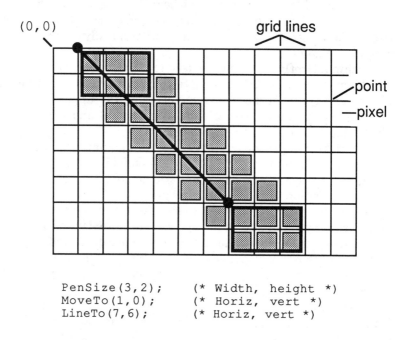

```
PenSize(3,2);      (* Width,  height *)
MoveTo(1,0);       (* Horiz,  vert *)
LineTo(7,6);       (* Horiz,  vert *)
```

Figure 2–8:   QuickDraw Pen

pixels, with a single bit per pixel for black and white displays. The bitmap also includes a Rect that specifies the boundaries of the bitmap. A bitmap that is implicitly used by many QuickDraw operations is referenced by QuickDraw's global variable ScreenBits, which corresponds to the primary display screen. Other operations are performed on an off-screen bitmap, with CopyBits later used to merge the data onto the screen or current GrafPort.

A simple and commonly used bit image is the 8 by 8 matrix known as a pattern, which is used by both QuickDraw primitives and as part of the QuickDraw pen. Other standard bit images include the 16 by 16 display cursor (e.g., the watch), and the 32 by 32 icon (such as the trash can in the Finder.)

Figure 2–9 shows examples to illustrate the capabilities of QuickDraw's primitive operations; each numbered example represents a separate primitive. The standard QuickDraw operations include drawing text, lines, and five geometric shapes: rectangles, rounded-corner rectangles, ovals, arc of an oval, and polygons. Note that oval operations allow you to draw a circle or elongated circle, but the latter shapes are not ellipses.

Operations on these standard shapes include drawing the boundaries (e.g., FrameRect), filling the interior with the background pattern (EraseOval), filling the interior with an arbitrary pattern (PaintRRect), or inverting the pattern of the interior (InvertPolygon). As shown in the figure, painting and framing a single shape actually represent two separate QuickDraw primitives.

Operations can also be performed on more arbitrary shapes known as regions. The simplest possible region is a rectangle, while complex regions can be defined in terms of individual pixels in a bitmap.

QuickDraw also provides primitive operations to draw text at the current pen location and to measure the size of characters and strings. The bitmap drawn for each character is prepared by QuickDraw using the Font Manager.

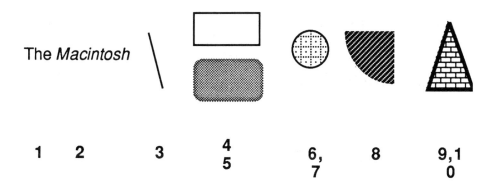

The primitive operations:

1. DrawString
2. DrawString
3. Line
4. FrameRect
5. FillRoundRect
6. FrameOval
7. FillOval
8. FillArc
9. FramePoly
10. FillPoly

Figure 2–9:   Ten QuickDraw Primitives

A series of QuickDraw primitive operations can be recorded and stored in a picture and then later displayed again. Such a QuickDraw picture is the standard format for interchanging graphics on the Mac between different programs. Often stored as a resource of type 'PICT', a picture allows a drawing to be included in a written report and an illustration prepared for screen display to be accurately reproduced on a laser printer. These pictures store a series of symbolic opcodes representing the QuickDraw operations needed to redraw the image. Pictures can be saved in a file or passed between applications using the clipboard.

DRAWING PORTS

Most applications will have multiple GrafPorts in use at any one time. Each new window opened using the Window or Dialog Manager allocates and initializes a new GrafPort data structure. GrafPorts are also used when drawing text and graphics that are being printed using the Printing Manager.

QuickDraw will normally have more than one port available for drawing but can only use one of those ports at any one time. This port is referenced by its global variable thePort, and changed by the SetPort and GetPort traps.

Each GrafPort includes a reference to a specific screen bitmap, such as a portion of the display screen. The port includes an indication of the corresponding device, usually either the screen or a printer. Each port has a boundary rectangle, current pen location, foreground and background colors, and patterns.

GrafPorts are allocated as nonrelocatable blocks on the heap. They are referenced by a GrafPtr pointer. Those created by the Window and Dialog Manager include additional information after the end of the port, as required by those managers.

A slightly different version of a GrafPort is used for drawing using color QuickDraw. Such color ports are indicated by a negative value of portBits.rowBytes field of a GrafPort, which otherwise would be a meaningless value.

COLOR QUICKDRAW

The Macintosh II includes a color version of QuickDraw, supported by two new managers and a new package to manage colors. In addition, the color graphics routines interact with color display devices and their corresponding drivers, as illustrated by Figure 2–10.

In the classic QuickDraw, each display pixel can have one of two possible values, white or black. Each pixel can thus be represented by a single bit.

In color displays, each pixel may require multiple bits. The number of bits used for each pixel is referred to as the pixel depth. Thus, bitmaps are

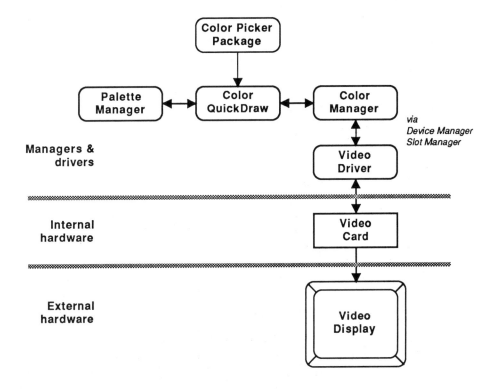

Figure 2–10: Macintosh II Color Graphics Interface

inadequate for color QuickDraw. Instead, to display an arbitrary screen image requires using pixel maps, provided by the PixMap data structure.

Cursors and icons are similarly extended to use multibit pixels. Patterns are also extended, but unlike their monochrome brethren, they can have a dimension of any power of 2, not just 8 by 8 pixel patterns. The classic QuickDraw bitmaps, cursors, icons, and patterns can also be used but are limited to only two colors.

Instead of the standard GrafPort, color QuickDraw operations normally allocate a CGrafPort. Although many of the fields have the same significance in the same place, a few fields are treated differently. Instead of embedding a screen bitmap and three pattern data structures, a CGrafPort uses handles to a PixMap for the screen and PixPat structures for the current patterns.

Colors are normally described by a 48-bit absolute specification, consisting of three unsigned 16-bit integers representing the red, green, and blue components, the three primary colors used in video displays. These three coordinates uniquely describe each possible color in RGB space. Figure 2–11 shows this coordinate system, including the eight possible extremes of the RGB color cube. As a subset of its capabilities, color QuickDraw can display

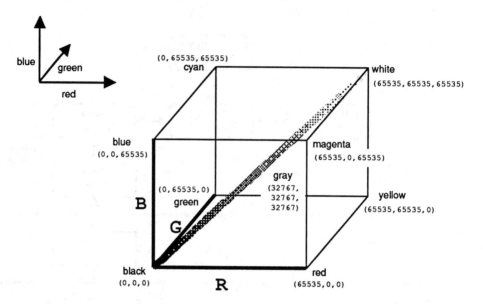

Figure 2–11: RGB Coordinate Space

65,536 possible gray levels, ranging from pure black to pure white, as represented by the diagonal of the RGB cube. This is the only option on video displays that support varying intensities but no colors.

The red, green, and blue coordinates are defined using a RGBColor data structure. RGBColor is used by most Color QuickDraw operations that set a color. The Pascal definition is equivalent to:

```
RGBColor = RECORD
    red, green, blue: INTEGER;
        { actually [0,65535] }
END;
```

while the C definition is equivalent to:

```
typedef struct RGBColor {
    unsigned short red, green, blue;
};
```

For example, the RGBForeColor trap sets the current drawing color and takes a single RGBColor parameter. The RGBBackColor parameter similarly sets the background color. Other operations implicitly define their own colors, such as those using PixMap and PixPat structures.

However, an absolute color is only used as a request specifying the ideal characteristics of the color to be displayed. QuickDraw chooses the closest available color, depending on the limitations of the device and the other colors currently being displayed. The most significant limitation is on the number of colors simultaneously displayed.

A Macintosh II with 4-bit color can only display 16 distinct colors at one time. A display card with 8-bit color can display 256 distinct colors at one time, but the RGB space defines more than 1014 possible colors. If your application were to successively call RGBForeColor with black and each of the 65,535 possible reds, there would be no way for color QuickDraw to display all distinct colors on display devices limited to 256 simultaneous colors.

Instead, each pixel in a pixMap contains an index into a Color Look-Up Table, or CLUT. The CLUT contains an index and the corresponding RGBColor value. No color can be displayed on the screen that does not correspond to a color in the CLUT, although some display cards may have fixed color assignments.

The depth of each pixel must be a power of 2: the Macintosh II implementation limits this depth to 1, 2, 4, or 8 bits per pixel. For a specific depth, the possible index ranges from 0 to 2depth-1. For example, an 8-bit depth allows indexes from 0 to 255. The first color index (0) should be white, while the maximum color index should be black.

A depth of 1 corresponds to a monochrome display. This corresponds to the classic QuickDraw GrafPort using the following two pixel values:

Color	Index	Red, Green, Blue
White	0	65535,65535,65535
Black	1	0, 0, 0

Note the difference in the sign convention—a pixel value of 0 is white, while in the RGB model, the coordinates (0,0,0) correspond to black.

The classic QuickDraw supports 8 possible colors using the ForeColor and BackColor traps. Although these calls had no effect with the monochrome display of the original Macintosh, they did allow color printing on the ImageWriter II. These 8 colors are predefined as part of the default color table, as shown in Table 2–6. Under color QuickDraw, both old- and new-style color traps—ForeColor and RGBForeColor—can be used with either a GrafPort or CGrafPort. Unless a new color trap is used to create a CGrafPort, however, drawing is limited to these 8 colors.

The default color table is 'clut' resource with ID No. 127. Applications that define their own 'clut' resources use IDs from 128 to 1023; the resource ID is used as a unique identifier to distinguish between multiple color tables in use. Dynamically allocated color tables have identifiers of 1024 or greater.

Color	ForeColor parameter	Equivalent RGBForeColor parameter		
		Red	Green	Blue
blackColor	33	0	0	0
yellowColor	69	64512	62333	1327
magentaColor	137	62167	2134	34028
redColor	205	56683	2242	1698
cyanColor	273	577	43860	60159
greenColor	341	0	25775	4528
blueColor	409	0	0	54272
whiteColor	30	65535	65535	65535

In a monochrome port, all but `whiteColor` are displayed as black.

Table 2–6:   RGB Values for Classic QuickDraw Colors

The color table resources are among several that are new to the color implementation of QuickDraw. Others include color palettes (used by the Palette Manager) and tables to correct for the nonlinearity of the display monitor. These resources are among those listed in Table 2–7.

For other types of resource a new color resource type replaces a standard Toolbox resource, with a color table implicitly included in the resource. For example, color programs might use a `'ccsr'` color cursor instead of the standard two-tone `'CURS'` resource.

Still other color resources provide a color table to supplement one of the standard Toolbox resource templates. This allows the resource template to be used with machines that do not support color, while at the same time allocating a color graphics port on machines that do support color.

For example, a `'WIND'` resource defines a Macintosh window, while a `'wctb'` defines the color table used to display that window. The system includes resources to provide default color mappings for all applications.

COLOR TABLE MANAGEMENT

The remaining two managers supplied with color QuickDraw allow complete control over the color table and thus the colors available to any program. They won't be needed by applications that use color for highlighting, such as a word processor, but may be required by programs that are primarily intended for graphics, such as painting or image processing programs.

The Palette Manager provides a mechanism by which applications may request a set of entries for a shared color table Each window has an associated palette of desired colors, which the Palette Manager uses to update the shared color table. Each color in a palette has a standard usage, which determines if (or when) the Palette Manager will reserve a corresponding entry in the color table.

New color resource types

Description	Color resource
Color look-up table	`clut`
Color (gamma) correction table	`gama`
Color palette	`pllt`

Color resource replaces standard resource

Description	Standard resource	Color resource
Cursor	CURS	`ccsr`
Icon	ICON	`cicn`
Pattern	PAT	`ppat`
Picture†	PICT	`PICT`

Color resource supplements standard resource

Description	Standard resource	Color resource
Alert template§	ALRT	`actb`
Control template§	CNTL	`cctb`
Dialog (alert) item template	DITL	`ictb`
Dialog template§	DLOG	`dctb`
Font§	NFNT	`fctb`
Menu	MENU	`mctb`
Window template§	WIND	`wctb`

† Version code within picture identifies it as color resource
§ Same format as a color look-up table

Table 2–7:   Color Resource Types

In specifying a window's palette, your program can specify a desired color and, optionally, a tolerance for how close a color must be to match an existing entry. If the approximate color is not already available, the Palette Manager will attempt to make a new entry in the color table for the desired color.

Once a window has a palette, color drawing in that window can set the foreground and background colors using indexes to the colors of the palette. Palette entries that request a matching color will be used by the Palette Manager in allocating colors between all open windows. Palette Manager routines also allow for the color table to be loaded from a palette and vice versa.

The lowest-level interface between color QuickDraw and color devices is handled by the Color Manager. Its primary function is managing entries in the color look-up table.

The Color Manager allows a program to replace color entries in the color table and allows you to directly look up the absolute RGB value for any pixel value in the current color table. More importantly, it provides a way to obtain the pixel value for the entry that is closest to a specified RGB value, which is used by QuickDraw to support drawing with absolute RGB values. To speed the look-up, the Color Manager builds an inverse color table that maps as many as 32,768 (215) of the possible RGB values to the nearest pixel value.

The color table has a finite capacity (256 entries for 8-bit pixels) that must be shared by all applications running simultaneously in a multitasking OS, as well as by desk accessories.

With 256 colors provided by 8-bit color, it's possible to support both the breadth of colors available from the monitor and at the same time provide application-specific colors. To provide breadth, the color table could be loaded with representative combinations of the three primaries. This is, in fact, the scheme used provided by the default color table.

All possible combinations of six intensities of red, green, and blue require 216 of the 256 available entries, assuring a reasonable approximation for most colors. The remaining 40 colors allow more precise pure hues or grays but are also the best candidates for replacement if your program requires its own color table entries.

With more restricted color tables, you may find that it doesn't make as much sense to try to develop application-specific palettes. For 4-bit (16-color) display, the default provides black, white, several shades of gray, and a representative assortment of hues. The 2-bit (4-color) color table provides black, white, light gray, and dark gray, although you might find it more satisfying to combine the two grays into medium gray and add one color— such as red—for emphasis.

Color QuickDraw also allows you to simulate other colors by combining available colors as part of a pixel pattern. This technique emulating available colors is known as dithering. The MakeRGBPat trap accepts a RGBColor parameter and returns a dithered PixMap pattern that emulates the specified color. Palette entries can also request a dithered color if no matching color is available.

The original QuickDraw did not include error handling, assuming beforehand that all requested operations are valid. The new color QuickDraw and Color Manager do include some error handling, and the QDError trap returns the error code for either.

ALTERNATE COLOR MODELS

The Color Picker Package provides a standard user interface for picking colors. It does not change the color table but instead supports a dialog that returns a specific selected color. This dialog can be called by your program to allow the user to select a color.

The Color Picker Package also provides conversion routines between RGB coordinates and three other standard specifications used in color graphics. One such model is Hue (combination of colors), Saturation (purity of color), and brightness (intensity Value), referred to as HSV. The package also provides conversion for Hue, Lightness, Saturation (HLS), and cyan-magenta-yellow (CMY) coordinates.

Like RGB values, all three coordinate systems use 16-bit unsigned values. However, the coordinates are interpreted with an implicit divisor of 216; therefore, values range from 0.0 to 0.99998 (65535/65536).

The HSV model more directly corresponds to the artist's view of color, with a pure hue combined with white to reduce saturation and black to reduce brightness. For example, pink is a red hue with less than 100 percent saturation. The user dialog displayed by the GetColor trap allows a color to be specified using either RGB or HSV values.

The three HSV coordinates correspond to a conical coordinate system, in which the hue is an angle on a color circle and brightness is the vertical coordinate. The saturation is a radial coordinate; zero saturation (S=0.0) corresponds to shades of gray, as shown by the center line in Figure 2–12. A brightness of V=0.0 is black, while S=0.0 and V=1.0 displays pure white.

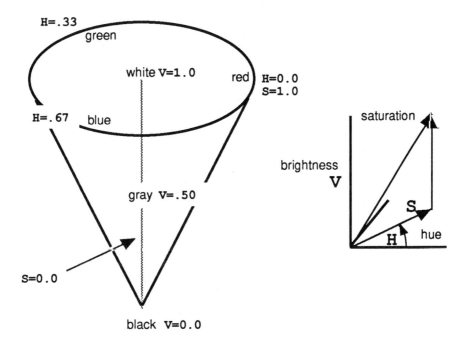

Figure 2–12: Hue, Saturation, Brightness (HSV) Coordinates

Colors with both 100 percent saturation and brightness represent the rim of the cone, with the hue coordinate specifying the combination of any two of the three primary colors. The sloping side surface of the cone also has 100 percent saturation but mixes these pure colors with black.

When compared to the RGB cube, the top surface of the cone (V=1.0) corresponds to three faces of the RGB cube, those shown with at least one of the RGB values = 65,535. The rim of the cone, with S=1.0, represents the six cube edges connecting red, yellow, green, cyan, blue, and magenta vertices. The cone's gray center line maps to the gray diagonal of the RGB cube.

As the name might suggest, the hue and saturation coordinates have similar meaning using the HLS model, with the hue an angular coordinate and saturation a radial coordinate in a circle of colors. However, in HLS coordinates, the circle of fully saturated colors is between a pair of cones with median lightness (L=0.5). These colors are diluted with black in one direction (toward L=0.0) and white in the other direction (L=1.0), which represent the vertex of each cone. Therefore, for L<0.5, increasing intensity from black increases color purity, as with HSV coordinates. For L>0.5, increasing intensity toward white decreases purity, as shown in Figure 2–13.

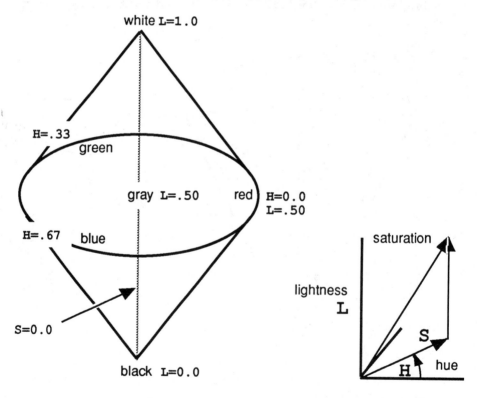

Figure 2–13: Hue, Lightness, Saturation (HLS) Coordinates

HLS coordinates are stored by the Color Picker as hue, saturation, and order to maximize the similarity to the HSV model. However, the abbreviation "HSL" should not be used with users as it is easily confused with "HSV" and does not conform to standard graphics terminology.

The CMY representation is the exact complement of the QuickDraw's standard RGB model. Red, green, and blue are additive primaries used for transmitted light, such as for a video display. Cyan, magenta, and yellow are the subtractive primaries used with reflected colors, such as combining paint pigments on paper. The CMY model corresponds to the standard color printing technique, such as the color ribbon of the ImageWriter II. Actual color printing often uses a fourth pigment, black, to assure neutral grays and maximum density for black.

The CMY coordinates are simply the complement of the RGB coordinates. They correspond to reversing the orientation of the axes in the RGB color cube, with the origin at the white vertex, and maximum saturation of all components corresponding to black.

FONTS

QuickDraw relies closely on the Font Manager to retrieve and preinterpret the resources that describe each font. The QuickDraw traps `TextFont`, `TextSize`, and `TextStyle` set the font family, size, and drawing style to be used for subsequent text operations in the current port, and QuickDraw uses the Font Manager to retrieve the appropriate font definition from the system.

Most fonts define the mapping of an 8-bit number (0 to 255) to one of the standard Macintosh display characters. Such fonts include the 95 printing characters (32 to 126 decimal) of the standard ASCII character set and usually include at least some of the 89 extended Macintosh characters defined by Apple. These characters support foreign languages, typographic symbols, and a limited set of mathematical symbols. Although this standard mapping is used by most fonts, it's only a convention, and the Font Manager doesn't really care whether character No. 48 is "0" or a "%".

Some special fonts will include none of the standard mappings. The pictographic Cairo and Tallesin fonts provide cute little houses and trees, while the Adobe Systems' Sonata font provides LaserWriter-quality musical notation. Fonts that require more than 256 characters, such as the Kanji font used in writing Japanese, define characters using two or more successive bytes.

Each character can be drawn with a particular character style. The most commonly used styles are italic, bold, underline, and plain—the absence of any style. Additional styles—outline, shadow, condensed, expanded—are less often used. All possible combinations of styles—bold italic, outline shadow expanded—are allowed.

All characters of the same font and size will have the same vertical spacing, but most fonts, the proportional fonts, have a different width for each character based on the character and style. A few fixed-width fonts, notably Monaco and Courier, are useful for program listings.

Fonts are described as a series of resources. When drawing a font, the Font Manager looks for a resource of type 'FOND', which describes a family of related fonts. The resource ID is the same as the family number, which is how the font is referenced by QuickDraw and TextEdit. The resource name is the same as the font family name; the Font Manager provides a trap to look for a specific font name and returns its corresponding number.

Two font families have a special predefined significance.

The system font is used to draw the menus and as the default display font for certain interactive windows, such as dialogs. The system global variables SysFontFam and SysFontSiz specify the system font and size, respectively. For U.S. Macintoshes, this will be Chicago (font 0) in 12 point. However, in Japan, the system font is Kyoto, while in Arabic countries it will be Al Qahira (Arabic for "Cairo").

The application font should normally be used as the default font for new documents. The font number is stored in system global ApFontId, although the constant applFont (1) is automatically equivalenced to the same font. The normal application font is Geneva, but it can easily be changed by any system.

Most font families include several sizes of the same font, such as Geneva-9, Geneva-12, Geneva-14, and so on. The 'FOND' resource should include character size and spacing information for all fonts in the family. These tables can include special spacing rules for overlapping certain character pairs, a simple form of kerning.

The font family may also reference several related fonts of different styles, such as Times Roman (plain), Times Bold, Times Italic, etc. The 'FOND' resource always includes a list of font sizes and styles with the resource ID for the appropriate font. The Font Manager first checks for a 'NFNT' resource, then a 'FONT' resource with the corresponding ID. The two resources have a similar format, containing the bitmap for each defined character.

What's the difference between 'FOND', 'FONT', and 'NFNT'? Applications that include a menu of fonts normally do so using the call AddResMenu ('FONT'), which will display all unique 'FOND' and 'FONT' names. It will ignore any 'NFNT' resource names, allowing resources such as Times Bold and Times Italic to be used as part of the Times resource family, without showing up in the font menu.

If there's an entry in the 'FOND' resource for the correct size but not the correct style, the Font Manager returns the necessary parameters to Quick-Draw for constructing the appropriate style from the nearest possible style, normally plain. These parameters are calculated with regard to the current

GrafPort device—typically the display or a printer—using Device Manager calls.

If the Font Manager does not find a font of the appropriate size, it will adapt another size of the same font. The exact approach has changed between revisions of the Font Manager. In the 128K ROM and later your program can use the SetFScaleDisable trap to disable the scaling of a different size. Instead, the Font Manager uses a smaller font, scaling the surrounding spaces (but not the characters) up to the appropriate size.

The later ROMs also include an option to space text using fractions of a QuickDraw coordinate. The 128K ROM rounds to the nearest half, while color QuickDraw allows an arbitrary fractional precision in a CGrafPort.

Color QuickDraw also allows an 'NFNT' resource to include a corresponding 'fctb' resource, which contains a standard QuickDraw color table to define a color for each pixel of a font pixmap. An important use for this is displaying gray scale fonts to reduce the jagged edges of characters and increase the apparent resolution. Using gray levels, a 72-dpi display screen can be made to look like a 300-dpi LaserWriter.

The Font Manager does not display the various nonprinting control codes that can be generated from the keyboard, including Backspace, Return, and the arrow keys. In fact, the Font Manager maps binary codes to displayed characters but has no role in translating the keys you press to those same codes. Understanding that translation requires examining how the Macintosh coordinates various types of external interactions as a series of "events."

2.4 The Toolbox

The Macintosh Toolbox provides the routines to implement the characteristics of what users have come to recognize as the Macintosh. This includes overlapping windows, pull-down menus, scroll bars, and dialogs. It also includes less visible but equally important parts of the Macintosh interface, such as mouse interactions (events) and transferring data between applications (the clipboard).

As we've already seen, graphics on the Macintosh are built around QuickDraw and the Font Manager portions of the Toolbox. The Toolbox managers are also very heavy users of the Memory Manager and Resource Manager.

EVENTS

Many computer programs have been built around modal interaction in which the program has several possible states and expects a certain user input at each state. For example, many mainframe programs designed for unsophisticated users present a list of a choices and require the user to choose from that list.

This makes it easy for the programmer—the only valid input is from the restricted list. Typically these programs are keyboard controlled, so it's merely a matter of checking the character (or word) against the list of valid responses and then branching to the appropriate logic. The display is never more complicated than a few lines of text. Many PC programs also exhibit this style of input, with the list selections made through cryptic key combinations, like Control-Q, Control-S to save a file.

Unfortunately, this interface is very counterintuitive because it is modal. Instead of telling the program what to do, first you must give the program the command to put it in the appropriate mode—and, of course, not all commands are valid in all modes.

To the degree it is possible, the Macintosh interface provides a modal-less interface. If a user wants to do something, he or she just does it. When you're driving a car, you don't go into "select radio mode" to change a station or "select transmission mode" to shift a gear; you just do it.

Providing such an interface is more akin to real-time programming. Rather than giving the user a short list of possible actions at any one time, your program must be prepared for the actions to come in any order. If certain actions are not possible at present, such as saving a document when none is open, the program should provide visual feedback to the user to indicate that the operation is not possible.

A Macintosh program is controlled by the user in one of two ways: by keystrokes or by mouse operations. These are but two of the possible interactions a program must deal with, interactions that are known as "events."

You could write your program to poll for events: check with one routine to see if a key has been pushed, a second to watch the mouse button, a third to check for any change in the desktop display. If your program took any significant amount of time to respond to one action (perhaps the user chose "Save" from the File menu), it might miss the next action, or, at the very least, get subsequent actions out of order.

Instead, the Macintosh OS and Toolbox keep track of all of these events for you; the list of pending events is known as the "event queue." The ROM includes separate event managers in the OS and the Toolbox for adding to and querying this event queue.

The Operating System Event Manager posts most types of events but is rarely called directly by an application. However, it may sometimes be necessary for your program to clear out any pending events, using the FlushEvents trap. For example, after a serious error, you might force the user to enter a new response to a warning message, cancelling any previous keystrokes or mouse clicks.

Most of the time, a program will use the Toolbox Event Manager (often referred to simply as the "Event Manager") to query the event queue. The GetNextEvent trap can be used to retrieve events, either by type or in the order received, and act on them one at a time; the WaitNextEvent trap is similar, but is designed to allow idle time to be reclaimed by other applications.

The capacity of the event queue is finite. If your program is not quick enough in servicing the events, events will be discarded if an event is generated when the queue is full. This is mainly a problem with interpreted programs handling keyboard events, for which a fast typist can generate 10 per second, but should not be a problem for programs written with a compiled language such as MPW C or MPW Pascal.

The events returned by GetNextEvent include the display-related events generated by other managers in the Toolbox, as well as the low-level keyboard, mouse, and I/O events. The Toolbox Event Manager is also used by programs to get the current state of the mouse or keyboard.

Along with the type of each event, the event managers will return the time of the event, the state of the mouse button, and the position of the Shift, Caps Lock, Option, and Command ("cloverleaf") keys. More recent keyboards (those using the Apple DeskTop Bus) use an open Apple symbol ⌘ in addition to the cloverleaf.

Some event types include additional information. For example, keyDown events will also include both the number of the key pressed and its corresponding extended ASCII value. Since Apple supplies one keyboard layout for the United States and Canada and a half-dozen different keyboards for foreign languages, the correspondence between these two values can vary, and you generally should use the ASCII value. Figure 2–14 shows the extended ASCII values for the Macintosh character set.

WINDOWS

Programs do their drawing within windows. The Window Manager creates and removes the windows, controls their ordering, and provides routines to allow you to determine which window a given point is in.

When creating a new window using the Window Manager, window parameters may be supplied directly to the NewWindow trap or by the GetNewWindow trap, which references a window template resource of type 'WIND'. The parameters include a location rectangle, a title, and a front-to-back position in relation to other windows. The type of window to be drawn is determined by numeric parameter, as shown by Figure 2–15.

The window type determines whether the window title is displayed and also whether the grow box (in the lower left corner) and zoom box (in the upper left corner) are shown. Symbolic names for these types include noGrowDocProc and ZoomDocProc. The display of the go-away (or close) box is determined by a separate parameter in a Window Manager call.

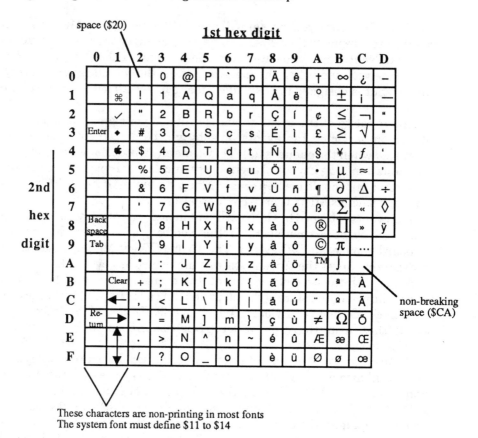

These characters are non-printing in most fonts
The system font must define $11 to $14

Figure 2–14: Extended Macintosh Character Set

Each displayed window is divided into two parts, the content region and the frame. The Window Manager draws the frame, and your program is responsible for filling the content region.

The content region of each window is a separate QuickDraw GrafPort or CGrafPort for color QuickDraw. Additional fields are allocated by the Window Manager after those defined for QuickDraw. As with a GrafPort (CGrafPort), a window is allocated as a nonrelocatable block on the heap, with a WindowPtr (CWindowPtr) returned by GetNewWindow or NewWindow to reference the window record.

A WindowPtr is an equivalent type to GrafPtr; therefore, this pointer must be typecast to the WindowPeek (CWindowPeek) type to access the window-specific fields. For example, the windowKind field is set to a negative value for a desk accessory, 2 for a window used by the Dialog Manager, and values greater than 7 to indicate application-specific types of windows.

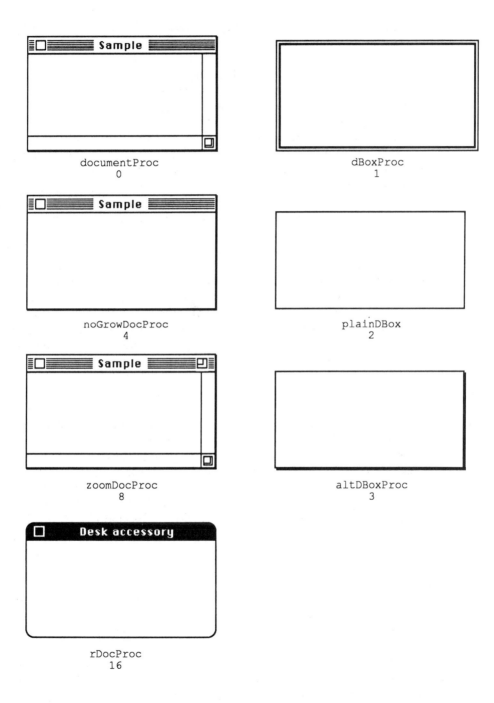

documentProc
0

dBoxProc
1

noGrowDocProc
4

plainDBox
2

zoomDocProc
8

altDBoxProc
3

rDocProc
16

Figure 2–15: Standard Window Types

Because the frame of each window is not within its corresponding port, the Window Manager creates a special GrafPort (CGrafPort) to draw the frames. This Window Manager port is the union of all available display screens, minus the menu bar, and corresponds to what the user sees as the desktop. A pointer to this port is returned by the GetWMgrPort (GetCWMgrPort) trap, but only the Window Manager (and the window framing procedures) draw in this port.

The most elaborate functions of the Window Manager involve the coordination of overlapping windows and their interactions. For each window, the manager will generate an activate event when the window becomes the frontmost (active) window and another such event when it is no longer the active window. This allows the program to give a distinctive appearance to the contents of the active window, as suggested by the user interface standard.

Separately, covering any displayable area of a window will add the missing area to the update region. When that window is uncovered, the Window Manager generates an update event, and your program must redraw that portion of the window contained in the update region. Creating a new window generates an update event for the entire window. For windows used to display a fixed contents, a program can store a QuickDraw picture in the window's data record, and the Window Manager will handle update events automatically.

DIALOGS AND CONTROLS

Displayed within a window, controls provide a way for the user to perform some well-defined action. Many controls display a current state, such as true, or 50 percent, and allow the user to change that state. The Control Manager takes care of drawing controls and interpreting mouse events.

Each control is handled by a control definition procedure, or 'CDEF' resource, which may support several different variant types of related controls. Two control definition procedures are predefined. One supports scroll bars, which return a value proportionate to the position of the indicator along the scroll bar.

The second standard procedure draws pushbuttons, check boxes, and radio buttons. For each of these three button variants the user clicks on the button to change a state. A pushbutton (or just "button") performs an immediate action, a check box displays a boolean value, and radio buttons are grouped to provide a list of mutually exclusive alternatives. Controls may be created by the Control Manager using values in a 'CNTL' resource template. One of the fields is an integer defining the control type—the definition procedure and variation—as shown in Figure 2–16. The Control Manager will also support other types of controls if you write your own definition procedure.

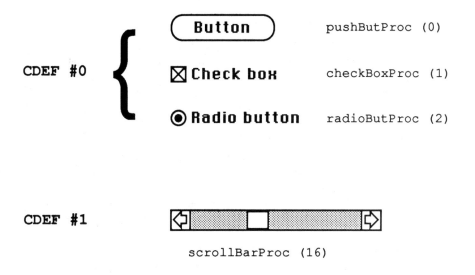

CDEF #0

Button   pushButProc (0)

☒ Check box   checkBoxProc (1)

◉ Radio button   radioButProc (2)

CDEF #1

scrollBarProc (16)

Figure 2–16: Standard Control Types

Controls are often used in conjunction with the Dialog Manager, which supports dialog boxes and alerts. As defined by the Macintosh user interface, these are special types of windows that are normally in front of all other windows and require some specific user response. Alerts are normally for errors or confirming user actions that might be irreversible. Dialog boxes can be used for any other operation for which a list of values and alternatives are appropriate.

The Dialog Manager displays a new dialog or alert based on parameters provided by a template resource. Each dialog template is a resource of type 'DLOG', while an alert template resource is of type 'ALRT'. Both contain information similar to that used by windows, such as the position of the dialog (alert) on the screen.

Both resources reference a dialog item list, a resource of type 'DITL'. Each item in the list may include a fixed text message, an editable text field, one of the three button controls, or direct references to a 'CNTL', 'ICON', or 'PICT' resource. If none of these types is appropriate, the programmer can define his or her own type of dialog item, known as a user item.

The boundaries of a dialog box (alert) are handled by the Window Manager. When a mouse event is detected in the dialog, or the entire dialog needs to be redrawn, the Dialog Manager calls on the Toolbox routine appropriate for updating each item.

Depending heavily on the Dialog Manager is the Standard File Package, which provides the standard interface for selecting a file. Routines from the package display two different types of dialogs: one (SFGetFile) corresponds to the "Open..." menu selection, the other (SFPutFile) to the "Save As..." function, as shown in Figure 2–17. The Standard File Package also makes extensive use of the File Manager.

To edit text items within a dialog box, the Dialog Manager uses TextEdit. TextEdit is the standard Toolbox Manager for displaying and editing text within a window.

The basic TextEdit routines are adequate for simple program source editors that use a single text font, size, and style and are limited to documents of 32K or less. The text is organized as a series of Return-delimited lines, which do not contain special characters, such as a Tab.

TextEdit provides text insertion, automatic word wrap and word breaking, scrolling, and cut and paste operations. All the operations associated with a particular block of text are performed using a TEHandle reference to a TERec structure, which contains current information about the text.

The extended TextEdit of the 256K ROM provides for different fonts and styles within the same document. The text is broken up into a series of runs, each of which contains one or more characters of the same font, size, and style. Each run references an entry in the style table, which defines the corresponding font information.

A program can determine whether it's using the new- or old-style text by examining the txSize field of the TERec. For the standard TextEdit, this is a positive integer specifying the font size; for the extended TextEdit, it's -1.

The extended TextEdit has also been enhanced to provide built-in text editing capabilities for foreign languages with dissimilar alphabets, as provided by the Script Manager.

INTERNATIONALIZATION.

The Macintosh includes the most elaborate effort to date by a U.S. computer manufacturer to isolate differences between various languages and national customs. Macintosh fonts include characters to display the standard European languages, while different keyboards correspond to national standards. A Dutch Macintosh includes a British keyboard, while French-speaking Canadians use a keyboard that is different from the one used in France.

Other differences require explicit logic on the part of your program. Most of these differences are parameterized by the International Utilities Package, which uses 'INTL', 'itl0', 'itl1' and 'itl2' resources stored in the System file to obtain the appropriate parameter.

These parameters include fairly obvious differences—such as the spelling of the days of the week and the months of the year or the symbols for the local currency.

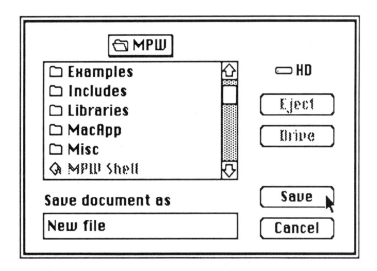

SFGetFile()

SFPutFile()

Figure 2–17: Dialogs from Standard File Package

However, Americans who have never studied a foreign language or traveled abroad may be unaware of the many other country-specific customs that we take as the norm. The value of π may be 3.14159 in the United States, but in France it's 3,14159. An evening show may begin at 8:00 P.M. here, but it's 20:00 in the United Kingdom and 20.00 Uhr in Germany. The U.S. date 7/4/76 would be 04/07/76 in most of Europe. If your program requires more specific information, the International Utilities will also return a code indicating the actual country for which the current system is configured.

A straightforward byte-for-byte comparison of two ASCII strings is adequate for English but won't work for most foreign languages, which include accents and diacritical symbols. You would want to sort "rêver" next to "révérence" in a French-English lexicon, despite the differing accents. The International Utilities include functions to order strings that are oblivious to accents and other diacritical marks.

Some national differences require even more significant changes. In particular, many languages use character sets that do not conform to the Indo-European norm. Several Asian languages require more than 256 characters, while Middle Eastern languages are drawn from right to left. The Script Manager, provided in the 256K ROM, provides for text input and display for such languages.

Each script is a writing system with a characteristic alphabet. The Latin-based languages of Western Europe use the Roman script. Other standard scripts include Japanese (Kanji), Arabic, and Hebrew. At startup time, the system has a standard script it uses by default. Each font is associated with a specific script, allowing text from different languages to be freely mixed.

The Script Manager has two dynamically selected scripts that affect other Toolbox routines. The font script is set to the script for the font used by the current GrafPort, is used to display characters, and also defines the script used by the International Utilities Package. The keyboard script determines what alphabet will be used to translate keyboard events. Most of the time, the two scripts will be the same.

Each script has a characteristic writing direction, left to right or right to left. The script supplies a standard mechanism for analyzing multibyte character codes, such as required by the Kanji alphabet used in Japan.

Several of the capabilities supplied actually make it easier to support text operations in Roman languages, while at the same time providing interfaces that will work with other alphabets. The Script Manager provides a routine, DrawJust, for displaying fully justified text, since not all languages justify text using spaces. It also supplies a standard routine to translate between a pixel position and the specific character of a string.

The Transliterate routine can be used to change a text between two alphabets, such as Potop in Cyrillic to Rotor in the Roman alphabet. It is also the preferred way to capitalize or lowercase ordinary text, since it won't mangle text in other languages.

OTHER TOOLBOX MANAGERS

The **Menu Manager** draws the menu bar at the top of the display. It allows your program to add new menus to the menu bar or add new items to an existing menu. Individual menu items can be enabled or disabled; their appearance can be changed. Specialized routines will build menus from a resource list (say of fonts or desk accessories) and will find the proper menu item for a Command key.

When a menu is pulled down, the pixels underneath the menu must be saved. The Menu Manager allocates temporary memory to save these pixels. For large menus, this can be a significant fraction of the size of a screen pixel map.

The enhanced version of the Menu Manager allows for hierarchical menus. When a specified menu item is selected, the Menu Manager displays a new menu, referred to as a submenu. Items on a submenu are selected in the same way as items on any other menu.

The **List Manager Package** makes it easy to display a list of icons, pictures, or text items in a window, for selection and scrolling. It is used, for example, by ResEdit to display a list of resources.

The **Desk Manager** controls the interactions between stand-alone applications and desk accessories. It allows an application to open or close a desk accessory and defines the interface for writing your own desk accessory.

Both applications and desk accessories exchange information through the clipboard (the "scrap") which is controlled by the **Scrap Manager**. The scrap can be stored either in memory or on disk in the "Clipboard File." The Scrap Manager allows your program to find out which scrap is being used and to read and write the memory version to or from disk so that it can be used by another program.

Programs should support cutting and copying data to the scrap and pasting data from the scrap to their program. The Scrap Manager indicates the type of data in the scrap by a four-character data type, which corresponds to a resource type of the same name. Each program is expected to be able read both of two standard data types, 'PICT' or 'TEXT', and be able to write at least one type.

The 'PICT' type is identical to a QuickDraw picture and is used for exchanging graphical information. Pictures created by QuickDraw in a CGrafPort have a slightly different format from those created in a GrafPort, but ROM patches are provided for the machines without color QuickDraw to allow them to read the newer format.

The 'TEXT' type contains unformatted ASCII text, complete with Return characters. When the scrap is created by the extended TextEdit, an additional 'styl' type is added to the scrap, which contains the formatting information for the associated 'TEXT'.

The same data can be stored in the scrap in more than one format, with a separate data type used for each format. For example, the original

MacWrite word processor copies two types of data to the scrap. The 'MWRT' data includes the text, rulers, styles, and formats but is intelligible only to MacWrite and other word processors. The 'TEXT' data includes only the text but can be read by any application.

The scrap can also be copied to and from the scrapbook. The format of the Scrapbook File is defined by the Scrapbook desk accessory, which is normally the only program that accesses the scrapbook directly. Clipboard data is stored with a resource type corresponding to its scrap data type (e.g., a 'PICT' resource). The resource ID is used in combination with an index resource to maintain the order of entries in the scrapbook; multiple resources with the same ID are used for different representations of the same item.

The Toolbox Utilities include miscellaneous low-level routines used by the remainder of the Toolbox. These include various resource utilities (to find a 'STR ' string resource, for example), as well as standard fixed-point arithmetic functions.

The Toolbox Utilities also include a strangely named function known as Munger—a general-purpose byte-manipulation function. This can be used to search and replace text substrings within a relocatable block.

2.5   The Operating System and Peripherals

The operating system provides the lowest-level building blocks for Macintosh operations.

The Memory Manager has already been introduced. The remaining OS routines are primarily associated with input/output devices. Any standard application will use the File Manager, which manages the unformatted disk space on an arbitrary disk device, and the Printing Manager, which provides a virtual interface to any printer.

An understanding of the details of other managers may be important when writing specialized software, such as low-level I/O drivers or communications programs.

DEVICES

As supplied, a Macintosh computer comes with one or more internal disk drives. On the back panel, there are connectors for printers, modems, or the AppleTalk local-area network. Other connectors support an external disk drive and, on the Macintosh Plus and later models, a high-speed SCSI bus for use with hard disks.

The Macintosh SE and Macintosh II allow for internally mounted hard disks and peripheral interface cards. They also use a more generalized interface for the keyboard and mouse.

A number of OS managers and drivers are provided for controlling these peripherals.

Most peripherals are controlled, either directly or indirectly, by the Device Manager. Figure 2–18 shows a simplified version of the interrelationship between the Device Manager, other OS managers and drivers, internal hardware, and various external peripherals.

All current models include two standard types of peripheral interface chips. The Zilog Z8530 (or equivalent) Serial Communications Controller provides an RS-422 serial port for modems, printers, and AppleTalk use. The Rockwell 6522 Versatile Interface Adapter controls the mouse and keyboard operations and, on some models, controls aspects of disk, sound, and real-time clock operations. Although direct access to these chips may be necessary when writing custom drivers, such references will likely cause portability problems with future machines.

More information can be found in the manuals describing specific models and their hardware interfaces, as well as documentation on specific peripherals, such as the *LaserWriter Reference Manual* .

FILES

As on other computers, the most used Macintosh peripheral is the disk drive used to hold programs and data. Each unformatted disk volume is structured into a series of named files through the File Manager.

There is an important difference between the original 64K ROM and later versions of the File Manager. The original Macintosh supported only one level of structure on each volume; this disk format is referred to as the Macintosh File System (MFS), and is normally used on single-sided (400K) floppy disks.

To more effectively organize hard disks of 20 Mb or more, the 128K ROM added a File Manager that also supports the Hierarchical File System. HFS is also the standard format for double-sided (800K) floppies.

The main advantage of HFS is that it divides each volume into a series of directories, which are shown as folders in the Finder. (Folders under MFS were just an elaborate illusion maintained only by the Finder.) Under HFS, the File Manager only has to maintain information about directories currently in use, such as those folders opened from the Finder. Unlike some file systems, folders are not a special form of file in HFS.

To improve compatibility with earlier applications, each directory is normally referenced by a number, which is used the same way as the earlier MFS volume number. Also, the folder containing the System and Finder that are used to boot the Mac is designated the "blessed" folder. When opening an existing file under HFS, the File Manager uses the Poor Man's Search Path to provide an extra way for files to be found. It first checks the specified

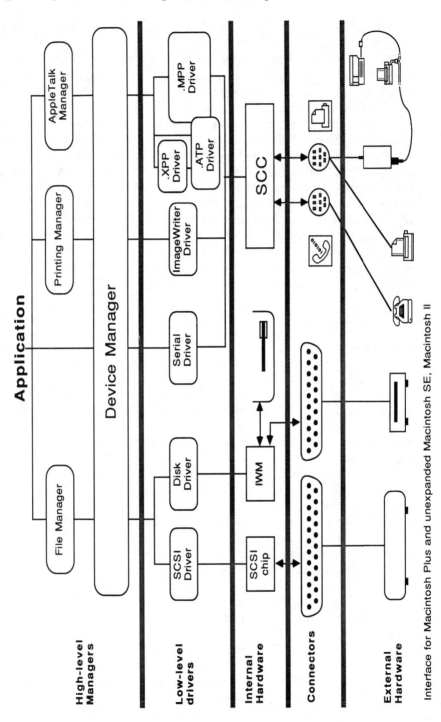

Figure 2–18: Software and Hardware Device Interface

directory. If that directory is on the boot volume, the topmost directory and (if different) the blessed folder are also searched. The blessed folder is the common location for separate files containing for printer drivers, other system software, and application-specific configuration files.

Each file (program or document) on the Macintosh has two four-character codes indicating its usage; these codes usually consist of letters only but may include one or more trailing spaces. The first code specifies the file type, which indicates the usage of the file; for example, 'TEXT' is an ordinary ASCII source file and supported by many applications.

The second code is the file creator, which indicates the application program associated with the file and controls which application is launched when the file is opened from the finder. For most documents, this is the same as the creator field for the application that created the file. However, some applications that export files set the document's creator to be the same as the target application.

Files of the same type but with different creators may be opened by any application that will read that type. Types and creators for a variety of files are shown in Table 2–8. Files created by MPW always have a creator 'MPS', with a trailing space.

Each file also has a creation date and a modification date. These dates are maintained if you copy a file using the Finder, such as when making a backup of your hard disk to floppies.

These files require a lower-level driver to control the underlying physical device. The Disk Driver will control internal and external 3-1/2-inch floppy drives, in 400K and 800K variations, as well as the original Apple Hard Disk 20. The SCSI Driver controls devices that conform to the American National Standard Committee specifications for the Small Computer Standard Interface, normally a hard disk attached to the SCSI port on the back of the computer. Later machines have both internal and external SCSI ports.

A particular desk accessory, the "Chooser," is used to select a driver corresponding to certain devices, such as printers. The chooser can also select remote file servers via AppleShare, which is used by the File Manager to implement an external file system, which allows access to files on disk volumes not directly connected to the Macintosh. Instead, these files are accessed via AppleTalk.

The Disk Initialization Package examines whether a newly mounted floppy disk is initialized in the Macintosh format. If not, it presents a dialog allowing the user to format the disk. Your program should call this package if a disk-insertion event indicates a disk was unsuccessfully mounted. The Disk Initialization Package is automatically called the one time disk insertions are most important—when the Standard File Package is offering the user a dialog for opening or saving a file.

Hard disks are normally formatted using a separate stand-alone utility provided by the disk manufacturer.

System Folder	*Type*	*Creator*
AppleShare	RDEV	afps
AppleTalk ImageWriter	PRER	IWRX
Clipboard File	CLIP	MACS
Finder	FNDR	MACS
ImageWriter	PRES	IWRT
LaserWriter	PRER	LWRT
Laser Prep	LROM	LWRT
System	ZSYS	MACS

Applications	*Type*	*Creator*
Edit (MDS)	APPL	EDIT
Excel	APPL	XCEL
MacDraw	APPL	MDRW
MacPaint	APPL	MPNT
MacWrite	APPL	MACA
MORE	APPL	MORE
MPW Shell	APPL	MPS

Documents†	*Type*	*Creator*
Edit	TEXT	EDIT
Excel	XLBN	XCEL
Excel (Text)	TEXT	XCEL
MacDraw	DRWG	MDRW
MacDraw (PICT Format)	PICT	MDRW
MacPaint	PNTG	MPNT
MacWrite	WORD	MACA
MacWrite (Text Only)	TEXT	MACA
MORE	MORE	MORE
MORE (Export Text)	TEXT	MORE
MORE (Export MacWrite)	WORD	MACA
MPW	TEXT	MPS
MPW (object)	OBJ	MPS
MPW (tool)	MPST	MPS

† Default format shown first

Table 2–8:   **File Type and Creator for Sample Files**

APPLETALK

Network communications for the Macintosh are controlled by the AppleTalk Manager. Implementation of the manager is handled by a series of data protocols, logically subdivided into "layers." These layers range from the electrical signals along the cables to the user-level interface.

The AppleTalk protocols conform to the Open Systems Interconnection (OSI) seven-layer reference model endorsed by the International Organization for Standardization (ISO). The standard AppleTalk protocols and their corresponding OSI layers are shown in Table 2–9. The advantage of this design is that a different protocol can be adopted at one layer without abandoning the capabilities provided at other layers. Just because the transfer rate to the printer is faster, for example, isn't a good reason to change the commands sent by a program to control the printer.

Most of these functions are handled by resources of type 'DRVR', some of which are contained in ROM in the later machines.

STANDARD PERIPHERALS

When it comes time for an application to print, the Printing Manager provides the interface for translating the screen display to the printed page. The Printing Manager calls a specific print driver stored in a separate file in the blessed folder, such as the ImageWriter or LaserWriter drivers. As when preparing a screen display, QuickDraw calls are the basis for preparing graphical output on paper.

The original Printing Manager did not have any traps but linked in calls to the printer drivers for each program that used it. A common printing trap is available on any machine running version 4 or later of the System file, and the trap should be used in all new programs.

The Macintosh can support a wide variety of other serial devices. This includes direct connections to other computers or connections via telephone modems. The Serial Driver controls transmission speeds, formats, provides a limited amount of I/O buffering, and will detect a limited number of transmission errors.

The Sound Driver controls output to the Macintosh speaker and the external output jack, providing a limited set of sound functions emulated through software. As a consequence, more elaborate sounds can require the full processing power of the Macintosh.

On the Macintosh II, the Sound Manager controls the Apple Sound Chip to provide sound synthesis capabilities in hardware. It defines standard resources for sounds and sound-generation algorithms and supports external MIDI polyphonic synthesizers, connected via a serial port. The Sound Manager incorporates the Sound Driver calls as a subset of its capabilities.

OSI Reference Model Layer	Description	AppleTalk Implementation
1. Physical	Hardware	SCC
2. Data Link	Data formats, bus contention	ALAP
3. Network	Addressing and routing	DDP
4. Transport	Error and flow control	ATP, NBP, RTMP
5. Session	Complete transactions	ASP, PAP
6. Presentation	Data conversion	AFP, PostScript
7. Application	Program-specific	printer drivers, applications

Hardware

SCC: Serial Communcations Controller
AppleTalk Personal Network cables

Contained in file System or ROM

DRVR '.MPP'
    ALAP: AppleTalk Link Access Protocol
    DDP: Datagram Delivery Protocol
    NBP: Name Binding Protocol
    RTMP: Routing Table Maintenance Protocol
DRVR '.ATP'
    ATP: AppleTalk Transaction Protocol
DRVR '.XPP'
    AFP: AppleTalk Filing Protocol (partial)
    ASP: AppleTalk Session Protocol

File Laser Prep

PostScript initialization

File LaserWriter

PAP: Printer Access Protocol
LaserWriter driver

File AppleTalk ImageWriter

PAP: Printer Access Protocol
ImageWriter driver

Table 2–9:   AppleTalk Protocol Layers

TIMING

The "heartbeat" of the Macintosh OS occurs when the video circuitry is has finished drawing one frame and is waiting to draw the next. As the electron beam moves from the bottom of the screen to the top, it is turned off (blank); hence this period is know as vertical blanking, abbreviated VBL.

This happens 60 times per second with the original Macintosh display. Although this is the same as the North American power frequency, this is also the vertical blanking rate in those countries in which the power frequency is 50 Hz. The period of this cycle, 1/60 second, is known as a tick.

The OS includes a provision for adding tasks to be performed during each of these interrupts or every second interrupt (30 times a second), every thirtieth interrupt (every half-second), and so on. The role of scheduling and starting each of these VBL tasks is managed by the Vertical Retrace Manager. The effective use of VBL tasks provides true real-time capabilities, including flicker-free animation. However, each task will gain control of the Mac at any time in your application; therefore there are major restrictions on exactly what each these VBL tasks can do.

On the Macintosh II, the actual vertical retrace period depends on the specific video display. The Vertical Retrace Manager is enhanced to provide separate VBL queues for each display device, as well as supporting the standard VBL task operations every tick.

For periods shorter than one-sixtieth of a second, the Time Manager provides a resolution of 1 millisecond (.001 seconds). As with the Vertical Retrace Manager, your program installs tasks that are woken up after a specified interval.

If resolution of the Time Manager is precise enough, the system global variable TimeDBRA provides an approximate scaling factor for assembly-code loops. Its value is directly proportional to the number of loops that can be executed per millisecond and is automatically initialized by the 256K ROMs of the Macintosh SE and Macintosh II.

NEWER PERIPHERALS

The Apple DeskTop Bus Manager handles devices connected using the Apple DeskTop Bus, which is a standard interface for all new Apple microcomputers, such as the Macintosh SE, II, and the Apple IIgs. ADB is a low-speed input-only peripheral interface, that is used for the keyboard, mouse, and similar devices, such as graphics tablets.

The Start Manager controls the operation of the Macintosh upon initial booting from disk. Both the Macintosh SE and II versions provide traps to set the default boot volume, and the Macintosh II version also controls the default video device.

The Slot Manager supports operations to manage the NuBus cards stored in the slots of the Macintosh II. This includes reading the card ROM, as well as control and status operations for the corresponding devices. The Slot Manager is not available on the Macintosh SE, which has a single Apple-specific internal expansion slot.

Each card must have a corresponding driver. The driver can be stored in ROM on the card and loaded into the system heap by the Start Manager, or it can be stored in the blessed folder along with other drivers. The driver, as with other drivers, is called via the Device Manager. A driver required by any Macintosh II is the Video Driver, which interfaces between QuickDraw and the video display device.

The Deferred Task Manager allows for tasks to be scheduled to respond to slot-related interrupts. Because some of these operations may be time-consuming, the OS defers initiation of the task until it can be run with all interrupts enabled.

OTHER OS MANAGERS

The Shutdown Manager provides two standard system termination routines: one that reboots the system and one that shuts it down without rebooting. On the Macintosh II, the latter routine powers off the system. It also allows you to add or remove tasks that will be performed if the system is shut down.

The System Error Handler assumes control when a fatal error is detected by the OS, including any unexpected 68000 exception. It presents the system error alert (also known as the "bomb" box), which indicates a numeric error code and allows the user to reboot the system. Your program can also supply a procedure (using the InitDialogs trap) that the System Error Handler will execute if the user selects the "Resume" button in the alert.

The Operating System Utilities include a set of routines to copy relocatable and nonrelocatable blocks. Also included are functions to fetch the current date and time (represented as a 32-bit integer) and convert them to and from their individual components: year, month, day, hour, minute, and second.

Certain system or user settings are saved when you turn off your Macintosh, even if you unplug it and take it somewhere else. These settings are saved in the parameter RAM, which is contained on the battery-powered clock chip of the original Macintosh and Macintosh Plus. The settings include the printer communications settings, the speaker volume, and the time the alarm clock is set to go off. Utility routines allow a Pascal or C routine to read and modify these values in low-memory system globals and write these updated values back out to the parameter RAM.

The OS Utilities also support a standard format for a linked list of data. This Operating System queue format is supported by traps to add or remove an entry from a queue. These queues are the heart of the OS Event Manager and Vertical Retrace Manager and are also used to maintain lists of requested I/O operations for the File and Device Managers.

But your most likely use of the OS Utilities will be for one of two miscellaneous routines involving time. SysBeep beeps the audio output for a specified period, while Delay merely pauses for a specified time.

2.6 Arithmetic

Any program will require some form of numeric calculation. The same numeric types and their corresponding operations are available to all MPW programs, whether written in C, Pascal, or assembler.

Simple integer types are directly supported in hardware by the 68000 processor. Fixed-point and floating-point types, as well as conversion to and from textual representations, requires use of one of the Macintosh managers or packages.

INTEGER ARITHMETIC

At this writing, there are 12 numeric formats supported by the 68000, the Macintosh OS and Toolbox, and related packages. When used from a higher-level language, notably MPW Pascal, these types of numbers can be mixed interchangeably, with conversions for many provided by the compiler. However, understanding these formats requires consulting various Macintosh technical documentation; the gradations also have differing performance implications.

The Motorola 68000 supports three sizes of integers: 8, 16 and 32 bits, referred to as byte, word, and long, respectively. Each size is available in both unsigned and 2s-complement signed representation. The resulting six integral formats are shown in Figure 2–19, along with their corresponding MPW Pascal and C declarations.

As suggested by the illustration, MPW Pascal does not completely support unsigned integer data types. Integer subrange types for the intervals 0...255 and 0...65535 will normally be mapped to the signed integer type that includes the upper bound, that is, an INTEGER or LONGINT. These can be used for unsigned byte and word variables when declared as part of a PACKED ARRAY or PACKED RECORD but cannot be effectively used as the domain of a pointer type.

MPW C defines an int to be the same as a long, i.e., 32 bits. However, you're safer using the long data type if you may be moving code to Apple II or other Macintosh C compilers, which may define int to be the same as short.

Integer types

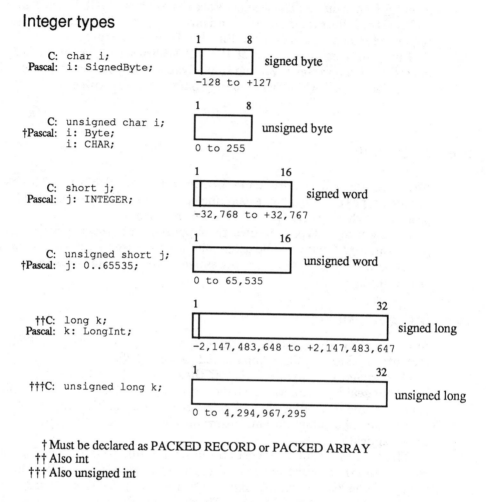

C: char i;
Pascal: i: SignedByte;

signed byte

-128 to +127

C: unsigned char i;
†Pascal: i: Byte;
       i: CHAR;

unsigned byte

0 to 255

C: short j;
Pascal: j: INTEGER;

signed word

-32,768 to +32,767

C: unsigned short j;
†Pascal: j: 0..65535;

unsigned word

0 to 65,535

††C: long k;
Pascal: k: LongInt;

signed long

-2,147,483,648 to +2,147,483,647

†††C: unsigned long k;

unsigned long

0 to 4,294,967,295

† Must be declared as PACKED RECORD or PACKED ARRAY
†† Also int
††† Also unsigned int

Figure 2–19: Macintosh Integer Numeric Formats

For customary arithmetic operators used in high-level languages, the Motorola 68000 instruction set directly supports integer arithmetic on the following types:

- 8-, 16-, or 32-bit add and subtract
- 16-bit multiply and divide
- 8-, 16-, or 32-bit shifts and rotates
- 8-, 16-, and 32-bit logical operations

Although 8-bit multiplies can be done using the 16-bit instructions, notably missing are the 32-bit multiply and divide instructions. Both MPW

Pascal and C use small subroutines to perform these operations on the 68000/68010, resulting in much slower performance than for 16-bit operations.

The Motorola MC68020 used in the Macintosh II and other processors directly supports 32-bit integer multiply and divide instructions. To take advantage of this, you would have to compile your Pascal or C program with the option specifying the MC68020 as the target processor; such code would also be compatible with later processors, such as the MC68030. However, programs with these instructions will not work on a MC68000 or MC68010 processor.

The Toolbox Utilities include so-called "bit functions" to shift, rotate, and perform logical arithmetic on 32-bit values.

These logical operations are also available as 68000 instructions. These instructions are generated by the MPW Pascal compiler when you use one of the extended in-line functions. Since each trap requires a dozen instructions of overhead to execute the one logical operation, Pascal programmers should use the Pascal in-line functions (BAND, BOR, BSL, BSET, etc.) instead of the equivalent traps (BitAnd, BitOr, BitShift, BitSet). Like all standard C compilers, MPW C supports the & and | bitwise logical operators and the << and >> shift operators as in-line instructions.

FIXED-POINT COMPUTATIONS

The Toolbox Utilities provide two signed fixed-point data types. These are used for nonintegral computations within a well-defined range of values and are considerably faster than corresponding computations for the floating-point numbers. The two formats are shown in Figure 2–20.

The original Macintosh Toolbox includes only the FIXED data type, which provides 16 bits of integer (±32768) and 16 bits (nearly 5 decimal digits) of fraction. The 128K ROM added the FRACT data type, which redistributes the same 32 bits to 2 bits of integer (±2) and 30 bits (9 decimal digits) of fraction.

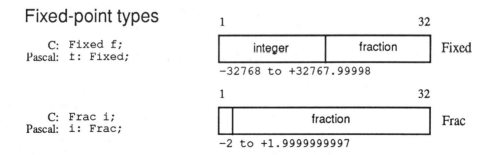

Fixed-point types

C: Fixed f;
Pascal: f: Fixed;

1		32
integer	fraction	Fixed

−32768 to +32767.99998

C: Frac i;
Pascal: i: Frac;

1	32
	fraction	Frac

−2 to +1.9999999997

Figure 2–20: Toolbox Fixed-Point Values

The implied decimal point within these 32-bit integers does not affect additive calculations; therefore, normal 32-bit addition and subtraction instructions will produce the correct results. Multiplication and division traps are provided for each type, as well as a routine to convert the ratio of two signed 16-bit words to the FIXED type.

The original ROM provides for functions to convert between a FIXED line slope and its corresponding angle (in degrees) from the 12 o'clock position. The 128K ROM also provides simplified transcendental functions for fixed-point data types. The square root function operates on FRACT data types. The sine and cosine functions take a FIXED angle and return a FRACT value (see the description of the routines for angles outside ±2π radians), while the arctangent function returns an angle from a ratio of two 32-bit integers. These functions are best used for calculating distances and angles for circles on the QuickDraw plane.

The Toolbox Utilities also include conversion routines between the two fixed-point types, between the FIXED type and 32-bit integers, and between either type and the standard 80-bit floating- point type.

SANE

The Standard Apple Numeric Environment (SANE) defines a standard library of floating-point functions with common characteristics on both the Macintosh and Apple II family of computers. Although the actual code implementing SANE is different for the 68000 and 6502-family microprocessors, the computational results seen by high-level language computations should be identical.

Originally written for the Apple III, SANE was one of the earliest complete software implementations of the Institute of Electrical and Electronic Engineers Standard 754 for floating-point arithmetic. IEEE-754 is also the basis for floating-point coprocessors, including the Intel 8087 used by the IBM PC family and the Motorola 68881 of the Macintosh II.

In addition to specifying precision and rounding characteristics, the IEEE-754 standard extends upon standard industry practices of the previous three decades by defining representations for positive and negative infinities and signed zero values. IEEE-754 also requires that certain calculations produce values referred to collectively as "Not a Number." For example, the quantity 0*Infinity produces the SANE quantity NANMUL, the multiplicative NaN. Comparisons or calculations with NaN values will normally produce an error.

All SANE calculations are performed using the 80-bit floating-point format defined by IEEE-754, the extended data type. The IEEE-754 standard also defines two more compact formats, corresponding to single and double (32- and 64-bit) representations. These formats, and the range of representable values, are shown in Figure 2–21.

SANE integer type

C: `comp m;`
Pascal: `m: comp;`

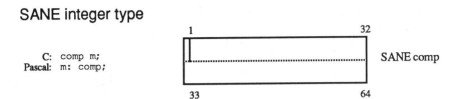

IEEE-754 floating-point types

C: `float r;`
Pascal: `r: REAL;`

C: `double d;`
Pascal: `d: DOUBLE;`

C: `extended e;`
Pascal: `e: extended;`

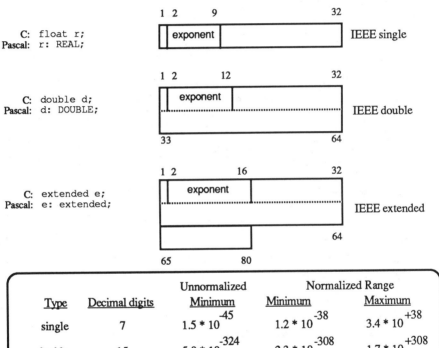

Type	Decimal digits	Unnormalized Minimum	Normalized Range Minimum	Maximum
single	7	$1.5 * 10^{-45}$	$1.2 * 10^{-38}$	$3.4 * 10^{+38}$
double	15	$5.0 * 10^{-324}$	$2.3 * 10^{-308}$	$1.7 * 10^{+308}$
extended	19	$1.9 * 10^{-4951}$	$1.7 * 10^{-4932}$	$1.1 * 10^{+4932}$

Figure 2–21: SANE Data Types

SANE also includes a 64-bit integer type `comp`, designed for exact integral calculations, such as those used in accounting applications. The range of this type is $\pm 9*10^{18}$, enough to handle the total U.S. government budget for the next few million years (not allowing for inflation).

A complete description of SANE is given in the three-part Apple *Numerics Manual*, which is must reading if you intend to use floating-point numbers on the Macintosh. The first part describes SANE, its data types, computations, exceptions, and associated functions. The second part describes the implementation for the Apple II family, based on the 6502 and 65816 processors, while the final part describes SANE for the Macintosh, including the necessary assembly-language calling sequences.

When writing floating-point calculations in MPW C or Pascal, the compiler will normally generate calls to the corresponding SANE routines, which are stored in three separate Macintosh packages.

The Floating-Point Arithmetic Package defines all the basic floating-point operations, such as addition, multiplication, and comparisons. It is referred to in the SANE references as "FP68K," which is also the name of its assembly-language macro.

The Transcendental Functions Package defines SANE's elementary functions, which include trigonometric, logarithmic, exponential, and financial functions. These make use of the floating-point arithmetic package. The 68000 SANE documentation refers to this as "Elems68k."

Numbers are not displayed or input in their binary form but instead must be converted to or from a string of ASCII characters. These conversions are handled by the Binary-Decimal Conversion Package. The package includes conversion routines for both 32-bit integers and SANE data types; the latter usage is referred to as "DecStr68k" in the SANE documentation. When converting from character (ASCII) to binary values, the SANE scanning routines provide an error indication, while the integer version does not.

Unlike the original Macintosh, which required the use of disk-based packages to keep the ROM size under 64K, all three floating-point packages are included in the 128K and later ROMs. However, these routines are still accessed through the Package Manager. Both the Floating-Point Arithmetic Package and Transcendental Functions Package use an operation code on the top of the stack to specify both the operation and the format of the operands. On the Macintosh II, the floating-point packages are programmed to take advantage of the built-in Motorola MC68881 floating-point coprocessor, which is many times faster than using the 68000 (or 68020) to emulate floating-point instructions.

Both the Pascal and C compilers also include options to generate code directly referencing the 68881. When this option is enabled, extended data types are stored in 96 instead of 80 bits, with 16 additional bits of zeroes.

Chapter 3

Structure of Macintosh Programs

THERE ARE A NUMBER OF DIFFERENT TYPES OF MACINTOSH PROGRAMS. Some stand alone, some can be used to assist stand-alone programs, and others perform one small task that can be used by many programs. MPW is a special stand-alone program, and it has its own format for building add-on utilities.

Each type of program has its own interface and associated programming approach. Even if two programs are designed to perform the same function, if one is an application and the other a desk accessory, there are major differences in the interface and structure of the program.

This chapter summarizes the difference between the types of programs, including the special characteristics of the MPW utilities.

3.1 Introduction

As shown in Table 3–1, there are (at least) 13 different types of code that can be written for the Macintosh. Three of these types correspond to the customary definition of a complete program, as in the Pascal definition of the same name: applications, MPW tools, and desk accessories.

The remaining types are more similar to subroutine libraries. Most implement or extend some aspect of the Toolbox or operating system. For example, device drivers are needed by the OS to interface to peripherals,

Code type	Resource	Found in	Called by
Application	CODE	File type 'APPL'	Finder
MPW Tool	CODE	File type 'MPST'	MPW Shell
Desk accessory	DRVR	System	Desk Manager
Driver	DRVR	System or another file	Device Manager
Package	PACK	System	Package Manager
Control defproc	CDEF	System	Control Manager
List defproc	LDEF	System	List Manager
Menu bar defproc	mbdf	System	Menu Manager
Menu defproc	MDEF	System	Menu Manager
Window defproc	WDEF	System	Window Manager
Function key Manager	FKEY	System	Toolbox Event
Initialization	INIT	File type 'INIT'	System startup
VBL task	CODE	any	same

Table 3–1:   Macintosh Code Types

while a definition procedure is needed to implement the interface for a window.

Each type of code has different characteristics, such as the resource type used to write the code. Those in the second group extend the functionality of a program rather than act as complete programs themselves. However, most are developed as separate programs using MPW; therefore, these will be discussed as "program types" throughout this chapter.

Examples of all 12 types are present in the Macintosh. Even if you won't be writing all the types, it's important to understand what they are and the role they play since many of these types will be used by your program. For example, an application will usually reference the window definition procedures and at least one of the packages supplied by Apple as part of the System file.

PROGRAM TYPES

To contrast the three different types of complete programs, we'll take a specific example. Suppose you want to write a program, say, to read an address list and convert it into mailing label form. The input would be a text file with each entry on a separate line, with fields separated by commas. The output would be a text file with each field on a separate line. While you're at it, you'd probably want to leave off the phone number. If a field is blank, such as the corporate title, you'd want to leave it off entirely.

If you wanted to make a standalone program, you would probably write a Macintosh application. Such a program takes complete control of the Macintosh, normally puts up menus and windows, and when it is finished, returns to the Finder. For this example, you might have a menu with "Open…" and "Save As…" items; each would put up Standard File Package dialog to select a file name.

If you are writing a one-time program to do a simple task or one that will be used (by yourself or others) for software development with MPW, you may want to consider writing an MPW tool. Although MPW tools can adopt all the complexity of a Macintosh application, generally they rely on a much simpler, line-oriented interface similar to MS-DOS or UNIX. MPW tools usually need two standard text files, one for input and one for output, which would be well-suited to the example.

Finally, the program could also be implemented as a desk accessory. Desk accessories are run from within any application, but generally can do everything a small application can. Although desk accessories can read and write files, a more appropriate approach would be to read and write the data in the clipboard. This data could be then moved directly into other applications.

Most of the remaining program types are not directly seen by the user; they more closely correspond to system libraries provided by other operating systems.

A package is a library of subroutines, grouped together through a common dispatch trap and thus available to all Macintosh programs. A total of 16 packages can be defined, of which 7 (0, 2 to 7, and 12) are used by System 4.1. Apple has reserved all package IDs for itself, so this is a program type you will more often study than write yourself.

Also available to all applications are the definition procedures (often called "defprocs") used by the Toolbox Managers to implement the user interface. They draw on the screen and accept input from the mouse or keyboard. For example, a window frame is drawn using a 'WDEF' resource, and its scroll bar is a control drawn by a 'CDEF' resource. The appearance of a menu bar is defined by an 'mbdf' resource, while the actions of an individual menu are handled by an 'MDEF' resource. Lists of items can be displayed using an 'LDEF' resource.

Currently, only two definition procedures are supplied by Apple for controls and windows, one each for menu bars, menus, and lists. However, each procedure can support a number of related variants, such as windows with or without the close box.

A VBL task performs a task at periodic intervals and is always started by another program type. For example, an application may require updating a clock on the screen once every second. It would use the Vertical Retrace

Manager to schedule a VBL task to occur, and the task would reschedule itself to occur every 60 ticks after that. VBL tasks are very limited in what actions they can perform; in particular, all memory must be allocated before the task is begun.

Drivers—used for disks, serial and network I/O, printers, and sound output—would seem to have little in common with desk accessories. However, both have the same resource type and format and are called using the same Device Manager calls.

The Macintosh normally performs a series of steps upon system startup. An important function is to load new versions of OS and Toolbox traps from disk into memory to correct bugs discovered after the ROM was built. Other steps may involve user-specific actions, such as installing a RAM disk. These tasks performed at the time of system initialization are normally stored in 'INIT' resources.

Finally, 'FKEY' resources are user-invoked subroutines to perform a specific function. They are called using the Command, Shift, and a single numeric key, with the number corresponding to the resource number of a resource of type 'FKEY'. Function keys 1 and 2 are built into ROM, ejecting floppy disks. However, keys 3 and 4 (which dump the screen) are contained as 'FKEY' resources in System. FKEYs can be used for purposes similar to those for desk accessories. However, unlike DAs, they enter and exit once and have no associated resources.

LOCATION OF PROGRAMS

Most Macintosh programs are stored in separate files on the disk. Applications always have file type 'APPL', while the creator type of an application is used to link it with associated documents. The Finder will run only files of type 'APPL', unless you force it to accept a file as a program by holding down Command-Option before you launch it.

One particular application, MPW Shell, has a creator type 'MPS'. MPW tools are a type of MPW document, so they have the same creator but always have file type 'MPST'. When using the MPW linker to build a Macintosh program, both the file type and creator are normally specified, thus allowing MPW to know how the program should be started. As of this writing, MPW tools can only be run from within the MPW Shell application.

Most other program types are installed in the file named System, usually in the System Folder of the boot disk. Desk accessories are resources of type 'DRVR', with the name of the desk accessory resource used to identify it in the apple-shaped menu. Desk accessories are installed using the Font / DA Mover application supplied by Apple to all users.

Drivers are also DRVR resources, normally located in the System file. However, certain drivers, such as those for printers or file severs, may be located in a separate file for each type of device, and the driver is selected through the "Chooser" desk accessory.

Also stored in the System file are Toolbox definition procedures (CDEF, LDEF, mbdf, MDEF, WDEF), packages and FKEY resources. If you write your own, you must install it yourself in the System file using a resource tool, such as ResEdit. All must use a unique resource ID for the corresponding type, including those resources defined in the ROM, so you should know which resource IDs are system defined.

For code being distributed to users, Apple recommends that such routines should be included as part of the resource fork of any application that uses them. For example, a CAD application might include a special control for rotating an object in two dimensions simultaneously, thus requiring a custom CDEF resource. Desk accessories and drivers can also be stored in an application rather than System, where appropriate.

If it is necessary to install these resources in a user's System file, the Apple-supplied Installer program will perform the update automatically. Writing such scripts is the subject of a *Macintosh Technical Note*.

From the resource fork of the file that contains them, how are these program types found? Applications and tools are run by name, the former via the Segment Loader, the latter by the MPW Shell.

Drivers and desk accessories are normally found by their resource name, which begins with a period (.) or null (00 hex), respectively. A package and Toolbox definition procedure is referenced by its resource number in any program that calls it; so the resource number should be chosen carefully and permanently. The number of an 'FKEY' resource corresponds to the numeric key used to call it and can be changed at will, as long as the user remembers what it is.

An INIT resource is normally stored in the resource fork of a file of type 'INIT'. If the file is in the blessed folder—the one with the System and Finder used to boot the system—it will be run at system startup.

Finally, a VBL task is a subroutine installed by another program in the vertical retrace queue. At the appropriate time, it is called by the Vertical Retrace Manager.

CHARACTERISTICS

There are a number of differences that distinguish the previously mentioned program types. They are given in Table 3–2.

The major distinction is between applications and programs that run under applications. A Macintosh application must initialize all of the Toolbox managers, which makes these managers available for use by desk accessories, drivers, and so on. An MPW tool must initialize QuickDraw if it uses any graphics, such as a window or the Standard File Package. The other program types should not initialize the Toolbox managers.

Most applications use the standard menu bar. By convention, a desk accessory may have a single menu, although this is optional. Similarly, many

	Application	MPW Tool	DA	Driver	VBL Task	Defproc	PACK
Toolbox Init's	•	1†					
Global Variables	•	•					
Memory Manager	•	†	•	•††		•	•
Resources	•	†	††	††		††	††
Menus	•		1†				
Windows	•		1				
Events	•		•				
Scrap	•		•				
Periodic Action	•		•	•	•		
Re-entrant			•	•	†	•	

† Optional
†† Restrictions on usage apply
* Except for initialization, an MPW Tool can do anything an application can do. Customary usage is shown.

Table 3–2:   Macintosh Program Characteristics

applications support multiple windows, while a desk accessory almost always has exactly one.

Both applications and desk accessories are event driven. That is, an application explicitly calls the Toolbox Event Manager to check for events, such as a mouse click or a key press. The structure of a desk accessory includes an entry point for event handling. Desk accessories and applications normally pass data via the Clipboard, as maintained by the Scrap Manager.

MPW tools do not initialize all the managers and rarely include menus, but they can otherwise include any of the characteristics of an application, such as putting up multiple windows and responding to events. However, this is not what MPW tools are best suited for. A program with a complete Macintosh interface is probably better suited to be an application separate from MPW.

An application will have periodic functions, such as in the main event loop; if the timing of the function is important, the application will install a VBL task. Both desk accessories and drivers can also request periodic time slices, such as to update the display of a clock DA or for a network driver to poll the status of the network.

Like most non-Macintosh programs, applications and MPW tools are run once, begin at the beginning and continue until processing is complete. If you run one of these programs twice, nothing is "remembered" between subsequent runs, except as stored on disk files.

However, desk accessories, drivers, and Toolbox defprocs are re-entrant, i.e., called more than once. These types are run multiple times to complete a series of related operations, such as display, resizing, and updating a specific window. These programs must preserve status information in memory between multiple calls.

Desk accessories and drivers have a specific entry point to perform initialization code, while definition procedures receive a specific control parameter that indicates this type of operation. Any remaining operations for these programs can count on the initialization code being run first, and later, clean-up logic will be run when the related operations are completed.

Take the example of a new window being created by the Window Manager. NewWindow calls the WDEF defproc to allocate memory defining the characteristics of the window, such as it location, size, whether it has a go-away box, and so on. Those characteristics are passed back to the WDEF code for use by the various Window Manager calls for this specific window until DisposeWindow or CloseWindow is called. The other calls can rely on the fields of the window record being set to reasonable values by the initialization code.

The approach for packages is specific to each package. Some packages (the List Manager) follow this re-entrant form, while others (Binary/Decimal Conversion) include routines that can be called a lá carte. Similarly, VBL tasks may be called once, or more than once, although any memory used to save status between multiple entries must be allocated by the application.

GLOBAL VARIABLES

There are restrictions imposed by each of the program types. Experienced programmers may find that the most severe restriction is that most program types do not allow use of global variables, as defined by the Pascal and C languages and as used by many of the libraries supplied with MPW. (In this chapter, the term "global variable" does not include the so-called "system global variables," which are stored at low memory locations below the system heap.)

In MPW release 2.0, only applications and MPW tools may have global variables. As with other Macintosh development systems, the MPW compilers reference such global variables using the 68000 register A5.

Customarily, applications store global variables at negative offsets from the address contained in A5, although this is not required by the ROM or system software. In addition, certain application-specific data is stored at positive offsets from the address contained in register A5. This data is initialized by the Segment Loader and described in the next section.

When an application is running, A5 must always point to its global variables. If more than one application is being run through multitasking system software, the software will load A5 with the appropriate value before staring (or resuming) the application.

An MPW tool is allowed to use A5 to reference its global variables without interfering with the application because the shell is careful to preserve its own value of A5. However, other programs that run at the same time as an application cannot use A5 to reference their own global variables, because they would corrupt the value of the application's variables.

Release 2.0 does not support global variables for desk accessories and drivers, although a solution (such as using another register) is expected in a future release. Until such a solution is provided, such programs must allocate a dynamic Pascal record (C struct) on the heap and use this to store the information used by the multiple entries in the code.

Other routines may need to reliably access global variables of the application. This might include a VBL task or a completion routine for an asynchronous File Manager call. The value of A5 at the time of such an interrupt is not reliable; instead, you must use the application's value for A5, as stored in the system global CurrentA5. If you're writing in Pascal (or C), the SetUpA5 routine in the OS Utilities will save the actual value of A5 and set A5 to CurrentA5, thus allowing you to directly reference application globals. RestoreA5 must be called before the end of the routine to reverse the process.

In addition to the variables declared at the outermost scope of a program, certain library routines will have their own global variables, such as those declared at the outermost level of a Pascal unit or the data used by C's standard I/O library. A special category of such libraries variables are the so-called "QuickDraw globals", which may be used by QuickDraw and various Toolbox routines.

There are two additional ways a program built with MPW can reference these QuickDraw variables, thus potentially corrupting an application's data. Your program can make direct reference to such a value, or it may find that one of the Toolbox traps is expecting to use such a value.

The layout of all these types of global variables is shown in Figure 3–1. The notation is slightly different than that used by some *Inside Macintosh* illustrations, with the notation (value) used to indicate the contents of the specified register or system global.

When a program is built by the MPW linker, the application (or tool) globals are loaded at negative offsets closest to the address referenced by A5. Next come the library globals, including the QuickDraw globals, which for Pascal programs are defined by a USES of the QuickDraw unit. The linker will complete a global variable reference in any routine linked at this time (yours or the library's) to be a specific negative offset from A5.

However, the QuickDraw globals may also be referenced by Toolbox traps, which must run with any application built by any development system. To allow these traps to locate the QuickDraw globals the 4 bytes addressed by A5 contains the *address* of the first of the QuickDraw global variables, which is thePort for Pascal programmers, qd.thePort for those using C.

The linker will automatically allocate space for QuickDraw globals when building applications and MPW tools. A call to InitGraf initializes these

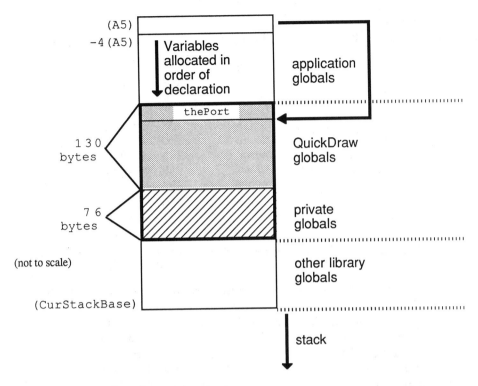

Figure 3–1:   Global Variables

globals to meaningful values, as must be used before any QuickDraw operation. Other types of programs will have to use the application's (or tool's) QuickDraw globals, saving and restoring the values if they are changed.

The Toolbox routines are not affected by where these variables are in memory, even if located on the heap or the stack, as long as the location referenced by A5 contained the address of the variables, and they were initialized before use by a call to InitGraf.

The QuickDraw globals, totalling 206 bytes, are summarized by Table 3–3. Of these, the first 130 bytes are used for nine variables that are directly available to applications. The remaining 76 bytes contain variables that are used by the QuickDraw implementation. Although the variable names are listed in the MPW assembler equates for QuickDraw, they are not officially documented by Apple, and thus could pose future compatibility problems if you were to use them in your program.

Because the variables are stored in descending order, as are other global variables, the first of the variables is the one stored at the highest location in memory. The first variable, thePort, is the most often used, and thus the most easily referenced of the QuickDraw globals.

Offset to thePort	Variable	Type	Usage
0	thePort	GrafPtr	Current drawing port
-8	white	Pattern	0% pattern
-16	black	Pattern	100% pattern
-24	gray	Pattern	50% pattern
-32	ltGray	Pattern	25% pattern
-40	dkGray	Pattern	75% pattern
-104	arrow	Cursor	Standard cursor
-122	screenBits	BitMap	Display screen
-126	randSeed	LongInt	Seed for Random function
-127 to -202			QuickDraw private variables

Table 3–3:   QuickDraw Global Variables

Two of the variables will change during the execution of an application or tool. A pointer to the current GrafPort being used for drawing by QuickDraw and all managers that use QuickDraw is contained in thePort, while randSeed is the seed for the Random pseudorandom number generator. Programs other than applications or tools cannot change these values permanently, or they will cause unanticipated side effects or crashes in the application. Any changes must be properly saved and restored.

For example, almost any desk accessory will draw in its own window. Any time the desk accessory is called, it would use GetPort to save the current value of thePort, SetPort to make its window the current drawing port, and then SetPort to restore the GrafPort when it is done drawing. The same restrictions would apply to a VBL task updating a clock on the screen or a package that organizes the display, such as the List Manager. The CDEF, LDEF, mdbf, MDEF, and WDEF routines are called with thePort already set to the appropriate GrafPort.

Another variable, screenBits, rarely changes. It is a bitmap representing the entire screen. Routines that perform direct operations on bitmaps (e.g., CopyBits) can perform direct transfers to the screen. Most often, the subfield screenBits.bounds is used as the official way to find the rectangle representing the screen size. Programs should not assume a particular screen size or layout.

The remaining six variables are actually constants used frequently by QuickDraw and thus can be easily shared by applications and desk accessories. Five of these are desktop patterns, defining 0, 25, 50, 75 and 100 percent grays. The sixth is the standard arrow cursor, pointing toward the upper-left corner.

Although you may be able to identify explicit references to QuickDraw globals, you should be alert for implicit references by Toolbox traps. For example, `InitCursor` in the 128K ROM uses variable arrow. Any program must assure that the QuickDraw globals referenced via A5 have been properly initialized before a call to any Toolbox routine.

For an application or MPW tool, this means a call to `InitGraf` before any Toolbox traps. For other programs, this means don't modify A5, even temporarily, since any Toolbox trap might need it to find the value of a QuickDraw global.

OTHER RESTRICTIONS

Other restrictions apply to some of the program types.

Although resources are strongly encouraged for most Macintosh programs, and difficult to avoid for some Toolbox calls (e.g., Alert), not all program types can include resources.

Applications (or MPW tools) can freely use a 16-bit positive resource ID greater than or equal to 128. Resource IDs 0 to 127 are reserved for system use.

Negative resource IDs are assigned to other program types. The resource IDs available are associated with resource numbers of the code resource that owns those resource, e.g., a DRVR or WDEF. The formula for computing the resource IDs of these "owned resources" is shown in Figure 3–2. This limits each such program to 32 resources of a given type.

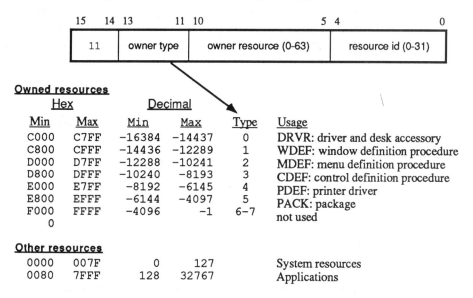

For example, a CDEF #1 (scroll bar) could use resources numbered from $D820 to $D83F, or -10208 to -10177.

Figure 3–2:   Owned Resource IDs

No resource types are available to either an 'FKEY' or 'LDEF' resource. For a List Manager definition procedure, you could define resource IDs allocated to 'PACK' #0, the List Manager Package, if you were careful to avoid existing resource IDs.

A VBL task can access resources of the application that launched it. However, a VBL task cannot directly call the Memory Manager and thus, cannot load a resource—unless it is guaranteed that the resource is in memory. Instead, any memory allocation must be performed by the application that launched the VBL task. If the application does a GetResource call to force the (nonpurgeable) resource into memory, then, of course, the VBL task can use GetResource or another routine (such as GetIcon) to access the resource, since no memory allocation will be required.

3.2 Applications

Applications are the most common and useful program type around, the most complete and thus the most complex. Most third-party software is sold in the form of one or more related applications.

An application should normally support the entire Apple User Interface and thus must handle menus, window interactions, the mouse, and so on. An application must also initialize and prepare certain aspects of the Macintosh environment, particularly the Toolbox and the Memory Manager, as desk accessories that run under the application cannot perform these operations directly.

INITIALIZATION

Each application will normally call initialization routines for six Toolbox managers:

- QuickDraw
- Font Manager
- Window Manager
- Menu Manager
- TextEdit
- Dialog Manager

Even if the application does not intend to use all six managers, if it supports the use of desk accessories, it must initialize all six, as DA's may use any routine in the Toolbox.

Example 3–1 shows the standard initialization sequence, which includes calls to initialize these six managers. The example is given in both C and Pascal, as are other examples in this chapter.

```
/* (C): Application initialization */

/* initialize QuickDraw variables */
InitGraf(&qd.thePort);
InitFonts();                    /* Font Manager */
FlushEvents(everyEvent, 0);
InitWindows();                  /* Window Manager */
InitMenus();                    /* Menu Manager */
TEInit();                       /* TextEdit */
InitDialogs(NULL);              /* Dialog Manager */
/* Perform application-specific initializations */
InitCursor();            /* Change watch cursor to arrow */
```

```
{ (Pascal): Application initialization }

InitGraf(@thePort);   { initialize QuickDraw variables }
InitFonts;                      { Font Manager }
FlushEvents(everyEvent, 0);
InitWindows;                    { Window Manager }
InitMenus;                      { Menu Manager }
TEInit;                         { TextEdit }
InitDialogs(NIL);               { Dialog Manager }
{ Perform application-specific initializations }
InitCursor;                { Change watch cursor to arrow }
```

Example 3–1:   Application Initialization

The routines should be called in the order specified. Application-specific initializations may be performed after the appropriate managers are initialized. For example, new windows could be created after the call to InitWindows.

The ordering of these Inits and other intialization steps will be based on style, structure of the initialization code, and overall strategy for memory management. However, the InitCursor should not be performed until the application-specific initialization is finished, as this removes the watch cursor and indicates to the user that the program is ready to go.

Included in the initialization code will be the first steps of the application's memory management. Prior to allocating relocatable blocks, or loading any code segments, the application should first allocate any antici-pated nonrelocatable blocks to avoid heap fragmentation. Such blocks include the master pointers allocated by calls to the routine MoreMasters; the number of master pointers needed should be established once the application is completely implemented and tested. Most applications will also call MaxApplZone to expand the size of the application heap.

Another common source of nonrelocatable blocks is the allocation of the records used by the Window Manager for each window. Many applications allocate one or more window records in the initialization code prior to actually using these records to display actual windows to reduce fragmenta-tion.

Finally, each application will also initialize its menus. GetMenu is used for each menu to build a list of menu handles, which are used for all future menu references.

MAIN EVENT LOOP

Once an application is started, it normally transfers control to the main event loop. This is a section of code that waits for user actions to control the application's behavior. The loop will continue until the program is ready to terminate, often indicated by changing the value of a boolean global variable.

The main event loop centers around a Toolbox Event Manager function, GetNextEvent. The routine checks for a pending event matching the mask of recognized types that is passed as a parameter. If such an event is found, GetNextEvent completes an EventRecord data type with the type of the event and other information that depends on the event type, such as the location of the mouse click or a pointer to a window to be updated.

To make maximum use of the available CPU cycles, later System file versions provide a trap patch for WaitNextEvent, which is similar to GetNextEvent. The new routine features two new parameters over its predecessor: it allows specification of a region in which your program wishes to detect the mouse pointer has entered; second, it specifies a maximum delay before returning if no events are available. The latter allows the program to release unused blocks of time to the system for other tasks. However, you cannot use WaitNextEvent without first checking for the availability of the trap.

You should be careful to distinguish between the two types of constants defined to reference event types. One corresponds to ordinal value of the type (0,1,2,3) and is used in the EventRecord. The other type is a bit mask used by GetNextEvent and FlushEvents (1,2,4,8). The constant keyDown (3) has a corresponding power of 2 for a mask keyDownMask (8).

The events customarily handled by an application are shown in Example 3–2. Their usages are suggested by the comments.

```
/* (C): Application event loop */

void MyEventLoop()
{ short code;                 /* significance of click */
  long vhcode;                /* v,h of a grown window */
  char c;                     /* the key pressed */
  Point click;                /* where mouse clicked */
  Rect newsize;               /* size of gorwn window */
  WindowPtr tempwindow;       /* window affected */
  EventRecord myevent;        /* the event returned */

  while (!quitSeen)   /* stopped by global boolean */
  { SystemTask();         /* give time where needed */
    if GetNextEvent(everyEvent, &myevent)
    switch (myevent.what) {
    case mouseDown:         /* mouse button pressed */
      click = myevent.where;
      code = FindWindow(click, &tempwindow);
      switch (code) {
      case inMenuBar:            /* the menu bar */
        DoMyCommand(MenuSelect(click), FALSE);
        break;
      case inDrag:               /* any title bar */
        DragWindow(tempwindow, click, &dragRect);
        break;
      case inGoAway:             /* any close box */
        if (TrackGoAway(tempwindow, click))
          CloseMyWindow(tempwindow);
        break;
      case inZoomIn:
      case inZoomOut:            /* any zoom box */
        if (TrackBox(tempwindow, click, code))
          ZoomWindow(tempwindow, code, TRUE);
        break;
      case inGrow:              /* any grow box */
        vhcode =
          GrowWindow(tempwindow, click, newsize);
        if (vhcode)             /* size changed */
          ResizeMyWindow(tempwindow, vhcode);
        break;
      case inSysWindow:         /* DA content region */
        SystemClick(&myevent, tempwindow);
        break;
      case inContent:    /* non-DA content region */
        DoMySelect(tempwindow, click);
      } /* switch */
      break;
```

```
      case keyDown:          /* key pressed */
      case autoKey:          /* key auto-repeating */
         c = myevent.message & charCodeMask;
         if (myevent.modifiers & cmdKey)
            DoMyCommand(MenuKey(c), TRUE);
         else
            DoMyKey(tempwindow, c);
         break;

      /* activate or deactivate a window */
      case activateEvt:
         ActivateMyWindow((WindowPtr)myevent.message,
            (myevent.modifiers & activeFlag) != 0);
         break;

      case updateEvt:    /* update a window's contents */
         UpdateMyWindow((WindowPtr)myevent.message);
         break;

      } /* switch */
   } /* while */
} /* MyEventLoop */


{ (Pascal): Application event loop }


PROCEDURE MyEventLoop;
VAR
   code: INTEGER;          { significance of click }
   vhcode: LONGINT;        { v, h of a grown window }
   c: CHAR;                { the key pressed }
   click: Point;           { where mouse clicked }
   newsize: Rect;          { size of gorwn window }
   tempwindow: WindowPtr;  { window affected }
   myevent: EventRecord;   { the event returned }
BEGIN
   WHILE NOT quitSeen DO    { stopped by global boolean }
      BEGIN
         SystemTask;        { give time where needed }
         IF GetNextEvent(everyEvent, myevent) THEN
            CASE myevent.what OF

            mouseDown:        { mouse button pressed }
               BEGIN
                  click := myevent.where;
                  code := FindWindow(click, tempwindow);
                  CASE code OF
                  inMenuBar:                { the menu bar }
                     DoMyCommand(MenuSelect(click), FALSE);
```

```
            inDrag:              { any title bar }
               DragWindow(tempwindow, click, dragRect);
            inGoAway:            { any close box }
               IF TrackGoAway(tempwindow, click) THEN
                  CloseMyWindow(tempwindow);
            inZoomIn, inZoomOut:    { any zoom box }
               IF TrackBox(tempwindow, click, code)
                  ZoomWindow(tempwindow, code, TRUE);
            inGrow:              { any grow box }
               BEGIN
                  vhcode :=
                     GrowWindow
                          (tempwindow, click, newsize);
                  IF vhcode <> 0 THEN { size changed }
                     ResizeMyWindow(tempwindow, vhcode);
               END;
            inSysWindow:      { DA content region }
               SystemClick(myevent, tempwindow)
            inContent:        { non-DA content region }
               DoMySelect(tempwindow, click);
            END; {CASE code}
         END; {mouseDown}

      keyDown,                { key pressed }
      autoKey:                { key auto-repeating }
         BEGIN
            c :=
               CHR(BAND
                    (myevent.message, charCodeMask));
               { n.b.: Use inline Bitwise-AND instead
                  of Toolbox BitAnd for speed }
            IF BAND(myevent.modifiers, cmdKey)<>0 THEN
               DoMyCommand(MenuKey(c), TRUE)
            ELSE
               DoMyKey(tempwindow, c);
         END;

      activateEvt: { activate/deactivate a window }
         ActivateMyWindow(WindowPtr(myevent.message),
            BAND(myevent.modifiers, activeFlag)<>0);

      updateEvt:        { update a window's contents }
         UpdateMyWindow(WindowPtr(myevent.message));

      END; {CASE what}
   END; {WHILE}
END; {MyEventLoop}
```

Example 3-2: Application Event Loop

Clicking in a menu, or in the go-away, zoom or grow boxes of a window produces a mouseDown event. The application uses Toolbox-provided routines to wait until the mouse button is raised and indicatesthe appropriate action. Resizing the window may involve application-specific actions to update the window contents.

Looking at the example, you may notice the psuedo part codes for the zoom box, which are not shown in early books on Macintosh development. Beginning with 128K ROM, the Window Manager supports two sizes for a window with a zoom box. A standard size is defined by the application when the window is created, and the user defines a second size, which is usually smaller. Clicking the zoom box toggles the window's size between the two. When the mouse is clicked in the zoom box, FindWindow returns two distinct part codes, depending on the current state of the toggle.

Applications must normally handle two types of events for its windows. When it receives an updateEvt, a program should draw the contents of a window. This is either the first time the window is drawn or after something that covered this window (such as a dialog) has been moved or eliminated.

The activateEvt is generated when a window either becomes the active window (activation) or is no longer the active window (deactivation). Thus, activateEvt events usually come in pairs: one to deactivate the old window and another to activate the new window. Your program should change the appearance of the window, such as drawing or erasing the scroll bars. You may also need to change the menus (or enable items within the menus) to correspond to the active window if your program has more than one type of window—such as a text window and a graphics window.

Note that both activation and deactivation of a window are reported as event type activateEvt, with the modifiers bit mask of the event record used to distinguish between the two. Similarly, the application needs to check whether the Command key was down for any keyboard event, because such keystrokes are normally used to indicate a menu selection.

If your program is running at the same time as other programs, the system provides a mechanism for informing it of a pending context switch. If the appropriate flags are set in the program's 'SIZE' resource, context-switching events are passed to the application as it gains control of the CPU and just before it loses it.

Other event types are defined and can be returned by GetNextEvent but are less often used. The event mask normally excludes keyUpMask, and so these won't be returned by GetNextEvent. The mouseUp events are rarely used, since most mouseDown events wait until the mouse button is up. Few applications handle networkEvt or driverEvt types, while GetNextEvent will attempt to resolve diskEvt (disk inserted) events.

Finally, the nullEvent type indicates that none of the defined types were found. WaitNextEvent differs the most dramatically from GetNextEvent here, in that it will attempt to wait the maximum specified delay before returning a null event—thus allowing the CPU time to be used by other programs.

The function GetNextEvent will return FALSE if it has already arranged for the event to be handled by a desk accessory. This will include activate and update events for the desk accessory window and mouse-up and keyboard events if the active window is a desk accessory.

Mouse-down events are always handled by the application, which in turn will defer a mouse-down in a desk accessory to the DA routine using SystemClick. Each application will handle mouse-down events for the window structure (dragging the title bar, clicking go-away, or zoom boxes, etc.) for both applications and desk accessory windows.

The principles behind the main event loop of an application are also applicable to other programs that handle events, such as a desk accessory handling events of a modal dialog.

SEGMENTATION

To reduce the amount of RAM needed at any one time, applications are built with multiple code segments. These correspond to multiple resources of type 'CODE'. Code segments are not normally read from disk until they are needed, and they are purged via calls to the Segment Loader trap UnloadSeg when no longer needed.

To define the beginning of a new segment or continue with a previously declared segment, the MPW Pascal compiler uses directives such as

```
{$S SegmentName}
```

MPW C uses preprocessor directives of the form:

```
#define __SEG__ SegmentName
```

and also provides a compiler option to define the segment name for an entire compile. (The word SEG is preceeded and followed by two underscores in the declaration.) For both Pascal and C, an individual routine cannot span segment boundaries.

For any program, the default segment name is Main. Upper- and lowercase segment names are distinct, and the segment name can be repeated more than once in the same source file or in multiple files. Segment names are not used by the compiler's lexical analysis and can be the same as a routine name or a reserved word. MPW reserves segment names beginning with "%" for its own use.

The segment name is later used as the resource name for the 'CODE' resource generated by the MPW linker for the segment. The linker also allows options to both number and name segments. Some of the MPW library code, such as the C standard I/O package, is compiled into separate named segments that will be included with any application that references that code.

Segment sizes are normally limited to about 32K, which is the maximum supported by the older 64K ROM. Larger segments can be used if you know you won't be running on an older machine, although this defeats the spirit behind segmentation to minimize memory requirements. They also require additional effort at link time to assure that no reference between two routines in the same segment is more than 32K from its destination.

'CODE' resource #1 is normally termed Main and is always the segment that is run first. The developer normally puts most one-time initialization code into another segment, often named Init.

As indicated in the previous chapter, calls between segments are normally resolved via the "jump table." A single jump table is used to resolve all references between the segments of the application. MPW tools have a separate jump table, as will be discussed later, but other program types can neither use the application jump table nor have their own jump table. Instead, other code resources (of type 'DRVR', 'MDEF', etc.) would have to be manually loaded—such as with GetResource—from these programs prior to being called, which would require a far more complicated and tricky scheme than the transparent mechanism provided for 'CODE' resources.

The jump table is initialized by the Segment Loader when an application is launched by reading 'CODE' resource #0, which contains the jump table data. Once loaded into memory, the address of the jump table is given by the 16-bit offset stored in system global variable CurJTOffset, added to the address in A5. The locations between the global variables (as shown in Figure 3–1) and the jump table are used to contain parameters passed by the Finder to the application.

Each routine referenced outside its own segment has a corresponding 8-byte entry in the jump table, and all entries for a segment are stored contiguously in the table. To call a routine in another segment, a procedure branches to the third byte of the routine's jump table entry. If the segment is not currently loaded, this code will cause a _LoadSeg trap to the Segment Loader, which will load the entire segment.

When it loads a segment, the Segment Loader changes all entries for routines in that segment to branch directly to the corresponding routine, as shown in Figure 3–3. If the segment is later unloaded, the entries for routines in that segment are restored to use the _LoadSeg trap.

The first entry of the jump table is always for the initial entry point of the application. Although that entry point is always in 'CODE' resource #1, it may be located anywhere within that resource.

Other segmentation information is stored in the first 16 bytes of the 'CODE' #0 resource, and the first 4 bytes of each of the other 'CODE' resources. This information is used by the Segment Loader but is not loaded as part of the jump table.

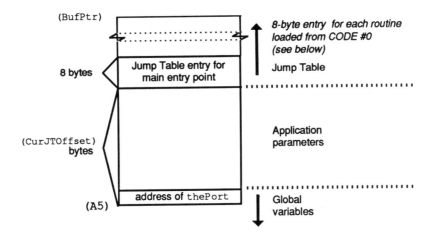

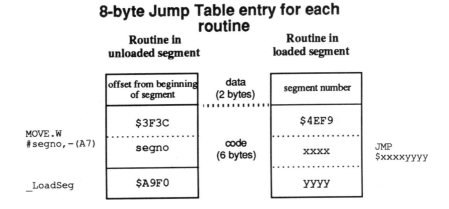

Figure 3–3:   Application Jump Table

All segments (or other code resources) must be locked when in use. Code resources can be stored in the application as unlocked (except when run on the 64K ROM, or 'CODE' #1 on any ROM), and the Segment Loader will use the MoveHHi and HLock Memory Manager calls to lock the code resource prior to execution at the top of the application heap. This approach reduces the fragmentation of contiguous free space in the heap into smaller blocks.

Segments are unlocked and marked purgeable through a call to UnloadSeg. UnloadSeg should not be called to unload the current code segment. If the segment being unloaded contains a routine that called the current segment, the program can crash. Calling a routine always goes through the jump table, thus checking whether the segment is loaded. Returning always assumes that the segment is still in memory, causing havoc if it is not.

One way to avoid these problems is to never call UnloadSeg from any segment except the Main segment, which always remains resident. As suggested by Apple, the main event loop should be in the main segment, which, as discussed in the next section, also contains a small part of the initialization logic. Other recurrent code segments are always unloaded by the main event logic when idle, and memory-intensive operations (such as printing) are not begun until after the segments are unloaded.

Applications (or MPW tools) written in release 2.0 of MPW Pascal or C will always include a segment named %A5Init, which includes code to initialize application global variables. This segment is automatically called before the first statement of the main routine and is loaded and locked into place. Your application must unload it before any memory allocation to avoid heap fragmentation.

POTENTIAL MEMORY MANAGEMENT PROBLEMS

Memory management is the most common cause of problems for an application. This is particularly true for an application well under development that fails only at odd, unpredictable times, or after long periods of use.

There are three levels of detail required when designing an application's memory management strategy. If you're writing a one-time application and you have plenty of memory available, you may be able to just worry about first- or second-order problems.

First, any memory allocation operation may result in a heap compaction. This will cause unlocked relocatable blocks to be relocated, resulting in garbage values if the handle to a relocatable block has been dereferenced. Such deferencing includes use of the Pascal WITH statement or converting the handle to a pointer (single-level indirection). It can also happen if the field of a relocatable block (as in hand^^.field) is passed by address to a subroutine, such as for a Pascal VAR parameter.

If compacting the heap fails, the Memory Manager will purge any purgeable blocks from memory. References to such a block (relocatable or nonrelocatable) will become invalid.

Second, it is still possible to run out of memory once the heap has been compacted and purged. A simple order-of-magnitude calculation will often indicate to the designer whether there will be enough memory. Some applications may require a certain fixed amount of memory, while others require a fixed amount per document or may have memory requirements that vary by the size of the document.

Applications should both estimate whether enough memory will be available before opening the document and check after each memory allocation for failure using function MemError.

Such checks can be very difficult to achieve in practice, since any operation which references a resource can fail due to lack of memory. This includes any transfer to a routine in another segment, since the segment may need to be loaded from disk. Memory allocations are also performed by Window, Control, and Dialog Manager traps, which will crash if the memory is not available, so your program would have to check before each trap to see if enough memory will be found by the trap.

A more sophisticated and foolproof approach is to allocate a reserved block of memory at initialization time and then install your own grow zone function using SetGrowZone. When the Memory Manager faces an out-of-memory condition, it will call your grow zone function, which would allocate the memory from the reserve. The function should then prevent the application from requesting further memory or take drastic steps to free up memory, such as closing desk accessories or asking the user to close documents.

A complete approach to preventing crashes would also install a function to handle Resource Manager errors, since many Toolbox routines also assume that resource requests will be successful. The address of such a function is stored in global variable ResErrorProc, and its use is documented by *Inside Macintosh*.

Third, even if there is enough memory available, the available space may not be in large enough blocks to allocate, say, a 30K byte TextEdit record for a large text file or a 100K pixel map for a color display. The compaction algorithm will slide relocatable blocks toward lower addresses but will not change the order of the blocks within the heap. If a nonrelocatable block (or a locked relocatable block) is in the middle of the heap, the space made available in the heap by the compaction is separated into two or more noncontiguous blocks, as shown by Figure 3–4.

Many memory management problems only manifest themselves after a complex series of actions or long use. The main goal of a memory management strategy during development should be to both anticipate these problems and, while testing, exacerbate the problems so they may be more easily discovered.

MEMORY MANAGEMENT STRATEGIES

The solution to these problems are interrelated. To determine whether the application is susceptible to heap compaction or purging problems, the development version of your application can call CompactMem and Purge-Mem explicitly. MacsBug and other debuggers also can simulate these actions.

To avoid unanticipated relocation during a compaction, relocatable blocks must sometimes be locked. This can contribute to heap fragmentation if the block is locked when memory is allocated, since the compaction will be incomplete. Try to avoid allocating new memory while a block is locked.

Only a minimum amount of memory need be used for disk-based data that can easily be recovered. Most resources are compiled as purgeable or

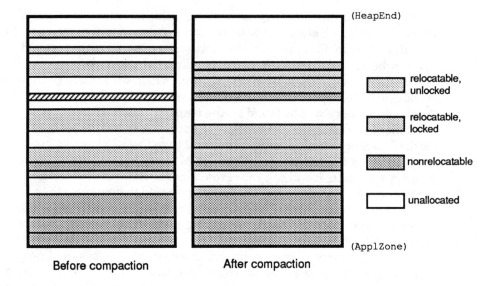

(HeapEnd)

☐ relocatable,
    unlocked

☐ relocatable,
    locked

☐ nonrelocatable

☐ unallocated

(ApplZone)

Before compaction   After compaction

Figure 3–4:   Compacting a Fragmented Heap

explicitly purged with HPurge once no longer needed. Code resources cannot be purgeable but are purged using calls to UnloadSeg.

Certain resources—such as the WIND and DITL template resources—can always be purgeable, since they are not used directly but instead provide instructions for the appropriate manager to build the actual data structures. Once the template has been used, it's no longer needed.

Any resource declared purgeable may be removed from the heap by the next PurgeMem, which disposes of as many blocks as necessary to satisfy the request. However, if a purge is not required by later allocations, the purgeable block will actually remain in memory and be available for the next usage without causing another disk access. Purging (or unloading) a resource should not be thought of as removing the block from memory, but as marking the memory as available in case it is needed.

Since the code segments must be locked when in use, any loaded segment can cause fragmentation. Some other types of blocks are always allocated as nonrelocatable blocks, such as for GrafPorts (or the derived window records or dialog records) Master pointers can also fragment the heap, though this is easily solved through enough calls to MoreMasters in the initialization logic.

There are only two safe locations for nonrelocatable blocks or locked relocatable blocks: at the top or the bottom of the heap. Nonrelocatable blocks are normally allocated at the lowest free address, moving relocatable blocks higher if necessary.

Nonrelocatable blocks, before they are locked, should be moved away from the center of the heap. The routine MoveHHi moves a relocatable block to the top of the heap and can be used before the resource is locked. This approach is used by the Segment Loader (except on the 64K ROM) for all unlocked 'CODE' resources when they are loaded.

Using MoveHHi and HLock on a block can actually tend to fragment the heap if used improperly. The heap starts out at a minimum size, and the address of the top of the heap (contained in system global HeapEnd) increases toward higher memory as more memory is needed until it reaches the maximum value given by system global ApplLimit. As shown by Figure 3–5, a locked block at the top of a small heap would be in the middle of the heap—causing fragmentation—if the heap were later grown. For example, this will always happen with a MPW Pascal or C application unless you explicitly unload the %A5Init segment, as discussed in the previous section.

To avoid this problem, your initialization logic should call MaxApplZone before performing any memory allocations. MaxApplZone grows the heap to the maximum allowed value so that a block moved to the top of the heap and locked will always be at the top. This should be done before any segment is loaded, or the loaded segment (which is automatically locked) will caused fragmentation.

If your program requires more than the default stack size provided by the Finder, it must first use GetApplLimit and SetApplLimit to adjust the value of ApplLimit downward by the necessary amount. The value of ApplLimit cannot be set less than HeapEnd, so once MaxApplZone has been called, ApplLimit cannot be changed.

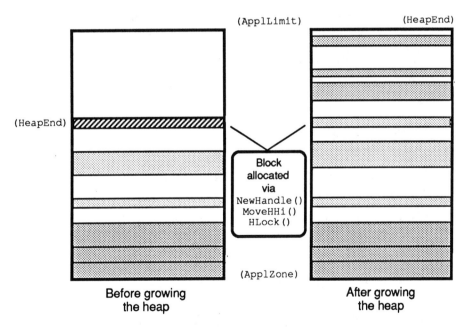

Figure 3–5:   Fragmentation After Growing Heap

Example 3–3 shows the correct ordering of the customary initialization steps for an application developed with MPW.

Debugging these subtle memory-management problems requires several long runs of the application while examining the state of the heap. This is made easier if the program can run unattended in a test mode. For example, many games have an autoplay feature (for demonstrations) which can be used to run the program for hours and catch such subtle bugs.

DOCUMENTS

The Macintosh file containing an application will have file type 'APPL'. Its four-character creator is its distinctive signature, which should be unique

```
/* (C): Unloading initialization segments */

extern void _DataInit();
  /* declared to unload %A5Init segment */
void MySetupMemory(), MyInitialize()

/* other declarations, etc. */

#define __SEG__ Main
main()
{ UnloadSeg(_DataInit);    /* purge %A5Init segment */
  MySetupMemory();         /* before loading segments */
  MyInitialize();
  UnloadSeg(MyInitialize); /* purge MyInit segment */
  MyEventLoop();
  MyQuit();
}

void MySetupMemory()
{ MaxApplZone();                   /* grow heap to maximum
*/
  /* 256 master pointers is a good first guess */
  MoreMasters();
  MoreMasters();
  MoreMasters();
  MoreMasters();
}

#define __SEG__ MyInit
void MyInitialize()
{
/* Initialize Toolbox managers, menus, windows, vari-
ables, etc. */
}
```

```
{ (Pascal): Unloading initialization segments }

PROCEDURE _DataInit;
    { declared to unload %A5Init segment }
EXTERNAL;

{ other declarations, code, etc. }

{$S MyInit}
  PROCEDURE MyInitialize;
  BEGIN
  { Initialize Toolbox managers, menus, windows,
    variables, etc.}
  END;

{$S Main}
  PROCEDURE MySetupMemory;
  BEGIN
    MaxApplZone;{ grow heap to maximum }
    { 256 master pointers is a good first guess }
    MoreMasters;
    MoreMasters;
    MoreMasters;
    MoreMasters;
  END;

BEGIN  { main }
  UnloadSeg(@_DataInit);   ....{ purge %A5Init segment }
  MySetupMemory;           ....{ before loading segments
}
  MyInitialize;
  UnloadSeg(@MyInitialize); ...{ purge MyInit segment }
  MyEventLoop;
  MyQuit;
END. { main }
```

Example 3–3 Unloading initialization segments

among applications on all the disks that you use. If you plan on selling your application to others, the signature must be registered with Apple's Technical Support group to avoid a conflict with another application.

   Most applications will allow creating or reading data files on disk, which are referred to as documents. Documents created by an application will normally have the same four-character creator type as the application's signature. Desk accessories and FKEYs that create files may use their own creation signatures, use the creator of an existing application, or leave the creator anonymous, as indicated by the reserved creator '????'.

The file type of a document describes the format of the file's contents, which normally indicates how the data fork should be interpreted. Many files with different creators can have the same type.

For example, MacWrite, Microsoft Word, Excel, MacTerminal, and MPW can all create files of type 'TEXT', as can many desk accessories. MacPaint, FullPaint, and SuperPaint all create 'PNTG' files, the bit-mapped format first used by MacPaint and also created by FKEY #3. MacDraw, PageMaker, and SuperPaint can all read files of type 'PICT', corresponding to a QuickDraw picture.

The format of each of these types is standardized. A file created by one application should be readable by all applications that support the type. There should be no differences between two files of the same type and different creators. The two files will be shown with different icons by the Finder, and a different application will be called when either "Open" or "Print" is selected for the document from the Finder. Other proprietary file types are used by specific applications, but are not readable—or readable with great difficulty—by other developers.

Some applications will store application-specific information as resources in the document, such as the font name and size used by MPW in editing a text file. If the document has been opened by more than one application—such as a 'TEXT' file edited by the MPW and MDS editors—it could conceivably include private information for multiple applications in its resource fork. In this case, the font size set when editing with MPW could be different than that set by MDS Edit, since this is represented by separate resources rather than through information in the data fork. These resources would, in turn, be ignored when reading the file into Excel.

An application normally selects documents, and actions on the entire document, through the "File" menu. A representative menu is shown in Figure 3–6, with the customary selections for Command-key equivalents. Also shown is the corresponding input source for MPW's standard resource compiler, Rez.

The **New** entry opens a new window, creating a corresponding document. The name of such a document will typically default to "Untitled" or "Untitled1." A few applications, including MPW, require names for all documents and will present a dialog similar to that used by "Save As."

Both the **Open** and **Save As** items use routines in the Standard File Package to allow the user to select a file name. The **Open** operation should use the SFGetFile routine of the Standard File Package. The **Save As** operation uses SFPutFile with the previous name (if any) selected as default. Two other routines, SFPGetFile and SFPPutFile, allow you to define your own dialog, but your program may require changes if the format of the standard dialog is changed.

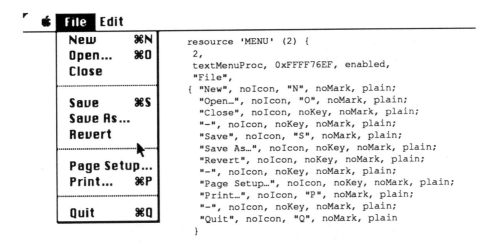

Figure 3-6:   File Menu and MPW Source

If a new file has never been named, some applications treat the **Save** operation like **Save As**. Other applications will disable **Save** until the name is specified. The application may also disable **Save** if the file has not been changed since the last **Save**.

Page Setup and **Print** both present Printing Manager dialogs for printing the document. **Page Setup** corresponds to routine `PrStlDialog` of the Printing Manager, while `PrJobDialog` is used by **Print**. Both dialogs modify the standard 120-byte print record. The print record may either be stored in the header block of the data fork or in the resource fork of the document in a resource of type `'PREC'`. Whenever a new document is created, the print record should be initialized using `PrintDefault`.

Close closes the active document or, if the top window is a desk accessory, the DA. If changes have been made to the document since it was opened, an alert should be presented to ask the user if the changes should be saved before closing the document. Example 3-4 shows the standard alert that should be shown for the **Close** operation in which the default (suggested) action is to save the changes. `Rez` source statements are shown as they might be compiled for use by your application.

Revert to Saved (or simply **Revert**) is similar to a **Close**, followed by an **Open** of the same file. It will also present a confirmation alert, which would ask the user if the changes should be discarded, the opposite wording (and default) from the **Close** alert.

Finally, **Quit** corresponds to a **Close** for each of the document windows, including the confirmation alerts. It might also save any user-specified

```
/* Close confirmation alert */

/* Rez resource compiler source */
resource 'ALRT' (501, purgeable) {
   { 100, 120, 220, 358},
   501,
   OK, visible, silent,
   OK, visible, silent,
   OK, visible, silent,
   OK, visible, silent
};

resource 'DITL' (501, purgeable) {
   { {58, 25, 76, 99},   Button { enabled, "Yes" };
   {86, 141, 104, 215},  Button { enabled, "Cancel" };
   {86, 25, 104, 99},    Button { enabled, "No" };
   {12, 20, 45, 223},
      StaticText { disabled,"Save changes to \"^0\"?" }
   }
};
```

Example 3–4:   Close Confirmation Alert

preferences in a separate document (hidden from the user) prior to quiting. It's not necessary to deallocate memory, since exiting the main program or using the ExitToShell trap to call the Finder will reinitialize the application heap.

Not all of these options are available at all times. If no more documents can be opened because of design or memory limitation, the **New** and **Open** options should be disabled. If no documents are open, only **New**, **Open**, and **Quit** would typically be enabled. Finally, if the top (active) window is a desk accessory, only the **Close** (which closes the DA) and **Quit** options should be enabled.

FINDER INTERFACE

When it launches an application, the Segment Loader passes certain information to an application. This information is stored in the application parameters, which are located between the global variables and the jump table, as shown earlier in Figure 3–3.

If the application was opened with one or more documents from the Finder, the parameters will contain the name of the file(s). The current Finder supports both opening and printing from the Finder, and routine CountAppFiles returns both the number of files and the operation requested. If opening or printing one or more documents was requested, the application uses `GetAppFiles` to find the name and volume for the document. A count of zero indicates that the application was opened without documents.

The application can determine its name using a call to `GetAppParms`. Since the user can change the application name, such as to include the release number, this should be used whenever the application name is needed.

The signature resource conventionally holds the version information for this application. For example, MPW has signature `'MPS '` and a string of the same name. The version data is stored as a text string.

An application bundle allows the desktop icons to be associated with an application and its related documents. A list of known file types and icons is declared that is used for files with a creator equal to the bundle's signature type.

Example 3–5 shows a sample application bundle for an application of type `'WXYZ'` in `Rez` source form. The bundle refers to the application, `'TEXT'`-type documents, and a special file used to store user preferences. The `'ICN#'` resource provides the 32 by 32 icon and mask for displaying the document on the desktop, while the `'FREF'` indicates the file types affected. Icons and file types are associated through a common "local id", in this case 0, 1, and 2. For each resource type listed in the bundle, a resource number corresponding to each local ID is given.

To tell the Finder that an application contains a bundle, the File Manager includes a "bundling" bit in each file entry. This is set by the linker for any application with a `'BNDL'` resource. This can be set using the `SetFile` command.

Finally, applications need a `'SIZE'` resource to indicate parameters to be used when the program shares the machine with other applications. First designed for Switcher, the resource is the standard format for indicating multi-tasking compatibility. In addition to the providing minimum memory the program requires, the `'SIZE'` resource also contains compatibility bits—such as whether the program wishes to receive events indicating that the program is about to become or finish being the currently running application.

3.3 MPW Tools

The MPW programming environment provides a line-oriented shell that supports a number of commands (known as MPW tools) that can be run from within that shell. The interface between a tool and the MPW shell is modeled after that provided by the command shell of the UNIX operating system, which makes it easy to move C programs from UNIX to MPW.

```
/* Application finder resources */

/* Rez resource compiler source */
data 'WXYZ' (0) {
  "Xyz v1.0 © 1987 Joe E. Developer"
};

resource 'BNDL' (128, purgeable) {
  'WXYZ',                    /* signature type */
  0,                         /* version */
  { 'ICN#',                  /* Desktop icons */
    { 0, 400;                /* local id, resource id */
    1, 401;
    2, 402
    };
    'FREF',   /* Files associated with those icons */
    { 0, 500;
    1, 501;
    2, 502
    }
  }
};

resource 'FREF' (500, purgeable) {   /* Application */
  'APPL',                      /* file type */
  0,                           /* local resource id */
  ""                           /* file name (not used) */
};
resource 'FREF' (501, purgeable) {   /* Document */
  'TEXT',                      /* file type */
  1,                           /* local resource id */
  ""
};
resource 'FREF' (502, purgeable) {   /* Preferences file
*/
  'WXYP',                      /* file type */
  2,                           /* local resource id */
  "Xyz Preferences"/* file name */
};

resource 'ICN#' (400, purgeable) {   /* Application icon
*/
  { /* icon */
    $"0001 0000 0002 8000 0004 4000 0008 2000"
    $"0010 1000 0020 0800 0040 0400 00AA BA00"
    $"012A 8900 0211 1080 0429 2040 0829 3820"
    $"1000 0010 2000 0008 4000 3F04 8000 4082"
```

```
        $"4000 8041 2001 3022 1001 C814 080E 7F8F"
        $"0402 3007 0201 0007 0100 8007 0080 6007"
        $"0040 1FE7 0020 021F 0010 0407 0008 0800"
        $"0004 1000 0002 2000 0001 4000 0000 8000";
        /* mask */
        $"0001 0000 0003 8000 0007 C000 000F E000"
        $"001F F000 003F F800 007F FC00 00FF FE00"
        $"01FF FF00 03FF FF80 07FF FFC0 0FFF FFE0"
        $"1FFF FFF0 3FFF FFF8 7FFF FFFC FFFF FFFE"
        $"7FFF FFFF 3FFF FFFE 1FFF FFFC 0FFF FFFF"
        $"07FF FFFF 03FF FFFF 01FF FFFF 00FF FFFF"
        $"007F FFFF 003F FE1F 001F FC07 000F F800"
        $"0007 F000 0003 E000 0001 C000 0000 8000"
    }
};
resource 'ICN#' (401, purgeable) {    /* Document icon */
    { /* icon */
        $"0FFF FE00 0800 0300 0800 0280 0800 0240"
        $"0800 0220 0800 0210 0800 03F8 0800 0008"
        $"0800 0008 0A24 4888 0942 8508 0881 0208"
        $"0942 8508 0A24 4888 0800 0008 0800 0008"
        $"0800 0008 0912 2448 08A1 4288 0840 8108"
        $"0840 8108 0840 8108 0800 0008 0800 0008"
        $"0800 0008 08F9 F3E8 0810 2048 0820 4088"
        $"0840 8108 08F9 F3E8 0800 0008 0FFF FFF8";
        /* mask */
        $"0FFF FE00 0FFF FF00 0FFF FF80 0FFF FFC0"
        $"0FFF FFE0 0FFF FFF0 0FFF FFF8 0FFF FFF8"
        $"0FFF FFF8 0FFF FFF8 0FFF FFF8 0FFF FFF8"
        $"0FFF FFF8 0FFF FFF8 0FFF FFF8 0FFF FFF8"
        $"0FFF FFF8 0FFF FFF8 0FFF FFF8 0FFF FFF8"
        $"0FFF FFF8 0FFF FFF8 0FFF FFF8 0FFF FFF8"
        $"0FFF FFF8 0FFF FFF8 0FFF FFF8 0FFF FFF8"
        $"0FFF FFF8 0FFF FFF8 0FFF FFF8 0FFF FFF8"
    }
};
resource 'ICN#' (402, purgeable) {    /* Preferences icon
*/
    { /* icon */
        $"0000 0000 0000 0000 0000 0000 0000 0000"
        $"0000 0000 0000 0000 0000 0000 0000 0000"
        $"0000 0000 0000 0000 0000 0000 0000 0000"
        $"0000 0000 0000 0000 0000 0000 0FFF FF80"
        $"0800 0040 0AAB 8020 0AA8 8010 0911 0008"
        $"0A92 0008 0A93 8008 0800 0008 0800 0008"
        $"0B33 BB88 0AAA 2208 0B33 3388 0A2A 2088"
        $"0A2B A388 0800 0008 0800 0008 0FFF FFF8";
        /* mask */
        $"0000 0000 0000 0000 0000 0000 0000 0000"
```

```
    $"0000 0000 0000 0000 0000 0000 0000 0000"
    $"0000 0000 0000 0000 0000 0000 0000 0000"
    $"0000 0000 0000 0000 0000 0000 0FFF FF80"
    $"0FFF FFC0 0D76 7FE0 0FD7 FFF0 0EEE FFF8"
    $"0DFF FFF8 0F6C 7FF8 0FFF FFF8 0FFF FFF8"
    $"0DED 6D78 0D55 DDF8 0ECE ECF8 0DFC DF78"
    $"0DD6 5C78 0FFF FFF8 0FFF FFF8 0FFF FFF8"
    }
};
```

Example 3–5:   Application Finder Resources

From a programming standpoint, tools are in some ways similar to a desk accessory. Like a DA, tools are run under an application . However, in most ways tools are more similar to a slimmed-down application. In fact, tools offer an easy way to prototype portions of an application from within MPW.

In particular, numerical and file-oriented (i.e., anything but event-oriented) algorithms are well-suited to testing as small tool prototypes, which are later fleshed out or added to an existing application. Of course, tools can become very large without becoming applications. The two best examples are the Pascal and C compilers.

RELATIONSHIP TO MPW

MPW tools are programs that are started by the main MPW application, which is called MPW Shell. Only one tool can be running at any time. Tools cannot be run without MPW.

Like a DA, a tool does not initialize the Toolbox Managers, nor does it perform the memory initialization steps to manage the size of the heap. However, it does have its own global variables which, like those of an application, are referenced using register A5. If the tool uses QuickDraw or any part of the Toolbox, either directly or indirectly, it will include an InitGraf call for thePort, as the QuickDraw variables must be initialized for a tool, as was described previously for an application.

In addition to global variables, a tool includes a jump table referenced via A5. The format and location of the jump table is the same as that for an application. Because it has its own jump table, a tool may be divided into multiple segments, in the same manner as an application.

The MPW Shell, of course, is an application, and like all applications built with MPW, it uses A5 to reference its global variables. How do MPW tools and the shell share the use of A5? They don't.

Instead, the MPW Shell has to perform many of the same steps in launching a tool that the Finder must do when launching an application. It reads the 'CODE' #0 resource to determine the size of the tool's globals and allocates the tool's globals as a nonrelocatable block on the application heap. The shell then sets A5 to point to these tool globals. It restores A5 to point to application globals when the tool completes or when it's used by the tool to perform some operation, such as update the output window.

In contrast, while the Finder launches an application, it allocates globals below the buffers (as given by BufPtr) and throws away its own value of A5.

A tool controls only a portion of its own memory management. The handling of out-of-memory conditions, as described for applications, is automatically provided by the shell.

This is both a blessing and a curse. It's a blessing, because it frees the tool writer from worrying about SetGrowZone, MaxApplZone, and ResErrorProc, making it easier and quicker to finish the task of writing the tool. The curse—perhaps a minor one—is that the tool does not have limitless flexibility in its memory management, and when a severe crisis comes, it can be abruptly terminated without warning by the shell. In particular, the shell shows no mercy when it is out of memory—the tool will be terminated so that the shell may live.

A tool starts with the same application heap being used by the shell. Certain key code segments of the shell—those that handle standard I/O, windowing, and memory—remain resident with the tool and are locked into low memory before the tool is launched. Many of the shell resources are purged, and other blocks that can be easily retrieved or reconstructed are subject to disposal if the tool requires additional memory.

The shell tags all of its memory blocks before launching the tool. When the tool completes execution, any memory blocks that were created by the tool can be identified as untagged and thus disposed.

The shell also purges all the tool's resources but does not dispose of them. If you are going back and forth between the shell and a tool and you have enough memory, resources for both will be purged but will stay in memory and not require reading the disk the second time around.

A tool does not have its own stack allocated but begins with what remains of the shell's stack. The tool has no control over the size of the stack, and if requires more stack than the default, you must adjust the initial stack size allocated for the MPW Shell application, as described in the *MPW Reference Manual*.

Without memory management hardware, it is impossible for the shell to completely protect itself from a tool that writes to random memory locations. An errant (or malicious) tool can effectively corrupt portions of the heap or stack used by the shell, and both will crash. The memory map of a tool and the shell are shown by Figure 3–7.

Unlike an application, a tool does not ExitToShell to return to the Finder. Instead, it would normally return to the shell by completing the main routine or outer PROGRAM of a Pascal tool. The MacsBug command

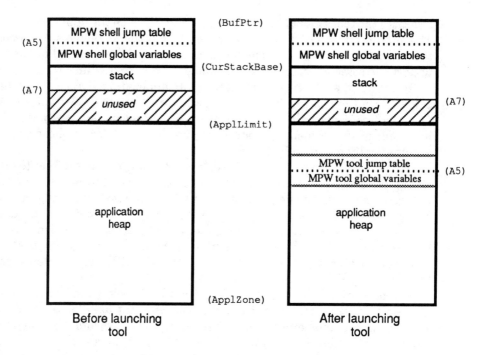

Figure 3–7:   Memory Map of an MPW Tool

G STOPTOOL

can be used to force a tool to terminate, much as the standard

ES

command forces an application to ExitToShell. Both actions are risky and will sometimes cause the Mac to produce the system error alert. This is because an MPW tool is subject to more strict memory management requirements than an application. When an application terminates, the application heap and stack are completely reinitialized. Because an MPW tool shares both the stack and the application heap with the shell, it must not corrupt the state of either, or the shell will likely crash when the tool terminates.

Finally, the shell patches certain Macintosh traps to intercept operations by MPW tools. These include File Manager traps, to allow integration of shell window I/O with the standard OS file I/O calls. This also allows it to close any open files when the tool terminates.

STANDARD I/O UNITS

Although there are some restrictions on tools that do not apply to applications, there are also several new capabilities not available to applications. Perhaps the most significant of these is the provision for standard input and output units.

A Macintosh application displays output in a window, writes it to a file, or uses one of the peripheral (modem, printer, AppleTalk) ports. The restrictions are similar for reading data.

However, line-oriented operating systems such as UNIX, MS-DOS, CP/M, etc., provide a far simpler interface mechanism, one that is assumed by programming languages such as C, Pascal, FORTRAN, and Basic. These languages define one or more character files that are automatically opened for each program.

The MPW environment emulates such a line-oriented environment and provides three standard text files that are opened by default for each tool. These should be familiar to the C programmer, since the usage and terminology for these files are the same as used by C programs under UNIX.

The two most commonly used files are the standard input and output files. These are represented in Pascal by the reserved names `Input` and `Output`; unlike the ISO Pascal standard, these names do not have to be included as parameters on the `PROGRAM` statement in MPW Pascal. These files are also used for I/O statements in which no file is specified.

MPW C programs use `stdin` and `stdout` for these two files. As with other C implementations, I/O calls that use an implied file—such as `getchar` or `printf`—also use these standard files.

These standard I/O files normally are associated with the display window. However, they can be easily reassigned to a specific file of type `'TEXT'`, a portion of a window, combined with other MPW tools to provide a chain of linked commands, or mapped to a null device (a "bit bucket").

The remaining file is another output file, which is normally used for displaying shorter diagnostic messages. This is often used when the standard output unit is producing a long output that is normally assigned to a file, while occassional error or progress messages must be given to the user. C programmers will recognize this as the customary description of file `stderr`. No such concept exists in standard Pascal, so MPW Pascal defines this as a `file Diagnostic`, which is defined in the `IntEnv` unit.

The standard error unit also differs from the other I/O units in the buffering of the I/O. Normally, I/O to standard input and output are buffered in 1024-character groups, while output to the diagnostic file is buffered a line at a time. If you want to write progress messages, you should do so using `stderr` or `Diagnostic`, or the messages will come out in groups of 10 lines or more.

Some programs may use line-at-a-time input/output interactions in which a message is printed and then an interactive response sought from the keyboard. This might be found with a program converted from another operating system. To handle these cases, a read request made by an MPW tool to the command line will automatically flush all output buffers. Also, any command line input is passed through directly to the tool when the Enter key is pressed.

The shell intercepts key File Manager traps while the tool is running, particularly those that open and close files. This allows the shell to recognize and handle special reserved file names (such as Dev:StdIn) that are available from shell commands but are not part of the file system defined by the Macintosh OS. It also allows the shell to close any files opened by a tool when the tool terminates.

SIMPLE TOOLS

If you're familiar with Macintosh development, you've surely heard the claim that "there's no such thing as a simple Macintosh program." An earlier section enumerated the initialization and other requirements of a Macintosh application, while the next section will demonstrate that desk accessories are not appreciably simpler.

On the other hand, an MPW tool can be very simple, although it does so by sacrificing the graphical, event-oriented Toolbox operations that characterize the Macintosh. In a sense, writing such an MPW tool is a step back to a simpler place and time, a step that is particularly appropriate when you're writing a program that you're going to use once and throw away.

The simplest possible MPW tool would be one that performs a single calculation and then prints out the result. An example of a tool written in Pascal illustrates the trivial case:

```
PROGRAM Add;
BEGIN
   WriteLn('2 + 2 = ', 2+2);
END.
```

The corresponding tool written in C is also simple:

```
#include <stdio.h>
main()
{ printf("2 + 2 = %d\n", 2+2);
}
```

Of course, this is not the sort of tool that one would develop for permanent use, but it might correspond to simple one-time programs written to answer an immediate question.

Perhaps more useful are tools that convert data to a different format. This data might be used by an application, edited using MPW, or the result of another MPW tool. Since the names of files used for standard input and output can be selected from the shell, all such a tool must do is to perform the appropriate transformation on the input data and output the result.

These files don't have to correspond to a problem related to programming. Figure 3–8 shows the input data format that might be used by a business cash expenditure journal or by a home budgeting system based on a personal checking account. Each line includes a check number, a date, an expenditure amount, and an account number to categorize the expenditure. It is desired to transform this to a spreadsheet format that can be used to calculate totals for each account (a ledger), as shown.

Example 3–6 is an MPW tool that transforms the data of Figure 3–8 by reading from standard input and writing to standard output. To allow the output data to later be read into separate columns by a spreadsheet, each output column is separated by tab (ASCII HT) character. Because it provides better built-in formatting routines, the C version is much simpler and would probably be the language you would use for such a problem if both languages were equally available and familiar.

Input Data

Check	Date	Account	Amount
232	1/31	4	$27.72
233	2/1	1	$200.00
234	2/3	5	$4.59
235	2/5	3	$117.75
236	2/5	5	$32.20
237	2/8	2	$65.22
238	2/10	5	$4.15

Output Data

	A	B	C	D	E	F	G
	Check	Date	1. Rent	2. Utilities	3. Taxes	4. Auto	5. Supplies
1							
2	232	1/31				$27.72	
3	233	2/1	$200.00				
4	234	2/3					$4.59
5	235	2/5			$117.75		
6	236	2/5					$32.20
7	237	2/8		$65.22			
8	238	2/10					$4.15

Expenditures

Figure 3–8:   Input and Output Data for Example 3–6

```c
/* (C): MPW tool using standard I/O units */

/* Reformat journal entries into a spreadsheet ledger */
#include <stdio.h>

main()
{ int account, col;
  char check[16], date[16], amount[16];
  while
     (scanf("%s %s %d %s\n", check, date, &account,
        amount)>0)
  { printf("%s\t%s", check, date);
    for (col = 1; col<=account; col++)
        printf("\t");
    printf("%s\n", amount);
  }
}
```

```pascal
{ (Pascal): MPW tool using standard I/O units }

PROGRAM ReFormat;
{ Reformat journal entries into a spreadsheet ledger }

TYPE
  BuffStringType = STRING[15]; {STRING is MPW-specific}

CONST
  Tab = $09;   { Ascii tab character }

VAR
  tabchar: CHAR;

  PROCEDURE MyReadString(VAR s: BuffStringType);
  VAR
    c: CHAR;
    newlen: INTEGER;
  BEGIN
    s := '';
    newlen := 0;
    WHILE NOT Eoln DO
      BEGIN
        Read(c);
        IF (c = ' ') OR (c = tabchar) THEN
          LEAVE; { Lisa/MPW extension to ISO Pascal }
        newlen := newlen+1;
        s[0] := CHR(newlen); { Manually set length }
        s[newlen] := c;       { and add character }
      END;
  END; { MyReadString }
```

```
PROCEDURE MyReadInt(VAR num: INTEGER);
VAR
  c: CHAR;
BEGIN
  num := 0;
  WHILE NOT Eoln DO
    BEGIN
      Read(c);
      IF (c = ' ') OR (c = tabchar) THEN
        LEAVE;
      num := num*10 + ORD(c) - ORD('0');
    END;
END; { MyReadInt }


VAR
  account, col: INTEGER;
  check, date, amount: BuffStringType;

BEGIN
  tabchar := CHR(Tab);
  WHILE NOT Eof DO
    BEGIN
      MyReadString(check);
      MyReadString(date);
      MyReadInt(account);
      MyReadString(amount);
      ReadLn;
      Write(check,tabchar,date);
      FOR col := 1 to account DO
        Write(tabchar);
      WriteLn(amount);
    END;
END.
```

Example 3–6: MPW Tool Using Standard I/O Units

SHELL INTERFACE

Not all tools have such simple requirements. In addition to the input and output files, more elaborate interfaces are available to allow a tool to communicate with the MPW environment. As with the standard file assignments, the interfaces are similar to those provided by UNIX.

MPW Pascal adopts the unit concept of UCSD Pascal. The USES statement is used to import the definition of a library module and its interface. In this case, `IntEnv` defines routines and variables used by a tool to interface with the MPW environment.

Each MPW tool may return an exit status to the shell. A status of 0 is considered successful and is the default returned when a program exits normally. Other values indicate varying warning or error levels. As with UNIX, C programs use the system subroutine `exit` to return a status code or use the return statement in `main()`. Pascal programs use a procedure `IEExit` defined in unit `IntEnv`.

Each tool can receive a list of parameters, normally either options (beginning with a -) or file names. This, again, is like UNIX, although the ordering, length, and case sensitivity for interpreting MPW options differs from UNIX.

C programs receive these parameters as two arguments to the `main` routine. The first argument (named `argc` in C programming books) is one more than the number of parameters. The second argument is the array (`argv`) of C strings, with `argv[0]` containing the tool name, and `argv[1]` through `argv[argc-1]` containing one parameter each.

The situation in Pascal is somewhat more complicated. MPW Pascal uses the same names as for C programs, but the variables require the `IntEnv` unit. While `ArgC` has the same meaning as its C equivalent, `ArgV` is a pointer to a zero-based ([0..8091]) array of `IEStringPtr` variables which are simply pointers to type `STRING`. These pointers must normally be dereferenced before being used.

Example 3–7 demonstrates the use of command parameters and exit status codes in a simple program that displays a file. After verifying that exactly one file name has been given, that name is used to open a file referred to as `newfile`. The file is copied, one line at a time, to the standard output file. If the number of parameters is incorrect or the file cannot be opened, an error message is printed on the standard output unit. The former error terminates with a status of 1 (normally reserved for syntax errors), while the latter terminates with a status of 2.

ADVANCED INTERFACE ROUTINES

To purchasers of the original 128K Macintosh, one aspect of the Mac's graphical interface became maddingly familiar. Instead of the hourglass used by the Xerox Smalltalk system, the Mac used a more modern watch-shaped cursor to indicate that the user must wait. Cute iconography, of course, did nothing to speed the wait.

Also, it was sometimes difficult to tell whether the program was working or had merely put up the advisory and "gone south." Bleary-eyed late-night hackers might also argue that the watch was small and hard to see.

MPW offers a larger, newly designed cursor, a checkered circle often referred to as the "beach ball." To provide more satisfying user feedback, an MPW tool can both display and spin the beach ball cursor. The direction of

```
/* (C): MPW shell interface */

/* Display the file given by parameter #1 on standard
      output
 Limitation: only works with lines of 255 characters or
      less
*/

#include <stdio.h>

main(argc, argv)
int argc;
char *argv[];
{ char line[256];
  FILE *newfile;

  if (argc != 2)    /* tool name and one parameter */
  { fprintf
       (stderr, "### Wrong number of parameters to
%s\n",
     argv[0]);
     exit(1);
  }

  if ((newfile = fopen(argv[1], "r")) == NULL)
  { fprintf(stderr, "### Unable to open %s\n", argv[1]);
     exit(2);
  }

  while (fgets(line, 256, newfile) != NULL)
     fputs(line, stdout);
}


{ (Pascal): MPW shell interface }

PROGRAM DisplayFile;
{ Display the file given by parameter #1 on standard
      output
  Limitation: only works with lines of 255 characters or
      less
}

USES
  PasLibIntf,            { required by IntEnv }
  IntEnv;                { Diagnostic, ArgC, ArgV }
```

```
VAR
  line: STRING[255];
  newfile: TEXT;    { text-only FILE }

BEGIN
  IF ArgC <> 2 THEN{ tool name and one parameter }
    BEGIN
      WriteLn
        (Diagnostic,
         '### Wrong number of parameters to ',
         ArgV^[0]^);
      IEExit(1)
    END;

  Reset(newfile, ArgV^[1]^);
  IF IOResult <> 0 THEN
    BEGIN
      WriteLn
        (Diagnostic, '### Unable to open ', ArgV^[1]^);
      IEExit(2)
    END;

  WHILE NOT Eof(newfile) DO
    BEGIN
      ReadLn(newfile, line);
      WriteLn(line)
    END;
END.
```

Example 3–7:   MPW Shell Interface

the spin can be changed to provide additional information. The routines to perform these operations are defined for Pascal programs by unit Cur-sorCtl.

Tools can also access symbolic name assignments defined via Set and Export MPW shell commands. This includes such information as the base directory used by MPW, the name of the current active window, and other user-controllable parameters, as will be discussed in later chapters.

C programs can use the same mechanisms as used to read UNIX shell variables. The (optional) third parameter to main is an array of strings (customarily named envp) containing all the environment variables, or the function getenv can be used to look up the value of a particular shell variable. Pascal routines would use the IEGetEnv function defined by the IntEnv unit.

MPW tools can define procedures to receive control when a particular condition is raised. The interface for C programs uses the same include file

(`<signals.h>`) as defined by the UNIX kernel; Pascal programs use unit Signal. At present, the only signal generated by MPW is the interrupt signal, which occurs when the user types Command-period.

Many tools may need to interpret OS and Toolbox error numbers into human-readable strings. MPW Pascal programs can use the same list of messages that are used by Apple's tools by initializing and calling the shell's error manager. These are defined by unit ErrMgr.

Finally, tools you write should provide interactive dialog help such as that provide by those supplied with MPW. To do so, you need to include a resource of type 'cmdo' in the resource fork of your tool.

This resource defines the size of the dialog displayed by the Commando tool, the user-selectable buttons, check boxes, pop-up menus and so on, and the corresponding shell command to be generated for each user selection. Building such resources is described in the *MPW Reference Manual*.

3.4 Desk Accessories

The interface used by the Toolbox for desk accessories is similar to that used by the OS for device drivers. The two program types share a common resource type ('DRVR'). A desk accessory uses a subset of the driver interface defined by the Device Manager and described in *Inside Macintosh*. There are also a few Toolbox operations particular to desk accessories, such as those involving the clipboard, which are described in the chapter on the Desk Manager.

STORING AND BUILDING

A desk accessory is a DRVR resource. The name of the resource is the name of the DA, which will be shown in Apple menu. Because the Device Manager and File Manager share a common _Open call (PBOpen from C or Pascal), a desk accessory must include a null character ($00) as the first character of the name. Otherwise, the DA "Chooser" would be confused with a file named "Chooser."

A desk accessory DRVR resource must be built using a reserved-format header, as must a device driver. This includes offsets for the three entry points used by desk accessories and two other entry points used only by drivers. All entry points return a function value of type OSErr, which for DAs should always be a constant noErr (0).

To allow desk accessories written in a higher-level language, such as Pascal or C, MPW provides a standard approach for building DAs without assembly language, using the MPW resource compiler Rez. To use this, you would

- Declare the 'DRVR' resource header in a Rez source file
- Include other related resources using the above formula
- Write the Pascal (C) code using five predefined routine names
- Link the Pascal (C) as a resource of type 'DRVW'
- Compile the 'DRVR' resources, merging in the 'DRVW' Pascal (C) code

The Rez command in the final step is used to set the file creator to 'DMOV' and the file type to 'DFIL', which will be recognized by the Font/DA Mover utility program as the appropriate file to find a desk accessory in.

CAPABILITIES

The capabilities of a desk accessory can be seen in the description of a 'DRVR' header, as shown in Table 3–4. This header is the standard format expected by the Device Manager for both desk accessories and device drivers, as discussed later. The table shows the flags defined for the first word of the header as they would be defined using a Rez input file. After the 'DRVR' header, many DAs will also include an 8-byte entry giving version information. This is used by the Installer to determine which is the latest version of a DA, as will be discussed in conjunction with Toolbox definition procedures.

The header includes offsets to five predefined entry points. Using the MPW 'DRVR' definition for higher-level languages, these entry points are declared as normal Pascal functions named DRVROpen, DRVRClose, DRVRControl, DRVRStatus, and DRVRPrime. The MPW C compiler allows defining routines that conform to the Pascal calling sequence, using the pascal storage class directive.

All operations for a desk accessory result in calls by the application (via Desk Manager traps) to one of the open, close, or control entry points. The remaining two routines are called only for drivers, but must be provided to avoid a link error. All three entry points accept two parameters, which are the same as those used for device drivers.

The first parameter is a pointer to a ParamBlockRec, which is the standard parameter block used for device manager and file manager calls. This is not needed for open and close calls, but the csCode and csParam fields are used by DA control calls, just as they are for device control operations.

The second parameter is a pointer to a device control block of type DCtlEntry. This block retains its contents for the DA as long as the DA remains open, and so is used to communicate values between the various entry points until the DA is closed. The fields of this block are shown in Table 3–5.

Offset	Name	Desk Accessories	Drivers††
0	drvrFlags	Flags (see below)	
2	drvrDelay	Ticks (1/60 second) between periodic action	
4	drvrEMask	Event mask for DA	
4	drvrMenu	Id of associated menu	
8	drvrOpen	Offset to DRVROpen†	
10	drvrPrime	—	Offset to DRVRPrime†
12	drvrCtl	Offset to DRVRControl†	
14	drvrStatus	—	Offset to DRVRStatus†
16	drvrClose	Offset to DRVRClose†	
18	drvrName	Name (Pascal string)	

Data after the name may include an 8-byte entry for the Installer application, as shown in Table 3–7.

Values for drvrFlags

Name*	Bit mask	Desk Accessories	Drivers††
needLock	$4000	lock DRVR when loaded	
needTime	$2000	periodic action per drvrDelay	
needGoodbye	$1000	Driver is open	
statusEnable	$0800	—	DRVRStatus is defined
statusEnable	$0400	—	DRVRControl is defined
writeEnable	$0200	—	DRVRPrime performs writes
readEnable	$0100	—	DRVRPrime performs reads

†   Relative to beginning of DRVR resource
††   Except as noted, same as for desk accessories
*   As declared in MPW resource source files

Table 3–4:   DRVR Resource Header

Offset	Name	Type	Usage
0	dCtlDriver	Ptr	Pointer or handle to DRVR
4	dCtlFlags	word	Flags (see below)
6	dCtlQHdr	QHdr	Queue header
10	dCtlPosition	long	Driver read/write current position
14	dCtlStorage	Handle	Private storage used by driver
18	dCtlRefNum	word	Reference number = -(resource id)-1
20	dCtlCurTicks	long	Tick count
24	dCtlWindow	WindowPtr	DA window
28	dCtlDelay	word	Ticks between periodic action
30	dCtlEMask	word	Event mask for DA
32	dCtlMenu	word	Id of associated menu

The values of the high byte of dCtlFlags are the drvrFlags from the resource header. The low byte contains:

Name*	Bit mask	Usage
iOpened	$20	Driver is open
iRAMBased	$40	dCtlDriver is handle to relocatable
idrvrActive	$80	Driver is currently running

*Suggested name; actual name not defined by MPW Release 2.0

Table 3–5:   Driver Control Block Fields

Of the values defined by the dctl pointer to a DCtlEntry, three are used directly by most desk accessories. The integer dctl^.dCtlRefNum (dctl->dCtlRefNum in C) contains the driver reference number, which is a negative integer, equal to one less than the negative of the actual 'DRVR' resource ID.

The handle dctl^.dCtlStorage is normally used to point to variables used by the desk accessory entry points, while dCtlWindow contains a pointer to the DAs window. The desk accessory should use GetPort to save the previous GrafPort and SetPort to assign the dCtlWindow as the drawing port before any QuickDraw operations.

None of these values are initialized by the Desk Manager, but must be assigned by the DRVROpen entry point.

THE DRVROPEN FUNCTION

The DRVROpen function is called by the application (via OpenDeskAcc) when the desk accessory name is selected from the Apple menu. This will start up the DA if it is not already present on the desktop. If the DA is already open (as may be deduced by examining dCtlWindow or dCtlStorage, as appropriate), it will normally bring the DA window to the front of the other windows. However, some DAs, such as those without windows (or without a go-away box in their window) will treat the second open call as a close request.

The resource IDs of a desk accessory are assigned by the Font/DA Mover when the desk accessory is installed in the System file to assure a unique resource number. Such DAs are currently limited to resource numbers 12 through 26. Apple reserves IDs 27 through 31 for desk accessories stored in the resource fork of an application.

As noted earlier, desk accessories may include resources limited to a particular range of resources IDs. Because the resource ID of a DA will likely be changed by installation, a DA must compute the resource numbers of its resources dynamically. However, when building a DA, an arbitrary resource ID must be chosen and used consistently for all the owned resources. This initial resource number is calculated as

```
resid := $C000 + 32*driverresno;
```

For example, a DRVR resource number 16 would use owned resources ranging from $C400 to $C41F at the time the desk accessory was built.

During execution, a DA must recalculate its actual resource ID, as set by the Font/DA Mover. No assumptions about an actual value can be made. This can be calculated from the reference number, as expressed by the formula:

```
driverno := -dctl^.dCtlRefNum - 1;
```

For example, dCtlRefNum set to -21 would indicate that the desk accessory was stored in the System file with a resource ID of 20. All references to owned resources should then range from $C280 to $C29F. The normal way is to use this to set a variable to the calculated base value ($C280) and then express all resource references in the DA as the base value plus a constant in the range [0,31]. For example,

```
yesno := Alert(resid);
msghand := GetString(resid+msgno);
```

A desk accessory that wishes to communicate data (such as the value of resid) between successive calls to the entry points will normally allocate a relocatable block in the application heap to hold that data. In MPW release 1.0, this data is normally declared as a Pascal record (C struct) and allocated by the DRVROpen routine using NewHandle, with the handle stored in dctl^.dCtlStorage. All references to these variables in the three DRVR routines are performed using this handle, although Pascal programmers would normally HLock the handle at the entry to each routine and then use a WITH statement to simplify references to the fields of the record.

Apple has indicated that a release of MPW after 2.0 will probably simplify the use of variables in DAs to be more like application global variables. As noted earlier, the lack of such variables prevents the use of library routines that require these variables. When using a later release of MPW, you should consult your reference manual to determine the current restrictions regarding the use of global variables.

The typical actions performed by a DAs DRVROpen routine are shown in Example 3–8.

THE DRVRCLOSE FUNCTION

As discussed earlier, the application will call CloseDeskAcc when the go-away box of a DA window is clicked or when Close is selected from the File menu with the DA window on top. This in turn calls the DRVRClose entry point of the desk accessory.

A DRVRClose routine should deallocate any memory allocated by the DRVROpen operation. It also closes the desk accessory window and performs any necessary cleanup operation. It should reset both fields in the DCtlEntry to NIL as a matter of form, so that a "smart" Desk Manager will not deallocate the memory a second time.

THE DRVRCONTROL FUNCTION

The DRVRControl function is used to handle all remaining DA operations. The first parameter to the function, csCode, indicates the operation to be performed, as summarized in Table 3–6.

Code	Name	Action
-1	goodBye	Application is about to ExitToShell
64	accEvent	csParam is pointer to an EventRecord
65	accRun	Perform periodic action
66	accCursor	Update cursor appearance
67	accMenu	csParam contains menu id and item
68	accUndo	Undo previous action
70	accCut	Cut selection to clipboard
71	accCopy	Copy selection to clipboard
72	accPaste	Paste clipboard to selection
73	accClear	Clear selection

Table 3–6:   Desk Accessory Control Parameters

Normally, when an application terminates (usually via ExitToShell), the current desk accessories are not closed, to speed up the termination process. Instead, the entire application heap will be reinitialized, and thus

```
/* (C): DRVROpen actions */

#include <Types.h>
#include <QuickDraw.h>
#include <OSUtils.h>
#include <Devices.h>
#include <Windows.h>

#define noErr 0     /* don't need entire <Errors.h> */

pascal OSErr DRVROpen(pb, dctl)
ParamBlockRec pb;
dCtlEntry dctl;
{ short drefno, dresid, baseres;
  WindowPtr mywind, saveport;

  drefno = dctl->dCtlRefNum;
  baseres = 0xC000+(~drefno << 5);

  if (dctl->dCtlWindow <> NULL)
  { GetPort(&SavePort);   /* protect application */
    mywind = GetNewWindow(baseres, NULL, (WindowPtr)-1);
    dctl->dCtlWindow = mywind; /* needed later */
    /* a DA window */
    ((WindowPeek)mypeek->windowKind = drefno;
    SetPort(SavePort);
  }
  else
    BringToFront(dctl->dCtlWindow);

/* Don't need to manually draw window, because both
    GetNewWindow and BringToFront will generate
    updateEvt forDRVRControl
*/

  return (noErr);
}


{ (Pascal): DRVROpen actions }

UNIT MyDA;

USES
  MemTypes, QuickDraw, OSIntf, ToolIntf;
```

```
FUNCTION DRVROpen
    (pb: ParamBlockRec; dctl: dCtlEntry):OSErr

VAR
    drefno, dresid, baseres: INTEGER;
    mywind, saveport: WindowPtr;
    mypeek: WindowPeek;

BEGIN
    drefno := dctl^.dCtlRefNum;
    baseres := $C000+BSL(BNOT(drefno), 5);

    IF (dctl^.dCtlWindow <> NIL) THEN
        BEGIN
            GetPort (SavePort);    { protect application }
            mywind :=
                GetNewWindow(baseres, NIL, WindowPtr(-1));
            dctl^.dCtlWindow := mywind  { needed later }
            mypeek := WindowPeek(mywind);
            mypeek^.windowKind := drefno;  { a DA window }
            SetPort (SavePort);
        END
    ELSE
        BringToFront(dctl^.dCtlWindow);

{ Don't need to manually draw window, because both
  GetNewWindow and BringToFront will generate
  updateEvt for DRVRControl
}

    DRVROpen := NOErr;
END; {DRVROpen}
```

Example 3–8:   DRVROpen for a Desk Accessory

any memory allocated will be freed automatically. Any windows will also disappear when the heap is reinitialized.

However, some desk accessories may need to update a configuration file to disk, ask the user to save a data file, or some other final action. If the DA has specified needGoodbye in its flags word, then DRVRControl will be called with the goodBye code, the so-called "goodbye kiss." For any action short of a crash, a DA can rely on receiving control one last time if this flag is set. This normally will call the same logic used by DRVRClose, although this is not the routine that will be called directly by the Desk Manager.

A desk accessory may also request control periodically. The resource header gives a delay in terms of ticks, one-sixtieth of a second. A zero delay corresponds to the maximum frequency of calls, which is once per tick. A delay of 1 is every other tick, 2 every third tick, while 59 would be once every second. When the periodic action is to be performed, DRVRControl is called with a code of accRun.

Such time requests are only as reliable as the calls to SystemTask by the application. If the application is performing a time-consuming operation (such as saving a file) without calls to SystemTask, the DA will not receive control until the next call to SystemTask. Therefore, a DA should not assume that the delay is as requested, but should instead use TickCount or GetDateTime to obtain the actual elapsed time. A VBL task is a more reliable, but less flexible way to perform a periodic task, as will be discussed later.

A DA will often include an associated menu. Selection of a DA's menu item causes a MenuSelect trap (called from the the application's event loop) which passes an accMenu code to the control routine. The value of csParam contains the menu number and menu item in a 32-bit longword. The DA would use the same logic as an application to separate the menu and item numbers.

The accCursor control call allows a DA to set the QuickDraw cursor to an appropriate value, using SetCursor. The call comes from SystemTask. It's up to the DA to determine if the mouse position is over the DA's window.

Five possible control codes—accUndo, accCut, accCopy, accPaste, and accClear—correspond to selections on the Edit menu. These allow a desk accessory to communicate information to the application through the clipboard. It is the responsibility of the application to put up an appropriate Edit menu (with the five items enabled) when a DA is the active window and to call SystemEdit to produce the control calls. A DA should probably beep if it receives an inappropriate edit operation.

All remaining events are passed to the DA using the accEvent control code. In such cases, csParam contains a pointer to the EventRecord passed by the application to SystemClick or SystemEvent. DAs that use the Dialog Manager to handle events will pass these events directly to DialogSelect.

Of the possible events, all DAs need to respond to an updateEvt for the DA window, which is used to redraw the DA window when it has been behind other windows. DAs also may also perform special actions for the activation (or deactivation) of the DA window. Finally, many DAs use either keyDown or mouseDown events in the DA to control the action of the DA.

3.5 Support Routines

The remaining types are not complete programs in themselves, but are normally used to support an application (or tool or DA). Many of these types were originally expected to be used only by Apple. Thus, developing such a program is the province of an experienced Macintosh programmer, and the documentation on these topics is somewhat sparse and scattered.

This section describes the capabilities of these types and provides an overview of their structure.

DRIVERS

A driver is a resource of type 'DRVR' with a resource name beginning with a period (.). Several drivers are built in, either in the ROM or in the System file. These include the floppy disk driver (.Sony), the sound driver (.Sound), as well as drivers for the serial ports, AppleTalk, and the printer. These drivers normally use reserved resource numbers in the range [0,11]. The eight possible SCSI devices use resource numbers in the range [32,39].

Other drivers may be stored outside the System file. The most common of these drivers are for printers, which are stored in separate files in the blessed folder. Each user can only use one printer at a time, so the appropriate printer is selected via the Chooser desk accessory, and the name of the device type is stored in a system resource. When an application calls the Printing Manager, it in turn uses this chosen name to find the corresponding printer driver file, which includes several DRVR resources to do the page setup and printing.

A 'DRVR' resource header is the same format for a driver as for a desk accessory, and the mechanism for building such a resource is similar. The DCtlEntry and ParamBlockRec parameters have been previously described, although the ParamBlockRec is more extensively used for device drivers.

A device driver is called by the _Open, _Close, _Control, _Status, _Read, and _Write Device Manager traps which select the indicated driver by its driver reference number. When called by Pascal and C programs, these traps are identified as PBOpen, PBClose, and so on. The FSOpen and FSClose routines perform a similar function but have a different calling sequence.

Open, Close, Control, and Status correspond to the four entry points of similar names. Read and Write map to calls on DRVRPrime, with pb^.ioTrap equal to one of the following two values:

```
aRdCmd Read  call
aWrCmd Write call
```

All five entry points are functions of type OSErr (a 16-bit integer) and, unlike a DA, may return an nonzero error code. Among the likely error codes are statusErr, controlErr, abortErr, and ioErr.

PACKAGES AND TOOLBOX DEFPROCS

Packages and the Toolbox definition procedures (resource types 'CDEF', 'LDEF', 'mbdf', 'MDEF', 'WDEF') are similar in several ways.

First, each of these programs has exactly one entry point, at the beginning of the corresponding resource. It's up to the program to determine the action to be performed by examining one or more of the parameters.

Second, each of the resources is normally stored in the System file. A resource is stored as unlocked to avoid heap fragmentation when it is read into memory; it is the responsibility of a package or defproc to lock itself if it performs memory allocations, including Resource Manager calls. Packages are normally stored as purgeable.

Third, each resource customarily includes a 12-byte header, as shown in Table 3–7. The format of the first word of the header is not important as long as it is a 68000 instruction to skip over the nonexecutable sections of the header.

Offset	Type	Usage	Comments
0	word	Branch over header	Usually BRA *+$0A
2	word	Flags	Usually 0
4	ResType	Resource type†	Same as for resource
8	word	Resource id†	Same as for resource
10	word	Version†	Unsigned integer
12	—	Beginning of code	

† Available for use by Installer application

This 12-byte header is customary format for the following resource types:

CDEF	Control definition procedure
LDEF	List definition procedure
MDEF	Menu definition procedure
PACK	Package
WDEF	Window definition procedure

Table 3–7:   Header for Packages and Toolbox defprocs

Such a header is not strictly required by the Toolbox or the corresponding manager. However, it is used to keep these resources up to date. An application supplied by Apple, the Installer, allows any user to take an installation script and update his or her System file to the latest version of the resource. The 8 bytes indicated are examined by the Installer, which gives preference to the largest version number.

Toolbox definition procedures are called indirectly by your program: the corresponding manager calls the appropriate Apple routine which supplies the standard Toolbox definition procedures that are used by all applications and documented in *Inside Macintosh*. You would write a new definition procedure if one of the existing ones did not suit your requirements. Each of the Toolbox definition procedures expects a series of parameters, including one that distinguishes what operation is to be performed for the control, window, etc.

Packages aren't something that you normally write yourself: the only exception is when designing a device driver selected by the Chooser desk accessory. However, your program will make frequent use of packages so it will be important to understand how they work when it comes time for debugging.

The protocol for a package is that the last parameter pushed onto the stack is a 16-bit "routine selector," indicating which routine in the package is to receive control; most packages number the selector sequentially from zero. Routine selectors for the SANE-related packages are different, and the actual values can be obtained from the *Apple Numerics Manual*.

The format of the remaining parameters depends on the routine selected. For example, NumToString and StringToNum are both called with the _Pack7 trap but use routine selectors 0 and 1 and have different parameter formats.

There is a considerable performance overhead associated with each package, as opposed to a direct subroutine call. Each package call involves code in the following order:

- Pushing parameters on the stack
- Pushing the routine selector
- The _Pack*n* trap
- The trap dispatcher
- The Package Manager to load and transfer to the package
- Decoding the routine selector by the package
- The actual routine

Despite the overhead, Apple's packages provide a standardized interface for a group of related routines that will be used by multiple applications. Also, packages overcome incompatibilities between the MPW and other linker formats, such as Lisa, MDS, Lightspeed, Turbo Pascal, Rascal, etc. A package written with MPW can be used from any language that supports calling the Macintosh ROM, even including languages such as Basic, FORTRAN, or Lisp.

OTHER PROGRAM TYPES

VBL tasks are installed and uninstalled using the Vertical Retrace Manager. A task is defined by a nonrelocatable record of type VBLTask, which includes a pointer to the task (vt^.vblAddr) and the number of ticks before it is to be run (vt^.vblCount).

The task is installed in the vertical retrace queue using trap VInstall. It will be executed when the value of vblCount reaches 0. If each entry to the VBL task resets `vblCount` to a nonzero value, it will be reinserted in the queue for future execution after the task completes. The trap `VRemove` is used to remove such an entry from the queue.

On the Macintosh II, the vertical retrace period depends on the specific video card and display. Old-style VBL interrupts are emulated by the Mac II, and you can also install tasks synchronized to the actual retrace period using `SlotVInstall`.

Initialization resources are executed at system startup time. They are contained in resources of type `'INIT'`. Those written by Apple are stored in the System file, while you should store yours in an initialization file of type `'INIT'` in the system folder; `'INIT'` resources can also be found in `'RDEV'` device driver files, such as the AppleShare workstation driver. The state of the memory management and various system globals is somewhat different from that when an application is running and is subject to change in the future.

An `'INIT'` resource should be marked as locked in the resource file so that it will not be relocated while it is running. This is reasonable to do, since memory availability and heap fragmentation won't usually be a problem at initialization time.

`FKEY` resources are similar to desk accessories, except that they have only a single entry point, and very little support is provided to the function key by the Toolbox. Unlike desk accessories, `FKEY`s do not have an associated window, storage, or owned resource IDs defined by the Toolbox. The `FKEY`s supplied by Apple are not reentrant, but perform only a one-time action. However, third-party `FKEY`s have been written that put up a window, modify the clipboard, etc.

MEMORY-RESIDENT CODE

Most program types are run for only one application. For example, desk accessories are automatically loaded by the `OpenDeskAcc` call into the application heap, and they are terminated when the application terminates (thus reinitializing the heap). A desk accessory can be designed to run cleanup code at this time.

Similarly, a VBL task may be installed only for the duration of an application and removed by the application prior to termination.

However, some code may need to remain memory-resident for longer periods of time, spanning multiple applications. For example, a disk driver— such as for a RAM disk—should probably be loaded once into memory and retained until the Macintosh is shut down. Some VBL tasks may be appropriately run under any application, such as one that draws a clock or the menu bar.

Such code can be installed in one of two ways. One involves using system heap, while the other uses memory outside any heap.

When calling a Memory Manager trap to allocate memory on the heap, an optional bit is available to indicate that the memory is to be allocated from the system heap. A resource stored in a file can also indicate that it should be loaded in the system heap via a bit in the resource attributes; this was used to load the AppleTalk driver resources before these drivers were built into the ROM.

The system heap is most often used by 'INIT' resources. If the resource is stored in the initialization file with the sysHeap resource attribute set, the system will load it into the system heap. Such resources may also contain code and data that is used later, such as for a VBL task installed as system startup. If the 'INIT' does a DetachResource call for itself (and any other resources) prior to exiting, the space will not be freed and will remain memory resident.

To assure adequate system heap space to run an 'INIT', the system looks for a 'sysz' resource #0 in the initialization file, which contains a 32-bit value indicating how much contiguous system heap space is required by all the 'INIT' resources in that file. The system heap will be expanded, if necessary, to guarantee that heap space.

System heap space prior to System version 4.1 is severely limited. If you will be distributing your software for such systems, Apple recommends using less than 100 bytes in the system heap for such configurations, as other software may also attempt to use the limited system heap space.

More memory is available by increasing the space between the system buffers and the application globals, adjusting the global space toward lower memory. This is done by decreasing the value of BufPtr by the number of bytes required and then placing the necessary code between the new and old values of BufPtr. This was used by the RAM Cache provided by the 128K ROM and by many third-party drivers, printer spoolers, etc.

Obviously, this can't be done while running an arbitrary application since the application might include pointers to the globals that would become invalid. However, an application could be written with the sole purpose of installing the code, and this is used by many RAM disk utilities. Another way is to use an INIT resource to do this at system startup.

Unfortunately, installing code this way has one major disadvantage— you can't easily remove it. Other programs may have changed the value of BufPtr themselves, so blindly restoring its previous value is a good way to crash. If removing the code is important, you should find enough room in the system heap, where blocks can be deallocated in the same way as on the application heap.

Chapter 4

The MPW Shell

MACINTOSH PROGRAMMER'S WORKSHOP IS AN INTEGRATED DEVELOPMENT SYSTEM that supports editing, compiling, and running Macintosh programs.

MPW operations revolve around a single Macintosh application called "MPW Shell." This shell includes a text editor and command interpreter and supports external tools and applications from within the shell, including the compilers and resource utilities.

This chapter describes the shell and its design, describing the shell's approach to windowing and commands. It also summarizes all the available shell commands and gives tips on how to perform simple customizations after installation. It concludes by describing the shell menus and simple MPW commands for examining and modifying files.

4.1 Introducing the Shell

The MPW Shell is a Macintosh application that remains running whenever you are using MPW. The shell provides an integrated programming environment to support everything you need to do while developing Macintosh programs. Every step can be performed from within the shell, whether editing, printing, renaming files, compiling, linking programs, or running them.

There are two ways to perform an operation within MPW. Commands can be selected from menus, as with other Macintosh applications. The MPW shell also has its own unique text commands. These two types of commands will be referred to as menu commands and shell commands.

145

MPW built-in editor supports multiple document windows controlled by menu commands. At any time, any given window can be used for data, commands, or both.

The shell commands have their own syntax and usage. The number of available commands exceeds 100, which can easily be extended to include your own commands.

This section talks about the shell and its design, concluding with a simple "hands-on" session.

DESIGN PHILOSOPHY

MPW is an integrated programming environment that combines the following three design concepts:

- A Macintosh-style text editor

- A UNIX-like line-oriented command language

- A window-based command interpreter reminiscent of Smalltalk.

The provision of a text editor within MPW is a necessity. Apple's Lisa Workshop, its Macintosh 68000 Development System (MDS), and various third-party development systems all included menu-driven editors since, unlike some systems, the Macintosh does not come with a text editor.

Thanks to the strong Macintosh interface guidelines, the MPW editor is so similar to that supplied with other development systems (and Mac word processors) that you should be able to sit down and use the editor without reading a single page of documentation. The menus, described later, are almost identical to those of other editors. It doesn't hurt that some of the MPW editor is adapted from the original MDS Edit application.

However, the two other aspects of the shell are not as obvious at first glance. From a description of MPW's numerous commands, a reader might note that the command language (if not the actual commands) parallels that of the UNIX operating system. The syntax for combining commands and specifying options is also similar to that of UNIX. In the internal implementation of commands, many C commands designed to run under UNIX can be easily modifed to run as MPW tools.

MPW also supports UNIX-style command procedures and there are a number of analogs to the various functions and special characters of the various UNIX command shells. (See Appendix F for a comparison of the commands.)

However, in its treatment of commands and how they are run, MPW is more similar to the Smalltalk programming environment in its approach.

MPW bears an intentional resemblance to the Smalltalk environment. To begin with, the original Macintosh design was heavily influenced by the Smalltalk workstations. Multiple windows, the selection of text, and use of the clipboard on the Mac are similar to Smalltalk, while the use of menus and scrolling bars is analogous, even though the design is different.

MPW adapts one more key concept from the Smalltalk environment. In MPW, commands are just like text until they are executed, and any piece of text can later be treated as a command.

In contrast, most interactive operating systems—such as UNIX, VAX/VMS, and MS-DOS—use a modal command intrepreter. Text is entered in one of two distinct modes. In one mode, the typing forms commands, which the system automatically executes when the typing is completed. In the other mode, your typing is just data and is stored without interpretation.

In MPW (and Smalltalk), commands are typed the same way as data. Then, once the command (or command list) is complete, a signal is supplied to indicate that the command should be executed. In Smalltalk, it's the "DoIt" menu command from the center mouse button. For MPW, it's the "Enter" key. Like Smalltalk, a shell command can be executed from within any of the MPW windows.

Each time you use Smalltalk, the system workspace window is opened to display a predefined list of commands. To execute one of these commands, you click to select the command(s) desired using the mouse and then DoIt. MPW always starts with the "Worksheet" window, which usually contains the commands you ran in a previous session. You can select any command in the worksheet and then Enter.

MPW actually supports both the Smalltalk and UNIX view of commands, but UNIX users will require some adjustment. You can't just type Return after entering a command, since the Return key is used to break up lines within a document. Instead, a command line is executed after typing a Command-Return or Enter.

DOCUMENTS

A key part of MPW is the integrated editor, which allows direct manipulation of multiple text documents.

As with other Macintosh software development systems, MPW uses documents of type 'TEXT'. These documents can contain program source, MPW commands, data, or program output. Such documents can be read and written by most word processors, database programs, and spreadsheets.

MPW's editing capabilities are robust. Document size is constrained only by available disk space, instead of the limit of 32,000 characters imposed by TextEdit on simple text editors. The number of documents open at one time is also memory limited, with 14 windows possible on a 1 Mb Macintosh Plus. The editor also includes special support for editing program source statements.

The text of the document is stored in the data fork of a Macintosh file of type 'TEXT'. The text can include printable characters, Tab and Return characters. Other nonprinting characters can be included but will not be displayed. This text is what is read by other MPW commands, for menu-based editing, the shell-based editing commands, the compilers, and so on.

The data fork of an MPW document can also be read by applications outside MPW, such as a database or a word processor. The MPW editor, in turn, can read text files from a third-party development system, converted from the Lisa Workshop or from other applications.

Other information about the document is stored in the resource fork of the file. Most of this formatting information is used only by the MPW editor. This information is summarized in Table 4–1.

Data Fork

    Text data, including Tab and Return characters
    No limit on length

Resource Fork (Resource type 'MPSR')

    Document formatting
        Font Name
        Font Size
        "Show invisibles" setting
        "Auto indent" setting
        Tab width
    Window contents
        Current selection
        Horizontal and vertical scrolling
    Window frame
        Window size
        Window location
        Zooming status (in or out)
    Printing (Page Setup)
        Paper size
        Orientation
        Reduction/Enlargement
        Special effects
    Markers
        Marker names
        Marker selection

Table 4–1:   Contents of an MPW Text Document

Three of the resource-based settings are used by some of the MPW commands. These correspond to parameters set by the Format menu, as described later in this chapter.

One of the settings, tab width, determines the interpretation of Tab characters. When included in an MPW document, each Tab skips to the next tab stop. Each document has a setting for the number of spaces between these uniformly spaced tab stops. As shipped, MPW assumes a value of 4, which means that tab stops are set at column 5, 9, 13, and so on. Source files from operating systems such as UNIX and VAX/VMS assume tab stops every

8 characters, so this is another common choice under MPW. The default tab size is a customizable environment parameter.

The other two format settings control the font name and size used for the document. You should choose a nonproportional font (Courier or Monaco) for your documents so that source code will line up in vertical columns. If you print listings on a LaserWriter, you normally will use the Courier font, although the document's font name and size used for displaying a document can be overridden when printing from within MPW.

Changes to the text of a document can be saved by the Save menu command or undone using the Undo or Revert to Saved menu commands. However, changes to the resource-based settings, such as the font size or current selection, are *always* saved in the document when it is closed, even if the changes to the text are not saved. If the document is opened read-only, editing and certain format changes are disabled, but changes in the selection and window appearance are saved nonetheless.

While you are editing the document, the integrated MPW environment automatically maintains the document consistent with any other MPW commands that affect it. If you edit a source file and then compile it, the compiler will use the current version displayed, even if the changes haven't been saved to disk. If you rename a document (or folder), the title of any open document window affected by the rename will automatically be updated and the new pathname shown.

COMMANDS AND WINDOWS

Like other programs that conform to the Macintosh user interface, the MPW editor uses the Window Manager to display multiple document windows. Both functionally and visually, the Window Manager makes an important distinction between the frontmost and all remaining open windows.

The front window is termed the "active" window by the Window Manager documentation, and has a distinctive appearance—including a "status panel" in the lower left corner of the window. Typing and menu commands are interpreted as affecting the active window. The active window remains frontmost until you click on another window or a menu command closes the window or brings another one forward.

As dictated by the standard user interface, the Window Manager considers the remaining windows displayed to be "inactive." Inactive windows have a distinct appearance, with their scrolling and title bar controls not drawn (see Figure 4–1). In the standard Macintosh interface, operations do not affect any inactive window, except for commands that may affect all windows, such as Save All or Quit. Instead, to change the contents of one of the inactive windows, you must first make it the active window.

MPW assigns a special significance to the frontmost inactive window, the second window from the top of the stacked window frames. This window is termed the "target window," because it is the target of many MPW shell commands.

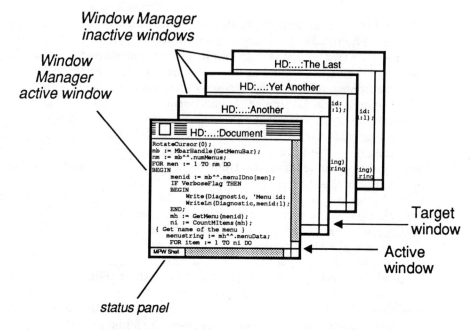

Figure 4–1:   MPW Document Windows

As is customary, MPW interprets keyboard and menu commands as changing the contents of the active window. Editing, save, clipboard operations, and typing all affect the topmost window, as one might expect.

However, shell commands must be entered in the active window. As will be described in the next chapter, many of these commands are intended for editing documents. If these commands were to operate on the active window, you would have to add them to your document each time you needed them—and the commands would even edit themselves!

Instead, most editing commands are performed using two windows, the command window and the document window. The commands are run in the active window, while the target window is assumed to hold the document. Most shell editing commands change the contents of the target window if no window is specified. Usually, the command (active) window will be the worksheet, with your document set as the target window. Since the worksheet is saved from session to session, if you find a particularly useful command, it will likely be there in the worksheet the next time you need it.

4.2 Shell Commands

Most of the functions of MPW are available only through the line-oriented shell commands which are selected in one of the open windows.

Each command may include options that modify the command operation and parameters to specify what the command should operate on. Additional syntax rules must be followed if the parameters include special characters, such as spaces.

The section concludes with a summary of the shell commands available from within MPW.

TYPES OF COMMANDS

There are actually four types of commands that can be executed from within MPW. Each of these commands can take parameters and follow the syntax rules described in the next subsection. MPW generally makes their differences transparent, although the implementation of each type is radically different.

The four types are:

Built in commands. These are commands that are compiled into the MPW Shell application, and, not suprisingly, are the quickest to execute. Most of the commands that come with MPW are built in. You can't modify built in commands, but you can replace them using command aliases, described later. An example of a built in command is `Help`.

Command files, also known as *scripts.* These contain a series of MPW shell commands in a text document. When you execute a command file, the individual commands are shown in the command window. How command files work and how to build your own is the subject of Chapter 6. An example of a command file is `Line`. Command files are easy to find because they are the only documents in the command folders that the editor will allow you to open.

MPW tools. As described in Chapter 3, tools are special compiled programs that are designed to run within MPW. Most of the larger components of MPW are tools, including the compilers, assembler, disassemblers, and the linker. An example of an MPW tool is `Pascal`.

Applications. Any Macintosh application—a program that can be run from the Finder—can be an MPW command. An example of an application run from MPW is ResEdit.

However, running applications is slower than running tools from within MPW, since there is a considerable delay in saving MPW's status information before running the application and restoring it afterward. No matter how excruciating, you can't stop an application once it's started; instead you must wait until it finishes initializing before your Quit will return you to MPW.

Applications designed to run as stand-alone programs are also not integrated with the MPW environment. The information displayed by MPW disappears from the screen when the MPW windows are replaced by those of the application.

You may find it inconvenient to run applications from within MPW or at least want to make sure that you don't accidentally run an application that guarantees your machine will be locked up for several seconds. For that, you need to know how MPW finds commands.

After checking to see if a command is built in, MPW searches in one or more folders on your disk to find a file corresponding to the command name. The list of folders is given by your Startup file and can easily be changed, as will be described in the next section.

The file type and creator determine how MPW will run the file, as shown by Table 4–2. Both command files and tools are expected to have MPW as its creator ('MPS' with a space) and the specified file type. Each application will have its own creator but must have a file type 'APPL'. If MPW finds a file in one of the command folders that does not match the known forms, the file is ignored.

Command type	Creator	File Type	Where
Built-in	—	—	MPW Shell
Command file	MPS	TEXT	{Commands}
MPW tool	MPS	MPST	{Commands}
Application	any	APPL	{Commands}

Table 4–2:   MPW Command Types

COMMAND SYNTAX

Each shell command line consists of a command name and one or more parameters, separated by a blank character. Between parameters, multiple spaces and tabs are considered equivalent to a single blank. For example, in the command line

```
Catenate First Second      Third
```

the command name is Catenate, and the three parameters are First, Second, and Third.

Command names must always be completely spelled out, although you can freely use upper- and lowercase letters. MPW does not recognize any abbrevations for its command names unless you define your own.

MPW recognizes two types of parameters. Options begin with a minus sign. Some options—but not all—require the next parameter to be associated with the option. These parameters do not have a minus sign.

For example, the Print command outputs one or more text files to the currently selected printer, as in

```
Print -copies 2 -h -font Courier MyFile
```

The -copies option takes a parameter specifying the number of copies to be printed; the parameter for the -font option is the name of the font to be used in printing. The -h option adds a heading to the top of each page and does not have an associated parameter. This command would print two copies of file MyFile with page headers using the Courier font.

As their name suggests, options are not required but suggest alternate interpretation for a given command. The use of options varies from command to command, and sometimes two MPW commands will use the same option (usually a single letter) for two separate purposes. Table 4–3 shows some of the commonly used options and their associated parameters, where appropriate.

Option	Explanation	Example
-c count	Repeat command count times	Replace -c 5 /the/ 'that'
-c creator	Specify file creator	Files -c 'MPS '
-c	Answer "Cancel" to dialog	Move -c Source.p Backup.p
-d name	Define symbol for compiler	Pascal -d DEBUG Demo.p
-font name	Specify font name	Print -font Courier
-h	Include (or suppress) headers	Print -h Sample.p
-i folder	Specify include directory	C -i HD:MyIncludes: hi.c
-l	Long format	Files -l
-l	Display line number	Search -l
-n	Answer "no" to dialog	Delete -n TheFolder
-o objfile	Output to objfile	Asm Demo.a -o Demo.o
-p	Display progress information to diagnostic output	Duplicate -p :Src: Back:
-p	Print (for applications only)	MacWrite -p UserManual
-t type	Specify file type	Files -t 'TEXT'
-y	Answer "yes" to dialog	Erase -y 1

Table 4–3: Sample Shell Command Options

All remaining words in the command line are considered "positional parameters." The remaining parameter in the above example—MyFile—is a positional parameter, as were all the parameters in the Catenate example. Most commands expect one or more positional parameters; usually these parameters are file or folder names, but not always.

Options and their parameters can be given before, in the middle, or after positional parameters; this ordering is not important according to the standards for MPW commands. If you write your own commands, allowing options and parameters in any order may require additional programming on your part.

The ordering of the different options is also not important. However, a few commands allow repeating the same option in the command line, such as to specify multiple folders in which to search for files. In those cases, the ordering of the option parameters may be significant to the command.

Distinctions between upper- and lowercase letters in command lines are usually not important. The differences are always ignored in command names and the names of options, so that the two commands

```
files -l
FILES -L
```

are treated identically. When indicating an error message, however, the command will print its name with the actual capitalization you used.

Positional and option parameters are often case insensitive. The File Manager ignores case when searching for an existing file, so file and folder name parameters can be specified without regard to case. MPW commands will usually ignore case when it is not significant, so that the command line

```
print -h -font couRIER MYFILE -COPIES 2
```

is equivalent to the earlier Print example.

However, case is important for some parameters. Several commands use option parameters to specify resource types, file types, and file creators as four-character codes, for which upper- and lowercase identifiers are distinct. These codes may also include spaces, which must be enclosed in quotation marks (quoted). For example, to list all applications in the current directory, the command

```
Files -t APPL
```

would be used. The command

```
Files -t appl
```

would produce a different list.

When defining a new name, the case of the parameter will be used for the name. This applies to file names, resource names, and segment names. You should not type

```
Duplicate myfile COPYOFFILE
```

if you wanted the new file to be named CopyOfFile.

Case distinctions will also be retained for human-readable text. Examples of this include page titles, the Echo command, and prompts in command files and dialog boxes.

SPECIAL CHARACTERS

Even before a command receives its parameter list, the shell analyzes the command line and interprets blanks as separating parameters. What do you do if you have a parameter that has a space in it, such as System   Folder?

Any parameter that includes a blank character must be *quoted* to make sure that the space or tab characters are recognized as part of the parameter rather than as separating consecutive parameters. Quoting is also used to prevent the shell from interpreting other special characters in a parameter. For example, the command

```
Files 'HD:System Folder:'
```

lists the files in the system folder.

The shell recognizes both apostrophes (single quotes) and quotation marks (double quotes) to delimit quoted strings. The two delimiters have a slightly different significance*, but for many purposes can be used interchangeably. The following two commands are equivalent:

```
Files 'HD:System Folder:'
Files "HD:System Folder:"
```

Note that the delimiters are the two standard ASCII characters. The Macintosh character set also includes opening and closing apostrophes and quotes (' ', " "), which are not treated in any special way by MPW.

The apostrophe and quotation mark are among those characters that have special meanings to the MPW shell. Sometimes, you'll need to actually pass these characters through the shell to a command. To indicate the actual meaning, a special character may be quoted in the same way as a blank character.

A quotation mark is always quoted between apostrophes and vice versa— "" or '''. If you need to include both, you can run several strings together. The parameter in the command

```
Echo '"I '"can't"' go," he said.'
```

is composed of three strings, delimited by apostrophes, quotation marks, and apostrophes, respectively.

Another way to prevent the shell from interpreting special characters is to "escape" the character, preceding it with a ∂ character (the Greek delta, Option d) in the command line. As an example, the Echo command merely takes its parameters and displays them in order, separated by a space. The command

---

* Apostrophes quote all characters to the next apostrophe. Paired quotation marks do not quote the shell interpretation of the symbols `, {, and ∂.

```
Echo My name    is      ∂"mud∂"
```

would produce the output

```
My name is "mud"
```

Sometimes it is necessary to continue long commands across multiple lines. If the last character of a command line is a ∂, the shell continues interpreting the command on the next line as though neither the ∂ nor end-of-line characters were present. The two command lines

```
Echo My name ∂
     is ∂"mud∂"
```

are considered equivalent to the previous command.

The ∂ character has a third significance to the shell: it is used to introduce certain nonprinting control characters, as shown in Table 4–4. The tab character is often needed when writing editing commands, while the return is important when MPW commands are used to display other commands.

Symbol†	Explanation
∂t	Tab character, ASCII HT
∂n	Return character, ASCII CR
∂f	Form feed, ASCII FF
∂<Return>	Ignore both ∂ and CR character
∂c	Display c

† The ∂ symbol is Option-D.
   ∂ is not recognized when quoted by apostrophes, e.g. '∂n'

Table 4–4:   Generating Special Characters

Quoting and escaping both override the interpretation of certain characters that are special to the shell. There are many characters considered special by the shell, as will be described in the next chapter. Fortunately for the novice MPW user, many of these characters are ones not commonly used, like ∂, ≈, ¬, and ∞.

If you want to include more than one command on the same line, the commands can be separated by a semicolon (;). As with any other special character, if the semicolon is quoted or escaped, it is not "seen" by the shell and has no special significance.

If you're not sure what the available options are, or aren't comfortable with the line-oriented syntax, you can use the Commando tool to present an interactive dialog. For example,

```
Files…
```

would offer a dialog showing the options and expected parameters for the Files command. Instead of an **OK** button, the action button is labeled **Files**; clicking on it will execute the command you have constructed. If, when clicking **Files**, you hold down the Option key, the constructed command will also be displayed on the command window; if you hold down Command-Option, the command will be displayed but not executed.

Finally, there will be occasions when you want to include information in a list of commands that is not an actual command. The shell command syntax allows for comments, much as with any other programming language. The number sign (#) indicates that the remainder of the line is a comment and should not be interpreted by the shell. The shell ignores the remainder of the line and any other special characters in it, including a ∂ at the end of the line.

A complete list of special shell characters is described in conjunction with shell programming in Chapter 6.

USING COMMANDS

A shell command is text in one of MPW's open document windows, with an indication to MPW that the text should be executed as a command. There are four ways you can signal this to the shell:

- Select the command(s) and click on the status panel (in the lower-left corner of the active window)
- Select the command(s) and press the Enter key
- Type the command into any window and then type Enter

Command-Return is equivalent to the Enter key, but may be awkward for some typists or keyboards. MPW 1.0 also provided an "Enter" menu item, but this was replaced by the status panel-click in 2.0.

In the remainder of this chapter, the phrase "Enter the command Do This" will be used as a shorthand notation for typing, selecting, and executing the command line "Do This." How the command is entered is up to you.

Starting the command will change the command display in the lower left corner of the active window to show the command name. If the command shown is anything other than MPW Shell, it can be aborted by Command-period.

Most commands will either display the "watch" delay cursor or MPW's own checkered circle, which is dubbed the "beach ball." Commands that use the beach ball cursor will spin the cursor periodically to let you know your Mac is still alive.

Most MPW commands will use textual input, output, or both. The MPW environment provides for three standard input and output streams for any command. These streams are assigned to the active window by default, but can be changed to another window or file via special command line characters.

Most MPW commands display some form of output. By default, this display will be placed in the active window. Because the output is inserted in the current window, it will always deselect the command and will be displayed after the commands. If you have selected multiple commands, the output for all commands will appear after all the commands.

As noted earlier in Chapter 3, the shell supports two separate output streams for each command. One stream is the standard output, which includes the normal display of a command. For a command that outputs the contents of the file, the output goes to the standard output stream.

Many commands also produce additional information that is not part of the standard output. Instead, it is sent to a second output stream, the diagnostic output stream. Any command that produces error messages will do so to the diagnostic output. Some commands include an option (usually -p) to display detailed progress reports, which also go to the diagnostic output.

These standard assignments for the diagnostic output apply to all commands and thus are not mentioned (except in their breach) in the description of specific MPW commands.

Although the two outputs are displayed the same way by default, they can be separated. Also, the diagnostic output is displayed after each line, instead of the larger buffer sizes used by standard output.

Figure 4–2 shows the diagnostic output from the MPW Pascal compiler, which is displayed after the command line. Note the beach ball cursor and the command display.

Like many MPW commands, the Pascal command produces output in the form of other MPW commands. In this case, selecting and entering the File and Line commands shown would cause the MPW shell to display the file in error at the appropriate line. The comment character on the remaining lines prevents them from being executed as commands.

Some commands also expect textual input. Most of these allow one or more file names to be given as positional parameters. Examples of such commands include the assembler and compilers. However, if no input file is specified, these commands read their input from the standard input file.

The mechanism for entering data in the shell is the same as for entering commands. Either you select the text you want and enter it, or you type one line at a time and type Enter anywhere on that line. In fact, it is possible to compile small programs directly from the worksheet.

When a shell command is waiting for input, each entered selection is passed to the command. You can tell a command is waiting for input because the name is shown in the command display, but the normal (I-beam) editing

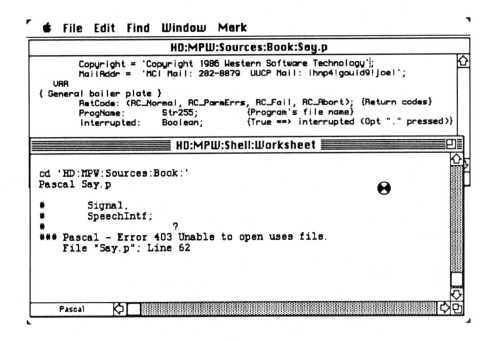

```
 ▄  File  Edit  Find  Window  Mark

╔═══════════════════ HD:MPW:Sources:Book:Say.p ═══════════════════╗
║        Copyright = 'Copyright 1986 Western Software Technology'; ⇧
║        MailAddr = 'MCI Mail: 282-8879  UUCP Mail: ihnp4!gould9!joel'; 
║    VAR
║ { General boiler plate }
║        RetCode: (RC_Normal, RC_ParmErrs, RC_Fail, RC_Abort); {Return codes}
║        ProgName:    Str255;         {Program's file name}
║        Interrupted: Boolean;        {True ==> interrupted (Opt "." pressed)}
╠══════════════════════ HD:MPW:Shell:Worksheet ═══════════════════╣
║                                                                 ⇧
║ cd 'HD:MPW:Sources:Book:'
║ Pascal Say.p                                        ⊗
║
║ #        Signal,
║ #        SpeechIntf;
║ #                  ?
║ ### Pascal - Error 403 Unable to open uses file.
║     File "Say.p"; Line 62
║
║                                                                 
║    Pascal   ◁▯▓▓▓▓▓▓▓▓▓▓▓▓▓▓▓▓▓▓▓▓▓▓▓▓▓▓▓▓▓▓▓▓▓▓▓▓▓▓▓▓▷▯
╚═════════════════════════════════════════════════════════════════╝
```

Figure 4–2:   Diagnostic Output in Active Window

cursor is shown instead of the watch or beach ball. To terminate the input stream, type Command-Enter.

However, the power of MPW's standard input/output streams—output, diagnostic output, and input—comes from their flexibility. Each stream can be reassigned to a specific file on the command line.

As shown by Table 4–5, the shell interprets certain reserved characters

Output

> file	send standard output to file
>> file	append standard output to end of file

Diagnostic output†

≥ file	send diagnostic output to file
≥≥ file	append diagnostic output to end of file

Input

< file	read standard input from file
cmd1	cmd2	use the output of cmd1 as the input of cmd2

† The ≥ symbol is Option-.

Table 4–5:   Command I/O Redirection

as reassigning one of the three standard I/O streams to refer to a specific file. This is referred to as a "redirected" stream.

The symbols for redirecting I/O are similar to command options in that they require a parameter to follow. Unlike options, a blank is not required between the redirection symbol and the file name parameter. And unlike options, I/O redirection is handled by the shell—not the command—and any command that reads or writes from one of the three streams can have the stream redirected.

The output and diagnostic output can be directed to overwrite the contents of a file. Each can also be directed to append the output to the end of an existing file, which is useful if you have several commands that output to the same file. For any of the four possible combinations, if the output file does not exist, it is created as an MPW document.

Redirection of output is important because it allows the output and diagnostic streams to be separated. For many commands, you will want to direct the output to a file but not redirect the diagnostic output, which would still be displayed in the active window.

Input can be taken from an arbitrary file by redirecting the input. If the file doesn't exist, the shell stops without executing the command.

If a command allows either a file name parameter or reads from standard input, you can read a file either by specifying the file name or redirecting input. The difference between the two commands

```
Pascal Sample.p
Pascal < Sample.p
```

is that the second Pascal command does not know the name of the file. This means that the second command will use a fixed name for its object file output. For the first command, the source file name is used to define the output name, in this case Sample.p.o.

As with other MPW operation, I/O redirection is integrated with the rest of the environment. If you redirect output to a document that you're currently editing, the version in the window will change as the command runs. If you redirect input from a file that's being edited, the version in the document window will be used, even if that version has not been saved.

Finally, a series of MPW commands can be chained together, with the output of one command used as the input of the next. The vertical bar character (|) separates a series of sequential commands, much as the semicolon (;) separates multiple commands. The difference is that the output of the first command is sent to the input of the second command; the default diagnostic stream for all commands remains the active window.

This "piping" of successive commands was one of the important innovations of the UNIX operating system. However, unlike UNIX, the standard Macintosh operating system does not support multitasking, so MPW cannot have the two commands running simultaneously. Instead, it stores the output of the first command in a temporary file, then uses the temporary file as input to the second command.

Input and output files can also be redirected using the Commando tool if you're not comfortable with the UNIX-like syntax of redirecting the I/O streams on the command line.

AVAILABLE COMMANDS

A complete copy of MPW includes more than 100 commands spread across MPW, the C and Pascal packages, and MacApp. Tables 4–6 through 4–9 subdivide the commands into four categories: file manipulation, editing, shell programming, and program development. Studying this list will give you some idea of MPW's capabilities. As indicated, several of the program development commands are only available in the optional C, Pascal, and MacApp packages.

A few of these commands—such as Commando—are rarely used directly, but are designed to be called by other commands. Many of the commands are useful only when writing a list of commands that will be used repeatedly.

Not shown is the single application included with MPW, the ResEdit resource editor. Most Macintosh developers will be familiar with ResEdit, as prerelease versions were distributed by Apple more than 2 years before MPW was released. ResEdit is described in Chapter 9.

Also not shown is the MacsBug debugger, which provides assembly-language debugging for programs built with MPW.

Once you've learned some of the MPW commands, you might occasionally forget and confuse the actual name with a similar command from another system. For example, many systems use Copy to mean copying an entire file; in MPW, this is the standard clipboard operation, while Duplicate copies a file. To look up the actual command, you first have to remember its name, since the reference manual lists the command descriptions alphabetically. Table 4–10 is supplied to jog your memory.

FILE PATHNAMES

Macintosh owners are used to selecting file names using the Standard File Package dialog boxes, as noted in Chapter 2. However, line-oriented MPW shell commands must specify a file using a written name. When you're typing commands, you can avoid this by using Commando to select your files, but if you're writing command files, you need to understand the syntax of the shell's file and folder names.

Often, you only need the name of the file. In some cases it will be necessary to specify the folder the file is stored in.

A complete Macintosh file specification is referred to as a "full pathname". A full pathname consists of a disk volume name, perhaps followed by one or more folder names, then optionally followed by a file name. A full

General use

Help	display command information

Disk Volumes and Folders

Directory	set or display the default directory
• DirectoryMenu	add standard menu for changing directory
Eject	eject volumes
Erase	initialize volumes
Mount	mount volumes
NewFolder	create directory (folder)
• SetDirectory	set the default directory
• SetPriv	set access privileges for file server folder
Unmount	unmount volumes
Volumes	list mounted volumes

File Properties

• Backup	selectively copy files and folders
Delete	delete files and directories
Duplicate	copy files and directories
• Exists	check for existence of a file or directory
Files	list names of files and directories
Move	move files and directories
• Newer	compare modification dates of files
Rename	rename files and directories
SetFile	set file attributes

File Contents

Catenate	concatenate multiple files into one
Compare	compare text files†
Count	count lines and characters†
Equal	compare files and directories
FileDiv	divide file into several smaller files†
Search	search files for pattern†

Formatting

Canon	map identifiers to canonical spelling†
Entab	convert runs of blanks to tabs
Font	set font and size for window
Print	print text files†
Tab	set tab positions
• Translate	translate character set†

Legend

†	MPW tool
	Except as noted, other commands are built in
•	Not included in MPW 1.0

Table 4–6:   File Commands

Clipboard Operations

Clear	delete the selection
Copy	copy selection to Clipboard
Cut	delete selection and save in Clipboard
Paste	replace selection with Clipboard contents

Windows

Close	close a window
• MoveWindow	change screen position of document window
New	open new file in window
Open	open file in window, or make active window
• Revert	revert window to saved state
Save	save contents of window(s)
• SizeWindow	change size of document window
• Stack Windows	rearrange windows to overlap
Target	make window the target window
• TileWindows	rearrange windows to not overlap
Windows	display window names
• ZoomWindow	zoom or unzoom document window

Markers

• Mark	assign a marker to a text selection
• Markers	display marker names
• Unmark	remove a marker

Other Editing

Adjust	shift lines left or right
Align	align left margin of source text
Find	find and select a text pattern
Replace	pattern-match text replacement
Undo	undo last editing operation

Legend

•   Not included in MPW 1.0
All commands are built in

Table 4–7:   Editing Commands

pathname is an unambiguous specification of a file or folder—unless there are two disks currently mounted with the same volume name, which you should make a point of avoiding.

In some cases, you might specify a file name (perhaps preceeded by one or more folder names) without a disk volume name. Any pathname without a volume name is considered to be a "partial pathname," and is interpreted relative to the current folder.

The HFS version of the File Manager uses the colon character (:) to separate the components of a pathname. If the first character of a pathname is a colon or if it contains no colons, the name is considered to be a partial pathname. Such examples include `Sample.c` and `:RIncludes:Types.r`.

Environment Variables

Alias	define or display aliases
Evaluate	calculate result of expression
Export	export shell variables or display exports
Set	define or display shell variables
Shift	renumber command file parameters
Unalias	remove aliases
• Unexport	delete shell variable from export list
Unset	remove shell variable definitions

Dialogs, Menus and Prompts

AddMenu	add or display menu item
Alert	display alert box
Beep	generate tones
• Commando	display dialog with command parameter help
Confirm	display confirmation dialog
Date	display the date and/or time
DeleteMenu	delete user- defined menu items
Request	request text from a dialog
• Select	display arbitrary selection dialog
StdFile	display file selection dialog

Command Files and Parameters

Echo	display parameters
Execute	run command file with current scope
Exit	return from command file
Parameters	display command file parameters
• Quote	display quoted parameters
• Which	indicate pathname of command

Control Flow

Begin	group commands for I/O redirection
Break	(un)conditional exit from For or Loop
Continue	(un)conditional iteration of For or Loop
Else	separate statements of If command group
End	terminate Begin, For, If or Loop command group
For	repeat commands once per parameter
If	conditionally execute commands
Loop	repeat commands indefinitely until Break
• Quit	leave MPW to finder
• Shutdown	power down or reboot the Macintosh

Legend

•   Not included in MPW 1.0
    All commands are built in

Table 4–8:   Shell Programming Commands

Shared Utilities

	CvtObj	convert Lisa object files to MPW object files
•	ErrTool	create an error message file
	Lib	combine object files in object library
	Line	find source line with error§
	Link	link object files into a program
•	PerformReport	generate a performance report
•	SetVersion	update program version resource
•	SysErr	display error message

Program Building

•	BuildCommands	display commands necessary to build program§
•	BuildMenu	add standard build menu§
•	BuildProgram	compile and link a program§
•	CreateMake	generate a Make dependency file§
	Make	display build commands based on dependency file

Assembler

Asm	Motorola 68000-family assembler
DumpCode	disassemble CODE resources
DumpObj	disassemble object files
MDSCvt	convert MDS assembler source to MPW
TLACvt	convert Lisa TLA assembler source to MPW

Resources

DeRez	resource decompiler
ResEqual	compare two resource forks (sample program)
Rez	resource compiler
RezDet	validate resource fork

Optional Components

Pascal

Pascal	Pascal compiler
PasMat	format Pascal programs
PasRef	cross reference Pascal programs
• ProcNames	display procedure and function names

C

C	C compiler

MacApp

MABuild	compile and link a MacApp program§
PostRez	build MacApp-compatible resources

Legend

§	Command file (script)
	"Except as noted, other commands are MPW tools"
•	Not included in MPW 1.0

Table 4-9:   Program Development Commands

AddMenu	DeRez	MABuild	Save
Adjust	Directory	Make	Search
Alert	DirectoryMenu	Mark	Select
Alias	DumpCode	Markers	Set
Align	DumpObj	MDSCvt	SetDirectory
Asm	Duplicate	Mount	SetFile
Backup	Echo	Move	SetPriv
Beep	Eject	MoveWindow	SetVersion
Begin	Else	New	Shift
Break	End	Newer	Shutdown
BuildCommands	Entab	NewFolder	SizeWindow
BuildMenu	Equal	Open	StackWindows
BuildProgram	Erase	Parameters	StdFile
C	ErrTool	Pascal	SysErr
Canon	Evaluate	PasMat	Tab
Catenate	Execute	PasRef	Target
Clear	Exists	Paste	TileWindows
Close	Exit	PerformReport	TLACvt
Commando	Export	PostRez	Translate
Compare	FileDiv	Print	Unalias
Confirm	Files	ProcNames	Undo
Continue	Find	Quit	Unexport
Copy	Font	Quote	Unmark
Count	For	Rename	Unmount
CreateMake	Help	Replace	Unset
Cut	If	Request	Volumes
CvtObj	Lib	ResEqual	Which
Date	Line	Revert	Windows
Delete	Link	Rez	ZoomWindow
DeleteMenu	Loop	RezDet	

Table 4–10:   Alphabetical List of MPW Commands

A complete pathname always begins with the volume name, followed by a colon, followed by any folder names, followed by the file name, if any. An example of a complete pathname is `HD:MPW:Libraries:Interface.o`.

Two successive colons skip back past a folder name. The names `HD::Sources:MPW:` and `HD:MPW:` both refer to folder `MPW` on volume `HD`.

Full pathnames are displayed by MPW in the title of each document window and in the Windows menu. In cases in which the pathname is too long, one or more middle components of the pathname will be omitted, replaced by the ellipsis (...).

Table 4–11 summarizes the different forms of pathnames. In some cases, MPW will recognize the name of a folder or file, depending upon which the name actually refers to.

A "directory" is either a specific disk volume or folder located on one of the volumes. Under HFS, folders can be on the desktop (directly in the volume)

Partial pathnames

F	File or folder F, relative to current directory
:F	Folder F, relative to current directory
:F:	Folder F, relative to current directory
:F:G	File or folder G in folder F, relative to current directory
::F	File or folder F in parent directory of current directory†
:::F	File or folder F in parent of parent directory†

Complete pathnames

V:	Disk volume V
V:F	File or folder F in volume V
V:F:	Folder F in volume V
V:F:G	File or folder G in folder F of volume V

†If the current directory is HD:MPW:Sources:, then the parent directory is HD:MPW:

Table 4–11:   Interpreting Pathnames

or within other folders. Moving a folder from within one folder to another doesn't change the folder name, but it does change the directory name.

The shell maintains a single current directory. The `Directory` command displays or sets the name of that directory, or you can use the `SetDirectory` command, which also adds entries to the optional Directory menu. Changes in the current directory will change the directory used by the Open and Save As dialogs, but not the other way around.

Any command that expects a file name can take either a complete or partial pathname, as can the shell's I/O redirection symbols. If a partial name is given, it is interpreted relative to MPW's current directory.

In most cases, you don't type full pathnames or even pathnames for MPW commands. Instead, many MPW commands display other commands referencing the file name. Alternately, MPW will display the file name, and you can edit the line containing the file name into a command. MPW includes a menu command to open the selected file name, and you may define your own menu commands that operate selected names.

However, you will make your life much easier if you avoid using spaces or other special characters in any folder or file name that will be regularly used with MPW. Although MPW allows using such names, they must always be quoted. This adds extra typing each time you use the name.

More significantly, the use of such names means any command that uses a file name parameter must quote the names. This includes your custom command files, menu commands, and the dependancy files used with Make to automate program building. While it's generally a good idea for these commands to quote any names, sometimes you may forget, and other times it may be syntactically awkward to combine a quoted name with other quoted parameters.

This use of prudent name choices begins with the name of the disk volume(s) you use for development, since this name will begin every pathname used by MPW. From the previous discussion of command syntax, you can see that volume names of the form ∂20, My Disk, and —Reliable would tend to confuse the shell when they appear in pathnames.

Directory names that will be used with the SetDirectory command are even more restrictive. They should not include any of the characters in ;^!< or a leading - or (.

If you want to use spaces in file or folder names to improve readability, there is one available option. The nonbreaking space (Option-spacebar) is not considered a blank. This space does not require quoting, and thus its use in a folder name will not require any path to be quoted. At the Finder, go ahead and change the name of System Folder to use a nonbreaking space.

When you select a name with a nonbreaking space, you'll get the proper file or folder. The Macintosh file system considers breaking and nonbreaking spaces to be the same, so if it represents the nonbreaking space, the commands

```
Files SystemFile
Files "System File"
```

would be considered equivalent. Either command would match System File and System File.

Certain pathnames are reserved by MPW. These pathnames all begin with Dev: as a psuedodevice instead of an actual volume name. Such names have a special meaning for files opened both by the shell (such as for I/O redirection) and by MPW tools. These special names are shown in Table 4–12.

Dev:StdIn	current assignment for standard input
Dev:StdOut	current assignment for standard output
Dev:StdErr	current assignment for diagnostic input
Dev:Console	default input (entered) and output (active window)
Dev:Null	empty input stream; first-in, never-out output stream

Table 4–12:   MPW Reserved Pathnames

They will most often be used when writing shell command files. However, there are two cases in which you may want to use such names when entering commands interactively.

One example is when either the diagnostic or standard output produces information that you don't really need. For example,

```
Command > Dev:Null
```

causes Command to be executed with the diagnostic output displayed in the active window, but with the standard output thrown away.

Second, you may want to reassign both output streams to a single file, with the streams intermixed. The command line

```
Command > OutputFile ≥ Dev:StdOut
```

means "send the standard output of Command to OutputFile and then send the diagnostic output at the same time to the same file as the standard output."

4.3 Customizing MPW

Much of the power of MPW is that it can be fully customized for your particular requirements. Making these custom changes is only a matter of editing a standard file of shell commands.

For example, the standard MPW configuration expects a particular directory structure for the MPW tools, source files, and libraries. However, this structure is defined using shell commands run when you launch the shell, and these commands can easily be changed.

In addition to modifying MPW's directory structure, you can also define your own symbolic names for directories and files. For commands you use frequently, you can define shell command abbreviations for existing MPW commands. As will be described in later chapters, you can also define your own menus and shell commands.

STANDARD COMMAND FILES

Under certain circumstances, MPW must execute a series of operations to set or save the state of the shell environment. These actions are controlled by a series of command files; the names of the command files are fixed, and they are expected to be in the same directory as the shell application. Table 4–13 lists these five special files and how they are used.

File	When run by MPW
StartUp	After launching shell
UserStartup	From the end of StartUp
Suspend	Before launching an application
Resume	After exiting from application
Quit	Before exiting to the finder

Table 4–13:   **Standard Command Files**

When the shell is launched, it executes the commands in the Startup command file, which set the shell's configuration. As the last command, the Startup command file supplied with MPW runs the commands in the UserStartup file. Both can be used to run initial commands.

Normally, you would modify the UserStartup file and leave Startup unchanged; when a new release of MPW is available, you will replace your Startup with the new version and leave your version UserStartup unchanged. However, there's nothing sacred about this arrangement. You could write your own Startup and throw away UserStartup, as long as the information that MPW expects is provided by your initialization.

As supplied, the Quit command file does nothing but save the current worksheet. If you want to save any information about your current context, you can add your own commands here.

Note that any commands placed in StartUp, UserStartup, or Quit will be executed each time you start or stop the MPW application. The more commands you have, the longer it will take to start and stop MPW. If your files grow to be quite long, you may want to keep another text editor around for those occasions when you just want to edit or print one source file.

MPW also runs the Suspend and Resume command files to save and restore its context when leaving the shell to run an application. They are used anytime you specify an application as a command name, such as ResEdit. These command files account for much of the overhead in running applications.

SHELL VARIABLES

The MPW shell includes its own programming language. Like any other programming language, it must have a way to store values. For this purpose, MPW has its own "shell variables," which are an important part of its current context.

Shell variables are often used to store the pathnames of files or folders, although that is not the only use for them. Many of the startup commands are used to set standard variable names to refer to specific directories.

The value of a shell variable can be modified or displayed using the Set command. The Unset command deletes a shell variable from the shell's list of known variables

Set, Unset

Define, display, or delete shell variable assignment

Syntax:

```
Set variable value        Define variable to mean value
Set variable              Display definition for variable
```

`Set`	Display all shell variables
`Unset` *`variable`*	Delete definition for *`variable`*
`Unset`	Delete *all* variable definitions

Input/Output:

Output	Displayed definitions as `Set` commands

Examples:

`Set MyDir "{MPW}My Dir:"`	Define variable `MyDir` for a folder
`Set MPW`	Display value for `MPW`
`Unset Libraries`	Delete value for `Libraries`

As you'll discover is true for many MPW commands, the `Set` command displays its output in terms of executable shell commands. As with other commands, the `Set` commands displayed will quote any parameters that include spaces or special characters.

If you enter the command

```
Set MyName 'Sam Smith'
```

the command

```
Set MyName
```

will display

```
Set MyName 'Sam Smith'
```

to the standard output. If you were to just enter

```
Set
```

a series of `Set` commands would be displayed for all the variables known by the shell.

Instead of using the `Set` command to display a shell variable's definition, the normal way of using a shell variable is as part of a command parameter. When the shell encounters the name of a shell variable surrounded by braces ({}), it will replace the variable name with its value or a null string if the variable is unknown.

The normal way to verify the interpretation of special characters in parameters, including shell variables, is through the `Echo` command. The `Echo` command displays each of its parameters in order, with each parameter separated by a space.

Echo, Quote

Display parameters to standard output

Syntax:

```
Echo value …          Display value
Quote value …         Display value, with special characters
                      quoted
```

Options:

```
-n                    Do not end display with a return charcter
```

Remarks:

The commands display the value of their parameters after evaluation by the shell. Quote also quotes any parameter against shell interpretation if it contains a special character that would otherwise be interpreted as special by the shell.

If no parameters are supplied, only a return is displayed.

Input/Output:

```
Output                Each value, separated by a space
```

Examples:

```
Echo Hi there         Display the message "Hi there"
Quote {Boot}          Display quoted value for variable Boot
```

The ... is used in the syntax diagrams to indicate that the additional parameters can be supplied, with each parameter handled in the same way as the first parameter of the group. It is never typed and should not be confused with the Commando help dialog suffix.

Echo is an easy way to check the shell's interpretation of parameters before using those parameters with another command. In particular, Echo is used to establish the shell's interpretation of a parameter involving a shell variable or other special shell characters. For example, before adding the command

```
          Set Sources {MPW}Sources:
```

to your list of UserStartup actions, you might wish to first try the command

```
          Echo {MPW}Sources:
```

to see the value that will be assigned to variable MPW.

The Quote command is the same as Echo, except that it quotes any special characters in the output, allowing you to use the result as the parameter to another command. As an example, the command

```
Quote Set MyName {MyName}
```

would display

```
Set MyName 'Sam Smith'
```

In this case, Quote displays the two literal parameters untouched; since the third parameter contains a space, it is quoted.

Although they've so far been treated as the same, the two types of quoting (quotation marks and apostrophes) have an important difference when it comes to shell variables.

Variable expressions enclosed in apostrophes will never be interpreted. So, for example, the commands

```
Echo '{MPW} =' "{MPW}"
```

might display

```
{MPW} = HD:MPW:
```

Note also that the { character is special to the shell, but the } has no such meaning, except after a {. That means that only the { character must be escaped, not the }. The following command produces the same display as the previous Echo command:

```
Echo ∂{MPW} =' "{MPW}"
```

Variable expressions enclosed within quotation marks will have the actual value substituted by the shell. This allows you to use the value of a variable, but quote it as a single parameter if that value includes blanks.

When writing command files, you should always quote file name parameters if they might contain spaces or other special characters. For example, the Startup command line

```
Set MPW "{Boot}MPW:"
```

sets MPW to a valid value even if {Boot} is the name My Hard Disk.

Variables initialized or modified by the Set command are only known in the current context. If the command is entered interactively, then that context is all the commands you enter interactively. If the Set command is in a command file, then this is the case only while that command file is running.

If you need to share variables between contexts, you must "export" each variable using (surprise) the Export command.

Export

Make variable assignment available by all contexts

Syntax:

Export *variable* ...	Make *variable* definition global
Export	Display all exported shell variables

Input/Output:

Output	Displayed list of exports as Export commands

Example:

Export MyDir	Make MyDir available globally

Any variable defined and exported interactively will be available to any command file you run interactively. Variables defined by the startup command files have the same context as those entered interactively.

These exported variables will also be available to any built in commands or MPW tools, including the various compilers. These are used, for example, to find the interface definition files used by the Asm, C, and Pascal commands or to set printing options for the Print menu command.

However, exported variables only go one way. If you enter the name of a command file or tool, it cannot change the shell variables and export them back to your interactive context. A special command (Execute) is provided for those cases in which you need to run a list of commands to change the current context.

STANDARD PATHNAMES

There are a number of exported shell variables that MPW either defines before it begins or that various MPW components expect to have defined later on. These variables give the full pathnames of certain folders or documents. Most of these variables are defined by the startup command files and can be set to any value you desire.

All of the values can be accessed from shell commands. If you use these symbolic names from within your command files and tools, your program won't break if you decide later on to rearrange the folders that contain your development software.

Table 4–14 gives a list of shell variables that define these pathnames.

Static Variables

Variable	Default value	Description
AIncludes	{MPW}AIncludes:	Asm include files folder
Boot†		Boot volume
CIncludes	{MPW}CIncludes:	C include files folder
CLibraries	{MPW}CLibraries:	C object libraries folder
Commands commands	":,{MPW}Tools:, {MPW}Applications:"	Folders with MPW {MPW}Scripts:,
Commando	Commando	Command to execute for ...
Libraries	{MPW}Libraries:	Common object libraries folder
MacApp	{MPW}MacApp:	MacApp base directory
MPW	{Boot}MPW:	Base MPW directory
PInterfaces	{MPW}PInterfaces:	Pascal USES files folder
PLibraries	{MPW}PLibraries:	Pascal object libraries
RIncludes	{MPW}RIncludes:	Rez include files folder
ShellDirectory†		Folder with MPW Shell
SystemFolder†		Folder with System and Finder
Worksheet†	{ShellDirectory}Worksheet	Pathname of worksheet

Dynamic Variables††

Variable	Description
Active	Pathname of active window
Aliases	List of alias names, separated by commas
Command	Pathname of last MPW command, or name if built-in
Target	Pathname of target window
Windows	List of open document windows, separated by commas

† Automatically set by MPW Shell at launch from system configuration
†† Automatically updated as needed by shell

Table 4–14:   Shell Variables for Pathnames

Some of the variables are defined automatically by the shell and cannot be overridden. The {Boot} and {SystemFolder} variables are automatically set to the disk volume and complete pathname of the folder than contains the System and Finder files.

Another name—{ShellDirectory}—is automatically set to be the pathname of the folder containing the MPW Shell application. This shell variable is used to find the Startup, UserStartup, Quit, Suspend, and Resume files. It's also used to find the Worksheet file, which has its own variable.

Most of the names are defined in terms of the variable {MPW}. This variable is set by the Startup file to be the MPW directory of the boot volume. If you want to change this assignment—such as define MPW as being within another folder of the boot disk—you must edit the Startup file. Another possibility is to define MPW as

```
Set MPW "{ShellDirectory}"
```

which defines the base directory to be the folder containing the MPW Shell application. The advantage of this is that any time you move the shell (or rename its folder), the new name will automatically be used.

Most of the pathnames are defined by commands in the Startup and UserStartup command files, which you can change. The startup files normally set the current directory to be {MPW}. The other pathnames expect other components of MPW to be stored in folders contained immediately within the MPW folder.

One of the shell variables defines not a single folder pathname but a list of folder pathnames, separated by commas. The {Commands} variable gives a list of pathnames to be searched for running command files, tools, or applications. The default list searches the current directory (whatever it might be), then searches the Tools, Scripts, and Applications folders of the MPW directory. You can use the Which command to determine which folder the command is in. Given a command name parameter, it displays the full pathname of the corresponding tool or command file. The command

```
Which Pascal
```

might display

```
HD:MPW:Tools:Pascal
```

The complete directory hierarchy supplied by default with MPW is shown in Figure 4–3.

This hierarchy means that the pathnames for many MPW files will usually have four parts—the boot volume, the MPW folder, another folder, and the file name. You'll probably add another folder in the MPW directory for any sources of your own. If you also purchased MacApp, the MacApp distribution is normally stored in folders of directory {MPW}MacApp.

This hierarchy is one that emphasizes breadth at each level rather than a structured depth. With all the optional components, the MPW directory has 13 folders and 8 files. If you list the files or search through the directory using one of the Standard File Package dialogs, you'll have to work your way through all 21 entries each time.

Another approach is to group several folders into other folders to add an extra level of indirection. Figure 4–4 shows this alternate hierarchy, which has only five folders in {MPW}.

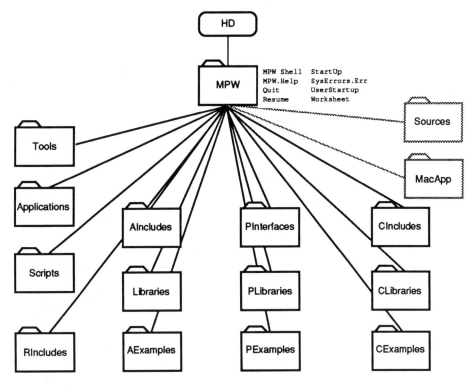

Figure 4–3:   Standard MPW Directory Hierarchy

Two other changes are made in the example. Although the shell is normally stored in the (MPW) directory, it can be stored in any folder as long as the related files are moved to the same folder. Second, you can move the scripts to the Tools folder.

The alternate hierarchy does require one additional folder selection in the standard file dialog box, but you'll have to scroll through fewer names. It also results in longer pathnames, which will be inconvenient to enter or display. Note that the source directory is at the same level, so the pathname of your files should be unaffected by the change.

Example 4–1 shows how the Set and Export commands to define this alternate structure. You would include these commands in the UserStartup file.

Since the Startup file predefines many of these names, you could speed up execution slightly by placing a comment character in front of the corresponding Set and Export commands to bypass those commands. If you leave them in, your later commands will automatically replace the Startup definitions.

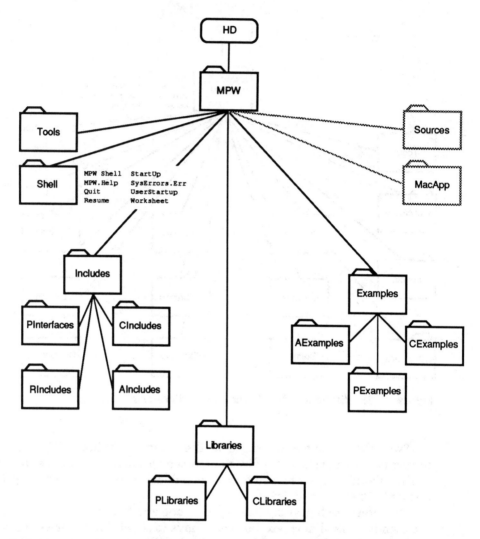

Figure 4–4:   An Alternate Directory Hierarchy

Another directory strategy is to nest folders based on languages. You might have folders in (MPW) entitled CFolder, PFolder, AFolder, and so on, with the libraries, include files and examples stored in their corresponding folder. This maps to the way that the software is distributed and also can be easily extended to include other languages. If disk space becomes tight and one of the languages isn't being used, you could back up and remove that folder.

```
# Example 4-1: Shell commands for alternate directory
# hierarchy

# Define the directory used by most of MPW
# Change this if you re-arrange your disk

  Set MPW "{Boot}MPW:";                        Export MPW

# Use a different hierarchy than provided by default MPW
# have Includes, Libraries off of {MPW}
# nest Asm, C and Pascal-specific folders below those

  Set Includes "{MPW}Includes:";      Export Includes

# Following directories are used by MPW:
#
# {AIncludes}    C       INCLUDE 'xxx.a'
# {CIncludes}    Asm     #include "xxx.h"
# {PInterfaces}  Pascal  USES xxxIntf;
# {RIncludes}    Rez     #include "xxx.r"
#
# {Libraries} Object libraries used by Assembler, C,
#             Pascal
# {CLibraries}Object libraries used by C
# {PLibraries}Object libraries used by Pascal
#
# {MacApp}  Base directory for MacApp

# Export AIncludes
  Set AIncludes "{Includes}AIncludes:";
# Export CIncludes
  Set CIncludes "{Includes}CIncludes:";
# Export PInterfaces
  Set PInterfaces "{Includes}PInterfaces:"
# Export RIncludes
  Set RIncludes "{Includes}RIncludes:";
# Export Libraries
  Set Libraries "{MPW}Libraries:";
# Export CLibraries
  Set CLibraries "{Libraries}CLibraries:";
# Export PLibraries
  Set PLibraries "{Libraries}PLibraries:";

# Export MacApp
  Set MacApp  "{MPW}MacApp:";
```

```
# Where to look for command files, tools and
# applications
  Set Commands ":,{MPW}Tools:,{Boot}Applications:"
  Export Commands

# These symbols are not used by MPW, but may come in
# handy in command files or Make sources
#
  Set Examples "{MPW}Examples:";    Export Examples
  Set Sources "{MPW}Sources:"; Export Sources
  Set Tools "{MPW}Tools:";      Export Tools
```

Example 4–1:   Shell Commands for Alternate Hierarchy

Also, depending on the development systems being used, you might want to separate your sources from MPW entirely. Instead, you would define a folder with:

```
        Set Sources "{Boot}Sources:"
```

One advantage is that the MPW folder (and other inner folders) would become read-only, with few (if any) changes requiring backup.

COMMAND ALIASES

Although the MPW command names are recognizable words, these long commands can sometimes be a pain to type if they're often used. MPW allows you to define a single keyword to represent a command name or any portion of a complete command. These abbreviations are called "aliases."

Alias, Unalias

Define, display, or delete abbreviations for commonly used commands

Syntax:

Alias *keyword word* ...	Define *keyword* as an alias for *word* ...
Alias *keyword*	Display definition for *keyword*
Alias	Display all defined aliases
Unalias *keyword*	Delete definition for *keyword*
Unalias	Delete *all* alias definitions

Input/Output:

Output	Displayed command as Alias commands

Examples:

```
Alias hc Help Commands    Define hc to list available commands
Alias File                Display abbrevation for File
Unalias hc                Remove alias for hc
```

A very commonly used shell command is `Directory`, which changes the shell's current directory if a parameter is specified. An alias to shorten this is

```
Alias cd Directory
```

where `cd` stands for "change directory."

The command defined can include space or other special characters. Any variables in the command will be evaluated at the time the `Alias` is entered unless the "word" is quoted with apostrophes.

Command aliases can only define a command name or a command followed by a fixed list of parameters. They won't work if you, say, wanted to always use the same command and second parameter, but specify the first parameter as a parameter to the alias. Instead, you would have to write a one-line command file.

The delay in interpreting an alias is negligible, so if the alias references built in commands, it will be just as fast to use the alias—unlike a command file, which is significantly slower because it must be interpreted line by line. Command aliases also execute at the current context and can change shell variables.

The context of the shell includes both its shell variables and its aliases. Unlike shell variables, aliases are always exported to inner contexts.

However, if you want to run a series of commands to define aliases (or shell variables), merely mentioning the name of the command file will create a new context. The commands in the command file will not change the state of the current context. Instead, you must run the command file using the `Execute` command so that it will modify the current context.

Execute

Run command file with current context

Syntax:

```
Execute command file      Execute commands in command file
```

Example:

```
Execute "{ShellDirectory}"UserStartup
```
                          Runs the commands in `UserStartup`

Any shell command file can be run in one of two ways. The Execute command is one way, e.g,. Execute Startup. The other way is to enter the name of the file; the full pathname (e.g., "{ShellDirectory}Startup}") must be used unless the file is within one of the directories specified by the {Commands} variable.

With Execute, any variables or aliases changed in the command file will change the current context. This is not true for commands called by their pathname, for which the changes *never* change the calling context.

This is why file Startup includes the line

```
Execute "{ShellDirectory}UserStartup"
```

instead of the shorter (but less useful)

```
"{ShellDirectory}UserStartup"
```

For the latter command, all of the Set, Export, and Alias commands contained in UserStartup would have no effect.

OTHER CUSTOM SETTINGS

There are several other shell variables not associated with pathnames that are also used by the MPW shell. Initial values are given to these variables by the startup command files, which you can change to suit your preferences. You can change the values to suit your preferences using a combination of Set and Export commands in your UserStartup file. These variables are listed in Table 4–15.

Variable	Default value	Description
CaseSensitive	0	Treat upper/lower differently
Echo	0	Show command before running
Exit	1	Command files terminate on error
PrintOptions	-h	Options for Print menu command
Tab	4	Spaces per tab stop
Test	0	Don't execute tools or applications
WordSet A-Za-z	0-9_	Define a "word" for double-clicking

Table 4–15:   Other Shell Variables

Four of the variables take boolean values, expressed as the integer 0 or 1. The {CaseSensitive} variable defines whether textual searches descriminate based on upper- or lowercase distinctions. The {Exit} variable determines whether the shell stops executing a list of commands (in the active window or in a command file) if it encounters a command error. The

{Echo} and {Test} variables control the display and execution of commands in command files, aliases, and menu commands, as will be described in Chapter 6. All except {Exit} have a default value of 0 (false).

The {Tab} variable gives the default setting for tab stops. This is used when creating new documents and by shell commands when no tab setting is available from the document's resource fork.

The {PrintOptions} variable defines the formatting options used by the printing menu commands.

The editor's response to double-clicking on text is to select the entire word, as is the standard for the Macintosh user interface. The definition of a "word" can be modified by changing the value of the {WordSet} shell variable. {WordSet} describes the alphabet of characters that comprise a complete "word" to the shell editor. When you double-click in a document window, the editor will create a selection that stops at the next character, on either side of the mouse location, that is not in the standard alphabet.

The variable includes each valid character, with ranges of characters separated by a minus (-) sign. The standard definition of {WordSet} is

```
Set WordSet 'a-zA-Z_0-9'
```

which means that a double-click selection would terminate on the next punctuation character (other than an underline) or a blank.

If you are frequently selecting file names, you may want to define the word set as

```
Set WordSet 'a-zA-Z_0-9:.Δ'
```

where Δ is the nonbreaking space, Option-spacebar. This would allow you to select the entire pathname of a document by double-clicking in the window in which the pathname is displayed.

4.4 Disk and File Commands

The shell provides a number of commands to manipulate the contents of Macintosh disks. These commands allow you to perform most of the functions of the Finder without leaving the shell.

One of the most common requirements is to set the shell's current directory, which is used by default with all partial pathnames.

As with the Finder, shell commands allow you to create new folders and copy files or entire folders. You can delete files or folders, move them to other directories, or change their names.

Like the Finder, several of these commands will confirm dangerous actions with an alert box, such as the one shown in Figure 4–5. These commands allow you to prespecify a "Yes," "No," or "Cancel" answer to the confirmation with the -y, -n, and -c options, in which case the alert will not be shown, with the intended response assumed. This is useful when you are making a command file to run unattended or one that involves many files—and thus many confirmation alerts.

However, there are a number of functions provided by the shell that are not available from the Finder. You can copy only the data or resource fork of one file onto another using the Duplicate command. You can change the modification date, the creator, or the file type for any file with the SetFile command. And the Catenate command allows you to merge the data fork from multiple files into one file.

Like many other MPW commands, several commands described here recognize the -p option. If you use this option, the command will display progress information to the diagnostic output as the command is being performed—such as when copying one disk to another.

DIRECTORIES

Most of the time you when are editing or compiling source files, you won't want to be forced to use the full pathname, which usually amounts to a fair amount of typing. Of course, if you have a separate disk volume named MPW and a source volume name Src, with source files such as f.c, perhaps it's not that bad.

Usually, you will want to use partial pathnames, such as the name of a file within the current folder. To do so, you must set the current directory to be folder containing your source. The shell's current directory is changed using the Directory command.

Figure 4–5:   Shell Command Confirmation Alert

Directory

Display or change current shell directory

Syntax:

```
Directory pathname
```
Change directory to *pathname*

```
Directory
```
Display current directory

Input/Output:

Output   Displayed directory

Example:

```
Directory {CIncludes}
```
Change directory to C #include directory

Changing the directory will affect the folders shown by the various Open and Save menu commands, but not the other way around.

MPW also provides another way to change the directory. The DirectoryMenu command script can be used to an optional Directory menu of directories you commonly use, while SetDirectory changes the current directory ands adds that name to the menu. The next time, you can either type a SetDirectory command or select the pathname directly from the Directory menu.

DirectoryMenu, SetDirectory

Update and use menu of directories in use

Syntax:

```
DirectoryMenu pathname...
```
Create a Directory menu, and add each *pathname*

```
SetDirectory pathname
```
Change directory to *pathname*

Remarks:

The DirectoryMenu command builds the Directory menu for the first time, including an item for adding new directories to the menus.

The SetDirectory command adds *pathname* to the menu (if not already present), and will create the Directory menu if necessary.

Example:

```
SetDirectory {ShellDirectory}
```
Initialize menu with a single directory entry

```
SetDirectory {MPW}Sources:
```
                                Change directory to source file directory

The Directory menu and entries in it are only created by the `Directo-`
`ryMenu` and `SetDirectory` commands. If you always wanted to have such
a menu available to get at folders you use all the time, you could modify your
`UserStartup` to include a command such as

```
DirectoryMenu "{MPW}" "{ShellDirectory}" "{MPW}Tools:" ∂
   "{PInterfaces}" "{CIncludes}" "{Sources}"
```

A menu built by these commands is shown in Figure 4–6.

If you will be typing `SetDirectory` frequently, you may find the alias

```
        Alias sd SetDirectory
```

a more appropriate shortcut.

When it's time to create a new folder (directory), you can do so within the
MPW shell, without exiting to the Finder. The command to create a new
folder is `NewFolder`.

NewFolder

Create a new folder (directory) or folders

Syntax:

```
NewFolder name ...
```
                        Create new folder *name*

Remarks:

Can only be used for HFS disk volumes.

Examples:

```
NewFolder :PExamples CExamples
```
                                Create two new folders in the current
                                directory
```
NewFolder {MPW}Sources
```
                        Create a new folder from the full
                        pathname

If you specify the partial pathname to create a new folder in the current
directory, the colons are optional. You can also specify a full pathname. If the
current directory is {MPW}, the following commands are all equivalent:

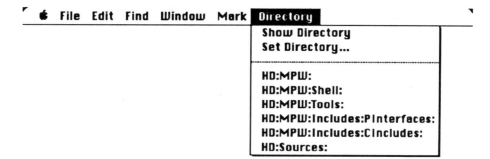

Figure 4–6:   Optional Directory Menu

```
NewFolder Sources
NewFolder :Sources
NewFolder :Sources:
NewFolder {MPW}Sources
NewFolder {MPW}Sources
```

DISK VOLUMES

If you need disk space information on your hard disk or just want to know the name of a newly mounted floppy, you can use the Volumes command to display information on all currently mounted disk volumes.

Volumes

Display mounted volume or volumes

Syntax:

Volumes	Display information about all disk volumes
Volumes *name*	Display information about volume *name*

Options:

-l	Display long output form

Remarks:

The value of *name* can either be a disk volume name terminated with a colon or a drive number: 1 for the first internal floppy, higher numbers for other floppy and hard disk drives. The default form displays only the volume name. The long form display includes the volume name, drive number, capacity, available capacity, and counts of the number of files and folders.

Input/Output:

Output   Displayed volume information

Example:

Volumes -1   Display information about all mounted
                          volumes

    MPW also supports additional File Manager calls that operate on disk volumes. The Erase, Eject, Mount, and Unmount commands are primarily useful when writing command files to copy floppy disks.

FINDING FILES

There are two shell commands that are very frequently used to manipulate files. One is the Directory command, used to change the current directory. The other is the Files command, used to list the files in the directory (or any other directory).

Files

Display list of files and directories

Syntax:

Files   Display files in current directory
Files *name* …   Display files specified by path*name*

Options:

-f		Display full pathname for all files
-i		List folder names, not contents
-l		Display long output form
-r		Recursively search each folder found
-s		Do not print directory name before its contents
-c	ABCD	List only files with creator ABCD
-t	WXYZ	List only files of type WXYZ
-x	attr	Selective extended information:
	a	Attribute flags: locked, visible, bundle, system
	b	Size in bytes
	c	File creator
	d	Creation date

j	Size in 1024 (K) bytes
m	Modification date
t	File type

Remarks:

The default form displays only partial pathnames. With -f, the full pathname for each file is given. Unless -i is used, Files will display the contents each folder (directory) matched by *name* rather than the folder name itself; the contents is preceeded by the folder name unless -s is used.

The long form display includes the file name, drive number, type, creator, size, attribute flags, modification, and creation dates. The selective long display allows any of these to be shown, in the order of the format flags.

Input/Output:

Output   Displayed file information

Examples:

```
Files -c 'MPS '    Display files created by MPW in current
Files -l -r {PExamples}
                   Display full information about Pascal examples
```

The long format display of the Files commands displays the size, creation, and modification dates and types for all the files and folders in the current directory. The size of a folder includes the size of all the files and folders contained within that folder. You can also use the -r option to recursively descend through all the folders.

Figure 4–7 shows using the Directory command to change the current directory and the long format display of the Volumes and Files commands.

PATHNAME WILDCARDS

Unlike the Finder, the shell allows you to specify search strings to match only a subset of file names. If such a string is in a command parameter, the shell will replace the string expression with the actual file names before the parameters are "seen" by the command. This allows any command that takes one or more pathnames as parameters to take advantage of the shell's file name expansion.

One wildcard will be used most often in specifying file names. That character is the ≈ symbol (Option-X), which MPW interprets to mean "match any series of zero or more characters."

It can be used at any point in a full or partial pathname. For example, the command

```
Files ≈
```

```
≡≡≡≡≡≡≡≡≡≡≡≡≡≡≡≡≡ HD:MPW:Shell:Worksheet ≡≡≡≡≡≡≡≡≡≡
Volumes -l

Name                     Drive    Size    Free  Files  Dirs
----                     ----     ----    ----  -----  ----
Floppy:                    1      785K    556K     2     0
HD:                        5    30811K    533K  2406   259

Directory "(MPW)"
Files -l
Name                 Type Crtr  Size   Flags     Last-Mod-Date      Creation-Date
-------------------- ---- ----  ----   -------   ----------------   ----------------
Examples             Folder     856K  lvbspold   1/31/87   9:54 AM   8/4/86  10:14 AM
Includes             Folder     612K  lvbspold   1/31/87   9:55 AM   8/4/86   3:03 PM
Libraries            Folder     541K  lvbspold   2/11/87   2:42 PM   5/27/86 11:26 AM
MacApp               Folder    2416K  lvbspold   2/12/87   1:30 PM   8/20/86   9:17 AM
Misc                 Folder     843K  lvbspold   1/31/87   9:02 AM   9/25/86   7:29 AM
'Official 1.0'       Folder      43K  lvbspold   1/31/87  11:25 PM   1/31/87   9:03 AM
Shell                Folder     221K  lvbspold   2/12/87   3:22 PM   1/28/87   1:47 PM
Sources              Folder    1881K  lvbspold   2/12/87   7:35 AM   8/4/86  12:57 PM
Tools                Folder    1695K  lvbspold   2/11/87   3:58 PM   5/27/86 11:12 AM



   MPW Shell
```

Figure 4–7:   Detailed Disk Volume and Folder Information

is similar to the Files command with no parameters; that is, it lists all the files in the current directory.

The command

```
Files ≈.o
```

would only list files whose name ended in .o, which is the suffix used by the MPW compilers and assembler for object files. This is similar to the command

```
Files -t 'OBJ '
```

which should produce a similar list, based on the type of the file rather than its name.

The wildcard character will match a file or folder name, but will not match the portion of a pathname that includes a colon. You can use multiple wildcards to search in multiple directories; the command

```
Files -l :≈:≈.p
```

asks the Files command to display any Pascal source files contained in any of the folders of this directory.

The question mark (?) character is also recognized as a wildcard, but it matches a single character. For example,

```
Files Jupiter.?
```

would match Jupiter.a, Jupiter.p, and Jupiter.r but not Jupiter. or Jupiter.p.o.

Pathnames with wildcards can be combined with other pathnames on commands that take multiple parameters, so the command

```
Print -h ≈.c :≈:≈.c
```

would print all the C source files in the current directory or in folders that are located in the current directory. If the shell can find no names that match a wildcard specification, it does not pass any parameters corresponding to those specifications to the command.

You must be very careful when using wildcards on disk volumes that do not support HFS, since all files on such volumes are stored in a single directory. A pathname on such a volume consists of the volume name and the file name, separated by a colon.

If you ask for a list of file names on a non-HFS volume (400K floppy), you could fill several screens. More importantly, if you make changes using wildcards, you could change all the files on a disk. You should use wildcards to selectively specify only certain files.

FILE CONTENTS

The Catenate command reads the data fork of a text document and displays its contents to the output stream. It can also be used to merge multiple files into one file.

Catenate

Merge multiple source files

Syntax:

Catenate	Display the input stream on the output stream
Catenate *name* ...	Display data forks of a list of files

Input/Output:

Output	Displayed output

Example:

Catenate ≈.p >Merged.Pas	Merge all the Pascal source files into one file

If no parameters are specified, the `Catenate` command will copy its input stream to the output stream. The command line

```
Files | Catenate
```

is just a slow way to list the files in the current directory.

The opposite of the `Catenate` command is the `FileDiv` command, which divides a single text file into to several files.

The `Duplicate` command is similar to the Finder command of the same name. If you're copying one file, unlike the Finder, it allows you to specify the name of the copy.

It also allows you to copy multiple files (or folders) into another directory, such as to a floppy disk. In this case, the original file names will be used for the duplicates.

Duplicate

Duplicate files or directories

Syntax:

Duplicate *name1 name2*	Copy file *name1* to file *name2*
Duplicate *name … targetfolder*	Copy list of files (or folders) to *targetfolder*

Options:

-d	Duplicate data fork only
-r	Duplicate resource fork only
-p	Display progress information
-y	Overwrite conflicting files or folders
-n	Skip conflicting files and folders

Remarks:

If the destination (last) parameter is a folder, the duplicate files (folders) will be placed within that folder. If more than one source parameter is specified, the destination parameter must be a folder name.

Normally, the data fork, the resource fork, and the file's Finder attributes are copied to the duplicate, as are the file's creation and modification dates. If only the data or resource fork is copied to an existing file, the remainder of the file will be unchanged.

Input/Output:

Diagonostic   Displayed progress information

Examples:

```
Duplicate -y MPW2: {MPW}
```
           Copy all files from disk volume to directory
```
Duplicate -r Foo.rsrc Foo
```
           Copy the resources in `Foo.rsrc` to `Foo`

A series of `Duplicate` commands necessary to copy an entire folder or hard disk can be generated using the `Backup` command. Files can be selected based on name, change date, creator, or type, among other criteria. `Backup` is primarily useful when maintaining copies of source files in two separate folders, such as one on your local hard disk and another in a remote AppleShare file server. As it name suggests, it can also be used to back up your hard disk to floppies.

FILE PROPERTIES

The `Delete` commands throws files into the trash, removing them permanently from a disk volume.

Delete

Delete files or folders

Syntax:

```
Delete name …
```
          Delete the named files

Options:

`-y`	Delete any folders
`-n`	Skip any folders
`-c`	Abort if any folders are listed
`-p`	Display progress information

Input/Output:

Diagonostic   Displayed progress information

Examples:

```
Delete This
```
          Delete the file `This`
```
Delete -y :≈:
```
          Delete all the folders in the current directory

The `Delete` command can be very dangerous. For example, the command

    Delete -y ≈:≈

will attempt to delete the contents of all mounted volumes. (Your Macintosh will probably crash first.)

For this reason, you should be careful in specifying file names for `Delete` commands—unlike the Finder, there is no way to pull files out of the trash can. Also, the `-y` option shouldn't be used unless you're absolutely sure of what you're doing. It always helps to do a `Files` command with the same parameters first, just to make sure you know which files will be deleted.

If you're creating a new copy of a file, but you want to keep the old one around, you can use the `Move` or `Rename` commands to move the file to another folder or to change its name.

Move, Rename

Change name or location of files and folders

Syntax:

Move *name1 name2*	Change name of file *name1* to *name2*
Rename *name1 name2*	Change name of file *name1* to *name2*
Move *name ... targetfolder*	Move list of files (or folders) to *targetfolder*

Options:

-y	Overwrite conflicting files or folders
-n	Skip conflicting files and folders
-c	Abort if there are any conflicts
-p (Move only)	Display progress information

Remarks:

For the Move command, if the destination (last) parameter is a folder, the moved files (folders) will be placed within that folder. If more than one source parameter is specified, the destination parameter must be a folder name.

The Rename command always leaves the file in the same directory.

Input/Output:

Diagonostic	Displayed progress information

Examples:

```
Move {MPW}Quit {MPW}Sources:
```
Move the command file to another folder
```
Rename myfile MyFile
```
Change the capitalization of MyFile

The Move command is generally more flexible than Rename, as it will allow you to move a file from one directory to another. If you've used another command shell, many operating systems only have one command, similar to MPW's Move. It also allows you to move multiple files from one folder to another.

However, the Rename command performs one important function that cannot be performed by Move. As far as the File Manager and the shell are concerned, if you use the name MyFile, it will match an existing file named myfile. Names containing other characters, such as nonbreaking spaces and foreign characters may also match different names, as determined by the International Utilities Package for comparing strings. (For example, "cote" would match "côté.") Changes between such equivalent names must be done using Rename.

The SetFile command modifies other properties of Macintosh files. Most of these correspond to the visual display of the file in the Finder or to information about the file that is displayed by the Finder's Get Info command.

SetFile

Change finder attributes of a file

Syntax:

```
SetFile name …
```
Display files specified by path name

Options:

-a	attrs	Change file attributes
-c	ABCD	Change file creator to ABCD
-t	WXYZ	Change file type to WXYZ
-d	date	Set the creation date to date
-m	date	Set the modification date to date

Remarks:

The attributes (as interpreted by the File Manager) are set by uppercase letters and reset by lowercase letters:

L	Locked
V	Invisible
B	Bundle
S	System
I	Inited
D	On Desktop
M	Shared (run multiple times from fileserver)

Attributes not mentioned are unchanged.

Date formats include the day in MM/DD/YY form, followed by an optional time specification in HH:MM:SS form; the seconds are optional, as are an AM or PM code word. The option parameter must be quoted if it contains blanks. A period (.) may be used to specify the current date and time.

Examples:

```
SetFile -c 'MPS ' Src.p    Change creator of Src.p to be MPW
SetFile -a L {PExamples}≈.p
                           Make Pascal example sources read-
                           only
SetFile -d '1/24/80 1:20 PM' Msg
                           Change the creation date to an
                           impossible value
```

SetFile can be used to establish a particular creator or type for a document during development. You won't normally need to use it with your own programs since the linker options specify the creator and type for programs. However, SetFile can be used to be set the bundling bit and to mark files and folders as locked (read-only).

The most likely reason for changing a file's dates is to reset them to correct values after you've run the Macintosh with the wrong date. If the clock battery fails or is removed, the OS Utilities will set the date to January 1, 1904, when the Mac is booted, and any files changed until you discover the problem will have a modification date of 1904.

Otherwise, this capability should be used with care. MPW does not check to see if the dates are meaningful, only that the syntax is correct.

4.5 Shell Menus

This section summarizes each of the available commands on the standard MPW shell menus. For advanced users, the final subsections provide shell commands equivalent to the menu items and also offer keyboard and mouse shortcuts.

Individual menu items are shown in **bold** in this section.

Several of the menu commands involve the current selection and are enabled only when there is a selection of one or more characters in the active window. Among these commands are the standard clipboard operations **Cut**, **Copy**, and **Clear**.

Both the **Open Selection** and **Find Selection** commands change their appearance depending on the selection. If less than a line is selected, a truncated form of the selection is shown in the menu. If the word "Foo" were selected, the menu items would read **Open Foo** and **Find Foo**, respectively. If the selection is more than one line, the word "Selection" is used instead.

Figure 4–8 shows the standard menu lists for the MPW shell version 2.0. Note that the actual contents of the **Mark** menu will depend on the current active document.

For those who previously used version 1.0 of MPW, there are three major differences in the menus of version 2:

- The Format menu has been consolidated into a dialog called by a single menu item;

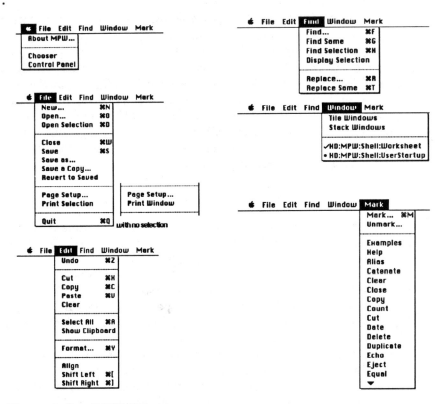

Figure 4–8:   MPW Menus

- Several items from the Find menu have been consolidated with the **Find** and **Replace** dialogs;
- A new menu, Mark, is provided, to name locations within a text file.

APPLE MENU

The **About MPW...** menu item gives the current version number and copyright notices.

Of course, the actual desk accessories will vary, but they are likely to include the two shown. The **Chooser** is used to select a printer if you have more than one. It also includes radio buttons to enable/disable AppleTalk.

The **Control Panel** is important to MPW for several of its functions. The RAM Cache setting controls how much memory is used for the cache and thus how much is available for MPW—in particular, the most memory-intensive operations, those involving compilations. A cache of 32K to 128K improves the speed of linking and other MPW functions, but on a 1 Mb machine, there's not a lot of room to spare, particularly if you have 50K of memory allocated by MacsBug. You'll have more room available for big compiles if you always close all your document windows first.

The **Speaker Volume** setting affects the output of the Beep MPW command, which may be included in some command scripts. The Control Panel also includes controls to set the time and to connect or disconnect AppleTalk.

Two other desk accessories may also be useful to some MPW owners. Many of the MPW shell commands involve unfamiliar special characters for file name and string pattern-matching characters, so having the **Key Caps** desk accessory will help—at least initially—if you're ever stuck for a character. And if you're using MPW to manipulate text data for another application, you may find that the **Scrapbook** is a more convenient way to transfer data than by creating new files.

FILE MENU

The File Menu includes operations for the current document or to create a new document; most have familiar usages. Open, Close, Save, Save as, Revert to Saved, Page Setup, and Quit have their customary usages.

New creates a new file and makes it the active window. The name of the file must be specified when the file is created.

Open offers a standard file dialog to open an existing file. Unless Cancel is selected, the new file becomes the active window. The selection within the file is remembered from its previous use by MPW.

Open Selection opens the file name that is selected if it exists; otherwise the editor will beep at you. If the name includes spaces or other special characters, you must select the surrounding quotes since the editor evaluates the name by the same rules as a shell command would.

Close closes the active window. If changes to the text were made, MPW displays the standard alert asking if the changes should be saved. Note that closing a document always saves the current formatting resources—such as the font name, font size, tab width, current selection, window size—even if no other changes have been made.

Save saves the active window; it is disabled if no changes have been made to the document's contents (text) since the last save. Changing the font size, for example, is not considered by the editor to be a change to the contents.

Save as asks for a new file name and saves the active window to a new name. Editing continues with the new document. **Save a Copy** is similar, except that editing continues with the original document. Both copy the formatting resources in addition to the text, which won't happen if you create a new document using New and copy the text using the clipboard.

Revert to Saved asks if the changes to the document are to be discarded. If so, the document is reopened with the same text as the last saved version. Revert does not affect the formatting resources.

Page Setup offers a style dialog that allows you to sets the paper size and orientation for any printing. This should be done after using the Chooser to change printers.

Print Window prints the current document. However, unlike most Macintosh applications, it does not offer a job dialog before printing. Instead, printing begins immediately with the previously stored print options.

Print options are controlled by the value of shell variable {PrintOptions}, and the format of the options is the same as for the Print command. Commonly used flags for {PrintOptions} are shown in Table 4–16. The default is -h, which displays the file name as a header at the top of each page, along with the date and page number.

If you normally print to an ImageWriter, you will want to include -q draft in your print options to speed the output.

If your default printer is a LaserWriter, the -r option prints the pages in reverse order, so that the top page is the first when printing completes. If you do not normally save your documents with the Courier font, you should also include the options -font Courier since the Print Window command does not perform font substitution. Similarly, if you're having trouble fitting an entire listing on a page, the option -size 7 should allow enough room for any MPW listing with adequate legibility.

When a selection is made in the active window, the Print Window command is replaced by **Print Selection**. The same print options are used, and the operation is similar to Print Window, except that the document title will be appended with .§, the MPW selection symbol. This can be used instead of a print job dialog to print only certain pages of a file.

The **Quit** item exits MPW for the Finder. Prior to completing, it executes any commands in the {ShellDirectory}Quit file, which you can modify to include your own commands. After that, the shell performs a Close for each

Option	Description	Default
-f [fontname] -font [fontname]	Select printing font	†
-h	Print page heading	
-l [lines]	Lines per page	
-ls [spacing]	Spacing per line	1
-n	Display line numbers	
-q [high] -q [standard] -q [draft]	ImageWriter "High" quality ImageWriter "Standard" quality ImageWriter "Draft" quality	
-r	Print pages in reverse order	
-s [fontsize] -size [fontsize]	Select printing font size	†
-t [tabwidth]	Spaces per tab stop	†
-lm [inches] -rm [inches] -tm [inches] -bm [inches]	Left margin Right margin Top margin Bottom margin	5/18" 0 0 0

† Default value is given by document resource fork

Table 4–16:   Print Options for the Menu Command

open window. As with a Close, each window that has changed contents prompts an alert asking if the changes should be saved.

EDIT MENU

The items of the Edit menu generally operate on the current selection in the active window.

The **Undo** command undoes the last operation for this window, whether it is a menu item, a command, or typing from the keyboard. Each separate window (document) has its own "memory," so the Undo is remembered until the next change to the document's contents. However, if a single shell command can include multiple actions, the Undo will reverse only the last one. For example, Undo will reverse only the last substitution in a `Replace -c ∞`, which replaces all occurrences.

As is customary, the **Cut** and **Copy** commands take the current selection and place it in the clipboard; Cut deletes the selection from the document as well. **Paste** takes the contents of the clipboard and replaces the current selection. **Clear** replaces the current selection with nothing. Cut, Copy, and Clear are disabled unless the current selection includes a range of one or more characters.

Select All makes the current selection the entire document. For example, Select All followed by Copy (Command-A,C) places the entire document in the clipboard, where it can be pasted into a new or existing document. **Show Clipboard** displays a window with those clipboard contents.

The **Format** command controls the display of the current document, as stored in the document's resource fork and also as used by shell and menu commands—such as printing—which need to know the format of the document. It produces a dialog box similar to that shown in Figure 4–9.

Within the dialog, dialog items set the font size and font name, using the standard Macintosh conventions. For the selected font, the actual sizes defined for the font will be shown in the list of available sizes, although any size can be entered textually in the box.

The other numeric field, Tabs, controls the interpretation of each tab character in the current document. The value given is the number of spaces between each tab stop, typically in the range 2 to 12. When a new document is created, the document has its tab stops set every {Tab} characters. You should set the value of Tab in your UserStartup file to be your most commonly used setting.

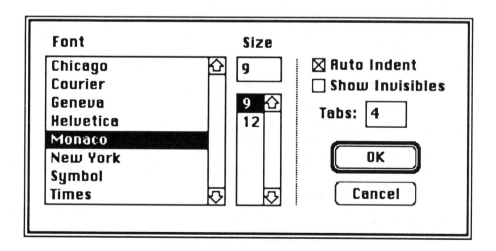

Figure 4–9:   Format Dialog

Although it's generally a good idea to use the same tab convention for every document, a few documents may require a different setting. For example, the MPW assembler works best with tabs set every 10 or 12 characters because some opcodes and identifiers are longer than 8 characters.

The Auto Indent setting controls the indentation of successive lines when you're typing. When Auto Indent is enabled, each new line typed will begin with the same left margin as the previous line. Show Invisibles displays special symbols for three normally invisible characters—space, tab, and return; all other control characters are represented by an inverted question mark. An example is shown in Figure 4–10.

Among the remaining menu commands, **Align** aligns the left-hand margins of the selected lines. All lines are aligned to the same indentation as the first line.

Adjust Left is equivalent to deleting a tab character (or the equivalent number of spaces) from the beginning of each line, up to the actual number of spaces. **Adjust Right** adds a tab character at the beginning of each line. Both work on the current line if no range is selected.

An **Enter** command was provided by MPW 1.0. In later versions, you should click on the status panel to execute a command or use the keyboard equivalent.

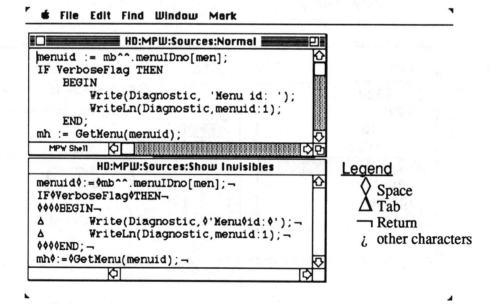

Figure 4–10: Showing Invisible Characters

FIND MENU

The Find menu includes commands to find and replace text strings in the active window. The interpretation of the Find and Replace commands are controlled by several option items included in find and replace dialogs.

Find puts up a dialog box to ask what string to search for, including a list of options for the search. The string used for the previous search is displayed by default. If the string is found, Find selects the text; it beeps if it is not found.

Find Same repeats the previous search. **Find Selection** (the actual title depends on the selection) searches for the string given by the currently selected text in the window. Immediately after a successful search, the desired string will be selected, so both Find Same and Find Selection will find the next occurrence of the same string.

Display Selection scrolls the window so that the current selection is visible. Unlike Find Selection, the appearance of the Display Selection menu item does not change depending on the word or lines selected.

Replace offers a dialog for both the search and replacement strings, which are remembered between commands. The dialog also includes settings that control the interpretation of the replacement command, as shown in Figure 4–11. You also have the option of replacing all remaining occurrences or of merely finding the first occurrence without replacement.

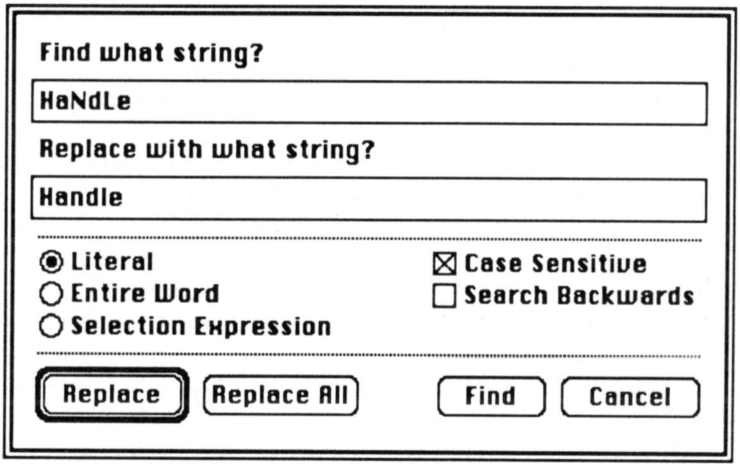

```
┌─────────────────────────────────────────────────────┐
│  Find what string?                                    │
│  ┌─────────────────────────────────────────────────┐ │
│  │ HaNdLe                                          │ │
│  └─────────────────────────────────────────────────┘ │
│  Replace with what string?                            │
│  ┌─────────────────────────────────────────────────┐ │
│  │ Handle                                          │ │
│  └─────────────────────────────────────────────────┘ │
│  ⦿ Literal              ⊠ Case Sensitive             │
│  ○ Entire Word          ☐ Search Backwards           │
│  ○ Selection Expression                               │
│  ┌─────────┐ ┌───────────┐   ┌──────┐ ┌────────┐     │
│  │ Replace │ │Replace All│   │ Find │ │ Cancel │     │
│  └─────────┘ └───────────┘   └──────┘ └────────┘     │
└─────────────────────────────────────────────────────┘
```

Figure 4–11: String Replacement Dialog.

The value of the search string is shared with the Find command, so changing the search string in the Find command changes it for Replace and vice versa. **Replace Same** repeats the most recent replacement. If you want either string to include a Tab character, you can type one in the Worksheet, copy it to the clipboard, and then paste it into the replacement dialog.

Both the Find and Replace dialogs offer similar settings. By default, the search and replacement commands operate from the current selection toward the end of the file, stopping either with the next match on the search string or at the end of the file. The Search Backward setting in either dialog allows you to search toward the beginning of the file.

The Case Sensitive check box determines whether the searches attempt to match the exact case specified. The default action is to ignore case. The value of this toggle corresponds to the shell variable {CaseSensitive}, and changing one will change the other. This setting also controls the default operation of the Find, Replace, and Search shell commands.

Within a Find or Replace operation, there are three possible interpreations of the search string. The default action is to look for the Literal matching characters. Entire Word selects whether the search string is expected to be a separate word. The definition of a "word" is the same as for double-clicking, that is, the range of characters specified by shell variable {WordSet}. With Entire Word enabled, a Find or Replace operation will not match a string in the document if either of the adjacent characters (before or after the string) is part of the word set.

The third alternative, Selection Expression, provides access to MPW's standard pattern-matching capabilities. When it is enabled, the normal Find and Replace commands instead expect MPWs special form of selection expressions to describe the search string. The appearance of the dialog box is changed to remind you of the difference, as shown in Figure 4–12.

The setting of Case Sensitive still applies when searching for selection expressions. However, Selection Expression disables the Entire Word option, which can be handled by complex selection expressions, as described in the next chapter. Also, the Find Selection command expects that the selected text is an expression rather than a simple string.

When Selection Expression is enabled, ordinary strings are no longer valid as search strings for the Find and Replace commands. Ordinary strings are still expected, however, for the replacement string of a Replace command.

To search for a particular string, surround it with slashes (/string/) to search forward or reverse slashes (\string\) to search backward. When Selection Expression is enabled, Search Backward is disabled. Any of the MPW string-matching special characters can be used within the slash delimiters, with useful values shown in Table 4–17.

About the only time you wouldn't use the slash delimiters is when you're looking for a particular line or range of lines. Typical line number expres-

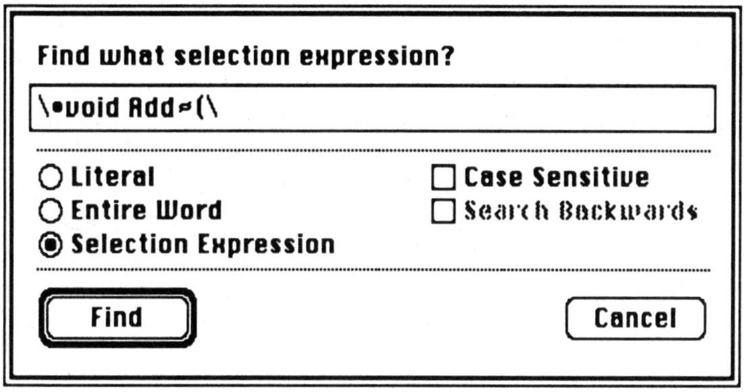

```
┌─────────────────────────────────────────────────────┐
│  Find what selection expression?                    │
│ ┌─────────────────────────────────────────────────┐ │
│ │ \•void Add≈(\                                   │ │
│ └─────────────────────────────────────────────────┘ │
│  ○ Literal                  ☐ Case Sensitive        │
│  ○ Entire Word              ☐ Search Backwards      │
│  ◉ Selection Expression                             │
│ ┌──────────────┐              ┌──────────────┐      │
│ │    Find      │              │   Cancel     │      │
│ └──────────────┘              └──────────────┘      │
└─────────────────────────────────────────────────────┘
```

Figure 4-12: Finding a Selection Expression

Expression	Description	Example
Strings		
/string/	Search forward	/integer/
\string\	Search backward	\typedef\
≈	Match any characters	/in≈Button/
•	Match at beginning of line	\•PROCEDURE\
∞	Match at end of line	/Point;∞/
∂	Match special character	/∂/∂*/
Line numbers		
n	Select entire line n	20
n:m	Select lines n through m	1:35
Δn	Beginning of line n	Δ123
n Δ	End of line n	123Δ
•	Beginning of document	•
∞	End of document	∞

Notes
1. Upper/lower case distinctions are ignored unless **Case Sensitive** is checked.
2. The special characters are generated (for US keyboard) using:

≈	Option-x
•	Option-8
∞	Option-5
∂	Option-d
Δ	Option-j

Table 4-17:   Common Selection Expressions

sions are shown in the table. Although entering a number will select the corresponding line, this selects the entire line; if you type a character, you will delete the selected line. If you use Selection Expression to find particular lines in your file, you should get in the habit of prefixing the line number with the Δ (Option-j) character to place the insertion point at the beginning of the line instead.

Note that the beginning and end characters (• and ∞ respectively) have a special meaning as both search strings and line number expressions. The difference is whether they are enclosed in delimiters. If so, they refer to a position within a line. If not, they refer to a position within a document.

More information on selection expressions is contained in the next chapter.

WINDOW MENU

The first two commands on the Window menu control the display of multiple windows on the screen. **Tile Windows** causes the windows to be made smaller and arranged so that they cover the display without overlapping. If you have more than two windows, you won't find them much use without a large screen display—although you can choose any window and make it larger by clicking in the zoom box. **Stack Windows** returns the windows to their default overlapping display.

The remainder of the window menu includes the list of all the documents currently open by MPW. The first of the documents is always the worksheet.

The name of the active window is checked, while the name of the target window is indicated by the "bull's-eye" (•) symbol. If the corresponding document has been changed since it was last saved, its name is underlined.

Selecting the name of the window makes the specified window the active window, and the previous active window becomes the target window.

MARK MENU

Version 2.0 includes the ability to assign named markers to locations in a source file, which is supported by a dedicated menu. This was a feature for the Lisa Workshop editor that was sorely missed by Lisa veterans when the original MPW was released.

Using the Mark menu, named context markers can be attached to a source file. Often the names will be the name of a routine, although it can be any valid MPW selection.

For a new document, the menu starts with only two items. The **Mark** command offers a dialog box to attach a name (the "marker") to the current selection in the active window. By default, the command will use the first word of a selection range as the name of the selection. If you want to use a longer name, you can copy it from the active window into the dialog box.

The **Unmark** command deletes a marker by its name. A list of the current markers is presented, allowing you to delete one.

The remainder of the menu will be the list of markers defined. As with other long Macintosh menus, if the menu list is longer than the height of the screen, an arrow will appear at the bottom of the menu list, and the list will scroll as you drag the menu toward the bottom. Selecting the marker name changes the selection in the current active window to the stored location, scrolling the window to display the selection if necessary.

The contents of the menu reflect the markers in the current active document, so as you change active documents, the menu will change. By default, the worksheet distributed by Apple contains some helpful tips, including sample commands, with the markers set so you can easily find those tips.

Figure 4–13 shows the Mark menu with a series of markers attached for a Pascal source program.

EQUIVALENT COMMANDS

Most of the menu items have equivalent shell commands, as shown by Table 4–18.

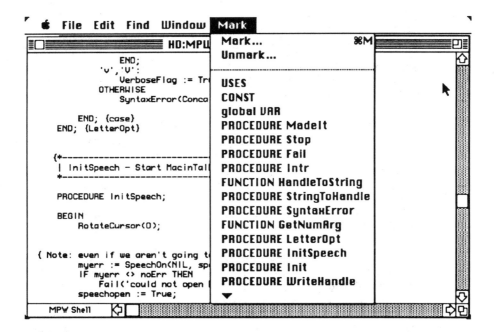

Figure 4–13: Sample Markers

Menu (Active Window)	Command (Target Window)	Command (Active Window)†
File Menu		
New	Open -t -n filename	New
Open	Open -t filename	Open filename
Open Selection	Open "`Catenate §`"	
Close	Close	Close "{Active}"
Save	Save	Save "{Active}"
Save as		
Save a Copy	Duplicate "{Target}" new	Duplicate "{Active}" new
Revert to Saved	Revert	Revert "{Active}"
Page Setup		
Print Selection	Print {PrintOptions} §	Print{PrintOptions}"{Active}.§"
Print Window	Print {PrintOptions} "{Target}	Print {PrintOptions} "{Active}"
Quit	Quit	Quit
Edit Menu		
Undo	Undo	Undo "{Active}"
Cut	Cut §	Cut § "{Active}"
Copy	Copy §	Copy § "{Active}"
Paste	Paste §	Paste § "{Active}"
Clear	Clear §	Clear § "{Active}"
Select All	Find •:∞	Find •:∞ "{Active}"
Show Clipboard		
Format††		
Align	Align §	Align § "{Active}"
Shift Left	Adjust -l -{Tab} §	Adjust -l -{Tab} § "{Active}"
Shift Right	Adjust §	Adjust § "{Active}"
Enter	Execute "{Target}".§	Execute "{Active}".§
††Format Dialog		
Tabs	Tab value	Tab value "{Active}"
(font names)	Font name size	Font name size "{Active}" sizes
Find Menu		
Find†††	Find /string/	Find /string/ "{Active}"
Find Same		
Find Selection	Find /`Catenate §`/	Find /`Catenate §`/ "{Active}"
Display	Find §	Find § "{Active}"
Selection		
Replace	Replace /old/ 'new'	Replace /old/ 'new' "{Active}"
	Replace Same	
†††Find Dialog		
Case Sensitive	Set CaseSensitive 1	
		Set CaseSensitive 0
Search	Find \string\	Find \string\ "{Active}"
Backwards		

Window Menu

Tile Windows	TileWindows	TileWindows
Stack Windows	StackWindows	StackWindows
(window name)	Target windowname	Open windowname

Mark Menu

| Mark | Mark § marker | Mark § marker "{Active}" |
| Unmark | Unmark marker | Unmark marker "{Active}" |

† Used for command files or custom menus

Table 4–18:   **Commands Equivalent to Menus**

The equivalencies are not exact. MPW-defined menu commands always operate on the active window. When you define your own menus, you should use the same convention for the sake of consistency. However, shell commands are always entered in the active window and change the contents of the target window and thus are not used in exactly the same way as the menu commands.

Most of these command equivalents require additional concepts not yet introduced and are presented for reference purposes only. The shell commands for editing are described in the next chapter. Some of these shell commands require use of some of the more intricate shell programming tricks.

KEYBOARD AND MOUSE SHORTCUTS

There are a number of shortcuts that, while not strictly necessary to make effective use of MPW, certainly can make your life a lot easier.

In addition to the Command-key equivalents shown in the menu bar, Command-Backspace deletes from the current position to the end of the file. This is primarily useful when you wish to delete the long output from the command you just entered—although, if you haven't made any other changes, Undo (Command-Z) also works.

The Command (apple) key can be used with the arrow keys to quickly move within the document. Command left arrow and right arrow move to the left and right margins of the document. Command-shift up and down arrow move to the beginning and end of the document, while Command-up- and down-arrow move one screen in the appropriate direction.

Typing the letter Y or N is a shortcut for clicking the Yes or No button of a confirmation dialog. Command period is a synonym for Cancel in any alert or dialog that contains a cancel button, in addition to its customary role in cancelling an executing MPW command.

Both the Adjust Left and Adjust Right menu commands will shift by a single space if the Shift key is held down when the menu is selected or if a

Command-Shift equivalent is used. For example, Command-Shift-[would shift the text left one sapce.

As noted earlier, the action of double-clicking can be modified by changing the WordSet shell variable. Triple-clicking (three clicks in rapid succession) always selects the current line.

When you double-click on a bracket, parenthesis, or brace character ([ ], ( ), { }), the editor will select all the text up to the matching character at the other end of the grouped expression. The delimiters are never included in the selection. The editor correctly counts nested grouping characters of the same type.

You can double-click on either the opening or closing delimiter to select the expression. The only difference is that the fixed point of the slection will be where you click, should you decide to extend the selection with a Shift-click.

When clicking on a quote or apostrophe, the editor will select everything up until the next such character. Unlike the grouping delimiters, you must always select at the beginning of a quoted string. Examples of these selections are shown in Figure 4–14.

If the matching delimiter is not found, the selection ends at the beginning (or end) of the document, depending on the direction of search.

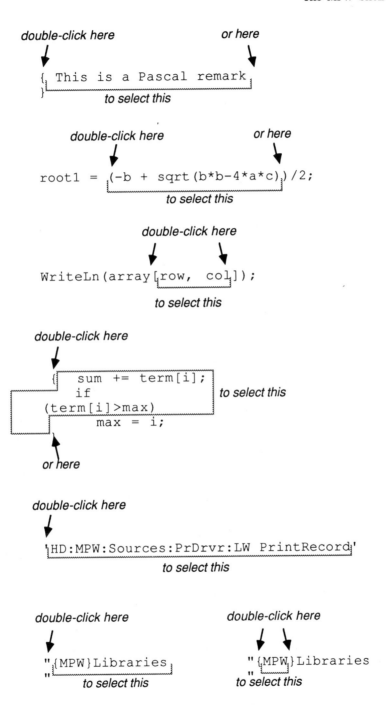

Figure 4–14: Double-Clicking on Delimited Text

Chapter 5

Command-Based Editing

As DESCRIBED IN THE PREVIOUS CHAPTER, MPW provides menu-based editing capabilities that parallel those of other text editors and word processors. These menu commands are suitable for making simple changes to your files and can be used without prior training or a manual. Most of these menu commands also have corresponding shell commands, which are described in this chapter.

More complex text operations can also be done using the menus if you understand MPW's standard form for selection expressions, which include pattern-matching regular expressions. These expressions, which were briefly introduced in the previous chapter, are fully described here.

However, many operations—particularly those involving repeated searches or replaces—require the use of shell commands. We'll call this approach "command-based editing," to distinguish it from the menu-driven alternative described in the previous chapter.

These commands can be entered interactively or built into command files that are used over and over again, as will be described in the next chapter. Combining selection expressions and shell commands allows you to perform almost any operation.

Other shell commands can also be used to change the formatting of text documents. These include commands to modify the indentation or spelling of source program text, as well as to print a formatted listing to the printer.

5.1   Documents

The commands described in this section involve the document windows opened by the shell. These commands generally do not change the contents of the window but may change its appearance on the screen.

SHELL WINDOWS

The MPW application supports a large number of concurrent windows, each referencing a text document. As described in the previous chapter, two of these windows have a particular importance for shell editing commands.

If you're entering a command interactively, it will always be selected in the active window. Normally, you'll use the worksheet as the active window for editing commands. This is not required (or expected) by MPW but means that all the one-time commands clutter up only one file. If you find particular commands that are useful over and over again, you might want to put them in a separate document, called, for example, "Tips". When you later encounter a similar situation, you can open that document and select the commands directly from the Tips window.

All of the commands described in this chapter will operate on the target window by default. Most allow you to specify any window to operate on—although it rarely makes sense to operate on the active window when entering commands interactively since that will include the selection command itself! However, the commands involving the active windows are often used when you are defining your own menus, as discussed in the next chapter.

As shown in Figure 5–1, the shell provides several visual clues that distinguish the active and target windows. These are in addition to the standard Macintosh user interface—as implemented by the Window Manager—which distinguishes the active window from all other windows.

The active window includes the name of the currently executing command (or "MPW Shell") in the horizontal scroll bar; for all other documents, this area will be blank. As with other editors, MPW shows the selected text in the active window in reverse video, white letters on a black background if you're using a monochrome display.

However, MPW also indicates the selection in the target window. This is the "current selection" used by shell editing commands. The selected area is shown outlined with a rectilinear border.

If a Macintosh text selection does not encompass any characters, the selection is known as an "insertion point." The insertion point in the target window is displayed in a dimmed fashion, as shown in Figure 5–2. The insertion point in the active window is, as is standard, shown as a blinking insertion point.

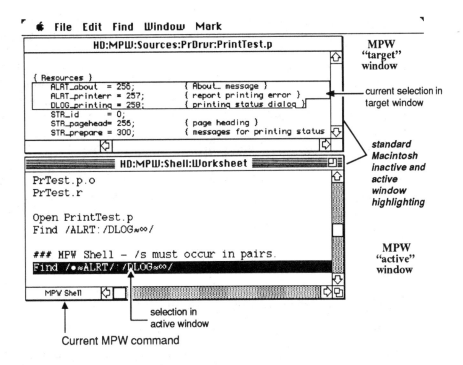

Figure 5–1: Active and Target Window Selections

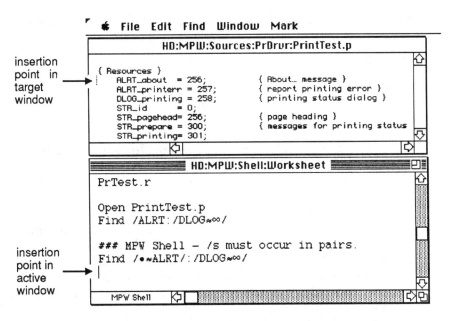

Figure 5–2: Active and Target Window Insertion Points

You normally activate document windows using the Windows menu or by clicking anywhere on the window. The previous active window becomes the target window.

There may be occasions when you want to adjust the position of the windows without changing which window is active. For example, you may want to move the target window to where it can be seen, underneath the active window. A little-known feature of the Window Manager allows you to drag an inactive window by its title bar without making it active if you hold down the Command key when clicking on the title bar.

To save the list of currently open windows and their ordering, MPW includes a shell command to display the window names. The output of the Windows command includes the complete pathnames of the corresponding documents. Unlike the titles displayed at the top of each window, the output of the Windows command never abbreviates long names.

Windows

Display a list of the currently open documents

Syntax:

Windows   Display the names of all the open windows

Remarks:

The windows are displayed from front to back, with the active window always last. The clipboard is never included in the list.

Input/Output:

Output   Pathnames of open documents, one per line

Examples:

Windows >> "{Worksheet}" Append the list of windows to the worksheet

Figure 5–3 shows the display from a sample Windows command and the corresponding Windows menu. Note that pathnames containing special characters—such as a space—are quoted so that they can be used as the input to other commands. Also note that the Windows menu shows the documents in the order they were opened, while the Windows command displays the window names from front to back. This allows you to reopen the same windows in the same order later on.

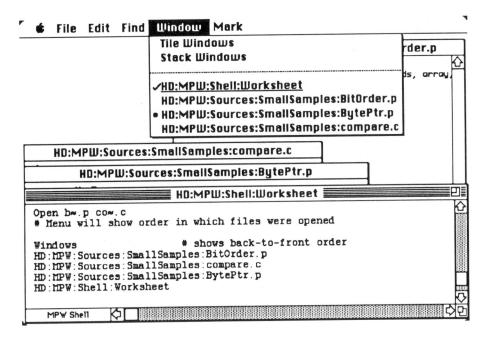

Figure 5-3:   Displaying Window Names

OPENING A DOCUMENT

MPW includes shell commands to open existing documents and create new ones. These provide additional capabilities beyond the corresponding menu's operations. They're also useful when you're already typing other commands—such as the Directory command—and you don't want your hands to leave the keyboard.

Open

Open a document and make it the active window

Syntax:

```
Open filename ...        Open filename and make it the active window
Open -n filename...      Open filename, creating it if it doesn't exist
Open -n                  Open a new document and assign it a name
```

Options:

```
-r                       Open the document read only
-t                       Make the document the target window
```

Remarks:

If -n is used without *filename*, Open assigns a name of the form "Untitled-n". An attempt to open an existing file fails if the file does not exist already. If the document is already opened by the shell, the existing window is used.

If successful, Open makes the document the active window; the previous active window becomes the target window. If more than one *filename* is specified, the documents are opened in the order specified and the last document becomes the active window. Open -t is similar to the Target command.

Examples:

```
Open "{ShellDirectory}Startup"
                    Open the standard startup command file
Open -r "{CIncludes}stdio.h"
                    Open the C standard I/O include file as read
                    only
Open -n
                    Create a new window and assign a file name
```

The Open command normally expects as a parameter either the full or partial pathname of an existing text document. When the -r option is used, you will not be allowed to change the document's contents, although the editor will save changes to the resource based formatting information described in Chapter 4.

Open can also be used to create a new file and give it a default pathname. If the file already exists, there's no error: instead the shell will open the existing file. For example, you might want to define in UserStartup the command alias

```
        Alias mm 'Open -n Makefile'
```

to make a new copy of the Make input file for a folder, if none exists already.

Open is also useful when writing command files that use a selected or derived name for the document name. For example, an assembly language source file Test.a will normally have a corresponding listing file Test.a.lst. It would be easier to open this listing file with the alias

```
        Alias OpenListing 'Open "{Target}.lst"'
```

The quotation marks are necessary to treat {Target}.lst as one parameter to Open, while the apostrophes prevent the value of {Target} from being evaluated when the alias is defined.

If you want to include an `Open` command in a command file but you don't know the name ahead of time, you could use `Commando` to present a file selection dialog. The command

Open...

would display a Commando dialog, allowing you to open one or more files.

New

Create a new document

Syntax:

`New` *filename*   Create *filename* and make it the active window

`New`   Create a new document and assign a name

Remarks:

If a document name is assigned by `New`, it will be of the form "Untitled-n", where n is a positive integer.

`New` is similar to `Open -n`, except that `New` returns an error if *filename* already exists.

Examples:

`New Test.p`   Create a new file `Test.p` in the current folder

`New` could be used in command files when you want to start editing an input file. It differs from the New menu command in that it never presents a file name selection dialog box.

If, in a series of commands, you are using `New` to create a specific file, you should either check to see if the file exists before using `New` or use the `Open -n` command to allow use of the file if it already exists.

ACTIVATING WINDOWS

As noted earlier, command-based editing will make frequent use of the two topmost documents displayed by MPW, the active and target windows.

The window you use for entering shell editing commands is always the active window, with those commands operating on the document in the target window. However, if you are typing new text for that document, you must make the document the active window. This sounds somewhat awkward, and it can be at times, although you'll generally find yourself "batch-ing" each type of editing rather than alternating back and forth, one operation at a time.

It's also helped by the existence of shell commands that will change the position of the windows. If you're going to go back and forth between selecting a list of shell commands and typing new data, it's just as easy to add a command at the end of the list to make the document (target window) the active window.

You would do this by adding (and selecting) an `Open` command. In addition to creating a new window, `Open` is also used to select one of the existing windows to become the active window. Although `Open` will indirectly determine the target window, the choice of the target window can also be controlled directly through the `Target` command.

Target

Make a window the target window

Syntax:

`Target` *window*   Make *window* the target window

Remarks:

If *window* is not an open document, the `Target` command will attempt to open an existing file before making it the target window. The command fails if the file does not exist.

If only one document (the worksheet) is open, the worksheet cannot be made the target window.

Examples:

`Target Math.c`   Open `Math.c` and make it the target window
`Target "{Worksheet}"`
                Make the worksheet the target window

The `Target` command is often the first in a series of commands to select the window that the remaining commands will operate on. `Target` will also open a document if it's not already open. However, as a matter of style, you may wish to use `Open -t` to open documents in any command files you write since it's more readily apparent (to others that might use your command files) that you are creating a new window. `Target` would be used for moving an existing window to the second position from the top.

If, as frequently is the case, you want to swap the order of the top two windows, the following two commands are equivalent ways of doing the same thing:

```
Open "{Target}"     # make target window the active
Target "{Active}"   # make active window the target
```

If no documents (other than the worksheet) are open, there is no target window, only the active window. The value of {Target} is undefined (and thus is null) and the Target command cannot be used, except to create a new window.

Finally, the File command is also used to change the target window and is displayed by the output of several MPW commands. File is defined as an alias for Target in the standard Startup file supplied with MPW.

The compilers and assembler display File commands with any error message, while the text search command uses them with matching lines. The File command can then be selected and used to open the specified source file as the target window for editing.

CHANGING WINDOWS

Once open, each document has a size and position on the screen. This information is stored in the resource fork of the document.

You can change the window's appearance with the mouse by dragging or resizing the window or through the MoveWindow and SizeWindow commands.

MoveWindow, SizeWindow

Reposition document window

Syntax:

MoveWindow *h* *v*	Move left, top corner of target window to *h, v*
MoveWindow *h* *v* *window*	Move left, top corner of *window* to *h, v*
SizeWindow *h* *v*	Make target window *h* wide by *v*] high
SizeWindow *h* *v* *window*	Make *window h* wide by *v* high

Remarks:

The MoveWindow parameters specify the location of the upper-left corner of the content region (window interior) in global (screen) coordinates. The SizeWindow parameters specify the exterior dimensions of the window.

Examples:

MoveWindow 3 40	Move target window to upper left corner

```
SizeWindow 500 30 "{Worksheet}"
```
                              Resize worksheet to a horizontal strip

For example, you might want to assign each newly created document to a standard position on the screen. To take the earlier alias for creating and opening a Makefile, the definition could be extended to include positioning the window at the bottom of the screen.

```
Alias mm 'Open -n Makefile;'∂
' MoveWindow 3 240 Makefile; SizeWindow 500 100'∂
  ' Makefile'
```

Of course, the actual parameters used for MoveWindow and SizeWindow will depend on your screen size.

Under the Macintosh Window Manager, every window can have two states. Under MPW, the user state is set by the MoveWindow and SizeWindow commands and their mouse equivalents.

Clicking in the zoom box will set the window to the standard state, which for MPW is the largest possible window. A second click will restore the window to the user state. Zooming never affects the user state, while moving or resizing the window always changes the user state.

The ZoomWindow command is similar to clicking in the zoom box. However, the command always sets the window to one state or the other.

ZoomWindow

Toggle window zooming

Syntax:

ZoomWindow   **Make target window maximum size**
ZoomWindow *window*   **Make *window* maximum size**

Options:

-s   **Size window to (smaller) user state**

Examples:

ZoomWindow -s "{Worksheet}"
                              Shrink worksheet to user state

When you have many documents open, the position of each document may become disorganized or haphazard. The StackWindows and TileWindows commands impose an order upon the desktop by reposition-ing all open windows according to standard algorithms; their effect is identical to the menu commands of the same names.

StackWindows, TileWindows

Reposition all open windows

Syntax:

StackWindows	Overlap and stagger windows
TileWindows	Position windows to avoid overlap

Remarks:

Both commands permanently change the user state for each of the open windows.

Examples:

TileWindows	Move windows to avoid overlap

For both commands, the window closest to the upper left corner is the first window opened—the first window in the Windows menu, the worksheet. The remaining windows are positioned in the order they were opened, which for the StackWindows command is slightly lower than and to the right of the preceding window.

The algorithm for TileWindows is more complex. With only a few windows, the command will position the windows as a series of horizontal strips the width of the screen. If this would produce windows that aren't tall enough, the windows are arranged in a horizontal grid, subdivided both vertically and horizontally. Figure 5–4 shows the result of TileWindows command with five open windows.

Neither the StackWindows or TileWindows command affect the front-to-back ordering of the windows. For StackWindows, the active window will remain on top when the command is complete.

SAVING A FILE

The Save command can be used to save one or more of the open documents. The shell also recognizes several other commands which, either directly or indirectly, close the open windows, possibly saving beforehand.

The Save command allows you to save a specific document, something that cautious programmers may wish to include in commonly used lists of commands. For example, if you're compiling a program, that's a good time to save the source code, as with the alias

```
Alias PasComp 'Save; Pascal "{Target}"'
```

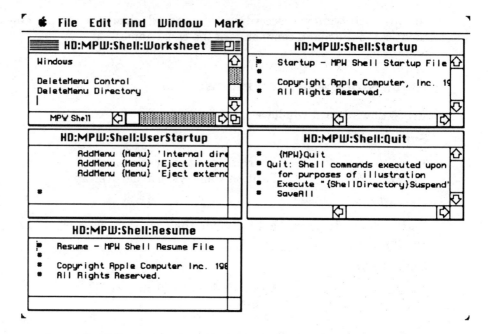

Figure 5-4:   Display After TileWindows Command

The Save command is similar to the Close shell command. Both have one additional capability beyond their menu equivalents—an option to save (close) all the open windows.

Save

Save the contents of a document or documents

Syntax:

Save	Save the contents of the target window
Save *window*	Save the contents of *window*
Save -a	Save the contents of all open windows

Remarks:

The command is ignored if contents of the window(s) have not been changed since the last save.

Examples:

Save "{Worksheet}"	Update the contents of the worksheet to disk
Save -a	Save all the open documents to disk

Close

Close an open window or windows, saving if necessary

Syntax:

`Close`	Close the target window
`Close` *window* ...	Close each *window*
`Close -a`	Close all open windows

Options:

`-y`	Save the window(s) if necessary before closing
`-n`	Don't save the window(s), discarding changes

Remarks:

If neither `-y` or `-n` is given for a window that has been changed, the shell will display a confirmation alert asking if changes should be saved. If the confirmation alert is cancelled, the window will not be closed.

`Close` will never close the worksheet.

Examples:

`Close -n`	Close the target window, discarding changes
`Close -y -a`	Close and save all the open documents

As with other MPW commands, the `-y` and `-n` options bypass confirmation alerts by forcing a response of yes or no, respectively. The `Close` command will save the document(s) for yes, and discard any changes for no.

One way to use the `Close` command is to discard the changes to the document:

```
Alias Discard ∂
'Set f "{Target}"; Close -n; Open -t "{f}"'
```

The `Set` command is used to assign a shell variable before the target window is closed so that it can be reopened immediately.

This can also be achieved using the `Revert` command.

Revert

Revert open window(s) to the saved version

Syntax:

`Revert`	Restore the target window to disk version
`Revert` *window* ...	Restore each *window*

Options:

-y	Do not present a confirmation dialog

Remarks:

If the -y is not given for a window that has been changed, the shell will display a confirmation alert asking if the changes should be discarded. If the confirmation alert is cancelled, the window will be unchanged.

Examples:

Revert -y	Reopen the target window, discarding changes

The Discard alias would then be defined as

```
Alias Discard 'Revert -y'
```

In this case, a yes to the Revert confirmation alert discards the changes.

Two shell commands are provided to exit MPW; one exits to the Finder, and the other shuts down the Macintosh and optionally reboots it. These commands would be used as the last command in a command alias or command file. For example, you may wish to define a special quit command that saves a list of open windows prior to exiting to the Finder.

Shutdown, Quit

Exit MPW

Syntax:

Quit	Exit to the Finder
Shutdown	Power off the Macintosh

Options:

-y	Save the window(s) if necessary before closing
-n	Don't save the window(s), discarding changes
-c	Don't exit if any window needs saving
-r (Shutdown only)	Reboot the Macintosh

Remarks:

If neither -y, -n, nor -c is given, the shell will display a confirmation alert for any window with changes, asking if changes should be saved. If the confirmation alert is cancelled, the command will be aborted.

By default, the Shutdown command will power off a machine that provides software control of the power, such as the Macintosh II; for other machines, a power-off alert will be displayed.

Examples:

`Quit -y`	Save all the open documents, exit to Finder
`Shutdown -n`	Turn of Macintosh without saving changes

5.2 Selection Expressions

Most MPW shell commands for finding, selecting, and changing text use a standard form of selection expression. These selection expressions include references to the current selection, specific positions within the file, or searching for particular strings, as well as combinations of all these types.

Selection expressions can be used with the `Find` shell command to change the current selection in an open window. These selection expressions are the same form used by the Find menu command when Selection Expression is enabled. A simplified version of this syntax was presented in the Chapter 4 description of the Find menu command, and a complete definition is provided here.

The selection expressions also include a category of expressions that form matching arbitrary string patterns. Since these expressions can be quite complex, the discussion of such patterns is deferred until the next section.

TYPES OF EXPRESSIONS

The shell recognizes a number of special characters as representing all or part of a selection expression. For those commands that require a selection expression parameter, a simplified syntax is summarized in Table 5–1.

The selection expressions can be broken into two categories. The first is those expressions that select a series of characters that can be copied to the clipboard, replaced, and so on. The second is the expressions that define only an insertion point or a space between characters.

If a shell command matches the specified selection expression, the syntax of the expression will always define whether the new selection is a range the current selection will remain unchanged

SELECTION AS A FILE NAME

One character shown in Table 5–1 also has a special meaning outside of selection expressions and can be used with commands that do not expect a selection expression as a parameter.

The § (Option 6) character indicates the current selection in the target window. This can be used as a parameter to any command that expects a file name. This works because MPW intercepts certain key File Manager traps

Expression	Selection Range Description	Example
§	Current selection	§
¡n	Select line n lines before §	¡2
!n	Select line n lines after §	!0
n	Select entire line n	22
/string/	Search forward for string	/END/
\string \	Search backward for string	\#include\
marker	Select named marker	"PROCEDURE Foo"
s1:s2	Select from selections s1 through s2, inclusive	\{\:/}/
(selection)	Group selection	(!0):(!10)

Insertion Point

•	Beginning of document	•
∞	End of document	∞
Δselection	Beginning of selection	Δ/BEGIN/
selection Δ	End of selection	123Δ
selection¡n	n characters before selection	\INTEGER;\¡4
selection !n	n characters after selection	Δ/int Foo()/!4

† The values of selection include any valid selection expression

Keyboard equivalents for special characters are:
- ¡   Option-1
- •   Option-8
- ∞   Option-5
- Δ   Option-j

From highest to lowest, the order of precedence is
/ or \
( )
Δ
! or ¡
:

Table 5–1:   Selection Expressions

and thus is able to open a "file" named § when so requested by an MPW tool. For example, the command

```
Duplicate § NewFile
```

would take as input the current selection in the target window and for output would create a file NewFile to hold the contents of that selection.

A more common use is to display the selection in the current output stream, as in

```
Catenate §
```

This form will often be used when programming the shell to implement your own version of Open Selection, Find Selection, and other such commands.

The current selection character can also be prefaced by the name of a window. For example, the command

```
Catenate "{Active}".§ § >>"{ShellDirectory}Tips"
```

would copy the current selections in the active and target windows to the end of a file called Tips in the same directory as the MPW shell. This is illustrated schematically by Figure 5–5.

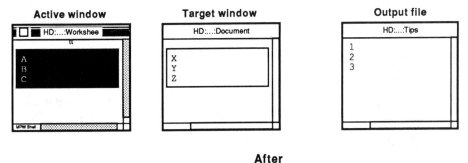

After

```
Catenate "{Active}".§ § >>"ShellDirectory}Tips"
```

 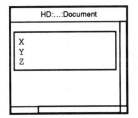 

Figure 5–5:   Appending Selections to an Output File

The selection can also be used as an output file. The command

```
Catenate "{Sources}Prototype.c" > §
```

replaces the current selection in the target window with the contents of a prototype file, which will become the new selection. To add to the selection, add the new contents to the end of the current selection.

Note that other selection expressions are *not* recognized as psuedo-file names, even if they include the § symbol. The command

```
Catenate "{Sources}Prototype.c" > §Δ
```

will faithfully create a document named §Δ.

CHANGING THE SELECTION

When editing text interactively, use the mouse to select text in the active window. When editing text using a series of shell commands, you will often select text using the Find command, usually in the target window.

Since selection expressions include both simple and pattern matching strings, the Find command is also used to find and select a specified string.

Find

Find and set selection in document window

Syntax:

Find *selection*	Find *selection* in the target window
Find *selection window*	Find *selection* in *window*

Options:

-c *count*	Repeat search *count* times

Remarks:

The Find command takes a standard shell selection expression as its first parameter and uses it to change the current selection in the specified window. When searching for a simple string, the string must be bracketed by the search string delimiters / or \.

Examples:

Find \BEGIN\	Find previous occurrence of BEGIN
Find -c 3 /PROCEDURE/	Find third occurrence of PROCEDURE
Find /•HD:/	Find next line beginning with HD:
Find •	Select top of target window

```
Find ∞ "{WorkSheet}"        Select bottom of worksheet
Find /∞/                    Select end of next line
Find Δ20                    Select beginning of line 20
```

The Find command is the most innocuous of all the shell commands that take a selection expression. Find does nothing but find the specified location and change the current selection, while commands such as Replace or Cut will generally change the text contained in the selection.

Note that the Find command does not work like the simple search commands of many editors. Commands such as

```
        Find int
        Find "PROCEDURE Alert"
```

will not be recognized because Find *always* expects a selection expression such as /int/.

FINDING STRINGS

An important class of selection expressions include those that specify search strings. Some characters of a search string are treated as special pattern-matching characters, but the remaining characters will be matched as is.

The delimiter used for the search string determines the direction searched. A slash character (/) leaning "forward" searches the document from after the current selection toward the end of the document, or forward in the file. A reverse slash (\) leaning "backward" searches back from before the current selection toward the beginning of the file.

Thus, if you want to select the next occurrence of the word "something," you must use a selection expression to indicate the search string, as in

```
        Find /Something/
```

The two selection delimiters quote strings from shell interpretation under rules similar to those for quotation marks. Only the ∂, {, and ` characters are treated as special within the string, as is, of course, the closing delimiter. If you want to search for one of these characters, you should precede it by the shell escape character ∂ (Option-D), as in:

```
        Find /1∂/2/
```

By default, strings will match without regard to case distinctions. The two commands

```
        Find /DEFINE/
        FIND /define/
```

would be interpreted identically with the default shell variable settings. You would normally use the command

```
Set CaseSensitive 1
```

when you want to match based on the exact capitalization used in your search strings. Setting CaseSensitive to a nonzero value does not affect the normal interpretation of command, option, and file name capitalization, for which case is always ignored.

POSITIONAL SELECTION

Two characters represent the beginning and end of the document. The character used to select the beginning of the file is the "bullet" character (•) (Option-8). This is often used before a text search or a search and replace to make sure the entire document is searched.

The ending character—the ∞ symbol (Option 5)—may be easier to remember. This is often used to append output to the end of a document.

For example, the {ShellDirectory}Quit command file includes a list of shell commands to be executed when you leave MPW. Modify the file to include the following commands at the beginning of the command file:

```
Find ∞ "{Worksheet}"      # set insertion point
Echo -n "Directory " > §# build partial command
Directory >> §           # append current directory
```

When you resume MPW, your worksheet always ends with a command to restore your current directory to the location you were at when you left, as in Figure 5–6. Hit Enter to restore the directory, backspace (or Clear) if you don't want to.

MPW also recognizes a line number as specifying a position within the file. When used with a Find command, the entire line is selected. So the command

```
Find '10'
```

selects the tenth line of the document, not the next occurrence of the number 10. If the line number is zero or greater than the length of the file, the selection is truncated to the beginning or end of the document.

Such numeric selections will often be seen in compiler error messages that include the Line command. Line is a simple command file (script) that selects an entire line in the target window, then makes that window the active window—so you can see it and edit it.

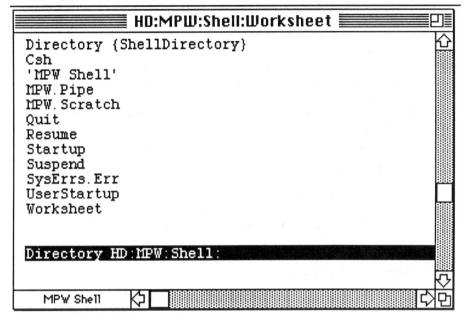

Figure 5-6:   A generated Directory Command

If the compiler outputs a message of the form

```
File "dumb.c" ; Line 20  # expected ";" got: int
```

you can select the error message line and enter it. The # causes the error message to be treated as a comment.

The equivalent commands executed will be

```
Target dumb.c # make source the target window
Find 20       # select the line with the error
Open dumb.c   # bring the selection to the front
```

As noted in the discussion of the Find menu in Chapter 4, using a line number as a selection can be dangerous since it selects the entire line. The next time you type a character, the selected text is deleted, and you'll lose the line. If you want to begin typing at the beginning (or end) of the line, you should precede (follow) the line number with a Δ (Option J) in the selection expression.

Finally, a positional selection expression can be the name of a marker set with the Mark menu. For example, if the marker #include has been set to refer to the header declarations in a C file, the command

```
Find '#include' # note quoting of # character
```

would be equivalent to selecting "#include" from the Mark menu with the target window.

If you intend to use markers in conjunction with shell commands, you should take care to avoid using any of the special selection expression characters (as shown in Table 5–1) as part of your marker names. Otherwise, marker names can include spaces and other punctuation characters as long as the name is quoted in a selection expression.

COMBINING SELECTIONS

Two or more selection expressions can be combined to form a compound selection, with each expression separated by a colon. The resulting selection range includes the characters in each selection and every character in between.

The most commonly used compound selection is the one that selects the entire document, as in:

```
Find •:∞
```

The individual expressions of the compound selection can be of arbitrary complexity. The command

```
Find 20:\#define\
```

would select from line 20 back to a preceding #define directive, inclusive.

When outlining the target selection, the editor will go through great contortions to indicate the exact portion of each line selected, as shown in Figure 5–7.

There are several other operators that can be combined with the previously defined selections.

The ∆ character has already been introduced to select at the beginning or end of a line, but it can be used with any selection expression to set the insertion point immediately before or after the selection.

Suppose you want to insert a comment line before each procedure in a Pascal program. Once you find the procedure heading, the current selection will be the heading. Outputting the comment to the current selection will delete the heading. Instead, you can put the insertion point before the selection and then output the new line, using the commands

```
Find /PROCEDURE/
Find ∆§
Echo "(* ---------------------------- *)" > §
```

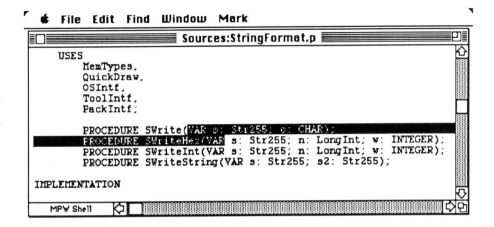

Figure 5–7:   Outlined Selection Range

When appended to a selection, the exclamation point and inverted exclamation point (¡) can be used to set an insertion point a specified number of characters away from that selection. For the exclamation point, the following integer specifies the number of characters before the beginning of the selection, while the inverted exclamation point is followed by the number of characters after the end of the selection. The command

                        Find §¡1

is equivalent to a left-arrow key, while

                        Find Δ/FooBar/!3

will find the next "FooBar" and position the insertion point before the word "Bar."

These two operators have a different meaning when they are not appended to another selection expression. The integer specifies the number of *lines* relative to the current selection, selecting the entire line. For example,

                        Find !10

skips down 10 lines from the current selection. A similar interpretation also holds when the ! or ¡ term stands alone as part of a selection range. The command

```
Find /PROCEDURE/:!10
```

will select the heading of the next procedure as well as the 10 lines following the heading, while

```
Find /PROCEDURE/!10
```

would set the insertion point 10 *characters* after the word PROCEDURE.

You can group individual components of a compound selection expression using parentheses. Although the shell defines a precedence for the order of evaluating operators, it's better to put the expression in parentheses if you have any doubt, since it makes it easier for you (or someone else) to understand how it works later on.

Example 5–1 shows sample Find with sample expressions and comments describing what they're searching for.

REPEAT COUNTS

Many of the commands described in this chapter also take repeat counts to indicate that the requested operation should be repeated an integral number of times. The repeat count is specified using the -c option, as in:

```
Replace -c 20 /This/ That
```

You can use a -c parameter of ∞ to indicate a very large repeat count, but it won't necessarily apply to the entire file. All commands start at the current selection in the specified window and stop at the beginning or end of the document, depending on the search direction. To search the entire document, you must first position the insertion point at the opposite end of the document.

For consistency's sake, the repeat count is recognized by all editing commands that operate on selections. Those commands that take repeat counts are Find, Replace, Cut, Copy, Paste, Clear, Align, and Adjust. The repeat count is crucial for Replace but is rarely used for the other commands.

If an editing command includes a repeat count, only the last operation can be reversed by the Undo menu. If you plan on making a global change to your file, you may wish to save it first. Then, if the change is not what was intended, the document can be reverted to its saved version.

```
# Example 5-1: Sample selection expressions


# Select line 20
Find 20

# Select beginning of line 20
Find Δ20

# Select beginning of document
Find •        # or Find 0 or Find Δ1

# Select entire document
Find •:∞

# Find next Pascal procedure heading
Find /PROCEDURE/

# Select line with previous Pascal procedure
Find \PROCEDURE\
Find !0

# Select last 10 lines of document
Find ∞:¡10

# Find Pascal global variables
Find •
Find /VAR/

# Find C variable definition in active window
Set CaseSenstive 1
Find Δ\int var\!4 "{Active}"

# Select current Pascal block, including BEGIN … END
Find \BEGIN\:/END/

# Select Pascal block that contains line 400
Find 400:\BEGIN\:/END/

# Select within current C block, excluding { }
Find \∂{\Δ:Δ/}/

# Select 101 through 200th characters
Find (•!100):(•!199)
```

Example 5–1: Sample Selection Expressions

5.3 Searching Documents

When you're writing a program, you'll often find yourself looking for the definition or use of a particular identifier among several source files.

With MPW C or Pascal, the `#include` and USES files each total more than 250K of declarations. When writing new code using these declarations, you will often find it easier to search the appropriate interface file than to grab a printed copy of *Inside Macintosh* and find the appropriate page among thousands—if you have an effective way of scanning all the files.

If you're working on an existing program, you may need to check the declaration of one of your own routines. With MacApp, much of your application will be defined by the library sources supplied with MacApp. Or you may wish to keep online sample programs, such as those distributed by APDA, so that you can look for a sample usage of a particular Toolbox routine.

The `Search` command allows you to scan a series of files to find lines that match a particular pattern. These patterns include simple text strings and a variety of pattern-matching characters, as described in this section.

SCANNING TEXT

The `Search` command has some similarities to the `Find` command. Like the `Find` command, `Search` is often used to scan a file to look for a particular word or line.

However, the purpose of the `Find` command is to leave the selection at a single location that matches the specified selection expression. The `Search` command does not change the selection, but displays a list of lines that match the specified expression; because it can match many lines (rather than one), it can also be used to scan several files.

Therefore, the parameter of a `Find` command is always a selection expression. The parameter to a `Search` command is always a string, which can be used as part of a selection expression. Both commands can use strings that include pattern matching expressions.

Search

Display lines matching search pattern

Syntax:

```
Search pattern file …      Scan file for pattern
Search pattern             Scan input for pattern
```

Options:

-q	Don't display file names or line numbers

-r	Display lines not matching pattern
-s	Dearch is always case sensitive
-i	Dearch is never case sensitive

Remarks:

The *pattern* can be a literal string or any pattern-matching regular expression. The *pattern* may optionally be delimited by /.../ characters; if so, the *pattern* is partially quoted against shell interpretation. The \...\ delimiters are not recognized.

Unless the -q option is used, Search displays its output with File and Line commands. The matching lines are included as a shell comments.

If neither -s or -i is used, Search will ignore case distinctions if shell variable (CaseSensitive) is zero (the default) or use them if it is nonzero.

Input/Output:

Output	Display of matching lines or list of commands

Examples:

```
Search PROCEDURE File.p   Display procedure declarations in File.p
Search -i/error/ "{Target}"
                          Search target for errors, showing line
                          numbers
Search -q ResType {CIncludes}≈
                          Display resource type in all C include
                          files
```

Search will scan the specified files for the string pattern and display the line containing that pattern. Whether the search is case sensitive is determined by the value of (CaseSensitive), although command options can be used to always make the search case sensistive or insensitive.

Search does not require the /string/ delimiters but will allow them for consistency with the Find and Replace commands. The following commands are identical in their effect

```
Search void Main.c
Search /void/ Main.c
Search "void" Main.c
Search "/void/" Main.c
Search 'void' Main.c
Search '/void/' Main.c
```

since the quotes and apostrophes are stripped by the shell.

For each match, Search normally displays the name of the file and the line number as a series of File and Line commands, with the actual source lines as comments. The `File` command will open the appropriate file as the target window, while `Line` will select the proper line and make the target window the active window.

If you have a small Mac display, you may need to use a small font for your worksheet to be able to see each `File` command, `Line` command and source line without horizontal scrolling.

Occasionally, you'll want to see only the matching lines from the input files without displaying shell commands. To do so, you would suppress the File and Line commands with the `-q` (quiet) option. For example, if you wanted to build a list of all the procedure declarations in a folder of Pascal files, you could use the command

```
Search -q PROCEDURE ≈.p
```

to produce a single output stream containing the matching lines. This is shown in Figure 5–8.

Unlike most of the commands described so far, `Search` does not operate on the target window by default. Instead, omitting any file name causes `Search` to scan its standard input stream. The command line

```
Set | Search -q include
```

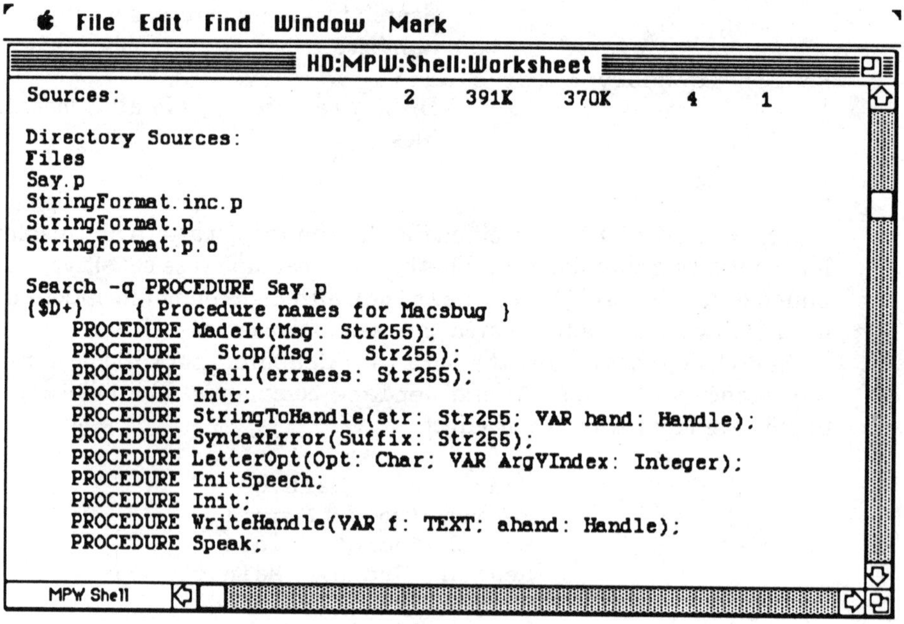

```
 ⚫ File  Edit  Find  Window  Mark
═══════════════════ HD:MPW:Shell:Worksheet ═══════════════════
 Sources:                    2      391K      370K      4      1
 Directory Sources:
 Files
 Say.p
 StringFormat.inc.p
 StringFormat.p
 StringFormat.p.o

 Search -q PROCEDURE Say.p
 {$D+}    { Procedure names for Macsbug }
   PROCEDURE MadeIt(Msg: Str255);
   PROCEDURE   Stop(Msg:    Str255);
   PROCEDURE  Fail(errmess: Str255);
   PROCEDURE Intr;
   PROCEDURE StringToHandle(str: Str255; VAR hand: Handle);
   PROCEDURE SyntaxError(Suffix: Str255);
   PROCEDURE LetterOpt(Opt: Char; VAR ArgVIndex: Integer);
   PROCEDURE InitSpeech;
   PROCEDURE Init;
   PROCEDURE WriteHandle(VAR f: TEXT; ahand: Handle);
   PROCEDURE Speak;

 MPW Shell
```

Figure 5–8:   Finding Procedure Names

would display a subset of the output of the Set command, such as:

```
Set AIncludes HD:MPW:AIncludes
Set CIncludes HD:MPW:AIncludes
Set RIncludes HD:MPW:RIncludes
```

If you want to search the target window, you can specify it as a file parameter, as in:

```
Search Copyright "{Target}"
```

If you intend to search the active window, be sure to redirect the output to a file. Otherwise, the list of previous matches will be matched as it is displayed, and this recursive scan will continue indefinitely.

REGULAR EXPRESSIONS

The MPW shell provides a standard facility for matching arbitrary string patterns. These strings are used by the Search command and by commands that recognize selection expressions, such as Find and Replace. A subset of these expressions can also be used for matching file names, as will be described in Chapter 6.

MPW's standard form for such pattern-matching strings are termed "regular expressions." Each regular expression can consist of a series of patterns. These patterns are shown in Table 5–2.

To match consecutive patterns, the patterns are listed in order, without separators. Previous examples have already shown the degenerate case of such expressions: a literal string—one without special characters—matches text with exactly the same series of characters. Letters, numbers, spaces, and most standard ASCII punctuation characters are treated literally.

As with other shell parameters, regular expressions containing special characters must be quoted. If unquoted, the shell will interpret many of the regular expression characters as indicating a pattern-matching string for file pathnames. Regular expressions that includes blanks must be quoted to prevent them from being treated as command separators.

Fortunately, the /.../ and \...\ delimiters used by selection expressions will quote the enclosed pattern-matching strings. As with quotation marks, all characters will be passed by the shell without interpretation except for the ∂, `, and { characters.

For the Search command, if you don't use the /.../ delimiters, you should use some form of quoting. The following commands will pass a pattern to Search

Character	Description
c	Match c as an ordinary character (unless special)†
'string '	treat string as ordinary characters
"string "	treat string as ordinary characters, except for ', {, ∂
?	match any single character
≈	match as many characters as possible (0 or more), except Return
[list]	match a single character in list ††
[–list]	match a single character not in list ††

† Character	Treated as special...
∂ (Option-D)	except within apostrophes('...')
? ≈ * + [« ( )	except within range ([...]), or quoted ("...",'...')
® (Option-R)	only after right parenthesis,)
• (Option-8)	only as first character
∞ (Option-5)	special as last character
/ \	special only if used as leading delimiter

†† *list* contains individual characters to be matched, or ranges separated by - signs. For example:

[013]	match 0, 1 or 3
[A-Z]	match uppercase letter
[+*/-]	match arithmetic operator
[]{}[()]	match grouping character

Table 5–2: Regular Expression Symbols

```
Search /PB≈Rec/ Files.h
Search "PB≈Rec" Files.h
Search 'PB≈Rec' Files.h
```

while

```
Search -l PB≈Rec Files.h
```

will allow the unquoted ≈ to be interpreted by the shell.

The differences between the types of quotation are important with two types of literal strings: those that include shell variables and those that include control characters.

Unless quoted by apostrophes, a shell variable expression in a search string will be replaced by the literal value of the variable. The command

```
Search /{MPW}/ {ShellDirectory}Startup
```

would search for the string represented by the {MPW} shell variable, such as HD:MPW:, while

```
Search '{MPW}' {ShellDirectory}Startup
```

searches for any references to the shell variable MPW, i.e., the literal characters {MPW}.

You may also wish to search for literal control characters, such as the tab character. The command

```
Search "END;∂t∂{" Proto.p
```

searches for a Pascal-commented END statement, in which the comment is separated from the END by a tab.

SIMPLE PATTERNS

More useful forms of regular expressions usually include pattern-matching terms in which the actual character to be matched is unknown.

Two regular expression characters represent wildcard patterns, matching any valid character. The ? character matches any single character, while ≈ (the familiar Option-X) matches a string of zero or more characters. For these wildcards, Return is not considered a valid character, but tab characters are treated as single characters.

You can be more selective in the characters matched by specifying a list of characters to be matched, enclosed in brackets. Such a list specification matches a single character at the corresponding position. The list can include a range of ASCII characters, separated by minus signs. For example,

```
Find /,[A-Z],/
```

would match a single letter, bracketed on either side by commas. If variable {CaseSensitive} is 0, it would match either an uppercase or lowercase letter.

You can also match any character not in the list by preceding the list with the logical not symbol ¬ (Option-L).

Most regular expression characters are not treated as special characters within a list. To match a right bracket or minus sign, the character must appear at the beginning or the end of the list, respectively. The logical not symbol has a special meaning only at the beginning of the list.

The ∂ symbol is, however, used to generate control characters within a list, even if the regular expression parameter is quoted by apostrophes. One expression you'll soon grow used to typing is a list of blank characters, as in the command:

```
Find /[∂t ]thewindow/
```

Example 5–2 shows pattern-matching commands using forms of regular expressions.

```
# Example 5-2: Simple pattern-matching commands

# Select the next Pascal procedure declaration, includ-
ing the name
Find /PROCEDURE[ ∂t]+([A-Za-z0-9]+)/

# Select next C procedure declaration
Find /void≈()/

# Search for Pascal declarations of the form
# cLetters =
# where 'c' is preceeded by a tab or space
Search -i "[∂t ]c[A-Z]≈=" UDrawShapes.p

# Scan assembler for reference to register A0
Find /MOVE≈A0,/

# Scan Rez source for a string resource definition
Search /resource≈'STR '/   "{Target}"

# Look for any procedure call beginning with Frame
Search -s /Frame≈∂(/   "{Target}"
```

Example 5–2: Simple Pattern-Matching Commands

COMPLEX PATTERNS

The individual patterns can be combined to form regular expressions to match just about any possible string. Table 5–3 displays the rules for combining these simpler regular expressions.
The syntax of regular expressions allows searching for a repeated pattern, such as a series of letters. These repeats are indicated by a notation suffixed to the pattern to be repeated.
   Standard symbols are provided for repeats of zero or more occurrences of a pattern (indicated by a * character) and for repeats of one or more occurrences (indicated by +). Arbitrary minimum and maximum counts can

Character	Description	Example
patt *	Match 0 or more of pattern *patt*	[A-Z]*
patt +	Match 1 or more of pattern *patt*	[∂t]+
patt «n,»	Match n or more of pattern *patt*	[∂t]«2,»
patt «n»	Match exactlyn of pattern *patt*	[∂t]«1»
patt «n,m»	Match n to m of pattern *patt*	[∂t]«0,1»
•*patt*	match *patt* at beginning of line	•[–∂t]+
patt∞	match *patt* at end of line	[–∂t]+∞
(*patt*)	Group *patt* for repeating or tagging	([–:]:)+
(*patt*)®n	Tag *patt* as expression number n	(≈)®1:(≈)®2

Special characters:
  ®   Option-R
  «   Option-\
  »   Shift-Option-\
  •   Option-8
  ∞   Option-5

From highest to lowest, the order of precedence is
  ( )
  [ ] « » ? ≈ * + ®
  • ∞

Table 5–3:   Combining Regular Expressions

also be specified. When the pattern is initially matched, the subsequent text is searched for repeats. If no maximum repeat count is specified, the pattern will match to the end of the line or to the end of the file if the pattern includes ∂n.

Every pattern should include at least one literal character or nonzero repeat count expression. A command such as

```
Find /X*/
```

will select an X (or series of Xs) if the current selection is immediately before an X. Otherwise, it will stop immediately on an insertion point since a null selection certainly satisfies the "zero or more X characters" condition.

A series of repeated strings can be combined in order, and the shell will search any series of text that matches all patterns. The command

```
Search /[∂t ]+[A-Za-z][0-9]*[∂t ]+/
```

will search for a line containing:

- A series of blank characters
- Followed by a digit
- Optionally followed by a series of letters
- Followed by a series of blank characters

You will often combine search string patterns with pathname patterns to scan a series of files for a possible match.

```
Files -l :≈:≈.c | Search -q '6/22'
```

lists detailed information for all the C files in the next subdirectories with creation or modification dates of June 22 (6/22).

The commands

```
Directory "{SrcMacApp}"
Search -s '[─A-Za-z]c[A-Z]' UMacApp.inc≈.p
```

would search for any MacApp command number constant. These constants all begin with the letter c, followed by a capital letter, followed by other letters (which are not important here). The not matched list prevents spurious matches of identifiers that include an embedded c.

An individual pattern can be anchored to the beginning or the end of a text line. The • symbol preceding a pattern indicates matching the beginning of the line, while a ∞ symbol after the pattern denotes matching at the end of the line. The command

```
Find /•(-)«40»∞/
```

looks for a line containing exactly 40 minus signs.

You can also search for the literal character as ∂n as part of a selection expression; the difference is that the Return will be part of the new selection. Literal return characters will never be matched by the Search command because it only scans each line between Return characters.

As with selection expressions, the pattern-matching characters of regular expressions can be grouped to build complex patterns. Grouping can be used to override the default precedence of pattern symbols and also to group smaller patterns into larger ones. The command

```
Find / [0-9]+(, [∂t∂n ]*[0-9]+)*/
```

would search for a list of one or more integers, separated by commas and optional blank characters.

Grouped expressions can also be tagged, which is equivalent to assigning the matched string to a variable. These named strings can be used in the replacement string of a Replace command, as described in the next section.

5.4 Replacing Text

MPW's `Replace` command can be used to make straightforward substitutions, similar to those provided by the Search menu of most Macintosh editors. It can also take advantage of more complex string pattern-matching expressions, including those that remember portions of the matched string for use as part of the replacement string.

SIMPLE REPLACEMENTS

The `Replace` command changes an occurrence of a specified selection expression to the indicated string. An optional repeat count allows the replacement to be repeated any number of times.

Replace

Change occurrence(s) of search string to replacement string

Syntax:

`Replace` *selection string*	Change next occurence of *selection* to *string*
`Replace` *selection string window*	Change next *selection* to *string* in *window*

Options:

`-c` *count*	Repeat the replacement *count* times

Remarks:

The search pattern *selection* is always a selection expression, while the replacement parameter *string* is normally an ordinary string.

If *selection* includes a string search pattern, the delimiters used indicate the direction of the replacement scan.

Examples:

`Replace /PROCEDURE/ Function`
> Change next `PROCEDURE` to `Function`

`Replace 100:101 ∂n∂n`
> Replace lines 100-101 with two blank lines

`Replace \FooBar\ "Fouled Up"`
> Change previous `FooBar` to `Fouled Up`

`Replace -c ∞ /EBCDIC/ ASCII`
> Change `EBCDIC` to `ASCII` until end of file

Note that there is an inherent asymmetry between the two parameters of a `Replace` command. The first parameter is a standard selection expression, which may include line numbers or selection ranges. The second parameter is a text string, which sometimes will contain special characters referencing parts of the search string.

If you merely wish to replace a string, you must always bracket the search pattern with the appropriate text delimiters, as in the command:

```
Replace -c /PROCEDURE/ PROCEDURE
```

Since the `Replace` command is also case insensitive by default, this would capitalize all occurrences of the keyword without regard to the original case.

An -c parameter of ∞ will only change from the current selection to the end (or beginning) of the file. To make sure that you change the entire file, you have to start the replacement at one end of the document, as in:

```
Find •
Replace -c /rlngt/ RunLength
```

With the exception of the repeat count, the `Replace` shell command works the same way as the Replace dialog when the Selection Expression button is checked. Any of the replacement strings described in this section can be used with the menu-driven replacement, although you must make the substitutions one at a time.

Note that `Replace` begins after the end of the current selection. If you've already used `Find` to locate the correct part of the file, you can perform the `Replace` starting in that part.

For example, suppose you want to change int functions to long functions in a C source file, prior to exporting an MPW C program for use with another C compiler. If you first used

```
Find /•int [A-Z]+(/
```

to select the correct line, the command

```
Replace /int/ 'long'
```

would match and change the *next* occurrence of int after the current one, which is not what is intended. However, the commands

```
Find Δ$
Replace /int/ 'long'
```

will position the insertion point before the current selection, thus assuring that the declaration in the current line is changed.

WILDCARD REPLACEMENTS

Pattern-matching search strings will often be used with the Replace command. One of the most frequent uses is matching blank characters, since as far as the human-formatted text is concerned, tabs and runs of spaces can be used interchangeably.

For example, to left-justify the comments in a Pascal program (such as after it has been indented by the PasMat command), you could use the command:

```
replace -c ∞ /•[ ∂t]+∂{/ '{'
```

This would only affect comments that are on lines without source statements.

Both the search expression and the replacement string can span multiple lines. The command

```
Replace -c ∞ /1987∞/:/•[∂t ]*-/ "1987∂n∂f∂n∂t∂t∂t    -"
```

looks for a footer at the bottom of every page ending in "1987" and then for an indented header several lines later that includes a centered page number. The replacement string leaves the header and footer as is but replaces the intervening lines with an ASCII form feed character followed by a return.

TAGGING REGULAR EXPRESSIONS

When performing a replacement with literal string, you know beforehand what strings will be matched. However, when using pattern-matching strings, there is no such guarantee.

Suppose you need to parenthesize every integer in a file. You can use the selection expression

```
Replace -c ∞ /[0-9]+/ /(?????)/
```

to find the integers, but how do you get that integer matched into the replacement string?

The Replace command allow you to tag any regular expression in your search string with a number. You can then reference this tag in your replacement string, which will be replaced by the text that matched the expression when the substitution is made.

In the selection expression, a tagged regular expression is always grouped by parentheses and followed by the ® symbol (Option-R) and a 1 to 3 digit integer. The ® and the number are repeated in the replacement string in the relative position in which the matched string should be inserted.

Thus, the integers could be parenthesized with the command:

```
Replace /([0-9]+)®1/   '(®1)'
```

Regular expressions are often used to reverse the order of two parameters. For example, the statement

```
Replace -c ∞ /∂{ (≈)®1, (≈)®2 ∂}/ ' { ®2,     ®1 }'
```

would reverse the order of two values delimited by braces and separated by a comma, such as found in a Rez resource source file.

Regular expressions can also be used to discard all but the interesting part of a line. The command

```
Replace -c ∞ /•≈(A???[ ∂t]+_[A-Z0-9]+)®1≈∞/ '®1'
```

would look for strings such as

```
A000   _Open
A810   _Unique1ID
```

while discarding any character preceeding or following such strings on the same line.

There's no reason Replace must be limited to program source or data. It also can come in handy when used with a word processor, moving data to and from other systems or assisting with other applications.

For example, suppose you have a file with lines of arbitrary length, such as produced by most word processors when you request a Return only at the end of each paragraph. You must transfer this file with a terminal program to a system that insists on lines of 60 characters or less. The command

```
Replace -c ∞ /(?«60»)®1/ "®1∂n"
```

would take 60 characters at a time and then start a new line, producing an output with fixed left and right margins.

What if the file is written English, and you want it to be intelligible when you're done? The command

```
Replace -c ∞ /(?«40»[¬ ∂t∂n])®1[ ∂t]/ "®1∂n"
```

looks for the first word break after the fortieth character on a line. Or, you can use

```
Replace -c ∞ /(?«40,60»)®1[ ∂t]/ "®1∂n"
```

to match 40 to 60 characters on a line, followed by a trailing blank character.

EXAMPLE: CONVERTING C TO PASCAL

Example 5–3 provides a lengthy example of combining pattern matching strings with tagged regular expressions. It shows an initial conversion that was used to take a C program and produce an initial draft of a corresponding Pascal program.

To run the program, you would select and enter it in the active window. It expects to find a C program in the target window and will create a new document containing the resulting Pascal source.

Because of the major differences in program structure between the two languages, it is impossible for such a simpleminded editing script to completely transform a C source program into Pascal. There is no doubt that the resulting output will produce a syntactically incorrect program. In at least several cases, common constructs—such as the ++ operator—are deliberately left alone so that the Pascal compiler will flag the statements that are incompletely translated. In other cases, it deletes a declaration that it is unable to handle and turns it into a comment.

However, many of the common replacements—including the more difficult inversions of keywords within a statement—will have been handled correctly.

With such an elaborate script, it is important to qualify regular expressions as much as possible to avoid unintended consequences. A good example is the use of the equals sign by the two languages. The C statements of the form

```
y = f(x);
if (y == 0)
```

should be transformed into

```
y := f(x);
if (y = 0)
```

When matching the = for the first transformation, it is vital to avoid matching another equals sign on either side. Also, there are a number of symbols such as <= which are the same in both languages, and others that don't have a translation and should be left as is so that the compiler will flag them. Thus, instead of the simple

```
Replace -c ∞ /=/ '=='
```

we must use

```
Replace -c ∞ /([¬!∂/<>=-]®1=([−≠])®2/ "®1:=®2"
```

```
# Example 5-3: Converting C source to Pascal

# This makes a rough attempt at converting C sources to
# Pascal
# There are many things it can't catch

Set Pfile "{Target}.p"
Duplicate "{Target}" "{Pfile}"

Target "{Pfile}"
Set Exit 0              # don't stop if we miss a match
Set CaseSensitive 1

# Convert delimiters
# Expects { at the beginning of next line; K&R uses
# { at the end of the previous line
Find •
Replace -c ∞ /([∂t ]*)®1∂{/ "®1BEGIN∂n®1"
# break line & indent
Find •
Replace -c ∞ /∂}/ "END"
Find •
Replace -c ∞ /END∞/ "END;"
Find •
Replace -c ∞ /∂/∂*/ "(*"
Find •
Replace -c ∞ /∂*∂// "*)"
Find •
Replace -c ∞ /∂"([—∂"]*)®1∂"/ "∂'®1∂'"

# Standard operators
Find •
Replace -c ∞ /!=/ "<>"
Find •
Replace -c ∞ /!/ "NOT "
Find •
Replace -c ∞ /&&/ " AND "
Find •
Replace -c ∞ /||/ " OR "
Find •
Replace -c ∞ / % / " MOD "
# must avoid printf("%s") etc.

# Pointer operators
Find •
Replace -c ∞ /∂*(([A-Za-z0-9])+)®1/ "®1^"
Find •
Replace -c ∞ /->/ "^."
```

```
Find •
Replace -c ∞ /([[(=,][∂t ]*)®1&([¬&=])®2/ "®1@®2"
# Cannot handle ++, --: leave as is for syntax errors

# Convert = to :=, then == to :=
Find •
Replace -c ∞ /([¬!∂/<>=-])®1=([¬=])®2/ "®1:=®2"
  # Note "-" must be at end of a scan set [...-]
Find •
Replace -c ∞ /==/ "="

# Handle some type and variable definitions
Find •
Replace -c ∞ /typedef (≈)®1∞/ "∂{ TYPE ®1 ∂}"
Find •
Replace -c ∞ /char ∂*/ "Str255 "
Find •
Replace -c ∞ /•(([ ∂t])*)®2Str255 (([¬;])+)®1;/∂
   "®2®1: Str255;"
Find •
Replace -c ∞ /•(([ ∂t])*)®2Handle (([¬;])+)®1;/∂
   "®2®1: Handle;"
Find •
Replace -c ∞ /•(([ ∂t])*)®2Rect (([¬;])+)®1;/∂
   "®2®1: Rect;"
Find •
Replace -c ∞ /•(([ ∂t])*)®2short (([¬;])+)®1;/∂
   "®2®1: INTEGER;"
# Some int's may actually be INTEGER not LONGINT
Find •
Replace -c ∞ /•(([ ∂t])*)®2int (([¬;])+)®1;/∂
   "®2®1: longint;"
Find •
Replace -c ∞ /•(([ ∂t])*)®2long (([¬;])+)®1;/∂
   "®2®1: LONGINT;"
Find •
Replace -c ∞ /•(([ ∂t])*)®2Boolean (([¬;])+)®1;/∂
   "®2®1: BOOLEAN;"
Find •
Replace -c ∞ /•(([ ∂t])*)®2char (([¬;])+)®1;/∂
   "®2®1: CHAR;"
Find •
Replace -c ∞ /∂[∂]: / ": ARRAY OF "
Find •
Replace -c ∞ /^: / ": ^"
Find •
Replace -c ∞ /NULL/ "NIL"

# Conditional compilation
```

```
Find •
Replace -c ∞ /•#include <((([¬.])+)®1.h>/ "USES ®1;"
Find •
Replace -c ∞ /•#[∂t ]*else/ "∂{$ELSEC∂}"
Find •
Replace -c ∞ /•#[∂t ]*endif/ "∂{$ENDC∂}"
Find •
Replace -c ∞ /•#[∂t ]*define (([¬ ]+)®1 ([¬
∂t∂n]+)®2(≈)®3∞/ "∂{$SETC ®1 := ®2∂}®3"
Find •
Replace -c ∞ /•#[∂t ]*ifdef/ "∂{$IFC UNDEFINED∂}"
Find •
Replace -c ∞ /•#(([∂t -∂}]*)®1∞/ "∂{$®1∂}"

# Hack at control flow
Find •
Replace -c ∞ /((([ ∂t])+)®2if (≈)®1∞/ "®2IF ®1 THEN"
Find •
Replace /;∂n((([ ∂t])*)®1else/ "∂n®1ELSE"
Find •
Replace -c ∞ /for ∂(;;∂)/ "WHILE TRUE DO"
Find •
Replace -c ∞ /for
∂((([¬;]*)®1;([-≺]*)<=(([¬;]*)®2;[-∂)]*∂)/∂
    "FOR ®1 TO ®2 DO"
Find •
Replace -c ∞ /for
∂((([¬;]*)®1;([-≺]*)<(([¬;]*)®2;[-∂)]*∂)/∂
    "FOR ®1 TO ®2-1 DO"

# Procedures
# Assume a C program has procedure declarations on the
#    left margin and the right parenthesis is flush to
#    the right margin, as in:void f(x,y,z)
# Also treat an untyped function as type 'void' rather
#    than 'int'
Find •
Replace -c ∞ ∂
   /•(void[∂t ]+)«0,1»([A-Za-z0-9]+)®2∂(([-∂)]*)®3∂)[∂t ]*∞/ ∂
   "PROCEDURE ®2∂(∂);  ∂{ Parms: ®3 ∂} "
# Now change functions
Find •
Replace -c ∞∂
   /•([A-Za-z0-9]+)®1[∂t ]+([A-Za-z0-9]+)®2∂(([-∂)]*)®3∂)[∂t ]*∞/∂
   "FUNCTION ®2∂(∂): ®1;  ∂{ Parms: ®3 ∂}"
# On C, you must always use () on function calls; Pascal
#    no
```

```
Find •
Replace -c ∞ /∂(∂)/ ""

# Specific procedures
Find •
Replace -c ∞ /([¬A-Za-z0-9_])®1exit[∂t ]*∂(/ "®1IEExit("
Find •
Replace -c ∞ /([¬A-Za-z0-9_])®1[f]«1,2»printf[∂t ]*∂(/∂
  "®1Write("
Find •
Replace -c ∞ /Write∂(stderr/ "Write(Diagnostic"

Set Exit 1
```

Example 5–3: Convert C source to Pascal

Figure 5–9 shows a C sample before translation, and Figure 5–10 shows the psuedo-Pascal output. The formatting of the output could be cleaned up even further by using the PasMat formatting utility for Pascal source once the syntax errors were corrected through a trial Pascal compilation.

There are some semantic differences that cannot be handled by such a simple script. Some #define statements are used to set conditional compilation flags, and this is the assumption made by the example. However, others should be replaced by CONST declarations of constants, while still others define text macros that cannot be translated into MPW Pascal.

Typecasting in both C and Pascal is difficult to catch, as the output shows. There are also some things that cannot be translated, such as the different approaches to I/O, including the provision of a hex format conversion option in C that's not available in Pascal.

The reverse changes would in some ways be easier to convert with such a line-at-a-time parser. Pascal is a more verbose language, with certain key reserved words indicating program sections. For example, the word PROCE-DURE designates the beginning of a new Pascal procedure, while the example has to make assumptions about parentheses and indentation to detect procedures in C.

USING THE CLIPBOARD

Four shell commands are provided to perform standard Edit menu operations involving the clipboard and the current selection—Cut, Copy, Paste, and Clear. A fifth menu operation, Select All, can be handled by:

```
Find •:∞
```

```
/*C source for Example 5-3*/

(* output from example 5-3 *)

/* Printer testing code, initial prototype*/

#include <Types.h>
#include <QuickDraw.h>
#include <Resources.h>
#include <Printing.h>

#include <stdio.h>

typedef unsigned char byte;

main()
{ Boolean b;
  int i;
  short rn;
  THPrint printhand;

    InitGraf(&qd.thePort);

#ifndef PRINTER
  PrOpen();
  printhand = (THPrint)NewHandle(sizeof(TPrint));

  PrintDefault(printhand);
  dumphand ("After PrintDefault()", printhand);

  for (;;)
    { b = PrStlDialog(printhand);
      if (! b)
        break;
      dumpPrint("After PrintStlDialog()", printhand);
    }

  for (;;)
    { b = PrJobDialog(printhand);
      if (! b)
        break;
      dumpPrint("After PrintJobDialog()", printhand);
    }

  DisposHandle(printhand);

  PrClose();
```

```
#else
  rn = OpenResFile(PRINTER);
  if (rn < 0)
    exit(3);                        /* file not found */

  printhand = GetResource((ResType)'PREC', 0);
  if (printhand == NULL)
    exit(4);                        /* no such resource */

  dumphand ("Contents of PREC #0', printhand);

  ReleaseResource(printhand);
  CloseResFile(rn);
#endif
}

/* Do a hex dump on the block referenced by the handle
*/
dumphand(msg, hand)
char *msg;
Handle hand;
{ int off,len,n;
  byte *p;

/* Some will object to the use of printf throughout, but
it reduces link size and speed, and run-time performance
is not an issue here */

  HLock(hand);
  p = (long *)(*hand);     /* pointer to first byte */

  len = GetHandleSize (hand);

  for (off = 0; off < len; off++)
    { if ((off % 16) == 0)
      fprintf(stderr, "\n%04X:", off);
                                    /* show offset */
      if ((off % 2) == 0)
      fprintf(stderr, " ");
       n = *p++;
      fprintf(stderr, "%02X", n); /* dump some bytes */
    }

  fprintf(stderr, "\n");

  HUnlock(hand);
}
```

Figure 5–9:   C source for Example 5–3

```
(* Printer testing code, initial prototype *)

USES Types;
USES QuickDraw;
USES Resources;
USES Printing;

USES stdio;

{ TYPE unsigned char byte; }

PROCEDURE main;   { Parms:  }
BEGIN
  b: BOOLEAN;
  i: longint;
  rn: INTEGER;
  THPrint printhand;

  InitGraf(@qd.thePort);

{$ifndef PRINTER}
  PrOpen;
  printhand := (THPrint)NewHandle(sizeof(TPrint));

  PrintDefault(printhand);
  dumphand('After PrintDefault', printhand);

  WHILE TRUE DO
  BEGIN
    b := PrStlDialog(printhand);
    IF (NOT  b) THEN
      break;
    dumpPrint('After PrintStlDialog', printhand);
  END;

  WHILE TRUE DO
  BEGIN
    b := PrJobDialog(printhand);
    IF (NOT  b) THEN
      break;
    dumpPrint('After PrintJobDialog', printhand);
  END;

  DisposHandle(printhand);

  PrClose;
{$ELSEC}
  rn := OpenResFile(PRINTER);
  IF (rn < 0) THEN
    IEExit(3);                        (* file not found *)
```

```
   printhand := GetResource((ResType)'PREC', 0);
   IF (printhand = NIL) THEN
      IEExit(4);                    (* no such resource *)

   dumphand('Contents of PREC #0', printhand);

   ReleaseResource(printhand);
   CloseResFile(rn);
{$ENDC}
END;


(* Do a hex dump on the block referenced by the handle
*)

PROCEDURE dumphand;                 { Parms: msg,hand }
msg: ^CHAR;
hand: Handle;
BEGIN
   off,len,n: longint;
   byte p^;

(* Some will object to the use of printf throughout, but
   it reduces link size and speed, and run-time
   performance is not an issue here *)

   HLock(hand);
   p := (long *)(hand^); (* pointer to first byte *)

   len := GetHandleSize(hand);

   FOR off := 0 TO  len-1 DO
   BEGIN
      IF ((off MOD 16) = 0) THEN
        (* show offset *)
        Write(Diagnostic, '\n%04X:', off);
      IF ((off MOD 2) = 0) THEN
        Write(Diagnostic, ' ');
      n := p^++;
      (* dump some bytes *)
      Write(Diagnostic, '%02X', n);
   END;

   Write(Diagnostic, '\n");

   HUnlock(hand);
END;
```

Figure 5-10: Pascal output from Example 5-3

Cut, Copy

Move the selection to the clipboard

Syntax:

Cut *selection*	Cut *selection* from target window to clipboard
Cut *selection window*	Cut *selection* from *window* to clipboard
Copy *selection*	Copy *selection* from target window to clipboard
Copy *selection window*	Copy *selection* from *window* to clipboard

Remarks:

The only difference between Cut and Copy is that Cut deletes the selection.

Examples:

Cut §	Move and delete current selection to clipboard
Copy 1:3 "{Active}"	Copy first three lines of active window to clipboard

Paste

Replace the selection with the contents of the clipboard

Syntax:

Paste *selection*	Copy clipboard to *selection* in target window
Paste *selection window*	Copies clipboard to *selection* in *window*

Options:

-c *count*	Repeat paste *count* times

Remarks:

  If the clipboard does not include data of type 'TEXT', Paste is equivalent to Clear.

Examples:

Paste §	Replace current selection in target window
Paste -c 5 /**TBD**/	Replace next five occurrences of string
Paste Δ100	Paste clipboard before line 100
Paste ∞ "{Worksheet}"	Append clipboard to end of worksheet

Clear

Delete the selection

Syntax:

Clear *selection*	Deletes the *selection* in target window
Clear *selection window*	Deletes the *selection* in *window*

Options:

-c *count*	Repeat paste *count* times

Examples:

Clear §	Delete the current selection
Clear -c ∞ /IBM/	Delete all occurrences of "IBM" to end of file

5.5 Formatting Commands

MPW includes a number of commands to format source files.

The most common is the Print command, which outputs a listing to the printer, with an optional header. By using wildcards for the file pathnames, you can print several files with a single shell command.

Other commands allow you to mark selections within a source file, change its indentation, or reformat the identifiers within it.

PRINTING

In conjunction with MPW pathname wildcards, the Print command can be used to print many files without manual intervention.

Print

Format text files to the printer

Syntax:

Print *file* ...	Print named files

Options:

-b	Add rounded-corner rectangle border to each page
-bm *inches*	Bottom margin is *inches*
-f *fontname*	Print using font *fontname*

```
-font fontname
-from firstpage        Start printing with page number firstpage
-h                     Include file name, date, and page number on each
                       page
-hf fontname           Print heading using font fontname
-l lines               Extra whitespace to print lines lines per page
-lm inches             Left margin is inches
-ls spacing            Print spacing lines per source line
-md                    Use the modification date in the header
-n                     Include line numbers before source lines
-p                     Display progress information
-page num              Start numbering pages at num
-q high                ImageWriter "High" quality
-q standard            ImageWriter "Standard" quality
-q draft               ImageWriter "Draft" quality
-r                     Print pages in reverse order (for LaserWriter)
-rm inches             Right margin is inches
-s fontsize            Print using font size fontsize
-size fontsize
-t tabwidth            Replace tabs using tabwidth spaces per tab stop
-tabs tabwidth
-tm inches             Top margin is inches
-title string          Use string as page title in heading
-to lastpage           Stop printing after page number lastpage
```

Remarks:

The Print command cannot take input from its standard input stream.

Default values for the font, size, and tab setting are taken from the resource fork of an MPW text document.

The -h option displays a page header at the top of each page, including the file name, current date and time, and the page number. The -hf, -hs, -md, and -title options have no effect without -h.

Page margins can be specified as decimal numbers. All default to 0, except for the left margin, which has a default value of .278 (5/18").

Examples:

```
Print -h Test.p        Print Test.p with a page heading
Print -c :≈:≈.c        Print C files in each folder with heading
```

One of the more common uses of Print is to print all the documents in the current directory. If you display a heading, the page title will be set to the document name for each new document, and the page number will be reset to 1.

The title will reflect the name used as a parameter. The command

```
Print -h {CIncludes}≈.c
```

will include full pathnames at the top of each page, while

```
Directory {CIncludes}
Print -h ≈.c
```

would include only the name of the file, without the volume and folder information. The date will be the current date, unless the –md option is used.

Like other MPW commands, printing can be interrupted by Command-period.

MARKING SELECTIONS

In addition to the Markers menu, shell commands are provided to display and change the selection markers for a given document. This allows you to automatically build a list of markers.

Mark, Unmark

Add or delete named selection markers in window

Syntax:

Mark *selection marker*   Define *marker* to refer to
                                        selection in target

Mark *selection marker window*   Define *marker* to refer to
                                        selection in *window*

Unmark *marker*   Delete definition of *marker*
Unmark *marker window*   Delete definition of *marker* for
                                        document *window*

Unmark -a   Delete all markers in target
                                        window

Remarks:

The -r option to the Mark command replaces an existing marker.

Examples:

```
Mark /PROCEDURE FX/ FX
```
                    Define marker for Pascal procedure FX
```
Unmark -a
```
                    Delete all markers for target window

Markers

Display current list of marker names

Syntax:

```
Markers                 Display marker list for target window
Markers window          Display marker list for document window
```

Remarks:

The names of the markers are displayed in the order in they are in the Mark menu, i.e., the order in which they were defined.

Examples:

```
Markers "{Active}"  Display all markers for active window
```

TAB INTERPRETATION

Many MPW owners will be converting the source code for existing programs from other development systems to MPW. (If you're still using the other system, you may also need to convert it back.) For large projects, this means changing several large files or many small files, a tedious task in either case.

This process is greatly speeded by the various MPW shell commands. The previously mentioned editing commands can operate with infinite repeat counts, and you can enter a list of changes to be performed, one after another. If you build a command file (as described in the next chapter), it's easy to also have them make changes on multiple files.

Other commands are provided to support certain standard changes to source files. One of the simplest changes is to reinterpret the use of Tab characters. If you're importing a source file from UNIX or VAX/VMS, for example, you must assume tab characters every eight columns. If you want to use a different style for your own development, the Entab command allows you to change the tabs.

Entab

Replace spaces with tabs

Syntax:

```
Entab file ...          Replace tabs in file
Entab                   Replace tabs from standard input stream
```

Options:

```
-d width                Assume input tab stops every width characters
-t width                Replace spaces with tabs set width apart
```

Remarks:

Entab always removes existing tab stops from a source file. An option of −t 0 prevents it from inserting new ones.

Normally, the output of Entab is directed to a file using output redirection. Do not attempt to Entab a source file onto itself.

Input/Output:

Output   Newly-tabbed version of input stream

Examples:

```
Entab -t 0 src.c >src.export
```
                  Format src.c to src.export without tabs

Like the Print command, Entab reads the resource fork of any documented edited by MPW and thus knows what the tab stop settings are for display purposes. You should not override this unless the file was not created by MPW, and thus has no tab stop settings.

CONVERTING SOURCE FILES

MPW also provides some assistance for more specific source conversion requirements.

MPW includes two specific utilities, TLACvt and MDSCvt, for converting Lisa and MDS assembler sources to MPW assembler. These are important because the format of many of the MPW psuedo-operands differs from those in the earlier assemblers.

Converting Lisa Pascal programs to MPW is very easy—the MPW Pascal compiler recognizes the full Lisa syntax and interprets it nearly identically. Most other Pascal compilers for the Mac implement a subset of the Lisa standard; so programs from those systems will also be easy to convert.

C programmers face more significant problems. Macintosh C compilers vary somewhat in their syntax and semantic interpretation of C programs. A good example of the latter is the size of an int variable, which is 32 bits in MPW C.

However, one problem common to both C and Pascal programs is the use of identifiers. The MDS and Lisa Workshop linkers were more lax than MPW, truncating all external names—such as procedure names—in object files to eight characters. In MPW, such names have essentially unlimited length.

This means that if a Lisa Pascal program uses the name of a "glue" (marked [not in ROM]) routine misspelled in the ninth character, that error will be ignored, while the MPW Pascal compiler and linker will catch the error. This name truncation also applies to Lisa Workshop C and development systems that used the MDS linker. It would not apply to the names of traps by those compilers that generated inline traps, since these would not generate external references.

This may not seem like a serious incompatibility. However, in programs of several thousand lines, there are bound to be a few minor typos, and this has proven to be the most significant problem in moving Pascal programs from the Lisa Workshop to MPW.

Also, not all programs use the "official" capitalization of the names defined by *Inside Macintosh*, which include both uppercase and lowercase letters in trap names, data structure types, and variable definitions. Instead, some programs use all caps or lowercase identifiers for these names. The MPW linker, unlike the Lisa Workshop and MDS linkers, is capable of recognizing both upper- and lowercase names.

This is a serious problem with MPW C since the compiler treats names of different case as distinct names: `initgraf` is not the same as `InitGraf`. If the capitalization is not exact, the compiler or linker will not match the names. At least one third-party C compiler was distributed with all libraries defined with lowercase names; therefore such programs must be converted to work under MPW.

Case errors are not a problem with MPW Pascal. Symbolic references in MPW Pascal are case insensitive, as the compiler automatically converts all identifiers to uppercase. However, Pascal programmers may wish to use the official names (`PBGetEOF` instead of `PBGeteof`) for improved readability.

The `Canon` command allows you to convert a text file to use the standard identifier names. By default, it will match the name without regard to case and convert it to the standard capitalization. It also includes an option to ignore parts of the identifier after a specified number of characters, normally eight.

Canon

Modify text stream to conform to standard spellings

Syntax:

Canon *dictionary file* ...	Modify spelling of *file*

Options:

-s	Treat upper- and lowercase input as distinct
-c *len*	Match only the first *len* characters

Remarks:

The most commonly used value for *dictionary* is {Tools}Canon.Dict, which contains all the MPW C identifiers, but it can also be used with Pascal and assembler source. The most common value for *len* is 8, which was the name-truncation length used by MDS and the Lisa Workshop linker.

Input/Output:

Output   Corrected version of input
                                    stream

Examples:

```
Canon {Tools}Canon.dict f.c >g.c
```
                                    Correct f.c and store new version in g.c

The Canon.dict dictionary includes a list of standard spellings for MPW C programs, with one identifier per line. Canon only modifies identifiers consisting of letters, digits, and the underscore character (_) .

The Canon command can also be used with your own renaming rules, such as when merging two source libraries with conflicting names. If you're writing your own dictionary, the first identifier on any line is the identifier to be matched, and the second identifier (if any) is its replacement. If only one name is specified, the name is assumed to be the canonical (standard) spelling before truncation or case variations.

The renaming rules also allow you to use special characters at the beginning of the name to establish a context. Suppose you wanted to convert the Pascal declarations of the form

```
a,b: INTEGER;
x,y,z: REAL;
```

to C declarations such as

```
int a,b;
real x,y,z;
```

Unfortunately, as demonstrated earlier when converting C to Pascal, there are far too many data types used by a typical Macintosh program to catch every one with Replace commands.

However, you could use a brief set of Replace commands, combined with a Canon dictionary. The command

```
Replace -c ∞ /(≈)®2:[∂t ]*([A-Za-z0-9]+)®3;/∂
  /®1:®3 ®2;/
```

would change the order of the types and variables to

```
:INTEGER a,b;
```

```
:REAL x,y,z;
```

Then, using `Canon` with a dictionary of the form

```
:INTEGER short
:REAL real
```

would allow you to specify all the possible data types using `Canon` rather than a bulky series of Replace commands.

DOCUMENT COMPARISON

We conclude with two commands that allow you to get summary information about the status of text files.

The `Compare` command can be used with any two text file to produce a list of differences.

Compare

Compare two text files and display difference information

Syntax:

Compare *file1 file2*	Compare *file1* to *file2*
Compare *file*	Compare *file* to the standard input

Options:

-t	Ignore trailing blanks
-b	Like -t, but also treat multiple blanks as one
-l	Ignore case distinctions
-h	Display result side by side
-x	Do not expand tabs before comparison
-v	Do not prefix data lines with line numbers
-h *width*	Display lines side-by-side using *width* columns

Remarks:

`Compare` checks for lines that do not match between the two input files. As the number of mismatched lines increases, the number of lines required to resynchronize the input streams also increases.

By default, the output includes a series of selection commands, with the unmatched data lines prefixed by line numbers; the -v option displays these lines as they were in the input file. The -h option displays corresponding lines side by side on the same output line, with line numbers for each line; –v is ignored.

Unless the –x option is used, each tabs in an input file is converted to a series of spaces, based on the MPW resource in the file specifying the tab width, or to 4 if there is none. For the –b and –l options, Compare converts blanks to a single space and letters to lowercase, respectively. Data lines outputted by the Compare command will show the result of these conversions.

Input/Output:

Output   Shell commands and mismatching
                                lines

Examples:

```
Compare -b Oldf.p F.p
```
                     Ignore spacing differences between two files
```
Compare -v -x main.c std.c
```
                     Display mismatches in same format s input
```
Compare -h Traps512 TrapsII
```
                     Display mismatches side by side

Figure 5–11 shows the result of a Compare command for two versions of the same file.

Many programmers measure their results by lines of code completed. The Count command allows you to measure the size of one or more text files, either in characters or in lines.

Count

Count the number of lines and characters in a text file

Syntax:

```
Count [file ...]
```
                                Count the lines and characters in
                                [file ...]

Options:

```
-c
```
                                Display character count only
```
-l
```
                                Display line count only

Remarks:

If multiple file parameters are given, display includes subtotals by file and a grand total. Only the number(s) is (are) displayed if a single file is given, or the input comes from the standard input stream.

Input/Output:

Output   Count of characters and/or lines

Examples:

Count ≈.p   Subtotals and totals for Pascal files in
                                        this folder
Count -c §   Number of characters in target selection
Count -l {CIncludes}≈.h   number of lines in all C header files

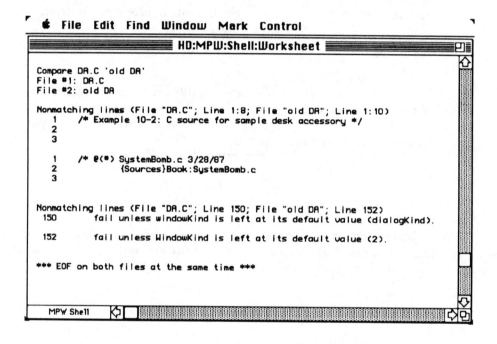

Figure 5–11: Comparing related files

Chapter 6

Shell Programming

MPW SHELL COMMANDS CAN BE COMBINED to perform operations that are repeated over and over again. Learning how to build shell commands is a crucial aspect of harnessing the power of MPW to meet your particular requirements.

The shell provides a complete interpretive programming language, one with heavy emphasis on string manipulation and dynamic command interpretation. You can easily define your own MPW commands by writing a command file that uses this language. A command file can be like a procedure with parameters, variables, looping constructs, and input/output. Because the commands are interpreted, debugging command files is quick and immediate.

Shell commands can also be used to build custom menus. These menus can scroll in the window, move data between the active and target windows, or change the current directory.

6.1 More Command Syntax

This section completes the description of the syntax of shell commands, covering features primarily related to command files that were omitted from the syntax discussion of Chapter 4.

The shell has many special characters that must be quoted to avoid interpretation when they are to be used literally. Among them are the

271

pattern-matching characters for pathname generation, similar to those used for search string regular expressions.

This section summarizes the complete syntax of shell commands.

SPECIAL CHARACTERS

When writing a command file, it is important to understand the impact of certain special characters in a command line, even if you don't use them deliberately. These special characters can cause your command files to fail the first time or unexpectedly when combined with unusual parameters.

Table 6–1 shows a complete list of characters with special interpretation by the shell.

Shell special characters

Character	Interpretaton
∂c	Treat c literally, unless ∂n (Return), ∂t (Tab), ∂f (Form feed)
'string'	Treat string literally
"string"	Treat string literally, except for ∂, ', { and `
> file	Send standard output to file
>> file	Append standard output to end of file
≥ file	Send diagnostic output to file
≥≥ file	Append diagnostic output to end of file
< file	Read standard input from file
/string/	Forward pattern-matching scan for string
\string\	Backward pattern-matching scan for string
{variable}	Replace with value of variable
`command`	Replace with output from command
cmd1 ; cmd2	Execute cmd1 and cmd2
cmd1 && cmd2	Execute cmd2 if cmd1 succeeds
cmd1 || cmd2	Execute cmd2 if cmd1 fails
cmd1 | cmd2	Redirect output of cmd1 to input of cmd2
(commands)	Group execution of commands
# comment	Ignore comment
...	Provide Commando interactive help

Table 6–1:   Shell special characters

The special significance of these characters can be overridden by quoting or escaping. When quoted by "...", /.../, or \...\, only the following characters have a special meaning:

∂   Escaping
{   Variable evaluation
`   Command evaluation

No characters have a special meaning between pairs of apostrophes ('...').

PATHNAME PATTERNS

As introduced in Chapter 4, the ≈ and ? wildcard characters can be used to match a series of one or more file names. The shell replaces parameters containing these characters with the list of matching file names; any name containing a blank or special character will be quoted by the shell automatically. If no names match the pattern, the shell will indicate an error.

Chapter 5 showed the use of other pattern-matching characters and regular expressions in shell commands for editing documents. The same expressions are available for specifying file pathnames.

Unless quoted—such as by the selection delimiters /.../ and \...\—these special characters in a parameter are interpreted by the shell as pattern-matching expressions for file names. Unless the parameter contains a colon (:) specifying a specific volume or folder, the shell will attempt to find the corresponding file name in the current directory. For example, in the command

```
Echo Enter a letter from [A-Z]?
```

the final parameter is interpreted as a path name pattern. The shell will attempt to find a file name consisting of a single letter, followed by any other character, even if this was unintended. If you wanted to display the literal prompt, you would use a command such as

```
Echo 'Enter a letter from [A-Z]?'
```

However, the consistency between editing and file name pattern evaluation means you only have to learn one expression syntax. This syntax can be used to your advantage when you want to use several files from among many in a crowded directory. For example, the command

```
Print ≈.[acp]
```

would only print files with names ending in .a, .c, or .p in the current directory. If no file names match, an error message is displayed and the command will not be executed.

The colon is a special character in name patterns, as it divides up the individual components of a pathname. It must be specified as a literal character in a pattern, so

```
Print -h :≈:≈.[acp]
```

would be valid but the recursive

```
Print -h (:≈)+:≈.[acp]
```

would not. Another way to print these files is provided by command substitution, discussed later in this section.

EXAMPLE: SCANNING MACAPP SOURCES

The structure of the MacApp library provides a good example of how more complex patterns can be used as file name patterns. Even if you don't have MacApp, the strict naming rules for file names and program source provide a structure for using pattern matching.

MacApp comes with Pascal source code to the libraries used to implement standard Macintosh operations. This source code is used to link with your programs and also provides the complete definition of the interfaces. The directory "{MPW}MacApp:MacApp Source Files" contains two types of MPW Pascal sources. One type of file defines the INTERFACE for a Pascal UNIT, while the other type contains the IMPLEMENTATION. The interface source files have names such as

```
UDialog.p
UMacApp.p
UPrinting.p
```

while the implementations have names like

```
UDialog.inc1.p
UMacApp.inc1.p
UMacApp.inc2.p
UMacApp.inc3.p
UPrinting.inc1.p
```

There are also a few assembler source files with names like UObject.a.

Suppose you wanted to search for a reference to constant cPaste. Assuming the constant is properly capitalized throughout, you could avoid spurious messages with the case sensitive search command:

```
Search -l -s cPaste ≈.p
```

If you will be making several consecutive searches, it's probably more convenient to make case-sensitive searches the default, as in:

```
Set CaseSensitive 1
Search -l cPaste ≈.p
```

If you only want to search the implementation files to see how the constant is used, that's nearly as easy, using only the simple wildcard characters. The command

```
Search -l cPaste ≈.inc?.p
```

will pass to Search only file names that end in .inc1.p, .inc2.p, and any other character between the .inc and .p suffix.

But if you're searching for the value defined for the constant, you would want to search only the interface files, which is not as easy. There's no simple wildcard character that would match, for example UMacApp.p and not UMacApp.incl.p. However, the pattern-list expressions introduced in Chapter 5 handle this nicely. The command

```
Search -l cPaste [A-Z]*.p
```

would match only names consisting of letters, followed by .p. This would match interface files but not implementation files.

Remember that pathname parameters are *never* case sensitive, no matter what the setting of the CaseSensitive flag. This also applies to the command and option names. In fact, in the command

```
Search -l '[¬A-Za-z]c[A-Z]' [A-Z]*.p
```

the first list matches any character not a letter (upper- or lowercase), the second list matches any capital letter, while the third list matches any series of letters in the file name.

You should also keep it clear in your mind how the two patterns are interpreted. Because it is quoted, the first parameter is passed intact to the Search command without interpretation. However, the shell scans the second parameter, finds the pattern-matching expression, and replaces that parameter with zero or more pathname parameters.

6.2 Combining Commands

When building longer alias and command files, you must be aware of the interactions of the various commands and how to control those interactions.

The shell allows you to combine the output of one command to define the parameters of another command.

COMMAND SUBSTITUTION

When defining a set of standard commands, it is often necessary to use one command to get the parameters of another. The MPW shell allows you to do this through a process known as "command substitution."

The accent character (standard ASCII ` character) delimits a series of one or more MPW commands. The value substituted for the delimited string is the output stream that would normally displayed by the command(s). This allows the output of the command to be assigned to a shell variable or combined as a parameter of another command.

If the concept seems foreign, this is perhaps best illustrated by a series of examples. The command

```
Directory `Echo MPW`
```

would be treated exactly the same as

```
Directory MPW
```

A more useful example is the command line

```
Print -h `Files -t TEXT`
```

which directs the shell to:

1) Figure out which files of type `'TEXT'` there are in the current directory
2) Build a list of the corresponding file names
3) Pass that list to the `Print` command, one file per parameter
4) Print each file with a header

Step 3 is actually the magic one. There is one additional step that is not immediately obvious unless you step back and look at it—or are familiar with one of the UNIX shells, which treat the `` `...` `` delimiters the same way.

The Files command generates a list of file names, with one file name per line. If the name includes blanks or special characters, it is quoted.

However, the `Print` command expects a list of file names, each separated by blanks. The output of the `Files` command does not exactly match the input expected by `Print`.

The shell allows for this and converts multiple lines of output from the evaluated command (in this case, `Files`) into blank-separated parameters to the new command (`Print`).

Command substitution explains why a number of commands, such as `Files` and `Volumes`, display quoted names when necessary. For example, the command

```
Files -r `Volumes 1`
```

would list the files in the disk currently mounted in the internal drive. When it displays a volume name, `Volumes` must quote any name that contains special characters (such as `'My Disk:'`), so that the appropriate device name will be passed to Files as a single parameter.

Figure 6–1 shows the `Files` command evaluated as a parameter to `Echo`.

Note that the evaluated `Files` output is quoted before being used as a parameter—otherwise, the shell would strip the quoting from the file names, and the `Echo`'d output would not show these quotes. The `Quote` command is similar to `Echo`, but will automatically requote its parameters, if necessary; so

```
Quote `Files`
```

would also produce a list of file names, quoted where necessary.

More elaborate commands can, of course, be substituted. A recursively generated printout of all C source files contained in any folder relative to the current one can be obtained from the substitution:

```
Print -h `Files -r -f | Search /≈.c∂'*∞/`
```

The `-f` option of the `Files` command displays the full pathname of a file, since the file could be in any directory. In order to match file names such as `Foo.c`, without matching `Foo.c.o`, the search pattern is anchored against the right margin with ∞. However, file names containing spaces will be quoted by an apostrophe; so the string also includes matching against an optional apostrophe at the end of the line.

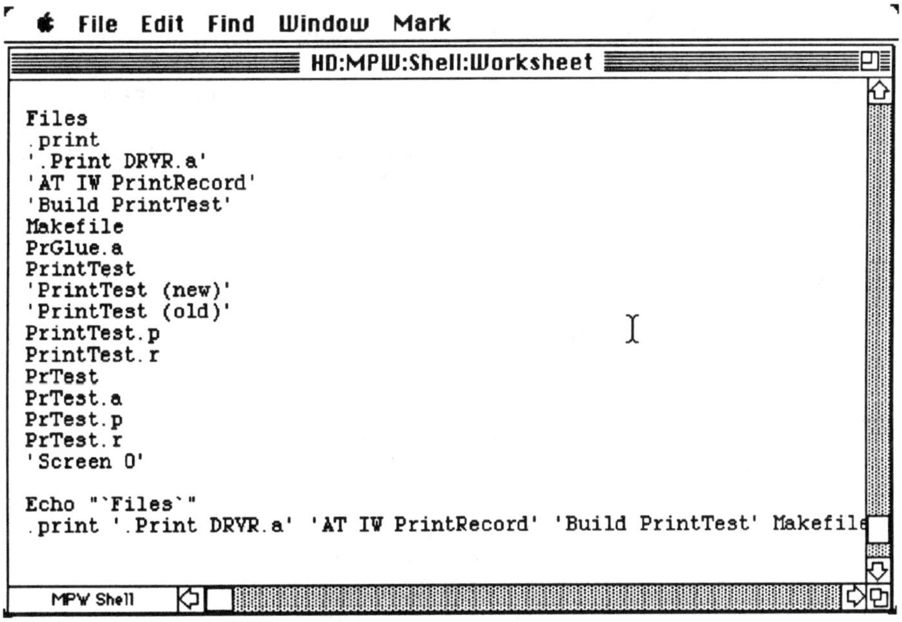

```
 ⌐  ⊛  File  Edit  Find  Window  Mark                          ¬
 ╔══════════════ HD:MPW:Shell:Worksheet ═══════════════╗
                                                       ⇧
 Files
 .print
 '.Print DRVR.a'
 'AT IW PrintRecord'
 'Build PrintTest'
 Makefile
 PrGlue.a
 PrintTest
 'PrintTest (new)'
 'PrintTest (old)'
 PrintTest.p                          I
 PrintTest.r
 PrTest
 PrTest.a
 PrTest.p
 PrTest.r
 'Screen 0'

 Echo "`Files`"
 .print '.Print DRVR.a' 'AT IW PrintRecord' 'Build PrintTest' Makefile
                                                       ⇩
 ┌─────────┐
 │MPW Shell│ ◁                                         ▷
 └─────────┘
```

Figure 6–1: Evaluation of Files command

It's a good idea to use `Echo` to test the result of a file substitution before using it as a parameter to a dangerous command (such as `Delete`) or a time-consuming one (such as `Print`).

Command substitution can also be used as a way to define a complete command and execute that command. If the value of symbol {MPW} is `HD:MPW::`, then

```
`Set MPW`
```

would execute the command

```
Set MPW HD:MPW:
```

While this particular subsitution would not make any significant change, it illustrates how an alias or command file can be used to generate a single-line shell command.

DISPLAYING MESSAGES

The substitution syntax is often used to build display messages on a single output line. Take the `Count` command, which displays the number of characters or lines in a document. The command line

```
Echo File "{Target}" is `Count -l "{Target}"` lines long
```

would display a single-line message, such as

```
File HD:MPW:Sources:Sample.c is 500 lines long
```

One command often used in building such prompts is the `Date` command, which displays the current date and time.

Date

Display date and/or time

Syntax:

`Date`	Display the date and time

Options:

`-a`	Use abbreviated date format
`-s`	Use short date format
`-d`	Display date only
`-t`	Display time only

Remarks:

The three date formats correspond to the country-specific formats, as documented for the International Utilities Package. In the United States, the default format is:

```
Monday, March 2, 1987 10:02:00 PM
```

The abbreviated format uses three-character abbreviations for all countries:

```
Mon, Mar 2, 1987 10:02:00 PM
```

while the short format uses numbers:

```
3/2/87 10:02:00 PM
```

The order of date fields and any words are country specific, as are the number of digits in the numeric fields.

The format of the time field is not controlled by an option and reflects the standard time format defined by the International Utilities. However, if a 24-hour clock is selected with the Control Panel, the default format will be:

```
Monday, March 2, 1987 22:02:00
```

Input/Output:

Output   Displayed date and/or time

Examples:

Date -a   Display abbreviated date, followed by time
Date -s -d   Display short date only

For example, the command line

```
Echo Compile begun at `Date -t` on `Date -s -a'
```

might display

```
Compile begun at 3:15:39 PM on Thu, Mar 19, 1987
```

You can also substitute commands to assign values to variables, as will be used in parsing pathnames later in this chapter. If you wish to have a shell variable with today's date, the command

```
Set Today `Date -s -d`
```

would allow you to include the variable {Today} where a date was required, such as in Make input files.

When using command substitution, you must be careful about quoting both the parameters to the command being substituted and the substituted result. Quoting characters are stripped each time the shell scans the input line, as will be explained later.

CONTROLLING COMMAND EXECUTION

Several of the standard variables are used by shell procedures for debugging and conditional execution. These variables are summarized in Table 6–2.

Variable	*Command Shell Variables* *Default Value*	*Description*
Active		Pathname of active window
Command		Pathname of last MPW command
Echo	0	Show command before running
Exit	1	Command files terminate on error
Status		Success status from last command
Target		Pathname of target window
Test	0	Don't execute tools or applications

Table 6–2:   Command shell variables

As with other variables, changing these values will only change the value in the current context. The value of the variable must be exported to change the value of the corresponding variable in a command file run from this context.

The Echo variable can be used for debugging aliases, custom menus, and command files. When set to a nonzero value, the shell displays each command after its parameters are evaluated but before the command is executed. This allows you to see exactly how the commands are being interpreted and, when running a command file, follow the control of execution within that file. Figure 6–2 shows the result of echoing commands during execution.

The Test variable can also be used for debugging command files. When set to a nonzero value, the shell will not execute MPW tools or applications. It will, however, execute built-in commands and command files. You normally would set Test in conjunction with Echo. If the commands are time-consuming or dangerous (such as Delete), this allows you to test a command file before using it.

Two variables are automatically set by the shell after the execution of each command. The Command variable is set to the full pathname of the previous tool or command file or to the name of any built in command.

The Status variable is the status value indicating the success of the command. A value of zero indicates normal completion, while a nonzero value indicates an error of some sort, as shown in Table 6–3. The actual return codes for each type of error will vary by command. See the latest edition of the MPW reference manual for more information on a particular command's return value.

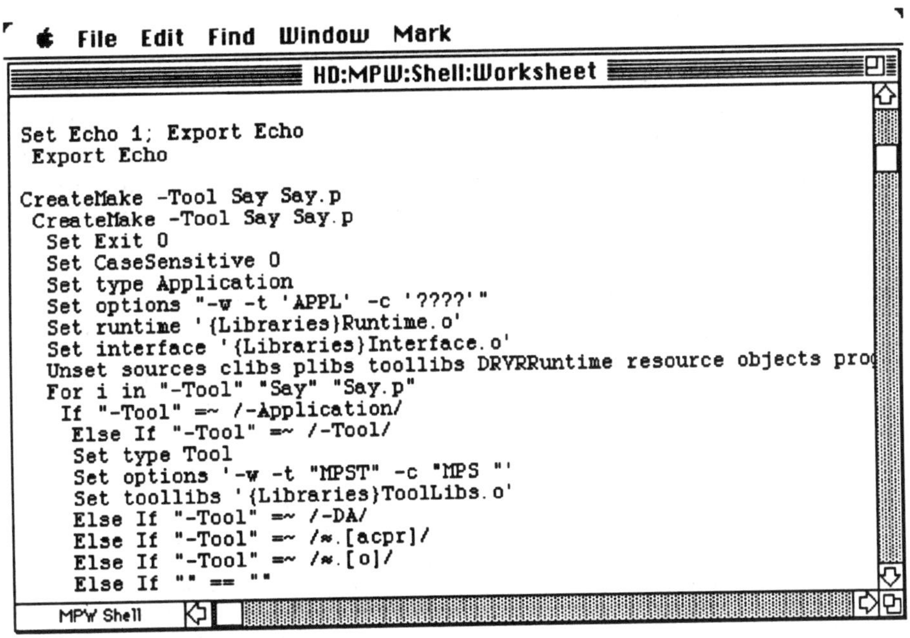

```
 File   Edit   Find   Window   Mark
═══════════════════ HD:MPW:Shell:Worksheet ═══════════════════

Set Echo 1; Export Echo
 Export Echo

CreateMake -Tool Say Say.p
 CreateMake -Tool Say Say.p
  Set Exit 0
  Set CaseSensitive 0
  Set type Application
  Set options "-w -t 'APPL' -c '????'"
  Set runtime '{Libraries}Runtime.o'
  Set interface '{Libraries}Interface.o'
  Unset sources clibs plibs toollibs DRVRRuntime resource objects pro
  For i in "-Tool" "Say" "Say.p"
   If "-Tool" =~ /-Application/
   Else If "-Tool" =~ /-Tool/
    Set type Tool
    Set options '-w -t "MPST" -c "MPS "'
    Set toollibs '{Libraries}ToolLibs.o'
   Else If "-Tool" =~ /-DA/
   Else If "-Tool" =~ /*.[acpr]/
   Else If "-Tool" =~ /*.[o]/
   Else If "" == ""

  MPW Shell
```

Figure 6–2:   Echoing commands

Status values

Value	Description
0	Successful completion
1	Syntax error
≥ 2	Other errors

Table 6–3:   Status values

If you are executing a series of commands, an error in one of the commands will normally terminate any remaining commands in the selection or command file. To disable this, enter

```
Set Exit 0   # normally 1
```

which disables this termination based on command failure.

As with other shell variable changes, note that these settings only affect the current context unless exported. This allows you to temporarily change the command interpretation without affecting command files. If you enter the command

```
                         Export Exit
```

the definition of Exit would be changed for command files as well.

You should use Exit to disable termination on error whenever you wish to use the value of {Status} in the next command, since the shell will otherwise terminate execution before it can reach that command.

GROUPING COMMANDS

MPW provides a number of symbols for grouping a series of two or more commands into a logical unit. It also provides the Begin command, which groups commands up until the corresponding End command (see Table 6–4).

Grouping operators

Command	Effect
cmd1 ; cmd2	Execute cmd1 and cmd2
cmd1 && cmd2	Execute cmd2 if cmd1 succeeds
cmd1 || cmd2	Execute cmd2 if cmd1 fails
cmd1 | cmd2	Redirect output of cmd1 to input of cmd2
(commands)	Group execution of commands
Begin commands End	

Table 6–4:   Grouping operators

The ; operator allows two or more commands to be placed on the same line, but the commands are otherwise interpreted the same as if they were on separate lines; that is, they are executed sequentially. This is primarily useful where commands must be on a single line—such as with Alias—or to save space in a command file.

The | piping operator combines the standard output of the first command with the standard input of the second. The diagnostic output can also be redirected at the same time with a command such as

```
        Cmd1 ≥ Dev:StdOut | Cmd2
```

which is interpreted as "pipe the output of Cmd1 to Cmd2 and direct the diagnostic output of Cmd1 to the same place as its standard output."

The Begin command indicates a block of commands that is later terminated by an End command.

Begin ... End

Bracket a group of commands

Syntax:

```
Begin
   commands ...
End                        Group the commands
```

Remarks:

The status value returned by the block of commands is the status value of the last command executed. Output and diagnostic output redirected for the block will be redirected for all the commands in the block.

Commands can also be grouped using the (and) delimiters.

Examples:

```
Begin; Set; Export; End > Vars
```
Output variable definitions and exports to *Vars*

The main use of Begin ... End is to redirect the output of a series of commands to a similar place, as in:

```
Begin
   Echo "-------------"
   Catenate ≈
   Echo "-------------"
End >"{Target}"
```

The Begin ... End blocks are similar to those grouped by parentheses characters, with only a minor difference in how they are used. The previous commands could be expressed as:

```
( Echo "----------"; Catenate ≈; Echo "-----------" ) ∂
>"{Target}"
```

or

```
Begin; Echo "-------------"; ∂
Catenate ≈; Echo "--------------"; ∂
End  >"{Target}"
```

Note that the Begin and End commands require a semicolon (;) to separate them from other commands on the same line, while the parentheses do not. Both types of groupings can be nested within other groupings.

Execution of all the preceding groups stops if there's an error and the value of {Exit} is true, i.e., nonzero. You can set Exit to 0 and then test the value of {Status} with an If command to see if the command has completed successfully.

However, there is an easier way to conditionally combine commands without having to directly test the value of the {Status} variable.

Two operators allow you to combine successive commands, with the execution of the second (or later) command contingent on the first. The && operator executes the second command only if the first is successful. The || operator executes the second command only if the first fails.

The different ways of combining commands can be illustrated by an example. Suppose that True and False are simple commands that return successful and unsuccessful error statuses, respectively. Then the commands

```
True && Echo "One"
True || Echo "Two"
True ; Echo "Three"
```

will display "One" and "Three," while

```
False && Echo "One"
False || Echo "Two"
```

will display "Two."

The command

```
False ; Echo "Three"
```

will display "Three" only if variable {Exit} is zero. The two conditional forms of combining commands are unaffected by the value of {Exit}.

HANDLING ERRORS

If you specify bad parameters to a shell command or an error occurs during the processing of the command, the command will terminate with an error status. Normally, it will display at least one line to the diagnostic output. Unless you override the shell's standard action, the error status will terminate execution of a list of commands, which the shell will indicate by displaying its own error message.

For example, the invalid command

```
Directory ..
```

will terminate with

```
### Directory - Unable to set current directory.
# File not found (OS error -43)
```

If it was part of a series of commands, you'll also see

```
### MPW Shell - Execution of input terminated.
```

This is a useful display to see if you are entering the command interactively in the worksheet. You can easily remove the clutter of error messages with the Undo menu item, Command Z.

However, you may wish to write command files that will continue running no matter what the error and without cluttering up the current active window. If the command file contains a loop you could get pages and pages of output when really all you wanted was a one-line message indicating the failure.

This requirement becomes even more important when you're defining your own custom menu commands. Normally, you'll be using these commands with a document in the active window and you don't want the failure of one of these commands to fill one of your source files with useless text.

A good place to start is by taking the diagnostic output and throwing it into the "bit bucket," the null device. All you need to do is to bracket your commands by

```
Begin

End ≥ Dev:Null
```

and any diagnostic output generated by your command will be discarded. The similar parentheses grouping characters are particularly useful when defining a one-line alias, as in:

```
Alias PrintDelete '(Print ≈; Delete -y ≈)  ≥ Dev:Null'
```

If you have only one command, it might seem unnecessary to group the single command before redirecting the diagnostic output. However, there are certain errors possible that will be caught by the shell before the command executes.

Suppose you are trying to display all the C source files in the current directory, but when you write the command file, you have no control over whether the command will be used in, say, a directory of Pascal library files. If your command file includes a statement such as

```
Files ≈.c
```

it will produce the message

```
### MPW Shell - No match for file name pattern "≈.c".
```

if used in a directory without C source files. Redirecting the diagnostic output of the `Files` command would seem to solve the problem. However,

```
Files ≈.c ≥ Dev:Null
```

will produce the same message because the file name interpretation is performed by the shell, not by the `Files` command. (Notice where the error message said it came from.)

Instead, the command

```
(Files ≈.c) ≥ Dev:Null
```

will throw away the shell message since it redirects the diagnostic before the shell interprets the command line. This is also useful if you have a substituted command that may or may not be written properly.

However, it's still necessary to trap the error status. Otherwise, the shell will print a message

```
### MPW Shell - Execution of input terminated.
```

when the command fails.

Setting {Exit} to 0 will prevent the error message from being displayed, but if you're writing a short command file, this is unnecessary. If you're writing a command alias or a custom menu, changing the value of {Exit} will change it for other commands as well.

Instead, you can follow any command that may fail with the | | command combining operator. If the first command fails, the shell will execute the second command rather than terminating with the error message. The second command can, in fact, be a null command, so the statement

```
(Files ≈.c || ) ≥ Dev:Null
```

would either display a list of files to the active window or execute the second (null) command and display nothing.

MUSIC-MAKING WITH THE SHELL

When writing a command file, you can use the previous techniques to suppress generation of text message in case of an error. However, you may want to provide a substitute indication of an error. In other cases, you will write command files that require a long period of time to complete, and you need a way to signal that it's time to return to the work.

The `Beep` command can be used to provide an audible indication from within a series of shell commands. In its simplest form, it makes a noise like that used by other Macintosh programs to signal an error, but it can also be used to play simple melodies (although no four-part harmonies) using the Sound Driver's square-wave synthesizer.

Beep

Sound a tone or melody

Syntax:

```
Beep                      Sound a standard tone
Beep note ...             Play the specific melody defined by note...
```

Remarks:

The standard tone is equivalent to the OS Utility call

```
                          SysBeep(8);
```

If specified, each note parameter consists of the following components:

```
              octave, PITCH, duration, level
```

where

   octave is an integer in the range 1 to 3, optionally preceded by a minus sign; indicating the number of octaves above or below the scale from middle C up to B;

   PITCH is a letter from A to G (upper- or lowercase), optionally followed by b or #;

   duration is a time value in ticks (one-sixtieth of a second); and

   level is an amplitude from 0 to 255.

PITCH is required; unrecognized values will produce no sound for the specified duration. If omitted, *octave* defaults to 0, *duration* defaults to 15 and *level* defaults to 128.

Examples:

```
Beep                          Sound a simple tone
Beep -1F,30 e,30 C,60         Play a three-note theme
```

Beep can be used to indicate success in a command file. If you're executing a time-consuming series of commands, it can bring you back from your coffee break. You can also use it to indicate failure, and you can use its melody-making capabilities to distinguish between the two.

In conjunction with Dev:Null, it's possible to make your command files and custom menus completely "clean," while at the same time indicating failure. The || grouping operator, combined with the Beep command, provides this capability. For example, the command

```
    Alias OM 'Open Makefile ≥Dev:Null || Beep'
```

would allow you to use OM to open the Makefile if it exists.

If it does not exist, the | | prevents an error status from the first command from terminating execution, even if {Exit} is 1. Instead, the Beep command is executed instead. This means you can trap failures without stopping the execution of your command file; if the second command is successful, the command file will continue executing.

Beep can also be used to generate more complex tunes using the square-wave synthesizer of the Sound Driver. It has a range of nearly seven octaves, from -3C (33 Hz) to 3B (3951 Hz), only a third of an octave less than that of a piano. The low end of the range is well beyond the limitations of the Mac's tiny built-in speaker, and the high end is very shrill, so as a practical matter, you will probably use the four-octave range -2C to 2C. Figure 6–3 shows musical notes corresponding to Beep parameters.

The standard duration of 15 ticks (one-quarter of a second) is equivalent to an eighth note in a brisk allegro, or a sixteenth note in a more leisurely adagio. When transcribing music, you may wish to adjust the tempo slightly to make it a multiple of 15 ticks so that some note values can be entered in the more compact form, without a duration.

The sharp indication (#) is, of course, the shell's comment character, so the parameter must be quoted (or the sharp sign within the parameter) must be quoted by apostrophes. The command

```
Beep D,60 C#,30 D,60
```

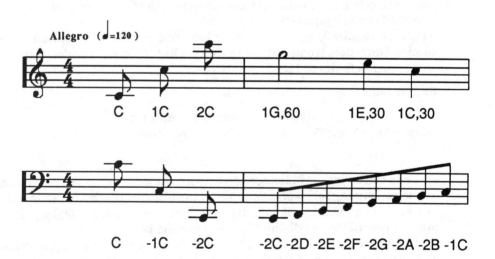

Figure 6–3:   Beep note values

would treat ", 30 D, 60" as a comment. The correct way to enter this would be:

```
Beep D,60 'C#,30' D,60
```

Since Beep uses the 12-tone tempered scale, you can also use the enharmonic equivalent flat pitch to avoid quoting:

```
Beep D,60 Db,30 D,60
```

Beep does not play a note for an unrecognized letter. You can use this to insert a rest in a melody, as in:

```
Beep D X Db D X Db D Db D Gb A
```

Playing melodies with Beep might seem like overkill for a development system (it is) and like the clever idea of someone who likes thinking up clever ideas (it was), but it also has a practical purpose. In a long command file, there may be several possible outcomes, ranging from complete success to partial failures anywhere along the way. You can give each alternative a distinctive leitmotif, allowing it not only to summon your attention back to the computer when the job is complete but to indicate the result at the same time.

If you want to test your musical prowess, see if you can identify the musical fragments provided in Example 6–1.

6.3 Custom Menu Commands

In addition to defining command files and aliases, MPW allows you to build your own custom menus and menu items. Unlike the line-oriented commands, these can be used to operate on the active window and make changes to it.

These custom menu-based commands are defined in terms of shell commands, which can use all the shell programming constructs available to command aliases and command files.

This section concentrates on building custom menus to operate on the active window. Custom menus can also be used to call command files, as described in the next section.

ADDING MENU ITEMS

MPW allows you to define your own menu commands. You can define your own menus or add items to some of the MPW-defined menus. Each of your

```
############## Classical ##############
# A choral work
Beep 1D,60 A,20 B,20 A,20 X,40 1D,60 A,20 B,20 A,20 X,40 ∂
A,10 A,10 B,20 A,20 X,40   A,10 A,10 B,20 A,20 X,40 ∂
1D,20 '1C#,20' 1D,40 '1C#,20' 1D,40

# A German song
Beep G,90 'F#' G B,105 A G,60 X,60 A,46 B,7 A,7 G 'F#' E 'F#' G,60

# Variations and Fugue
Beep X,5  D,60 F,60 A,60 1D,30 1E 1F 1G 1F 1E 1D '1C#,60' ∂
1A,30 1D 1F 1A 1F 1D,30 1Bb,60 1G,30 1C 1E 1G 1E 1C,30 1A,60 ∂
1F,30 Bb 1D 1F 1D 1G,30 1E,30 A '1C#' 1E '1C#' 1F 1E 1F 1E 1D ∂
'1C#,30' 1F,30 1E 1F 1E 1D A,30 1D,30 '1C#' 1D 1E 1D 1D,60

# A famous canon
Beep 'F#,50' E,50 D,50 'C#,50' -1B,50 -1A,50 -1B,50 'C#,50'

# March music
Beep 1E '1G#' '1G#' '1G#' '1F#,8' 1E,7 1B,45 ∂
1B,8 1A,7 '1G#' '1G#' '1G#' '1F#,8' 1E,7 1B,45 ∂
1B,8 1A,7 '1G#' 1A,8 1B,7 1A '1G#' '1F#'  B,30


############## Traditional ##############
Beep G,20 A,20 B,20 1C,40 1C,60 1C,20 G,20 A,20 B,40 B,60
```

Example 6-1:   Name that tune

menu items will correspond to a shell command line to be executed when the menu item is selected.

Menu commands are defined with AddMenu, which takes a menu title, a menu item, and the command to be executed when that item is selected. As with the Set command, if one (or more) of the parameters is omitted, AddMenu will instead display the current definition(s).

AddMenu, DeleteMenu

Define, display or delete user-defined menu commands

Syntax:

AddMenu *menu item command*	Add user-defined *menu item*
AddMenu *menu item*	Display user-defined *menu item*
AddMenu *menu*	Display user-defined *menu*
AddMenu	Display all user-defined *menus*

DeleteMenu *menu item*	Delete definition for *menu item*
DeleteMenu *menu*	Delete user-defined *menu*
DeleteMenu	Delete *all* user-defined *menus*

Remarks:

If the *menu* and *item* are already defined, the *command* replaces any previous user definition. If the user-defined menu exists, the item is added to the end of it; otherwise, the menu is created with the single item. User commands can also be added to the end of the File, Edit, and Find menus.

The *item* can include formatting metacharacters, as defined for the AddMenu trap of the Menu Manager. These characters include:

(	Disable (dim) menu item
/c	Define keyboard equivalent as Command-c
<s	Set display style; B Bold, I Italic, U Underline, O Outline, S Shadow
!	Check the menu item

Formatting codes can be used to change the appearance of an existing menu item, but *command* must be specified.

Input/Output:

Output	Displayed menu items as AddMenu commands

Example:

AddMenu	
AddMenu Control	Display user-defined Control menu
DeleteMenu Control	Remove user-defined Control menu

If the command includes any blanks, it must be quoted so that the shell treats it as a single parameter. Additionally, the normal action is to interpret any shell variables at the time the AddMenu is entered, usually in a startup file. If the value of a variable is to be interpreted *at the time the menu item is selected,* the command must be quoted using apostrophes. Any menu item that includes spaces or metacharacters should also be quoted.

This comes up frequently for menus that manipulate the active and target windows. In the definition

```
AddMenu File 'DraftPrint/P'∂
'Print -h -q Draft "{Active}" '
```

the command is quoted with apostrophes to prevent interpretation until it is used. The window name is quoted with quotation marks so that if it includes a space, it will be treated as a single parameter by the Print command.

The menu command line specified in AddMenu can be as complex or as long as you like. Multiple commands will be executed if the command parameter is properly quoted and the commands are separated by a semicolon.

AddMenu always insists on a command parameter, even if the menu item is not intended to be executed. Any command can be used; for example, the definition

```
AddMenu File '(-' Beep
```

adds a dimmed line to the end of the File menu. Since the item is disabled, it will never be executed.

AddMenu will replace the existing command definition for the menu and item unless the item is the "-" item separator, which is always appended to the menu. AddMenu cannot be used to display or change a built in menu definition.

If DeleteMenu is used to delete a single menu, any user-defined menus to the right of that menu are shifted to the left.

ACTIVE AND TARGET WINDOWS

As described in the previous chapter, most of the editing commands accept a parameter to specify the window to be changed. This allows custom menus to be defined to operate on the active window, target window, or any other window.

The simplest examples illustrating this principle are two simple extensions to the Find menu. The following commands define menu operations to position the active window to the beginning or end of the file:

```
AddMenu Find '(-' beep
AddMenu Find Top 'Find • "{Active}"'
AddMenu Find Bottom 'Find ∞ "{Active}"'
```

These are primarily intended for illustration only, since MPW provides Command-Shift equivalents using the up and down arrow keys.

More complex operations can be performed using the selection in the active or target window. As indicated in the previous chapter, the psuedo-files § and "{Active}.§" can be used to represent the value of the selection in either the target or active windows, respectively.

For example, you might have a series of constant references in one of your source files that you'd like to look up in the library interfaces. Certainly, you could use a series of Find menu commands or Find shell commands. However, there's no need to reenter the keywords to be found, when they are already entered in your source file.

Instead, the following menu definition would take the currently selected text in the active window and search for the first reference in the target window. Next, it makes the target window the active window. If the first reference is not the one desired, the Find Same menu item can be used to find the appropriate one. The definition is:

```
AddMenu Find 'Find Selection in Target' ∂
 'Find •;Find /`Catenate "{Active}.§"`/;Open "{Target}"'
```

How does it work? After positioning at the top of the document to be searched, the currently selected string in the active window (the "{Active}.§" selection psuedo-file) is substituted for the Catenate command and, in turn, is used as the search string for the Find command.

If you recall the menu equivalents shown in Chapter 4, it's possible to define commands equivalent to almost all of the built in menu items. One such command is Open Selection. Of course, there's no need to define the same command again, but a similar command—such as opening the selected name read only—can be easily defined. With the proper error handling, this definition is

```
AddMenu File 'Open Selection Read-only' ∂
 '(Open -r `Catenate "{Active}.§"` || Beep) ≥ Dev:Null'
```

As with the standard Open Selection, the selected name must be quoted if it includes blanks or other special characters.

An even more useful definition is one that opens a referenced include file. For example, if you normally use C, the definition

```
AddMenu {Menu} 'Open Include/I' ∂
 'Open -r {CIncludes}`Catenate "{Active}".§`'
```

would allow you to double click on a file name and then type Command-I to open the file, as shown in Figure 6–4.

If you normally use Pascal or a variety of languages, the problem is slightly more complex. Pascal USES declarations do not include the .p suffix, while a variety of languages will have the include files in several different folders.

However, multiple languages can be easily handled you use the alternate directory structure shown in Chapter 4, in which

```
Set AIncludes    "{Includes} AIncludes:"
Set CIncludes    "{Includes} CIncludes:"
Set PInterfaces  "{Includes} PInterfaces:"
```

The Pascal suffix can be optionally included using a filename pattern. Thus, the custom menu definition

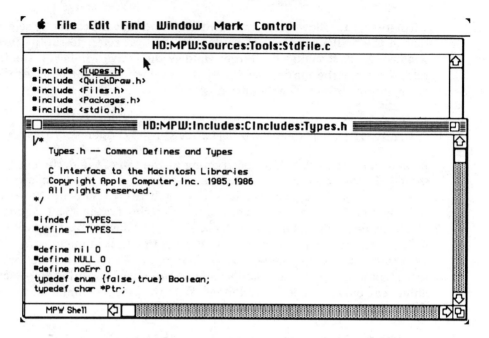

Figure 6–4:   Opening an Include file

```
AddMenu {Menu} 'Open Include/I' ∂
  'Open -r {Includes}≈:`Catenate "{Active}".§`(.p)*'
```

would allow you open any type of file. Double click on the actual name of an assembler, C, or resource include file or on the name of a Pascal unit and the corresponding definition will be opened read only.

MOVING DATA BETWEEN WINDOWS

The Macintosh defines a standard format for moving data between documents using the clipboard.

However, if you're moving several fragements between two documents, the multiple operations required to move data using the clipboard can be inconvenient. With the power of MPW custom menus and selection expressions available to you, it's easy to define operations to move the data directly. The command

```
AddMenu Control Grab 'Catenate §'
```

defines a new menu item that copies data from the current selection in the target window to the active window.

Figure 6–5 shows an example of what the active and target window might look like before using Grab. As always, the boxed area in the target window is the current selection in that window. After the menu command, Figure 6–6 shows the selected text transferred to the active window.

Similarly, you can define a command to take the selection in the active window and place it in the target window. This would be more useful if you're taking many fragments out of one document and adding them, one after the other, to another file. An example would be if you're building a rought draft of a new program by combining pieces of older programs.

The corresponding command, Shove, would be defined by the AddMenu command:

```
AddMenu Control Shove ∂
'Find §∆; Catenate "{Active}.§" >§'
```

These two commands defined for Shove can be interpreted as:

- Move to the end of the current selection in the target window and make an insertion point.

- Read the text from the current selection in the active window and display it to the current selection in the target window.

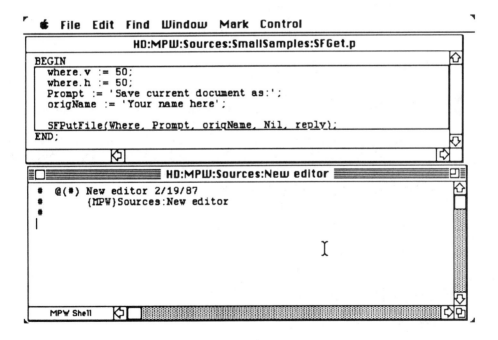

Figure 6–5:   Active and target windows before Grab

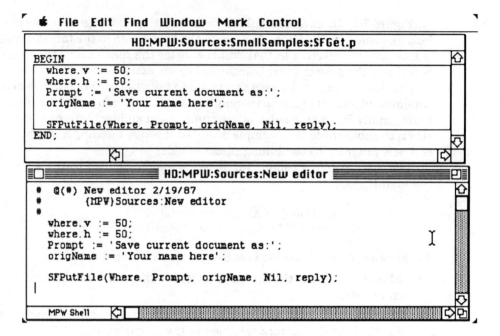

Figure 6–6:   Active and target windows after Grab

PROMPTS

The shell also includes commands to present standard Macintosh alerts and dialogs. These can be used as prompts within custom menus and command files.

The Alert command presents an alert to display a single message, which is acknowledged by the Ok button. The Confirm command presents an alert with a two- or three-way choice, with the choice indicated by the exit status of the command. Finally, the Request command displays a dialog with a fixed text string and an editable text string and then displays the edited string on the standard output.

Alert

Display alert with message

Syntax:

```
Alert prompt          Display prompt
Alert                 Display standard input
```

Remarks:

The single parameter is displayed as part of a standard Dialog Manager alert, which contains a single Ok button.

Examples:

```
Pascal "{Target}" || Alert "Compile failed"
                    Display a prompt if compilation fails
```

Confirm

Display alert and request selection

Syntax:

```
Confirm prompt       Display prompt and ask for response
Confirm              Display standard input and ask for response
```

Options:

```
-t                   Include three-way choice
```

Remarks:

The single parameter is displayed as part of a standard Dialog Manager alert, which by default contains two buttons, Ok and Cancel. The optional three-way choice displays buttons Yes, No and Cancel.

The selected button is indicated by return status of the Confirm command. The default status values are:

    0   Ok
    4   Cancel

The optional status values returned are

    0   Yes
    4   No
    5   Cancel

Examples:

```
Confirm "Delete {F}" && Delete "{F}"
                    Delete file {F} only if Ok clicked
```

Request

Display dialog and request text

Syntax:

```
Request prompt       Display prompt and ask for response
Request              Display standard input and ask for response
```

Options:

-d *default*   Initialize response text to *default*

Remarks:

The single parameter is displayed as the static text of a standard Dialog Manager dialog. If the optional parameter is given, it is used to set the default value of the editable text. The final value of the edited text is displayed on the standard output.

The selected button is indicated by return status:

0	Ok
2	Cancel

Input/Output:

Output   The edited response string

Examples:

```
Set N "`Request 'Enter name:'`"
```
                Define variable N to be the entered name

All three commands accept parameters to specify a prompt; if none is given, they read the prompt from standard input. This allows you to generate the prompt from the output of another command.

Figure 6–7 shows the displayed dialogs for examples of the Alert, Confirm, and Request commands.

Request can be used with command substitution to allow an interactively entered string to complete a shell command. For example, the definition

```
AddMenu Find 'Goto…' ∂
'Find ∆`Request "Go to line?"` "{Active}" || Beep'
```

would select the beginning of a specified line number in the active window.

More user inputs are possible from two additional prompt commands. The first, Select, presents a dialog with a scrolling list of multiple items, allowing you to select zero or more. As with Request, a default can be specified.

Select

Display dialog allow multiple selection of arbitrary items

Syntax:

Select *item* …	Display each *item*
Select	Display items read from standard input

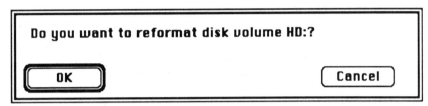

Alert 'Something serious has happened'

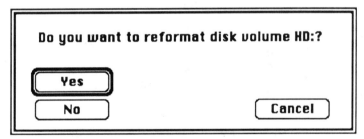

Confirm 'Do you want to reformat disk volume HD:?'

Confirm -t 'Do you want to reformat disk volume HD:?'

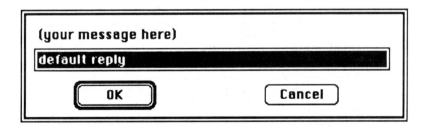

Request -d 'default reply' '(your message here)'

Figure 6-7:   Alert, Confirm and Request prompts

Options:

-d *defitem*	Select *defitem* by default
-m *message*	Use *message* as user prompt
-r *rows*	Display *rows* items in list
-w *width*	Display items in list as *width* pixels wide

Remarks:

The items specified as parameters are displayed in a scrolling list, with the size of the display area controlled by the -r and -w options. If no parameters are given, items are read from standard input, one item per line. The -d option may be specified more than once, with each *defitem* automatically added to the list of items.

The user may select a range of items, using Shift-click, or several discontinuous items using Command-click. The items selected (if any) are displayed on standard output, one per line, quoted if necessary.

The selected button is indicated by return status:

        0   Ok
        2   Cancel

Input/Output:

Output	The item(s) selected

Examples:

```
Set Compiler ∂
"`Select -m 'Choose a language' -d Cobol Asm C Pascal`"
```
                        Define variable Compiler to language selected

Figure 6–8 shows a Select dialog produced for a list of windows.

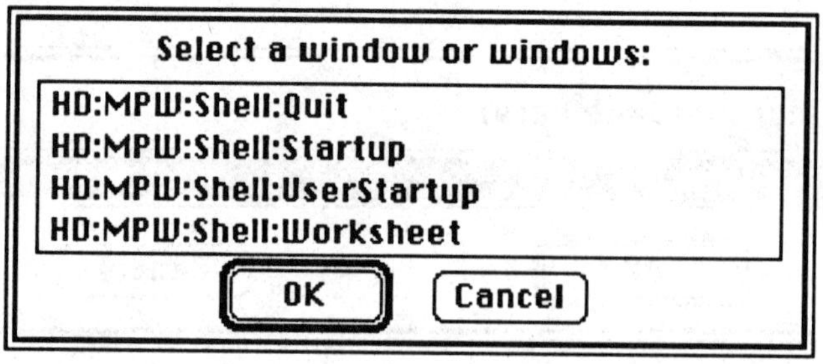

```
Select -w 300 -m 'Select a window or windows:' `Windows`
```

Figure 6–8:   Select prompt

There's another way to produce the same result. The output of the `Windows` command can be piped to the input of `Select`, with one line used for each window, as in:

```
Windows | Select -w 300 -m 'Select a window or windows:'
```

However, the `Windows` command (like `Files`, `Volumes`, `Select`, and many other MPW commands) normally quotes any file names containing special characters. This quoting is to prevent interpretation in shell parameters, but in this case, the `Windows` output won't be seen by the shell and thus quoting is not needed—in fact, the quotes will show up in the dialog.

`Windows` (like the other commands mentioned) has a rarely used option, `-q`, that solves this problem. When it is used, the output is never quoted, as in:

```
Windows -q | Select -w 300 -m ∂
    'Select a window or windows:'
```

We can use this as part of a command to, for example, select the target window:

```
Target `Windows -q | Select -w 300 -m ∂
    'Select window to be edited:'`
```

MPW also provides a way to select an arbitrary file using the Standard File Package. The `StdFile` tool displays a file dialog to select an existing file, define a new file, or select a directory. As with `Request` and `Select`, the selected name is displayed to the command's standard output.

StdFile

Display dialog to select file or directory

Syntax:

`StdFile`	Display a standard file selection dialog
`StdFile` *pathname*	Display dialog with default *pathname*

Options:

`-d`	Display dialog to select an existing directory
`-p`	Display dialog to select a new file name
`-m` *message*	Use *message* as user prompt
`-b` *name*	Default button is named *name*
`-t` *TYPE*	Display only files of the given *TYPE*

Remarks:

By default, StdFile displays a dialog to select any existing file: the -t option limits the file types that will be shown and may be repeated up to four times. The -d and -p options change the dialog to select a directory or new file name ("put" dialog).

With -p, *pathname* specifies the default pathname to be selected. For other dialogs, *pathname* is used to set the default directory only. The -b option can be used to override to the default button name.

The selected button is indicated by return status:

0	Default button: Open, Directory, Save, or user-specified name
4	Cancel

Other status values indicate an error.

Input/Output:

Output   The pathname selected, quoted if
                                      necessary

Examples:

```
Directory `StdFile -d`      Select a new directory
```

EXAMPLE: CUSTOM MENUS

The techniques for building custom menus are summarized by the series of menu definitions shown in Example 6–2.

The AddMenu commands append four new commands to the standard Find menu. The commands have been explained before, although "Find §" is used as a compact shorthand for "Find Selection."

A new menu, Control, defines a series of new menu items. The first group of commands extends the capabilities of the File menu. The commands open a file read only using the StdFile prompt, close all the open documents, or save all the open documents.

The next group of commands—Shove and Grab—moves selected text between the active and target windows, as described earlier.

The next two commands activate either the worksheet or the target window and include command equivalents to make them easier to use.

The fourth group offers three file-related commands. One uses StdFile twice to move an arbitrary file from one directory to another. The second changes the default directory using the selected directory name. A third displays a list of files in the current directory, a frequent requirement.

The final group of commands is intended for those who must continue to struggle with floppy disks, such as those containing source archives (or the original MPW distribution). The first two commands will change the directory to the mounted disk and list the files at the desktop—allowing you to

```
# Append these to the end of shell-defined menu
AddMenu Find '(-' dmy                          # 'dmy' just a placeholder
AddMenu Find Top 'Find • "{Active}"'
AddMenu Find Bottom 'Find ∞ "{Active}"'
AddMenu Find "Goto..." ∂
    '(Find ∆`Request "Go to line?"` "{Active}"|| Beep) ≥ Dev:Null'
AddMenu Find 'Find § in Target' ∂
    'Find •; Find ⌐Catenate "{Active}".§`/; Open "{Target}"'


# Define a new custom menu
AddMenu Control 'Open Read-only...' '(Open -r `StdFile -t TEXT`)≥Dev:Null'
AddMenu Control 'Close All' 'Close -a ≥ Dev:Null'
AddMenu Control 'Save All/E' 'Save -a ≥ Dev:Null'


AddMenu Control '(-' dmy
AddMenu Control 'Shove/-' 'Find §∆; Catenate "{Active}".§ > §; Find §∆'
AddMenu Control 'Grab/=' 'Catenate § '


AddMenu Control '(-' dmy
AddMenu Control 'Activate Worksheet/\' 'Open "{Worksheet}"'
AddMenu Control 'Swap Active & Target/ ' 'Open "{Target}"'


AddMenu Control '(-' dmy
AddMenu Control 'Move...'∂
    '(Set F `StdFile -m "Move what file?"`; ∂
    'Move "{F}" `StdFile -p -b Move -m "Move {F}:"`)≥Dev:Null'
AddMenu Control 'Directory §' ∂
    '(Set D `Catenate "{Active}".§`; Directory "{D}") ≥Dev:Null || ∂
    'Alert "Unable to set current directory as ∂"{D}∂"."'
AddMenu Control 'Display Files/L' 'Files -L'


AddMenu Control '(-' dmy
AddMenu Control 'Internal floppy directory' ∂
    'Set V "`Volumes 1`"; Directory {V}; Files'
AddMenu Control 'External floppy directory' ∂
    'Set V "`Volumes 2`"; Directory {V}; Files'
AddMenu Control 'Eject internal/1' ∂
    '(Set V "`Volumes 1 ||(Beep; Exit 1)`"; Eject {V}; Directory "{Sources}") ≥ Dev:Null'
AddMenu Control 'Eject external/2' ∂
    '(Set V "`Volumes 2 ||(Beep; Exit 1)`"; Eject {V}; Directory "{Sources}") ≥ Dev.Null'
```

Example 6–2:   Menu definitions for UserStartup

change directories to look through the volume further. The last two commands eject the appropriate disk, which normally causes the File Manager to unmount the disk volumes. Since the disk is no longer available, the default directory is changed to a typical value to prevent MPW errors. The menus built by this example are shown in Figure 6–9.

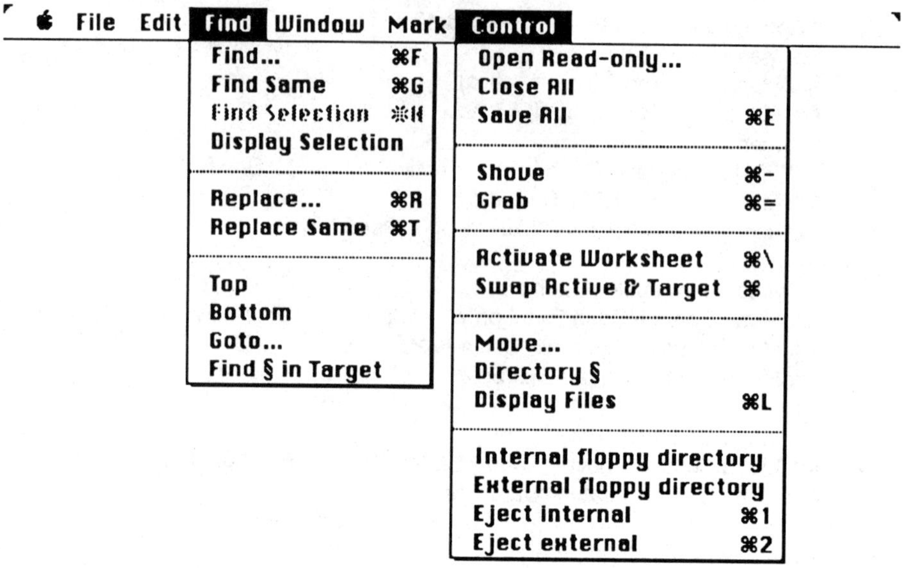

```
      File   Edit   Find   Window   Mark   Control

              Find...          ⌘F      Open Read-only...
              Find Same        ⌘G      Close All
              Find Selection   ⌘H      Save All            ⌘E
              Display Selection
                                       Shove               ⌘-
              Replace...       ⌘R      Grab                ⌘=
              Replace Same     ⌘T
                                       Activate Worksheet  ⌘\
              Top                      Swap Active & Target ⌘
              Bottom
              Goto...                  Move...
              Find § in Target         Directory §
                                       Display Files       ⌘L

                                       Internal floppy directory
                                       External floppy directory
                                       Eject internal      ⌘1
                                       Eject external      ⌘2
```

Figure 6-9:   Menu built by Example 6-2

6.4 Command Files

A series of MPW shell commands are often combined into a command file. Although command files can be run using the Execute command, this section focuses on running command files using the name of the file as the command name and passing parameters to that file as part of the command line.

The number of parameters and the values assigned to these parameters are available to commands within the command file. MPW provides commands to modify those parameters and to check how those parameters will be interpreted.

Command files can contain any valid shell command. Some of the changes made by command files will not affect the execution of other command files but instead are local to that command file. The complete scoping rules for these changes are described in this section.

EXECUTING COMMAND FILES

As noted in Chapter 4, when you enter a command line, the shell will search for a built in command, alias, command file, or MPW tool. The latter two are sought in one of the directories defined by shell variable {Commands} directories. The definition of {Commands} normally includes a colon (:) as the first directory, which directs the shell to search in the current folder.

When you write your own command file, you must place the file in one of these directories. One choice is directory "{MPW}Tools:." You can also create a new folder and make the name of the corresponding directory part of the Set Commands definition in your UserStartup file.

If you're having trouble getting your command file recognized by the shell, the Which command can be used to analyze the shell's interpretation of command names.

Which

Display name of command to be executed

Syntax:

Which *name*	Display pathname for command *name*
Which	Display pathnames of all command directories

Options:

-a	Display all matching commands
-p	Display progress information

Remarks:

If *name* is a built in command, Which displays *name*; if it is an alias, it displays the alias equivalency. Otherwise, Which searches the directories defined by {Commands} and displays the full pathname of the first command file *name* found in those directories.

With the -p option, Which displays the directories as they are searched to the diagnostic output, while the -a option displays the pathnames of all matching command files.

Input/Output:

Output	Pathname of matching command

Examples:

Which Line	Display definition for Line command

Which complements the {Command} (*not* {Commands}) shell variable. {Command} indicates the pathname of the last command executed, while Which displays the command that would be executed, without actually executing it first.

PARAMETERS

Each command file will have a series of shell variables defined that specify the parameters to the command. These variables are used by commands in the file to represent the parameters used when the command file is called.

These parameter variables are represented by integers. The variable {1} references the first parameter, {2} the second, and so on. To take a simple example, if the file {Tools}ForceDup contained the line

```
Duplicate -y "{1}" "{2}"
```

the command

```
ForceDup Source 'Old Source'
```

would execute

```
Duplicate -y "Source" "Old Source"
```

The variable {#} is replaced by the number of parameters; so if command file also contained

```
Echo There are {#} parameters.
```

it would display

```
There are 2 parameters.
```

for the previous ForceDup command.

The variable {Parameters} is replaced by the current list of parameters. The variable {"Parameters"} is a special variable that is replaced by the same list of parameters, but each of the parameters is quoted against interpretation. This allows the same parameters to be passed to another command or command file without reinterpretation.

Shift

Remove command file parameters from the beginning of the list

Syntax:

Shift	Renumber parameter {2} to {1}, etc.
Shift *n*	Renumber parameter {*n*+1} to {1}, etc.

Remarks:

This also changes the definitions of the variables {#}, {Parameters}, and {"Parameters"}. If *n* is greater than {#}, the command eliminates all parameters.

Example:

```
Shift 2
```
Renumber parameter {3} to {1}, {4} to {2}, etc.

The `Shift` command would be used after your command file has analyzed one or more of the initial parameters and will treat the remaining parameters in the same way. After the `Shift`, the initial parameters would be removed from the {"Parameters"} shell variable, which could then be used to refer to all the remainining parameters. An example of a standard MPW command that works this way is the `Search` command, in which the first parameter is a search string and all the remaining parameters are document names.

For example, if the command file {Tools}StoreIn contained

```
Set V "{1}"
Shift
Duplicate {"Parameters}" "{V}"
```

the command

```
StoreIn {MPW}Sources main.c sample.c sample.r
```

would be the intepreted as

```
Duplicate main.c sample.c sample.r {MPW}Sources
```

QUOTED PARAMETERS

As suggested in Chapter 4, there are elaborate rules for quoting and combining parameters to MPW commands. Parameters must often be quoted to prevent interpretation of special characters, but at the same time, parameters will often contain an evaluation of shell variables, such as {MPW}, that must be interpreted by the shell.

The `Parameters` command—not to be confused with the {Parameters} shell variable—will display the interpretation of its parameters and can be used to verify that interpretation when you are attempting to construct a quoted string.

Parameters

Display command parameters

Syntax:

```
Parameters parm ...
```
Display each *parm*

Remarks:

This command can be used to test the interpretation of command parameters, as would be seen by an MPW command.

Input/Output:

Output   Displayed parameters

Examples:

```
Parameters {MPW}
```
Display interpretation of {MPW} as parameter
```
Parameters {"Parameters"}
```
Display parameters to current command file

Several examples will serve to illustrate both `Parameters` and ideas for combining and quoting parameters.

```
Parameters First Second Third Fourth
```

is a simple version of the command that illustrates the use of multiple parameters and displays:

```
{0} Parameters
{1} First
{2} Second
{3} Third
{4} Fourth
```

(The `{0} Parameters` line is always displayed and will not be shown for the remaining examples.)

Of course, quoting of parameters only affects the interpretation of those parameters by the shell prior to being passed to the command. The outer apostrophe and quotation mark characters are always stripped before the parameter is made available to the command, as illustrated by the command

```
Parameters '{MPW}' is "{MPW}"
```

which would quote the first {MPW} and interpret the second, displaying

```
{1} {MPW}
{2} is
{3} HD:MPW:
```

Within quoted strings, these characters are passed intact. The commands

```
Parameters "They can't"
Parameters "Use ResType of 'BNDL'"
```

would display

```
{1} They can't
{1} Use ResType of 'BNDL'
```

When you must display one of the quoting characters within a string delimited by the same characters, you can escape it, as shown by the command and its corresponding display:

```
Parameters "Use ∂{MPW∂} for ∂"home∂" directory."
{1} Use {MPW} for "home" directory.
```

You can also concatenate multiple quoted strings. If they are not separated by a blank, they will be treated as a single parameter. In the command

```
Parameters 'Oh say can'"'"'t you "see"?'
{1} Oh say can't you "see"?
```

the parameter is built from three concatenated quoted strings:

```
'Oh say can'
"'"
'you "see"?'
```

while

```
Parameters "Oh say can't you "'"'"see"'"'"?"
{1} Oh say can't you "see"?
```

combines five quoted strings to form a single parameter.

SCOPE OF PROPERTIES

When writing and using command files, you should be aware of the scope of certain state information between multiple levels of those files.

If command file A calls command file B, A will be referred to as the outer context and B the inner context. The outer context can (and often will) be commands entered interactively in the worksheet.

Each type of information available to a command file has its own scope. For some types of information, if a value is defined or changed in either context, it is passed to the other. Other types of information flow from the outer context to the inner context but not the other way around. Still other types are never shared between contexts.

The following information is always local to the current context:

- Unexported variable definitions
- Command file parameters

This means that any command file can freely redefine these values without regard to the impact on other command files.

The following information will go from an outer command to an inner command but never in the other direction:

- Exported variable definitions
- Aliases

This means that a command file must allow for definitions from its outer context but can freely change those definitions without effecting the outer context. The Unalias command at the beginning of a command file will eliminate the effect of any predefined aliases.

The following information can be changed at either level, and it always affects the other context:

- Current directory
- Custom menus
- Active and target window assignments
- Open windows and their positions
- All files on disk

These rules are illustrated by Figure 6–10.

If a command file is run using the Execute command, it will not receive command parameters. Instead, it runs with the same scope as the context it is run from. So if command file Outer contains the command

```
Execute Inner
```

the values for {Parameters}, {1}, aliases, etc., will be same in Inner as for Outer. This approach is required when using a command file to define variables or aliases to be used by the outer context. Thus, there's no point in exporting shell variables in a command file unless the inner command file calls other command files or is run using Execute. Unlike UNIX, Execute always returns after completing execution of the command file.

If you prefer to run the command file without typing the Execute command, you can, of course, define an alias to abbreviate the usage for you, as in:

```
Alias SetAliases 'Execute {ShellDirectory}UserAliases'
```

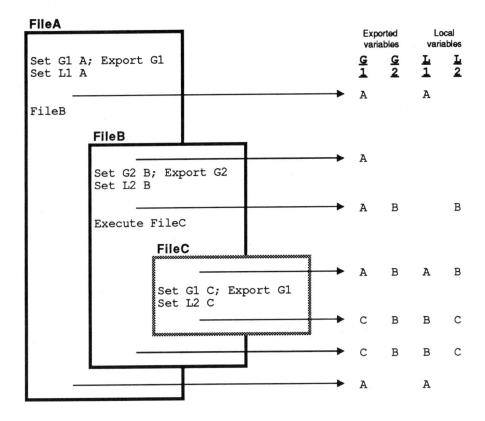

Note: command aliases have the same scope as exported shell variables

Figure 6–10: Scope of nested command files

6.5 Expression Evaluation

Several shell commands recognize a syntax for evaluating certain expressions. These expressions can include numeric and boolean terms and a wide variety of operators. The syntax also directly supports literal and pattern-matching string comparison.

As with other programming languages, these expressions can be used to assign values to variables or used for the conditional execution of statement blocks.

EXPRESSIONS

The standard form for expressions is used by the Evaluate command, the If command, and by the optional If clauses of the Exit, Break, and Continue commands. These expressions are not interpreted by the shell, but are an expected part of the syntax of these five commands.

These expressions can include a wide range of operators for combining terms, as summarized by Table 6–5. Most of the operators will be familiar to C programmers; they closely follow those of the UNIX "C shell," csh. Where not contradictory, the shell also recognizes some of the Pascal operators.

Expression operands are normally 32-bit signed integers. These integers can be used with the four standard arithmetic operations or with bitwise logical operators. Integer constants can also be expressed in hex by beginning the constant with the prefix $ or 0x. For example, both $10 and 0x10 would be interpreted as 16.

The shell also supports the standard six relational operators to compare two integers and produce a boolean result, as well as boolean operators to combine boolean results. Like C, boolean results in the MPW expressions are represented by the integers 0 and 1, with any nonzero value treated as True.

Any operand not recognized as an integer is treated as a character string. Character strings can be compared with the same six relational operators. There are also two special operators to test regular expression equality and inequality, which allows use of pattern matching, as will be described later. If a string is used as a numeric or boolean operand, it is assigned a value of 0 if a null string, otherwise a 1.

USING EXPRESSIONS

Expressions can be directly evaluated using the Evaluate statement, which displays the result of an expression calculation.

Evaluate

Display the evaluation of an expression

Syntax:

Evaluate *expression*   Display evaluation of *expression*

Remarks:

If *expression* is a nonnull string, the result is 1. A null string is evaluated as 0.

Input/Output:

Output   Displayed result of evaluation

Algebraic	Pascal	C	Description (in order of precedence)
( )	( )		Group expressions
	-	-	Integer negation
¬	NOT	!	Logical NOT
		~	Bitwise NOT
	*	*	Integer multiplication
+	DIV		Integer division§
	MOD	%	Integer remainder
	+	+	Integer addition
	-	-	Integer subtraction
		<<	Bitwise shift left
		>>	Bitwise shift right (sign-extend)
	<	<	Less than†
≤	<=	<=	Less than or equal to†
	>	>	Greater than†
≥	>=	>=	Greater than or equal to†
		==	Equal to†
≠	<>	!=	Not equal to†
		=~	String equal to regular expression
		!~	String not equal to regular expression
		&	Bitwise AND
		^	Bitwise exclusive OR
		|	Bitwise inclusive OR
	AND	&&	Logical AND
	OR	||	Logical OR

Integer and bitwise expressions operate on signed 32-bit integers

Logical expressions return integer 0 (FALSE) or 1 (TRUE), and
    • Treat zero operands as FALSE, non-zero operands as TRUE
    • Treat null string operands as FALSE, other strings as TRUE

Non-integral operands are treated as character strings

† Integer or character string operands
§ The / character is always used to delimit regular expressions

Table 6-5:   Evaluation expression operators

Example:

```
Set X `Evaluate {X} + 1`  Increment value of variable {X}
```

Note that Evaluate does not directly change the value of any shell variable or return a value by its status. Instead, the result of an Evaluate calculation is displayed on its standard output. The only way to take advantage of this result is to use command substitution to make the result a parameter of another command.

In conjunction with command substitution and the Set command, Evaluate can be used as the equivalent of the assignment statement in other programming languages. For example, the statements

```
Set Len1 `Count -l file1`
Set Len2 `Count -l file2`
Set Total `Evaluate {Len1} + {Len2}`
```

would set shell variable {Total} equal to the sum of the two lengths.

Sometimes, the actual result of the expression is not important, but the side effects of the evaluation are. Evaluate may be used with regular expression comparisons to set shell variables to reference the matched patterns, as will be described later in this section.

Figure 6–11 shows the Evaluate command used with a series of sample expressions.

Note from the results that TRUE and FALSE are just strings that have no special significance. When evaluated by itself, such strings evaluate to 1 (truth) if they have a nonzero length, no matter what the characters in the strings. Note also that TRUE does not compare equal to true, but it is considered equivalent in a pattern match—assuming {CaseSensitive} is 0.

CONDITIONAL EXECUTION

The If command conditionally executes a series of commands, based on the evaluation of an expression.

If ... Else ... End

Conditionally execute statement block

Syntax:

```
If expression          Execute commands if expression nonzero
  commands
End
```

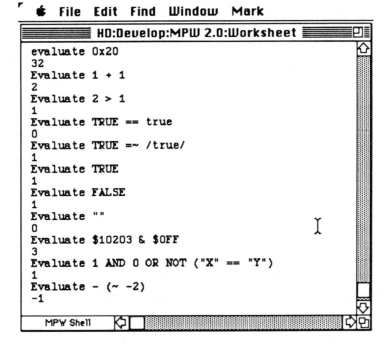

Figure 6-11: Sample expressions

```
If expression
    truecommands        Execute truecommands if expression
                        non-zero,
Else
    falsecommands       Otherwise execute falsecommands
End
```

Remarks:

Any number of commands may be included in the groups delimited by If, Else, and End. If ... End blocks can be nested.

Examples:

```
If ¬ "{MacApp}"      Define {MacApp} if not already defined
    Set MacApp "{MPW}MacApp:"
End
```

Instead of displaying the result of the evaluated expression, the If command conditionally executes statements up until the next corresponding End statement. Any nonzero value is treated as a boolean TRUE.

A special `Else If` statement can be used to construct a structure functionally similar to the Pascal `CASE` or C `switch` statements. Only one `End` statement is required for an if statement that contains multiple `Else If` statements.

For example, the statements

```
If {#} == 1
    Set V "{1}"
Else If {#} == 2
    Set V "{2}"
Else If {#} == 3
    Set V "{3}"
Else
    Echo "### {0} -- wrong number
                     -- of arguments
    Exit 1
End
```

would require one, two, or three parameters to the command and would set variable {V} to the value of the last parameter.

LEAVING THE COMMAND FILE

As with procedures in a compiled language, it will sometimes be more convenient to leave a command file in the middle when an error is detected.

The `Exit` command will terminate the execution of a command file; it allows an optional clause to make that termination conditional on the evaluation of a shell expression.

Exit

Return from command file

Syntax:

Exit *status*	Return with *status*
Exit	Return with status from last command
Exit *status* If *expression*	Return with *status* if *expression* nonzero
Exit If *expression*	Return with last status if *expression* nonzero

Remarks:

A *status* of 0 indicates successful completion of the command. Without any parameters, `Exit` is equivalent to

```
Exit {Status}
```

Examples:

`Exit 0`	Leave command file with no error
`Exit 1 If {Status}`	Leave with status 1 if last command failed

`Exit` can also be used interactively, such as in a series of selected commands, much as `break` might be used in a C program or LEAVE in an MPW Pascal program.

The `Exit` command can be conditionally executed based on the value of an expression. The expression can be the result of command substitution, can be a shell variable, or can be a shell expression, as with the `If` command.

The same rules for If also apply to the interpretation of an expression on the `If` clause of an `Exit` statement. The command

```
Exit 2 If {#} ≠ 2
```

is an abbreviated notation for

```
If {#} ≠ 2
    Exit 2
End
```

PATTERN MATCHING

The same pattern-matching strings used by the `Find` and `Search` commands can also be used with evaluation expression involving the `=~` and `!~` string comparions operators. The expressions are subject to the same terms as are other regular expressions, as described in the previous chapter.

Figure 6–11 illustrated this when comparing two text strings. The comparison between two literal strings will be false unless the strings are identical; however, a comparison to a string pattern will be case insensitive, by default, and thus will match names of different cases.

More complex pattern-matching expressions can also be used. For example, the command

```
Alias FindTarget ∂
'If "{Active}" !~ /≈:Worksheet/;
    Echo "{Active}";
Else;
    Echo "{Target}";
End'
```

would display the name of the active window unless it is the worksheet, in which case it would display the name of the target window.

This is extremely useful for command substitution with commands when you know the worksheet is not a valid target. The custom menu command

```
AddMenu Control "Pascal compile"  ∂
    'Target "`FindTarget`"; Pascal "{Target}"'
```

would compile the active window if it is not the worksheet or the target window if the active window is the worksheet. Of course, the commands

```
AddMenu Control "Pascal compile"  ∂
    'Open "{Worksheet}"; Pascal "{Target}" '
```

would have a similar result but wouldn't make as interesting an example.

Pattern matching can also be used with tagged regular expressions. Unlike the Replace command, the tagged expressions are not used within the same command. Instead, tagged expressions in statements such as Evaluate or If are set as a shell variable of the same name if the strings match.

For example, for the default directory structure, the command

```
Evaluate "{MPW}" =~ /{Boot}(≈)®1/
```

would display 1 (true) as its result. As a side effect, it also sets the shell variable {®1} to the tagged pattern. Then, the command

```
Echo {®1}
```

would then display

```
MPW:
```

EXAMPLES: PATHNAME PARSING

The use of these expressions with pattern matching is illustrated by two command files to parse full pathnames and display components of the name.

The DirName command shown in Example 6–3 takes a single argument and displays the directory specification from the pathname. It uses an Evaluate command to match a regular expression, disposing of the actual (boolean) result of the evaluation. The matched string is then displayed.

DirName, as shown in Example 6–4, displays the file name, optionally removing a specific suffix (such as .o or .p) if found. The directory name is first stripped using pattern matching. Then, if a suffix must be stripped, it is removed if present. The example sets the variable {®1} twice, once with each pattern matching.

```
# SYNTAX
# DirName pathname
#
# DESCRIPTION
# "DirName" delivers all but the last level of the
# pathname in string, that is to say, everything up to
# the last ":". If the last level includes a
#
# NOTE
# UNIX System V has a comparable command named "dirname"
#
# SEE ALSO
# BaseName
#
# EXAMPLE
# Directory `DirName "{Target}"`
#
# Changes the directory to that of the default target
# window.


If {#} != 1
  Echo
    "### {0}-Wrong number of parameters were specified."
  Exit 1
End

( Evaluate "{1}" =~ /((([¬:]+:)+)®1?+/ ) > Dev:Null
Echo "'{®1}'"
```

Example 6–3:   Parsing directory from pathname

Both commands always quote their output, so it can be used with other commands; this could be done only when necessary but would require additional computation without a comparable benefit.

The `DirName` command can be extremely useful in conjunction with a custom menu to set the current directory. This can be defined using the command

```
AddMenu Control 'Make Default/,' Directory
        `DirName "{Active}"`'
```

The new menu item allows you to quickly change your current directory to be the folder containing the source file you are currently editing, using the Command-, equivalent from the keyboard. This is a must before running a compilation or command file that expects the current directory to be set to the file's folder.

```
# SYNTAX
# BaseName pathname [ suffix ]
#
# DESCRIPTION
# "BaseName" deletes any prefix ending in ":" and the
# suffix (if present in pathname) from string, and
# prints the result on the standard output.  If the
# pathname is a folder or volume, the last component of
# the name is retained.
#
# NOTE
# UNIX System V and BSD 4.2 have a comparable command
# named "basename".
#
# SEE ALSO
# DirName
#
# EXAMPLE
# rename {Target}.exe "{MPW}Tools:`BaseName {Target}.c`"
#
# If the name of the target window is Foo.c, then it
# does
#    Rename Foo.c.exe {MPW}Tools:Foo

If {#} < 1 OR {#} > 2
  Echo "### {0} - Wrong number of parameters specified."
  Exit 1
End


# Try to remove directory, if successful, then try
# suffix
If "{1}" =~ /([¬:]+:)*(≈)®1/
  Set n "{®1}"
  If {#} == 2 AND `Evaluate "{n}" =~ "/(≈)®1{2}/"`
    Echo "'{®1}'"
  Else
    Echo "'{n}'"
  End
Else
  Echo "'{1}'"
End
```

Example 6–4: Parsing file from pathname

EXAMPLE: STANDARD SOURCE FILE HEADER

The problem of adding a standard-form source file header, with some fields
fixed and others variable, is an excellent example of combining the power of
the shell and the editor using a custom menu and evaluation expressions.

Suppose your company has a policy of including a copyright notice in every source file. The corporate lawyers say it must go in before any original expression is added.* This can get pretty tedious after a while.

To make matters worse, one of your ace programmers was lured away to a higher-paying job writing billing packages for funeral homes and left behind 10,000 lines of undocumented spaghetti code. Your vice president of R&D has decreed that a standard block of comments will be added to the top of every source file, in the form of:

```
File:
Procedure:
Author:
Date:
Description:
```

Meanwhile, the problem of supporting the Swedish and Japanese versions of "SuperGraph" has gotten to be incredibly tedious, so one of the apprentice programmers has offered to help out by installing a source code control system. Unfortunately, it, too, requires a standard header, one that has an inflexible form and must contain a date and the name of the file.

You could enter these lines by hand or use a static prototype file that you copy this from each time. For example, the command

```
Open -r {Sources}Copyright
```

could be part of your UserStartup to have the text ready to go or just leave it in the Scrapbook.

It sure will be tedious to manually add the file name and the date each and every time. Given that you're a versatile programmer, you use Pascal, C, and Assembler, occasionally mess with resource files; and when forced, write MPW shell scripts. Since each has a different syntax for comments, you would need a different prototype for each.

However, a combination of a command file and a menu command will perform this automatically. The command file, because the changes will require more than a simple one-line command and a menu command to add the text to the active window, the one you're currently looking at.

Example 6–5 shows a command file to perform just such a function. If it is stored in the file AddCopyright, the custom menu definition

```
AddMenu 'Control' 'Add Header' AddCopyright
```

could be used to add the standard header to the current active file.

---

* Some say that copyright notices actually reduce your protection under trade secret law, but the author is not licensed to practice law in any jurisdiction. See *Legal Care for Your Software* by Daniel Remer (Nolo Press).

```
# DESCRIPTION
# Adds a copyright and brief description to the current
# active document.  It understands the comment format
# for Pascal, C, MPW assembler, Rez input files, and for
# MPW command files.
#
# NOTE
# Must be called as a menu command, with a custom menu
# definition such as
#    AddMenu Control 'Add Copyright' AddCopyright

Unalias  # delete any aliases, particularly for Date
If "{Active}" =~ "/≈.([ACPRacpr])®1/"
  Set MidRem ''
  If {®1} == "p"
    Set OpenRem '(*'; Set CloseRem '*)'
  Else If {®1} == "a"
    Set OpenRem '; '; Set CloseRem '; '; Set MidRem '; '
  Else # c or r
    Set OpenRem '/*'; Set CloseRem '*/'
  End
Else { MPW commands }
  Set OpenRem '# '; Set CloseRem '# '; Set MidRem '# '
End

Set N "{Active}"
If "{N}" =~ "/{MPW}(≈)®1/"
  Set N "∂{MPW∂}{®1}"
End

Set F `BaseName "{Active}"`
Find • "{Active}"
echo "{OpenRem} @(#)" "{F}" `date -s -d` ∂
  > "{Active}".§
echo {MidRem} "∂t{N}" >> "{Active}".§
echo {MidRem}>> "{Active}".§
echo {MidRem} "∂t{Copyright}∂n" >> "{Active}".§
echo {MidRem} "∂tFile:∂t∂t{F}" >> "{Active}".§
echo {MidRem} "∂tProcedure:∂t" >> "{Active}".§
echo {MidRem} "∂tAuthor:∂t∂t{MyName}" >> "{Active}".§
echo {MidRem} "∂tDate:∂t∂t`Date -a -d`" >> "{Active}".§
echo {MidRem} "∂tDescription:∂t***UNSPECIFIED***" >>∂
 "{Active}".§
echo "{CloseRem}∂n" >> "{Active}".§
Find §∆ "{Active}"
```

Example 6–5: Adding a standard header

The command file expects two symbols to be defined. Symbol {MyName} allows every programmer to share the same command file, while {Copyright} parameterizes the copyright by project. The following commands in the UserStartup would define these symbols:

```
Set MyName "Dave Smith"; Export MyName
Set Copyright "© 1987 Exceptional Software";
Export Copyright
```

The command file first looks to identify the type of file and its appropriate comment character. If no known suffix is used, it assumes it is an MPW shell command file (or a Make dependency file, which has the same comment syntax). These are used to set the opening and closing comment delimiters for those that require such delimiters or the line-at-a-time comment characters for other languages.

Before building the actual name of the source file, the shell command checks to see if its pathname includes {MPW}, in which case that part of the name is instead represented symbolically. Of course, if you normally store your source files in subdirectories of {Sources}, you can use this instead to make the name shorter and more meaningful.

Finally, the command file adds the header to the top of the active window and deselects the header using a final Find command. One possible header generated by the command file is shown in Figure 6–12.

6.6 Repeating Commands

MPW provides two standard statement blocks for looping within a series of commands. The For command begins a list of commands executed for each parameter in a list, while Loop will continue the execution of the commands indefinitely.

The Break and Continue commands can be used to override the normal action of a loop.

These looping commands are summarized in Table 6–6. Together, these commands allow you to program a series of commands to repeat actions unattended.

The entire For … End or Loop … End block is interpreted as one unit by the shell. If you enter the For (or Loop) interactively, the shell will wait until you enter the corresponding End before executing the loop. For and Loop blocks can be nested within each other and with If … End blocks.

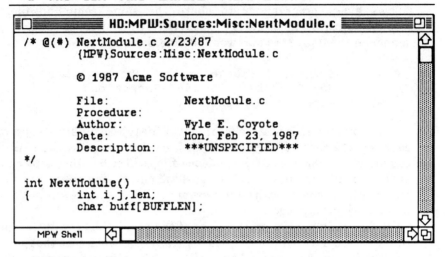

Figure 6–12: Generated header

Looping constructs

Construct	Description
For var In parm ... commands End	run commands with var set to each parm
Loop commands End	run commands indefinitely
Break Break If expression	transfer after End transfer after End if expression nonzero
Continue Continue If expression	transfer to beginning transfer to beginning if expression non-zero

Table 6–6:   Looping constructs

LOOPING WITH PARAMETERS

Unlike its namesake in procedural programming languages, the shell's For command does not iterate a numeric counter through a specific range. Instead, it repeats a block of commands (statements) for each parameter in a list. This reflects the normal use of iteration in a command file, with a list of command parameters or an expanded list of file names.

For

Repeat block of commands for each item in list

Syntax:

```
For var In parm ...
  commands
End
```
Execute *commands* with *var* set to each *parm*

Remarks:

The *commands* are executed with shell variable *var* set to the value of each parameter in the list. If no parameters are specified, the block is skipped entirely.

The loop can be abnormally terminated by a Break command. Continue skips to the beginning of *commands* with the next parameter.

Example:

```
For F in ≈.p ≈.c
  Open -r "{F}"
End
```
Open every Pascal or C file read-only

The For command is often used to operate on a series of parameters passed to a command file. The commands

```
For F In {"Parameters"}
  If "{F}" =~ /≈.p/
    Pascal {F}
  Else If "{F}" =~ /≈.c/
    C {F}
  Else If "{F}" =~ /≈.a/
    Asm {F}
  End
End
```

could be used as the starting point for a command file Compile, which would run the appropriate compiler on each in a list of file names.

For is also used with command substitution. The command

```
For W in `Windows`
  Echo Open {W}
End > "{ShellDirectory}UserStartup"
```

would erase the old contents of UserStartup (not necessarily a good idea) and replace it with a series of commands to open the documents now in use. An obvious place to put such a series of commands is in {ShellDirectory}Quit, to be performed when you leave MPW. The Suspend and Resume files use a similar construct to save and restore documents when you leave MPW to run an application.

Example 6–6 shows the use of command substitution to build a menu with a list of source files that you regularly work on. No matter what directory you are currently in, selecting the corresponding menu item would open the indicated source file.

```
# Expects file {ShellDirectory}ProjectList to contain
# a list of file names, in the form:
# :Shell:UserStartup
# :Shell:ProjectList
# (-
# :Sources:Demo.p
# :Sources:Demo.r
# (-
# :Sources:Main.c
# :Sources:Util.c
# :Sources:Init.c
#

If "{MPW}" =~ /(≈)®1:/
    Set MPWBase "{®1}"
End

For F in `Catenate "{ShellDirectory}ProjectList"`
    AddMenu Project "{F}" 'Open "'"{MPWBase}{F}"'"'
End
```

Example 6–6: Building a project menu

These commands would normally be included as part of the StartUp or UserStartup command files. Figure 6–13 shows a custom menu constructed by Example 6–6.

Another important use of the For command is to operate on a series of file names that are expanded by the shell. This is an important area in which the shell can be used to perform a repeated series of tasks. For example, the commands

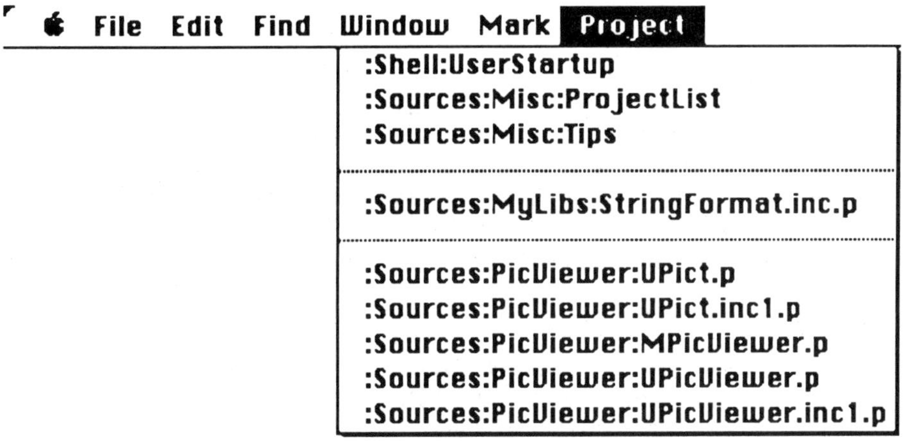

```
 ┌                                                                    
   ⌘   File   Edit   Find   Window   Mark   Project
 ──────────────────────────────┬──────────────────────────────────
                               │  :Shell:UserStartup
                               │  :Sources:Misc:ProjectList
                               │  :Sources:Misc:Tips
                               │ ..........................................
                               │  :Sources:MyLibs:StringFormat.inc.p
                               │ ..........................................
                               │  :Sources:PicViewer:UPict.p
                               │  :Sources:PicViewer:UPict.inc1.p
                               │  :Sources:PicViewer:MPicViewer.p
                               │  :Sources:PicViewer:UPicViewer.p
                               │  :Sources:PicViewer:UPicViewer.inc1.p
                               └──────────────────────────────────
```

Figure 6–13: A project menu

```
For F in ≈
    Open -t {F}
    Find •
    Replace /4-([0-9])®1/ /3-®1/
    Close -y {F}
End
```

could be used to rename the first comment in a series of sample programs (such as for this book) from 4-*n* to 3-*n*.

A series of commands can also be used to change the actual names of the files. Example 6–7 shows a command file which renames the source files in the current directory from the naming convention used by the Lisa Workshop to that of MPW. It changes names of the form `Sample.C.Text` to `Sample.c` and several other names as indicated. If it encounters an unrecognized name, it leaves it unchanged and displays an error message.

OVERRIDING LOOP CONTROL

The `For` and `Loop` control blocks can be prematurely exited using the `Break` command. The `Continue` command can be used to resume the execution of the block at its next iteration.

As with the `Exit` command, `Break` and `Continue` recognize an optional `If` clause to specify conditional execution of the command.

```
# Convert names
# From     To
# ----     --
# FOOR.TEXT    FOO.R      RMaker resource source
# FOOASM.TEXT  FOO.A      TLA (assembler) source
# FOO.C.TEXT   FOO.c      C source
# FOO.TEXT     FOO.p      Pascal source
#

For F in ≈
  If "{F}" =~ /(≈)®1.TEXT/
     Set N "{®1}"
     If "{N}" =~ /(≈)®1R/
        Rename "{F}" "{®1}.R"   # resource source
     Else If "{N}" =~ /(≈)®1ASM/
        Rename "{F}" "{®1}.A"   # assembler source
     Else If "{N}" =~ /(≈)®1.C/
        Rename "{F}" "{®1}.c"   # C source
     Else
        Rename "{F}" "{N}.p"    # Pascal source
     End
  Else
     Echo Unable to convert name "'{F}'"
  End
End
```

Example 6–7:   **Renaming Lisa Workshop files**

Break, Continue

Leave or cycle in `For` or `Loop` iteration

Syntax:

Break	Transfer after `End` of enclosing `For` or `Loop`
Break If *expression*	Transfer after `End` if *expression* nonzero
Continue	Transfer to beginning of enclosing `For` or `Loop`
Continue If *expression*	Transfer to beginning if *expression* nonzero

Remarks:

The shell indicates an error if a `Break` or `Continue` are found outside a loop.

Examples:

```
Break If {X} < 1        Define variable MyDir for a folder
Continue                Go to next iteration of For or Loop
```

Example 6–8 shows a command file to allow you to run applications from within the shell by specifying only part of the name of the application. It will search for the application in one of a list of directories.

If you give your applications names such as ResEdit 1.1, it would allow you to enter

```
Run ResEdit
```

without having to remember the version number.

The command file uses the For command to search each directory for a file of type 'APPL' that matches the name. If no files match for the current directory, a Continue skips to the next directory. If more than one name matches, the command file terminates with an error.

Otherwise, a confirmation dialog is presented to give you one last chance to change your mind. The command file then runs the application using the shell's standard syntax for doing so.

INDEFINITE LOOPING

Unlike the For command, the Loop command will continue a block of commands indefinitely. It can be used for iterations that have arbitrary termination conditions or to implement an iteration for a specific number of times.

Loop

Repeat commands until Break

Syntax:

```
Loop                    Execute commands until terminated
  commands
End
```

Remarks:

The block commands will normally include either Break or Exit.

Example:

```
Loop                         Repeat melody indefinitely
  Beep Gb,50 E,50 D,50 Db,50 ∂
   -1B,50 -1A,50 -1B,50 Db,50
End
```

```
# SYNTAX
# Run application [ filenames ]
#
# DESCRIPTION
# "Run" attempts to find an application in one of many
# predefined directories that match the name application
# which can be a partial name specification.
#
# If it finds only one such application it runs it using
# the remaining parameters as document names.
#
# EXAMPLE
# Run Write "{Book}Chapter 7"

Set name "{1}"
Shift 1
Set Exit 0     # suppress termination

Set dirlist "'{Boot}Applications:' '{MPW}Applications:'"

For dir In {dirlist}
    Begin      # give me a list of 'name1' 'name2'
        Set prog "`files -t APPL {dir}≈{name}≈`"
    End ≥ Dev:Null    # suppress no-match message

    Continue If ¬ "{prog}"   # go on if null

    If "{prog}" =~ /∂'≈∂' ≈/ OR "{prog}" =~ /[¬∂']* ≈/
        # multiple names, separated by spaces
        Alert ∂
    "Cannot run "{name}"; multiple names matched: {prog}"
        Exit 2
    End

    Confirm "Starting {prog}" || ( Beep; Exit 0)

# Launch it as MPW command, using full pathname
    {prog} {"Parameters"}
    Exit
End

Alert ∂
""{name}" does not match any application in folders
{dirlist}."
```

Example 6–8: Running an application

Because every Loop ... End block will continue without interrruption, you would not use this construct without a Break (or Exit) command within the loop to terminate on some condition, unless you want to tie up your Mac until someone presses Command-period.

Example 6–9 shows the use of a Loop ... End block to scan a pathname. The command file converts a name of the form /dev/null to dev:null by replacing each occurrence of a slash with a colon until no more are found.

```
# SYNTAX
# CvtPath pathname
#
# DESCRIPTION
# "CvtPath" tries to convert a UNIX-style path string to
# one compatible with MPW.
#
# It also supports
#    ~/xyz      {MPW}xyz
#
# NOTE
# Unfortunately, "/" is a special character to the
# shell.
# Failure to quote the name will give the error:
#    ### MPW Shell - /s must occur in pairs.
#
# SEE ALSO
# BaseName (Example 6-4)
#
# EXAMPLE
# Directory `CvtPath "~/Sources"`


If {#} != 1
  Echo "### {0} - Wrong number of parameters were speci-
fied."
  Exit 1
End

Set P "{1}"
Set C 0   # no path separators seen
# Scan through the name, converting '/' to ':'
Loop
  Break If "{P}" !~ /(≈)®1∂/(≈)®2/
  Set P "{®1}:{®2}"
  Set C 1
End
```

```
If {C}              # path separator seen
  If "{P}" =~ /:(≈)®1/
    Echo "'{®1}'"          # /a/b -> a:b
  Else # no leading / means leading :
    If "{P}" =~ /~:(≈)®1/
      Echo "'{MPW}{®1}'"        # ~/a -> {MPW}a
    Else
      Echo "':{P}'"      # a/b -> :a:b
    End
  End
Else
  Echo "'{P}'"       # a -> a
End
```

Example 6–9:   Converting pathname syntax

This command file can be used as part of a simple series of commands to make a flat directory hierarchical. Suppose you had a series of file names of the form Project1/Main.p, Project2/Main.p. If Example 6–9 is stored in command file CvtPath, the commands

```
For F in ≈
    Move {F} `CvtPath {F}`
End
```

would rename these files into separate folders :Project1:, :Project2:, and so on. Needless to say, if your file name syntax included – as a name separator instead of /, a slightly modified CvtPath could be used to transform these names.

The Loop command can also be used to construct more conventional iterations for a specific number of trips. The following commands illustrate such a loop, using the Break, If, and Evaluate commands:

```
# Perform FOR i := 1 TO n
Set i 0
Loop
    Set I `Evaluate {i} + 1`
    Break If {i} > {n}
    # commands
End
```

Example 6–10 uses a similar construct to count the number of disks duplicated.* However, instead of terminating after a particular number, the

---

* It also uses the Eject command, not previously introduced, to eject and unmount the disk in drive no. 1, the internal floppy.

loop continues until the Cancel button of a Confirm dialog is clicked. The entire output of the loop is directed to a disk file that provides a log of the contents of each disk.

```
# Note: Only Finder can create a DeskTop file
#
# To avoid long delays when the duplicate is used, use a
# master floppy that already includes a DeskTop file
#

Set C 0Set Vol "Distrib"
Loop
  Confirm "Insert a blank disk in internal drive." ||
Break
# Disk Initialization Package will put up initialization
# dialog

  Rename `Volumes 1` "{Vol}":  # change name from
                                 #'Untitled'
  Delete -y "{Vol}":≈   # in case the disk isn't new
  Duplicate ≈ "{Vol}":

  Set C `Evaluate {C} + 1`
  Echo ∂f-----------------------------------------------
  Echo At `Date -a`, disk #{C}
  Files -l "{Vol}":
  Echo

  Eject 1
End >> "{MPW}Duplication Log"

Alert "A total of {V} disks were duplicated"
```

Example 6-10: Duplicating disks

Chapter 7

Pascal

THIS CHAPTER DESCRIBES USING THE OPTIONAL PASCAL COMPILER for MPW and the tools and libraries supplied with it. It does not attempt to teach Pascal, which, for first-time users of the language, can be learned from one of the standard texts listed in the Bibliography. Instead, it describes the differences between MPW Pascal and other Pascal implementations and how to use MPW Pascal to build Macintosh programs.

The MPW Pascal compiler is an outgrowth of the Lisa Pascal crosscompiler used for most of the early Macintosh development. Like its Lisa predecessor, MPW Pascal supports full access to the Toolbox and OS traps. The compiler also includes many C-like features that make it easier to use for systems programming.

Other MPW extensions include the use of the units for separate compilation, a standard string data type, and a wide range of embedded compiler options. The compiler comes with a complete set of libraries used for building MPW Pascal programs.

The `Pascal` compilation command and the additional formatting tools included with MPW are also described. The chapter concludes with a sample MPW tool.

7.1 Getting Started

This section contains just enough information about the Pascal compiler and linker to get started. A complete discussion of the compiler options is

335

deferred to the final section of this chapter, while the linker is the primary topic of Chapter 10.

THE COMPILATION PROCESS

Developing a program in MPW Pascal is not much different than with most compiled programming languages. You edit a source program in one or more text files, compile it, link the compiled object files into an executable program, and then run the program.

By convention, MPW Pascal expects the source file names to end in .p, as in Sample.p, but there is nothing to enforce this convention. Each file must define a single Pascal PROGRAM (or library unit), although sometimes the source is split across several files and automatically merged through directives to the MPW Pascal compiler.

Programs are compiled by the Pascal command. If you had a file Sample.p, the command

```
Pascal Sample.p
```

would compile the Pascal source statements in Sample.p and report any errors to the diagnostic output unit. Unlike mainframe compilers you may be familiar with, the compiler does not produce a formatted source listing, although separate commands provide a decent substitute.

When it encounters a syntax error, the compiler normally displays the line with the error and the preceding line, followed by the error messages and then a shell command to select the line with the error. Figure 7–1 shows Pascal error messages from source text entered interactively to the compiler.

If it does not detect any errors, the compiler produces an object file containing the compiled program. The file name will be the same as the source name with .o appended. If the source program is Sample.p, the compiled code will go to Sample.p.o—*not* Sample.o, as on many systems.

If you've compiled source for a library, you can save the object file for later use with other programs. If you have several such object files, you may wish to merge them into a single object file using MPW's Lib command.

To build a program, you must link it into a form suitable for use by the Macintosh Segment Loader (an application) or the shell itself (an MPW tool). In the simplest case, you take a single compiled program file and merge it with MPW Pascal libraries using the Link command.

Link allows you to specify the name of the program to be created, any object or library files to be used in linking, the type of program to be created and a variety of diagnostic and formatting options. Link and the standard object libraries are described in this chapter from a "cookbook" standpoint to put together a few sample programs, with a more complete discussion deferred until Chapter 10.

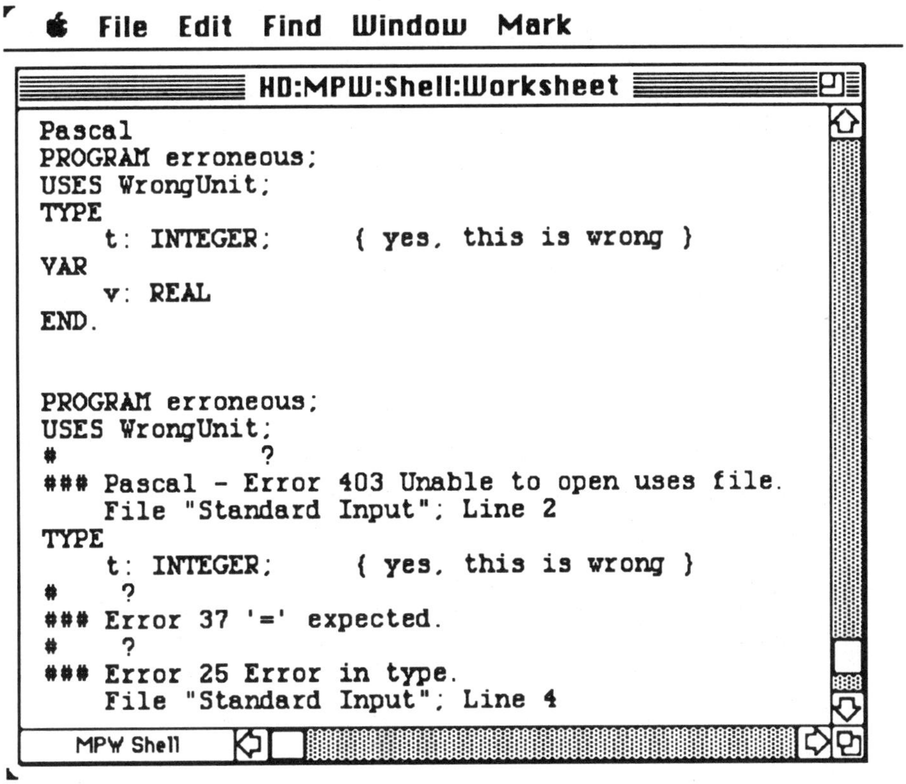

```
 r  É  File  Edit  Find  Window  Mark
```

```
═══════════════ HD:MPW:Shell:Worksheet ═══════════════
Pascal
PROGRAM erroneous;
USES WrongUnit;
TYPE
      t: INTEGER;        { yes, this is wrong }
VAR
      v: REAL
END.


PROGRAM erroneous;
USES WrongUnit;
#              ?
### Pascal - Error 403 Unable to open uses file.
    File "Standard Input"; Line 2
TYPE
      t: INTEGER;        { yes, this is wrong }
#     ?
### Error 37 '=' expected.
#     ?
### Error 25 Error in type.
    File "Standard Input"; Line 4
   MPW Shell
```

Figure 7–1:   Pascal compiler error messages

A SAMPLE PROGRAM

To illustrate building an MPW program requires a sample program. Example 7–1 shows a short program to display information about the current memory status. It uses standard Memory Manager calls to obtain the size of standard RAM and the available space on the stack and the heap, then frees space on the heap and lists the available space again.

If the program is stored in file MemStatus.p, it would be compiled by the command:

```
Pascal MemStatus.p
```

Since it produces textual output, MemStatus is more suitable to run underneath the MPW shell (which provides text display and redirection capabilities) than as an application, which should be more graphical and

```
{ Example 7-1: Simple MPW Pascal program }

(* MPW tool to display current memory status -
   Requires 128K ROM
*)
PROGRAM MemStatus;

USES
  MemTypes, QuickDraw,  { required for use with OSIntf }
  OSIntf;        { for Memory Manager routines, maxSize }

CONST
  OneK = 1024;
  OneMeg = OneK * OneK;


PROCEDURE WriteSymbolic(num: LONGINT);
BEGIN
  Write(num:0,' bytes(');  { no leading spaces }
  IF num >= OneMeg THEN
    Write((num/OneMeg):0:1, ' Mb) ')
  ELSE
    Write((num DIV OneK):0, 'K) ');
END;


BEGIN
  WriteSymbolic(ORD(TopMem));
  WriteLn('of RAM is installed.');
  WriteSymbolic(StackSpace);            { 128K ROM only }
  WriteLn('is available on the stack.');
  WriteSymbolic(FreeMem);
  WriteLn('is available on the heap.');
  PurgeMem(maxSize);    { purge all shell resources }
  WriteSymbolic(FreeMem);
  WriteLn('is available after purging the heap.');
END.
```

Example 7–1: A simple Pascal program

Mac-like. From a development standpoint, this is also fortunate since the shell can run tools within its own environment more quickly than exiting and launching a separate application.

To build an MPW tool, you tell the linker to build a program with the appropriate file type and creator. These are done using Link options. The Link command also requires the list of object files and libraries to be used; so the complete command to build the program looks like:

```
Link -o MemStatus -t MPST -c 'MPS ' MemStatus.p.o ∂
    "{Libraries}Runtime.o" "{Libraries}Interface.o" ∂
    "{PLibraries}PasLib.o"
```

When you run the program, it runs within the MPW shell, as does `Pascal` and a number of other commands supplied with MPW. Much of the shell also stays in memory, as long as there's room. The `PurgeMem` call in the example gets rid of the shell resources being kept around. As the output in Figure 7–2 shows, this makes a sizable difference in the amount of memory available, although such calls will be performed automatically by the Memory Manager if a tool is running low on space.

7.2 Language Overview

This section describes features of MPW Pascal not found in all Pascal implementations. Many of these extensions are intended for Macintosh systems programming, such as direct access to the ROM or low-memory globals, and were present in the Lisa Pascal cross-compiler. These extensions give MPW Pascal a C-like flavor, allowing direct manipulation of pointers, as well as other isolated extensions.

This section also compares MPW Pascal with the ISO Pascal standard, describing the few areas in which it does not conform to the standard. MPW Pascal is also compared to UCSD Pascal, as it includes many of the features first implemented there.

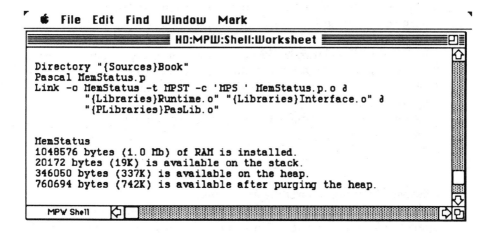

Figure 7–2:   Sample program results

DIFFERENCES FROM STANDARD PASCAL

A descendant of Algol, Pascal was designed by Niklaus Wirth and first implemented in 1970. The language proliferated in the early and mid-1970s, prompting two important efforts to standardize the language. The ISO Pascal standard (1982) was documented in a revised edition of the original *Pascal User Manual and Report*. A joint effort of the American National Standards Institute and the IEEE resulted in the ANS Pascal standard (1983).

This subsection summarizes the differences that would cause a Pascal program written to the ISO standard to be rejected or interpreted differently by MPW Pascal. MPW Pascal also has a number of characteristics that typically vary between implementations and thus should not be relied upon if portability is important. It also includes significant extensions to the language. Both are summarized in later subsections.

The ISO standard defines procedures `Pack` and `Unpack` to convert between packed and unpacked arrays. These are not available in MPW Pascal.

The standard also optionally defines a type of array parameter that allows the size of the array to be determined at run time by the routine using the parameter. These "conformant" arrays pass the upper and lower array bounds as implicit named parameters to a procedure. In the declaration

```
PROCEDURE Sum
    (arr: ARRAY[lodim..hidim: INTEGER] OF REAL);
```

`lodim` and `hidim` are variables that can be used in `Sum` to obtain the actual size of the `arr` array. A version of Pascal that does not support conformant arrays is considered a Level 0 implementation of the ISO standard.

One of the important needs for conformant arrays, to obtain the length of a character string, is handled by MPW Pascal's built-in `STRING` data type, which is described later. MPW Pascal does not interpret string literals (e.g., 'this message') as `PACKED ARRAY[lo..hi] OF CHAR` but instead as `STRING` data. However, string literals are assignment compatible with packed arrays, described later.

As defined by standard dialects, MPW Pascal accepts parameters on a program declaration, such as:

```
PROGRAM Sum(Input, Output);
```

However, they are ignored by MPW Pascal.

The standard also defines the @ and ^ characters as synonyms for the uparrow (↑) pointer symbol. However, in MPW Pascal, as with Lisa Pascal, the ^ is used as the standard Pascal pointer referencing operator. The @ sign is defined as the "take the address of" operator, similar to C's & operator. This can be best illustrated by a simple example:

```
TYPE
   IntPtr = ^INTEGER; { declare; not @INTEGER }
VAR
   i: INTEGER;
   p: IntPtr;
BEGIN
   p := @i;      { address of i; ^i is a syntax error }
   p^ := 2;      { dereference p; p@ is a syntax error }
```

Among the various Pascal dialects, one of the most influential was developed for use by students at the University of California at San Diego. UCSD Pascal featured several important enhancements, including support for separate compilation and a string primitive data type.

Apple historically has shown a preference for the UCSD Pascal dialect. Apple Pascal (for the Apple II) is a version of UCSD Pascal with the UCSD p-System interpreter, and Apple later adapted a native-code 68000 compiler for UCSD Pascal for use on the Lisa.

The MPW Pascal compiler, in turn, is derived from release 3.1 of Lisa Pascal, although it includes a number of additional features beyond Lisa Pascal. The final release of Lisa Pascal (3.9) was later updated with many of the features found in release 1.0 of MPW Pascal.

Among the extensions of the Lisa compiler were changes to Pascal to support object-oriented programming. This extended Pascal language was referred to as Clascal. In conjunction with Wirth, Apple refined the Clascal syntax into a simpler design known as Object Pascal, which is directly supported by the MPW Pascal compiler.

The important differences between MPW Pascal, Lisa Pascal (2.0 and 3.9), UCSD Pascal* and the ISO standard are summarized in Table 7–1.

IMPLEMENTATION CHARACTERISTICS

For any programming language, a number of features will naturally vary from one compiler to the next. If you've ever ported a program from one machine to another, you know this is the "fine print" that can pose the greatest obstacle to portability.

Only the first 63 characters of an identifier are unique in MPW Pascal. As with most Pascal implementations, the language is case insensitive. Identifiers can also include an underscore (_) and % character, although the latter is reserved by Apple for special uses.

The INTEGER data type is 16 bits, with the value of MaxInt defined as 32,767. This is the natural size for the MC68000 processor and is also consistent with UCSD Pascal and its PDP-11 heritage.

---

*As defined by *The UCSD Pascal Handbook* by Randy Clark and Stephen Koehler, Prentice-Hall (1982)

	MPW Pascal	Key Pascal differences Lisa Pascal	UCSD Pascal	ISO Pascal
Conformant arrays				•
Pack, Unpack				•
Direct Real arithmetic	•	†	•	•
Units	•	•	•	
SIZEOF (type) function	•	•	•	
STRING data type	•	•	•	
LONGINT data type	•	•		
OBJECT data type	•			
Pointer type coercion	•	•		
EXIT, HALT	•	•	•	
CYCLE, LEAVE	•	†		
Extended CASE	•	•		
Embedded compiler options		•	•	•
Conditional compilation	•	•	•	
Include files	•	•	•	
Range checking	•	•	•	
Segmentation	•	•	•	
** operator	•	†		
| and & operators	•	†		
Bit-manipulation routines	•	†		
Inline machine code	•	•		
External routines	•	•	•	
C routines	•	†		
Routines as parameters	•	•		•

† Later releases only

Table 7–1: Key Pascal differences

However, many of the Macintosh Toolbox and OS routines operate on larger quantities—such as the size of a memory block, resource, or file. The LONGINT (or, if you prefer, LongInt) data type is a full 32-bit integer, with the value of MaxLongInt defined as 2,147,483,647. The MPW compiler automatically decides between INTEGER and LONGINT data types in constants and data types. For example, in the declaration

```
UnsignedInt: 0..65535;
```

the variable is automatically defined as a subrange of a LONGINT type. Any integral constant not in the range of INTEGER will be treated as a LONGINT.

Binary operations (including multiplication) on two INTEGER values will produce an INTEGER; if either operand is a LONGINT type, the operation will be performed using 32-bit arithmetic. An integer can be forced to type LONGINT using the ORD4 intrinsic function. However, this is not necessary for assignment or parameter passing by value, as the compiler automatically converts between the two types by sign extension or truncation, as appropriate.

MPW Pascal supports three floating point data types:

- REAL is 32 bits and is implemented as SANE's Single, as described in Chapter 2; SINGLE is accepted as a synonym;

- DOUBLE, 64 bits, corresponding to SANE Double;

- EXTENDED, 80 bits, corresponding to SANE Extended; this data type is represented using 96 bits when code is generated for direct access to the Motorola MC68881 floating point coprocessor.

By default, MPW Pascal programs perform all floating point calculations using SANE. Expressions are evaluated by converting REAL and DOUBLE values to 80-bit EXTENDED quantities and then converting the final result back to the variable type, if necessary.

For the Macintosh II, a compiler option (described later in the chapter) allows you to directly perform floating point calculations using the MC68881. In this case, all calculations are performed using the 68881's 96-bit extended values, although the accuracy and range of values are the same as for SANE's 80-bit type.

The data type COMP (alias COMPUTATIONAL) is the SANE 64-bit integer format. Although it's not a floating point type, computations with COMP are also performed by conversion to EXTENDED. As described in Chapter 2, all four types include Not a Number values, while the three floating point types include positive and negative infinities.

Sets in MPW Pascal are limited to 2040 elements (as in s: SET OF 0..2039;) or 255 bytes. Dynamically allocated and local arrays are limited only by the size of available memory; in particular, they are not restricted by the 32K addressing limitation found in some compilers.

The control variable of a FOR block must be local in scope, i.e., must not be accessible at an outer scope. This allows the compiler to perform certain loop optimizations without regard to unanticipated side effects. In the statement

```
FOR count := 1 to limit DO
```

the variable count must be declared in the current procedure, not in any unit. If the loop is in a local procedure (nested within another procedure), count must be declared in that procedure and not as part of the enclosing procedure. Variable count can only be declared as a PROGRAM global variable if the loop is in the (unnamed) main program block.

MPW Pascal uses the Macintosh's extended ASCII character set. Printable characters from 32 to 126 correspond to the ASCII definition, one of the approved variants for the ISO standard character set. Characters greater than 127 are not syntactically significant but can be included as part of character literals or comments.

The implementation-specific special characters of MPW Pascal are shown in Table 7–2.

Implementation-specific special characters

Characters	Equivalent	Description
[ ]	(. .)	Array indexing or set construction
{ }	(* *)	Comments
{$ }	(*$)	Embedded compiler option
^		Pointer symbol
@		Address of unary operator†
**		Exponentiation operator
&		Short-circuit AND
|		Short-circuit OR
_		Valid identifier character
%		Valid identifier character
$		Begin hex constant

† Unlike ISO standard, @ is not equivalent to ^

Table 7–2:   Implementation-specific special characters

Note that MPW Pascal reserves comments beginning with a $ as embedded compiler options, as will be discussed later in this chapter.

STRINGS

Standard Pascal implementations manipulate character strings as PACKED ARRAY ... OF CHAR data types. However, MPW Pascal uses a built in data type STRING for variable-length character string manipulation, similar to that of UCSD Pascal.

Each string has two lengths, a logical length and a physical length. The logical length is the actual number of characters in the string, which will be used when the string is assigned, displayed, or otherwise used. The physical length is the amount of memory allocated for the string characters and thus the maximum logical length. When range checking is enabled, MPW Pascal checks to make sure that all logical lengths are within the physical limit.

The declaration of a string variable can include the physical length, as in:

```
msg: STRING[20];
```

This would declare a data structure to represent strings of 0 to 20 bytes in length. If no length is specified, the maximum possible length (255 bytes) is assumed.

As with any data type, strings can be assigned, compared, and passed as value or VAR parameters. MPW supports the standard UCSD functions for strings. The most commonly used are Length, which returns the logical length of a string, and Concat, which combines two strings to form a new one. Substrings are manipulated using the Pos and Copy functions and the Insert and Delete procedures, which are described later.

The actual implementation of a string is equivalent to a declaration of:

```
msg: PACKED ARRAY[0..20] OF CHAR;
```

The characters of msg can be indexed directly, as if declared as an array. For example,

```
IF msg[1] = 'x' THEN
    msg[1] := 'X';
```

would check and modify the first character of the string. This syntax should not be used to add characters to the end of the string since the length will not be automatically updated.

The value msg[0] contains the logical length. Since this is of type CHAR, numeric manipulation of the length requires the use of CHR and ORD functions. Normally, the Length function is used instead. The layout of a Pascal string is summarized in Figure 7–3.

In MPW Pascal, character constants are automatically interpreted as STRING rather than PACKED ARRAY ... OF CHAR. The null string literal can be used to set the logical length of a string variable to zero, as in:

```
msg := '';
```

Longer constants can be used to set by the characters and the logical length of a string variable. For example,

```
cr := 'M';              { placeholder to set length }
cr[1] := CHR($0D);      { ASCII CR character)
```

would set the length of the string to 1 using a string constant, then change the value of the first character to be a nonprinting character.

String constants can also be assigned to a PACKED ARRAY ... OF CHAR with the appropriate length. Arrays can also be assigned to each other and

```
s: STRING[12];

s := 'This';
```

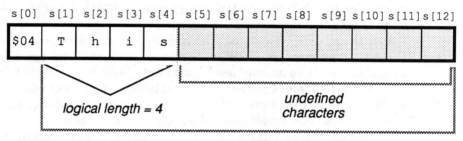

Figure 7–3:   String representation

compared for equality and inequality. When mixing packed arrays and strings, you should be aware the two types are not equivalent—the first byte of a string is a length, not a data character.

Most of the Macintosh Toolbox procedures and data structures use a data type Str255, which is not built in to the compiler. Instead, it is declared by unit MemTypes as equivalent to STRING[255].

POINTER MANIPULATION

MPW Pascal includes a number of important extensions that were provided by Lisa Pascal to allow manipulation of pointers. Nearly as powerful as those of C, these extended pointer capabilities allow direct access to arbitrary memory locations (such as low-memory globals) needed for Macintosh programming. They are also essential when using pointers to the variant or embedded data structures of the Macintosh ROM, such as those defined by the Window Manager or File Manager.

The @ unary operator is used to take the address of a variable. This creates a value of a type compatible with *any* pointer type: there is no type checking to verify that the variable matches the pointer type. For example, the statement

```
VAR
    gp: GrafPtr
. . .
gp := @record;
```

will be accepted no matter what the type of record.

There are some restrictions on taking the address of an element of a PACKED ARRAY or a field of a PACKED RECORD. The @ operator can always be used with unpacked component variables since these are customarily aligned to word (16-bit) boundaries or, in the case of a BOOLEAN, byte boundaries.

However, when MPW Pascal is directed to pack a data structure, it will not take up an entire byte for a component variable if several such variables can be stored in successive bits. Since 68000 addresses are the address of a byte, there is no valid address for such variables.

This means the @ operator cannot be used with such variables, and they also cannot be passed as a VAR parameter. The compiler will give an error message to let you know the usage is invalid, and the cure is to not pack the data structure or to use a temporary local variable to hold the value.

MPW Pascal supports several type coercion functions for making pointer values assignment compatible without changing the actual value, including POINTER, ORD, and ORD4. These functions allow you to bypass Pascal's strict type checking when performing systems programming operations, although they also bypass the safeguards provided by that type of checking. Normally, they are used in certain well-defined circumstances in which you deliberately coerce or reinterpret the type of a value; the remainder of the time, the normal type compatibility rules should be observed.

The function POINTER changes the type of a scalar value (such as an integer) to be compatible with any pointer type. For example,

```
TYPE
   WordPtr = ^INTEGER;
CONST
   Rom85 = $28E;        { system global, a word }
VAR
   Rom128k: BOOLEAN;    { 128k ROM features available }
   romp: WordPtr;       { pointer to signed integer }

...
   romp := POINTER(Rom85);
   IF romp^ < 0 THEN
      Rom128k := TRUE;
```

uses an integer constant as a pointer to a low-memory system global variable, in this case the variable that indicates the availability of the new traps introduced with the Macintosh Plus (and 512Ke) ROM.

Pointer types can be used as 32-bit integers after conversion with the ORD (or ORD4) functions. This can be used to perform arithmetic on pointers, such as testing to see whether a pointer is odd or incrementing through a series of bytes in memory.

Each new type in MPW Pascal automatically defines a *type coercion function* of the same name. These functions allow the transfer of an arbitrary bit pattern between two variables while overriding Pascal's normal type compatibility checks. These functions are normally used on pointers and handles but are defined for any type.

The safest and cleanest way to manipulate pointer types is with the type coercion functions rather than with the completely untyped POINTER function. They are often used to convert the type of pointers in the Toolbox's related data structures. For example, the Window Manager's WindowRecord is by default equivalenced to a QuickDraw GrafPort since it's most often used as a GrafPort. To get at the WindowRecord-specific fields, a type coercion is necessary, as in:

```
PROCEDURE MyNewTextWindow(thetext: TEHandle);
CONST
   WINDdoc = 128;
VAR
   w: WindowPtr;            { equivalent to GrafPtr }
   wp: WindowPeek;         { pointer to WindowRecord }
   r: Rect;
...
   w := GetNewWindow(WINDdoc, NIL, NIL);
   r := w^.portRect;       { field of GrafPort }
   wp := WindowPeek(w);   { coerce the pointer to
                             another type}
   wp^.refCon := ORD(TEHandle);{ field of
                                  WindowRecord }
```

As illustrated by the example, type coercion is also used on Macintosh handles, which, as noted in Chapter 2, are nothing more than pointers to other pointers.

The coercion functions are also used to restore the type of a pointer after it has been used in an arithmetic expression, such as when scanning through successive memory location. For example,

```
VAR
   bytep: Ptr;            { standard pointer to a byte }
   i, len, sum: INTEGER;
...
FOR i := 1 to len DO
BEGIN
   sum := sum + bytep^;    { add next byte }
   bytep := Ptr(ORD(bytep) + 1);
END;
```

adds the contents of a series of bytes, such as for a checksum.

Finally, the SIZEOF function can be used to determine the actual size of a variable or type. This is useful when indexing through memory locations or when copying a record to memory or to or from disk. The result of SIZEOF is always treated as a constant by the compiler since the size of a data type is fixed at compile time.

In the statements

```
VAR
   thep: Ptr;
   r: Rect;

BlockMove(thep, @r, SIZEOF(Rect));
thep := Ptr(ORD(thep) + SIZEOF(Rect));
```

the SIZEOF value is used both to transfer the data from memory and to update the pointer. The SIZEOF (Rect) reference could also be written SIZEOF (r) since the function will accept either a type or a variable of that type.

You might be tempted to rewrite this example as:

```
VAR
   rp := RectPtr;
...
rp := RectPtr(thep);
r := rp^;
thep := Ptr(ORD(thep) + SIZEOF(Rect));
```

Although this works well on the MC68020 processor of the Macintosh II, it will fail miserably on the MC68000 of the Macintosh Plus and SE if the value of thep is odd. If you're using a pointer to scan through an arbitrary section of memory, direct transfers through dereferencing should be limited to data types of a single byte.

CONTROL STRUCTURES

MPW Pascal includes several important extensions for structuring the control flow of a program. Two are built in pseudoprocedures to control execution of routines, while another two statements modify the execution of the current loop. MPW Pascal also extends to the CASE selection statement, while offering new interpretations of boolean expressions, normally used in IF and WHILE statements.

From UCSD Pascal, MPW inherits two procedures to handle routine and program termination, EXIT and HALT. EXIT will leave the current procedure or function. When used with a local routine (a procedure or function within another routine), it can also be used to exit the outer routine.

EXIT requires a single parameter, which is the identifier of the procedure or function to exit. In the following example

```
FUNCTION WriteFile: OSErr;
...
   PROCEDURE CheckErr(errnum: OSErr);
```

```
VAR
   alertitem: INTEGER;
BEGIN
   IF errnum <> noErr THEN
   BEGIN
      alertitem := Alert(128, NIL);      { complain }
      WriteFile := errnum;
      EXIT(WriteFile);
   END;
END;         {CheckErr}
BEGIN
   ...
   CheckErr(SetFPos(docrefnum, fsFromStart, 0));
   CheckErr(FSWrite(docrefnum, txtlen, txtptr));
   ...
END;         {WriteFile}
```

the local procedure CheckErr is used by function WriteFile to check for an error after any OS or Toolbox call. If an error is found, the error status is set for the function and then the inner procedure exits from the outer function to the routine that originally called WriteFile.

The reserved identifier PROGRAM can be used with MPW tools to exit to the shell. The statement

```
EXIT(PROGRAM);
```

will terminate the tool with {Status} set to 0. HALT is the same as EXIT(PROGRAM) for MPW tools, except that {Status} is set to 1.

As a matter of style, you will use the IEExit procedure defined by the MPW tool unit IntEnv, which takes any status value as its single parameter. Macintosh applications normally use the trap ExitToShell.

Two new statements are provided by MPW Pascal for modifying the action within a FOR, WHILE, or REPEAT loop. Together with EXIT, these eliminate the most common need for the dreaded GOTO statement in a well-structured program.

LEAVE exits the current loop and continues after the end of the loop; it can be used when an additional termination condition is required. CYCLE transfers to the beginning of the the loop, which will be at the next iteration for a FOR loop; it is useful when no further processing is required for the current iteration.

Unlike EXIT, both LEAVE and CYCLE are limited to the current (inner) loop only. Any outer loop must be terminated (or continued) using a GOTO statement.

The CASE statement has two small extensions. A range of values can be specified on a case label, with the bounds separated by the .. range separator. The CASE can also include a term specifying the alternative if none of the terms matches, which is indicated by the OTHERWISE reserved word. Both are illustrated by the statement:

```
CASE c OF
   '0'..'9':              Write('digit');
   'A'..'Z', 'a'..'z':    Write('letter');
   OTHERWISE              Write('Unknown');
END;    {CASE}
```

As with other case terms, the OTHERWISE must be followed by a BEGIN … END block if it is followed by more than a simple statement.

By default, AND and OR boolean operators will evaluate all operands before computing the result. However, two special operators will produce the same result but will evaluate the operands left to right only as necessary.

The short-circuit boolean operators & and | are equivalent to AND and OR. If the first operand is false for & or true for |, the second operand need not be evaluated. This is usually quicker and more compact than the standard form but will have different side effects on rare occasions.

If you want to use the traditional AND and OR for readability or portability, the compiler option {$SC+} can be used to interpret these as short-circuit operators.

OTHER DIFFERENCES

There are numerous other features provided by MPW Pascal, most of which are described in later sections.

MPW Pascal organizes the standard Pascal, Macintosh, and MPW libraries into UCSD Pascal-style units of related procedures and functions. The use of these units is the topic of the next section.

The compiler recognizes several directives—keywords used after the declaration—to describe different types of procedures and functions. These directives—FORWARD, C, EXTERNAL, and INLINE—are also described in the next section.

The compiler supports special functions for logical operations on LONGINT values. These are similar to a number of traps originally provided by the Toolbox Utilities but, like the corresponding C operators, map directly into single 68000 instructions. They are described later in the chapter.

The compiler allows integer constants of either INTEGER or LONGINT type to be entered in hexadecimal notation. The constant begins with a $ symbol and is followed by a series of 1 to 8 digits. Each digit can be a number from 0 to 9, a capital letter from A to F or a lowercase letter from a to f.

In addition to the predefined constants MaxInt and MaxLongInt, MPW also recognizes MaxComp, Pi (3.141592653589793 etc.) and Inf, which is the SANE (IEEE) positive infinity. Predefined string constants

CompDate and CompTime specify the compilation date and type and allow you build version information into your compile programs.

The Object Pascal syntax of MPW Pascal includes a number of new keywords, including OBJECT, INHERITED, SELF, and OVERRIDE. These extensions and the use of Object Pascal with the MacApp library are fully described in Chapter 11.

7.3 Separate Compilation

The major innovation of UCSD Pascal was its provision for separate compilation of Pascal programs. This extended the use of Pascal from writing simple classroom exercises to use with large systems. It also also allows Pascal programs to reference standard libraries of previously compiled code.

MPW Pascal includes these separate compilation features: declaration of externally implemented procedures and grouping programs into units. MPW Pascal also includes the Lisa Pascal extensions to directly access the ROM and C programs. These are used extensively to implement the standard libraries needed for Macintosh development.

ROUTINE DIRECTIVES

MPW Pascal allows special procedures and functions to be declared with corresponding directives immediately following the declaration. These are summarized by Table 7–3.

Directive	Description
FORWARD	Routine will be defined later
INLINE	Insert inline 68000 instructions for each routine call
EXTERNAL	Routine is implemented outside source file
C	Routine conforms to C calling sequence

Table 7–3:   Routine directives

The EXTERNAL directive declares the routine but indicates that an implementation of the routine will not be included in this compilation. This is the simplest solution provided by MPW Pascal to support separate compilation. Normally, EXTERNAL is used for routines written in other languages, such as assembler. However, it can be used for any procedure (including one written in Pascal) for which you have an MPW object file, such as in a library.

The C directive indicates that the routine conforms to the MPW C calling sequences. The main difference is that the order of parameters on the stack is reversed; C functions also return their result in registers rather than the stack as Pascal does. C routines will always be declared as EXTERNAL as well since they're presumably written and compiled separately in C.

The INLINE directive is followed by a series of one or more INTEGER constants, normally coded in hex. These represent 68000 machine instructions that will be inserted whenever the routine is referenced.

Normally, the INLINE directive is used to call Toolbox or OS traps, which are represented by a single constant in the range $A000 to $AFFF. MPW provides standard library declarations for all of the routines defined by *Inside Macintosh*. For example,

```
PROCEDURE MoveTo(h, v: INTEGER); INLINE $A893;
```

is used to define the QuickDraw procedure MoveTo.

However, INLINE directives can also be used to insert any series of 68000 machine instructions, as long as you understand the Pascal calling sequence and are willing to enter the instructions in hex. The best way to do this is to first write the code as a separate EXTERNAL routine in MPW assembler, and then link and test it. You would then replace the EXTERNAL directive with INLINE constants corresponding to the machine instructions shown in the assembler listing.

MPW Pascal also supports the standard Pascal directive FORWARD. A procedure declared FORWARD must be implemented later in the same compilation unit.

Example 7–2 includes examples of each of these directives.

THE UNIT CONCEPT

MPW Pascal allows (in fact, encourages) large programs and libraries to be broken up into separate components of related operations. These components are known as "units." If you're familiar with Modula-2, units are similar to Modula-2's modules, except that they cannot be nested. Units are considerably simpler than the packages used in Ada programs.

A unit is used to define a portion of a library, which is how units are used to support the *Inside Macintosh* interface to the Macintosh ROM. Units can also be used to define a section of the program using the library. Each unit normally includes many procedures or functions. It may also declare new data types, variables, and constants that are shared by those routines and by the routines that use the unit.

The unit is divided into two parts, the interface and its implementation. The unit's routines are generally declared twice, once in the interface and the second time in the implementation. As the name suggests, the implementation contains the actual body of code to implement the routine. The interface declares the public specifications for the routine, which includes its name, the number, and types of its parameters and the type of the function result, if any.

```
{ Routine defined in assembly language }
FUNCTION NewHandleClear(s: Size): Handle;
  EXTERNAL;

{ Routine to be defined later }
FUNCTION GetMenuColor(item: INTEGER): RGBColor;
  FORWARD;

{ MacsBug debugging breakpoints implemented through trap
  words }
PROCEDURE Debugger;
  INLINE $A9FF;
PROCEDURE DebugStr(astring: Str255);
  INLINE $ABFF;

{ Use C for unsigned arithmetic }
FUNCTION RGBDiff(r1,r2: RGBColor): LONGINT;
  C; EXTERNAL;
```

Example 7–2:   Procedure and function directives

The interface must declare any data types that are parameters to those routines. The interface also declares any global variables (more accurately, "unit variables") that are accessible to programs that use the unit.

You can, of course, define your libraries with EXTERNAL directives and without using units. The important advantage of using units is that the same interface declarations are read when compiling the unit and programs that use the unit. This allows the compiler to verify that both the use and the implementation of any routine match the declaration—and thus match each other.

REFERENCING UNITS

To reference units in your program, you must include a single USES statement listing each of the units required. This must be the first actual statement following the PROGRAM declaration, excluding comments and embedded compiler options.

The compiler has standard rules for finding the Pascal source files that define any referenced unit. In the declaration

```
PROGRAM MyApp;
USES
     MemTypes,
     QuickDraw,
```

```
                OSIntf;
```

the compiler would look for files `MemTypes.p`, `QuickDraw.p`, and `OSIntf.p` to contain the definition of the corresponding units' interface. These will normally be found in the directory defined by shell variable `{PInterfaces}` but other directories can be specified as options to the `Pascal` compilation command.

Existing source files from Lisa Pascal may include embedded compiler options of the form

```
          USES
          {$U obj/MemTypes} MemTypes,
          {$U obj/QuickDraw} QuickDraw,
```

to declare the actual name of the interface files. However, this will not normally be necessary with MPW Pascal programs. To improve portability, you should not "hardwire" the names of the interface files in your programs but instead should use the compiler option to specify any nonstandard directory.

Since each unit is a Pascal text file, using multiple units can slow down compilation significantly as the compiler reads the interface declarations before parsing your program. The MPW compiler provides a `{$LOAD}` embedded compiler option to save and reuse the symbol table built from these unit declarations, as described later in this chapter.

MACINTOSH INTERFACE UNITS

MPW Pascal structures access to its standard libraries using a series of units. These standard units include those for the Macintosh ROM routines, and the libraries supplied with MPW Pascal, including those for standard Pascal programs and for constructing MPW tools.

If you use a unit that in turn requires a second unit in its interface, that second unit must also be declared in your program prior to declaring the first unit. For example, unit `ToolIntf` includes the Window Manager declaration:

```
          PROCEDURE InvalRect(badRect: Rect);
```

So that the compiler will understand the `Rect` data type, you must also use the `QuickDraw` unit, which defines the `Rect` data type, prior to using `ToolIntf`. These dependency relationships impose restrictions on the order of the unit declarations in your programs.

The MPW Pascal units and their dependencies are summarized by

Figure 7–4. Not shown are the five units that don't have any dependencies: DeclROM, ObjIntf, SANE, Signal, and VideoIntf.

From the figure, the following order of unit references would be valid:

```
USES
     MemTypes,
     QuickDraw,
     OSIntf,
     ToolIntf,
     AppleTalk,
     PrintTraps;
```

As noted earlier, QuickDraw must come before ToolIntf, as must OSIntf. However, the dependency chart indicates that AppleTalk and PrintTraps

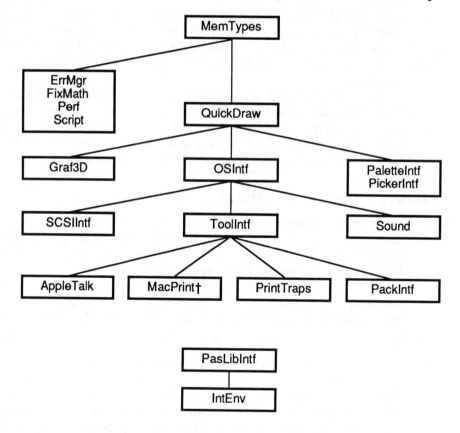

† Use MacPrint instead of PrintTraps only if target configuration includes System Version 3.2 or earlier

Figure 7–4:   Overall unit dependencies

can come in either order because neither depends on the other. Units that don't depend on any unit—such as ObjIntf—can be used in any order.

In fact, the most-often used units are those for the Toolbox and OS routines defined by *Inside Macintosh*. The names of the routines and data types in these units are not documented by the MPW manuals because it is assumed that you have the *Inside Macintosh* documentation. The early editions of *Inside Macintosh* describe how to use the various managers with Lisa Pascal examples. For all practical purposes, the Lisa and MPW implementations of these interfaces are the same and all editions since the release of MPW have been designed with the MPW—not Lisa Pascal—developer in mind.

However, *Inside Macintosh* does not detail which Pascal unit contains which managers. In addition, there is one standard unit—MemTypes—which does not correspond to any manager. Table 7–4 summarizes the usage of the various units for the Macintosh Toolbox and OS.

The MemTypes unit includes definitions for the most common standard data types that are not built in to the compiler, including Byte, SignedByte, Ptr, Handle, Fixed, Str255, and StringHandle. This will be required for all but the simplest of Macintosh programs and libraries.

Unit QuickDraw contains the interface for the Toolbox manager of the same name, as well as the closely related Color Manager. The unit defines certain basic data types used by most units, such as Point, Rect, BitMap, GrafPort, and GrafPtr. Although it is part of the Toolbox, it is also required for the OS interface declarations because the EventRecord data type defined by the OS Event Manager includes a Point field.

Unit OSIntf defines the interfaces for most of the OS managers, while ToolIntf defines them for the Toolbox. As you can imagine, most programs will require both of these units. Since they cover most of the ROM interfaces, parsing these two unit declarations will delay a compilation considerably.

The rules for the Printing Manager are more complex than for other managers. There are actually two units for the Printing Manager, one that calls the Print driver via glue, and another that uses a trap. Any program that performs printing should use one or the other—but not both, since the units mostly define the same procedures.

The PrintTraps unit should be chosen in preference for most new programs as it provides the latest functionality and long-term compatibility. However, it requires that anyone using the program have System file version 3.3 or later to provide the _Printing trap. (The Macintosh SE and later machines have the trap in ROM but these require system 4.0 or later; see Appendix D for trap compatibility information.)

Other aspects of the Toolbox and OS not used by most programs—SCSI, AppleTalk, various packages—are defined by separate units that require OSIntf and (usually) ToolIntf. Three units—DeclROMDefs, IndVideoIntf, and PickerIntf—are specific to the Macintosh II.

Macintosh Units

OS Units	Description	
AppleTalk	AppleTalk Manager	
MacPrint	Printing Manager (glue-based)	
OSIntf	ADB Manager	Serial Driver
	Deferred Task Manager	Shutdown Manager
	Desk Manager	Slot Manager
	Device Manager	Sound Driver
	File Manager	Start Manager
	Memory Manager	System Error Handler
	OS Event Manager	Time Manager
	OS Utilities	Vertical Retrace Manager
	Segment Loader	
PaletteMgr	Palette Manager	
PrintTraps	Printing Manager (trap-based)	
ROMDefs	NuBus declaration ROMs	
SANE	Standard Apple Numeric Enironment:	
	Floating Point Elements Package	
	Transcendental Functions Package	
	MC68881 support	
SCSIIntf	SCSI Manager	
Sound	Sound Manager (Macintosh II only)	
VideoIntf	Macintosh II video drivers	

Toolbox Units	Description	
FixMath	Fixed-point math (Toolbox Utilities)	
Quickdraw	QuickDraw, Color Manager	
PackIntf	Package Manager:	
	Binary/Decimal Conversion Package	
	Disk Initialization Package	
	International Utilities Package	
	List Manager Package	
	Standard File Package	
PickerIntf	Color Picker Package	
Script	Script Manager	
ToolIntf	Control Manager	Scrap Manager
	Dialog Manager	TextExit
	Event Manager	Toolbox Utilities
	Menu Manager	Window Manager
	Resource Manager	

Other units	Description
Graf3D	Three-dimensional graphics
MemTypes	Memory types: Byte, Ptr, Handle, Str255
ObjIntf	Standard Object Pascal definitions
Perf	Performance measurement procedures

Table 7–4: Macintosh units

Also in separate units are two sets of numerical routines, the fixed-point arithmetic of the Toolbox Utilities and the SANE floating point arithmetic. Although the compiler may generate references to SANE for floating point arithmetic, it is not necessary to include this unit unless you are directly referencing routines in it, such as trigonometric functions not predefined by Pascal.

Finally, release 2.0 of MPW includes libraries for measuring the performance of any program. The MPW Pascal run time interfaces are defined by unit Perf. Your program calls one routine to initialize the performance library, which establishes initial parameters and allocates a large block of memory to contain an array of "buckets," representing a series of evenly spaced memory addresses. The libraries then use Macintosh timers to periodically note the current program counter and increase the counter for the corresponding bucket.

The library is designed to sample any type of program—application, desk accessory, driver—and can include an analysis of the use of ROM routines. To improve the reliability of the results, your program would turn off sampling during idle times, such as when it is waiting for user input. When the measurements are done, the library writes raw sampling data to a text file, which can be later formatted into a procedure-by-procedure analysis using the PerformReport tool.

WRITING YOUR OWN UNIT

When building a unit, the interface and implementation are compiled together to produce an MPW object file containing the code that implements that unit. This object code is then linked with programs that reference the unit.

The general structure of a unit is:

```
UNIT MyUnit;
INTERFACE
  USES
     AStandardUnit,
     { other units }
  . . .
        { declarations }
  . . .
IMPLEMENTATION
  { implementation of the unit}
  . . .
END.
```

Units can, of course, reference other units. The USES must immediately follow the INTERFACE declaration.

USES cannot be included in the IMPLEMENTATION section; instead, any unit required for the implementation must be listed in the USES of the

INTERFACE. In the example above, suppose unit MyUnit references OtherUnit for its implementation but not for its interface. This means that one of the routines in IMPLEMENTATION of MyUnit references a routine in OtherUnit, but none of the data types of OtherUnit are required by the INTERFACE of MyUnit. In this case, OtherUnit does not have to be listed by a program that references MyUnit, such as

```
PROGRAM AnyProgram;
USES MyUnit;
```

since OtherUnit is not actually required to interpret the MyUnit interface when compiling AnyProgram.

The INTERFACE section will normally include a declaration of constants, data types, and routines. Routines are declared as though through a forward declaration, although the FORWARD directive is not used. If the interface includes a declaration of variables, the values of those variables are accessible to any routine and to any program using that unit. The interface cannot include either FORWARD or EXTERNAL declarations.

Except for routines declared as INLINE, the IMPLEMENTATION section includes the definition of most routines declared in the interface section— either as a series of Pascal statements or an EXTERNAL directive. It may also include constants, data types, or variables, which will be available to the routines in the unit but *not* to any program that uses that unit.

MPW Pascal does not allow an unnamed BEGIN ... END block as part of the IMPLEMENTATION section, as is defined by UCSD Pascal implementations (including Apple Pascal) and Modula-2 to automatically initialize a unit. Instead, you must write a separate procedure to initialize the unit and call it from your initialization code. The variables of a unit are initialized to zero by default.

To make the source code more manageable, you may wish to break the interface and implementation into separate source files. One way to do this is by placing the implementation code in a separate file and including it in the compilation using a {$I } compiler directive in the interface file. You can then print the interface for others to use, which shows the formal definition of the unit without detailing the actual implementation.

Only the INTERFACE section is necessary for compiling a Pascal program using that unit; the IMPLEMENTATION statement and any code following it will be ignored when the unit is used. If you wish to write your own units for use by other programmers, you must supply them with the Pascal source code for the INTERFACE and the MPW object code you obtained when compiling the entire unit. When defining compilation dependencies, other programs will require recompilation when the interface changes but will only require relinking when the implementation changes.

Example 7–3 shows the interface for a complete Pascal unit for formatted output appended to STRING variables instead of files. The implementation of the unit is shown in Example 7–4.

```
(* StringFormat.p: Interface definition *)
UNIT StringFormat;

INTERFACE

USES
  MemTypes,
  QuickDraw,
  OSIntf,
  ToolIntf,
  PackIntf;

  PROCEDURE SWrite(VAR s: Str255; c: CHAR);
  PROCEDURE SWriteHex
    VAR s: Str255; n: LongInt; w: INTEGER);
  PROCEDURE SWriteInt
    (VAR s: Str255; n: LongInt; w: INTEGER);
  PROCEDURE SWriteString(VAR s: Str255; s2: Str255);

IMPLEMENTATION

(* Include the actual implementation source *)
{$I StringFormat.inc.p}

END.
```

Example 7–3: Interface for string format unit

```
(* StringFormat.incl.p: Unit implementation *)

{ This source is compiled where included from the inter-
face file, StringFormat.p
}


{ As with all the Pascal equivalents, output the speci-
fied field width or the minimum necessary number of
digits, whichever is greater. Does not check for the
output string > 255 characters
}

{*----------------------------------*
 | SWrite -- format a character     |
 *----------------------------------*}

PROCEDURE SWrite(VAR s: Str255; c: CHAR);
```

```
VAR
  i : INTEGER;
BEGIN
  i := ORD(s[0]) + 1;
  s[0] := CHR(i);
  s[i] := c;
END;(* SWrite *)

{*--------------------------------------------------*
 | SWriteHex -- format a number in hex              |
 *--------------------------------------------------*}

PROCEDURE SWriteHex(VAR s: Str255; n: LongInt; w: INTE-
GER);
VAR
  d  : INTEGER;
  s2 : Str255;
BEGIN
  s2[0] := CHR(w);
  WHILE w > 0 DO
  BEGIN
    d := BAND(n,$F);
    n := BSR(n,4);
    IF d < 10 THEN
      s2[w] := CHR(ORD('0') + d)
    ELSE
      s2[w] :=  CHR(ORD('A') - 10 + d);
    w := w-1;
  END;
  SWriteString(s, s2);
END;(* SWriteHex *)

{*--------------------------------------------------*
 | SWriteInt -- format a number in decimal          |
 *--------------------------------------------------*}

PROCEDURE SWriteInt
  (VAR s: Str255; n: LongInt; w: INTEGER);
VAR
  i  : INTEGER;
  s2 : Str255;
BEGIN
  NumToString(n, s2);
  i := w - Length(s2);
  WHILE i > 0 DO
    BEGIN
      SWrite(s, ' ');                    (* Leading spaces *)
      i := i - 1;
    END;
```

```
      SWriteString(s,s2);
END; (* SWriteInt *)


{*-------------------------------------------*
 | SWriteString -- format a character string |
 *-------------------------------------------*}


PROCEDURE SWriteString(VAR s: Str255; s2: Str255);
BEGIN
   s := Concat(s,s2);
END;(* SWriteString *)
```

Example 7–4:   Implementation for string format unit

To build the unit, you would enter:

```
        Pascal StringFormat.p
```

The StringFormat interface file automatically includes the source from the separate implementation file as part of the compilation, using the {$I} compiler directive.

If you own the optional MacApp component of MPW, the MacApp sample programs and libraries provide good examples of the structure of complete MPW Pascal units. Even if you don't own MacApp, the MacApp source listings are available separately.

7.4 Predefined and Library Routines

This section summarizes the standard functions and procedures available with MPW Pascal, beyond those described by the *Inside Macintosh* specification.

These routines are used when writing MPW tools, and converting Pascal programs from other systems. They also included common utilities useful for all Pascal programs.

This section describes the routines predefined by the Pascal compiler, without using any unit interface. Other routines are defined in several of the standard units, and these units are summarized at the end of the section.

ROUTINE PARAMETERS

As with most Pascal implementation, VAR parameters are passed by including the address of the parameter in the actual stack frame. However, parameters longer than 4 bytes are always passed by address, whether declared as VAR or not.

For example, a variable declared as `Str255` is not copied to the stack; instead, the address of the variable is passed. What is the difference between the following declarations?

```
PROCEDURE F1(s: Str255);
PROCEDURE F2(VAR s: Str255);
```

Both would be called with the same calling sequence, the same series of machine instructions. However, the compiler would not allow the implementation of the procedure `F1` to modify `s`, while `F2` could.

These rules are normally transparent to the Pascal programmer, but may become important when mixing Pascal programs with routines written in other languages, where a detailed understanding of the respective calling sequences is required.

Parameter types can be declared as `UNIV` in MPW Pascal. Such a declaration provides some relaxation of type checking. A type prefixed by `UNIV` allows the actual parameter to be of any type of the same size. This is normally used with pointers. For example, a procedure declared as

```
PROCEDURE WriteHex(p: UNIV LONGINT);
```

could accept parameters of type `LONGINT`, `Ptr`, `GrafPtr`, and `Handle`, among others.

MPW Pascal allows passing functions and procedures as parameters, as does standard Pascal. For example, the procedure defined by

```
PROCEDURE Assign
   (FUNCTION SomeFunc(x:INTEGER): INTEGER);
VAR
   i: INTEGER;
BEGIN
   i := SomeFunc(i);
END
```

would allow the name of a function to be passed to procedure Assign, as with the statement:

```
Assign(Factorial, j);
```

Several Macintosh Toolbox and OS traps accept procedural or functional parameters. However, these parameters are normally defined in terms of type `ProcPtr`, defined in unit `MemTypes`. Such parameters can't be used by another Pascal program but can be used by assembly language programs written with a Pascal interface.

An example of this usage is a dialog event filter procedure used by several routines in the Dialog Manager. To pass a `ProcPtr` parameter, you evaluate the address of the procedure, as in:

```
ModalDialog (@MyFilterProc, itemno);
```

INLINE ROUTINES

In addition to procedures and functions defined via the standard interface units, the MPW Pascal compiler has built-in defintions for many routines. These are available for use by MPW Pascal programs without using any of the Pascal library units.

Some of these routines are not routines in the customary sense, in which the compiler generates a call to a function or procedure. Instead, the compiler generates direct 68000 code inline to implement these routines. The inline functions are summarized by Table 7–5, while Table 7–6 lists the inline routines. The parameter names are used in the definition to indicate the type of parameter allowed, as will be done throughout the remainder of this chapter.

Many of the inline functions are actually type transfer functions, which do not change the actual value of a variable but are used to change the type of the value. These are used to get around the type-checking features of Pascal. MPW Pascal includes more type transfer functions than most implementations. These functions are often used to manipulate pointers, as discussed earlier.

In addition to the procedures, MPW Pascal also recognizes four inline procedures. Two are actually control statements for exiting a procedure or program, as described earlier. The remainder are part of an extended set of bit-manipulation routines provided with MPW Pascal and later releases of Lisa Pascal.

Each of these routines correspond to a single Motorola 68000 instruction that operates on a 32-bit quantity. As such, they are subject to the limitations of those instructions.

For example, the shift count for both the shift and rotate instructions are evaluated modulo 64; the sign of the shift count cannot be used to set the shift/rotate direction. The shift functions correspond to the 68000's logical shift instructions, in which the sign bit is treated the same as any other bits.

These routines are not generally part of other Pascal compilers, either for the Macintosh or other computers. If you're writing code that may be used by another Pascal compiler for the Mac, you may wish to instead use the corresponding routines in the Toolbox Utilities, which are slower but available to any language. In most cases, the names are similar and the parameter usages the same.

However, the BSL and BSR inline functions map onto a single Toolbox function BitShift. Unlike the two inline functions, BitShift uses the sign of the shift count to determine the direction of the shift.

The BClr and BSet routines and the BTst function use the 68000 opcodes to operate on 32-bit integer, with bits numbered from 0 to 31, from the least

Predefined Inline Function

Function	Result	Description
Abs(n)	same as n	Absolute value
BAND(j1,j2)	LongInt	Bitwise AND
BNOT(j1,j2)	LongInt	One's-complement
BOR(j1,j2)	LongInt	Bitwise inclusive OR
BSL(j,i)	LongInt	Logical shift j i bits left
BSR(j,i)	LongInt	Logical shift j i bits right
BRotL(j,i)	LongInt	Rotate j i bits left
BRotR(j,i)	LongInt	Rotate j r bits right
BTst(j,i)	Boolean	Is bit i (0-31) of j set?
BXOR(j1,j2)	LongInt	Bitwise exclusive OR
Chr(i)	Char	Equivalent character
HiWrd(j)	Integer	Upper 16 bits of j
LoWrd(j)	Integer	Lower 16 bits of j
Odd(j)	Boolean	Is j odd?
Ord(v)	Integer	Numeric value of v
Ord(p)	LongInt	Same as Ord4(p)
Ord4(p)	LongInt	Numeric value of p
Pointer(j)	same as NIL	Convert j to pointer type
Pred(v)	same as v	Previous value of its type for v
Sizeof(t)	Integer	Size of type t in bytes
Sqr(n)	same as n	n^2 (n*n)
Succ(v)	same as v	Next value of its type for v
type(p)	*type*	Coerce value p to *type*

Variable	Type
i	Integer
j	LongInt, Integer or any integral subrange
n	any integral or floating-point type
v	Char or enumerated type
p	any pointer, numeric, character or enumerated type
t	any type or variable

Table 7–5:   **Predefined inline functions**

Predefined inline Procedures

Procedure	Description
BClr(L,i)	Clear bit i of L
BSet(L,i)	Set bit i of L
Exit(ident)	Leave routine ident. If ident is PROGRAM, leave program
Halt	Terminate program with error status

Variable	Type
i	Integer
L	VAR LongInt

Table 7–6:   **Predefined inline procedures**

significant bit (1) to the most significant bit (2^{31}). In comparison, the Toolbox Utilities BitTst, BitSet, and BitClr use a pointer to any series of bytes and number the bits 0 to 7 within each byte, from most significant (2^7) to least significant (1).

The alternative is to implement MPW's inline routines in the other Pascal. This allows you to use the most efficient routines when compiling with the MPW compiler and simulate their use when using the other compiler. Example 7–5 shows a series of bit routines that use Toolbox Utilities to implement MPW's inline routines.

The example assumes the availability of the INLINE directive in the target compiler. Some of the definitions directly call the corresponding Toolbox trap, as the parameters and function results are the same for both the MPW and trap version of the function.

If the other Pascal does not support INLINE, you would call the trap directly, as in:

```
FUNCTION BAND (n1,n2: LONGINT): LONGINT;
BEGIN
   BAND := BitAnd (n1,n2);
END;
```

The Toolbox does not include routines corresponding to BRotL and BRotR; so these would best be implemented using short assembly-language functions.

PREDEFINED LIBRARY ROUTINES

In addition to the inline routines, the MPW Pascal compiler predefines a series of procedures and functions that are referenced through MPW libraries. These routines are listed in Tables 7–7 and 7–8.

Many of these routines correspond to the standard Pascal definition. For example, New and Dispose can be used to allocate and deallocate memory from the Pascal heap. As is standard, these procedures accept optional parameters (not shown in Table 7–8) to distinguish between variant records; such parameters are also accepted by the SIZEOF function listed earlier.

Several of the routines are used to manipulate strings, character arrays, or an arbitrary series of bytes. The purpose of these routines overlaps somewhat.

The Concat function combines two (or more) strings into a value that can be assigned to a third string. The Copy function extracts a series of characters from one string to form a new string, while Insert and Delete are used to add or subtract characters from the middle of an existing string.

The procedures MoveLeft and MoveRight also transfer a series of characters but can operate on any data type, not just on strings. The two

```
PROCEDURE BClr (VAR num : LONGINT; bitno : INTEGER);
BEGIN
  BitClr (@num, 32-bitno);
END;


PROCEDURE BSet (VAR num : LONGINT; bitno : INTEGER);
BEGIN
  BitSet (@num, 32-bitno);
END;


FUNCTION BTst (num : LONGINT; bitno : INTEGER);
BEGIN
  BTst := BitTst (@num, 32-bitno);
END;


FUNCTION BSL (num : LONGINT; count : INTEGER);
BEGIN
  IF (count MOD 64) < 32 THEN
     BSL :=
        BitShift (num, count)    { BitShift uses MOD 32 }
  ELSE
     BSL : = 0;                  { 32-63 always 0 }
END;


FUNCTION BSR (num : LONGINT; count : INTEGER);
BEGIN
  IF (count MOD 64) < 32 THEN
     BST := BitShift (num, -count)
        { BitShift uses MOD 32 }
  ELSE
     BST : = 0;                  { 32-63 always 0 }
END;


FUNCTION BAND (n1,n2 : LONGINT) : LONGINT;
  INLINE $A858;                  { _BitAnd trap }
FUNCTION BOR (n1,n2 : LONGINT) : LONGINT;
  INLINE $A85B;                  { _BitOr trap }
FUNCTION BXOR (n1,n2 : LONGINT) : LONGINT;
  INLINE $A859;                  { _BitXOr trap }
FUNCTION BNOT (num : LONGINT) : LONGINT;
  INLINE $A85A;                  { _BitNot trap }
FUNCTION HiWRD (num : LONGINT) : INTEGER;
  INLINE $A86A;                  { _HiWord trap }
FUNCTION LoWRD (num : LONGINT) : INTEGER;
  INLINE $A86B;                  { _LoWord trap }
```

Example 7–5:   Substitute bit-manipulation routines

Predefined Library Functions

Function	Result	Description
Arctan(n)	Extended	Arctangent of n, in range $[-\pi/2, \pi/2]$
BlockRead(fu,b,i1,i2)	Integer	Read i1 blocks, return number transferred
BlockWrite(fu,b,i1,i2)	Integer	Write i1 blocks, return number transferred
ByteRead(fu,b,j1,j2)	LongInt	Read j1 bytes, return number transferred
ByteWrite(fu,b,j1,j2)	LongInt	Write j1 bytes, return number transferred
Concat(s1,s2,...)	String	Combine s1 and s2 to make newstring
Copy(s,i1,i2)	String	Return i2 characters from s[i1]
Cos(n)	Extended	Cosine of n (value in radians)
Eof(f)	Boolean	Is f at end of file?
EoLn(ft)	Boolean	Is ft at end of line?
Exp(n)	Extended	e^n
HeapResult	Integer	Status of last Pascal heap request
Length(s)	Integer	Length of s
Ln(n)	Extended	Natural log of n
MemAvail	LongInt	Available memory in Pascal heap
Member(P,T)	Boolean	Is object P of type T or a descendant?
Pos(s1,s2)	Integer	Position of string s2 within s1
Round(r)	LongInt	Round to nearest integer
ScanEQ(i,c,a)	Integer	Search i bytes of a for character c
ScanNE(i,c,a)	Integer	Search i bytes of a for character not c
Sin(n)	Extended	Sine of n (value in radians)
Sqrt(n)	Extended	$\sqrt{n}$
Trunc(r)	LongInt	Convert to integer, discarding fraction

Concat takes any number of parameters

The fourth parameter to BlockRead, BlockWrite, ByteRead, ByteWrite is an optional parameter to specify the starting block or byte.

Variable	Type
a	Packed array ... of Char
b	Buffer data type (usually an array or record)
c	Char
f	any file type: structured, untyped or text
ft	textfile (ft: TEXT;)
fu	untyped file (fu: FILE;)
i	Integer in range 1.255
j	LongInt, Integer or any integral subrange
n	any integral or floating-point type
P	object reference variable
r	real, double, extended or comp floating-point types
s	String
T	type of OBJECT

Table 7–7: Predefined library functions

Predefined Library Procedures

Procedure	Description
Close(f)	Close file f
Delete(s,i1,i2)	Delete substring at index i1 of length i2 from s
Dispose(p)	Deallocate memory referenced by p
FillChar(a,i,c)	Fill a with i copies of character c
Get(fs)	Read next record to buffer variable fs
Insert(s1,s2,i)	Insert substring s2 in string s1 at position i
Mark(p)	Mark location in Pascal heap
MoveLeft(b1,b2,i)	Move i bytes from b1 to b2
MoveRight(b1,b2,i)	Move i bytes from b1 to b2
New(p)	Allocate memory and assign result to p
Open(f,s)	Open file f named s
Page(ft)	Insert page break in ft
Put(fs)	Write buffer variable fs as next record
Read(F,v...)	Read variables from file F
ReadLn(ft,v...)	Read variables to end of line from file ft
Reset(f)	Position f for writing at beginning of file
Reset(f,s)	Open file f named s for reading
Rewrite(f)	Position f for writing at beginning of file
Rewrite(f,s)	Open file f named s for writing
Seek(f,j)	Position file f at j bytes from the beginning
Write(F,e...)	Write values to file F
WriteLn(ft,e...)	Write values to file ft, followed by return

Variable	Type
a	Packed array ... of Char
b	Buffer data type (usually an array or record)
c	Char
e	Optional list of expressions; each expression can be of the form *expression* : *width* : *decimal*
f	any file type: structured, untyped or text
F	structured file or textfile
fs	structured file (fs: FILE OF ...)
ft	textfile (ft: TEXT;)
i	Integer in range 1.255
j	LongInt, Integer or any integral subrange
p	any pointer type
s	String
v	Optional list of variables, separated by commas

Table 7–8:   Predefined library procedures

procedures have the same effect, unless used on overlapping memory blocks, such as sliding characters left or right within a packed array of characters.

Three routines operate only on a PACKED ARRAY ... OF CHAR. FillChar copies the same character repeatedly to a packed array of characters. ScanEQ searches the array for the first character in the array matching the specific character, while ScanNE searches for the first character not matching the character.

The Pos function searches a string value for the first occurrence of a desired substring. The substring can be of any length and if a single character, Pos is similar to ScanEQ but for a different parameter type.

STANDARD LIBRARY UNITS

The previous section summarized the MPW Pascal units used to access the Macintosh Toolbox and OS. The remaining units included with MPW Pascal extend the standard Pascal definitions for I/O and heap management and are also used to support MPW tools. These units are summarized in Table 7–9.

Standard Pascal and Tool Units	
Unit	*Usage*
PasLibIntf	Standard Pascal I/O and memory management
CursorCtl	Cursor control: RotateCursor, SpinCursor
ErrMgr	Error manager: GetSysErrText
IntEnv	Shell environment: ArgV, Diagnostic, IEExit
Signal	Signal handler: IESetSig

Table 7–9:   **Standard Pascal and tool units**

The names of the routines often include a prefix to avoid conflicts with names defined by Pascal or the Macintosh ROM. Routines in the PasLibIntf unit are prefixed with PL, as in PLPurge, while the IntEnv unit includes IE routines such as IEExit.

The PasLibIntf unit includes several procedures used to manipulate the Pascal heap, as referenced by New and Dispose. However, new Macintosh programs should normally be written to call Memory Manager routines to allocate and deallocate relocatable blocks, such as NewHandle and DisposHandle. If nonrelocatable blocks are required, use NewPtr and DisposPtr instead.

PasLibIntf also includes routines to control textfile I/O buffering and to perform additional operations beyond the standard Pascal definition. Again, you're better off using the File Manager directly if you're writing a new program for the Mac.

The remaining units define routines used when writing MPW Tools.

Unit IntEnv is the standard unit for accessing the MPW shell environment. It includes definitions of the variables ArgC and ArgV, which contain a Pascal tool's parameters and the file Diagnostic, which is the diagnostic error unit for an MPW tool.

IntEnv also contains routines that are used by a tool to communicate with the shell. IEExit terminates the tool; its single parameter is the command status to be passed to the shell. IEGetEnv can be used to get the value of a shell variable, while IEStandAlone returns false if called from a tool running under the MPW shell.

Unit Signal allows your tools to trap software interrupts through the use of "signals," similar to those defined by the BSD UNIX C library. In particular, function IESigSet is used to install your procedure as a handler, which obtains control if a particular signal is generated. Initially, the only signal defined for MPW tools is sigInt, which indicates the Command-period interrupt.

The CursorCtl unit defines procedures used by MPW tools to display and rotate the beach ball cursor. Both RotateCursor and SpinCursor will rotate the cursor in either direction but use different strategies for determining how often the cursor should be rotated. However,

```
        RotateCursor (0);
```

will always display the beach ball cursor (if not already displayed) and rotate it 90° in the clockwise direction.

Finally, unit ErrMgr is used by a tool to obtain a string description corresponding to an OS error number. It must first be initialized by a call to InitErrMgr, as in:

```
    InitErrMgr ('','',TRUE); { want error numbers }
```

Then, the procedure GetSysErrText can be used to obtain the corresponding text for a variable of type OSErr (INTEGER), as in:

```
        errnum := FSWrite(refnum, bufflen, buffptr);
        IF errnum <> noErr THEN
            BEGIN
                GetSysErrText(errnum , msg);
                WriteLn('###  ', msg);
                IEExit(2);
            END;
```

This would check and format the error message if an I/O transfer failed. The IEExit procedure is used to terminate the tool with an abnormal exit status.

INPUT/OUTPUT

Three types of files are defined by MPW Pascal. Two are part of the Pascal standard:

Structured files. These are files that are defined as referencing a particular type of data, using the notation FILE OF type, as in:

```
DataFile: FILE OF INTEGER;
```

which could be used to read and write 16-bit integers. The *type* will often be a RECORD.

Textfiles. These are used for ASCII character I/O, separated into lines. Textfiles are declared as type Text, as in:

```
MsgFile: TEXT;
```

The textfiles Input and Output are predefined for all programs and units. The textfile Diagnostic is defined by unit IntEnv and refers to the shell's diagnostic output. These three files are normally used only in MPW tools.

MPW Pascal also defines a third type of file that is not included in the standard but is often used for application programming in UCSD Pascal implementations:

Untyped files. These are files that have no associated type or structure and are declared like a structured file without its type, as in:

```
BlockFile: FILE;
```

The ByteRead and ByteWrite (BlockRead and BlockWrite) functions are used to transfer a series of bytes (512-byte blocks) to an arbitrary data structure. This circumvents the type checking provided by the structured files and is both an advantage and a hazard. Because the reserved word FILE cannot be used as a parameter type, the PasLibIntf unit defines an equivalent type, PASCALFILE.

Several of the predefined I/O functions and procedures have optional parameters. The Eof and EoLn functions and the Page procedure each accept a single optional parameter. If omitted, it defaults to Input for the functions and to Output for the procedure. Similarly, the first parameter to Read, ReadLn, Write, and WriteLn is optionally either a structured file or, in the case of ReadLn and WriteLn, textfile. If omitted, it defaults to Input or Output, as appropriate.

The fourth parameter to `BlockRead, BlockWrite, ByteRead, ByteWrite` is an optional parameter to specify the starting block or byte. If omitted, the current position is used.

The rules for input and output formatting to textfiles follow the Pascal standard. Each expression in a `Write` or `WriteLn` to a textfile can optionally include a field width. The field width is taken as a minimum value for numeric output, with numbers never truncated, so a field width of 0 will always display the shortest possible representation.

For a floating point expression, this field width can optionally be followed by a number of decimal places for a fixed point representation. Otherwise, the number is displayed in exponential notation.

Sample formats and the corresponding display for the `Write` statement are shown in Example 7–6.

```
PROGRAM WriteTest;

VAR
    i: INTEGER;
    r: REAL;
    c: CHAR;
    s: STRING [20];

BEGIN
    i := 123;
    Write(i);        { "     123"  8 characters default}
    Write(i:0);      { "123"minimum possible            }
    WriteLn;

    r := 123.45;
    Write(r);        { " 1.234e+2   "10 characters default
    Write(r:0);      { " 1.2e+2   "short E-format        }
    Write(r:6:2);    { "123.45"}
    Write(r:6:3);    { "123.450"   more space if needed}
    Write(r:0:0);    { "123"minimum possible, 0 d.p.}
    WriteLn;

    c := 'X';
    Write(c);        { "X" }
    Write(c:4);      { "   X" right-adjusted }
    Write(c:1);      { "X" }
    WriteLn;

    s := 'A string.';
    Write(s);        { "A string." actual length is default }
    Write(s:12);     { "   A string." }
    Write(s:3);      { "A s" truncate from left }
    WriteLn;
END.
```

Example 7–6:   Sample write formats

These routines can be used with existing Pascal programs from another computer or when writing MPW tools. Normally, Macintosh applications (and desk accessories) will use the high-level File Manager functions, such as FSOpen and FSWrite, or the lower-level parameter block functions PBOpen and PBWrite. These are defined by the OSIntf unit and documented in *Inside Macintosh*.

LINKING LIBRARIES

The MPW linker is used to take a compiled Pascal program and link it into the appropriate program type. Each MPW Pascal program must be linked against several object libraries. These libraries are summarized in Table 7–10.

Object library files	
All Programs	*Description*
{Libraries}Runtime.o	Standard run-time initialization
{PLibraries}PasLib.o	Standard Pascal libraries
Macintosh Interface	
{Libraries}Interface.o	Glue and RAM-based Macintosh routines
MPW Tools	
{Libraries}ToolLibs.o	Support for MPW tools
Optional Libraries	
{PLibraries}SANELib.o	SANE (USES SANE)
{PLibraries}SANELib881.o	Floating point interfaces for MC68881
{Libraries}DRVRRuntime.o	Desk accessory/driver support
{Libraries}ObjLib.o	Object Pascal support (USES ObjIntf)
{Libraries}PerformLib.o	Performance measurement (USES Perf)

Table 7–10:   Pascal object libraries

The library {Libraries}Runtime.o is required by any Pascal or assembler program. If any part of the program being linked is written in C, {CLibraries}CRuntime.o must be linked instead. {PLibraries}PasLib.o is also required by all programs, as it provides the standard Pascal libraries described earlier in this section.

Programs that use *Inside Macintosh* routines not called via traps or called via traps that require "glue" to load the appropriate registers (including most of unit `OSIntf`), must be linked against {Libraries}Interface.o.

Most of the remaining libraries may be required for some MPW Pascal programs. The linker will indicate if any routine references are unresolved and will also indicate if a library is unnecessary, so it's fairly easy to come up with the minimum list of libraries necessary to satisfy all references.

The following definitions in `UserStartup` could be used to link most MPW tools:

```
Set PLibs "{Libraries}Interface.o {PLibraries}PasLib.o"∂
   " {PLibraries}SANELIB.o {Libraries}Interface.o"
Alias LinkTool ∂
   'Link -o "{Target}.tool" -t MPST -c "MPS " "{Target}.o" {PLibs}'
```

Applications or desk accessories involving resource source (`Rez`) compilations should normally have their own `Link` commands, such as generated using `Make`.

Special guidelines apply when linking with libraries to support SANE. There are two SANE run-time libraries, and only one (at most) is used in linking any program. The file {PLibraries}SANE.o is used by most programs that use unit SANE. File {PLibraries}SANE881.o is used for programs targeted to run only with the MC68881 floating point coprocessor and compiled using the corresponding directive, as described in the next section.

7.5 Compiler Directives

Most language compilers support options to control the interpretation of the source text. The MPW Pascal compiler is no exception, and it recognizes a series of options as part of the shell command line used to run the compiler.

However, the MPW Pascal version of the language differs significantly from the Pascal standards in that compiler options can be directly embedded in the program source file. To avoid requiring statements that would be rejected by other compilers, MPW Pascal follows the UCSD Pascal (Apple Pascal) convention of "hiding" these "compiler directives" in a special form of comment.

These embedded options are indicated by a dollar sign (`$`) immediately after the opening comment delimiter , as in:

```
{$S Init}
(*$R-*}
```

Unlike UCSD Pascal, multiple options cannot be included in the same comment. A directive such as

```
{$R-,D-}
```

would be rejected.

Table 7-11 summarizes the compiler directives recognized by MPW Pascal. The most commonly used are described in the remainder of this section.

The support for compiler directives was an important characteristic of the Lisa Workshop compiler, and most of the MPW Pascal directives were originally part of the Lisa Pascal language. Many directives, in fact, make more sense when used with the Lisa Workshop than with MPW. The {$E file} directive is used to redirect error messages in a Lisa Workshop compilation, but MPW users will find it more convenient to use shell I/O redirection, as in:

```
Pascal Source.p ≥ file
```

Other directives correspond to options that can be specified on the Pascal command line. If file Source.p includes the compiler directive

```
{$R-}
```

at the beginning of the file, the same result could be obtained (without the directive) by the shell command

```
Pascal -r Source.p
```

For those options that will be changed frequently—such as the inclusion of run-time checking in the development versions, but not in versions released to user—it may be more appropriate to use the command-line options rather than modifying the source each time the option changes.

CONDITIONAL COMPILATION

MPW Pascal includes four compiler directives to selectively merge Pascal source during a compilation. This can be used to build different versions of a program (U.S., Japanese, etc.), enable or disable debugging code, or to isolate dependencies in separate files.

The {$SETC} compiler directive is used to define a class of identifiers known as "compile-time variables." These variables are, in turn, used to control conditional compilation of Pascal source statements.

The variable can be assigned to an expression involving constants or other compile-time variables within the {$SETC} directive in a syntax reminiscent of the Pascal assignment statement. The directives

```
{$SETC level := 5}
{$SETC kernel := level > 3}
```

MPW Pascal compiler directives (1 of 3)

Conditional compilation	Description
{$SETC var := expression}	Set compile-time variable var to value expression
{$IFC expression}	Compile following source if compile-time boolean expression is true
{$IFC UNDEFINED var}	Compile following source if compile-time variable var not defined by $SETC
{$ELSEC}	Compile following source if previous $IFC was false
{$ENDC}	End of conditionally compiled source
{$I filename}	Include source text from filename

Units

{$U filename}	Load next unit in USES from filename
{$LOAD filename}	Save symbol table for following units to filename
{$LOAD}	End of units saved in symbol table

Error handling†

{$D+}	Insert 8-character routine names in generated code for debugger
{$D++}	Like $D+, except insert 16-character names for Object Pascal methods
{$D−}	Do not insert debugger names
{$H+}	Compile-time check for unsafe use of object reference variables (handles)
{$H−}	Do not check object handles
{$OV+}	Check for arithmetic overflow
{$OV−}	Don't check for overflow
{$R+}	Range check references to array, strings and sets, and subrange assignments

{$R-}	Don't check for range errors

† First option of group is default

MPW Pascal compiler directives (2 of 3)

Code generation†	Description
{$A1}	Interface and implementation globals stored non-contiguously
{$A5}	Store unit globals below register A5
{$B+}	Same segment routine address PC-relative
{$B-}	Same segment routine address A5-relative
{$C+}	Generate object code
{$C-}	Check for syntax errors only; do not generate object code
{$SC-}	Fully evaluate boolean expressions
{$SC+}	Treat AND, OR as short-circuit operators

Code generation for Macintosh II†

{$ALIGN-}	Normal data alignment
{$ALIGN+}	Align data to 32-bit boundaries
{$MC68020-}	Generate code for any 68000 processor
{$MC68020+}	Generate 68020-specific code
{$MC68881-}	Floating-point arithmetic uses SANE
{$MC68881+}	Floating-point arithmetic uses 68881

Linker interface†

{$J-}	Global variables must be defined in source
{$J+}	Global variables can be resolved by linker
{$N-}	Do not identify routines to linker
{$N+}	Pass all routine names to linker
{$Z-}	Disable identifying routines to linker
{$Z+}	Identify variables and routines until {$Z-}
{$Z*}	Identify outer routines only

† First option of group is default

MPW Pascal compiler directives (3 of 3)

Other options	Description
{$E *filename*}	Write compiler error messages to *filename*
{$S *name*}	Add following code to segment *name*
{$P}	Begin new page in PasRef output
{$PUSH}	Save current option settings
{$POP}	Restore saved option settings

Table 7–11:   MPW Pascal compiler directives

would define an integer compile-time variable level and a boolean compile-time variable kernel. Other variable types are not allowed.

The {$SETC} directive has a corresponding command option that can be used to set boolean variables. The command

```
Pascal -d aVar=TRUE Test.p
```

would compile Test.p as though

```
{$SETC aVar := TRUE}
```

were the first statement. Command line options will often be a more convenient way to control conditional compilation than changing the source for each compile.

Conditional compilation is controlled by the {$IFC} compiler directive. {$IFC} can include compile-time variables or expressions involving compile-time variables. As with the Pascal IF statement, the final result of any expression in {$IFC} must be boolean.

The structure of the {$IFC} conditional compilation block is similar to the shell's IF ... ELSE ... END commands. In the statements

```
{$IFC kernel}
   PROCEDURE KernelEntry;
{$ELSEC}
   PROCEDURE Entry;
{$ENDC}
```

the name of the next block would be KernelEntry if variable kernel were true, and Entry if not. The {$ELSEC} directive is optional but the {$ENDC} is not. Conditional compilation directives can be nested with the same rules against overlapping blocks as for the Pascal IF statement.

A special form of the {$IFC} directive can be used to check for compiler variables that are not yet defined. For example, code bracketed by the directives

```
{$IFC UNDEFINED qProdVers}
(* include debugging code here *)
{$ENDC}
```

would compile the debugging code by default but would not compile the code if the shell command

```
Pascal -d qProdVers=TRUE Source.p
```

were used to compile the program. The option parameter qProdVers=FALSE would produce the same result since the directive tests for the defintion—not the value—of the compiler variable.

The {$IFC} directive can also be used to test the settings of any of the standard compiler directives. The compiler function OPTION, surrounding the name of a boolean directive, can be used to test the setting of the compiler directive. In the source

```
{$IFC OPTION(R) }
(* code if range checking is enabled *)
{$ELSEC}
(* code if range checking is disabled *)
{$ENDC}
```

the first group of statements will be used if {$R+} has been set previously, the second if {$R-} is set.

In addition to conditional compilation, the {$I} directive can be used to include source from another file as part of the current compiliation. The directive includes the name of the source file to be read. For example,

```
{$I Foo.p}
```

will cause the compiler to compile the text in Foo.p at the point the {$I } is enountered. The directive is often handy when you need to break a large source file (such as a Pascal unit) into more manageable pieces.

The name specified in a {$I } directive can be a full pathname, but this is usually a bad practice. If you change the name of your folders or the organization of your hard disk, all of a sudden you will be unable to compile your programs.

However, it is much less troublesome if you use an MPW shell variable in an {$I } directive to specify a folder name. If the variable is one you normally set in your UserStartup command file, the current value will automatically be available to your program. For example, the source loaded by the directive

```
{$I $$SHELL(Sources)Prog.p}
```

is the file that would be edited by the shell command

```
Open "{Sources}Prog.p"
```

If you use only a partial pathname, the compiler will first search in the same directory as the current source file. The -i option of the Pascal command specifies additional directories that will be searched for by the {$I } compiler directive. For example,

```
Pascal -i "{MPW}MyIncludes" Source.p
```

would add the specified directory to the search list for Foo.p. More than one -i option can be specified.

After searching these directories, the compiler will search the directory (or directories) defined by the shell variable {PInterfaces}. In both the definition of {PInterfaces} and the parameters to the -i option, multiple directory pathnames can be separated by commas, as in:

```
Pascal -i "::MyIncludes:,::StdIncludes:" Source.p
```

These rules for finding an include file are also used in searching for units referenced by a USES statement.

The {$I } directive is not allowed as part of the INTERFACE section of a Pascal unit but can be used after the IMPLEMENTATION statement to separate the interface from its implementation. This technique was illustrated by Example 7–3, and is also used extensively by the MacApp Pascal libraries.

Include and unit (USES) references can be nested up to a limit of five files deep.

SEGMENTATION

Most large applications are split into segments to make effective use of the memory. The beginning of each segment in a Pascal program is indicated by the compiler directive:

```
{$S segmentname}
```

Routines following this directive are compiled as part of segment *segmentname*. If *segmentname* is omitted, the default segment name Main is used. This is also the initial segment name (prior to any {$S} directive) for any MPW Pascal compilation and is normally mapped onto CODE resource #1 by the MPW linker.

The same segment names can be used in more than one compilation, in which case each segment of the same name will be linked together into a single resource of type 'CODE'. Segment boundaries cannot be specified within any procedure or function; so

```
FUNCTION WriteFile: OSErr;

{$S Errors}

    PROCEDURE CheckErr(errnum: OSErr);
    VAR
        alertitem: INTEGER;
    BEGIN
        IF errnum <> noErr THEN
```

would not be valid.

The Link and Lib commands can be used to reassign segment names and numbers after a program has been compiled.

ERROR HANDLING

The {$D} directives control debugging symbols placed in the object code for debuggers such as MacsBug. The {$D+} directive identifies the name of each routine in the compiled code, truncated to 8 characters (and mapped to all capital letters), and is the default. The {$D++} directive, used by MacApp programs, is the same as {$D+}, except it includes 16-character names with Object Pascal method routines. {$D-} suppresses all symbols and is the same as the Pascal -z command.

The {$R} directives determine whether the compiler generates run time code to check that certain references are within a valid range. By default, the compiler performs range checking on Pascal operations; these checks are disabled by the {$R-} directive.

These checks include checking array and string indexes to verify that the references are within the bounds defined for the array or string. When a string value is assigned to a string variable, the (logical) length of the string is checked to see if it is less than or equal to the phyiscal (maximum) length of the variable. In the program fragment

```
msg: STRING[5];
longmsg: STRING[40];
...
longmsg := 'This is a long message';
msg := longmsg;
```

the constant string is short enough to be stored in the `longmsg` variable but too long for the `msg` variable.

Range checking also includes assignments to variables of subrange types of the form `lo..hi`, which will be checked to make sure the new value is between `lo` and `hi`, inclusive. Sets involving subranges will also be checked.

`{$R-}` disables this checking at run time and also disables compile time range checking for the same data types. In the statements

```
byt: SignedByte; { -128..127 }
...
  {$R-}
  byt := 512;
```

the `{$R-}` would suppress the compile time error that would otherwise be generated by the compiler for the assignment.

Code compiled with range checking enabled uses the CHK instruction of the Motorola 68000 to test for an out-of-range condition. If the value is outside the CHK range, the instruction generates a 68000 exception, which, in turns displays the System Error alert with ID=05, as illustrated by Figure 7–5.

The System Error Handler will allow you to resume execution after a

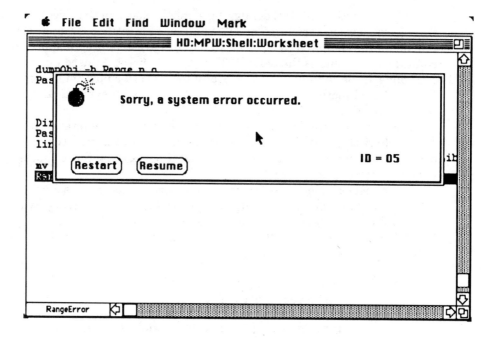

Figure 7–5:   Range checking system error

range-checking error when running under the MPW shell.

You may wish to temporarily disable range checking for a statement or series of statements, when Pascal's strong type checking gets in the way of what you know to be a valid usage. For example, a string in a dynamically allocated record may have an indeterminite length. If the string is declared as STRING[255], no range error is possible but each new record will allocate 256 bytes (255 plus the length) for the variable. In the statements

```
TYPE
   MyRecord = RECORD
      field1: INTEGER;
      aString: STRING[0];
   END;
   MyRecordPtr = ^MyRecord;
VAR
   myrec: MyRecordPtr;
...
myrec := MyRecordPtr(NewPtr(SIZEOF(MyRecord));
...
SetPtrSize(myrec, SIZEOF(MyRecord) + bufflen);
FOR i := 1 TO bufflen DO
{$R-}
   myrec^.aString[i] := ' ';
{$R+}
```

range checking is suppressed for the string accesses, since the compiler would otherwise reject a value for i greater than 0.

When generating your final production code, you would normally disable both range checking and debugging symbols with the directives

$$\{\$R-\} \quad \{\$D-\}$$

at the beginning of the source file to produce smaller, faster code. These options can also be specified on the Pascal command line by -r and -z, respectively.

The {$OV+} directive can be used to check for integer overflow in calculations. This will produce significantly longer and slower code and should be used only when debugging numeric algorithms where such overflows are important. Each calculation that could produce an error is followed by a TRAPV instruction, which will produce a system error alert with ID=06 in the event of a failure. The -ov option of the Pascal command can be used to insert the same overflow checks.

By default, the compiler will perform compile time checks to catch some unsafe usages of handles when referencing Object Pascal objects. The declaration

```
TYPE
   TFoo = OBJECT
```

```
      field: INTEGER;
    END;
VAR
  foo: TFoo;
  PROCEDURE AnyProc(VAR num: INTEGER); FORWARD;
...
AnyProc(foo.field);
```

would produce an error message:

```
#       AnyProc(foo.field);
#                        ?
### Pascal - Error 815 Unsafe use of a handle as a var parameter.
    File "HandleTest.p"; Line 36
```

Why? Variable field is in a relocatable block and is referenced through a doubly indirected pointer, as are all objects. The compiler assumes that AnyProc may allocate memory, which in turn can compact the heap and cause any relocatable block to relocate. The address of field (indicated by VAR) might become invalid (after such compaction) before it is used to store the result of AnyProc.

If you're sure the reference is safe, the {$H-} directive tells the compiler to ignore such errors. The following is certainly a brute-force approach that will always be safe at run time, while suppressing compile time error messages:

```
        HLock(Handle(foo));
    {$H-}
        AnyProc(foo.field);
    {$H+}
        HUnlock(Handle (foo));
```

CODE GENERATION

MPW Pascal's extensions for short circuit boolean operators—the & and | symbols—were introduced earlier. When these operators are used in a boolean expression, the compiler generates code that evaluates only the operands necessary—taking the "short-circuit" path where available. This is often faster than the corresponding AND and OR, which will always evaluate both operands.

For example, in

```
    IF (hte <> NIL) & (myport <> 0) THEN
        hte2^^.viewRect := myport^.portRect;
```

the value of myport will not be tested if hTE is NIL.

Unfortunately, the & and | operators are not standard Pascal symbols and may cause portability problems if you later use another compiler. The {$SC+} option forces AND to be treated the same as & and OR to be treated as |. This allows you to use the faster operations without changing standard Pascal source. You can include {$SC+} at the beginning of any program to speed all calculations so long as your code never relies on any side effects of evaluating the operands in a boolean expression. The statement

```
{$SC+}
. . .
IF (hte <> NIL) AND (myport <> 0) THEN
    hte2^^.viewRect := myport^.portRect;
```

would generate the same code as the previous example but would be portable to other compilers.

You should use {$SC+} only to speed your run-time execution, not where the interpretation of the statement would be invalid if {$SC-} were ignored. For example, the statements

```
{$SC+}
. . .
IF (hte <> NIL) AND (hte^^.txLen <> 0) THEN
    hand := hte^^.hText;
```

would be compiled by MPW Pascal into valid code. However, with a compiler that ignored the {$SC+} compiler option, the code would be prone to crashing; both expressions would be evaluated and handle hte would be used in the second expression, even if invalid.

MACINTOSH II CODE GENERATION

MPW Pascal includes several options to generate code specific to the Motorola MC68020 processor and the MC68881 floating point coprocessor. You would use these options if you wanted to improve the speed of programs that would run on a Macintosh II or other machines with such processors, such as the Levco Prodigy SE.

Such a program could not be run on a machine with only a 68000 and without a 68881, such as a standard Macintosh Plus. A well-designed program would use the SysEnvirons call to test for the 68020 (or 68881) and present an alert telling the user that the program can proceed no further.

Two of the compiler directives relate to the 68020, while a directive and command option target code for the 68881.

Using the {$MC68020+} directive modifies the generated object code to take advantage of some extended instructions only available on the 68020 and later processors. The most important are 32-bit multiply and divide instructions, rather than the much slower subroutines used by other MPW Pascal programs. The new instructions also include a faster way of unstacking parameters before returning from a procedure, direct conversion between signed bytes and LONGINT types, and bit-manipulation instructions for inserting and extracting data from packed data structures.

Since the 68020 has a 32-bit data bus, it works best when LONGINT and pointer values are stored on 32-bit boundaries (addresses divisible by 4). The {$ALIGN+} directive inserts extra space to provide this alignment before variables and data structures and can be safely used on systems that do not include a 68020. The option does not change the layout within a data structure, such as a record, as this would create incompatibilities with library interfaces. Instead, records should be designed from the start to provide such alignment by explicitly declaring filler bytes where necessary.

The {$MC68881+} directive generates code for the 68881 and defines all EXTENDED vaues as being the 96-bit quantity expected by the 68881, rather than the 80-bit quantity used by SANE. It should be listed before the USES statement for any program or any variable or procedure declaration. If your program USES SANE, this directive will automatically change the interfaces declared by the SANE unit.

With this directive enabled, the compiler generates 68881 instructions for the four basic operators, comparisons, and conversions between different sizes of floating point values. It also attempts to assign any EXTENDED local variables to one of the 68881's eight floating-point registers. Algorithms that use EXTENDED data will be considerably faster than those using REAL or DOUBLE values—to an even greater degree than with SANE—and, of course, more accurate as well.

The numeric results using the 68881 for basic arithmetic are identical to those produced by SANE. However, if your program makes use of any advanced SANE interfaces, such as those involving exception conditions, you should consult the Pascal documentation for a discussion of the differences.

A program that uses the {$MC68881+} directive can be further sped up using a compilation command such as

```
Pascal theprogram.p -d Elems881=TRUE
```

Such a compilation option causes the compiler to generate direct 68881 instructions for trancendental functions. These include trigonometric, inverse trigonometric, hyperbolic, logarithmic, and exponentiation functions. However, the results will be slightly different from (and less accurate than) those produced by SANE.

Since the choice of the {$MC68881+} directive affects the size of the EXTENDED data type, you may need to convert between the 80-bit data type used by SANE and the 96-bit type used by the 68881. With the 68881 code generation disabled, the Extended96 data type is defined as a 96-bit array, as are two functions:

```
FUNCTION X96toX80 (x: Extended96): EXTENDED;
FUNCTION X80toX96 (x: EXTENDED): Extended96;
```

These could be used to prepare a parameter for a call to an assembly-language function that invokes the 68881 directly.

Similarly, if you've enabled 68881 code generation, the Extended80 data type is an 80-bit array, and the SANE unit defines the functions:

```
FUNCTION X96toX80 (x: EXTENDED): Extended80;
FUNCTION X80toX96 (x: Extended80): EXTENDED;
```

You might need these if your standard file format included an 80-bit floating point value, although your program used the 68881 for computations.

The {$MC68020+} and {$MC68020-} directives can be used on a procedure-by-procedure basis, but Apple recommends that any program should be consistent in its choice of whether or not to use the 68881. If you choose to disregard the recommendation, you should allow for possible incompatibilities in calling sequences, global variables, and incompatible object library requirements. A better approach would be to write 68881-specific code in assembly language and then call it where appropriate.

SPEEDING UNIT COMPILATION

Compiling a program that uses the standard Macintosh interface units can be very time-consuming. Even the tiniest of programs will require reading more than 125K of unit interfaces each time the program is compiled so that the compiler can build a symbol table of the identifiers declared in those units.

MPW Pascal allows you to speed compilation by saving the symbol table built from a series of units and then automatically reloading that symbol table when that program is next compiled.

When it includes a file name, the {$LOAD} directive specifies the name of the saved symbol table, which includes the definitions of all the units mentioned until the next {$LOAD}. If no file name is specified, the compiler terminates the previous symbol table without starting a new one. In the source

```
USES
    Unit1,
    {$LOAD SymbA.LOAD}, Unit2, Unit3,
    {$LOAD SymbB.LOAD}, Unit4,
    {$LOAD} Unit5;
```

the file SymbA.LOAD contains the definitions of Unit2 and Unit3, while

SymbB.LOAD contains the definitions of Unit4. These symbol tables cannot be used for anything other than speeding compilations referencing Pascal units.

The same directives are used to write a symbol table the first time the program is compiled and to read it in subsequent compilations. What is the difference? If the $LOAD file is present, the Pascal compiler skips the units until the next load, instead reading the prebuilt symbol table. If the $LOAD file is not present, the compiler reads the sources and writes the symbol table to disk.

The -k option of the Pascal command specifies the directory to be used for both writing and reading the $LOAD file. The same $LOAD files can be shared by more than one program if they reference the same units, and you'll want to do so since the files can be quite large.

The optional MacApp component of MPW provides a good example of how to use {$LOAD} directives which can be adopted by your other Pascal programs. MacApp stores a symbol table for units MemTypes, QuickDraw, OSIntf, ToolIntf, and PackIntf in {LoadMacApp}MacIntf.LOAD.

Since this symbol table is larger than 100K, you could save disk space by referencing this same $LOAD file in your Pascal compiles both with and without MacApp. You would include {$LOAD} compiler directives around these standard USES in your source program, as in:

```
USES
   {$LOAD MacIntf.LOAD}
     MemTypes, QuickDraw, OSIntf, ToolIntf, PackIntf,
   {$LOAD}
     MacPrint, MyUnit;
```

Your compilation would then be run with a -k option to place the symbol table in the appropriate directory. The alias

```
Alias pc 'Pascal -k "{LoadMacApp}" "{Target}"'
```

would always compile the target window with the symbol table directory predefined.

If you're using {$LOAD} directives with units that may be changing, strange things can happen. If any changes are made in the source that is precompiled, the $LOAD file is no longer valid—the compiler won't tell you this—and you will probably see strange compilation errors from text that worked perfectly well earlier. This is true even if the files themselves are unchanged, but different text is selected through conditional compilation and compiler variables set by the -d compiler option.

In these cases, you must delete the $LOAD file to force it to be rebuilt with the new text or conditional compilations.

The Make command can be used to somewhat simplify the process of keeping these files up to date. However, $LOAD is best used with files that aren't changing frequently, such as the standard Macintosh interfaces. In that case, you would only have to delete your $LOAD files when you install a new release of MPW.

OTHER DIRECTIVES

As noted earlier, the {$U filename} directive specifies the name of the source file containing a Pascal unit; normally, filename will include the suffix .p. This directive is provided for compatibility with the Lisa Workshop compiler, but, in general, the -i pathname compiler option should be used instead to reference a particular directory.

The {$N} and {$Z} directives can be used to help track down linking problems. Normally, the object files do not include information identifying the routine names to the linker, except for identifiers declared in the INTERFACE of a Pascal unit. {$N+} can be used to force the compiler to include routine names in the object code, while {$Z*} and {$Z} can be used to selectively turn these names on and off. {$Z+} forces variable, global routine, and local routine names to be written to the object file.

The {$N} and {$Z} directives should not be confused with the {$D+} directive, which includes 8-character routine identifications in the object code but in binary form for run time use by debuggers.

The {$S+} directive directs the compiler to unload its segments frequently, which slows the compilation, but allows it to run with less memory. Again, the -s command line option may be more appropriate. Either may be necessary when compiling on a system with less that 1 megabyte of available RAM.

Several other special comments are not used by the Pascal compiler but instead are interpreted by related tools. The {$P} directive forces a new page in the formatted listing produced by the PasRef command. Comments of the form

```
{[directives] other text}
```

control the formatting of programs by the PasMat tool.

7.6 Building Pascal Programs

Once you have written a valid MPW Pascal program, you will, of course, want to compile and link that program into executable code, most like an MPW tool or a complete application.

The Pascal command is used to compile Pascal source to object code. This object code can be combined with other MPW object files by the MPW linker into one of the program types described in Chapter 3. The compiler is itself an MPW tool that is run from within the MPW shell environment.

Two other MPW tools are provided with the optional Pascal component of MPW. Both `PasMat` and `PasRef` are used to format a Pascal source file. `PasMat` reformats the source to a standard style of indentation and naming that is suitable for later compilation. `PasRef` produces a formatted cross-reference listing that you would normally print for future reference.

COMPILATION OPTIONS

The Pascal command is used to run the MPW Pascal compiler with one or more source documents and to produce object file(s) suitable for use with the `Link` or `Lib` commands.

Pascal

Compile a Pascal program

Syntax:

`Pascal file …`	Compile each source `file`
`Pascal`	Compile interactively entered source

Options:

`-align`	Align data to 32-bit boundaries (`{$ALIGN+}`)
`-d name=TRUE`	Compiler variable `name` is true (`{$SETC name := TRUE}`)
`-d name=FALSE`	Compiler variable `name` is false (`{$SETC name := FALSE}`)
`-i pathname,…`	Use each `pathname` directory to find unit and include files
`-k pathname`	Dump and load `{$LOAD}` symbol tables to directory `pathname`
`-mc68020`	Generate 68020 code (`{$MC68020+}`)
`-mc68881`	Generate 68881 code for standard operators (`{$MC68881+}`)
`-d Elems881=TRUE`	Generate 68881 code for trancendental functions
`-o objfile`	Output compiled object code to file or directory `objfile`
`-ov`	Enable overflow checking (`{$OV+}`)

-p	Display compilation progress report
-r	Suppress range checking ({$R-})
-t	Display compilation time
-z	Do not generate debugger names ({$D-})

Remarks:

By default, the compiled object code goes to file *file.*o for each *file.* Interactively entered source is terminated by Command-Enter, and the compile output is sent to file p.o by default. If more than one *file* is specified and the -o option is used, *objfile* must be a directory pathname.

More than one -i option may be used; each should include one or more option parameters, separated by commas. The directories specified by -i *pathname* are searched after the folder containing *file*, but before the directories defined by {PInterfaces}.

Input/Output:

Diagnostic	Compiler error messages

Examples:

Pascal Src.p	Compile Src.p and leave object in Src.p.o

Many of the compiler options correspond to compiler directives described in the previous section. The command line forms are often more convenient, as they can be used without changing the program source.

The compiler can be used interactively, which, if you're learning Pascal (or the MPW dialect), is an easy way to try out the syntax of declarations or programs. The compiler will normally create a file p.o in the current directory, so you should enter the command

```
Pascal -c
```

to use the compiler to syntax check interactively entered source.

The default Pascal options are suitable for most compilations unless you are using {$LOAD} directives to speed compilation of unit references. A simple menu command can be defined by the UserStartup commands:

```
Set POpts "-k {MPW}LoadDir"; Export POpts
AddMenu Control "Pascal compile" ∂
   'Open "{Worksheet}"; Pascal {POpts} "{Target}"'
```

The commands would define a custom menu to compile the Pascal program in the target window and display any error messages to the active window.

More elaborate compilation commands might involve a custom menu that references a command file. For example, you might wish to compile directly from the active window, but you must redirect any error messages to another window, such as the worksheet. You might also test that the active window is, in fact, a Pascal source file. The following commands

```
Open -t "{Worksheet}"
Find §Δ
Begin
  If "{Active}" =~ /≈.p/
    Save "{Active}"
    Pascal "{Active}"
  Else
    Beep
  End
End ≥ §
```

could be used in a command file PCompileActive, which would then be referenced by the custom menu definition:

```
AddMenu Control "Pascal compile" PCompileActive
```

Alhough both examples do so, it is not necessary to save the program source prior to compilation. If you wish to test-compile a small change without committing to it, you may not want to save the file first. On the other hand, the commands force you to save your source frequently, which is a good idea to protect against a crash, power failure, or some other unexpected calamity.

Linking Programs

As with other MPW programs, compiled MPW Pascal programs are linked using the Link tool supplied with MPW. This subsection presents enough options to allow you to build most simple applications and tools.

Link accepts any number of object files as input. For a Pascal program contained in a single source file, this will mean the file.p.o file produced by the Pascal compilation of that source. As described in an earlier section, the link command will also include one or more MPW (or MPW Pascal) object libraries, depending on what sort of program it is and which RAM-based libraries it references.

Linking is not necessary to resolve the *Inside Macintosh* routines defined as INLINE, since the compiler generates direct trap references for these routines. However, the default output of Link is Link.Out. Normally you will specify another name using the -o option, as in:

```
Link -o Mine Mine.p.o "{Libraries}Runtime.o"∂
     "{PLibraries}PasLib.o"
```

By default, if the output file (Mine) already exists, Link will replace the 'CODE' resources while leaving the remainder of the file unmodified. This allows you to use Link to build an application's code resources after Rez has compiled the other resources.

If the output file does not exist, a new file is created corresponding to a generic application: a file type of 'APPL' and a creator of '????'. The -t and -c options can be used to specify different types and creators. If you are building an MPW tool, you would use a command such as:

```
Link -o Mine Mine.p.o  -t 'MPST' -c 'MPS ' ∂
    "{Libraries}Runtime.o" "{PLibraries}PasLib.o"
```

When writing a menu command or alias designed to compile any possible program, you may end up including all the libraries you normally use. The linker will display diagnostic messages for any library that was unnecessarily included in the link. These messages are suppressed by the -w option.

A complete description of the Link command is provided in Chapter 10.

FORMATTING PROGRAMS

The PasMat command is used to reformat Pascal source statements. It has options to convert arbitrary Pascal source statements to almost every possible style, with particular emphasis on indentation and capitalization of statements.

PasMat

Format a Pascal program in the standard style

Syntax:

PasMat *file output*	Format Pascal source *file* to file *output*
PasMat *file*	Format Pascal source *file* to standard output
PasMat	Format Pascal source from standard input to standard output

Options:

-a	Disable CASE label bunching
-b	Enable IF statement bunching
-c	Place BEGIN on same line as previous word
-d	Don't change (* ... *) comments to { ... }

-e	Capitalize initial letter of identifiers
-h	Disable FOR, WHILE, and WITH bunching
-i *pathname*,...	Use each *pathname* directory to find unit and include files
-in	Process {$I *includefile*} directives; implied by -i
-k	Indent statements between BEGIN ... END
-l	Leave identifier case as is (overrides -l)
-o *width*	Format output to fit in *width* columns; default is 80
-p	Display progress information
-q	Treat ELSE IF the same as other ELSE constructs
-r	Map reserved words to uppercase (default is lowercase)
-rec	Indent declarations between RECORD ... END
-t *tab*	Each indentation is *tab* spaces wide
-u	Use first occurrence to determine identifier capitlization
-v	Place THEN on a separate line from IF
-w	Convert identifiers to uppercase (default is lowercase)
-x	Suppress spaces around +,-,*,/, <, <=, <>, >=, >, =
-y	Suppress spaces on either side of :=
-z	Suppress space after commas
-@	Force multiple tags in CASE group to separate lines
-_	Delete underscores from identifiers for portability

Remarks:

The interpretation of the -i option is the same as for the Pascal command.

   The -e, -l, -u, and -_ options all override -w (uppercase identifiers). All but -l also override -l (leave identifiers as is). The -r option combined with -l converts reserved words to uppercase while other identifiers are left unchanged.

   The shell variable {PasMatOpts} is checked by PasMat for a standard set of options that are used prior to any options specified on the command line.

Input/Output:

Output

Formatted Pascal source if *output* omitted

Examples:

PasMat Src.p

Format Src.p to standard output

Several of the PasMat options are used for bunching, which attempts to place multiple statements or keywords on the same line if there's room. For example, THEN is normally placed on the same line as the corresponding IF (the bunched form), but the -v option places it on the next line. Other options control the indentation of block structures, such as IF statements, FOR loops, and other BEGIN ... END blocks.

PasMat can also be used to set the capitalization of reserved words and other identifiers. The standard form recommended by Apple sets reserved words to all uppercase, while other identifiers are capitalized based on their first use. PasMat can also be used to rename identifiers, although the Canon tool (described in Chapter 5) provides both renaming and standard capitalization formatting.

Similarly, although PasMat can be used to insert tabs into the output, it may be more appropriate to combine it with the Entab command, as with:

```
PasMat OldSource.p  | Entab -t 4 > NewSource.p
```

To avoid strange results, you should always build the Tabs commands into your command files (or aliases) to make sure the tab spacing used by MPW to read the file is the same as that used to write the file.

The capabilities and use of the PasMat command are best illustrated by sample output. Example 7–7 shows a simple unformatted Pascal program prior to formatting, while Figure 7–6 shows the output produced by PasMat without any options.

Figure 7–7 shows the output when using options to bunch and uppercase the input source. The -b and -n options bunch IF statements and routine parameters, while -x removes spaces on either side of operators. The -r option maps reserved words to uppercase, while -u uses the first usage of other identifiers to establish their capitalization. The -d option disables subsitution of (* ... *) comment delimiters, while -t is used to set a different width for each indentation level.

Figure 7–8 shows a different output using options that demonstrate PasMat's optional indentation rules. The -h option disables bunching of FOR statements, -k indents statements within BEGIN ... END blocks, -v puts THEN on a separate line, and -q disables bunching ELSE IF on the same line. The -w option forces identifiers (rather than keywords, as in the previous example) to uppercase.

```
program anyprog;
type
StdArray = array
[1..100] of integer;
function SumThem(arr: stdarray; dim: integer): integer;
var
i,sum:
integer;
begin
sum:=0;
for i
:= 1 to dim
do begin
if arr[i] > 0 then
sum := sum+arr[i] else if
arr[i] = -maxint then
leave;
end;
sumthem := sum;
end; (* SumThem *)
var
a: stdarray;
begin
writeln(sumthem(a,20));
end.
```

Example 7-7:   Input for PasMat command

If PasMat reaches an unexpected syntax error in the source file, it will stop immediately. You would normally use PasMat after Pascal has verified that the program has a valid syntax.

Several of the PasMat options are not shown. PasMat also accepts formatting options embedded with a syntax similar to compiler directives. A complete explanation of PasMat options and directives is provided by the *MPW Pascal Language Reference* manual.

CROSS-REFERENCE INFORMATION

Two commands provide cross-reference information about a Pascal source program. The PasRef command produces a formatted listing and a cross-reference listing, while the ProcNames command lists the procedure names within the program.

PasRef

Produces cross-reference listing for Pascal program

```
PasMat -b -d -n -r -t 4 -u -x 'Example 7-7'

PROGRAM anyprog;

TYPE
    StdArray = ARRAY [1..100] OF integer;

    FUNCTION SumThem
      (arr: StdArray; dim: integer): integer;

    VAR
      i, sum: integer;

    BEGIN
      sum := 0;
      FOR i := 1 TO dim DO
         BEGIN
            IF arr[i]>0 THEN sum := sum+arr[i]
            ELSE IF arr[i]=-maxint THEN LEAVE;
         END;
         SumThem := sum;
    END; (* SumThem *)

VAR
    a: StdArray;

BEGIN

    writeln(SumThem(a, 20));

END.
```

Figure 7–6:   Default PasMat output from Example 7–7

Syntax:

PasRef [file …]	Format each Pascal source [file]
PasRef	Format Pascal source from standard input

Options:

-d	Cross-reference each [file] separately.
-i [pathname,...]	Use each [pathname] directory to find unit and include files
-ni	Do not process include files
-nl	Do not display input source, only cross-reference
-nu	Do not process units

```
PasMat -h -k -q -t 4 -v -w 'Example 7-7'

program ANYPROG;
type
   STDARRAY = array [1..100] of INTEGER;

   function SUMTHEM
      (ARR: STDARRAY; DIM: INTEGER): INTEGER;

   var
      I, SUM: INTEGER;

   begin
      SUM := 0;
      for I := 1 to DIM do
         begin
            if ARR[I] > 0 then
               SUM := SUM + ARR[I]
            else
               if ARR[I] = - MAXINT then
                  eave;
         end;
         SUMTHEM := SUM;
   end; { SumThem }
```

Figure 7–7:   PasMat output with bunching and uppercase

-o	The program includes OBJECT declarations
-p	Display progress information
-w [width]	Set maximum width of output listing; default is 110

Remarks:

By default, PasRef produces both a formatted source listing (with line number and indentation counters displayed in the left margin) and a cross-reference listing. It ignores conditional compilation directives.

Input/Output:

Output	Formatted cross-reference listing

Examples:

PasRef Src.p	Display cross-reference for Src.p to standard output

```
PasMat -b -d -n -r -t 4 -u -x 'Example 7-7'
PROGRAM anyprog;

TYPE
    StdArray = ARRAY [1..100] OF integer;

    FUNCTION SumThem
        (arr: StdArray; dim: integer): integer;

    VAR
        i, sum: integer;

    BEGIN
        sum := 0;
        FOR i := 1 TO dim DO
            BEGIN
                IF arr[i]>0 THEN sum := sum+arr[i]
                ELSE IF arr[i]=-maxint THEN LEAVE;
            END;
            SumThem := sum;
    END; (* SumThem *)

VAR
    a: StdArray;

BEGIN
    writeln(SumThem(a, 20));
END.
```

Figure 7–8:   PasMat output using indentation options

Figure 7–9 shows a PasRef source and cross-reference listing for Example 7–7.

The ProcNames command is used to list the procedure names defined by a Pascal source file. These include globally defined procedures and local procedures nested within other procedures. The command can be used with both programs and Pascal units.

ProcNames

List procedure names from a Pascal program

Syntax:

ProcNames *file* ...   List procedures from each Pascal source

```
    1  1     1 -- { Example 7-7: Input for PasMat command
}
    2  1     2 --
    3  1     3 --
    4  1     4 -- program anyprog;
    5  1     5 -- type
    6  1     6 -- StdArray = array
    7  1     7 -- [1..100] of integer;
    8  1     8 -- A function SumThem(arr: stdarray; dim:
integer): integer;
    9  1     9 -- var
   10  1    10 -- i,sum:
   11  1    11 -- integer;
   12  1    12 0- A begin
   13  1    13 -- sum:=0;
   14  1    14 -- for i
   15  1    15 -- := 1 to dim
   16  1    16 1- do begin
   17  1    17 -- if arr[i] > 0 then
   18  1    18 -- sum := sum+arr[i] else if
   19  1    19 -- arr[i] = -maxint then
   20  1    20 -- leave;
   21  1    21 -1 end;
   22  1    22 -- sumthem := sum;
   23  1    23 -0 A end; (* SumThem *)
   24  1    24 -- var
   25  1    25 -- a: stdarray;
   26  1    26 0- begin
   27  1    27 -- writeln(sumthem(a,20));
   28  1    28 -0 end.
   29  1    29 --
```

1. Example 7-7

```
-A-
  a            25*( 1)    27 ( 1)
  anyprog       4*( 1)
  arr           8*( 1)    17 ( 1)    18 ( 1)    19 ( 1)

-D-
  dim           8*( 1)    15 ( 1)

-I-
  i            10*( 1)    14=( 1)    17 ( 1)    18 ( 1)    19
( 1)
  integer       7 ( 1)     8 ( 1)     8 ( 1)    11 ( 1)

-M-
  maxint       19 ( 1)
```

```
-S-
  StdArray     6*( 1)
  stdarray     8 ( 1)    25 ( 1)
  sum         10*( 1)    13=( 1)    18=( 1)    18 ( 1)    22
( 1)
  SumThem      8*( 1)
  sumthem     22=( 1)    27 ( 1)

-W-
  writeln     27 ( 1)

*** End PasRef: 13 id's   31 references
```

Figure 7–9:   PasRef listing of Example 7–7

	file
ProcNames	List procedures from standard input

Options:

-c	Process USES and include only once
-f	Format output compatible with PasMat
-i *pathname,…*	Use each *pathname* directory to find unit and include files
-n	Do not display line numbers and nesting levels
-o	The program includes OBJECT declarations
-p	Display progress information
-u	Processes USES statements

Remarks:

By default, ProcNames displays the list procedures in the files, preceeded by the line number. The name is also preceded by an integer that starts at zero for a UNIT or PROGRAM name, increasing by one for each level of nesting of one procedure within another. It ignores conditional compilation directives.

Input/Output:

Output	List of procedure names

Examples:

ProcNames -n Test.p	Show procedure names for Test.p to standard output

Figure 7–10 shows a ProcNames listing for a sample program.

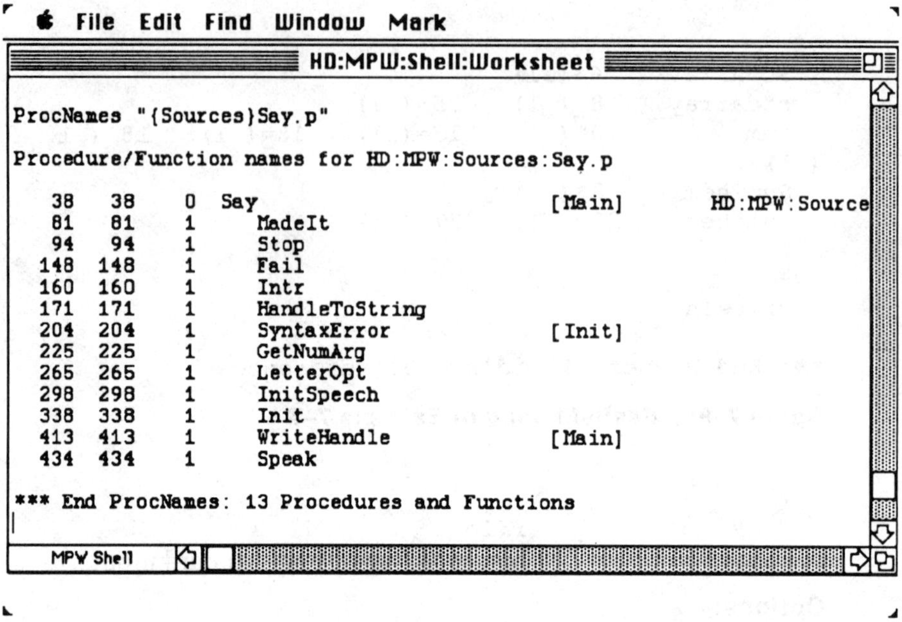

```
  File   Edit   Find   Window   Mark
╔══════════════════ HD:MPW:Shell:Worksheet ══════════════════╗
ProcNames "{Sources}Say.p"

Procedure/Function names for HD:MPW:Sources:Say.p

    38    38   0   Say                        [Main]        HD:MPW:Source
    81    81   1     MadeIt
    94    94   1     Stop
   148   148   1     Fail
   160   160   1     Intr
   171   171   1     HandleToString
   204   204   1     SyntaxError              [Init]
   225   225   1     GetNumArg
   265   265   1     LetterOpt
   298   298   1     InitSpeech
   338   338   1     Init
   413   413   1     WriteHandle             [Main]
   434   434   1     Speak

*** End ProcNames: 13 Procedures and Functions

 MPW Shell
```

Figure 7–10: Sample ProcNames listing

EXAMPLE: THE TALKING TOOL

The Example 7–8 displays a complete MPW tool, which accepts command parameters and uses the tool libraries to control the cursor and intercept Command-period interruptions.

```
{ Example 7-8: Talking MPW tool }

{-------------------------------------------------------------
NAME
  Say -- speak something

SYNOPSIS
  Say [-v] [-m] [-f freq] [-r rate] [-q] [-p] message

DESCRIPTION
  "Say" uses the MacinTalk driver, if present, to ar-
ticulate
  a message.
```

```
     -f freq gives intonation pitch (Hz)
     -r rate gives speaking rate (words/minute)
     -m      machine-like monotone
     -p      message is already phonetically spelled
     -q      don't talk, show phonetic equivalent on std
output
     -v      output verbose information to diagnostic output

DIAGNOSTICS
   0  Normal termination.
   1  Syntax error.
   2  An error occurred.
   3  Execution aborted.


------------------------------------------------------------}
{$R-}    { No range checking }
{$D+}    { Procedure names for Macsbug }

{$P}
{==========================================================}
{ By default, segment 'Main' }
PROGRAM  Say;

{ Must run as MPW tool. Will not run stand-alone }

USES
  MemTypes,     { OS & Toolbox }
  Quickdraw,
  OSIntf,
  ToolIntf,
  PackIntf,
  PASLIBIntf,   { Pascal stuff }
  IntEnv,       { MPW Tool interfaces }
  CursorCtl,
  ErrMgr,
  Signal,
  SpeechIntf;   { Macintalk interface file }

CONST
  Version = '1.0';

VAR
  { General boiler plate }
  RetCode: (RC_Normal, RC_ParmErrs, RC_Fail, RC_Abort);
{Return codes}
  ProgName: Str255;      {Program's file name}
  Interrupted: Boolean;
                  {True ==> interrupted (Opt "." pressed)}
```

```
      { Here are some options }
      PhoneticFlag, FreqFlag, RateFlag, MachineFlag, Ver-
    boseFlag,
         QuietFlag: Boolean;
      Freq,Rate: INTEGER;
      { These handles have to be de-allocated upon exit }
      speech: SpeechHandle; { for MacinTalk driver }
      msgH: Handle;
      phonH: Handle;
      { Other variables }
      myerr: INTEGER;
      speechopen: Boolean;
         { MacinTalk was successfully started }
      msgLen: LongInt;


    {*-------------------------------------------*
     | MadeIt -- print progress information |
      *------------------------------------------*}

    PROCEDURE MadeIt (Msg: Str255);
    VAR
       i: INTEGER;
    BEGIN
       IF VerboseFlag THEN
          WriteLn(Diagnostic,Msg);
    END;


    {*-------------------------------------*
     | Stop  -  terminate   execution    |
      *-----------------------------------*}

    PROCEDURE Stop(Msg:    Str255);

    VAR
       Len: Integer;
       errmsg: Str255;
       p: StringPtr;

    BEGIN {Stop}

       RotateCursor(0);

       { Print the supplied message }
       Len := Length(Msg);
       IF Len > 0 THEN
          WriteLn(Diagnostic,  Msg);
```

```pascal
  { Now check if the problem needs an explanation }
  IF myerr <> noErr THEN
    BEGIN
      InitErrMgr('',  '',  True);
        { Show error numbers }
      p := @errmsg;
      GetSysErrText(myerr,  p);
      WriteLn(diagnostic, '# ',  errmsg);
      CloseErrMgr;
    END;

  { Clean up everything that's pending }
  IF speechopen THEN
    { We succeeded in opening driver }
    BEGIN
      SpeechOff(speech);
        {Turn it off; deallocates handle}
      MadeIt('MacinTalk driver closed.');
    END
  ELSE
    BEGIN
      IF speech <> NIL THEN
        DisposHandle(speech);
          { manually clear handle }
    END;
  IF msgH <> NIL THEN
    DisposHandle(msgH);
  IF phonH <> NIL THEN
    DisposHandle(phonH);

  RotateCursor(0);

  IF Interrupted THEN
    RetCode := RC_Abort;
  IEexit(Ord(RetCode)); { Well,  that's that... }
END; {Stop}

{*--------------------------------------------*
 | Fail - Report a failure during processing |
 *--------------------------------------------*}

PROCEDURE Fail(errmess: Str255);

BEGIN {Fail}
  RetCode := RC_Fail;
  Stop(Concat('### ', progName, ' - ', errmess, '.'));
END; {Fail}
```

```
{*--------------------------------------*
 | Intr   - Process external interrupt |
 *--------------------------------------*}

PROCEDURE Intr;

BEGIN {Intr}
   Interrupted := True;
      {test this switch wherever appropriate to do so}
END;   {Intr}

{*------------------------------------------------*
 | HandleToString - Convert a Handle to a Str255 |
 *------------------------------------------------*}

FUNCTION HandleToString
   (hand: Handle; offset: LongInt; VAR str: Str255):
   LongInt;
   { Returns # of characters unconverted }
VAR
   len, x: LongInt;
   p: Ptr;

BEGIN {HandleToString}
   len := GetHandleSize(hand) - offset;
   IF len <= 0 THEN
      str := ''
   ELSE
      BEGIN
         IF len < 255 THEN
            x := len
         ELSE
            x := 255;
         HLock(hand);
         BlockMove
         (Ptr(ORD(hand^) + offset),
            Ptr(SUCC(ORD(@str))), x);
         HUnlock(hand);
         str [0] := CHR(x);    { set length byte }
         HandleToString := len - x;
            { number left undone }
      END;
   END; {HandleToString}

{$P}
{=========================================================}
{$S Init}
{*---------------------------------------------------------
*
```

```
  | SyntaxError-Report syntax error for the command line
  |
  *---------------------------------------------------------
*}

  PROCEDURE SyntaxError(Suffix: Str255);

  VAR
    Len: INTEGER;

  BEGIN {SyntaxError}
    Len := Length(Suffix);

    IF Len > 0 THEN
      WriteLn
        (diagnostic, '### ',
         progName, ' - ', Suffix, '.');

    RetCode := RC_ParmErrs;
    Stop
      (Concat
        ('# Usage - ', progName,
         ' [-v] [-m] [-f freq]
            [-r rate] [-q] [-p] message'));
  END; {SyntaxError}

  {*---------------------------------------------------------*
   | GetNumArg - Get int argument after letter option |
   *---------------------------------------------------------*}

  FUNCTION GetNumArg
    (VAR ArgVIndex: Integer;
     Name: Str255;
     Low, High: INTEGER
    ): INTEGER;
  VAR
    i: INTEGER;
    num: LongInt;

  BEGIN
    i := ArgVIndex + 1;
    IF i >= ArgC THEN   { Need another parm }
      SyntaxError
        (Concat
          ('The "', ArgV^ [ArgVIndex]^,
            '" option requires a parameter'));

    WriteLn
      (diagnostic, '### ', progName, ' - ',
```

```
              'The "', ArgV^[i]^, '" option has invalid '
          Name,  '.');

        StringToNum(ArgV^ [i]^,  num);

        IF(num < Low) OR(num > High) THEN
          BEGIN
            WriteLn
               (diagnostic, '### ', progName, ' - ',  '"',
               ArgV^ [ArgVIndex]^,  '" option requires ',
               Low, ' <= ',  Name,  ' <= ', High, '.');
            SyntaxError('');
          END;

      ArgvIndex := i;
      GetNumArg := num;   { Give back the value }

    END; {GetNumArg}


    {*----------------------------------*
     | LetterOpt - Set a letter option  |
     *----------------------------------*}

    PROCEDURE LetterOpt
       (Opt: Char; VAR ArgVIndex: Integer);

    BEGIN
      CASE Opt OF
        'f', 'F':
        BEGIN
          FreqFlag := True;
          Freq :=
            GetNumArg(ArgVIndex, 'freq',  65,  500);
        END;
        'm', 'M':
          MachineFlag := True;
        'p', 'P':
        PhoneticFlag := True;
        'q', 'Q':
          QuietFlag := True;
        'r', 'R':
        BEGIN
          RateFlag := True;
          Rate :=
            GetNumArg(ArgVIndex,  'rate',  85,  425);
        END;
        'v', 'V':
          VerboseFlag := True;
```

```
        OTHERWISE
            SyntaxError
                (Concat
                    ('"',  ArgV^ [ArgVIndex]^,
                     '" is not an option'));
    END; {case}
END; {LetterOpt}


{*----------------------------------*
 | InitSpeech - Start MacinTalk driver |
 *----------------------------------*}

PROCEDURE InitSpeech;

BEGIN
    RotateCursor(0);

{ Note: even if we aren't going to say text,  we need
    SpeechOn for Reader }
    myerr := SpeechOn(NIL,  speech);
    IF myerr <> noErr THEN
        Fail('could not open MacinTalk driver');
    speechopen := True;
    MadeIt('MacinTalk driver opened.');

    RotateCursor(0);

    IF MachineFlag THEN
        BEGIN
            SpeechPitch(speech,  0,  robotic);
            MadeIt('Set Robotic intonation.');
        END;
    IF FreqFlag THEN
        BEGIN
            SpeechPitch(speech,  Freq,  noChange);
            IF VerboseFlag THEN
                WriteLn
                    (Diagnostic,  'Pitch set to ',
                     Freq,  ' Hz.');
        END;
    IF RateFlag THEN
        BEGIN
            SpeechRate(speech, Rate);
            IF VerboseFlag THEN
                WriteLn
                    (Diagnostic,  'Rate set to ',
```

```
                        Rate,  ' words/minute.');
          END;

     END; {InitSpeech}


     {*--------------------------*
      | Init - Tool initalization |
      *--------------------------*}

     PROCEDURE Init;

     VAR
        IORslt,  ArgVIndex,  FileCount,  HoldIndex:
          Integer;
        PrevSig: SignalHandler;
        Arg: Str255;
        limit: INTEGER;

     BEGIN {Init}

     { Initialize values }
        progName := ArgV^ [0]^;
        myerr := noErr;
        RetCode := RC_Normal;

        { install handler }
        PrevSig := IEsigset(SIGALLSIGS,  @Intr);

        ArgVIndex := 0;
        limit := ArgC -1;      {ArgC is num args plus one}
        WHILE ArgVIndex < limit DO
        BEGIN
           ArgVIndex := ArgVIndex + 1;
           Arg := ArgV^ [ArgVIndex]^;
           IF(Length(Arg) <> 0) THEN
           BEGIN
             IF Arg [1] = '-' THEN     { we have an option }
                BEGIN
                   HoldIndex := ArgVIndex;
                   LetterOpt(Arg [2],  ArgVIndex);
                   IF ArgVIndex <> HoldIndex THEN
                   Cycle;
                      { so that LetterOpt skipped an arg }
                END
             ELSE         { must be the message }
                BEGIN
                   IF msgH = NIL THEN
                   BEGIN
```

```
                      {Grab the string and stuff it into a
                       relocatable block }
                      msgLen := Length(Arg);
                      msgh := Handle(NewString(Arg));
                  END
              ELSE        { Already have a message }
                  SyntaxError
                      ('Too many parameters were specified');
              END;
          END;
      END;


      IF msgH = NIL THEN
          SyntaxError
              ('Not enough parameters were specified');

      IF VerboseFlag THEN
          BEGIN
              WriteLn(Diagnostic);
              WriteLn
                  (Diagnostic,  progname,  '(Version ',
                   Version,  ')');
              WriteLn(Diagnostic);
              IF QuietFlag THEN
                  WriteLn
                      (Diagnostic,
                       'Output phoneme equivalents.');
          END;

      IF Interrupted THEN
          Stop('');

      InitSpeech;    { Fire up those drivers }

      IF Interrupted THEN
          Stop('');

   END; {Init}



{$P}
{=======================================================}
{$S Main}
   {*-------------------------------------------------*
    | WriteHandle- like Write(str), but handle to text |
    *-------------------------------------------------*}
```

```
PROCEDURE WriteHandle(VAR f: TEXT; ahand: Handle);

VAR
   str: Str255;
   off, len: LongInt;

BEGIN
   off := 0;
   REPEAT
     len := HandleToString(ahand,  off,  str);
     Write(f,  str);
     off := off + Length(str)
   UNTIL len <= 0;        { no more characters left }

END;       {WriteHandle}

{*--------------------------------*
 | Speak -- speak our piece       |
 *--------------------------------*}

PROCEDURE Speak;

VAR
   talkstat: INTEGER;

BEGIN {Speak}

   RotateCursor(0);
   { The user may claim to have given us phonetic
     speech. Humor him. }
   IF PhoneticFlag THEN
     BEGIN
       phonH := msgH;
       msgH := NIL;
     END
   ELSE
     BEGIN
       phonH := NewHandle(0);
       IF phonH = NIL THEN
         BEGIN
           myerr := ResError;
             { for decoding of text }
           Fail('unable to allocate memory');
         END;

       HLock(msgH);
       myerr :=
         Reader(speech,  msgH^, msgLen,  phonH);
       HUnlock(msgh);
```

```
            IF myerr <> noErr THEN
               Fail('could not translate to phonetic');

            IF VerboseFlag THEN
               BEGIN
                  WriteLn(Diagnostic);
                  WriteLn(Diagnostic,  'Phonetic text:');
                  WriteHandle(Diagnostic,  phonH);
                  WriteLn(Diagnostic);
                  WriteLn(Diagnostic);
               END;

         END;

      RotateCursor(0);
      IF QuietFlag THEN              { Unspeakable text }
         BEGIN
            WriteHandle(Output,  phonH);
            WriteLn;
         END
      ELSE
         BEGIN
            talkstat := MacinTalk(speech,  phonH);
            IF talkstat <> 0 THEN
               BEGIN
                  IF talkstat < 0 THEN   { OS error }
                     BEGIN
                        myerr := talkstat;
                        Fail('can''t say message');
                     END
                  ELSE                { offset of bad phoneme }
                     Fail
                        ('can''t say message: phoneme
                          error');
               END;

            MadeIt('Wrote to MacinTalk driver.');
         END;

      RetCode  := RC_Normal;
      Stop('');
   END; {Speak}


{*--------------------------------*
 | Say -- main program            |
 *--------------------------------*}


BEGIN {Say}
   Init;               { parse params,  fire up driver }
```

```
{ Leave room for phonetic/speaking buffers }
UnloadSeg(@Init);
Speak;                   { do the work }
END. {Say}
```

Example 7–8:   Talking MPW tool

When compiled, the Say tool accepts a single parameter, an English-language message to be spoken. Say opens the MacinTalk driver and uses it to generate spoken messages.*

Instead of the earlier compilation menu, you might wish to redefine your standard compilation menu to take advantage of Say:

```
AddMenu Control "Pascal compile" ∂
'Pascal "{Target}"; Say `BaseName "{Target}" .p`" is
compiled"'
```

BaseName is a command file described in Chapter 6. After compiling file Test.p, for example, Say would announce "Test is compiled." Say can also be used with the standard rules for building Pascal files in Makeinput files.

---

* The MacinTalk driver and interfaces are available from APDA as part of the "Macintosh Development Package." Because of the extensive use of timeing-dependent code, it is not compatible with the Macintosh II.

Chapter 8

C

THE OPTIONAL C PACKAGE FOR MPW contains three basic components:

- The compiler itself, an MPW tool named C
- A series of header files for the Macintosh and standard C interfaces
- Object libraries used in building C programs

The compiler implements the complete C language defined by Brian Kernighan and Dennis Ritchie in *The C Programming Language* (1977). It also includes most of the standard extensions developed since the Kernighan and Ritchie (K&R) text.

MPW C is also designed to be used in writing Macintosh-specific programs, including applications and desk accessories. In fact, most of the MPW shell is written using MPW C, a convincing testimonial to its suitability for large projects.

However, the standard Macintosh interfaces are documented and implemented using Pascal calling conventions. Some translation is required to use these interfaces from C, and this chapter includes a summary of the rules for making such translations.

The chapter includes several examples demonstrating the Macintosh interfaces and concludes with a complete MPW tool that converts a File Manager file specification to its complete textual pathname.

8.1 Getting Started

This section is intended to get you started on the MPW C compiler and on linking a program written on MPW C. More detailed information about compiler options and C header files are contained later in this chapter, as is introductory information on the selection of standard library files for linking. A complete description of the Link command can be found in Chapter 10.

THE COMPILATION PROCESS

If you've written C programs on a UNIX system, the process of building programs using MPW isn't dramatically different. You still edit source files, compile them, and link them. Unlike UNIX, you never leave the editor to do the compile, so you don't have to save the file first if you don't want to. Also, the MPW C programmer has to contend with more separate libraries and linking options than is typical under UNIX.

As with UNIX, MPW C programs are contained in source files that include the suffix .c. The compiler does not enforce this convention and will gladly compile and file of type 'TEXT'. Each file normally includes a series of #include preprocessor commands and one or more C functions.

The C command (not cc) compiles a C program. If you had a file main.c, you would compile it with:

```
C main.c
```

Unlike the UNIX cc command, the C command does not link the program for you. Also, the object code (if no errors are found) would be placed in main.c.o, not main.o.

When it encounters a syntax error, the compiler normally displays the line with the error and the preceding line, followed by the error messages and then a shell command to select the line with the error. Figure 8–1 shows C error messages from source text entered interactively to the compiler.

The Link command allows you to link an application in the form that can be launched by the Segment Loader or a tool to be used within the MPW shell. Link allows you to specify the name of the program to be created, any object or library files to be used in linking, the type of program to be created, and a variety of diagnostic and formatting options.

A SAMPLE PROGRAM

Although not included in the MPW definition, the standard UNIX shell command "sleep" is among the easiest to implement. It takes a single parameter that is a period in seconds, delaying execution of the next command for the specified period. Since you usually want compiles to go

```
 r    🍎  File  Edit  Find  Window  Mark
┌────────────────────────────────────────────────────────┐
│▒▒▒▒▒▒▒▒▒▒▒▒▒▒▒▒▒▒▒ HD:MPW:Shell:Worksheet ▒▒▒▒▒▒▒▒▒▒▒▒▒█│
├────────────────────────────────────────────────────────┤
│ C                                                     ⇧ │
│                                                         │
│ main(argc,argv)                                         │
│ int argc;                                               │
│ char **argv;                                            │
│ {   int i;                                              │
│                                                         │
│     for (i=0; i<argc; i+)                               │
│         printf("argv[%d] = \"%s\"\n", i, argv[i];       │
│ }                                                       │
│                                                         │
│ File "<stdin>" ; line 6 # Illegal variable or expression│
│ File "<stdin>" ; line 7 # Type mismatch                 │
│ File "<stdin>" ; line 7 # expected: ')' got: name       │
│ File "<stdin>" ; line 7 # expected: ']' got: ')'        │
│ |                                                     ⇩ │
├────────────────────────────────────────────────────────┤
│        C        ◁▯                        ▒▒▒▒▒▒▒▒▒  ⇨▯  │
└────────────────────────────────────────────────────────┘
```

Figure 8–1:   C compiler error messages

faster—not slower—this won't be needed most of the time, but might come in handy if, for example, you wanted to wait for a floppy disk to be inserted during disk duplication.

Example 8–1 shows the source for this command. It uses standard C library functions to validate and convert the command parameter and the Operating System Utilities trap `Delay` to do the actual work.

With the program stored in `sleep.c`, it is compiled by the command:

```
C sleep.c
```

As with most UNIX-style commands designed to be run from a shell, this program is most suitably built as an MPW tool. Besides being faster to launch than an application, a tool can accept arbitrary parameters (such as the delay time), while applications are limited to file names only.

Linker options are used to specify the appropriate file type and creator for an MPW tool. The `Link` command also requires the list of object files and libraries to be used, so `sleep` would be linked using the commands:

```
Link -o Sleep -t MPST -c 'MPS ' Sleep.c.o ∂
    {CLibraries}CRuntime.o {CLibraries}StdCLib.o ∂
    {CLibraries}CInterface.o {CLibraries}CSANELib.o
```

The number of libraries required by `Link` is increased by the use of the standard I/O function `printf`, which implicitly references floating point conversion routines as well.

```
/* Usage:
    sleep time
    where time is a positive integer, delays execution
    for time seconds.
*/

#include <OSUtils.h>              /* for Delay() */
#include <stdio.h>
long atol();
int strspn(),strlen();

main(argc, argv)
int argc;
char **argv;
{ int len;
  long tickcount, dmydelay;

  if (argc == 2)            /* must have single parameter */
  { len = strlen(argv[1]);       /* validate parameter */
    if (len && len == strspn(argv[1], "0123456789"))
        /* Toolbox uses 1/60ths */
    { tickcount = 60 * atol(argv[1]);
      Delay(tickcount, &dmydelay);
      exit(0);
    }
  }
  fprintf(stderr, "# %s - invalid syntax.\n", argv[0]);
  fprintf
    (stderr,
     "# %s - usage:  %s time\n", argv[0], argv[0]);
  exit(1);     /* indicate syntax error to shell */
}
```

Example 8–1:   A simple C program

To try the command, you would type (and enter)

```
sleep 10
```

which should display the command name in the lower left corner of the active
window for 10 seconds before continuing.

8.2 Language Differences

This section describes implementation-dependent features that generally differ from one C compiler to another, as well as most of the language enhancements specific to the MPW C compiler. Those language constructs used in defining the Macintosh interface are described in the next section.

MPW C includes integer data types compatible with most other 68000 C compilers, including other C compilers for the Macintosh. A few of these characteristics, such as pointer size and byte order, are dictated by the Motorola 68000 architecture, while others may vary from compiler to compiler.

MPW C defines the two standard C floating point types, as implemented by SANE. It also defines two additional SANE types generally not found in other C compilers.

The overall characteristics of the language recognized by MPW C are summarized by Table 8–1.

INTEGERS AND POINTERS

In MPW C, pointers such as

```
char *string;
```

are represented by 32-bit values. As with most C implementations, the size and representation of all pointers are the same. This is the only reasonable choice for the 68000 architecture and the most common choice for other C compilers. Programs compiled for the PDP-11 and "small model" 8086 programs use 16-bit pointers.

Most C implementations standardize on 8 bits for char, 16 bits for short, and 32 bits for long. The only latitude is in choosing the size of an int; is the natural size, a short, or a long? This has important implications for the entire program since int is used as the default type for untyped functions and constants.

MPW C chooses the longer representation, in which an int is the same as a long. This means undeclared functions, as well as constants passed as parameters, default to 32 bits. Also, many standard library functions (such as strlen) are defined as accepting int parameters or returning int values, and thus MPW C allows these functions to use the full 32-bit range.

Another advantage is that some archaic C code assumes that the size of a pointer is the size of an int. The 32-bit size is also appropriate for the Motorola 68020 architecture that will become increasingly important for Macintosh programs.

Data Types	Size	Minimum	Maximum
char	8	-128	+127
unsigned char	8	0	+255
short	16	-32,768	+32,767
unsigned short	16	0	+65,535
long	32	-2,147,483,648	+2,147,483,647
unsigned long	32	0	+4,294,967,295
int	32	-2,147,483,648	+2,147,483,647
unsigned	32	0	+4,294,967,295
char *	32		
comp	64	$-(2^{63}-1)$	$+(2^{63}-1)$
real	32		
double	64		
extended	80		

Post-K&R extensions

enum	yes
void	yes
struct by value	yes

Other characteristics

character set	ASCII with 8–bit extensions
byte order	most significant to least significant
char	signed
bit fields	unsigned

Table 8–1:   MPW C characteristics

However, a case can also be made for 16-bit int values, the definition used by many other C compilers for the Mac. This is actually the most efficient and natural size for the MC68000 of the original Macintosh, since the MC68000 does not include a 32-bit multiply or divide. More significantly, the ROM interfaces designed for Lisa Pascal make extensive use of the Pascal INTEGER type, which is 16 bits.

If you're writing new code for the Mac, you should avoid using int for parameters or data structures and might consider avoiding direct use of short and long. Code generally takes on a life of its own and will be used with projects and compilers unanticipated when originally written. You should take steps to avoid having the code blow up later when used with a C compiler that has 16-bit ints, such as LightspeedC or Apple (IIgs) Programmer's Workshop C.

Instead, the use of declarations such as

```
typedef short Integer;   /* or Half or Word */
typedef long LongInt;    /* or Full or LongWord */
```

will allow you to easily move your MPW C program to and from other C compilers. You would then declare all larger variables as either `Integer` or `LongInt`, which would also make it easier to compare your code to the *Inside Macintosh* Pascal definitions.

When passing an integer parameter to another C routine, you may wish to declare the parameter type as `int` if the size is not important. This takes advantage of the fact that untyped constants are always passed as an `int`, as well as any `char` or `short` variable. Then

```
int sum(x,y)
int x,y;
...
short total;
val = sum(total,2);
```

is safe with MPW C (32-bit `int`) and other Cs that use 16-bit `int`.

However, a less convenient approach is to use the same size variable for all compilers. In the statements

```
Integer sum(x,y)
Integer x,y;
...
val = sum(total, (Integer) 2);
```

the result will always be treated as a 16-bit integer on any Macintosh C compiler; so fewer side effects will be seen in moving from one compiler to another.

MPW C recognizes the data types `unsigned char` and `unsigned short`. The type `unsigned` is treated the same as `unsigned int` or `unsigned long`. However, the current implementation treats decimal integer constants larger than the maximum `int` as extended (floating point), even if they are less than the maximum `unsigned`. Hex constants (such as `0x10000000`) are handled properly.

FLOATING POINT

MPW C performs floating point arithmetic using the three standard data types defined by SANE. These types are:

- `float`, 32-bits, implemented as SANE's Single
- `double`, 64-bits, corresponding to SANE Double
- `extended`, 80-bits, corresponding to SANE Extended

Two of the types—float and double—should produce the same results as other C compilers using IEEE-conforming arithmetic, such as the 80287 of the IBM AT or the 68881 used by many UNIX workstations. The range and accuracy of these types are also similar to 32- and 64-bit floating point values for other C compilers.

MPW C differs slightly from most C compilers in that it performs all floating point calculations using the extended type rather than double. All floating point arguments are also converted to extended before being passed by value, and all functions returning a floating point type actually return an extended value. In contrast, the standard K&R definition is for values passed as double.

As part of SANE, MPW supports IEEE-conforming infinities and Not-a-Number (NaN) values, as described in Chapter 2. If the value of a variable is a NaN, any comparison involving that value will be false.

MPW C programs can also use the comp SANE data type to hold 64-bit integers. Although comp does not represent a floating point number, expressions involving comp variables are always handled by conversion to extended. This includes passing comp arguments and function results.

POST-K&R EXTENSIONS

MPW C includes the three standard post-K&R extensions: enum, void, and using structures by value.

The type enum is an enumerated data type, similar to Pascal's scalars. An enumeration type is a sequence of related constants that are associated with an indentifier. The constants are integers that by default increase from 0.

Normally, enum is used to declared a new type using a typedef statement. For example

```
typedef enum {false, true} Boolean;
```

is a standard type declared for all C programs by the Types.h header file. From this declaration, the value of false is 0 and true is 1.

Like a struct, an enum can be declared without defining a new type, as in:

```
enum xfermode {copy, or, xor };
...
MyBlit(bm, mode)
BitMap bm;
enum xfermode mode;
```

In this case, copy would correspond to the constant 0, or to 1, and xor to 2.

Unlike the case in Pascal, more than one constant can have the same value. Also, enumeration constants can be declared to have nonsequential values. The definition

```
typedef style
   {normal, bold, italic, underline=4, outline=8,
   shadow=16, condense=32, expand=64} style;
```

could be used for the QuickDraw text style. However, the enumeration types are not extensively used in the Macintosh interfaces.

By default, MPW C represents enum variables using the smallest type that can represent the range of the enumeration constants: char, unsigned char, short, unsigned short, long, or unsigned long.

However, the standard C representation of an enum is an int, and the MPW C compiler includes an option to use this interpretation. Using this option will not allow you to use the Macintosh interface headers, as they assume the enum variables use the more compact allocation.

The keyword void is used to declare a new type—or lack thereof. Its use is best illustrated by an example from pure K&R code:

```
transpose(len, arr)
int len,arr[][];
{
   ...
   return;
}
```

The declaration of a function without specifying a function type was a stylistic convention (prior to void) that indicated that the type of the result was irrelevant. However, transpose is not a procedure, as with Pascal, but implicitly a function of type int. A statement such as

```
i = transpose(100, thearray);
```

could be used, even though transpose did not return a valid value.

The post-K&R type void can be used to formally declare procedures that don't return a value. The declaration

```
void transpose(len,arr)
```

would cause

```
i = transpose(100, thearray);
```

to be rejected as an error.

Void is also used as a matter of style to indicate that the return value of a function is ignored. The Dialog Manager trap Alert returns the push button selected, as in:

```
item = Alert(128, NULL);
```

If you know that alert has only one button, you don't need to know which button was selected. The statement

```
Alert(128, NULL);
```

ignores the value, but

```
(void) Alert(128, NULL);
```

formally acknowledges that the return value is being discarded. This is helpful if you ever examine your source code with a fastidious checker such as the UNIX utility lint.

A variable declared as void * is a pointer to an unknown type and thus a completely untyped pointer. Of the statements

```
char *p;
int i,*q;
void *v;
  v = p;
  q = v;
  i = *v; /* error: unknown length */
```

the first two assignments are valid, but the last assignment is an error because the type of the value referenced by v is undefined. However, you could write

```
i = *( (int *) v);
```

to cast the pointer to a known type before dereferencing.

Finally, MPW C allows full use of data structures by value, as do most recent C compilers. One structure can be assigned to another, passed as an argument (without using & to pass a pointer to a struct) or be used as the result type of a C function.

PREPROCESSOR LINES

MPW C recognizes the standard K&R preprocessor lines, but the implementation of those lines often varies from compiler to compiler. MPW C also predefines several preprocessor identifiers and uses one identifier to implement segmentation of a Macintosh program.

The search path for any MPW header (#include) declaration such as

```
#include <Types.h>
```

is specified by MPW shell variable {CIncludes}, which may reference one or more directories. Additional directories can be specified with the -i compiler option, described later in this chapter. The name search is made by the Macintosh File Manager and thus is case insensitive.

If the reference is of the form

```
#include "Something.h"
```

the compiler will search the directory containing the current source file prior to searching the standard directories.

Preprocessor lines are used in MPW C programs to implement segmentation in applications and larger tools. The reserved preprocessor identifier __SEG__ (the characters _, _, S, E, G, _, _) is used to set segment names within MPW C programs. Where a Macintosh application written in MPW or Lisa Pascal would use the compiler directives

```
{$S Init}
...
{$S Main}
```

a C program would use

```
#define __SEG__ Init
...
#define __SEG__ Main
```

It's tempting to convert existing line-oriented C programs from UNIX and MS-DOS to MPW tools, as is. However, larger programs should probably have some Macintosh-specific segmentation added. The MPW application will take care of most memory management, but some segmentation (and calls to UnloadSeg, as described in Chapter 3) will allow the program to process more data or run with more MPW windows open before running out of memory.

If the program is organized into separate source files, the -s compiler option can also be used to define the segment name for each file without modifying the source code. If no segment name is specified by either an option or preprocessor line, the compiler begins placing compiled code in segment Main.

Two other preprocessor symbols, __FILE__ and __LINE__, can be referenced from within a C program, indicating the current source file name and source line being compiled. These are often referenced by internal error messages, such as defined by the macro:

```
#define assert(num)  { if (! (num)) {                    \
   fprintf
    (stderr,
     "Assertion failed, file %s, line %d\n",        \
    __FILE__, __LINE__); exit(1); } }
```

This allows you to include code of the form

```
assert(strlen(oldstr) < sizeof(newstr));
strcpy(newstr, oldstr);
```

to assure that any unlikely errors will be trapped before they can cause any damage. This sort of display is suitable for a UNIX program or an MPW tool but is inappropriate for a Macintosh application.

MPW C also provides several predefined preprocessor identifiers that can be used to isolate nonportable constructs. One such identifier is `macintosh`. You could use this to isolate Toolbox dependencies on a program that runs on both the Mac and line-oriented UNIX systems. For example, the previous macro can be generalized to display a standard Macintosh alert for errors while compiled as part of a Macintosh program:

```
#ifdef macintosh
# define assert(num)  { if (! (num)) {            \
  char buff[12];                          .......\
  sprintf(buff, "%d", __LINE__);               .\
  ParamText(__FILE__, buff, NULL, NULL);       \
  (void) Alert(ALRT_assert, NULL);             .\
  ExitToShell(); } }
#else
# define assert(num)  { if (! (num)) {                  \
  fprintf
    (stderr,
     "Assertion failed, file %s, line %d\n",          \
     __FILE__,__LINE__); exit(1); } }

#endif
```

An MPW tool that used this macro must first initialize QuickDraw using an `InitGraf(&qd.thePort)` call, as described in Chapter 3.

Another predefined symbol is `mc68000`, used by other C compilers for the Motorola 68000 family, such as on UNIX workstations. Suppose you wanted to unpack 32-bit words into 16-bit components, but your code would also be used with another machine that uses the reverse byte order. The definition

```
typedef short Half;
#ifdef mc68000
# define unpackword(fullptr,hiptr,loptr) \
    (*hiptr = *( (Half *)fullptr)++, \
     *loptr = *( (Half *)fullptr)++)
#else
# define unpackword(fullptr,hiptr,loptr) \
    (*loptr = *( (Half *)fullptr)++, \
     *hiptr = *( (Half *)fullptr)++)
#endif
```

would conditionally define the macro for the appropriate byte order, which then could be used by a statement such as:

```
long n;
Half hi,lo;
...
unpackword(n,&hi,&lo);
```

If you were using the code on many different machines, you would probably have a series of #ifdef groups defining the macro, one for each possible machine, and then indicate a compilation error if none of the machine identifiers were defined.

The MPW C compiler was developed by Green Hills Software, Inc., and thus it also predefines the ghs symbol. This can be used if you're prototyping software or developing libraries that are compiled by more than one Macintosh C compiler. For example,

```
#ifdef ghs   /* MPW C */
typedef short Half;
#else        /* Some other Macintosh C compiler */
typedef int Half;
#endif
```

would work for a C compiler that expected an int to be 16 bits.

OTHER PORTABILITY CONSIDERATIONS

There are two size-related limitations that can affect moving large C programs from mainframe implementations.

MPW C programs are currently limited to a maximum of 32K in global and static variables and in string constants. This is because all are addressed via 68000 instructions using a 16-bit signed displacement to register A5, ranging from 0 to -32,768.

If your program exceeds this limit, the obvious first approach to correcting the problem is to allocate any large arrays dynamically. Next, you might check for duplicate string constants in all your source files, replacing them with a reference to a common initialized global variable. Finally, some (or all) of your string references could be replaced by fetching the strings from the resource fork.

Each MPW C program (like any other Macintosh program) is also limited by default to 32K of code. To exceed this limit, you should include segmentation. If you're porting an existing program, you can mark all segments as preloaded (using ResEdit or Link) as part of an initial segmentation strategy. It's the size of each segment—not the overall size—that's important.

You can also override the linker's settings to allow for longer segments, using the Link -ss option, with the functions ordered such that no branches are greater than 32K between routines in the same segment. However, this will produce programs that may not work correctly with 64K ROM machines.

As with all C implementations, the ordering of bytes within a word may occasionally be important, such as when reading binary data from a byte-by-byte data network. As noted in the previous section, the Motorola 68000 is considered a "big-endian" machine, in that bytes are address from most significant to least significant. The code

```
long num; /* emphasize 4 bytes */
int i;
char *p;
    num = 0x01020304;
    p = (char *) &num;
    for (i = 0; i<4; i++)
        printf("%02X", (int) *p++);
```

is just a long-winded way of displaying the string "01020304."

Because of restrictions of the 68000 architecture, MPW C aligns most variables or members on short (16-bit) boundaries. The only exception is for 1-byte data types such as char. In a struct such as

```
typedef struct {
    char c;         /* byte 0 */
    short i;        /* bytes 2-3 */
    char d;         /* byte 4 */
    long j;         /* bytes 6-9 */
} foo;
```

two bytes are wasted preserving alignment. As a matter of style, you should either pair 1-byte members (such as char c, d) or include explicit filler char members to account for the alignment. This prevents misinterpretation by those who might use your code from other languages and also makes it more likely (although not guaranteed) that a binary write of the struct will store the same values on different implementations.

MPW C uses the register declarations to assign integer and pointer variables to among the 68000's eight data registers and eight address registers. The C compiler should normally have six data registers (D2 through D7) and three address registers (A2 through A4) available for assignment within any function, but the number depends on registers modified in calling other functions: transient registers (such as D0 and D1) may also be used if no functions are called.

The data registers are best used for char, short, and long (int) data types, with the address registers used for pointers. However, the compiler uses a heuristic algorithm to allow the maximum and most efficient use of registers, since both types of registers can be freely used for assigning integer and pointer values. Some operations require more restrictive assignments. The data registers must be used for multiply and divide instructions, while indirect pointer references require the address registers.

After allocating any manually declared `register` variables, MPW C attempts to assign any remaining automatic variables, not including floating point values and those that are referenced by & within the function. Multiple variables can be assigned to the same register if the variables do not overlap in usage.

MACINTOSH-SPECIFIC DIFFERENCES

MPW C recognizes the standard escape notation, \c, for representing special characters in strings. However, \n maps to the return character (ASCII CR, 0x0D, same as \r) when compiled by the MPW C compiler, instead of the line feed character (ASCII LF, 0x0A) used by UNIX implementations.

Purists might object to this difference, but the most common use of \n is in strings output to an I/O stream. Unlike UNIX, the Macintosh file system uses the return character as its line delimiter. If you really want a line feed, you should use the octal notation \012 instead.

MPW C also differs from many implementations in that it allows character constants to range in length from 1 to 4 bytes, with all character constants treated as type int. The following two statements

```
i = 'ABCD';
i = 0x41424344;
```

are equivalent. This is important when referencing resource types and the creator and type of files: each are normally four-letter codes.

Differences in the MPW standard C libraries from other implementations are described later.

8.3 Using the Macintosh Library

MPW C provides a standard set of interfaces to the Macintosh libraries. These include direct calls to Toolbox traps, as well as a library of entry points for those functions that cannot be called directly. MPW C also provides a mechanism that allows you to declare new traps and Pascal-compatible functions.

Since all of the interfaces are documented in *Inside Macintosh* in their Pascal form, these interfaces must be mentally translated by the C programmer, particularly when it comes to the type of arguments to the function. This section describes the rules for translating those interfaces, as well as the specific header files required for each manager. It also provides enough information for you write your own interfaces.

ROUTINE INTERFACE

The Macintosh Toolbox was originally written to be called from Lisa Pascal programs, although experience since then has shown C to be an efficient choice for writing Macintosh programs. However, these Toolbox interfaces have been firmly defined as using the Pascal calling sequence.

MPW C provides extensions for calling functions that conform to the Pascal calling sequence (such as RAM-based packages) and for directly calling Macintosh traps. It also allows you to write your own routines that conform to the Pascal calling sequences, which is necessary for Toolbox and OS interfaces that expect to call a Pascal-style function that you provide.

The declaration pascal is a new storage class for function declarations and, as such, comes before the type of the function. For example,

```
pascal short PrError()
    extern;
```

declares a function PrError that conforms to the Pascal calling sequence. Pascal external names are generated all uppercase since the Pascal compiler is case insensitive.

This declaration changes the arguments and function results to correspond to the Pascal calling sequence and modifies the order of the arguments. Unlike C, MPW Pascal passes function results on the stack. Therefore, you *must* declare any function result for a Pascal function, even if you intend to ignore it, since this affects the stack frame built by the compiler when generating the call. If the function returns no value, it should be declared as void.

The pascal storage class can also be used with functions you write to have the function mimic the Pascal standards. This is important for those traps, such as ModalDialog, which expect a pointer to a function you supply. Any such function called by the ROM *must* conform to the Pascal calling sequence.

To declare a Pascal function implemented in another file, an extern storage class keyword follows the procedure declaration, indicating that the function is not implemented in this source file, as in:

```
pascal void AnyGlue()
    extern;
```

For direct calls to the Macintosh ROM, this extern can include a 16-bit integer specifying an in-line machine instruction to be generated. The declaration

```
pascal short ResError()
    extern 0xA9AF;
```

defines a function returning a 16-bit integer called using the Pascal calling sequence and opocde A9AF, hex.

The declaration of Pascal interfaces also has provisions for parameter checking, as in:

```
pascal void FrameRect(r)
    Rect *r;
    extern 0xA8A1;
```

The type of arguments are validated by the C compiler during compilation. This allows the compiler to distinguish between statements such as:

```
Rect myrect;

FrameRect(myrect);   /* wrong */
FrameRect(&myrect);  /* right */
```

Some conversions are automatically applied. The provision of parameter conversions is an important consequence of the choice of integer sizes. In the declaration

```
pascal void MoveTo(h,v)
    short h,v;
    extern 0xA893;
```

the MoveTo trap expects two 16-bit integers. If not for automatic conversion by the compiler, the statement

```
MoveTo(100,200);
```

would produce unexpected results, as each parameter would be interpreted as a 32-bit integer.

This use of integer constants is rampant throughout Macintosh programs, particularly with QuickDraw coordinates and resource numbers.

Example 8–2 shows examples of each of these declarations. They correspond to the declarations used in Example 7-2.

As detailed in Chapter 2, some interfaces between higher-level languages and the Macintosh ROM require the use of glue routines, tiny pieces of code that bind programs written in such languages to the traps.

For example, the register-based traps of the Memory Manager require glue to remove the arguments from the stack and place them in registers. Glue for the function SetHandleSize might be implemented as:

```
#include <Types.h>
#define __ALLNU__
#include <QuickDraw.h>

/* Routine (with C calling sequence) defined in assembly
   language */
extern Handle NewHandleClear();

/* Routine (with Pascal-style calling sequence) defined
   in Pascal code
   C correctly handles pushing a pointer to a 48-bit
   function result */
pascal RGBColor GetMenuColor(item)
  short item;
  extern;

/* MacsBug debugging breakpoints implemented through
   trap words */
pascal void Debugger()
  extern 0xA9FF;
pascal void Debugger(astring)
  Str255 astring;          /* a Pascal string */
  extern 0xABFF;

/* Externally-defined C routine (called by Pascal) */
extern long RGBDiff();
```

Example 8–2:   Examples of Pascal interfaces

```
MOVE.L 8(A7),D0  ; load D0 with size
MOVEA.L 4(A7),A0  ; load A0 with handle
_SetHandleSize
MOVE.W D0,MemErr ; save for later MemError() call
RTS
```

Different library glue routines are used for MPW C than for MPW Pascal. C programs call glue written to the C calling sequence.

The MPW C header files take advantage of one of the documented shortcuts for C function declarations. If a function is never declared before its use, it is assumed to return an int. As noted earlier, this can also be used for functions that return no values at all since C— unlike Pascal—allows to you ignore the return value.

MPW C uses glue routines for functions that return a 16- or 32-bit integer or any pointer type. Most of these functions are not declared in headers but instead are implicitly used as functions of type int.

For example, most of the File Manager calls return an OSErr value, which is equivalent to a 16-bit short. By writing the glue to return a 32-bit int instead, these functions do not have to be declared. Nor do the Memory Manager functions that return a pointer or handle. This makes the header files shorter and speeds compilation. If you were using a syntax checker such as lint on the source, you might wish to have a separate set of headers (or conditionally compiled headers) that included the more strongly typed function results.

DATA TYPES

The correspondence between fundamental Pascal and C data types is summarized by Table 8–2.

Fortunately, once a Pascal function or data structure is properly declared, MPW C will take care of the conversions for you. Understanding the translation rules is important when writing your own declarations or when comparing how the MPW C headers correspond to the *Inside Macintosh* Pascal interfaces. If you're writing code in both languages, you should fully appreciate the subtleties in the parameter and data structure type representations.

Many of the data types are identical in name and usage, including the fixed point integers and most of the floating point types. All of the data structures declared by the Macintosh interfaces, such as Rect and Window-Record, have the same name and usages, as do the pointer types, such as Handle and WindowPtr. The correspondence between the Pascal LONGINT and C's long is easy to remember, and the REAL versus float types correspond to the standard terminology for short floating point numbers.

There are several cases in which the corresponding type is not what you might first expect. The most important is that a Pascal INTEGER is not a C int but a short. Most of the Toolbox is oriented toward these 16-bit integers, so the short is a data type you'll use a lot, whether directly or typedef'd through Half or Integer.

Another important variance is the string data type. Versions 1.0 and 2.0 of MPW provide special rules for handling string parameters and struct member variables, as discussed later in this section.

A Pascal SignedByte (range [-128,+127]) corresponds to a C char; both represent a signed 8–bit quantity. The <Types.h> header declares an enumeration type Boolean which has two values, false and true. Of course, you would use the standard (and quicker) C notation for boolean tests:

```
if (boolvar)
```

rather than the more cumbersome:

```
if (boolvar == true)
```

Pascal Type	C Type
Integer	short
LongInt	long
Str255	char * or Str255†
Byte††	short
Char††	short
SignedByte	char
Boolean	Boolean
real	float

Same data types

double
extended
comp
Fixed
Fract
Handle
OSErr
Ptr
ProcPtr

† See text
†† Except when declared as part of a packed array or record

Table 8–2:   Pascal equivalent data types

This is also less desirable because the Toolbox, as with C, may use other nonzero values to represent true. For example, the Window Manager sets the `visible` member of a `WindowRecord` structure to `0xFF` for true.

The use of the Pascal data types `CHAR` and `Byte` will definitely be counterintuitive for the C programmer. Unlike C, a `CHAR` is not an integer type but is its own separate type. However, both `CHAR` and `Byte` represent values in the range [0,255]. To make things complicated, a single byte in Pascal (represented by the Macintosh type `SignedByte`) is limited to the range [-128,+127].

As such, Pascal normally stores each `CHAR` and `Byte` variables as a [0,255] subrange of [32768,+32767], allocating a 16-bit word. Therefore, you would use a `short` or an equivalent type for any Pascal global or parameter declared as `CHAR` or `Byte`.

However, Pascal arrays and records (`structs`) declared as `PACKED` will be stored in the more compact form. The *Inside Macintosh* declaration

```
TYPE
Int10Rec = PACKED RECORD
   decimalPt: CHAR; { 1 byte }
```

```
    thousSep: CHAR;   { a byte, etc ... }
    currSyml: CHAR;
...
    metricSys: Byte; { also 8 bits }
    intlOVers: INTEGER;    { 16 bits }
END;
```

in the C header <Packages.h> becomes:

```
typedef struct IntlORec {
   char decimalPt;
   char thousSep;
...
   unsigned char metricSys;
   short intlOVers;
} IntlORec;
```

When in packed records, you should realize that the rules are:

CHAR becomes char
Byte becomes unsigned char

However, if the previous Pascal record had not been declared as packed, it would be equivalent to the C type:

```
typedef struct IntlORec {
   short decimalPt;
   short thousSep;
...
   short metricSys;
   short intlOVers;
} IntlORec;
```

A few of the interfaces described in *Inside Macintosh* make extensive use of Pascal's variant records, which are different variants of a single record type. For example, the File Manager parameter block has four variants and is partially described in Pascal as:

```
ParamBlockRec = RECORD
   ...
   CASE ParamBlkType OF
     ioParam:
        (ioRefNum: INTEGER;
        ...);
     fileParam:
        (ioFRefNum: INTEGER;
```

```
                ...);
            volumeParam;
                (long filler2;
                short ioVolIndex;
                ...);
        END; (* ParamBlockRec *)
```

These declarations *could* be partially emulated as a C union of `struct` types, as in:

```
        typedef struct {
            ...
                            union {
                struct {
                    short ioRefNum;
                    ...
                } IOParam;
                struct {
                    short ioFRefNum;
                    ...
                } FileParam;
                struct {
                    long filler2;
                    short ioVolIndex;
                    ...
                } VolumeParam;
            }
        } ParamBlockRec;
```

Unfortunately, this would require each member to be fully qualified with the name of the type within the union. With the declaration

```
        ParamBlockRec pb;
```

`pb.ioRefNum` is not a valid member reference, but instead the qualified syntax `pb.IOParam.ioRefNum` is required.

Instead of imposing this unwieldy requirement on each use, MPW C gives each named variant a separate type with the corresponding name. The different types share some members with the same name for the same variables at the same offset (declaration order) in each structure.

For example, the File Manager types `IOParam`, `FileParam`, `VolumeParam`, `HFileParam` (for HFS), and `HVolumeParam` all begin with the common member declarations:

```
        typedef struct {
            struct QElem *qLink;
            short   qType;
```

```
        short  ioTrap;
        Ptr ioCmdAddr;
        ProcPtrioCompletion;
        OSErr  ioResult;
        StringPtr ioNamePtr;
        ...
    } eachParam
```

followed by the members specific to the corresponding structure.

If you wanted to use a parameter block for I/O calls, you would instead declare the block as

```
        IOParam pb;
```

and no additional qualifiers would be required (pb.ioRefNum) to get at the members of the structure.

Whenever you see a variant record listed in *Inside Macintosh*, you should examine the corresponding header file to determine the appropriate C usage, although each will generally follow this form.

ARGUMENT TYPES

Even after you have the appropriate data type for calling one of the Macintosh interface routines, you still must be aware of when to pass the argument by pointer and when to use the default pass by value.

For any data type longer than 4 bytes (32 bits), MPW Pascal passes the address of the variable rather than its value. This includes the larger floating point types and most data structures. In addition, any parameter declared as VAR (returning a value) is also passed by address. However, in MPW C, as in most Cs, all variables and structures are passed by value unless an explicit & operator is used.

This means when calling a Macintosh function from MPW C, any of these larger parameter types must be passed with the address of the parameter taken by the & operator. Arguments passed by address include:

- comp, double, and extended

- Strings, such as Str255, but not including four-character ResType

- Any VAR parameters, such as
  PROCEDURE GetDateTime(VAR secs: LONGINT)

- Any struct, including Point and Rect

MPW Pascal and the Toolbox expect any small array or record (such as the 4-byte Point) to be passed by value. By default, version 2.0 of MPW C defines all Macintosh interfaces so that any struct is passed by pointer. The difference between the interface and what the Toolbox trap expects is fixed up through the use of glue.

When a Pascal program expects the types CHAR and Byte as unsubscripted parameters, these types are actually 16-bit values. As indicated earlier, such arguments should be declared as short or unsigned short.

STRINGS

MPW C programs will often use both C-style and Pascal-style character string types. The former is terminated by a null byte, while the latter is prefixed by a single-byte (0-255) length. Each string has a maximum length corresponding to the number of bytes allocated. (Figure 7-3 illustrates the layout of a Pascal string.)

Pascal strings are defined by <Types.h> as:

```
#define String(size) struct {\
    unsigned char length; unsigned char text[size];}
```

This header file also defines the Str255, StringPtr, and StringHandle standard Pascal string types:

```
typedef String(255) Str255, *StringPtr, **StringHandle;
```

To use Pascal string, you may wish to have the Pascal string length function defined as a macro that operates on Str255 variables:

```
#define LENGTH(s255) ( (short) (s255).length )
```

When calling an OS or Toolbox function that expects a string argument, the default glue routines in the version 1.0 and 2.0 interfaces automatically convert a C string argument to the Pascal string expected by the trap. The order of these steps is:

- Convert C string to Pascal
- Call the trap
- Convert the string back to a C string

The last step is necessary in case you need to use the string again as a C string.

However, in many cases your program will be taking a Pascal string directly from a resource file and passing it to a Toolbox trap. If you want to avoid the conversion steps, it's easy for you to define your own trap interfaces to call the Toolbox traps directly. Example 8–3 gives several sample declarations, with the prefix P prepended to each trap name to avoid conflicts with the standard interface declarations.

```
pascal void DrawPString(s)
  Str255 *s;
  extern 0xA884;

pascal short PStringWidth(s)
  Str255 *s;
  extern 0xA88C;

pascal void PParamText(p1, p2, p3, p4)
  Str255 *p1,*p2,*p3,*p4;
  extern 0xA98B;
```

Example 8–3:   Pascal string traps

For example, the function

```
void DispErr(errno)
int errno;
{ StringHandle sh;
  sh = GetString(1000+errno);
  PParamText(*sh, NULL, NULL, NULL);
  (void) Alert(ALRT_err, NULL);
}
```

could be used to display a standard error alert, with the error message selected by number from a list of 'STR' resources. This is the proper approach to displaying error messages in Macintosh programs, rather than embedding the English-language strings in the middle of your source code.

For those who are writing new code starting with version 2.0 of MPW C, direct Pascal trap routines are also declared to replace most Toolbox glue. These traps—distinguished by identifiers in all caps—can be used to replace glue routines that would otherwise perform string conversion. For example, NumToString() is a glue routine that returns a result in a C-style string, while NUMTOSTRING is a trap using a Pascal string that is declared as:

```
pascal void NUMTOSTRING(theNum, theString)
  long theNum;
  Str255 *theString;
  extern;
```

Such glue-bypass alternatives also apply to routines that use glue to convert small (4 bytes or less) structures passed by address (as declared by MPW C) to those passed by value (as expected by Pascal and the Toolbox). For example, the Toolbox trap `EqualPt` expects two 4-byte QuickDraw Point structures passed on the stack:

```
Boolean EQUALPT(pt1, pt2)
    Point pt1, pt2;
    extern 0xA881;
```

It's likely that a future version of MPW will make the default (mixed-case capitalization) name be the nonglue variant.

If you wish to explicitly convert any string in place, the conversion functions used by MPW are declared in `<strings.h>` as:

Version 2.0 also allows you to declare Pascal-style string literals by prefixing the string with `"\p"`; then the call

```
DRAWSTRING("\pHello");
```

would pass the address of a five-character Pascal literal string to the QuickDraw ROM trap `_DrawString`.

```
char *p2cstr();
char *c2pstr();
```

Each takes a single argument, the string (pointer) to be converted. The function p2cstr converts a Pascal string to a C string, while c2pstr goes the other way. The type of c2pstr is declared as `char *`, but the result is actually a `Str255 *`; both functions are likely to be used with the same pointer declared as `char *`.

MPW never converts strings embedded in other data structures. For example, header `<Packages.h>` defines the data structure:

```
typedef struct SFReply {
    Boolean good;
    Boolean copy;
    OSType fType;
    short vRefNum;
    short version;
    String(63) fName;
} SFReply;
```

SFReply is used by the routines of the Standard File Package. The value of fName is always a 63-character Pascal string, which is used like any other Pascal string: it is not a C string. Similarly, the ioNamePtr in parameter blocks used for File Manager calls is a pointer to a Pascal string, not a C string.

When performing string conversion, it may be advantageous to keep both the Pascal and C version around to avoid having to convert the string back. Also, this allows you to use distinct typing of your variables between C strings (`char cstr[20]`) and Pascal strings (`String(20) pstr`). If you're converting in place and forget which is currently being used, using a C string as a Pascal string (or vice versa) will create extra debugging grief.

Example 8–4 shows functions to convert between separate C and Pascal string arguments, modeled after the standard `strcpy` function defined for two C strings. If you will be performing other operations directly with Pascal strings, you may wish to define `strcat`, `strchr` (index), and similar functions for Pascal strings.

HEADER FILES

Using the OS and Toolbox routines requires `#include` directives for one or more appropriate header files. Unlike the Pascal interfaces, the C headers are generally organized with one manager per file, as indicated by Table 8–3

As you might expect, some of the upper-level Toolbox interfaces require use of the lower-level Toolbox definitions. These dependencies are shown by Figure 8–2.

However, the headers are designed to automatically include any missing header files; therefore

```
#include <Dialogs.h>
```

would automatically include `<Windows.h>`, `<QuickDraw.h>`, and `<Types.h>`. At the same time, each header file is set up to ignore redundant `#include` directives for the same file.

Most of the files require `<Types.h>`, which defines a series of data types and constants, as described in Table 8–4.

Two of the types take advantage of a Macintosh-specific interpretation of character constants. Both `OSType` and `ResType` are usually defined using four-character constants. These types use a 32-bit value containing four characters (indicated by the constant `'ABCD'`) rather than a pointer to a string of characters (`"ABCD"`).

In the example

```
OSType filetype, creator;    /* 4-character int */
    filetype = 'TEXT';
    creator = 'MPS ';
    err :=
        Create(filename, volno, creator, filetype);
```

the function call to `Create` passes an absolute hex value `0x54455854` (`'TEXT'`) for `filetype` instead of the address of a string containing the 5 bytes `"TEXT\000"`.

Two different header files are shown for the Printing Manager. `PrintTraps.h` should be used on programs designed to run on System 3.3

```
/*-------------------------------------------------------

    StringLib - convert separate C and Pascal strings


SYNOPSIS
    int strcpy_c2p(pstr, cstr)
    int strcpy_p2c(cstr, pstr)
    int strncpy_p2c(cstr, pstr, n)
    char *cstr;
    Str255 *pstr;
    int n;

DESCRIPTION
    The parameter cstr points to a C string (array of
    characters termianted by a null character). The
    parameter pstr points to a Pascal string (unsigned
    byte holding string length, followed by the
    characters).

    Function strcpy_c2p copies string cstr to string
    pstr, converting from C-style strings to Pascal-
    style strings.

    Function strcpy_p2c copies string
    pstr to string cstr, converting from  Pascal-style
    strings to C-style strings.

     Function strncpy_p2c copies exactly n characters
    from pstr, truncating pstr or adding null characters
    to s1 if necessary; the result will not be null-
    terminated if the length of s2 is n or more.

{***NOTE***}
    All return the number of characters copied.
    However,
        since a C string can theoretically be longer than a
        Pascal string, strcpy_c2p returns -1 if the string
        was too long to be copied.

    ----------------------------------------------------*/


#include <Types.h>

/* Note: strcpy_c2p(), strcpy_p2c(), and strncpy_p2c()
    must know about Apple's clever but perverse scheme for
    defining a Pascal string, a.k.a. Str255.
```

They assume that Str255 looks exactly like
```
   typedef struct {
      unsigned char length;
      unsigned char text[255]
   } Str255
*/
```

```
#define min(x, y) ( (x)<(y) ? (x) : (y) )
```

```
/* Note on transferring data:
   BlockMove
      is a glue routine that loads 3 registers
      then calls a ToolBox trap to a ROM routinememcpy
      is some tight C-callable (RAM-based) assembly code

   we could, of course, add our own code in-line if we
   wanted
*/
```

```
/* Convert a Pascal string to a C string
   Return the actual length
*/
int strcpy_p2c(cstr, pstr)
char *cstr;
Str255 *pstr;
{ int len;
  char *p;

  if (len = pstr->length)
    memcpy(cstr, (pstr->text), len);
  cstr += len;   /* assure null-terminated */
  *cstr = '\0';
  return (len);
}
```

```
/* Convert a Pascal string to a C string, copying
     specified # of chars
   Return the actual length
*/
int strncpy_p2c(cstr, pstr, n)
char *cstr;
Str255 *pstr;
int n;
{ int len;
  char *p;
```

```
    if (len = pstr->length)
        memcpy(cstr, (pstr->text), min(len, n));
    if (len < n)
    {   cstr += len;/* null-terminate remainder */
        *cstr = '\0';
    }
    return (len);
}


/* Convert a C string to a Pascal string
   Return -1 if too long
   Else return the actual length
*/
int strcpy_c2p(pstr, cstr)
char *cstr;
Str255 *pstr;
{ long len;

    len = strlen(cstr);
    if (len > 255)
        return (-1);
    else
    {   if (len)
        memcpy(pstr->text, cstr, len);
        pstr->length = len;
        return (len);
    }
}
```

Example 8–4:   String-to-string conversion functions

or later as these programs will then use the _Printing trap to call the latest version of the Printing Manager. Printing.h provides the original glue-style interfaces to the ".Print" DRVR resource and must be used for programs to run under earlier System versions.

OTHER CONSIDERATIONS

Some of the Macintosh traps perform trivial functions, while the basic overhead of the trap interpretation is considerable, as much as 5 or 10 C statements. An excellent example is the SetRect trap, which merely assigns 4 integers to the members of a Rect struct.

Since C programmers are traditionally concerned with performance, you may wish to replace these simpler traps with C macros, which will be nearly as compact and considerably faster. The use of macros is also important

File	Use
AppleTalk.h	AppleTalk Manager
Controls.h	Control Manager
Desk.h	Desk Manager
DeskBus.h	Apple DeskTop Bus Manager
Devices.h	Device Manager
Dialogs.h	Dialog Manager
DiskInit.h	Disk Initialization Package
Disks.h	Disk Driver
Errors.h	OS and system error constants
Events.h	Toolbox Event Manager
Files.h	File Manager
FixMath.h	Fixed-point arithmetic
Fonts.h	Font Manager
Graf3D.h	Three-dimensional QuickDraw graphics library
Lists.h	List Manager Package
Memory.h	Memory Manager
Menus.h	Menu Manager
OSEvents.h	OS Event Manager
OSUtils.h	OS Utilities
Packages.h	Package Manager
Palette.h	Palette Manager
Perf.h	Performance measurement functions
Picker.h	Color Picker Package
Printing.h	Printing Manager (glue-based)
PrintTraps.h	Printing Manager (trap-based)
Quickdraw.h	QuickDraw and Color Manager
Resources.h	Resource Manager
Retrace.h	Vertical Retrace Manager
ROMDefs.h	NuBus declaration ROMs
SANE.h	Standard Apple Numeric Environment
Scrap.h	Scrap Manager
Script.h	Script Manager
SCSI.h	SCSI Manager
SegLoad.h	Segment Loader
Serial.h	Serial Driver
ShutDown.h	Shutdown Manager
Slots.h	Slot Manager
Sound.h	Sound Driver and Sound Manager
Start.h	Start Manager
Strings.h	C-to-Pascal string conversion utilities
TextEdit.h	TextEdit
Time.h	Time Manager
ToolUtils.h	Toolbox Utilities (see also FixMath.h)
Traps.h	List of available traps

Types.h	fundamental data types
Values.h	SANE constants
Video.h	Macintosh II video interfaces
Windows.h	Window Manager

Table 8–3:   Macintosh interface header files

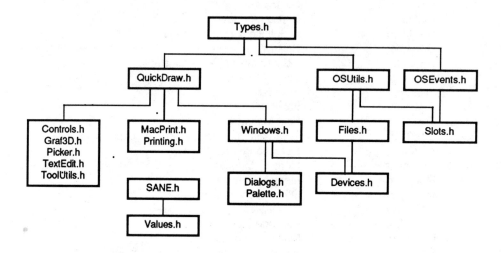

Figure 8–2:   Macintosh header dependencies

because it isolates the dependencies on such tricks. If a later Macintosh system makes your trick obsolete, you can easily change the macro to a call to the appropriate trap, as long as you keep the interface for your macro the same as the trap.

Constants	Description
NULL	zero pointer
noErr	successful OS return

Macro	Description
String(n)	Declare a Pascal n-byte string (STRING[n])

Types	Description
Boolean	unsigned byte, equivalent to logical enumeration
Ptr	pointer to arbitrary byte
Handle	pointer to master pointer
Fract	small fixed-point integer
ResType	four-character resource type, e.g. 'STR#'
OSType	four-character file creator or type, e.g. 'APPL'
Point	QuickDraw point (h,v)
Rect	QuickDraw rectangle (top, left, bottom, right)
Str255	Maximum-length Toolbox string
StringPtr	Pointer to Str255
StringHandle	Handle to Str255

Table 8–4: Standard identifiers declared by `<Types.h>`

Example 8–5 shows several such definitions for the most innocuous operations. The SetRect and SetPt have no side effects, merely changing values in the data structure you supply, while the remaining traps have documented assembly-language interfaces and thus are unlikely to change.

```
#define MEMERROR()  ( *((short *) 0x220) )

#define RESERROR()  ( *((short *) 0xA60) )

#define SETPT(pointptr, ch, cv)          \
   { (pointptr)->h = (ch);  \
   (pointptr)->v     = (cv); }

#define SETRECT(rectptr, cleft, ctop, cright, cbottom)
   { (rectptr)->left = (cleft);  \
   (rectptr)->top      = (ctop);  \
   (rectptr)->right    = (cright); \
   (rectptr)->bottom   = (cbottom); }

#define SETPORT(port)   qd.thePort = (port)
#define GETPORT(portptr)  *(portptr) = qd.thePort
```

Example 8–5: Trap macro equivalents

Note the type cast of a int constant (32 bit) to be the absolute memory address used as a pointer to a short value. This approach can be used to access any system global variable, but such a symbolic definition (defined in your own header file, such as SysGlobals.h) will make it easier to fix your code later if one of these references must be changed.

A few of the header files are MPW-specific, relating neither to the Macintosh ROM nor the standard C/UNIX libraries. Among these is <Perf.h>, for the MPW performance measurement library. As described in Chapter 7, the library measures the performance of a program by periodic sampling of the program counter value. The library can sample any type of code, including drivers and ROM code. and can include an analysis of the use of ROM routines. After sampling, raw sampling data written to a text file can later be formatted using the PerformReport tool.

The Macintosh interfaces also include definitions for the three-dimensional graphics library in <Graf3D.h>. This is the same library long-distributed with Lisa Pascal and is documented in the *MPW C Reference* manual.

OTHER C COMPILERS

MPW C was introduced after many other C compilers were offered for the Macintosh by third-party development companies. Because it was not the first C compiler for Mac development, Apple's compiler did not have the standard-setting impact of its Lisa Pascal compiler, and thus there is more variation between the available C compilers.

As noted earlier, the choice of the size for an int varies between implementations. Mac C by Consulair uses 32 bits, as does MPW, while both LightspeedC by Think Technologies and Aztec C by Manx Software Systems use 16-bit int values. Mac C also has a 16-bit int option. Some variations are also evident in the size of floating point types, although most use 32- and 64-bit sizes for float and double.

The names of the Macintosh interface headers may vary between implementations. The MPW C header references

```
#include <Types.h>
#include <Memory.h>
#include <Files.h>
```

in Mac C might be:

```
#include <MacDefs.h>
#include <Memory.h>
#include <PBDefs.h>
```

in Aztec C:

```
#include <types.h>
                /* of course, <Types.h> will work */
#include <memory.h>/* ditto <Memory.h> */
#include <pb.h>
```

and in LightspeedC:

```
#include <MacTypes.h>
#include <MemoryMgr.h>
#include <FileMgr.h>
```

All three implementations listed generally share the one file-per-manager approach, however.

The treatment of QuickDraw global variables differs slightly. MPW C declares variable qd as an externally defined struct that contains the global variables, and then the variables are referenced as fields within that struct. Therefore, application programs written in MPW C begin with:

```
InitGraf(&qd.thePort);
```

Some C compilers redefine the QuickDraw variables—thePort, white, black, gray, ltGray, dkGray, arrow, screenBits, and randSeed to directly reference the memory location (as in MPW Pascal); so initialization with these compilers is defined using:

```
InitGraf(&thePort);
```

Other differences typically include in-line assembly code (which MPW C lacks), C string conversion for Toolbox routines (most use Pascal strings instead), and the provision for post-K&R extensions.

8.3 Converting UNIX Programs

Table 8–5 shows the standard data types of MPW C compared to standard UNIX implementations.

STANDARD C LIBRARY

Apple uses the term "Standard C Library" to refer to the functions supplied with MPW C that are similar to other C implementations. Not suprisingly, these definitions generally conform to the C library under A/UX, Apple's implementation of UNIX System V for the Macintosh II.

After Kernighan & Ritchie

	MPW	DEC VAX	DEC PDP-11
character set	ASCII	ASCII	ASCII
char	8	8	8
int	32	32	16
char *	32	32	16
short	16	16	16
long	32	32	32
float	32	32	32
double	64	64	64
extended	80	—	—
maximum range†	±10±4932	±10±38	±10±38

† MPW range is for extended; float is ±10±38, double is ±10±308

Table 8–5:   MPW types compared to standard implementations

For those with prior C experience under UNIX, the definitions should be very familiar. Most of the library is a common subset of the two standard UNIX implementations, System V and BSD 4.3, with a few unique functions from each thrown in as well. In particular, MPW includes most of the C library (Chapter 3 of the *UNIX Programmer's Reference Manual*) and I/O functions of the system calls (Chapter 2) from UNIX.

The functions common to MPW's standard C library and the two major UNIX families are shown in Figure 8–3.

Not shown are the many UNIX system calls that don't make sense under the Macintosh OS. There's no point in having a `fork` if you don't have multitasking, and the `chmod` function would not work well with the different approach to file protection used by the Macintosh File Manager.

Among the minor differences, the `cfree` function is mentioned in K&R as the inverse of `calloc`, but is not part of the standard UNIX libraries.

The header files used by MPW C programs to access the standard library are summarized by Table 8–6.

The headers declared by Apple use mixed capitalization for the file names. However, the Macintosh File Manager ignores capitalization when searching for an existing file, so the statement

```
#include <stdio.h>
```

will match file {CIncludes}StdIO.h supplied MPW C. This usage (as opposed to #include <StdIO.h>) will also be portable to C compilers where case distinctions are important to the file system.

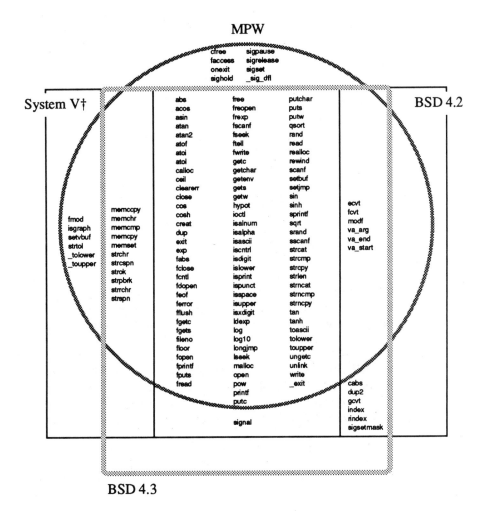

Figure 8–3:   Standard C library compatibility

† System V Interface Definition, Issue 2 (Release 2.0)

INPUT/OUPUT

MPW C provides the standard system call (open, read, write) and stdio.h (fopen, scanf, printf) functions common to most UNIX implementations. These can be used to port existing C programs or to build new

File	Use
CType.h	Classify and convert characters
CursorCtl.h	MPW tool cursor control
ErrMgr.h	MPW tool error manager
ErrNo.h	Standard library error numbers
FCntl.h	File control function `fcntl`
IOCtl.h	Device control function `iocntl`
Math.h	Standard mathematical functions
SetJmp.h	Non-local goto functions
Signal.h	Software signal and interrupt handling
StdIO.h	Standard I/O formatting functions
String.h	C string routines
VarArgs.h	Implement variable-length calling sequence

Table 8–6:   Standard C header files

Macintosh programs. A program can, for example, use both the File Manager and `stdio` functions in the same program, but for each file that's open, you should stick to one approach or the other to avoid the potential side effects of the two implementations.

The standard `fopen` (or `open`) call can be used with a full Macintosh pathname, with one of MPW's pseudo-file names (such as `Dev:StdErr`) or when running as an MPW tool, with reserved names such as § (described in Chapter 5.) A partial pathname will open the file in the current directory.

The Standard File Package can be combined with the UNIX I/O calls to use a Macintosh interface to select a file. After calling `SFGetFile` (or `SFPutFile`) to put up the dialog, you can change the default volume to be that of the file (probably an HFS directory) and then use the standard C `open` or `fopen` function, as in:

```
char name[64];

SFGetFile( ...
   &reply);
if (reply.good)
{ strcpy_p2c(name,reply.fName);
  SetVol(reply.vRefNum);   /* make its directory
                            default */
  infile = fopen(name, "r");
}
```

In MPW C, as with all Macintosh file names, file names are case insensitive: you don't have to get the capitalization right to open an existing file.

As noted earlier, the constant `\n` is same as `\r`. Macintosh files created using standard I/O have a return character at the end of each line.

MPW C includes the standard printf and scanf format string syntax of System V. The use of l for long arguments in format strings, as in %lX, is not important under MPW, since the size of a long is the same as the size of an int. This distinction may be important if you later move your code to other machines.

Because of the IEEE-style arithmetic supported by SANE, MPW C extends the floating point formatting routines to support infinities and Not-a-Number values. The letters INF or NAN can be produced in a floating point printf and are recognized by scanf. The infinity can be preceded by a sign, while the NaN will be followed by a parenthesized integer indicating which NaN value it represents.

In addition to MPW tools, which provide a UNIX-like line-oriented stream I/O, the C standard I/O functions can also be used with simple applications. These functions then provide console I/O functions emulating a very spartan glass teletype, with standard output printed directly on the desktop. Upon completion of the program, the MPW library code will wait for the Enter key before terminating the application (and erasing the screen), as shown in Figure 8–4.

In addition to the standard functions such as strlen, strcpy, strcmp, and strcat, the MPW library includes strchr and strrchr to search for a single character in a string. BSD programs have traditionally used a different set of functions, which can be defined by the macros:

```
#define index(s,c)  strchr(s,c)
#define rindex(s,c) strrchr(s,c)
```

BSD 4.3 also supports strchr and strrchr directly.

All of the strname functions operate on a zero-terminated string of ASCII characters. MPW includes several functions from System V/BSD 4.3 that operate on arbitrary memory blocks. For example, memset is the easy way to zero out (or blank out) a block of memory under MPW and UNIX, while memcpy can be used as a substitute for the BlockMove trap.

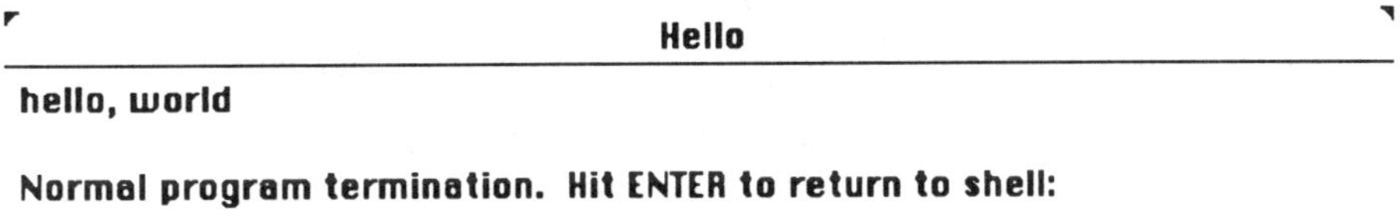

Hello

hello, world

Normal program termination. Hit ENTER to return to shell:

Figure 8–4:   Application output to the desktop String and Memory Functions

8.4 Building C Programs

This section describes how to compile and link MPW C programs. It includes a description of the most common options to the C command and the libraries used when building C programs with the Link command.

Also included are a command file and a custom menu definition to simplify compiling C programs. The chapter concludes with a complete MPW tool to select a file using a standard dialog and to display the corresponding pathname to the standard output.

COMPILING PROGRAMS

The MPW C compiler translates C source code into MPW object files, which are linked into an application or other program type using the Link command.

C

Compile a C program

Syntax:

C *file*	Compile source *file*
C	Compile interactively entered source

Options:

-align	Align data to 32-bit boundaries
-c	Include comments in preprocessor output
-d *name*	Define preprocessor symbol *name* to be 1
-d *name=string*	Define preprocessor symbol *name* to be *string*
-e	Display preprocessor translation without compiling source
-elems881	Generate 68881 code for trancendental functions
-g	Generate debugger names in code (forces -ga)
-ga	Generate complete stack frames for every function
-i *pathname,...*	Use each *pathname* directory to find header files
-mc68020	Generate 68020 code
-mc68881	Generate 68881 code for standard operators
-o *objfile*	Output compiled object code to file *objfile*
-p	Display compilation progress report

`-q`	Optimize object code for speed at the expense of size
`-s segname`	Name first segment *segname*
`-u name`	Make the preprocessor symbol *name* undefined
`-w`	Suppress warnings
`-x55`	Interpret bitfield members as signed
`-z6`	Make all `enum` variables the same size as `int` variables

Remarks:

By default, the compiled object code goes to file `file.o` for `file`. Interactively entered source is terminated by Command-Enter, and the compile output is send to file `c.o` by default. More than one `-i` option may be used; each should include one or more option parameters, separated by commas. The directories specified by `-i pathname` are searched after the folder containing `file` but before the directories defined by `{CIncludes}`.

If the `-e` option is used, the compiler passes the source through the preprocessor and displays the result to standard output. The program is not compiled. This is the only case in which information is displayed to standard output.

Input/Output:

Diagnostic	Compiler error messages
Output	Expansion of source after preprocessor substitutions

Examples:

`C Src.c`	Compile `Src.c` and leave object in `Src.c.o`

COMPILER OPTIONS

Many of the MPW C compiler options parallel those of the cc UNIX compiler command. Two important differences are that the C MPW command does not accept multiple source files and does not link the resulting program.

Also, the options to the C command are case insensitive and can consist of multiple letters, as is true for all MPW commands. For those options that overlap with cc, those options are described with the capitalization used by the cc command.

As with cc, the `-g` option adds debugging symbols to the compiled code. These symbols can be used with MacsBug and other debuggers to identify functions as they are being executed.

The `-D` and `-U` options can define and undefine preprocessor symbols, similar to the #define and #undefine lines. The `-E` option is also customary, displaying the result of the preprocessor translation to standard output without compiling the program. The preprocessor strips any comments from its output unless the -C option is used.

The -I option specifies directories for #include header files. Unlike UNIX commands, the parameter for this option must be separated by a space from the option itself and may also include a list of directories separated by commas, as in:

```
C -i "{Sources}CIncludes",{StdLib}CIncludes:"
```

The compiler recognizes the -o option as specifying the output of the compilation. Unlike cc, MPW C does not link the final result of the compilation for you; so this specifies the name of the object file, not the executable program.

Other compiler options are Macintosh-specific.

The -s option can be used to assign a segment name for an entire source file. The segment name specified with the option will be the default for the compilation, which will remain in effect until the first #define __SEG__ line.

By default, the C compiler will build a complete stack frame for each function only when necessary, making it more difficult to trace back through the stack to find each in a series of calls. The MPW -ga option includes entry code in each function to build a complete stack frame. This additional code is automatically enabled by the -g option as well.

MACINTOSH II CODE GENERATION

As with MPW Pascal, MPW C includes several options to generate code for the Motorola MC68020 processor and the MC68881 floating point coprocessor, as found on the Macintosh II. As described in the previous chapter, programs built using these options cannot be run on a machine with only a 68000 and without a 68881.

Two MPW C options relate to the 68020, while two target codes are for the 68881.

The -mc68020 option causes the compiler to take advantage of some extended instructions that are only available on the 68020 and later processors. As with MPW Pascal, these include 32-bit multiply and divide instructions, a shorter return sequence for most functions, direct conversion between signed char and long types, and bit-manipulation instructions for inserting and extracting data from bit fields.

To improve performance with the 32-bit data bus of the 68020, the align option aligns data on 32-bit boundaries. The compiler inserts extra space before variables and data structures. The option does not insert extra space within a struct—instead, a struct should be aligned through explicit filler members. Unlike -mc68020, the option can be safely used for programs that will run on other computers.

For the Macintosh II, the SANE packages are implemented to use the floating point operations of the 68881 coprocessor, instead of software emulation using integer instructions of the 68000 (or 68020) CPU.

For even faster results, the mc68881 option causes the compiler to directly generate 68881 instructions (instead of SANE calls) for the basic operators, comparisons, and conversions between different floating point types.

The compiler defines all extended variables, functions, members, etc. that are defined as being the 96-bit quantity expected by the 68881, rather than the 80-bit quantity used by SANE. It also attempts to assign any extended automatic variables to one of the 68881s 8 floating point registers. As is true for SANE, programs that use extended data will be considerably faster than those using float or double values.

This option also sets the preprocessor symbol mc68881, equivalent to

```
#define mc68881
```

which is used by the SANE.h header file to modify its declarations.

The numeric results using the 68881 for basic arithmetic are identical to those produced by SANE. However, if you're using SANE's exception condition handling or other advanced SANE features, you should consult the MPW C reference manual for a discussion of the differences.

By default, transcendental functions will be evaluated by SANE rather than the 68881. To further speed up any program, a compilation command such as

```
C transform.c -mc68881 -elems881
```

will direct the compiler to generate direct 68881 instructions for transcendental functions. These include trigonometric, inverse trigonometric, hyperbolic, logarithmic, and exponentiation functions, both those declared in SANE.h and those defined in math.h. However, the results will be slighlty less accurate than those of SANE.

The -mc68881 option affects the compilation of an entire file, but Apple recommends that any program should be consistent in its choice of whether or not to use the 68881. Failure to do so requires that you must manually allow for possible incompatibilities in calling sequences, global variables, and different library requirements.

LINKING C PROGRAMS

Table 8–7 lists the object libraries used in linking MPW C programs.

Any MPW program that includes even a single C function must be linked against {CLibraries}CRuntime.o. This code is required to properly

All Programs

{CLibraries}CRuntime.o	Standard run-time initialization
{CLibraries}CInterface.o	Glue and RAM-based Macintosh routines

Standard C library

{CLibraries}StdCLib.o	Standard C libraries
{CLibraries}CSANELib.o	SANE (referenced by standard I/O)
{CLibraries}Math.o	Standard C math library

Optional Libraries

{Libraries}DRVRRuntime.o	Desk accessory/driver support
{Libraries}PerformLib.o	Performance measurement (USES Perf)
{Libraries}ToolLibs.o	Support for MPW tools

Macintosh II Libraries (compiled with -mc68881 option)

{CLibraries}CLib881.o	Instead of StdCLib.o
{CLibraries}CSANELib881.o	Instead of CSANELib.o
{CLibraries}Math881.o	Instead of Math.o

Table 8–7:   C library files

initialize the program, global, and static preinitialized data, and it, in turn, references {CLibraries}CInterface.o, which also must be included.

If the program uses the standard C library, additional files must be included. The standard I/O routines reference floating point conversion functions in the CSANELib.o, which then must be included.

If you are linking a small MPW tool, you may be able to take advantage of Stubs.c (likely to be found in the CExamples folder) to shorten the size of your program. It provides empty stub functions for the console I/O routines (used only by applications) and the floating point conversion functions (used only when formatting floating point numbers), thus reducing the size of the linked tool considerably.

A much easier way to link small C programs is to combine it with the compilation step, as in the *cc* UNIX command. Example 8–6 shows a command file implementing a simplified version of that command.
For example, if K&R's introductory program

```
main()
{
    printf("hello, world\n");
}
```

```
# Example 8-6: cc command file

# Compiles and links a C program that runs under the MPW
# shell
#
# Syntax:
#    cc -o toolname file.c
#

If {#} != 3 || "{1}" != "-o" ||∂
 "{2}" =~ /•-≈/ || "{3}"=~ /•-≈/
  Echo "### {0} - Wrong parameters."
  Echo "# Usage - {0} -o toolname file.c"
  Exit 1
End

Set CLibs "{CLibraries}CRuntime.o"∂
" {CLibraries}StdCLib.o"∂
" {CLibraries}CInterface.o"∂
" {Libraries}ToolLibs.o"∂
" {CLibraries}CSANELib.o"∂
" {Libraries}Interface.o"

C "{3}"

Link -w -o "{2}" -t MPST -c 'MPS ' "{3}.o" {CLibs}
Delete "{3}.o"
```

Example 8–6:   cc command file

were stored in the file Hello.c, entering the MPW shell commands

```
            cc -o Hello Hello.c
            Hello
```

would compile and run this program, displaying the one-sentence message.

Menu-based compilation may also be very handy, particularly when iteratively adding (and checking) new source code prior to linking. The UserStartup commands

```
    Set COpts "-ga"; Export COpts
    AddMenu Control "C compile" ∂
      'Open "{Worksheet}"; C {COpts} "{Target}"'
```

would define a custom menu command appropriate for debugging compiles during development.

EXAMPLE: BUILDING FILE SPECIFICATIONS

The Macintosh file system may not be familiar to many C programmers that have not programmed for the Macintosh before. Example 8–7 lists a complete MPW tool which uses the Standard File Package to produce a complete file pathname. It is similar to the `StdFile` tool of version 2.0 of MPW C, which was developed independently.

The example displays one of the standard file selection dialog boxes and, if a file name is selected, outputs the full pathname of the file to its standard output. Clicking the "Cancel" button is indicated by the tool's return status.

`StdFile` uses the `strcpy_p2c` function supplied earlier in this chapter to convert the Pascal string in the standard file `SFReply` structure to a C string. It also uses the standard UNIX System V `getopt` function provided in Appendix F to parse the command options.

The custom menu definition

```
AddMenu {Menu} 'Open Read-only…' ∂
'Begin; Open -r "`StdFile -t TEXT -r`"|| Beep; End
    ≥Dev:Null'
```

would add an MPW shell menu item to open an existing text document read only. As described in Chapter 6, command substitution uses the standard output of `StdFile` to supply the file name for the Open command, while the remaining commands are used to trap the errors (and error message) generated if the file dialog is cancelled by the user.

```
/*------------------------------------------------------

NAME
   StdFile -- count lines and characters

SYNOPSIS
   StdFile [-r] [-t type] [-d filename] [prompt]

DESCRIPTION
   "StdFile" asks the user to select a file name, using
   the Standard File Macintosh package. The syntax and
   usage are slightly different than the command of the
   same name provided in version 2 of MPW.

   The interface to "StdFile" is similar to that for
   "Request".
   Without the -r option, it asks the user to designate a
   new file name. The message gives the prompt. The -d
   option may be used to provide a default file name.
```

The -r option indicates that an existing file should
be selected. If -t is given, only files of the specified type are shown. Other options and parameters are
not used.

DIAGNOSTICS
    0 "Save" (or "Open" for -r) button was selected.
    1 Syntax error.
    2 The default pathname was invalid.
    4 The "Cancel" button was selected.

NOTE
    It might be desirable to have StdFile quote the
    strings it outputs if they contain any spaces or
    special characters.

```
----------------------------------------------------*/


#include <Types.h>
#include <QuickDraw.h>
#include <Files.h>
#include <Packages.h>
#include <stdio.h>
#define Length(str255) ( (int) str255.length )
extern char *GetSysErrText(errNbr,errMsg);


#define BFSIZE 256
#define NAMELEN 64
#define PATHLEN 1024

#define STAT_OK 0
#define STAT_SYNTAX 1
#define STAT_ERR 2
#define STAT_CANCEL 4

#define FSFCBLen 0x3F6
        /* Global variable for HFS; see Tech Note #66 */

typedef short half;
        /* 16-bit integer; some call this an int */


Boolean dflag,rflag,tflag,errflag,hfsflag;
char filename[NAMELEN];
int makepath();
```

```
/* getopt() interface */
extern int optind;          /* last unparsed parameter */
/* parameter string for an option */
extern char *optarg;

main(argc, argv)
int argc;
char **argv;
{ int c,stat;
  char *filetype=0;
  char pathname[PATHLEN],buff[BFSIZE];
  OSErr err;

  /* Initialization*/
  InitGraf(&qd.thePort);
  *pathname = *buff = '\0';

  /* Scan command options */
  while ((c = getopt(argc, argv, "rt:d:")) != EOF)
  { switch (c)
    { case 'r':
         if (rflag)
            errflag = true;
         else
            rflag = true;
         break;
      case 't':
         if (tflag)
            errflag = true;
         else
            { tflag = true;
              filetype = optarg;
            }
         break;
      case 'd':
         if (dflag)
            errflag = true;
         else
         { dflag = true;
           strcpy(pathname, optarg);
         }
         break;
      case '?':
      default:
         errflag = true;
         break;
    }
  }
```

```
   switch (argc-optind)  /* Number of remaining parms */
   { case 1:               /* A message is given */
       strcpy(buff,argv[optind]);
       break;
     case 0:               /* No message given */
       break;
     default:              /* Must be > 1 */
       errflag = true;
       fprintf
         (stderr,
         "### %s-Too many parameters were specified.\n",
         argv[0]);
   }

   if (errflag)            /* Previous option error */
   { fprintf
       (stderr,"# Usage - %s [-r] [-t type] [-d filename]
       [message]\n",
       argv[0]);
     /* MPW convention: syntax error */
     exit (STAT_SYNTAX);
   }

/* Do actual work; Return 1 for cancelled; <0 for an
   error */
   if (rflag)                         /* Want existing file */
     /* return name, type (if any) */
     err = getafile(pathname,filetype);
   else                               /* Specify a new file */
     /* default/return name, prompt */
     err = putafile(pathname,buff);
   if (err < 0)
   { fprintf
       (stderr,"### %s - Error specifying file.\n",
       argv[0]);
     GetSysErrText(err, buff);
     fprintf(stderr,"# %s.\n", buff);
     exit (STAT_ERR);
   }
   else
     if (err)
       return (STAT_CANCEL);
     else
     { printf("%s\n",pathname);
       exit (STAT_OK);
     }
}
```

```
/* Standard file dialog for existing files
   Returns 1 if cancelled, 0 if OK
   <0 if OSErr detected
*/
getafile(name,types)
char *name,*types;
{ SFReply    reply;
  Point      dlgorig;
  SFTypeList typelist;    /* long integers */
  Str255     volfilname;
  int        volrefno;
  int        ntype = -1,  /* required for SFGetFile */
                    len;

    if (types && *types)
       /* a non-null typelist given */
       /* This may include more than one type; or a 3-
          character type
          Fill list with spaces first and calculate the
          number used */
    {  len = strlen(types);
       ntype = (len+3)/sizeof(typelist[0]);
       memset((char *)typelist, (int) ' ', (int) 4*ntype);
       memcpy((char *)typelist,types,len);
    }

    dlgorig.v = 100;        /* calculate this */
    dlgorig.h = 85;

    SFGetFile(&dlgorig,     /* coordinate of display */
       " ",                 /* Prompt not used */
       NULL,                /* No file filter */
       (half) ntype,        /* Number of file types */
       typelist,            /* List of file types */
       NULL,                /* No dialog hook */
       &reply);             /* where the result goes */

    if (reply.good)
       return (makepath(name,&reply));
    else
       return (1);          /* cancelled */
}

/* Standard file dialog for new files
   Same returns as for getafile()
*/
putafile(name,prompt)
char *name,*prompt;
```

```
{ SFReply    reply;
  Point      dlgorig;
  SFTypeList typelist;    /* integers */
  Str255     volfilname;
  int        volrefno;

  dlgorig.v = 100;        /* calculate this */
  dlgorig.h = 85;

  SFPutFile(&dlgorig,     /* coordinate of display */
     prompt,              /* Prompt used */
     name,                /* Default name value */
     NULL,                /* No file filter */
     &reply);             /* where the result goes */

  if (reply.good)
     return (makepath(name,&reply));
  else
     return (1);          /* cancelled */
}

/* Figure out the actual path name from a Std File reply
   record This works under HFS (128k ROM or RAM-based)
   and MFS (64k ROM) Returns 0 or a (negative) OSErr
   value

   Caution: This may produce a C string > 255 characters
   long If recoded into Pascal, paths will be limited to
   255 characters.
*/
makepath(name,rep)
char *name;
SFReply *rep;
{ char buff[PATHLEN],*p;
  Str255 vnambuff;
  int err,len;
  DirInfo pbbuff;
     /* n.b. sizeof(DirInfo) >= sizeof(VolumeParam) */

  *name = '\0';                   /* clear string */

  SetVol(NULL, rep->vRefNum);  /* make default volume */
  pbbuff.ioVRefNum = rep->vRefNum;
     /* WD (HFS) or volume (MFS) selected */
  pbbuff.ioNamePtr = &vnambuff;
```

```
    /* This trick from Tech Note #66 catches 128k ROM and
       RAM-based HFS */
      if (*((half *)FSFCBLen)>0)

   /* HFS available: The only way to build a complete
      directory is to trace back the parent folders until
      you reach the root directory First convert a 16-bit
WD
      number to a 32-bit DirID
   */
      {  ((WDPBRec *)&pbbuff)->ioWDIndex = 0;      /* use
ioVRefNum */
         if (err = PBGetWDInfo(&pbbuff,false))
            return (err);         /* FAILED */
         /* DirID in pbbuff.ioWDDirID, used by GetCatInfo()
            as pbbuff.ioDrDirID */

         /* fill buffer right to left */
         p = buff+sizeof(buff);
         *--p = '\0';
         do                       /* Continue to the root... */
            /* info on this DirID */
         { pbbuff.ioFDirIndex = -1;
           if (err = PBGetCatInfo(&pbbuff, false))
              return (err);       /* FAILED */
           len = Length(vnambuff);
           *--p = ':';
           p -= len;
           /* copy dir name */
           strncpy_p2c(p, &vnambuff, len);
         } while ((pbbuff.ioDrDirID = pbbuff.ioDrParID) !=
              fsRtParID);
         /* Quit at parent of Root directory */

         strcpy(name, p); /* Could be > 255 characters */
      }

   else       /* Get name of MFS volume */

   /* use ioVRefNum */
   {  ((VolumeParam *)&pbbuff)->ioVolIndex = -1;
      if (err = PBGetVol(&pbbuff,false))
         return (err);            /* FAILED */
      strcpy_p2c(name,pbbuff.ioNamePtr);
      strcat(name,":");
   }
```

```
    /* Convert to C-string */
    (void) strcpy_p2c(buff,&(rep->fName));     strcat(name,buff);
       /* Add file name */
    return (0);
}
```

Example 8–7:   StdFile tool

Chapter 9

Resources

Resources will be required to complete most Macintosh programs. Resources are expected by many of the Toolbox traps (such as in the Dialog Manager) and are also required to define desktop icons for an application and its documents.

When it comes to defining or examining resources, MPW has a major advantage over earlier development systems. MPW comes with a complete set of tools for manipulating resources and is fully user-extensible to handle any new resource type.

Resources can be compiled using the MPW resource compiler Rez or built using the ResEdit resource editor included with MPW. Also included are tools for decompiling resources back into Rez source or assembly code and a tool that analyzes the contents of the resource fork and checks it for validity.

9.1 Defining Resources

MPW includes both resource compiler and resource decompiler tools, which share a common syntax for specifying resource contents.

Rez compiles a text source file into a resource fork, much as a C or Pascal compiler compiles program source into object code. DeRez decompiles any resource fork back into source form. Both are user extensible through common files defining the format of the resources to be compiled or decompiled.

The Rez source format is described in this section after a quick review of the format of the desired result—i.e., the resource fork of a program or document.

471

RESOURCES REVISITED

Every Macintosh file can have a resource fork and a data fork. Within the resource fork, each resource is referenced by a four-letter type and a 16-bit ID and may optionally include a resource name and a series of resource attributes.

The resource type indicates the format of the data stored in the corresponding resource: resources of the same type will usually have the same layout. A list of standard Macintosh resource types is given in Table 9–1.

A Macintosh program—such as an application or MPW tool—is defined by the resource fork of the corresponding file.

The MPW Link command outputs the actual 68000 machine code for a program, producing resources of type 'CODE' by default. This code often references other resources through calls to the Resource Manager, either directly (e.g., GetResource) or indirectly (GetNewWindow).

The remaining resources in a program may be compiled using a resource compiler, which takes a text file and builds a corresponding resource fork. MPW includes the Rez resource compiler, which is similar in function to the RMaker resource compiler included with the Lisa Workshop, MDS, and many third-party development systems.

Resources can also be be built directly using a resource editor. MPW includes the standard ResEdit resource editor. A variety of specialized resource editors are also available from Apple and third parties, such as REdit and Dialog Creator.

Both resource editors and resource compilers will create resources in the resource fork of an application or other file, but Rez has some advantages. The important difference is that the resource compiler works from source—and thus you can recreate that resource at any time. With a resource editor, if your only copy of the resource is in the application, and if you accidentally delete the old one before creating a new one, there is no way to regenerate that resource.

Rez also solves the one major failing of its RMaker predecessor, which was limited to only a subset of the available resource types—and would not conveniently support user-defined resource types. As new managers are added to the Macintosh software architecture, new resource types are also added, which makes the need for extensibility even greater.

In contrast, the rules used by Rez for compiling resource types are fully defined by text file(s) used as input with the Rez compiler. You can modify those files to define new resources not yet supported by MPW or to define the format for your own type of resources.

The common syntax for defining resource type and data definitions is shared between Rez and DeRez, the MPW resource decompiler. When applied to the resource fork of a Macintosh file, DeRez can decompile most

Type	ROM	Description	Requires	Used By
actb	Color	Alert color table	ALRT	Dialog Manager
acur		List of cursors	CURS	MPW Shell
ADBS	256K	Apple DeskTop Bus		ADB Manager
ALRT		Alert template	DITL	Dialog Manager
BNDL		Application bundle	FREF	Finder
ccrs	Color	Color 16x16 cursor		QuickDraw
cctb	Color	Control color table	CNTL	Control Manager
CDEF		Control definition procedure		Control Manager
cdev		Control item		Control Panel
cicn	Color	Color 32x32 icon		QuickDraw
clut	Color	Color lookup table		Color Manager
cmdo		Interactive help for MPW tool		MPW Shell
CNTL		Control template		Control Manager
CODE		Application or tool machine code		Segment Loader
crsr	Color	Color 16x16 cursor		QuickDraw
CURS		Cursor 16x16		QuickDraw
dctb	Color	Dialog color table	DLOG	Dialog Manager
DITL		Dialog item list		Dialog Manager
DLOG		Dialog template	DITL	Dialog Manager
DRVR		Driver or desk accessory		Device Manager
FCMT		Finder comment		Finder
fctb	Color	Font color table	FONT	Font Manager
finf		Font information		Control Panel
FKEY		Function key		OS Event Manager
FMTR	128K	Floppy disk formatter		Disk Initialization Package
FOND	128K	Font family	FONT	Font Manager
FONT		Font		Font Manager
FREF		File reference		Finder
FRSV		Reserved font list	FONT	Font/DA Mover
FWID		Font width table		Font Manager
GNRL		General-purpose resource		
ICN#		Desktop icon (32x32) and mask		Finder
ICON		Icon (32x32)		QuickDraw
ictb	Color	Dialog item color table		Dialog Manager
INIT		Initialization code		system startup
insc		Installer script		Installer
INTL		Country-specific parameters		International Utilities
itl0		'INTL' resource #0		Script Manager
itl1		'INTL' resource #1		Script Manager
itl2		'INTL' resource #2		Script Manager
itlb		Table of 'itl' resources		Script Manager
itlc		'INTL' configuration		Script Manager
KCHR		Virtual key mapping to ASCII		Toolbox Event Manager

Type	ROM	Description	Requires	Used By
KMAP		Hardware to virtual key mapping		Toolbox Event Manager
KSWP		Key remapping		Script Manager
LAYO		Desktop layout		Finder
LDEF	128K	List definition procedure		List Manager
mach		Machine compatibility		Control Panel
MBAR		Menu bar	MENU	Menu Manager
mbdf		Menu bar def. procedure	MDEF	Menu Manager
mcky		Mouse-tracking parameters		
mctb	Color	Menu color table	MENU	Menu Manager
MDEF		Menu definition procedure		Menu Manager
MENU		Menu lists		Menu Manager
MMAP		Mouse-tracking code		
MPSR		MPW editor configuration		MPW Shell
NFNT	128K	Expanded font definition		Font Manager
nrct		List of rectangles		Control Panel
PACK		Code package		Package Manager
PAPA		Printer Access Protocol attributes		AppleTalk Manager
PAT		Pattern (8x8)		QuickDraw
PAT#		Pattern list		Toolbox Utilities
PDEF		Printer definition procedure		Print Manager
PICT		QuickDraw picture		QuickDraw
pllt	Color	Color palette		Palette Manager
POST		PostScript		LaserWriter
ppat	Color	Color pixel pattern		QuickDraw
PREC		Printing-related resource		Printing Manager
PTCH		ROM patch code		system startup
ROv#		Override ROM resource		Resource Manager
scrn	MacII	Screen configuration		Startup Manager
SERD		Serial Driver		Serial Driver
SICN		Small (16x16) icon		Finder
SIZE		Switcher size and options		Switcher
snd	MacII	Stored sound		Sound Manager
snth	MacII	Executable synthesizer code		Sound Manager
STR		String		Toolbox Utilities
STR#		String list		Toolbox Utilities
TMPL		Resource template		ResEdit
wctb	Color	Window color table	WIND	Window Manager
WDEF		Window definition procedure		Window Manager
WIND		Window template		Window Manager

128K	Requires 128K ROM or later	
256K	Requires 256K ROM or later	
MacII	Requires Macintosh II	
Color	Requires Color QuickDraw	

Table 9-1:   Standard resource types

resources built by `Rez` or `ResEdit` back into a form suitable for later (re)compilation using `Rez`.

SOURCE FILES

The source format used by `Rez` (and `DeRez`) is a user-extensible programming language with a C-like flavor.

Like C, statements may span multiple lines and are terminated by a semicolon. Braces ({ item1, item2 }) group blocks of data, while the standard C delimiters group comments (/* remark */). As with C programs, input files to `Rez` can include preprocessor directives to merge other source files or conditionally compile some statements. The rules for constructing integers and strings are generally similar to C, with some extensions. Like Pascal and unlike C, the language is case insensitive, except within literal and character strings.

The special characters recognized by `Rez` are summarized by Table 9–2. `Rez` also recognizes the standard C unary and binary operators, but these are more often used when defining custom resource formats, as described later.

Delimiters	*Description*
,	separate items in a statement
;	end of a statement
{ }	group multiple items in statement
/* */	comments

Series of arbitrary bytes	
"string"	string of ASCII characters
$"A1A2A3"	string of hex digits

32-bit signed integers	
'abcd'	character literal (resource type)
123	decimal integer
0x7B	hex integer
$7B	hex integer
0173	octal integer
0b1111011	binary integer

Other	
#directive	pre-processor directive
$$func	built-in function

Table 9–2:   Rez special characters

There are two kinds of statements in a `Rez` source file: those that define the format of resource data and those that define the actual resources. The format of a resource is usually fixed by the resource type.

Although the two kinds of statements can be freely mixed, the statements defining types and the files defining resource data are usually split into separate files, with the type declarations normally preceeding the source files in a compilation. This allows the type-defining files (or "resource description files") to be used with more than one source file. The same definition files can also be used to decompile the same resources, as shown by Figure 9–1.

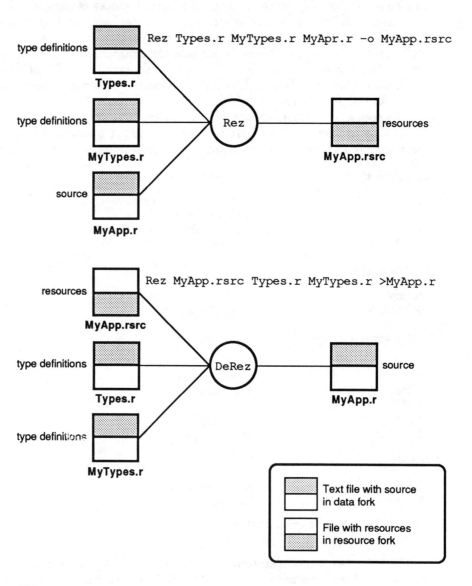

Figure 9–1:   Input and output files for resource tools

Statements in a `Rez` source file begin with one of five reserved keywords—data, include, read, resource, or type. As its name suggests, type defines the format of a resource type; the remaining statements are used to define resource data.

The statement keyword is followed by a series of required and optional parameters, depending on the keyword. The type, resource, and data statements include a list of items, delimited by braces.

The format of `Rez` statements is summarized by Table 9–3.

MPW comes with standard type definitions for the most commonly used resources. These are contained in the files included in the {RIncludes}

Type Definitions

```
type 'atyp' { declarations  … };
```
format for all resources of type 'atyp'

```
type 'atyp' (id) {declarations  … };
```
format for 'atyp' resources number id only

```
type 'atyp' as 'btyp';
```
format for 'atyp' resources is the same as for 'btyp'

Data Declarations

```
resource 'atyp' (id, "name", attributes…) { data … };
```
define 'atyp' #id using type format

```
data 'atyp' (id, "name", attributes…) { literal };
```
define 'atyp' #id using unformatted data

```
read 'atyp' (id, "name", attributes…) file;
```
define 'atyp' #id using data fork of file

```
include file;
```
merge all resources from file

Symbol	Description	Example
'atyp'	four-character resource type	'DLOG', 'STR#'
id	integer in range [-32768, +32767]	128, 0xFFC0
"name"	optional resource name	"X", "\000Chooser"
attributes	optional resource attributes	purgeable, preload
file	name of a file	"Text", "data.rsrc"

For other forms of include, see Table 9–4

Table 9–3:   Rez source statements

directory, which are updated with each release. To get a current list of the resource types available for use with `Rez` and `DeRez` commands, you could use the shell commands:

```
Directory "{RIncludes}"
Search /•[∂t ]*type≈∂'/ ≈.r
```

to list each line containing a type definition.

One way to define resources is to merge previously compiled resources from the resource fork of another file. The `include` statement provides several variations that select different resources from the resource file, as summarized by Table 9–4. The resources merged from the resource fork can be copied as is or their type (or resource ID) redefined in the new output.

```
include file;
```
merge all resources from file

```
include file 'atyp';
```
merge all resources from file of type 'atyp'
```
include file not 'atyp';
```
merge all resources from file not of type 'atyp'

```
include file 'atyp' (idrange);
include file 'atyp' ("name");
```
merge specified resource from file

```
include file 'atyp' as 'btyp';
```
merge all resources from file of type 'atyp' and include them in output file as resources of type 'btyp'

```
include file 'atyp' as 'btyp';
```
merge all resources from file of type 'atyp' and include them in output file as resources of type 'btyp'

where
   idrange is either `id` or `firstid:lastid`

Table 9–4:   Including compiled resources

DEFINING YOUR OWN RESOURCES

For programs that require resources, you will normally edit a `Rez` source definition into a document with a name ending in .r. The actual syntax rules for your file are contained by the type definitions of `Types.r` and other files in `{RIncludes}`. If you understand the type definition syntax, these files precisely spell out the rules for composing your input.

If you prefer a more "cookbook" solution to building resources, the syntax of commonly used resource types is given by example in Appendix D. It's easy enough to get by with the cookbook and an understanding of a few simple rules. This will also help when it comes time to define your own resource types.

Each formatted resource is defined using a resource statement that specifies the type, the resource ID, and other resource attributes. Next comes a list of values that correspond to the description within the type definition, bracketed by braces ({ }). The entire statement is terminated by a semicolon.

Probably the simplest of the standard resources is the string resource, type 'STR ' (note the required space). The syntax

```
resource ('STR ', 128)    { "This is a string" };
```

shows the definition of a resource containing a single value.

Each value in a resource statement will normally be an integer or string constant, depending on the data type specified for the field in the type definition. Where a string is expected, multiple strings that aren't separated by commas are treated as part of the same string. The source

```
resource 'STR ' (1000) {
    "When in the Course of human Events, it becomes "
    "necessary for one People to dissolve the Political "
    "Bands which have connected them with another … "
    "they should declare the causes which impel them "
    "to the Separation."
};
```

defines a single long string.

If you need to insert unprintable characters, such as the return character, Rez recognizes special escape sequences similar to those allowed in C strings. Within a string (or literal), a \ character can follow the numeric equivalent of the character to be compiled. The number can be specified in more than one base, but the number of digits is fixed by the base so that Rez knows where the next "normal" character begins. For example, characters specified in octal are always three digits so that

```
\0001
```

specifies two characters, an ASCII NULL (octal value 000), followed by the ASCII character 1.

The escape character can also be followed by one of several predefined characters. For example, The\rEnd would produce seven characters, with the middle character a Return character.

The escape sequences recognized by Rez are summarized by Table 9–5.

Most types will require more than one value for each resource. The fields in the resource input generally have a one-to-one correspondence to the fields in the generated resource; a few entries may be generated for you and thus do not require values to be specified in your input. The order of the fields is always the same as the order of the bytes in the resource, with bits within a byte ordered from most significant to least significant.

Values for the fields are separated by commas. Take, for example, the

Numeric Escapes

The escape character can be followed by a format and a fixed number of digits indicating the ASCII value. The following are all equivalent to "0":

"\060"	octal (3 digits)
"\0d048"	decimal (3 digits)
"\0x30"	hex (2 digits)
"\$30"	hex (2 digits)
"\0b00110000"	binary (8 digits)

Single-character escapes

"\b"	backspace	"\0x08"
"\t"	tab	"\0x09"
"\v"	vertical tab	"\0x0B"
"\f"	form feed	"\0x0C"
"\n"	newline	"\0x0D"
"\r"	return	"\0x0D"
"\""	quotation mark (")	"\0x22"
"\'"	apostrophe (')	"\0x27"
"\\"	backslash (\)	"\0x5c"
"\?"	rubout	"\0x7F"

These sequences apply both within string ("x\ty") and literal ('x\ty') constants.

Table 9–5:   Inserting special characters in strings and literals

'FREF' resource used as part of an application bundle. The type definition specifies three fields: a resource type (four characters stored in a 32-bit integer), an icon number, and a file name. The source

```
resource ('FREF', 0)   { 'APPL', 0, "" };
resource ('FREF', 1)   { 'TEXT', 1, "" };
```

would be part of the bundle for an application that created documents of type 'TEXT'.

Many of the types expect lists of simpler formats repeated over and over. These lists are implemented as arrays in the Rez syntax. Each array element can be a single data type, such as with a pattern list, icon list, or string list, which are defined as an array of patterns, icons, or strings. Elements can also include multiple fields, such as the rectangle and item type in a dialog item list. Other information may precede or follow the array: a 'MENU' contains a menu title, among other values, prior to an array of menu items.

You don't have to specify the length of the array: the type definition includes a declaration that automatically inserts the length (usually a 16-bit word) at the beginning of the resource. This length will be in the format expected by the corresponding manager, usually the number of elements or one less than the number of elements.

You indicate the length of the array implicitly in your source. Each array must be defined by an open brace and a list of array elements separated by semicolons and must be terminated by a closing brace, although Rez generally treats commas and semicolons the same. The number of array elements defined is thus implicitly given by the number of items in the source. For example, the source

```
resource ('STR#', 128)  { { "Undo"; "Redo" } };
```

might be used with the Toolbox Utility GetIndString to define two strings used to change the title of the Undo menu item.

Two QuickDraw types are defined as primitive data types in the Rez source format. A rect is specified as a series of four integers separated by commas and surrounded by braces ({top, left, bottom, right}.) Less often used is the point type, which contains two integers instead of four.

Many of the resources include symbolic definitions of alternate values. These symbolic definitions are enumeration constants, similar to Pascal scalers or C enum values. For example, a 'WIND' resource includes the window type, the initial visibility flag, and the close (go-away) box flag. A window definition might look like

```
resource 'WIND' (256) {
  {46, 8, 327, 507},
   zoomDocProc,
   visible,
   goAway,
   0,        /* user-defined constant */
   "Untitled"
   };
```

where zoomDocProc is the type of window to be drawn, and visible and goAway are symbolic names for the flag values.

Some of the symbolic definitions only apply to one common value, such as the "not used" case. For example, in the menu definition

```
resource 'MENU' (3) {
    3,                      /* Menu ID */
    textMenuProc,           /* definition procedure */
    0x7FFFFF51,             /* enabling flags for menu items */
    enabled,                /* enabling flag for entire menu */
    "Edit",                 /* menu title */
    { "Undo",    noIcon, "Z", noMark, plain;
      "-",       noIcon, noKey, noMark, plain;
      "Cut",     noIcon, "X", noMark, plain;
      "Copy",    noIcon, "C", noMark, plain;
      "Paste",   noIcon, "V", noMark, plain;
      "Clear",   noIcon, noKey, noMark, plain;
      "Select All", noIcon, "A", noMark, plain;
      "-",       noIcon, noKey, noMark, plain,
      "Show Clipboard", noIcon, noKey, noMark, plain
    }
};
```

the Command-key equivalent is specified by a single character, or the symbolic value noKey indicates the lack of an equivalent. Similarly, a menu with an icon would include the ID of the corresponding 'ICON' type resource, while other menus would use noIcon.

A few types will use symbolic references to define alternate formats for the resource, usually for elements of an array of items. The one you'll encounter most often is the dialog item list, in which each item in the list may have a different format. This can perhaps best be illustrated by an example:

```
resource 'DITL' (256) {
    { {60, 105, 80, 175}, Button { enabled, "OK" };
      {10, 20, 42, 52}, Icon { disabled,  0 };
      {10, 64, 42, 264}, StaticText { disabled, "^0" }
    }
};
```

Each item begins with a boundary rectangle and is followed by a symbolic constant indicating the type of item. The fields appropriate for that type are given within braces; the format of the fields depends on the item type, with some (Button) requiring a string for the item title and others (Icon) expecting an integer resource ID referencing another resource. This syntax—symbolic name, braces, list of fields—is common to all resources that use such alternate formats (Pascal variant records), although 'DITL' is the only such resource commonly used.

SPECIAL RESOURCE FORMATS

Although most of the standard types should be easy to use if you've used another resource compiler or editor, two of the standard resource types have quirks that might not be immediately obvious.

As shown earlier, the 'MENU' type includes a field that defines which menu items are enabled when the menu is displayed. This corresponds to 31 bits of the 32-bit enabling LONGINT expected by the Menu Manager; the last bit enables or disables the entire menu and is represented by Rez using a separate field.

You must manually build a mask (usually in hex) for the list of menu items enabled. Starting with the least significant bit for the first menu item, adding the bit only if the item is enabled. Once you get to the end of the menu, all the remaining items should be enabled. Figure 9–2 illustrates an example of how this arithmetic is done.

If hexadecimal subtraction doesn't faze you, you could also start with all 31 possible menu items enabled—a mask of 0x7FFFFFF—then subtract the corresponding bit for each disabled menu item. Note that if your menu has more than 31 items, the remaining items will always be enabled.

The other resource type that requires a word to the wise is 'ALRT'. As described in the Dialog Manager chapter of *Inside Macintosh,* the four stages of an alert template are defined from the least significant to most significant nibbles (4-bit groups) of a 16-bit word. These stages determine the noise that will be made (if any), whether the alert will be displayed, and, if displayed, which button will be outlined as the default button.

However, Rez always stores a series of bit fields from most significant to least significant. This means that when defining an 'ALRT' resource, you must list the actions in the reverse order that they will be performed. Take the example:

```
resource 'ALRT' (256) {
  {40, 131, 140, 381},
  256,
  { Cancel, visible, silent; /* fourth or later time */
    OK, visible, sound3;      /* third time */
    OK, invisible, sound2;    /* second time */
    OK, invisible, sound1     /* first time */
  }
};
```

In this case, the first two times Alert was called, the Macintosh would beep once and then twice but would not display the alert. The third time, the alert

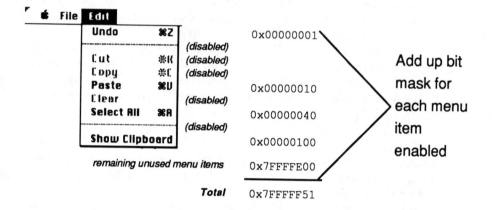

Figure 9–2:   Enabling menu items

would be displayed with three beeps. After that, the alert would be displayed silently, but the default action would become Cancel.

RESOURCE ATTRIBUTES

Additional information may be included for some resources outside the resource description: a resource name and resource attributes. The resource name, if any, is a string that follows the resource ID, as in:

```
resource 'TRAP' ($893, "MoveTo") { "QuickDraw", $A893 };
```

Drivers and desk accessories require a resource name. For other resources, the name is used for your convenience as an alternate way of finding a resource.

Anything following the resource ID (or name) that's not a string is assumed to be a resource attribute. The symbolic names for these attributes are shown in Table 9–6.

By default, all the resource attributes are zero; you enable specific atttribute bits by specifying the symbolic names, separated by commas. Most resources (with the notable exception of menus) are specified as `purgeable`. The `preload` attribute is useful if you expect the resource to be used immediately by the program. For example, if you display a standard alert (the copyright notice) upon starting your program, you might specify it as:

Value	Symbol	Description	Default
2	changed	Resource has been changed†	unchanged
4	preload	Load when resource fork opened	nonpreload
8	protected	Cannot be modified on disk	unprotected
16	locked	Do not relocate within heap	unlocked
32	purgeable	Purge from heap at any time	nonpurgeable
64	sysheap	Load into system heap	appheap

† Not valid for Rez input; used by DeRez output

Table 9–6:   Resource attributes

```
resource 'ALRT' (256, preload, purgeable) {
   {40, 131, 140, 381},
   256,
   { OK, visible, silent;
     OK, visible, silent;
     OK, visible, silent;
     OK, visible, silent
   }
};
```

The names for the default values will rarely be used—since that's the value that will be taken if you specify nothing. However, if you merge a resource from another file using an `include` statement, you have the option of overriding the resource attributes, and thus you might want to "unset" one of the bits.

9.2 Resource Commands

The `Rez` command is an MPW tool used to compile one or more source files into a resource fork. `DeRez` decompiles any resource fork back into source form.

Other resource-related MPW tools include `RezDet`, which analyzes the resource fork of any MPW file and displays information about its consistency. `DumpCode` can be used to dump the code resource fork of an MPW program as 68000 assembly language statements.

COMPILING RESOURCES

The `Rez` command uses type and resource definition text files to produce a single Macintosh file containing the compiled resources in the resource fork.

Rez

Compile resource descriptions

Syntax:

Rez *file* ...   Compile each source *file*
Rez   Compile interactively entered source

Options:

-a	Append resources to existing resource fork
-align WORD	Align each resource to 2-byte boundary
-align LONGWORD	Align each resource to 4-byte boundary
-d *name*	Define preprocessor symbol *name* to be ""
-d *name=string*	Define preprocessor symbol *name* to be *string*
-i *pathname*	Use *pathname* directory to find #include source files
-o *output*	Output compiled resources to file *output*
-p	Display compilation progress report
-rd	Don't print an error if a type is redeclared
-ro	Mark resource map as read only
-t *type*	Set output file type to four-character *type*

Remarks:

By default, the compiled object code goes to file Rez.out. If the output file does not exist, it is created with the default type and creator of 'APPL' and '????'. The output normally replaces the entire resource fork of the output file, unless the -a option is used, in which case any existing resource not redefined by the source input is left unchanged.

Interactively entered source is terminated by Command-Enter.

If a *file* is not found in the current directory, the directories defined by {RIncludes} are also searched. This allows the standard definition files, such as Types.r, to be specified without using a full pathname.

Input/Output:

Diagnostic   Compiler error messages

Examples:

Rez Types.r Data.r -o Data.rsrc
                      Compile Data.r; leave resources in Data.rsrc

The list of input files should include a file defining the resource formats prior to any use of those formats. The file Types.r includes most of the resource types you'll ever use.

Rez normally overwrites all the resources in the file and thus is normally used prior to the Link command. For example, an MPW tool might be built using:

```
Rez Types.r MyTool.r -o MyTool
Link -o MyTool -t MPST -c 'MPS ' MyTool.p.o {PLibs}
```

The file type and creator can be specified on either the Rez or the Link command. You can also append resources to a previously linked file, as in:

```
Link -o MyTool -t MPST -c 'MPS ' MyTool.p.o {PLibs}
Rez -a Types.r MyTool.r -o MyTool
```

However, with this approach, any resource definitions deleted from MyTool.r will remain in MyTool until MyTool is deleted or its resource fork is reinitialized, such as by a Rez without the -a option.

As with other MPW compilers, Rez accepts source compiled interactively.

DECOMPILING RESOURCES

Those who have used other Macintosh development systems before MPW will already have a series of resources defined for their programs. Some may have been built with RMaker, others with ResEdit.

It would be possible to convert RMaker source to Rez source using an editing script. But the syntax rules for RMaker are so *ad hoc* that a very complex script would be required to handle all the customary types. Of course, if the resources were built with ResEdit, there is no available source.

However, the DeRez command will take the resource fork of any file and decompile the resources into Rez source. The process is completely reversible—any source file compiled into resources can be decompiled and vice versa. The only difference will be the formatting of the Rez source.

DeRez

Decompile resource descriptions

Syntax:

```
DeRez resfile file ...
```
                    Decompile *resfile* using the definitions in
                    each *file*

Options:

-d *name*	Define preprocessor symbol *name* to be ""
-d *name=string*	Define preprocessor symbol *name* to be *string*

`-i pathname`	Use `pathname` directory to find `#include` source files
`-m size`	Maximum string width on output is `size` characters per line
`-only type`	Only decompile resources with type of `type`
`-only typeexpr`	Only decompile resources corresponding to `typeexpr`
`-p`	Display compilation progress report
`-rd`	Don't print an error if a type is redeclared
`-skip type`	Skip all resources with type of `type`
`-skip typeexpr`	Skip all resources corresponding to `typeexpr`

Remarks:

The output is a series of `resource` statements suitable for use with `Rez`. If a resource is encountered that does not have a known format, it is output as a `data` statement.

More than one `-only` or `-skip` option can be specified, but the two cannot be mixed. Two forms exist for their corresponding option parameters. The first form takes a single four-character resource type and applies to all resources of that type. When `typeexpr` is used, it is one of the following:

`"'[type]' ([id])"`	Specific resource type and ID
`"'[type]' ([id1:id2])"`	Specific resource type and range of IDs
`"'[type]' (∂"[ResourceName]∂")"`	Specific resource type and resource name

The apostrophes are necessary to treat the resource type as a 32-bit integer (rather than a string), while the quotation marks prevent the apostrophes from being stripped by the shell. `ResourceName` can include special characters, such as ∂"\000Chooser∂" for the desk accessory named Chooser.

If a `file` is not found in the current directory, the directories defined by {RIncludes} are also searched. This allows the standard definition files, such as `Types.r`, to be specified without using a full pathname.

Input/Output:

Output	Resource description

Examples:

```
DeRez Data.rsrc Types.r >Data.r
```
                        Decompile `Data.rsrc`; leave source in `Data.r`

The decompiled values will generally be displayed with one value per line. If the values are part of an array, comments will indicate the number of each array element, as in:

```
resource 'DITL' (256, purgeable) {
    { /* array DITLarray: 2 elements */
    /* [1] */
    {60, 105, 80, 175},
    Button {
        enabled,
        "OK"
    };
    /* [2] */
    {10, 64, 42, 264},
    StaticText {
        disabled,
        "^0"
        }
    }
};
```

The output normally will use symbolic values where defined. However, if the field can be expressed as the sum of a series of values rather than enumerated constants, the value will be shown as an integer. The two most common examples are font style (bold+italic) in a menu and an event mask (mDownMask+keyDownMask) in a desk accessory.

The format of unrecognized resources will be data statements, with the resource dumped in hex. The ASCII characters corresponding to the resource will be shown as comments, as in:

```
data 'FOO ' (1, preload) {
    /* This resource is */
    $"5468 6973 2072 6573 6F75 7263 6520 6973"
    $"204A 554E 4B"                    /*  JUNK */
};
```

Of course, a resource compiled using data statements will be decompiled in formatted form if you write its type statement prior to using DeRez. This is the easiest way to reformat Rez source if you add or change the type definition.

DeRez allows you to selectively specify only certain resources by type and optionally by resource ID or resource name. Two examples will help illustrate this. The command

```
DeRez -only DLOG "{SystemFolder}System" Types.r
```

would decompile all dialog template resources in the System file, using the standard 'DLOG' definition in Types.r. Meanwhile, the command

```
DeRez -only "'DLOG' (-16384:-14437)"
"{SystemFolder}System" Types.r
```

would only show dialogs within the specified range of resource IDs. These correspond to the owned resources for drivers and desk accessories and would not include other dialogs (such as for the Standard File Package) stored in the System file.

OTHER RESOURCE TOOLS

When you need to discover hard-to-find information on private parties, you would use a private detective. For hard-to-find information about resources, MPW programmers will use RezDet, the Resource Detective.

RezDet

Analyze consistency of resource fork

Syntax:

RezDet *resfile*...   Analyze the resource map of each *resfile*

Options:

-d	Dump information on header and each resource
-l	List each resource defined
-q	Quiet: display no information
-r	Raw dump: maximum information about each resource
-s	Show more detailed analysis of each resource than -l

Remarks:

The value of {Status} will be 2 if an error in the resource format was detected.

The output options, in increasing order of detail, are:

-q	no output; success indicated by {Status} only
(default)	two lines unless errors found
-l	same as default, but with one line per resource
-s	approximately eight lines per resource

-d	same as -s, plus format of resource header
-r	same as -d, with hex dump of each resource

Input/Output:

Output   Information about the resources

Examples:

RezDet -l MyApp   Display a list of all the resources in MyApp

RezDet analyzes and validates resources far more rigorously than any other program because that is its sole function, to validate resources. This means it's possible to manipulate a resource with DeRez or ResEdit or for your program to use any of the various ROM implementations of the resource manager. However, if RezDet takes a look, it may object to something the others have overlooked.

It enforces a canonical (standard) form on the resource map, header, and data. Of course, it checks for invalid resource types, IDs, names, and attributes. It looks for extra or missing data, inconsistent sizes (between the map and the resource), and duplicate resource IDs or names.

It has several output modes. At one extreme, the "quiet" mode returns a success/failure status to the MPW shell. At the other extreme, the error messages are printed above a dump of the resource data. Other options allow inclusions of information on each resource; no option prints only error messages.

Figure 9–3 shows five levels of output for RezDet when used on a file containing a single resource. The sixth level includes a hex dump of the resource data in addition to the information shown at the fifth level. If you get to this point, you probably should be using DeRez instead.

RezDet -q Rez.out

RezDet Rez.out
"Rez.out: The resource fork of Rez.out appears to be OK. RezDet -l Rez.out Rez.out:
'PICT' (-32768, Purgeable) [412] The resource fork of Rez.out appears to be OK.
RezDet -s Rez.out Rez.out: Type 0x50494354 'PICT': There is one item of this type.
Re"

Figure 9–3:   Increasingly detailed RezDet output

For a large application, an analysis of the entire resource fork may provide too much information. Instead, you may need to only check to see what resources (if any) have changed from a previous version. The ResEqual

command can be used to compare the resource forks of two files—much as the
Equal command can be used to compare their data forks.

ResEqual

Compare resource forks of two files

Syntax:

ResEqual *file1 file2*   Compare resource forks of *file1* and
                                file1

Options:

-p   Display progress information

Remarks:

The value of {Status} will be 0 if the resource forks compare equal and 2
if they compare unequal. Other values indicate a syntax error or an
interrupted comparison.

Input/Output:

Output   Description of the resource differences
                                (if any)

Examples:

ResEqual foo oldfoo

                                Compare the resources in foo and
                                oldfoo

One class of resource that hasn't been mentioned is that of executable
code. This includes 'CODE', 'DRVR', 'INIT', 'WDEF', and all the other
program resource types listed in Chapter 3.

DumpCode is designed to disassemble such executable resources. It
knows the special rules for 'CODE' resources and jump tables and will
disassemble any resource you ask it to (whether containing 68000 code or
not).

DumpCode

Disassemble executable resources

Syntax:

DumpCode *resfile*   ...

                      Decompile each *resfile* into assembly code

Options:

-d	Suppress disassembly, listing only resource information
-h	Suppress header information for each resource
-jt	Don't display a dump of the jump table ('CODE' #0)
-rt *type*	Only disassemble resources with type of *type*
-rt *type=id*	Only disassemble *type* resource with resource number *id*
-p	Display progress report
-s *segment*	Dump only the resource named *segment*

Remarks:

The output is similar to that produced by DumpObj.

Input/Output:

Output	Formatted assembly listings

Examples:

```
DumpCode -rt CODE=0 'MPW Shell'
                Display only the jump table of the shell
DumpCode -rt DRVR=20 "{SystemFolder}System"
                Format desk accessory #20 from the system
DumpCode -s %A5Init MyApp
                Show only the segment named %A5Init
```

9.3 Custom Resource Formats

More complicated Rez source files are possible than the simple examples shown earlier.

The source can use directives to the Rez preprocessor to merge source with the compilation. This allows you to automatically include the necessary type definition files without specifying the files each time in the Rez command.

Rez also recognizes several built-in functions and a standard suite of operators.

More significantly, all the rules for defining Rez input and DeRez output are determined by type statements. Once you understand the syntax of those statements, you can add declarations for your own files or modify the existing declarations to suit your requirements.

PREPROCESSOR DIRECTIVES

Rez recognizes preprocessor directives comparable to those used in C programs, as listed in Table 9–7.

#include "file"	Merge source from file
#define symbol value	Define preprocessor symbol to value
#undef symbol	Delete definition of symbol
#if expression	Conditionally include text if expression non-zero
#else	Invert sense of previous conditional inclusion
#endif	Terminate #if, #ifdef or #ifndef
#ifdef symbol	Conditionally include text if symbol defined
#ifndef symbol	Conditionally include text if symbol not defined
#elif expression	Conditionally include text if expression non-zero; use same #endif with preceding #if
#printf(fmt, arg, …)	Error messages using C-style printf function

Table 9–7:   Rez preprocessor directives

Symbols can be defined as constants or C-style expressions. These symbols can be used to fix the value of fields or used to evaluate conditional compilation statements. The definitions

```
#define false 0
#define true 1
```

are pre-defined.

The #if directive is used to conditionally include source text based on an expression. If the expression is 1, all the text to the next corresponding #else (if any) or #endif is included in the compilation, and any text between the #else and #endif is omitted. If the expression is 0, only the source between the #else and #endif will be included. Blocks of #if and #endif directives can be nested within other blocks.

The #ifdef and #ifndef directives are similar to #if except that the result of the logical comparsion depends on whether the symbol is defined at all, not its actual value. The statements

```
#ifdef false
#  if false
   resource 'STR ' (128) { "false is true" };
#  else
   resource 'STR ' (128) { "false is not true" };
#  endif
#else
   resource 'STR ' (128) { "false not defined" };
#endif
```

should compile a single string "false is not true."

The #elif statement can be used to build case-like structures; #elif is like an #if that does not require an #endif. Using the < and == comparison operators, the statements

```
#if symb < 0
   resource 'STR ' (128) { "negative" };
#elif symb == 0
   resource 'STR ' (128) { "zero" };
#else
   resource 'STR ' (128) { "positive" };
#endif
```

would again assemble a single string.

The #include directive merges source from another file. The remainder of the line is treated as a Rez string specification which, in its simplest form, means a single string with the file name. Rez will automatically search the path {RIncludes} for the file if it's not found in the current directory.

It is most useful to include the resource definition file in your source, thus eliminating the need for specifying it on your command line. If you normally would use the command

```
Rez -o Foo Types.r Foo.r
```

adding

```
#include "Types.r"
```

to file Foo.r would allow you to instead use

```
Rez -o Foo Foo.r
```

The #include directive—which merges Rez source prior to compila-tion—should not be confused with the include statement, which merges already compiled resources from the resource fork of another file directly to the Rez output file. Of course, if you have both the source and compiled resources for the same data, you can merge either one.

Finally, the #printf directive provides a flexible way of generating error messages based on arbitrary arguments and formats. It has the same capabilities as the C formatting function of the same name, with the same format characters and conventions as for the printf function in the MPW C library.

DEFINING RESOURCE FORMATS

The format for defining data types for Rez resembles the variable and type declaration section of any programming language. The Rez syntax predefines certain fixed data types (most significantly, integers and strings) and then allows you to define structured resources as a series of one or more of those types. The syntax also supports arrays, variant records, and enumerated values.

The predefined data types are summarized by Table 9–8. There are four categories of types: integers, strings, predefined data structures, and filler types.

The integral data types support sizes from 1 to 32 bits, including the three standard 68000 data types: byte, 16-bit word, and 32-bit long. The names—byte, integer, and longint—correspond to the Pascal types SignedByte, INTEGER, and LONGINT, and to the C types char, short, and long.

The bitstring data type represents an arbitrary number of bits from 1 to 32, although it's usually 1 or 2 bits. The bits are assigned from most significant to least significant in successive bytes. No alignment of other data types is assumed, such as to the nearest byte. Instead, alignment must be explicitly specified.

Each of the integer formats can have a display format (radix). These determine the format that will be used by DeRez to display the number. Four standard bases—2, 8, 10, and 16—are available. These numbers can also be designated as unsigned; signed decimal is default if no display format is specified.

The fifth format is to display the number as a series of ASCII bytes. This is used for resource types, file types, application signatures, and the like. For example, the resources

```
resource ('FREF', 0)   { 'APPL', 0, "" };
resource ('FREF', 1)   { 'TEXT', 1, "" };
```

might be compiled using the type definition

```
type 'FREF' {
    literal longint;
```

Declaration	Bytes	Description

Integer types†

bitstring[size]	size bits	series of bits
byte	1	signed 8-bit integer
integer	2	signed 16-bit integer
longint	4	signed 32-bit integer

String types††

string[size]	size	series of ASCII characters
pstring[size]	size+1	Pascal string (with length byte)
cstring[size]	size	C string
wstring[size]	size+2	string preceded by length word
hex string[size]	size	series of hex digits

Data structures

rect	8	four integers
point	4	two integers

Filler types††

fill type[size]		zero-fill specified length
align type		zero-fill to next type boundary

where type is nibble (4 bits), byte, word or long; fill bit is also allowed

Notes

†   Integer types can be preceded by an optional display format:

decimal	base 10 (default)
hex	base 16
octal	base 8
binary	base 2
literal	ASCII characters

and optionally by unsigned. These formats affect DeRez only.

††   [size] is optional for string and filler types

The following equivalences are pre-defined:

boolean	unsigned decimal bitstring[1]
char	string[1]

Table 9–8:   **Rez data types**

```
        integer;
        pstring;
}
```

The display formats only affect DeRez. Any of the five formats can be used for input, depending on the special characters used. To assure compatibility between DeRez output and its subsequent use as Rez input, the output will always include the appropriate base indicator (e.g., 0x7B, 0173, or 0b1111011) unless the radix is decimal.

The type boolean is predefined as an alias for an unsigned single-bit field. It is similar to a Pascal BOOLEAN (when declared as part of a PACKED RECORD) or C bit fields and can also be used for Pascal sets.

The string data types are used to hold strings of printable text, delimited by quotation marks. There are three types: an arbitrary series of characters, a Pascal string preceded by a length byte, or a C string terminated by a null byte.

By default, these strings only allocate the bytes necessary to represent the string. A value of hi entered for a pstring or a cstring would require 3 bytes; 2 bytes would be required for a string.

Going in the other direction, DeRez will interpret a pstring or a cstring using the actual length of the string stored in the resource fork and then continue formatting the resource with the next data type. Unfortunately, there's no way to tell how long an ordinary string is supposed to be, so DeRez will always continue to the end of the resource.

Consider decompiling resources using the following two resource definitions:

```
type 'STR ' {
    pstring;
};
type 'TEXT' {
    string;
};
```

The string type 'STR' would use the first byte of the resource as a length of 0 to 255 bytes, displaying the following bytes. Any additional data would be displayed by DeRez as a Rez comment. The text type 'TEXT' would display the entire resource as an unbounded series of characters; this corresponds to the standard resource format to be found in the scrapbook, as in:

```
DeRez -only TEXT "{SystemFolder}Scrapbook File"∂
    MyTypes.r
```

Fixed sizes for strings can be optionally supplied in brackets. This means that the actual size of the field is always the same for compiling or decompiling, no matter what data is used. For a string or cstring, the number is the actual length in bytes, while the actual length for pstring is one number longer to allow for the length byte. This treatment of pstring might seem inconsistent with the cstring convention, but both are consistent with their corresponding language definitions.

Such fixed-length strings are more convenient to use with a higher-level language definition than are variable length strings, particularly if they are followed by other fields.

For example, a program might expect to have a resource defining a file path such as:

```
type 'MFRF' {
   pstring[255];    /* folder path */
   pstring[31];     /* file name */
   literal longint; /* file type */
}
```

This could be declared in Pascal as:

```
MyFileRef = RECORD
   mfrFolderPath: Str255;
   mfrFileName: STRING[31];
   mfrFileType: OSType;
END;
```

For a C program, you might use a Rez definition

```
type 'MFRF' {
   cstring[256];    /* folder path */
   cstring[32];     /* file name */
   literal longint; /* file type */
}
```

which would correspond to the C source:

```
typedef struct MyFileRef {
   char mfrFolderPath[256];
   char mfrFolderPath[31];
   OSTypemfrFileType;
};
```

Rez also recognizes a hex string type. This is the same as the string type, except that DeRez displays the contents as a series of hex digits, delimited by $" … ".

The predefined type char is the same as string[1]. What's the difference between literal byte and char, both of which allow a single ASCII character? The first difference is the choice of delimiter, '…' versus "…". The second is that data for literal byte, like any other byte field, can be defined as a decimal integer, hex, etc., while strings must be escaped. If you wanted to specify a null value, it would be 0 for a literal byte but \000 for a char.

The two predefined structured data types have already been encountered. No format variations are possible for point and rect—DeRez always displays such fields as a series of decimal integers, surrounded by braces.

Finally, there are two filler types. The filled areas are always set to zero during compilation and ignored during decompilation. These types are used to assure the proper alignment of fields when mixing different data sizes. In particular, a bitstring followed by a byte or larger type should always be aligned to a byte boundary. In some cases, an integer or longint should also be aligned to an even address (word) boundary.

The use of fill or align are essentially interchangeable; in one case, the fill length is explicit, in the other case, it is implied. For example,

```
boolean;          /* most significant bit of byte #0 */
boolean;          /* next bit of byte #0 */
fill bit[6];      /* skip 6 low order bits of byte #0 */
byte;             /* byte #1 */
byte;             /* byte #2 */
fill byte;        /* skip byte #3 */
integer;          /* bytes #4-5 */
```

is equivalent to the definition:

```
boolean;          /* most significant bit of byte #0 */
boolean;          /* next bit of byte #0 */
align byte;       /* skip to byte #1 */
byte;             /* byte #1 */
byte;             /* byte #2 */
align word;       /* skip to byte #4 */
integer;          /* bytes #4-5 */
```

Fill can also be used for unused sections of memory within a byte. For example, if only the most and least significant bits of a byte are used, the Rez input would look like:

```
boolean;
fill bit[6];
boolean;
```

To summarize the rules for constructing type statements, let's look at an example of a simple resource format not included with the standard definitions. The Edit application that came with MDS (and third-party systems) placed two resources in any document that it edited. The format of those resources, 'EFNT' and 'ETAB', is defined by a *Macintosh Technical Note*. The corresponding Rez definition would be:

```
type 'EFNT' { /* MDS Edit text fonts */
    integer;    /* Font size */
```

```
    pstring;      /* Font name */
    };
type 'ETAB' {  /* MDS Edit tab stops */
    integer;      /* width of space in pixels */
    integer;      /* width of tab stops in spaces */
    };
```

You could then decompile the resources in all `Edit` documents in the current directory using the commands:

```
For F in `Files -c EDIT -t TEXT`
    DeRez "{F}" MyTypes.r
End
```

RESOURCE EXPRESSIONS

The `Rez` language supports definition of symbolic values for a particular field in a resource through enumeration lists. These symbolic values will be recognized when input during compiling a resource and will be output when decompiling a resource.

These symbolic values are specified by a list of enumeration values after the field type; by default, the names are assigned values sequentially from zero.

One common use is for boolean values. The `type` declaration for a `'WIND'` resource includes:

```
    byte        invisible, visible;
    fill        byte;
    byte        noGoAway, goAway;
    fill        byte;
```

where the symbolic values correspond to 0 and 1, respectively. C programmers should not read this as "define two `byte` variables named `invisible` and `visible`," etc.

The constant values can also be noncontiguous. For example, the `'WIND'` definition includes symbolic values for the field defining the shape and appearance of the window. These are:

```
integerdocumentProc, dBoxProc, plainDBox,
    altDBoxProc, noGrowDocProc, zoomDocProc=8,
    zoomNoGrow=12, rDocProc=16;
```

Symbolic values can also be defined for string constants. The `'MENU'` type definition includes

```
char noMark = "\0x00", check = "\0x12";
```

for the character used to mark a menu item. Normally, either noMark or check will be used, with the latter corresponding to the familar check mark (ʙ). The only time you'd use an actual string would be to precheck the item with some other symbol, specified as a string constant, e.g., •.

Fields can also be predefined with fixed values in the type definitions. If such a value is defined in a type statement, Rez will not expect a corresponding value in its resource statement, while DeRez will expect the resource to contain that value when decompiling the resource.

To automatically define a value for a resource field, the field type is followed by an equals sign and the value, as in:

```
byte = $FF;
```

The value can be either a constant or a complete expression. Rez recognizes a category of both string and integer-valued functions, as summarized in Table 9–9.

These functions can be used in any Rez source statement, including type, resource, and preprocessor directives. For example,

```
#include $$Shell("MPW") "Source:MyTypes.r"
```

would merge the source from file {MPW}Source:MyTypes.r.

The most versatile function allows the construction of arbitrary text strings as input to resource statements. The $$Format variable allows formatting using the C printf formatting function. For example, if you wanted to have the version string for a file have a particular format, you could use $$Format to construct the string using other variables, as in:

```
#define FILENAME "SomeFile"
data 'STR ' (0) {
   $$Format("%s as of %d/%d", FILENAME, $$Month, $$Year)
};
```

All the functions can also be combined as part of expressions involving the Rez operators, as shown in Table 9–10. Again, the operators can be used as part of an expression in any statement.

Structured Data Types

The Rez syntax also includes definitions for arrays and variant records. These include a list of one or more fields and may also be nested within each other.

The array type declares a list of fields (delimited by braces) that are repeated for each element of the array. This general form is:

Functions used for string fields

```
$$Date                            Today's date, as returned by        IUDateString
$$Resource("file", 'atyp', ID)    Merge specified resource from file
$$Resource("file", 'atyp', "name")
$$Shell("Var")                    Value of shell variable {Var}
$$Time                            Current time, as returned by        IUTimeString

$$Format(fmt, arg, …)             format each arg using printf function

$$Type                            Resource type
$$Id                              Resource id
$$Name                            Resource name
$$Attributes                      Resource attributes
```

Functions used for integer fields

```
$$Day                             day of the month
$$Hour                            hour of the day, 0 to 23
$$Minute                          minute of the hour
$$Month                           month of the year
$$Weekday                         day of week, with 1=Sunday
$$Year                            four-digit year

$$CountOf(array)                  number of elements in array
```

Table 9–9:   Rez functions

```
array {
    /* field definitions */
    ...
};
```

Such an array can be repeated over and over again until the end of the resource. For example, suppose you need a resource containing a list of several resources of the same type. Such a resource might be defined using:

```
type 'RES#' {
  literal longint;      /* resource type */
  array {
    integer;            /* each resource id */
  };
};
```

Operator	Description (in order of precedence)
( )	Expression group delimiters
-	Unary negation
!	Unary logical NOT
~	Unary bitwise NOT
*	Integer multiplication
/	Integer division
%	Integer remainder
+	Integer addition
-	Integer subtraction
<<	Bitwise shift left
>>	Bitwise shift right (sign-extend)
<	Less than
<=	Less than or equal to
>	Greater than
>=	Greater than or equal to
==	Equal to
!=	Not equal to
&	Bitwise AND
^	Bitwise exclusive OR
|	Bitwise includes OR
&&	Logical AND
||	Logical OR

Integer and bitwise operators operate on signed 32-bit integers, and are binary operators unless otherwise noted

Logical expressions return integer 0 (FALSE) or 1 (TRUE). Zero operands are treated as FALSE, non-zero operands as TRUE

Table 9–10:   Rez operators

The wide keyword causes DeRez to use a more compact display format but does not affect Rez. The corresponding change would be:

```
type 'RES#' {
    literal longint;        /* resource type */
```

```
wide array {
   integer;                   /* each resource id */
};
};
```

Since the DeRez output can be quite voluminous, this option is normally used for any array.

Such an array is useful for simple data structures, but in many cases you will need to define the number of array elements. This allows the program using the resource to easily find out how many are present and also makes it much easier for DeRez to decompile the resource.

The count is specified by naming the array and then using the $$CountOf function to enter the count as an expression in a specific field. A simple example is the standard string list, which is defined by:

```
type 'STR#' {
   integer = $$CountOf(StrArray);
   array StrArray {
        pstring;
   };
};
```

This generates a single 16-bit word with a string count, followed by a series of Pascal strings.

Rez also recognizes variant records, similar to the Pascal usage. A switch type introduces the beginning of a list of variants, and each variant is named by a case followed by a symbol. The format for each case continues until the next one is defined.

Each case must also contain a constant field that will be compiled by Rez into the resource to identify the variant. This is also used by DeRez to decode the variant upon decompilation. This field is declared like any other field, but the type is preceded by the reserved word key.

Having trouble following this? An example should make it much clearer. Suppose you wanted to have a general-purpose resource to store one of several types of data. You might allocate the initial byte of the resource to indicate the type of the data and then follow it with the actual contents. Such a definition is:

```
type 'DTA ' {
   switch {
     case Integers:
       key byte=$00;
       align word;
       integer=$$CountOf(IntArray);
       wide array IntArray {
          integer;
       }
```

```
        case PasString:
           key byte=$01;
           pstring;
        case CString:
           key byte=$02;
           cstring;
        case Rect:
           key byte=$03;
           align word;
           rect;
      };
   };
```

Note the 16-bit integers and the `Rect` data types are aligned to even addresses. Without the alignment, referencing the data in Pascal or C could produce a 68000 odd–address exception.

The `switch` types are also often used within arrays to define a list of different items. A good example is to look at the format of a `'DITL'` resource, as defined by file `{RIncludes}Types.r`. Each dialog item is a different variant, and the `'DITL'` resource is defined as an array of dialog items.

EXAMPLE: DECODING PICTURES

The rules for constructing custom resource definitions can be illustrated by a single type definition file. Example 9–1 defines a format that can be used to compile the standard QuickDraw picture format and to decompile a large subset of possible pictures. The example handles "classic" QuickDraw pictures rather than the extended format produced by color QuickDraw on the Macintosh II.

Each `'PICT'` resource consists of an array of 1-byte opcodes indicating the operation to be performed. Each opcode is followed by additional data which depends on the opcode. This is a perfect example of `Rez`'s support for variant records, with each opcode a different `case`. It also shows nested variants, as the picture comment opcodes ($A0 and $A1) have a number of different subcodes.

Although resources of type `'PICT'` are used by a few programs, the most common place to find them is in the Scrapbook File. The Scrapbook desk accessory stores clipboard data in the resource fork of the file. The resource type corresponds to the type of data originally copied to the clipboard*.

Figure 9–4 shows a MacDraw picture displaying sample QuickDraw primitives.

When this picture is copied to the clipboard and then pasted to the scrapbook, the resource fork of Scrapbook File will contain the picture in one

---

* Clipboard File contains a single entry in its data fork, while Scrapbook File contains multiple entries in its resource fork.

```
/* {RIncludes}Pict.r */


/* Decode QuickDraw pictures that predate the new format
   associated with Color QuickDraw. Valid pictures are
   distinguished by a version field of 1.


   This is based on three Macintosh Technical Notes:
       TN #21, QuickDraw's Internal Picture Definition
       TN #27, MacDraw's PICT File Format and Comments
       TN #91: Optimizing for the LaserWriter -- Picture
               Comments

   It also relies on empirical results from MacDraw 1.9.
*/


type 'PICT' {
  integer;       /* overall size, truncated to 16 bits */
  rect;          /* picture frame */
  wide array {
    switch {  /* one-byte opcode */
/* -------------------------------------------------------
-

  $00-$0F: Control Info
*/
    case NOP:
      key byte=$00;
    case clipRgn:
      key byte=$01;
      integer=10+             /* length of region data */
        $$CountOf(RegionData);
      rect;                     /* boundary box */
      wide array RegionData {
        unsigned hex byte;    /* region def */
      };
    case bkPat:
      key byte=$02;
      hex string[8];
    case txFont:
      key byte=$03;
      integer                     /* font name */
        Chicago, ApplFont, NewYork, Geneva, Monaco,
        Venice, London, Athens, SanFrancisco, Toronto,
        Cairo=11, LosAngeles,
        ZapfDingbats, Bookman, NHelveticaNarrow,
        Palatino, ZapfChancery,
```

```
            Times=20, Helvetica, Courier, Symbol, Mobile,
            AvantGarde=33, NewCenturySchlbk;
      case txFace:
        key byte=$04;
        byte;
      case txMode:
        key byte=$05;
        integer srcCopy, srcOr, srcXor, srcBic,
            notSrcCopy, notSrcOr, notSrcXor, notSrcBic;
      case spExtra:
        key byte=$06;
        unsigned hex longint; /* fixed point fraction */
      case pnSize:
        key byte=$07;
        point;                        /* width, height */
      case pnMode:
        key byte=$08;
        integer srcCopy, srcOr, srcXor, srcBic,
            notSrcCopy, notSrcOr, notSrcXor, notSrcBic;
      case pnPat:
        key byte=$09;
        hex string[8];
      case thePat:
        key byte=$0A;
        hex string[8];
      case ovSize:
        key byte=$0B;
        point;                        /* width, height */
      case origin:
        key byte=$0C;
        integer;                    /* dh */
        integer;                    /* dv */
      case txSize:
        key byte=$0D;
        integer;
      case fgColor:
        key byte=$0E;
        longint;                    /* color */
      case bgColor:
        key byte=$0F;
        longint;                    /* color */

/* ------------------------------------------------------
    $10-$1F: Misc. headers
*/
      case txRatio:
        key byte=$10;
        point;                        /* numer */
```

```
         point;                          /* denom */
    /* 'PICT' resources with a version > 1 are color, with
       16-bit opcodes.  Force us to dump remainder
       unformatted if we see a version code of 2; quit
       with error if we see any other version code. */
    case picVersion1:
      key integer=$1101;
    case picVersion2:
      key integer=$1102;
      hex string;


/* ------------------------------------------------------
-
   $20-$27: Lines
*/
    case line:
      key byte=$20;
      point;                          /* pnLoc */
      point;                          /* newPt */
    case line_from:
      key byte=$21;
      point;                          /* newPt */
    case short_line:
      key byte=$22;
      point;                          /* pnLoc */
      byte;                           /* dh */
      byte;                           /* dv */
    case short_line_from:
      key byte=$23;
      byte;                           /* dh */
      byte;                           /* dv */


/* ------------------------------------------------------
-
   $28-$2F: Text
*/
    case long_text:
      key byte=$28;
      point;                          /* starting location */
      pstring;
    case DH_text:
      key byte=$29;
      unsigned byte;                  /* dh */
      pstring;
    case DV_text:
      key byte=$2A;
      unsigned byte;                  /* dv */
```

```
      pstring;
    case DHDV_text:
      key byte=$2B;
      unsigned byte;              /* DH */
      unsigned byte;              /* DV */
      pstring;

/* ------------------------------------------------------
    $30-$3F: Rectangles
*/
    case frameRect:
      key byte=$30;
      rect;
    case paintRect:
      key byte=$31;
      rect;
    case eraseRect:
      key byte=$32;
      rect;
    case invertRect:
      key byte=$33;
      rect;
    case fillRect:
      key byte=$34;
      rect;
    case frameSameRect:
      key byte=$38;
    case paintSameRect:
      key byte=$39;
    case eraseSameRect:
      key byte=$3A;
    case invertSameRect:
      key byte=$3B;
    case fillSameRect:
      key byte=$3C;

/* ------------------------------------------------------
    $40-$4F: Round Rectangles

  BUG: Tech Note #21 (6/20/86) lists oval width, height
       are parameters; actually, width and height set by
       ovSize
*/
    case frameRRect:
      key byte=$40;
      rect;
    case paintRRect:
      key byte=$41;
```

```
      rect;
    case eraseRRect:
      key byte=$42;
      rect;
    case invertRRect:
      key byte=$43;
      rect;
    case fillRRect:
      key byte=$44;
      rect;
    case frameSameRRect:
      key byte=$48;
    case paintSameRRect:
      key byte=$49;
    case eraseSameRRect:
      key byte=$4A;
    case invertSameRRect:
      key byte=$4B;
    case fillSameRRect:
      key byte=$4C;

/* --------------------------------------------------------
   $50-$5F: Ovals
*/
    case frameOval:
      key byte=$50;
      rect;
    case paintOval:
      key byte=$51;
      rect;
    case eraseOval:
      key byte=$52;
      rect;
    case invertOval:
      key byte=$53;
      rect;
    case fillOval:
      key byte=$54;
      rect;
    case frameSameOval:
      key byte=$58;
    case paintSameOval:
      key byte=$59;
    case eraseSameOval:
      key byte=$5A;
    case invertSameOval:
      key byte=$5B;
    case fillSameOval:
      key byte=$5C;
```

```
/* ----------------------------------------------------------
   $60-$6F: Arcs
*/
    case frameArc:
      key byte=$60;
      rect;
      integer;                    /* startAngle */
      integer;                    /* arcAngle */
    case paintArc:
      key byte=$61;
      rect;
      integer;                    /* startAngle */
      integer;                    /* arcAngle */
    case eraseArc:
      key byte=$62;
      rect;
      integer;                    /* startAngle */
      integer;                    /* arcAngle */
    case invertArc:
      key byte=$63;
      rect;
      integer;                    /* startAngle */
      integer;                    /* arcAngle */
    case fillArc:
      key byte=$64;
      rect;
      integer;                    /* startAngle */
      integer;                    /* arcAngle */
    case frameSameArc:
      key byte=$68;
    case paintSameArc:
      key byte=$69;
    case eraseSameArc:
      key byte=$6A;
    case invertSameArc:
      key byte=$6B;
    case fillSameArc:
      key byte=$6C;


/* ----------------------------------------------------------
   $70-$7F: Polygons
*/
    case framePoly:
      key byte=$70;
      integer = $$CountOf(polyPoints)*4+10; /* size */
      rect;                       /* polyBBox */
```

```
       wide array polyPoints{ point; };
    case paintPoly:
      key byte=$71;
      integer = $$CountOf(polyPoints)*4+10; /* size */
      rect;                    /* polyBBox */
      wide array polyPoints{ point; };
    case erasePoly:
      key byte=$72;
      integer = $$CountOf(polyPoints)*4+10; /* size */
      rect;                    /* polyBBox */
      wide array polyPoints{ point; };
    case invertPoly:
      key byte=$73;
      integer = $$CountOf(polyPoints)*4+10; /* size */
      rect;                    /* polyBBox */
      wide array polyPoints{ point; };
    case fillPoly:
      key byte=$74;
      integer = $$CountOf(polyPoints)*4+10; /* size */
      rect;                    /* polyBBox */
      wide array polyPoints{ point; };
/*********************************************
    TN #21 says $78-$7C not implemented
    case frameSamePoly:
      key byte=$78;
    case paintSamePoly:
      key byte=$79;
    case eraseSamePoly:
      key byte=$7A;
    case invertSamePoly:
      key byte=$7B;
    case fillSamePoly:
      key byte=$7C;
*******************************************/


/* -----------------------------------------------------
 -
    $80-$8F: Regions
*/
    case frameRgn:
      key byte=$80;
      integer=10+              /* length of region data */
        $$CountOf(RegionData);
      rect;                    /* boundary box */
      wide array RegionData {
        unsigned hex byte;     /* region def */
      };
    case paintRgn:
      key byte=$81;
```

```
          integer=10+           /* length of region data */
            $$CountOf(RegionData);
          rect;                  /* boundary box */
          wide array RegionData {
            unsigned hex byte;   /* region def */
          };
      case eraseRgn:
        key byte=$82;
        integer=10+             /* length of region data */
          $$CountOf(RegionData);
        rect;                   /* boundary box */
        wide array RegionData {
          unsigned hex byte;    /* region def */
        };
      case invertRgn:
        key byte=$83;
        integer=10+             /* length of region data */
          $$CountOf(RegionData);
        rect;                   /* boundary box */
        wide array RegionData {
          unsigned hex byte;    /* region def */
        };
      case fillRgn:
        key byte=$84;
        integer=10+             /* length of region data */
          $$CountOf(RegionData);
        rect;                   /* boundary box */
        wide array RegionData {
          unsigned hex byte;    /* region def */
        };
      case frameSameRgn:
        key byte=$88;
      case paintSameRgn:
        key byte=$89;
      case eraseSameRgn:
        key byte=$8A;
      case invertSameRgn:
        key byte=$8B;
      case fillSameRgn:
        key byte=$8C;


/* -------------------------------------------------------
   $90-$9F: Bit Maps
*/
  /* Unfortunately, due to a limitation of the picture
     design the four bit map opcodes
     BitRect    $90
     BitsRgn    $91
     PackBitsRect$98
```

```
      PackBitsRgn $99
       do not have an easily interpreted length. If we
       encounter one such field, we must quit.

      Of course, on input, we can specify the information.
*/

      case BitsRect:
         key byte=$90;
         integer;                   /* rowBytes */
         rect;                      /* bounds */
         rect;                      /* srcRect */
         rect;                      /* dstRect */
         hex integer;               /* transfer mode */
         hex string;                /* bit map */

      case BitsRgn:
         key byte=$91;
         integer;                   /* rowBytes */
         rect;                      /* bounds */
         rect;                      /* srcRect */
         rect;                      /* dstRect */
         hex integer;               /* transfer mode */
         integer=10+                /* length of region */
            $$CountOf(RegionData);
         rect;                      /* region boundary */
         wide array RegionData {
            unsigned hex byte;      /* region def */
         };
         hex string;                /* bit map */

      case PackBitsRect:
         key byte=$98;
         integer;                   /* rowBytes */
         rect;                      /* bounds */
         rect;                      /* srcRect */
         rect;                      /* dstRect */
         hex integer;               /* transfer mode */
         hex string;                /* bit map */

      case PackBitsRgn:
         key byte=$99;
         integer;                   /* rowBytes */
         rect;                      /* bounds */
         rect;                      /* srcRect */
         rect;                      /* dstRect */
         hex integer;               /* transfer mode */
         integer=10+                /* length of region */
            $$CountOf(RegionData);
```

```
          rect;                    /* region boundary */
          wide array RegionData {
            unsigned hex byte;     /* region def */
          };
          hex string;              /* bit map */

/* ------------------------------------------------------------
-

   $A0-$AF: Picture Comments

   The long comments are more suitable for decompiling
   than compiling
*/
     case shortComment:     /* comments without data */
       key byte=$A0;
       integer picDwgBeg=130, picDwgEnd,
         picGrbBeg=140, picGrpEnd, picBitBet, picBitEnd,
         TextEnd=151, StringBegin, StringEnd,
         PolyBegin=160, PolyEnd, picPlyByt, PolyIgnore,
           picPlyClo=165,
         picArrw1=170, picArrw2, picArrw3, picArrwEnd,
         DashedStop=181,
         PostScriptBegin=190, PostScriptEnd,
         TextIsPostScript=194,
         RotateEnd=201;
     case longComment:             /* comments with data */
       key byte=$A1;
       switch {
         case TextBegin:      /* beginning of text */
           key integer=150;
           integer=6;              /* length */
           /* 0-4 are documented, but 5-7 are used */
           byte noJust, JustLeft, JustCenter,
             JustRight, JustFull,
             DrawLeft, DrawCenter, DrawRight;
           byte noFlip, FlipHoriz, FlipVert;
           integer noRotation;     /* rotation */
           byte Space1=2,          /* TLine */
             Space1_5, Space2;
           unsigned hex byte;      /* comment */
         case TextCenter  /* text centering offset */
           key integer=154;
           integer=8;              /* length */
           unsigned hex longint;   /* y: Fixed */
           unsigned hex longint;   /* x: Fixed */
         case PolySmooth: /* smoothing algorithm */
           key integer=164;
           integer=1;              /* length */
           fill bit[5];
```

```
            boolean no_fPolyClose, fPolyClose;
            boolean no_fPolyFill, fPolyFill;
            boolean no_fPolyFrame, fPolyFrame;
          case DashedLine:
            key integer=180;
            integer =   /* length of picture comment */
              $$CountOf(TDashedLine);
            wide array TDashedLine {
              unsigned hex byte;
            };
/* alternate way to specify, requires as much work: **
            integer; /* length of remaining **
            byte;   /* offset **
            byte;   /* centered flag **
            byte = /* length of array **
              $$CountOf(dashed);
            wide array dashed {
              unsigned hex byte;
            };
*/
          case PostScriptHandle:
            key integer=192;
            integer =   /* length of picture comment */
              $$CountOf(PSData);
            wide array PSData {
              char;
            };
          case PostScriptFile:
            key integer=193;
            integer =   /* length of picture comment */
              $$CountOf(FileName);
            wide array FileName {
              char;
            };
          case RotateBegin:
            key integer=200;
            integer =   /* length of picture comment */
              $$CountOf(TRotation);
            wide array TRotation {
              unsigned hex byte;
            };
          case RotateCenter:
            key integer=202;
            integer =   /* length of picture comment */
              $$CountOf(Center);
            wide array Center {
              unsigned hex byte;
            };
          };
```

```
/* ------------------------------------------------------------
-
    $FF: End Marker
*/
    case EndOfPicture:
      key byte=$FF;
    };
  };
}; /* 'PICT' */
```

Example 9–1:   Type definition for PICT resources

of its 'PICT' resources.

The resource can be decompiled using the command:

```
DeRez -only PICT "{SystemFolder}Scrapbook File" Pict.r
```

The output of the command should resemble Figure 9–5.

The major limitation of the definition file is that it is unable to decompile bit maps and will stop when it reaches one. Unfortunately, the definition of a QuickDraw picture does not include an explicit length associated with each variable-length opcode. In the case of bitmaps, the rules to deduce the

Some shapes and text

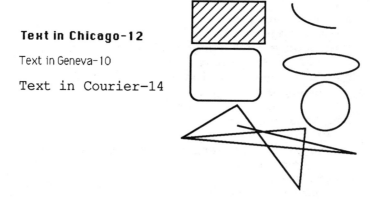

Figure 9–4:   Sample picture

```
resource 'PICT' (-32768, purgeable) {

    412
    {7, 7, 239, 348},
    {       /* array: 58 elements */
            /* [1] */
            picVersion1 {

            };
            /* [2] */
            shortComment {
                    picDwgBeg
            };
            /* [3] */
            longComment {
                    TextBegin {
                            DrawLeft,
                            noFlip,
                            noRotation,
                            Space1,
                            0xC
                    }
            };
            /* [4] */
            longComment {
                    TextCenter {
                            0xFFFD0000,
                            0x480000
                    }
            };
            /* [5] */
            shortComment {
                    StringBegin
            };
            /* [6] */
            clipRgn {
                    {7, 7, 239, 348},
                    {
            /* array RegionData: 0 elements */
                    }
            };
            /* [7] */
            txFont {
                    Helvetica
            };
            /* [8] */
            txFace {
                    1
            };
```

```
/* [9] */
txSize {
        14
};
/* [10] */
DHDV_text {
        135
        21
        Some shapes and text
};
/* [11] */
shortComment {
        StringEnd
};
/* [12] */
shortComment {
        TextEnd
};
/* [13] */
longComment {
        TextBegin {
                DrawCenter,
                noFlip,
                noRotation,
                Space1,
                0xC
        }
};
/* [14] */
eraseRect {
        {83, 46, 99, 173}
};
/* [15] */
longComment {
        TextCenter {
                0xFFFC0000,
                0x3D0000
        }
};
/* [16] */
shortComment {
        StringBegin
};
/* [17] */
txFont {
        Chicago
};
```

```
/* [18] */
txFace {
      0
};
/* [19] */
txSize {
      12
};
/* [20] */
long_text {
      {95, 49},
      Text in Chicago-12
};
/* [21] */
shortComment {
      StringEnd
};
/* [22] */
shortComment {
      TextEnd
};
/* [23] */
longComment {
      TextBegin {
            DrawLeft,
            noFlip,
            noRotation,
            Space1,
            0xC
      }
};
/* [24] */              .
eraseRect {
      {109, 64, 122, 163}
};
/* [25] */
longComment {
      TextCenter {
            0xFFFD0000,
            0x310000
      }
};
/* [26] */
shortComment {
      StringBegin
};
```

```
/* [27] */
txFont {
        Geneva
};
/* [28] */
txSize {
        10
};
/* [29] */
DHDV_text {
        16
        24
        Text in Geneva-10
};
/* [30] */
shortComment {
        StringEnd
};
/* [31] */
shortComment {
        TextEnd
};
/* [32] */
longComment {
        TextBegin {
                DrawRight,
                noFlip,
                noRotation,
                Space1,
                0xC
        }
};
/* [33] */
eraseRect {
        {131, 10, 146, 163}
};
/* [34] */
longComment {
        TextCenter {
                0xFFFD0000,
                0x440000
        }
};
/* [35] */
shortComment {
        StringBegin
};
```

```
/* [36] */
txFont {
      Courier
};
/* [37] */
txSize {
      14
};
/* [38] */
long_text {
      {142, 19},
      Text in Courier-14
};
/* [39] */
shortComment {
      StringEnd
};
/* [40] */
shortComment {
      TextEnd
};
/* [41] */
thePat {
      $0102 0408 1020 4080
};
/* [42] */
fillRect {
{56, 181, 97, 253}
};
/* [43] */
frameRect {
      {56, 181, 98, 254}
};
/* [44] */
ovSize {
      {18, 18}
};
/* [45] */
frameRRect {
      {102, 180, 153, 250}
};
/* [46] */
frameArc {
      {36, 279, 82, 365},
      180
      90
};
```

```
/* [47] */
frameOval {
     {106, 271, 128, 346}
};
/* [48] */
frameOval {
     {133, 289, 181, 337}
};
/* [49] */
shortComment {
     PolyBegin
};
/* [50] */
short_line {
     {188, 172},
     121
     -10
};
/* [51] */
short_line_from {
     -5
     58
};
/* [52] */
short_line_from {
     -62
     -80
};
/* [53] */
short_line_from {
     -54
     32
};
/* [54] */
line_from {
     {202, 343}
};
/* [55] */
short_line_from {
     -116
     -26
};
/* [56] */
shortComment {
     PolyEnd
};
```

```
/* [57] */
shortComment {
    picDwgEnd
};
/* [58] */
```

Figure 9-5:   DeRez output for sample picture

implicit length are too complex to express using Rez type definitions. When used with a bitmap, DeRez will print the header of the bitmap opcode and then follow it with a hex dump of the remainder of the resource.

9.4 ResEdit

In addition to providing a complete set of the line-oriented resource, MPW also comes with a windowing application for editing resources, ResEdit.

ResEdit handles certain types of resources—particularly icons and cursors—much better than do line-oriented Rez descriptions. Each has its advantages: Rez has a more powerful and flexible programming language but with only a few caveats, ResEdit can be customized to handle most resource formats.

Since you're likely to be working with both Rez and ResEdit for any resource you plan to edit, the ResEdit syntax for defining custom resource formats is described in terms of the Rez format.

CHANGING FILE AND RESOURCE ATTRIBUTES

ResEdit should be very familiar to experienced Macintosh owners. Several versions were released by Apple to developers prior to the completion of MPW.

Like most Macintosh applications, ResEdit is pretty easy to use without any formal explanation—which was proven by its popularity with end users well before the documentation was available. However, a few features may not be obvious to even the most seasoned ResEdit veteran, particularly since new features were added as it evolved.

The standard ResEdit menus are shown in Figure 9-6. Editing some resources will cause an additional menu to be added; also, not all menu items are enabled for all types of operations. Several of the items—**New**, the **Open** items, **Get Info**, and all the items in the **Edit** menu—have multiple usages, depending on whether you've currently selected a file, folder, a resource type, a particular resource, or even a component within a resource.

Figure 9–6:   ResEdit menus

When you start ResEdit, it shows a window for each mounted disk volume. In each window is a list of file and folder names, with a small icon indicating application, document, or folder. As with all such ResEdit windows, the window scrolls vertically if there are more items than can be shown at once.

To select a particular file, you select each folder in the path and open it either by double clicking or with the **Open** menu item. Opening a folder creates a new window with a new list of items.

Each of the files and folders can also be manipulated using ResEdit. For example, **New** will create a new file or folder in the folder corresponding to the active window. If a file (or a range of files) is selected, **Clear** will delete the file(s). ResEdit will not allow you to delete a folder that contains any files.

ResEdit also allows you to change some of the finder information about a file, such as the file type and modification date. Select the file and use **Get Info**. The resulting dialog allows you to change the file name, the file type, and the file creator, as well as the standard finder attribute bits documented in the File Manager chapter of *Inside Macintosh*. Figure 9–7 shows the result of opening the System Folder, and then doing **Get Info** on file System.

If you've selected a folder, an abbreviated dialog will be shown that contains only those attributes (such as "Locked" and "On Desk") that make sense for folders.

Double clicking on a file will cause ResEdit to check and see if the file has a resource fork. If it does, ResEdit will create a new window with a list of the four-character resource types contained in the resource fork. If you wish to add a resource type that's not shown, **New** will display a dialog asking for the resource type.

Double clicking on a particular type will create a new window with the list of resources of that type. Usually, one resource will be shown per line, with the type, ID, and resource name (if any) shown as text.

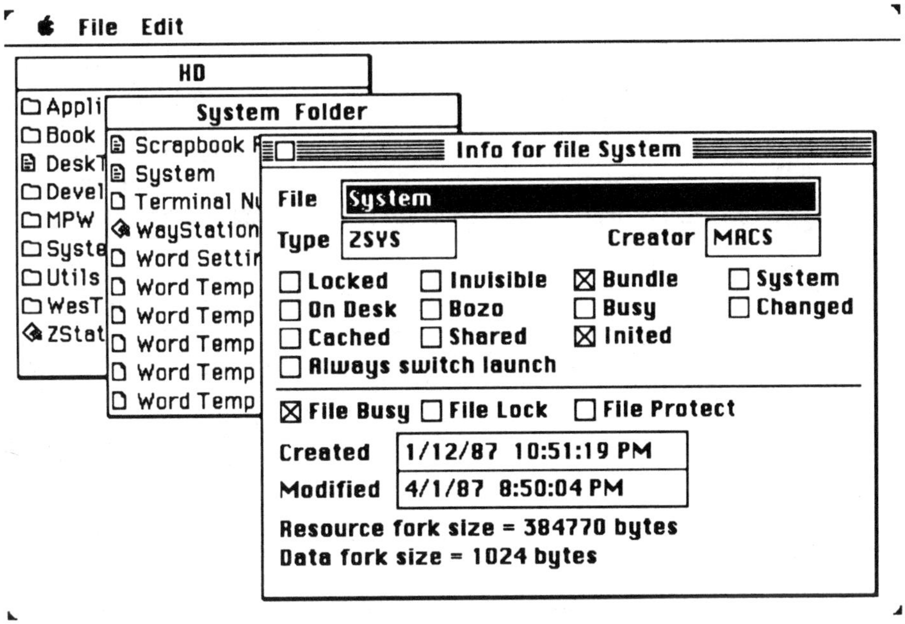

```
 ┌ É  File  Edit                                                    ┐
 ┌──────────────────────────────┐
 │            HD                │
 ┌──────────────────────────────────────────┐
 │◻ Appli│      System Folder              │
 │◻ Book │▣ Scrapbook F═════ Info for file System ═════
 │▣ DeskT│▣ System    ◻═══════════════════════════════
 │◻ Devel│◻ Terminal N│ File  System                  │
 │◻ MPW  │◈ WayStation│ Type  ZSYS            Creator  MACS │
 │◻ Syste│◻ Word Setti│                               │
 │◻ Utils│◻ Word Temp │ ◻ Locked    ◻ Invisible  ⊠ Bundle    ◻ System  │
 │◻ WesT │◻ Word Temp │ ◻ On Desk   ◻ Bozo       ◻ Busy      ◻ Changed │
 │◈ ZStat│◻ Word Temp │ ◻ Cached    ◻ Shared     ⊠ Inited    │
 │       │◻ Word Temp │ ◻ Always switch launch    │
 │       │◻ Word Temp │ ─────────────────────────────────── │
 │                      ⊠ File Busy ◻ File Lock  ◻ File Protect │
 │                      Created   │1/12/87 10:51:19 PM│ │
 │                      Modified  │4/1/87  8:50:04 PM │ │
 │                      Resource fork size = 384770 bytes │
 │                      Data fork size = 1024 bytes │
 └──────────────────────────────────────────┘
```

Figure 9–7:   Changing file attributes with ResEdit

If you select one of these resources, **Get Info** can be used to display and change information about the resource. The command displays a dialog with the resource name and ID, and the standard resource attributes. If you modify the resource ID, be careful not to change it to the same value as for another resource of the same type.

ResEdit nicely handles desk accessories, offering a button to insert the required null in the resource name. It also automatically supports owned resources, allowing you to specify such resources either by a 16 bit (negative) resource ID or by a combination of the owning resource type, the owning resource ID, and the sub ID (0-31), as shown in Figure 9–8.

Within the list of resources (DLOGs from System), **New** in the latter window will create a new resource of the appropriate type. If you've selected a particular resource, **Duplicate** will create a copy of that resource. A unique ID will be automatically assigned, which you'll probably need to change to some meaningful value using **Get Info.**

An individual resource or all resources of a particular type may also be moved between two files using the clipboard. **Cut** or **Copy** the resource (or list of resources) and **Paste** to the destination file; any existing resources with the same type and ID will be replaced.

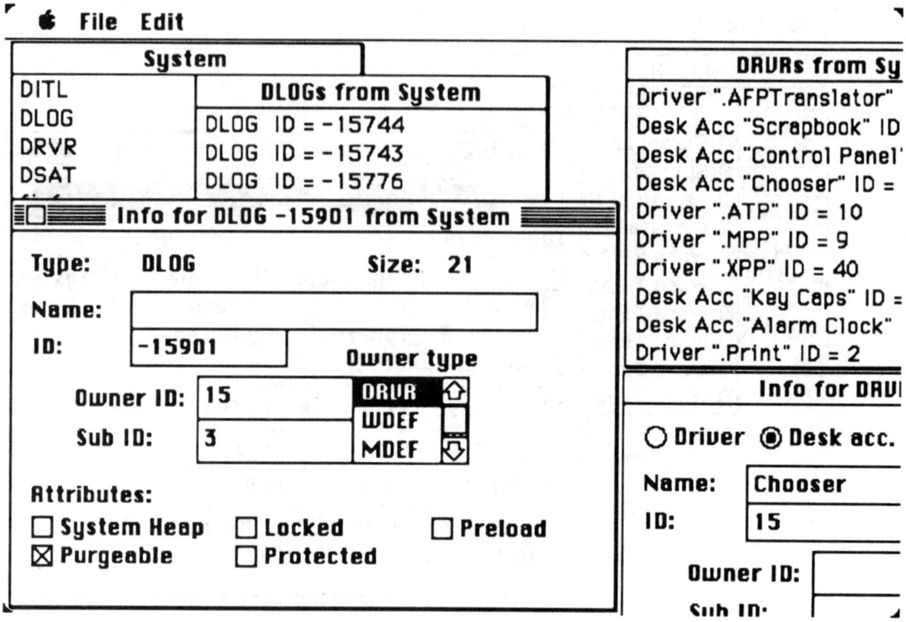

Figure 9–8:   Changing resource attributes with ResEdit

EDITING RESOURCES

ResEdit allows you to edit any type of resource. However, the approach you use to build a resource will differ, depending to a large degree on the type of the resource.

These four approaches are:

1   Certain key resources, such as icons and dialogs, are edited using special graphical interfaces built in to ResEdit

2   Most resources are edited using a dialog that contains editable text and boolean controls

3   Use it as another type; you can edit one resource using the format known for another*

4   Using a general format that shows hex and ASCII.

---

* Why would you want this? Each Application should have an application signature resource (say 'FOOB') that is a string containing version information. You would create a new 'FOOB' resource, then use Open As... to edit it as type 'STR', a Pascal string.

By default, if you double click on a resource, you will be offered either approach 1 or 2 for any type of resource that ResEdit knows how to edit. You can use **Open As...** to use another existing format. **Open General** or Option-click will use the general format, as will opening an unknown resource type.

Cursors, icons, and patterns are edited with an enlarged pixel-by-pixel display, similar to the "Fat Bits" format of various painting programs. When you open one of these types, such as 'CURS' or 'PAT#', ResEdit will show the resources graphically so that you can easily find the right cursor or pattern. **Open General** on the resource type will display the standard line-oriented list of resources.

ResEdit also supports graphical editing of fonts, alerts, dialogs, and dialog item lists. However, the list of resources in a window is displayed in the normal line-oriented fashion when you open the type.

The remaining types are edited using a window that contains a list of controls and editable text items. The window is similar to a dialog, except that the Dialog Manager does not directly support dialogs that scroll, moving the dialog items up, down, or off the screen.

Most of the data is entered into text boxes, which are used for both numbers and strings. In the former case, ResEdit will check to make sure the number is valid, depending on the size of the data (1 to 4 bytes) and whether it should be entered in decimal or hex. In the latter case, ResEdit supports the customary Pascal and C strings, hex strings similar to those defined by Rez, and also one- and four-character fixed-length strings. The text box will grow automatically to fit the size of the string being entered.

Some of the items are more restrictive. Boolean values are always controlled by a pair of radio buttons to toggle the value on and off. A few items—such as the number of elements in array—cannot be edited directly but are automatically generated for you.

Figure 9–9 shows an example of most of the item types in the dialog defining a window template. The window requires two numeric fields—the window type (procID) and reference constant—and a string specifying the window title. Two fields are boolean values, which are always controlled by a pair of radio buttons to toggle the value on and off.

The window also contains a rectangle field, which can be specified by entering the four numbers defining the boundaries in the text boxes for the top, left, bottom, and right coordinates. However, if you click on the Set pushbutton, ResEdit will expect you to define the rectangle's location by dragging its outline using the mouse. This is true of any such rectangle reference you might see, such as in a 'CNTL' resource.

Open As... will always use such a dialog-oriented format if it is available. In fact, several resource types have both graphical and dialog-oriented forms predefined. For example, if you open an 'ALRT' using **Open**, you will use the graphical interface. If you use **Open As...** to open it as ALRT, you will see a dialog similar to the Figure 9–9, except with information appropriate for the

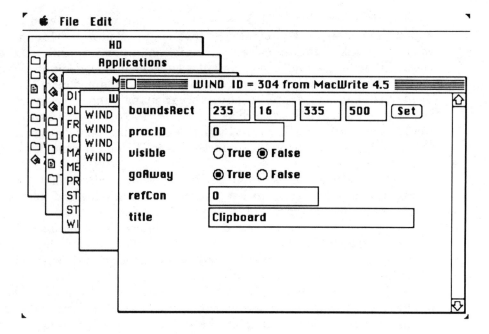

Figure 9–9:   Resource editing dialog

alert. This same choice of dual approaches is also available for resources of type 'DLOG' and 'DITL'.

The meaning of one item in the dialog format may not be immediately obvious. Some resource types will include separator lines (usually ✱✱✱✱✱) such as shown in Figure 9–10. They might seem to be unimportant, since there's no editable item associated with them.

However, these are part of the standard ResEdit approach to editing lists of items. In the dialog shown, a list of strings contains only a single string, which can be edited in the normal fashion. Suppose you want to add another string?

Select the separator before where the new string should go. In this case, to put a string at the end of the list, select the last separator. Now choose the **New** menu item. The display should now look like Figure 9–11, with an empty string added to the end. Note that the number of strings has been automatically updated by ResEdit.

To delete an item, select the separator before the item to be deleted and select **Clear**. The item will disappear.

Such lists can be nested, such as in editing resources of type 'BNDL'. ResEdit uses the indentation of the items to indicate the nesting relationship. Different separator lines are also used for each level, usually ✱✱✱✱✱ and ------.

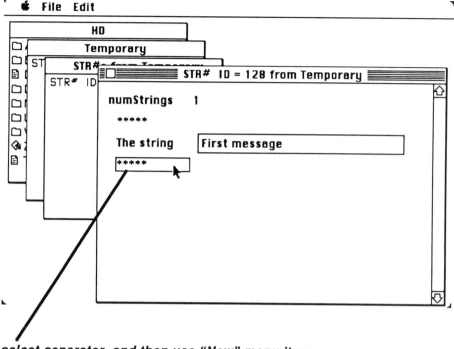

select separator, and then use "New" menu item

Figure 9–10: Before adding new item to string list

New and **Clear** are also used to add and delete items in the graphically edited resource types. The best example of this is adding and deleting items in a dialog item list.

CUSTOMIZING RESEDIT

A major strength of ResEdit is that it is an extensible resource editor. You can easily define the format of a new type of resource for ResEdit to edit. Not surprisingly, these formats are defined using resources.

These resources are of type 'TMPL' and must be stored in ResEdit's resource fork. Many such resources are built in to ResEdit and, in fact, are used for any resource that it edited using the dialog-oriented format. 'TMPL' resources are a nonalgorithmic interpretive programming language and in many ways parallel the Rez definition syntax.

Each 'TMPL' resource consists of a list of field names and types. Each field name is a Pascal string, which is displayed on the left margin when you're editing the resource. The type is a four-character code specifying how the data is to be formatted. The Rez definition for such a resource is:

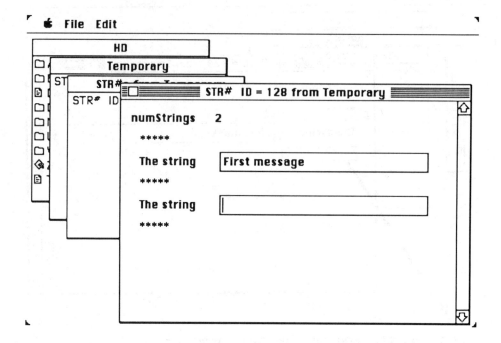

Figure 9–11: After adding new item to string list

```
type 'TMPL' {    /* ResEdit resource templates */
   wide array {
   pstring;    /* Field name */
   literal longint; /* 4-character type */
};
};
```

The resource name for a 'TMPL' resource is the same resource as the type it is used to edit. For example, a string might be edited using a

```
resource 'TMPL' (1000, "STR ", purgeable) {
  { "A string", 'PSTR',
  }
};
```

The resource ID is not important as long as it is unique. You should probably use larger numbers (say from 1000 on) to avoid conflicting with 'TMPL' resources predefined in ResEdit.

Most of the types recognized by ResEdit have directly corresponding types in Rez, as shown by Table 9–11.

ResEdit	Rez
DBYT	decimal byte;
DWRD	decimal integer;
DLNG	decimal longint;
HBYT	hex byte;
HWRD	hex word;
HLNG	hex byte;
BOOL	byte False, True;
BBIT	boolean False, True;
CHAR	literal byte; /* or char */
TNAM	literal longint;
PSTR	pstring;
ESTR	pstring; align word;
CSTR	cstring;
ECST	cstring; align word;
WSTR	wstring;
RECT	rect;
HEXD	hex string;
Hnnn	hex string[$nnn];

No exact equivalent:

OSTR	Pascal string, odd-aligned
OCST	C string, odd aligned

Table 9-11:   ResEdit 'TMPL' data types

Two of the field types are used for displaying long fields in hex. One displays a fixed-length field, while the other displays all the remaining bytes in hex. The latter is used at the end of a resource when a fixed-form header is followed by variable-length data, such as a 'DRVR' resource.

ResEdit also has rules for defining lists of items: special types bracket the series of items to be repeated. These groups parallel the use of arrays in Rez source files. Corresponding definitions are shown in Table 9-12.

How do you define a 'TMPL' resource? One way is to compile them using the Rez source definition. You can also use DeRez to display existing 'TMPL' resources and then modify those resources. DeRez is the only practical way to get a printed listing of a 'TMPL' resource.

ResEdit ('TMPL')	*Rez*

Length of array

"Count", 'OCNT';	integer=$$CountOf(StrArray);
"*******", 'LSTC';	array StrArray{
"The String", 'PSTR';	pstring;
"*******", 'LSTE'	};

Length of array less one

"Count", 'ZCNT';	integer=$$CountOf(StrArray)-1;
"*******", 'LSTC';	array StrArray{
"The String", 'PSTR';	pstring;
"*******", 'LSTE'	};

Stop at end of resource

"*******", 'LSTB';	array {
"The String", 'PSTR';	pstring;
"*******", 'LSTE'	};

Stop with zero byte

"*******", 'LSTZ';	array {
"The String", 'PSTR';	pstring;
"*******", 'LSTE'	};
byte=0;	

Table 9–12:   ResEdit 'TMPL' arrays

There is, in fact, a 'TMPL' resource defined by ResEdit for editing 'TMPL' resources. You can use the DeRez command

```
DeRez -only "'TMPL' (∂"TMPL∂")" ResEdit MyTypes.r
```

to display that resource. This would produce a display such as:

```
resource 'TMPL' (11, "TMPL", purgeable) {
    { /* array: 4 elements */
        /* [1] */
        "*****", 'LSTB';
        /* [2] */
        "Label", 'PSTR';
        /* [3] */
        "Type", 'TNAM';
        /* [4] */
```

```
        "*****", 'LSTE'
    }
};
```

What does this mean? The format of a 'TMPL' resource consists of an array of strings and field types. The 'TMPL' resource used in editing 'TMPL' resources has four entries: two that bracket the array and the two fields that are repeated over and over again.

'TMPL' resources can, of course, be edited directly with ResEdit. Figure 9–12 shows the template for editing the 'TMPL' resource, corresponding to the Rez source above.

ResEdit does not place restrictions on which files you can modify; it will allow you to open any file and make any changes you like. Most of the time, it's reliable enough to use on the current system disk or even ResEdit itself. However, editing 'TMPL' resources while they are being used as templates is foolhardy and just plain dangerous. You should close any open resources of the corresponding type before changing its 'TMPL'.

Example 9–2 contains a sample list of 'TMPL' resources in Rez source form. These could be compiled using Rez and then pasted into ResEdit by using ResEdit itself.

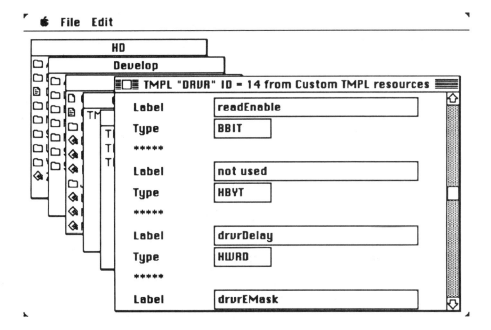

Figure 9–12: ResEdit templates

```
/* Example 9-2: Sample ResEdit templates */

type 'TMPL' {              /* ResEdit resource templates */
  wide array {
    pstring;               /* Field name */
    literal longint; /* 4-character type */
  };
};

resource 'TMPL' (1001, "TMPL", purgeable) {
  { "*****", 'LSTB';
    "Label", 'PSTR';
    "Type", 'TNAM';
    "*****", 'LSTE'
  }
};


resource 'TMPL' (1002, "EFNT", purgeable) {/* MDS Edit
text fonts */
  { "Font size", 'DWRD';
    "Font name", 'PSTR'
  }
};


resource 'TMPL' (1003, "ETAB", purgeable) {/* MDS Edit
tab stops */
  { "Space width (pixels)", 'DWRD';
    "Tabs", 'DWRD'
  }
};

/* Used to build a 'PREC' resource #4, for the
ImageWriter
  page size dialog */
resource 'TMPL' (1004, "PRC4", purgeable) {
  { "Number buttons", 'DWRD'; /* 1 to 6 */
    "Vert #1 (1/120ths)", 'DWRD';    /* paper dimensions
*/
    "Horiz #1 (1/120ths)",    'DWRD';
    "Vert #2 (1/120ths)", 'DWRD';
    "Horiz #2 (1/120ths)",    'DWRD';
    "Vert #3 (1/120ths)", 'DWRD';
    "Horiz #3 (1/120ths)",    'DWRD';
    "Vert #4 (1/120ths)", 'DWRD';
    "Horiz #4 (1/120ths)",    'DWRD';
    "Vert #5 (1/120ths)", 'DWRD';
```

```
        "Horiz #5 (1/120ths)",      'DWRD';
        "Vert #6 (1/120ths)", 'DWRD';
        "Horiz #6 (1/120ths)",      'DWRD';
        "Title #1", 'PSTR';   /* Title for Page Setup */
        "Title #2", 'PSTR';
        "Title #3", 'PSTR';
        "Title #4", 'PSTR';
        "Title #5", 'PSTR';
        "Title #6", 'PSTR'
    }
};

/* Detailed DA/driver header */
resource 'TMPL' (1005, "DRVR", purgeable) {
    { "not used", 'BBIT';
        "needLock", 'BBIT';
        "needTime", 'BBIT';
        /* truncate to fit display area */
        "needGoodby", 'BBIT';
        "statusEnabl", 'BBIT';
        "ctlEnable", 'BBIT';
        "writeEnable", 'BBIT';
        "readEnable", 'BBIT';
        "not used", 'HBYT';
        "drvrDelay", 'HWRD';
        "drvrEMask", 'HWRD';
        "drvrMenu", 'HWRD';
        "drvrOpen", 'HWRD';
        "drvrPrime", 'HWRD';
        "drvrCtl", 'HWRD';
        "drvrStatus", 'HWRD';
        "drvrClose", 'HWRD';
        "drvrName", 'ESTR';
        "Driver", 'HEXD'
    }
};

/* Resources for color QuickDraw and Toolbox */
/* Variable-length color lookup table */
resource 'TMPL' (2000, "clut") {
    { "CTSeed", 'DLNG',
        "transIndex", 'DWRD',
        "ctSize", 'ZCNT',
        "*****", 'LSTC',
        "value", 'DWRD',
        "red", 'HWRD',
        "green", 'HWRD',
        "blue", 'HWRD',
        "*****",  'LSTE'
```

```
        }
    };

    /* Color lookup table with fixed assignment for windows;
       shared by windows, dialogs, alerts
       Uses space in prompt, followed by Option-spaces, to
       present a visual break in the editing dialog
    */
    #define WCTB                                    \
    { "CTSeed", 'DLNG',                             \
      "transIndex", 'DWRD',                         \
      "ctSize (4)            ", 'DWRD',             \
      /* space Option-spaces */                     \
      "Content (0)", 'DWRD',                        \
      "red", 'HWRD', "green", 'HWRD',               \
      "blue               ", 'HWRD',                \
      "Frame (1)", 'DWRD',                          \
      "red", 'HWRD',                                \
      "red", 'HWRD', "green", 'HWRD',               \
      "blue               ", 'HWRD',                \
      "Text (2)", 'DWRD',                           \
      "red", 'HWRD',                                \
      "red", 'HWRD', "green", 'HWRD',               \
      "blue               ", 'HWRD',                \
      "Hilite (3)", 'DWRD',                         \
      "red", 'HWRD', "green", 'HWRD',               \
      "blue               ", 'HWRD',                \
      "TitleBar (4)", 'DWRD',                       \
      "red", 'HWRD', "green", 'HWRD',               \
      "blue               ", 'HWRD'                 \
    }

    resource 'TMPL' (2001, "wctb") { /*Window color table*/
      WCTB
    };

    resource 'TMPL' (2002, "actb") { /*Alert color table*/
      WCTB
    };

    resource 'TMPL' (2003, "dctb") { /*Dialog color table*/
      WCTB
    };


    resource 'TMPL' (2004, "cctb") {
      /* Control color table */
      { "CTSeed", 'DLNG',
        "transIndex", 'DWRD',
```

```
        "ctSize (3)                ", 'DWRD',
        "Frame (0)", 'DWRD',
        "red", 'HWRD', "green", 'HWRD',
        "blue                      ", 'HWRD',
        "Body (1)", 'DWRD',
        "red", 'HWRD',
        "green", 'HWRD',
        "blue                      ", 'HWRD',
        "Text (2)", 'DWRD',
        "red", 'HWRD', "green", 'HWRD',
        "blue                      ", 'HWRD',
        "Elevator (3)", 'DWRD',
        "red", 'HWRD', "green", 'HWRD',
        "blue                      ", 'HWRD'
    }
};
```

Example 9–2:   Sample ResEdit templates

Several tricks are illustrated by the example. First, the format of the 'wctb', 'actb', and 'dctb' color table resources are the same, and thus a preprocessor macro is used to define all three.

Second, these three resources are a subset of the 'clut' type, which represents an arbitrary color table with a variable number of color specifications. For ease of editing, however, the 'wctb' and related types are defined with the five fixed color specifications expected for those types, which allows a descriptive name to be associated in the template with each RGB value. A similar approach is used for a control color table, which has only four entries.

Third, with this fixed format, certain values are expected for several of the fields of the resource. These expected values are shown in parentheses in the prompt, making it easier to validate an existing resource or create a new one using the template.

Finally, special characters in the prompt strings can be used to influence the visual formatting of the dialog produced by the template. In this case, a series of nonbreaking spaces (Option–space) are used to provide a blank line after the ctSize value and each blue value. To make sure these blank "words" end up on a separate line, they are separated from the remainder of the line using a customary space. If _ represents a nonbreaking space and X an ordinary space, the prompt for the blue color is stored as:

blue_XXXXXXXXX

and a two-line prompt is given, one with blue and the other with XXXXXXXXX. The net result is shown in Figure 9–13, with a vertical break between each color specification.

ResEdit can also be extended with custom pickers, as provided with MPW Pascal. These allow you to run your own code within ResEdit to handle a particular resource type.

The code is built as a Pascal unit and compiled into a resource of type 'RSSC'. The resource name is the name of the type to be edited, prefixed by an @ sign. As distributed, ResEdit contains many such resources, as you can determine by the command

```
RezDet -l ResEdit | Search RSSC
```

The resource is built using an assembly language header that defines entry points at fixed locations from the beginning of the resource, much like the header of a desk accessory.

Sample code to extend ResEdit is included as an example with MPW Pascal, and further documentation is contained in the *MPW Pascal Reference Manual*

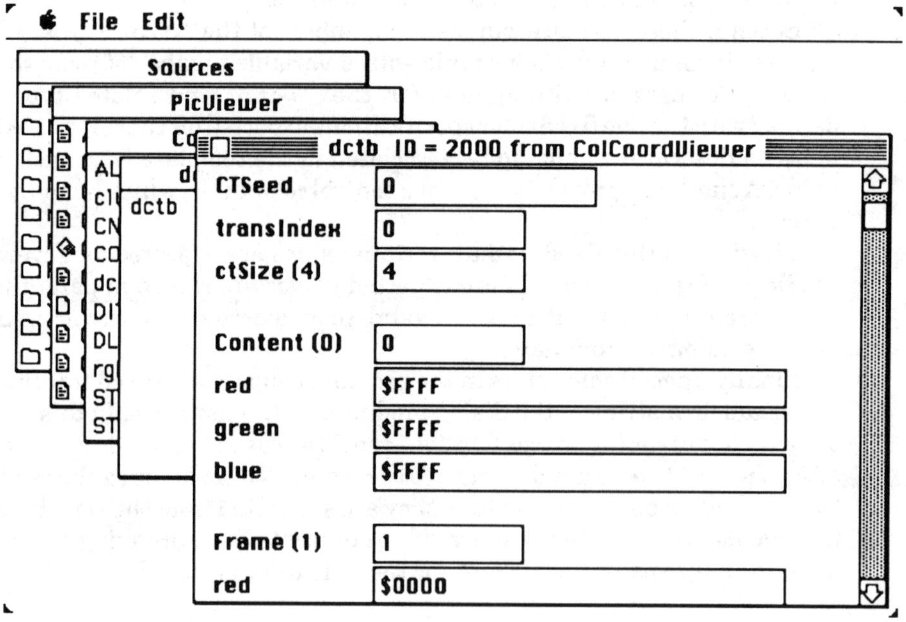

Figure 9–13: Editing a resource using Example 9–2

Chapter 10

Building MPW Programs

THE FINAL VERSION OF ANY COMPILED MPW PROGRAM is linked using the Link command. The MPW linker takes a series of MPW object files, such as these produced by the Pascal and C compilers, and builds one of the standard Macintosh program types.

Although you can specify every possible library in your Link command, making effective use of the linker requires an understanding of the different libraries supplied with MPW and how they are appropriate. The linking steps for applications, tools, desk accessories and other program types are different, requiring different Link options and different libraries. Complete examples are provided for linking a desk accessory and 'INIT' resource.

When working on a particular project, the same series of steps—edit, compile, link—will occur over and over again. One way to automate this is to write a command file. However, MPW also includes the Make command, which will generate a list of necessary commands based on a dependency file. This is particularly helpful when the source is split between several files, with only a few files changing each time the program is built.

10.1 Linking Applications and Tools

The final step of building an MPW program is normally a Link command, which combines compiled code into an executable program.

541

The MPW assembler and each of the MPW compilers produce object code in the data fork of files that have the suffix .o. In addition to your compiled program, libraries of compiled routines are provided with MPW and are used to implement ROM interfaces, language-specific operations (e.g., WriteLn, printf), and normal program initialization.

The linker selects only those components of the object files necessary to build the completed program. All of the Macintosh program types are stored as resources in the resource fork, either of a separate file or of the System file. The linker builds the resource fork of the program, the jump table, and any finder attributes, such as the file type or creator.

LINKING PROGRAMS

One or more MPW object files can be combined into an executable program using the Link command. The result should be one of the standard program types described earlier in Chapter 3.

Link

Link object files into an executable program

Syntax:

Link *file* …	Link each MPW object *file*

Options:

-b	Increase limits to do a big link
-c *type*	Set output file creator to four-character *type*
-d	Suppress warnings for duplicate symbols
-m *name*	Set main entry point to module or entry point *name*
-l	Display symbolic map of linked program
-o *outputfile*	Output linked program to *outputfile*
-opt	Optimize Object Pascal program
-p	Display progress report
-ra *seg=nn*	Set resource attributes of segment named *seg* to value *nn*
-ra *=nn*	Set resource attributes of all segments to *nn*
-rt *type =ID*	Output code as resource type *type* and ID *ID*
-sg *new=old,* …	Rename list of *old* segment names to *new*
-ss *limit*	Increase maximum segment size to *limit*
-t *type*	Set output file type to four-character *type*
-w	Suppress all warning messages
-x *mapfile*	Display cross-reference listing to *mapfile*

Remarks:

By default, the compiled object code goes to file `Link.out` and a series of resources of type `'CODE'` are produced. The maximum segment size defaults to 32760, but larger segment sizes can be set for programs that will not be used with the 64K ROM.

If the link is unsuccessful, the modification date of *output file* is set to 0 (1 Jan 1904). The MPW shell will refuse to execute such a program.

Input/Output:

diagnostic	Linker error messages
output	Linker map

Example:

```
Link -o Foo Foo.o {LibList}
```
Compile Data.r; leave resources in Data.rsrc

Among the most commonly used options are those that specify the type and creator for the output file. The standard values for programs contained in separate files are summarized by Table 10–1.

Description	*Type*	*Creator*
default	APPL	????
Application	APPL	*anyt*
Desk accessory	DFIL	DMOV
MPW tool	MPST	MPS
'INIT' resource	INIT	*n.a.*
Serial printer driver	PRES	*anyt*
Network printer driver	PRER	*anyt*
Other network driver	RDEV	*anyt*

n.a.   not necessary
anyt   program-specific type: should be reserved from Macintosh Technical Support

Table 10–1: Program creator and type values

By default, `Link` builds a series of resources of type `'CODE'` corresponding to the program's code segments. Resource ID No. 1 contains the initial entry point for the program and all other routines in the same segment, normally `Main`. Other segments are stored with resource IDs from 2 on up.

The linker also creates the application (or tool) jump table to resolve intersegment references, as 'CODE' resource No. 0.

The -rt option puts all the code in a different resource type instead of 'CODE' and suppresses creation of the jump table; the program should have only one segment. The resource type might be 'INIT' for initialization code and 'MDEF' for a menu definition procedure. The first word of the resource will be the initial entry point. Because they have a header referencing multiple entry points, linking desk accessories and drivers require additional steps described later.

Link replaces only those resources that are generated by the link. Other resources in the file are not disturbed. This allows you to link to a file that was generated as the output of a Rez resource compilation. If both Rez and Link are being used on the same file, either can be used to set the type and creator.

The -ra option can be used to set the resource attributes for the program resources. By default, the resources are marked purgeable—except for 'CODE' segment no. 1, which is locked and preloaded. The Segment Loader in the 64K ROM expects segments to be locked, so you would use -ra 48 (set to locked and purgeable) for any program intended to run on an old-ROM machine. Explicit resource attributes never affect 'CODE' resources 0 or 1.

If you are writing programs that won't run on the 64K ROM, the -ss option allows larger segment sizes. Such segments are likely to cause problems on a Macintosh 512, because of a bug in the Resource Manager that incorrectly handles some resources longer than 32K.

The -l option will produce a formatted listing of the layout of a linked program, broken down by segment. The map is ordered by segment number and offset within the segment, shown in the first two columns. Sample output for a trivial C program is shown in Figure 10–1.

The -x option can also be used to display a cross-reference listing of modules and entry points. Unlike the -l option, the output goes to a specified file rather than the standard output stream.

RESOLVING REFERENCES

The MPW linker is a "smart" linker that includes only the code necessary to build the resulting program. It is also smart about handling object files in any order.

Some linkers care about the order in which the object files are referenced in the link command. Some also make distinctions between object files—produced directly by compilers—and object libraries, merged from multiple object files and supplied for your use.

The Link command makes no such distinction. The linker merges only the code that is required from each of its input files. Code is included in units of modules, which correspond to procedures and functions in Pascal and C. If you write five routines in one of your source files and four are unreferenced anywhere, they will not be included in the output resources.

Link map produced from

```
main() {
}
```

and

```
Link -1 -c 'MPS' -t 'MPST' -o main main.c.o ∂
     {CLibraries}CRuntime.o {CLibraries}CInterface.o
```

```
  seg Main 1
main                 Main      1,0
CMain                Main      1,2       @22         #
_RTInit              Main      1,30
exit                 Main      1,212
_RTExit              Main      1,232
Save0                Main      1,284                 #
Save                 Main      1,286                 #E
NewPtr               Main      1,28E
c2pstr               Main      1,298
p2cstr               Main      1,2CA
  size Main 2E8

  seg %GlobalData 0
_SAGlbls             %GlobalData          0,0        #
_IntEnv              %GlobalData          0,56
StandAlone           %GlobalData          0,8A
  size %GlobalData 8E

  seg %A5Init 2
_DATAINIT            %A5Init   2,0
_DataInit            %A5Init   2,0       @2A         E
#0001                %A5Init   2,C8                  #
_A5Init              %A5Init   2,C8                  E
  size %A5Init C8
```

Figure 10–1:   Simple C Link map

  The order of the object files is normally unimportant, since the linker uses all the files simultaneously to resolve external references. It thus can resolve a reference in the fourth object file to a routine defined in the first one. A linker that processes the object files sequentially would require that the first file be repeated in the file list, as is true for many mainframe linkers.

  MPW object files contain one or more modules. Each module will normally consist of a single routine. The name of the module will be the same as the routine name; since the Pascal language is case insensitive, all such names are mapped to uppercase. Thus, a C function named `foo` would be stored in an MPW object module `foo`, but a Pascal function named `foo` would be stored in `FOO`.

Each compiler allows you to reference a routine written in the other language and allows for the naming rules to be interpreted accordingly. Thus, the C source

```
pascal foo() {
}
```

would generate a module named `FOO`.

The MPW object file format includes a provision to indicate that a particular module is the main entry point. When building an application (or an MPW tool), the linker must have such an entry point to know where to set the main entry point in the jump table. This is the address used by the finder (MPW shell) to transfer control when the program is launched (run from the shell).

More significantly, the linker uses this main entry point to build a tree of necessary modules from all the modules in the object files. It loads the module containing the main entry point, then loads all modules (routines) referenced by that module, continuing recursively until no more references can be resolved. If any unresolved references remain, it prints an error message and quits.

If a module is defined more than once, an error message is displayed by default and only one of the modules is used. The order of the file names on the `Link` command determines which module is used in the event of a tie.

ENTRY AND EXIT CODING

In an MPW Pascal program, the main entry point is the section of the code commencing with the PROGRAM statement, as illustrated by Figure 10-2.

To make sure the Pascal entry and exit coding are run, the Pascal compiler automatically includes "hidden" routine calls before and after any statements you might include in your PROGRAM.

In C, the mechanism is slightly different. The standard C program behaves as if its `main()` were a function called from the shell. For an MPW tool, for example, the arguments to `main()` will the be command line parameters used to launch the tool.

So that a C program can be built to follow this model, an MPW C program does not include `main()` as its main entry point, as one might expect. Instead, the module `CMain` in library `{CLibraries}CRuntime.o` is declared as a main entry point, as shown in Figure 10-3. `CMain`, in turn, calls `main()` after the appropriate entry coding; if `main()` returns, `CMain` transfers to the exit coding.

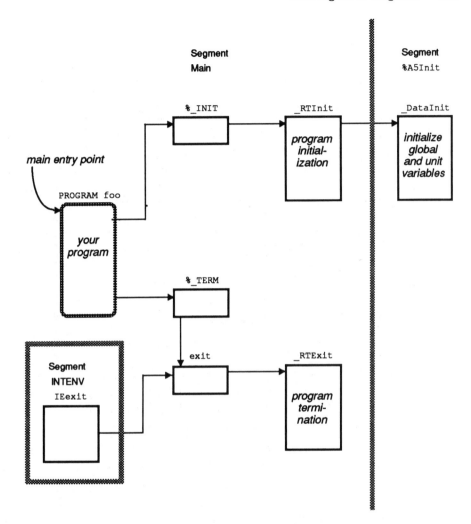

Figure 10-2:   Pascal standard entry and exit coding

Both languages share common routines for initialization and termination. For example, either type of program terminates using _RTExit, which may be reached via either the Pascal routine IEexit or the C library function exit. Both call _RTInit to initialize the program.

_RTInit in turn calls _DataInit to initialize values for global variables and other data not stored on the stack, such as C static variables and strings. _DataInit is loaded into its own segment %A5Init, which also contains the constants (indicated by entry %GlobalData) necessary to initialize the global data. If the program is written with both C and Pascal, %GlobalData will include the initial values necessary for both types of

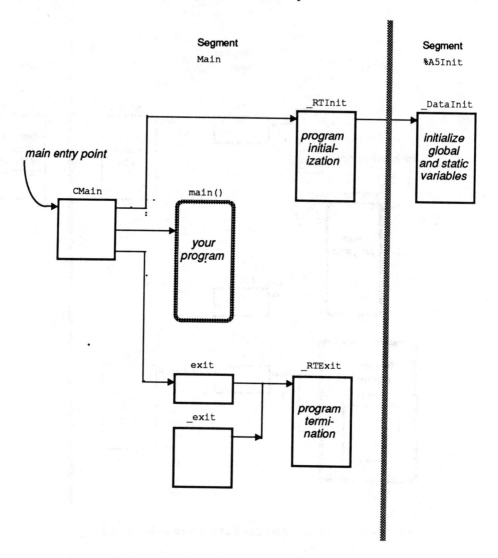

Figure 10–3:   C standard entry and exit coding

variables.

Initialization also sets up the application or tool parameters, the ones passed directly to C's main() or stored in ArgV for Pascal programs.

As with any other interface not formally documented by Apple, the names of the various entry and exit routines could potentially change in a future release. However, the initialization and termination steps performed for Pascal and C programs are a requirement that will remain fixed.

Other program types do not use the standard initialization and termination code, and thus there's less going on "behind your back." Desk accessories and drivers enter through one of five standard entry points. The remaining program types begin at the beginning of the corresponding resource.

STANDARD LIBRARIES

Library files are merged from one or more object files using the Lib command. These libraries will speed the linking of commonly used routines with other programs and also reduce the number of files required for the Link command.

Three folders of standard libraries are supplied with MPW. Folders {PLibraries} and {CLibraries} include library files intended for Pascal and C, respectively. Folder {Libraries} includes several files required by Pascal, used sometimes in assembly-language programming, but rarely used for C programs.

The libraries supplied with MPW are described in Table 10–2.

The actual libraries for any program can be established by trial and error. The linker will complain if it is unable to resolve a reference because you omitted a library, and it will also advise you if a library was not needed. However, certain general guidelines can be used to determine which libraries should be mentioned when linking a program.

Applications, tools, desk accessories, and drivers should be linked against one of the Runtime.o files to provide the initialization and termination code described earlier. A program containing any C code should be linked with {CLibraries}CRuntime.o, while Pascal programs are linked with {Libraries}Runtime.o.

These libraries also include several of the commonly used routines, such as the 32 bit multiply and divide subroutines for the MC68000 (which aren't needed if the -mc68020 C or Pascal compiler options is used.) It also includes several Integrated Environment routines similar to standard UNIX kernel functions, such as open, close, read, write, and ioctl.

Assembly language routines are linked with either if they include initialized data areas (any DS or DC). Desk accessories and drivers are linked with {Libraries}DRVRRuntime.o and may also need to be linked with CRuntime.o or Runtime.o.

Two of the standard libraries—{Libraries}Interface.o and {CLibraries}CInterface.o—provide the interface routines for the *Inside Macintosh* routines described as [Not in ROM]. These usually correspond to operations that can be easily implemented in assembly language, such as routine TopMem, which returns the value of the 32-bit long at location MemTop. These also include a few longer routines that are called from assembly language programs—although many of these routines are included as traps in later versions of the ROM.

```
{Libraries}Runtime.o
```
Pascal and assembler initialization and termination
```
{CLibraries}CRuntime.o
```
C initialization and termination
```
{Libraries}DRVRRuntime.o
```
Initialization for drivers and desk accessories

```
{Libraries}Interface.o
```
Interface routines ([Not in ROM]) for assembler and
Pascal;
Pascal OS glue for register-based traps
```
{CLibraries}CInterface.o
```
C interface routines and glue for OS and Toolbox traps

```
{PLibraries}SANELib.o
```
SANE floating-point libraries for Pascal
```
{CLibraries}CSANELib.o
```
SANE floating-point libraries for C

```
{PLibraries}PasLib.o
```
Built-in Pascal libraries; units `PasLibIntf` and `IntEnv`

```
{CLibraries}Math.o
    Standard C math library
{CLibraries}StdCLib.o
    Other C libraries, include stdio, memory and strings
```

```
{PLibraries}SANELib881.o
```
Use instead of `SANELib.o` when compiled for MC68881
```
{CLibraries}CSANELib881.o
```
Use instead of `CSANELib.o` when compiled for MC68881
```
{CLibraries}Math881.o
```
Use instead of `Math.o` when compiled for MC68881
```
{CLibraries}CLib881.o
```
Use instead of `StdCLib.o` when compiled for MC68881

```
{Libraries}ObjLib.o
```
Object-oriented procedures for type TObject
```
{Libraries}PerformLib.o
```
Performance measurment libraries
```
{Libraries}ToolLibs.o
```
MPW tool libraries: Error manager, cursor control

Table 10–2:   Standard MPW libraries

The interface libraries also include routines that are never used from
assembly language. These glue routines are necessary for calling certain
traps from C or Pascal. Most of the OS traps, such as in the Memory Manager

or the File Manager, expect parameters to be loaded into registers before being called. These glue routines unload the stack-based parameters into registers before calling the trap. Other glue routines are used to add the routine selector before calling one of the standard packages, such as SFGetFile. For each of the glue routines, the name of the routine is the same as the name of the trap.

The two interface libraries have separate glue routines for Pascal and C, each conforming to the appropriate naming and calling conventions. Take the BlockMove trap as an example, which expects parameters in registers A0, A1, and D0 and returns a function result in D0. Library Interface.o contains module BLOCKMOVE, which unloads the parameters from right-to-left, and returns a result on the stack for Pascal programs. Library CInterface.o contains module BlockMove, which unloads the parameters from left to right, and returns a result in a register for C programs.

The CInterface.o also includes glue routines specific to C. These include routines to convert struct arguments shorter than 5 bytes long, usually a Point or Rect. As noted in Chapter 8, the ROM usually expects the value of such a structure to be passed as an argument, while MPW C programs pass the address of the structure. Finally, glue routines are required to implement C-to-Pascal string conversion.

Pascal programs should link with {PLibraries}PasLib.o, which includes all the library procedures predefined by the Pascal language. These include procedures in the standard math and I/O libraries, such as sin, cos, WriteLn, and concat. PasLib.o also includes the implementations of units PasLibIntf and IntEnv.

Programs that use floating point functions will probably require {PLibraries}SANELib.o or {CLibraries}CSANELib.o. Pascal programs that call SANE floating-point routines directly through unit SANE must be linked with SANELib.o.

C programs that #include <math.h> or <SANE.h> must link to CSANELib.o. This library includes the standard (math.h) C functions implemented by SANE, such as sin, cos, sqrt. The library also includes SANE functions such as getround and getprecision.

The remaining math library functions defined by <math.h> are included in {CLibraries}Math.o. They include inverse trignometric functions and hyperbolic functions.

Other standard C libraries are in {CLibraries}StdCLib.o. These include the standard I/O (getchar, printf), the string (strcpy, strchr), and byte manipulation (memchr, memset) functions. Also included are setjmp/longjmp and the standard C memory allocation functions (malloc, free).

As shown, several of the libraries come in a separate version to be used with programs compiled to use direct MC68881 floating-point coprocessor instructions. As noted in the discussion of the –mc68881 compiler option to both the C and Pascal commands, the option replaces some SANE calls with direct 68881 instructions and changes the representation of an extended floating-point quantity from 80 to 96 bits. As a result, different glue routines are required for any routine involving floating point for either language.

The remaining libraries are specialized and used less often.

File {Libraries}ObjLib.o contains support procedures for object-oriented programming in Object Pascal and Object Assembler—when it's *not* being done as part of a MacApp program. This basically consists of four method procedures for type TObject, as well as several hidden routines used to implement method tables and method dispatching. A MacApp program will always be linked with the MacApp libraries, as described in the next chapter.

Performance measurement routines can be found in {Libraries}PerformLib.o and are used when analyzing the performance of a program under development. Since Apple strongly advises against shipping a program that calls these routines, this library is one that should always be omitted from linking a released version of any program.

File {Libraries}ToolLibs.o contains the error manager (GetSysErrText) and cursor control routines (RotateCursor) for MPW tools. The remaining MPW tool support routines (such as Pascal's IEExit or C's exit) are contained in the standard initialization or language libraries.

For MPW tools written in C, MPW C also includes the source to a stub library (in :CExamples:Stubs.c) that allows sophisticated programmers to Link smaller tools. As the name suggests, the routine supplies null (stub) substitute routines for several library functions unused by most tools — notably console I/O for stand-alone applications and all floating-point formatting. If you link with Stubs.c.o, you should list it before other libraries and use the Link -w option to suppress the warnings about duplicate symbol definitions.

The compatibility rules for mixing libraries are shown in Table 10–3. The only hard-and-fast rule is that Runtime.o should not be used with C code.

The segments used by the library routines, of course, will correspond to code resources in the linked program—any reference to another segment can cause a heap compaction. Since many of the interface routines are to traps that don't normally cause a heap compaction, the entire Interface.o and CInterface.o libraries are loaded in segment Main to avoid introducing additional compaction problems. Many of the shorter routines in the other libraries are also loaded in Main.

However, several other segments are also defined in the libraries, notably for initialization and the standard line-oriented I/O of C and Pascal. If the size of the Main segment is not a limiting factor in your memory management strategy, the -sg option can be used to merge multiple segments into one. The command

	Assembler	Pascal	C
{Libraries}			
Interface.o	*	*	
ObjLib.o	*	*	
PerformLib.o	*	*	*
Runtime.o	*	•	no
ToolLibs.o	*	*	*
{PLibraries}			
PasLib.o		•	
SANELib.o		†	
SANELib881.o		††	
{CLibraries}			
CInterface.o			•
CRuntime.o			•
CSANELib.o			†
CSANELib881.o			††
Math.o			†
Math881.o			††
StdCLib.o			†
CLib881.o			††

•	Required for all applications and tools
*	Required for some programs
†	Required for some programs compiled without −mc68881 option
††	Required for some programs compiled with −mc68881 option
no	Prohibited
	Other combinations are allowed, but not necessary

Table 10–3:   Library compatibility

```
Link −o PrintTest −sg Main=STDIO,SANELib PrintTest.p.o ∂
   {Libraries}Runtime.o {Libraries}PasLib.o {PLibraries}SANELib.o
```

would include code from the Main, STDIO, and SANELib segments of the
program and library as part of the main code segment.

10.2 Linking Other Programs

Other program types require different steps for building a complete program. Examples of an 'INIT' resource and a desk accessory are included to
show how to build such programs.

For further understanding of how to link programs, the DumpObj command allows you to analyze the exact contents of any MPW object file, either

your own or the libraries supplied with MPW. This allows you to see the module names, external references, and even the actual assembly code. An example is provided of preparing an index to all the MPW-supplied libraries.

LINKING AN INIT RESOURCE

Program types other than tools or applications should not use the standard initialization and termination code, but each program linked by the Link command must have a main entry point. To get around this, the -m option of the Link command can be used to set any linker name (module or entry point) as the initial entry point.

For a C program, this name can be any function. Since all Pascal procedures must be part of either a PROGRAM or UNIT, the normal approach is to write a stand-alone unit and use a procedure within that unit as the main entry point. The procedure must be declared in the INTERFACE of the unit so that the Pascal compiler will generate a named module that can be found by the linker.

The linker will start with this routine and follow the reference tree until all references are resolved. You won't normally need Runtime.o or CRuntime.o, since your program skips the standard initialization (and, in fact, cannot have any global variables).

Such program types will normally begin executing at the beginning of the resource. You must make sure that your entry point is the first thing loaded by the linker into memory. One way to do so is to specify your object file as the first one on the Link command.

Example 10–1 shows a very simple resource of type 'INIT'. It does one thing—sets the application heap to be the same size as on a 512K machine.

When installed in the system folder, this code changes the value of BufPtr after MacsBug has been installed but before the RAM cache is opened. If the RAM cache is off and the program is run on a Macintosh Plus, it will produce a machine that's fully software equivalent to a Macintosh 512K Enhanced, both in the ROM functionality and the size of the application heap.

Since many of us can't afford to have one of every type of machine, this provides an easy way to test code against smaller configurations. Such code could also be used to make a machine with expanded memory—such as a 2Mb Mac 512K or Mac Plus—emulate the standard configuration. BufPtr would be set to the value of scrnBase on the target machine, which is contained in *Inside Macintosh*.

The program is built using the commands

```
Delete "{SystemFolder}Mac512INIT"
Pascal Mac512INIT.p
Link -o Mac512INIT -t INIT -c MACS -rt INIT=0 Mac512INIT.p.o
Move Mac512INIT "{SystemFolder}"
```

```
{ Example 10-1: INIT to emulate a 512K machine }

UNIT Mac512INIT;
{$D-}            { Delete MacsBug symbols for space }

  INTERFACE

  PROCEDURE SysBeep(duration: INTEGER);
    INLINE $A9C8;

  PROCEDURE MoveBufPtr;

  IMPLEMENTATION

{ BufPtr points to the bottom of the screen and sound
  buffers, which is always the top of the application
  heap. The value of BufPtr might be decreased before we
  get here, such as to install a RAM disk or allocate
  memory for the RAM cache
}
  PROCEDURE MoveBufPtr;
  CONST
    BufPtr = $10C;          { bottom of buffer area }
    { BufPtr value on 512K machine }
    Mac512BufVal = $7A700;
  TYPE
    LongPtr = ^LONGINT;
  VAR
    lp: LongPtr;
  BEGIN
  { Set BufPtr to the standard (no-debugger)
    configuration for a 512K machine. Make sure that
    we're moving it down (which is always legal) rather
    than up (which is not). Beep to remind the user
    we're stealing the memory.
}
    lp := LongPtr(BufPtr);
    IF lp^ > Mac512BufVal THEN
      BEGIN
          lp^ := Mac512BufVal;     { move BufPtr down }
          SysBeep(1);              { remind we're here
}
      END;

  END; (* MoveBufPtr *)

END. (* Mac512INIT *)
```

Example 10-1: Pascal source for INIT resource

The `Link` step requires no libraries, only the `'INIT'` code itself. The program uses only one trap and no procedure calls. The trap is defined in line to save on compilation time but could also be defined by using units `MemTypes`, `QuickDraw`, and `OSIntf`.

Note that the commands first delete the old version, if any. The "poor man's search path" automatically supplied by HFS means that searching for a file in the current directory may find it anyway, even if it's in `{SystemFolder}`. The MPW 2.0 `Link` command will use an existing `Mac512INIT`, even if it's in the system folder and not the current directory; so the old one is deleted before the compile.

At startup time, the system searches for files of type `'INIT'` in the system folder and then runs initialization resources such as ours. The file creator is not important for execution, but using `'MACS'` as the creator automatically displays our file in the desktop using the standard Macintosh icon used for the System, Finder, Clipboard File, and Scrapbook File.

As discussed in Chapter 3, many program resources will include an optional header to identify the code type and version information. Because program execution begins at the beginning of the resource, the first bytes of the resource must be a jump around the header. The standard mechanism for linking desk accessories shows how `Rez` can be used (instead of assembly code) to supply a similar header.

LINKING DESK ACCESSORIES

Both desk accessories and drivers must be built as resources of type `'DRVR'`. The name of the resource is the name of the DA or driver. The DA name begins with a null; the driver name begins with a period.

The `'DRVR'` resource must begin with a header that includes several reserved fields and the offsets to the five standard entry points. This is used by the Device Manager to transfer control to the desk accessory or driver.

The standard MPW solution for building `'DRVR'` resources uses both the resource compiler and the linker. The `Rez` portion allows the individual bytes of the header to be exactly specified, while `Link` symbolically resolve code references to the five standard routines. The structure of the completed `'DRVR'` resource is illustrated by Figure 10–4.

The use of `Rez` input for the `'DRVR'` header allows someone who's not comfortable with assembly language to easily specify the header value.

The standard resource format includes symbolic names for the standard boolean control flags described in Chapter 3. Does the `'DRVR'` need time for a periodic action or a "good-bye kiss" if the application terminates? The header specifies whether the `'DRVR'` is loaded in a relocatable or nonrelocatable block, the latter normally used for drivers. Which of the optional functions are defined?

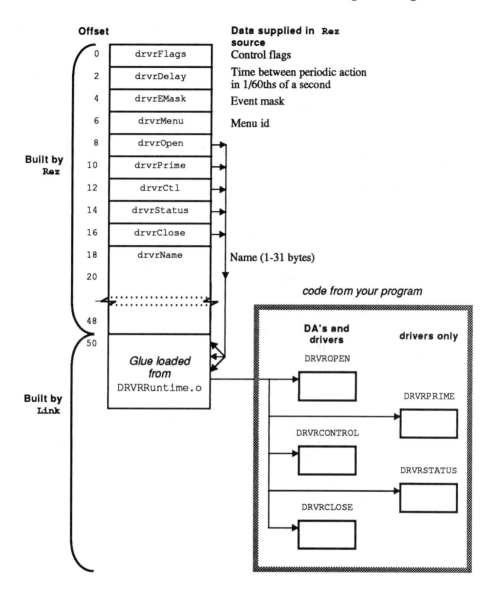

Figure 10–4:   Linking a desk accessory or driver

A numeric field indicates how often the periodic action be performed. For a desk accessory, the header will also include a mask of the events that are recognized by the DRVRControl routine. If it has a menu, the resource ID of the menu is listed. For both types of 'DRVR', the final field is the name repeated (without the null but with a period, if any).

All the configuration parameters are in the Rez source file—not the Rez or Link command or in the program source. The resource format is built using the type definition in file {RIncludes}MPWTypes.r.

Whether written in Pascal or C, a 'DRVR' resource is linked with {Libraries}DRVRRuntime.o, the standard 'DRVR' glue. This glue performs several functions.

First, it provides definitions at fixed locations for the five standard routines. These locations are expected by the standard resource header. If the glue file (DRVRRuntime.o) is listed first in the Link command, it assures the exact layout of the first few words of the linked code, which follows immediately after the data built by Rez.

Second, because the glue is resolved by the linker, it can join the fixed displacements required by the Device Manager with the symbolic linker names generated by the compilers. The glue references modules DRVROPEN, DRVRPRIME, DRVRCONTROL, DRVRSTATUS, and DRVRCLOSE. The modules can be in any order in any of the object files used in the link.

Third, the Device Manager calls to 'DRVR' resources are register based, like most OS traps. The Device Manager expects to call one of the five routines with the arguments in registers A0 and A1; the glue converts this to a series of standard Pascal parameters. C programs must declare these routines using the pascal storage class.

Example 10–2 shows the C source for a very simple desk accessory. When it is opened, the DA only displays two dialog boxes—the first one unsettling, the second one reassuring. As such, it only implements one of the five standard entry points, DRVROpen. However, it does serve to illustrate the complete structure of 'DRVR' resources, including owned resources, the resource header, and the commands to build it. It can also serve as an amusing program to give to unsuspecting friends.

er versions of the ROM. display a cross-reference listing of modules and ent y points. Unlike the -l option, the output goes t of the unit so that the Pasca compiler will generate a named module that can be found by the linker. Th linker will start wit?

It would be possible to produce the dreaded "bomb" box by calling the System Error Handler directly, using the OS trap SysError. However, to retain control in the DA (and provide a more representative example), the Dialog Manager is used to display a modal dialog imitating the real thing. Once the dialog is displayed, another modal dialog is displayed, telling your victim that the system error was just a fake.

Alert calls in the Dialog Manager could be used to display both dialogs. However, using the Alert trap on the first dialog would draw one of the pushbuttons with a bold outline—not a very good imitation of the real thing. Such outlining would be useful for the reassuring dialog. However, to draw one of the lines in italics, the dialog must be preloaded (invisible) to install a user-defined item in the dialog's item list, something that can't be done with an alert.

```
/* Example 10-2: C source for sample desk accessory */

/* Bomber.c */

/* This DA puts up a phony dialog box to scare the user     .
*/

/* Only show those headers we use directly; others
   automatically included. Some of these aren't strictly
   necessary, since the glue functions are not defined,
   but used as implicit type int
*/
#include <Types.h>
#include <QuickDraw.h>

/* required for DRVR parameter types */
#include <Devices.h>

#include <Dialogs.h>
#include <OSUtils.h>
#include <TextEdit.h>
#include <ToolUtils.h>
#include <Windows.h>


/* Note: This code is designed to bypass MPW C's
   automatic conversion between C and Pascal strings.
   Here are two Toolbox traps to directly call the ROM
   without string conversion.
*/
pascal void PParamText(p1, p2, p3, p4)
  Str255 *p1,*p2,*p3,*p4;
  extern 0xA98B;
pascal void PGetCTitle(theControl, title)
  ControlHandle theControl;
  Str255 *title;
  extern 0xA95E;


#define
  JOKEDAY(month,day) ((month==4) && (day==1))
#define
  OWNEDRESID(drvrresid) (0xC000 | ((~(drvrresid)) << 5))

/* This is instead of errors file */
#define noErr 0
```

```
/* Resource constants: relative to a calculated base
resource id */
#define DLOG_bomb          baseresid
#define DLOG_justjoking    baseresid+1
#define STR_jokeday        baseresid
#define STR_italictext     baseresid+1
#define item_italictext    3           /* item in a DITL
*/


/* Implementation-independent types */
typedef char Byte;
typedef short Half;
typedef long Full;


/* A UserItem for a dialog item list to draw italicized
text  */
pascal void DrawItalics(thewindow, itemno)
WindowPtr thewindow;
short itemno;
{ Rect itemrect;
  Half baseresid,dmyint;
  Handle dmyhand;
  StringHandle titlehand;
  StringPtr titleptr;

  baseresid =((WindowPeek) thewindow)->refCon;
  titlehand = GetString(STR_italictext);
  GetDItem
     (thewindow, itemno, &dmyint, &dmyhand, &itemrect);

  /* Now draw the string in italics */
  TextFace(italic);
  HLock(titlehand);
  titleptr = *titlehand;
  /* skip Pascal string length */
  TextBox((Ptr)(((Full)titleptr)+1),
     titleptr->length, &itemrect, teJustLeft);
  HUnlock(titlehand);
  TextFace(normal);
}

/*** Define the five standard 'DRVR' entry points ***/

/* Open the desk accessory: for this DA, the only
   functional entry point. Put up the bomb dialog and
   then the explanation dialog. Assume the resources are
   present and can be loaded into memory; the dialog can
```

```
      fail due to lack of memory for the window record.
*/
pascal short DRVROpen(ctlPB, dctl)
CntrlParam *ctlPB;
DCtlPtr dctl;
{ WindowPtr saveport, adialog;
  Handle itemhand;
  Half baseresid, whichitem, itemtype;
  Rect itemrect;
  DateTimeRec today;
  String(20) aparm;
  StringHandle msgh;
  StringPtr msgp;

  GetPort(&saveport);   /* every DA should do this */

/* Compute the resource id of the owned resources */
  baseresid = OWNEDRESID(dctl->dCtlRefNum);
  GetTime(&today);

  while(1)
/* Pascal string with 2-digit system error # set to
   today's date */
  { aparm.length = 2;
    aparm.text[0] = '0' + (today.day / (Half)10);
    aparm.text[1] = '0' + (today.day % (Half)10);
    PParamText(&aparm, NULL, NULL, NULL);

/* Display the fake bomb dialog. It would be nice to use
   Alert, but it outlines the default button, which
   would be a tip-off. There's still a tip-off:
   ModalDialog beeps if you click elsewhere, but the
   alternative is a lot of code.
*/
    if
      (adialog =
        GetNewDialog(DLOG_bomb, NULL, (WindowPtr) -1))
    { ModalDialog(NULL, &whichitem);
      /* Now get the name of the button selected before
         dropping dialog */
      GetDItem
        (adialog, whichitem,
         &itemtype, &itemhand, &itemrect);
      PGetCTitle(itemhand, &aparm);
      DisposDialog(adialog);
    }
    else               /* GetNewDialog failed */
```

```
            { SysBeep(1);
              break;
        }


    /* Display a message indicating the real purpose
       Mention button pushed in the message, and add a
       special message on April 1. Install a user item to
       draw italicized text
    */
      if
        (adialog =
          GetNewDialog
            (DLOG_justjoking, NULL, (WindowPtr) -1))
      {if (JOKEDAY(today.month,today.day))
        {msgh = GetString(STR_jokeday);
         HLock(msgh);
         msgp = *msgh;
         PParamText(&aparm, msgp, NULL, NULL);
         HUnlock(msgh);
        }
        else                                /* no special day
    */
            PParamText(&aparm, NULL, NULL, NULL);


    /* Normally, one would use the code
       ((WindowPeek)adialog)->windowKind = dctl->dCtlRefNum;
       to properly identify a DA window. However,
       ModalDialog/IsDialogEvent fail unless windowKind is
       left at its default value
       (dialogKind).

       We could change it (for ModalDialog) and change it
       back later, but for our purposes we can pass the
       owned resource id using the refCon instead.
    */
        ((WindowPeek)adialog)->refCon = baseresid;
        GetDItem
          (adialog, item_italictext, &itemtype,
            &itemhand, &itemrect);
        SetDItem
          (adialog, item_italictext, itemtype,
            DrawItalics, &itemrect);
        ShowWindow(adialog);

        ModalDialog(NULL, &whichitem);
        DisposDialog(adialog);
        if (whichitem == ok)
          break;                /* punish 'im unless it's OK */
      }
```

```
   else       /* GetNewDialog failed */
      { SysBeep(1);
       break;
       }
   }

   SetPort(saveport);
   return(noErr);
}


/*Remaining entry points just to satisfy Link command */

pascal short DRVRControl(ctlPB, dctl)
CntrlParam *ctlPB;
DCtlPtr dctl;
{
   return(noErr);          /* not implemented in this DA */
}

pascal short DRVRClose(ctlPB, dctl)
char *ctlPB;
DCtlPtr dctl;
{
   return(noErr);          /* not implemented in this DA */
}


/* These are required for Link, but are never called for
   a DA (just drivers)  */

pascal short DRVRPrime(ctlPB, dctl)
CntrlParam *ctlPB;
DCtlPtr dctl;
{
   return(noErr);       /* Not used in a desk accessory */
}

pascal short DRVRStatus(ctlPB, dctl)
CntrlParam *ctlPB;
DCtlPtr dctl;
{
   return(noErr);       /* Not used in a desk accessory */
}
```

Example 10–2: C source for sample desk accessory

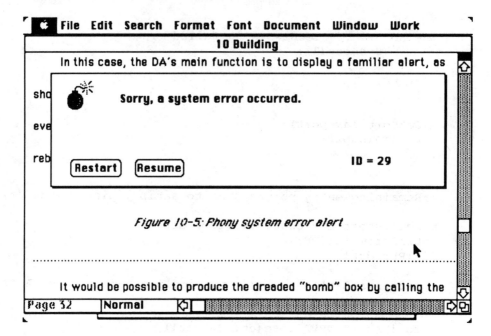

Figure 10-5:   **Phony system error alert**

To build this desk accessory, the following three shell commands are required:

```
C Bomber.c
Link -o Bomber.DRVW -rt DRVW=0  "{Libraries}DRVRRuntime.o" ∂
  Bomber.c.o "{Libraries}CInterface.o"
Rez -o Bomber -t DFIL -c DMOV Bomber.r
```

The Link commands combines the 'DRVR' glue with the standard entry points:

```
        Link -o Bomber.DRVW -w -rt DRVW=0 ∂
           "{Libraries}DRVRRuntime.o"      ∂
           Bomber.c.o ∂
           "{CLibraries}CRuntime.o" ∂
           "{CLibraries}CInterface.o"
```

In this particular example, none of the standard CRuntime.o functions are required. If some of these are required, a different Link command would be needed. The corresponding Pascal 'DRVR' would be linked with DRVRRuntime.o, Interface.o and possibly PasLib.o and Runtime.o.

The -w option suppresses the warning message that Link would otherwise produce, warnings for combining the run time files, such as:

```
### Link: Warning
   More than one starting entry point. module = %DRVRMain
```

Link: Warning
   More than one starting entry point. module = CMain

The messages indicate that both DRVRRuntime.o and CRuntime.o define initial entry points.

The Link command builds the program as a single resource of type 'DRVW', resource ID no. 0. The actual resource type and ID are arbitrary, since they're only referenced in the Bomber.r source. However, using this option eliminates the jump table ('CODE' no. 0) and puts all the code in a single resource.

The Rez source to build the standard 'DRVR' header is shown in Example 10–3. The output of the Rez command is a desk accessory file (type 'DFIL') appropriate for the Font/DA Mover (creator 'DMOV'.)

The Rez source merges the standard type files using preprocessor directives, much as a C program includes its definition files; the type definitions could also be specified as parameters to Rez. The source defines not only the 'DRVR' header but also the other resources used by the DA. The corresponding owned resource value is calculated for an arbitrary initial resource ID chosen for the 'DRVR' resource. Both will be renumbered by the Font/DA Mover when the desk accessory is installed in the System file.

The name of the desk accessory is defined symbolically in the resource definition file. The name is conditionally defined only if it is not previously defined. This allows you to change the DA name using a Rez command line option without modifying the source file. You could even build more than one copy of the DA, each with different names.

An alternate name is particularly appropriate for this example. It might be amusing to give it a name implying a useful function prior to giving it to an unwitting victim. For example, if the name "Undelete" would raise expectations and increase the surprise, the command

```
Rez -o Bomber -d ∂
   'drvrName="Undelete"' -t DFIL -c DMOV Bomber.r
```

would build a desk accessory that was otherwise identical, except for the name. The quotation marks are necessary for Rez to treat the name as a string, while the apostrophes prevent the quotation marks from being stripped by the shell.

When you're ready to install the DA, you can run the Font/DA Mover directly from the shell, with the DA file specified as a parameter:

```
"Font/DA Mover" Bomber
```

```
/* Bomber.r */

/* Any desk accessory is a 'DRVR' resource with an #id
   from 12 to 26. The resource name is the name of the
   DA shown in the Apple menu, except that it includes a
   leading null. Command options can be used to change
   the name, as in
     Rez -d 'drvrName="Tricky"'
*/
#ifndef drvrName
#define drvrName "Bomber"
#endif

/*
  The initial resource id is unimportant, since the
  Font/DA Mover assigns the actual id when installing
the
  DA in the System file. However, any resources used by
  the DA must use an owned resource id's corresponding
to
  this initial id. All resources in this file (other
  than 'DRVR') must have values in the interval
  [BaseResId, BaseResId+31]
*/
#define drvrResId    20
#define BaseResId (0xC000 | (drvrResId << 5))

#include "Types.r"
/* Includes 'DRVW' type for DA header */
#include "MPWTypes.r"

/* Compile 'DRVR' using 'DRVW' Rez format */
type 'DRVR' as 'DRVW';

resource 'DRVR' (drvrResId, "\0x00" drvrName, purgeable)
{
/* Build the standard header for a desk accessory or
driver */
   dontNeedLock,        /* relocatable between calls  */
   dontNeedTime,        /* no periodic action */
   dontNeedGoodbye,     /* no goodBye kiss required */
   noStatusEnable,      /* only for drivers */
   ctlEnable,           /* DA's do Control */
   noWriteEnable,       /* only for drivers */
   noReadEnable,        /* only for drivers */
   0,                   /* simple DA: no periodic */
   0,                   /*  events */
```

```
   0,                        /* menu */
   drvrName,     /* drvrName - This isn't used by the DA */

/* Now merge the actual compiled code here */
   $$resource("SystemBomb.DRVW", 'DRVW', 0)
};

resource 'DLOG' (BaseResId, purgeable) {
   {64, 32, 190, 480},
   altDBoxProc,
   visible,
   noGoAway,
   0,
   BaseResId,
   ""
};

resource 'DITL' (BaseResId, purgeable) {
   { {96, 22, 116, 81},
   Button { enabled,      "Restart" };
   {96, 97, 116, 153},
   Button { enabled,      "Resume" };
   {8, 18, 40, 50},
   Icon { disabled,          BaseResId };
   {20, 78, 36, 320},
   StaticText
      { disabled, "Sorry, a system error occurred."};
   {90, 341, 110, 401},
   StaticText
      { disabled, "ID = ^0" }
   }
};

resource 'DLOG' (BaseResId+1, purgeable) {
   {60, 106, 230, 406},
   dBoxProc,
   invisible,                /* to install UserItem */
   noGoAway,
   0,
   BaseResId+1,
   ""
};

resource 'DITL' (BaseResId+1, purgeable) {
   { {140, 70, 160, 140},
      Button { enabled,          "OK" };
```

```
      {140, 160, 160, 230},
      Button { enabled,           "Not OK" };
      {64, 36, 96, 280},
      UserItem { disabled };
      {8, 20, 40, 280},
      StaticText
        { disabled, "^0 isn't necessary.^1" };
      {48, 20, 64, 280},
      StaticText
        { disabled, "An example from Chapter 10 of" };
      {96, 36, 112, 360},
      StaticText { disabled,      "(Bantam Books)" }
    }
};

/* The dreaded 'bomb' */
resource 'ICON' (BaseResId, purgeable) {
  $"0000 0808 0000 0010 0000 0420 0000 8040"
  $"0000 2200 0000 0800 001F 002A 0020 C700"
  $"0040 3800 0040 0020 0040 0910 03F8 1008"
  $"03F8 2104 03F8 0000 0FFE 0100 3FFF 8000"
  $"3FFF 8000 7FFF C000 7FFF C000 FFFD E000"
  $"FFFF E000 FFFE E000 FFFE E000 FFFE E000"
  $"FFFF E000 FFFD E000 7FFF C000 7FF7 C000"
  $"3FFF 8000 3FFF 8000 0FFE 0000 03F8 0000"
};


resource 'STR ' (BaseResId, purgeable) {
  "\rApril Fools!"
};

resource 'STR ' (BaseResId+1, purgeable) {
  "Programming with Macintosh Programmer's Workshop"
};
```

Example 10–3: Resource source for desk accessory

However, it's much quicker to use one of the public domain desk accessory runners that allow you to open any desk accessory file without installing the DA in the System file. These programs—such as **Other...** by Loftus Becker or by Stefan Blaniuk—are readily available from user groups or electronic bulletin board systems.

ANALYZING OBJECT FILES

The DumpObj command can be used to analyze the contents of object files and libraries prior to being linked. It will disassemble the machine code in the file, either for the entire file or for a single module. It can also be used to display a summary report of the file contents.

DumpObj

Display analysis of object files

Syntax:

DumpObj *file* ...   Display formatted list of each object *file*

Options:

-d	Suppress assembly code
-h	Display assembly code unformatted
-m *module*	Display information only for module *module*
-n	Display only a list of names
-p	Display progress report

Remarks:

DumpObj normally produces a listing that includes headers for each file and module and a formatted assembly listing for each module. The assembly listing includes program counter offsets and a hex dump of the corresponding bytes.

Input/Output:

Output   Formatted listing

Examples:

DumpObj sample.c.o Format contents of object file sample.c.o

By default, DumpObj disassembles the entire file. The display includes a formatted 68000 assembly listing for each module. This listing includes a binary dump of the bytes next to the 68000 assembly instructions. If you will later be debugging your program with a machine language debugger such as MacsBug, you'll find that having a DumpObj listing of the routines you're working on will save a lot of time.

DumpObj also displays headers with additional information stored in the object code for each module. The exact format of the object code is contained in an appendix to the *MPW Reference* Manual, and should be consulted if you need to know exactly what the headers mean. Take, for example, a simple Pascal program:

```
PROGRAM noise;

    PROCEDURE Delay
        (numticks: LONGINT; VAR howlong: LONGINT);
        EXTERNAL;
    PROCEDURE SysBeep(numticks: INTEGER);
        INLINE $A9C8;

VAR
    i,j: INTEGER;
    len: LONGINT;
BEGIN
    i := 1;
    j := i*5;
    Delay(j, len);
    SysBeep(j);
END.
```

This program compiles into 68000 machine instructions to do the arithmetic, a call to the glue routine for `Delay`, and a direct trap to the `SysBeep` procedure. The `DumpObj` display for this program is shown in Figure 10–6.

The listing beings with a list of the symbol dictionary defined for the file and then is followed by a module header. Note that the names of procedures called are listed in Reference lines rather than where they are called. This also shows the entry and exit procedures automatically generated by MPW Pascal for a PROGRAM.

You can dump assembly code without the formatted bytes using `DumpObj -h`. However, most modules will include some data before or after the code, which will be disassembled into meaningless instructions. If you use `DumpObj -h`, you won't have the actual hex to tell what it's supposed to be.

The most common form for this data is the inclusion of debugger symbol names at the end of the module. MacsBug looks for the 68000 instructions

```
                    UNLK  A6
                    RTS
```

followed by the eight-character name of the routine. The first character of the name has 128 added to it (the high order bit) to help differentiate the name for the MacsBug scan.

An assembly language driver or other program type may also include a header at the beginning of the code. Again, using `DumpObj -h` formats the header as assembly code, losing the actual data values.

Since `DumpObj` produces detailed headers and listings for each module, the size of the `DumpObj` listing will be many times the size (in bytes) of the original object file. For a library, this can be useful to keep on disk, but because it may be 10,000 lines long or more, it is probably impractical to print

Dump of file p.o

First: Kind 1 Version 1

Dictionary: FirstId 2
      2: Main
      3: %_EXITMAIN

Module: Flags $10 ModuleId 1 SegmentId Main
EntryPoint: Flags $08 Offset $00000034 EntryId
  %_EXITMAIN
Reference: Flags $10 Id: %_END Short Offsets
                       003A
Reference: Flags $10 Id: %_TERM Short Offsets
                       0036
Reference: Flags $10 Id: DELAY Short Offsets
                       002C
Reference: Flags $10 Id: %_INIT Short Offsets
                       000C
Reference: Flags $10 Id: %_BEGIN Short Offsets
                       0002
Content: Flags $00
Contents offset $0000 size $004C
000000: 4EBA 0000   'N...'   JSR
*+$0002   ; 00000002
000004: 4E56 0000   'NV..'   LINK
A6,#$0000
000008: 2C5F   ',_'   MOVEA.L
(A7)+,A6
00000A: 4EBA 0000   'N...'   JSR
*+$0002   ; 0000000C
00000E: 3B7C 0001 FFFC ';|....'   MOVE.W
#$0001,$FFFC(A5)
000014: 7005   'p.'   MOVEQ
#$05,D0
000016: C1ED FFFC   '....'   MULS.W
$FFFC(A5),D0
00001A: 3B40 FFFE   ';@..'   MOVE.W
D0,$FFFE(A5)
00001E: 302D FFFE   '0-..'   MOVE.W
$FFFE(A5),D0
000022: 48C0   'H.'   EXT.L   D0
000024: 2F00   '/.'   MOVE.L   D0,
  -(A7)
000026: 486D FFF8   'Hm..'   PEA
$FFF8(A5)
00002A: 4EBA 0000   'N...'   JSR
*+$0002   ; 0000002C
00002E: 3F2D FFFE   '?-..'   MOVE.W

```
$FFFE(A5),-(A7)
000032: A9C8               '..'                 TOOLBOX
$A9C8        ; SysBeep
000034: 4EBA 0000          'N...'               JSR
*+$0002             ; 00000036
000038: 4EBA 0000          'N...'               JSR
*+$0002             ; 0000003A
00003C: 4E75               'Nu'                 RTS
00003E: 4E5E               'N^'                 UNLK        A6
000040: 4E75               'Nu'                 RTS
000042: CE4F               '.O'                 AND.W
A7,D7
000044: 4953               'IS'                 $$$$
000046: 4520               'E '                 CHK.L       -
(A0),D2
000048: 2020               '  '                 MOVE.L      -
(A0),D0
00004A: 0000               '..'


Dictionary: FirstId 9
     9: __NOISE

Module:       Flags $19 ModuleId __NOISE Size 8

Dictionary: FirstId 4
     4: %_END
     5: %_TERM
     6: DELAY
     7: %_INIT
     8: %_BEGIN

Last
End of file p.o
```

Figure 10–6:   DumpObj display for Pascal program

out.

The -m option displays information only for a particular module. The module name is case sensitive. In Pascal, it will always be all caps, but in C the name typically uses mixed or lowercase letters.

How do you know what modules are in an object file? DumpObj -n produces a list of linker names defined in the object file. This includes all module names but also includes additional entry points within a module. Entry points are not normally used for Pascal or C routines but are easy to use in assembly language programming. Some of the standard MPW libraries use entry points to cluster several related routines into one module.

A more useful and detailed report is produced by DumpObj -d. This displays the summary headers for each module, including the segment the module was compiled in and any entry points.

In fact, DumpObj and a simple editing script can be used to produce a complete table of modules and entry points in the MPW-supplied libraries. The shell commands to do this are shown in Example 10–4.

The commands use a For loop to dump each of the standard libraries. A series of If statements is used to change the full pathname (such as 'HD:MPW:Libraries:Runtime.o') back to a more meaningful symbolic name ({Libraries}Runtime.o). A DumpObj -h is used to display the module headers.

When applied to an entire library, DumpObj -h is still quite verbose. A Search command is used to selectively extract lines containing ModuleId and EntryId for the module and entry point information, respectively. The format of this output is shown in Figure 10–7 for one of the smaller library files.

```
{CLibraries}Math.o
Dictionary:  FirstId 1
Module:      Flags $01 ModuleId   Size 0
Module:      Flags $01 ModuleId   Size 0
Module:      Flags $01 ModuleId   Size 0
Module:      Flags $01 ModuleId   Size 0
Module:      Flags $01 ModuleId   Size 0
Module:      Flags $01 ModuleId   Size 0
Module:      Flags $01 ModuleId _seam Size 0
Module:      Flags $00 ModuleId _fixexceptions SegmentId
Main
Module:      Flags $00 ModuleId _dirrnd SegmentId Main
Module:      Flags $08 ModuleId floor SegmentId Main
Module:      Flags $08 ModuleId ceil SegmentId Main
Module:      Flags $08 ModuleId fmod SegmentId Main
Module:      Flags $08 ModuleId tanh SegmentId Main
Module:      Flags $08 ModuleId sinh SegmentId Main
Module:      Flags $08 ModuleId cosh SegmentId Main
Module:      Flags $00 ModuleId _atrigcommon SegmentId
Main
Module:      Flags $08 ModuleId asin SegmentId Main
Module:      Flags $08 ModuleId acos SegmentId Main
Module:      Flags $08 ModuleId atan2 SegmentId Main
Module:      Flags $08 ModuleId hypot SegmentId Main
```

Figure 10–7:   Display from Example 10–4 before editing

This list is still unwieldy and contains a lot of redundant information. Ideally, we would like a list of modules (and entry points) in tabular form.

```
# Example 10-4: Displaying library modules and entry
points

# Create a new file and use it as the target window
New 'Modules & entry points'
Target "{Active}"

# Format the DumpObj for each of these files to target
Set CaseSensitive 1
For F in {Libraries}≈.o {CLibraries}≈.o {PLibraries}≈.o
# Find a more meaningful pathname
  If "{F}" =~ /{CLibraries}(≈)®1/
    Set Name '{CLibraries}'"{®1}"
  Else If "{F}" =~ /{PLibraries}(≈)®1/
    Set Name '{PLibraries}'"{®1}"
  Else If "{F}" =~ /{Libraries}(≈)®1/
    Set Name '{Libraries}'"{®1}"
  Else If "{F}" =~ /{MPW}(≈)®1/
    # in case the list is changed
    Set Name '{MPW}'"{®1}"
  Else
    Set Name "{F}"
  End
  Echo "---------------------------------------------"
  Echo "{Name}"
  # Look for 'ModuleId' or 'EntryId'
  DumpObj -d "{F}" | Search /Id /
  Echo
End > "{Target}"

# Save output in case there are problems
Save "{Target}"

# Reformat in tabular form
Find •
Replace -c ∞ ∂
  /•Module:≈ModuleId[∂t ]+([—∂t ]+)®1[∂t ]SegmentId[∂t ]+(≈)®2/ ∂
  "®2∂t®1"
Find •
Replace  -c ∞ /∂nEntryPoint:≈EntryId[∂t ](≈)®1∞/ "∂t®1"

# Remove any other lines left by DumpObj
Find •
Replace -c ∞  /•[A-Za-z]+: ≈∂n/ ""
```

Example 10–4: Displaying library modules and entry points

The remaining commands in Example 10–1 delete any meaningless lines and rearrange the information into the form:

    segment   module   entry entry   …

where any entry points following a module definition are cascaded at the end of the line. The edited version of Figure 10–7 is shown in Figure 10–8.

```
{CLibraries}Math.o
Main _fixexceptions
Main _dirrnd
Main floor
Main ceil
Main fmod
Main tanh
Main sinh
Main cosh
Main _atrigcommon
Main asin
Main acos
Main atan2
Main hypot
```

Figure 10–8:   Display from Example 10–4 after editing

When you have the edited library inventory, you can take the data to a spreadsheet or database to be sorted or used for further reference.

As with any commands that edit the result of an MPW tool, the Search and Replace commands are very sensitive to the exact format of the DumpObj output. If the format of DumpObj changes, the final result may not be meaningful. If you have any problems, revert the output file to see what the output was like before the Replace commands.

Also, because of the amount of data being manipulated, these commands can take several minutes. If you're starting up the example, now might be a good time to have a leisurely meal or read the Sunday *Times*.

10.3 Automating Program Build

MPW provides a range of tools to systematize the process of building programs.

The cornerstone of these tools is the Make command, which uses a list of dependencies to generate a list of shell commands to be performed. If several source files are used but only one is changed, Make will generate only the commands to compile the changed files. To quickly take advantage of Make, the CreateMake command can be used to create an initial list of dependencies.

MPW also includes a series of commands that work with an existing dependency file. BuildCommands provides a simple shortcut to the Make process, while BuildProgram both lists the necessary commands and executes them. Finally, BuildMenu creates a standard menu to access these build commands.

THE MAKE COMMAND

When supplied with the appropriate information, the Make command displays the minimum commands necessary to build a program compiled and linked using MPW.

Make can be used to simplify and shorten the process of program regeneration and to assure consistency among all the components of an MPW program. It is particularly useful when multiple source files are required to build a program and only some need recompilation each time.

The input to Make is a file defining the dependency relationships between the source files, the end result (such as an application), and any intermediate products. The output from Make is the list of commands to be performed. By default, Make only lists those commands it determines to be necessary by looking for any prerequisite file (such as a source file) that has been modified more recently than its resulting product (such as an object file). It uses the modification date recorded for each file by the File Manager but can also be forced to ignore those dates and either rebuild everything or modify them to make everything seem up to date.

Make

Display commands necessary to build program

Syntax:

Make *file* …   Generate commands to build each *file*

Options:

-d *name=string*	Define variable *name* to be *string*
-e	Rebuild everything, ignoring change dates
-f *makefile*	Read dependency rules from *makefile*
-p	Display progress report
-t	Bring files up to date by changing modification Dates only
-v	Suppress all warning messages

Remarks:

If no *makefile* is specified with a -f option, the file Makefile in the current directory is used.

Input/Output:

Output   Shell commands to be executed

Examples:

Make   foo

> Generate commands to rebuild foo from rules
> in Makefile

Make Test -f Test.make

> Generate commands to rebuild Test from rules
> in Test.make

If you're familiar with its UNIX namesake, Make under MPW works slightly differently. Make does not automatically execute the commands necessary to build the program. Instead, it displays the commands in the active window, which you then select to rebuild the program.

The -t option can be used when you know nothing needs to be changed, such as when you modify the comments in a source file. The -e option ("everything") will rebuild the program from scratch, which makes a good step of last resort if your program is crashing and you suspect (or hope) something was fouled up during the build process.

MPW provides an easy way to build Make input files using default dependency rules. The CreateMake command will generate an input file using Pascal, C, assembler, resource files, and object files. It will conclude with a Link command using the appropriate options and libraries.

CreateMake

Generate a default Make input file

Syntax:

CreateMake *program file* ...   create rules to *program* from
                                       each *file*

Options:

-Application   create rules to build *program* as an application
-DA   create rules to build *program* as a desk
                          accessory
-Tool   create rules to build *program* as an MPW tool

Remarks:

The output is a file *program*.make containing suitable dependency rules for use in a subsequent Make command. The CreateMake command includes rules for each *file* in *program* .make according to the following guidelines:

file .a   Assemble *file* .a to *file* a.o; link *file* .c.o as part of *program*

file .c   Compile *file* .c to *file* .c.o; link *file* .c.o as part of *program*

file .p   Compile *file* .p to *file* .p.o; link *file* .p.o as part of *program*

file .o   Link *file* .o as part of *program*

file .r   Compile resources in *file* .r to resource fork of *program*

By default, CreateMake assumes that *program* will be built as an application, and links in all the libraries necessary for the source files used. Other options will change the libraries used and the Link options generated.

Examples:

```
CreateMake Test Test.p
```
                create Test.make to build Pascal program Test

The command

```
CreateMake Sketch Sketch.c Sketch.p Sketch.a Sketch.r
    SketchLib.o
```

builds a Make dependency file named Sketch.make. It defines an application program Sketch built from C, Pascal, and assembly sources compiled into object files, a Rez input file, an application specific object file, and whatever libraries are likely to be needed to make the complete application. The file Sketch.make created by this command is shown in Figure 10-9.

To use this file, you would then type

```
Make Sketch -f Sketch.make
```

which would display the list of commands necessary to compile and link Sketch. The commands would be selected and entered, as with any other generated MPW commands.

To understand how these rules work, it is necessary to examine the syntax of the dependency rules used by Make.

```
#    File:        Sketch.make
#    Target:      Sketch
#    Sources:     Sketch.c Sketch.p Sketch.a Sketch.r
#    Created:     Tue, Jun 9, 1987 11:19:35 AM

Sketch.c.o ƒ Sketch.make Sketch.c
  C Sketch.c
Sketch.p.o ƒ Sketch.make Sketch.p
  Pascal Sketch.p
Sketch.a.o ƒ Sketch.make Sketch.a
  Asm Sketch.a
Sketch ƒƒ Sketch.make Sketch.r
  Rez -append Sketch.r -o Sketch
Sketch ƒƒ Sketch.make SketchLib.o Sketch.c.o Sketch.p.o
Sketch.a.o
  Link -w -t APPL -c '????' ∂
    SketchLib.o ∂
    Sketch.c.o ∂
    Sketch.p.o ∂
    Sketch.a.o ∂
    "{Libraries}"Interface.o ∂
    "{CLibraries}"CRuntime.o ∂
    "{CLibraries}"StdCLib.o ∂
    "{CLibraries}"CSANELib.o ∂
    "{CLibraries}"Math.o ∂
    "{CLibraries}"CInterface.o ∂
    "{PLibraries}"PasLib.o ∂
    "{PLibraries}"SANELib.o ∂
    -o Sketch
```

Figure 10–9:   Sample dependency file from CreateMake

MAKE DEPENDENCY RULES

The rules used by Make to determine what commands should be run are contained in a dependency file, normally `Makefile` in the current directory or a program-specific file of the form `program.make`. The syntax for the statements parallels that for MPW commands, including quoting, comments, the use of shell variables, and line continuation.

Each rule has the general form:

> *newfile* ƒ *oldfile* ...
>   *commands*
>
>   ...

where each of the *commands* is preceded by either a space or tab.

Make examines these rules, builds a dependency tree, and determines which rules are relevant to building the requested program. It may need to use several rules if, for example, building the program requires preprocessor, compile, resource compile, and link steps.

If *newfile* is needed but doesn't exist or *oldfile* has been changed since *newfile* was built, Make will display the series of commands specified in the particular rule.

Suppose you are working on an MPW tool called Add, written in Pascal. As has been discussed earlier, you would first compile the Add.p source file into an object file, then link the object file to provide executable code. These two sequential dependencies are diagramed in Figure 10–10.

These dependency relationships are easily defined using the Make syntax. Your Makefile (or Add.make file) might look like

```
Add.p.o ƒ Add.p
    Pascal Add.p
Add ƒ Add.p.o
    Link -o Add Add.p.o -t MPST -c 'MPS ' ∂
        {Libraries}Runtime.o {PLibraries}PasLib.o
```

Assuming Add.p had not been compiled since it was last changed,

```
Make Add
```

would display the commands

```
Pascal Add.p
Link -o Add Add.p.o -t MPST -c 'MPS ' ∂
    HD:MPW:Libraries:Runtime.o
    HD:MPW:Libraries:PLibraries:PasLib.o
```

in the active window. If it had been compiled—that is, the modification date for Add.p.o is more recent than that for Add.p—only the command

```
Link -o Add Add.p.o -t MPST -c 'MPS ' ∂
    HD:MPW:Libraries:Runtime.o
    HD:MPW:Libraries:PLibraries:PasLib.o
```

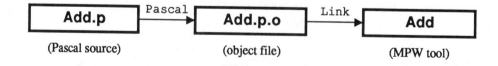

| **Add.p** | Pascal | **Add.p.o** | Link | **Add** |

(Pascal source)   (object file)   (MPW tool)

Figure 10–10:   Single dependency path

would be displayed. In either case, you would select the command(s) and then execute them.

Two quick caveats for the example. First, the `Make` command knows by default how to compile a Pascal program, so the first rule is not strictly necessary and thus will be omitted for the remainder of this example. Also, the `Makefile` for an application Add would be very similar, but the `Link` options and libraries used would differ slightly.

`Make` recognizes symbolic names in the commands to refer to the files mentioned in the dependency list. The previous rule could be restated as

```
Add ƒ Add.p.o
    Link -o {Targ} {NewerDeps} -t MPST -c 'MPS ' ∂
        {Libraries}Runtime.o {PLibraries}PasLib.o
```

where {Targ} refers to the target to be built (Add) and {NewerDeps} is the list of prerequisite files newer than the target. If the `Link` command is being run, we know Add.p.o is newer, since it's the only prequisite.

However, the target can also be described as depending on multiple prerequisites, if necessary. For example, some programs may require linking with more than one file. Suppose you decide to add floating-point arithmetic to Add but define the source for that arithmetic in a separate file, AddFloat.p. This second file would be compiled separately and linked together in the final step, as illustrated by Figure 10–11.

In this case, the dependency rules would look like

```
Add ƒ Add.p.o AddFloat.p.o
    Link -o
        {Targ} Add.p.o AddFloat.p.o -t MPST -c 'MPS ' ∂
        {Libraries}Runtime.o {PLibraries}PasLib.o
```

Make would generate commands to relink the program if either Add.p.o or AddFloat.p.o were changed.

Finally, there will be occasions in which there are multiple dependency paths, but each path terminates in a separate command rather than being

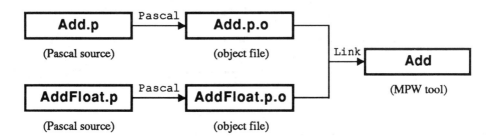

Figure 10–11:   Merged dependency paths

part of the same final command (typically Link) that constructs the target. The best example is when resources are used to build a program, since both a Rez and a Link are typically used.

For example, Add may instead depend on Pascal source in Add.p and resource source contained in Add.r. Separate Link and Rez commands terminate each dependency path, as shown in Figure 10–12.

To express such disjointed paths, a special form of dependency rule is used. This uses a *ff* symbol and was, in fact, shown in the earlier CreateMake example. For our Add program, the rules might look like:

```
Add ff Add.p.o
    Link -o {Targ} Add.p.o -t MPST -c 'MPS ' ∂
        {Libraries}Runtime.o {PLibraries}PasLib.o
Add ff Add.r
    Rez -a -o {Targ} Add.r
```

We can read these rules as saying:

- If Add.p.o is newer than Add, link Add.p.o and place the 'CODE' resources in Add

- If Add.r is newer than Add, compile the resources defined in Add.r and append them to Add.

Make may generate commands necessary for both steps if both are out of date. Note that the analysis of the dates takes place before the actual building commands—otherwise, linking a new Add would always make Add newer than Add.r, and thus Add.r would not be compiled.

DEFAULT DEPENDENCY RULES

Make also recognizes rules that do not mention specific targets by name but define default operations based on file name suffixes, such as .p and .p.o. These rules take effect only if a specific rule for the desired file is not given.

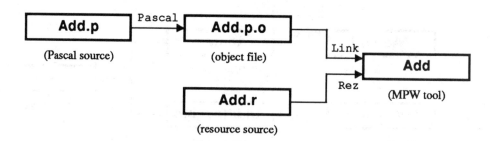

Figure 10–12:   Separate dependency paths

Some of these rules are built in. For example, Make knows how to compile Pascal and C programs. By default, Make can build [*file*].p.o from [*file*].p using a command equivalent to

```
Pascal {POptions} [file].p
```

It also knows how to make [*file*].c.o from [*file*].c using the command

```
C {COptions} [file].c
```

Variables such as {COptions} and {POptions} can be defined as exported shell variables, as in

```
Set COptions '-g'
Export COptions
```

and Make will automatically use their value.

Alternately, variables can be defined in the Make dependency file using lines of the form:

```
COptions = -i "{MPW}MyIncludes:"
POptions = -k "{MPW}LOAD_Files"
```

You should not use both ways to define the same symbol since Make will complain about a duplicate definition.

Such symbolic names are often used to define the list of standard libraries to be used in linking a program since you may have a separate rule for each program name. A definition such as

```
CLibs ={CLibraries}CRuntime.o ∂
   {CLibraries}StdCLib.o ∂
   {CLibraries}CSANELib.o ∂
   {CLibraries}CInterface.o
PLibs ={Libraries}Runtime.o ∂
   {PLibraries}PasLib.o ∂
   {PLibraries}SANELib.o ∂
   {Libraries}Interface.o
```

would allow the earlier Link rule to be rewritten as

```
Add ƒ Add.p.o
   Link -w -o
     {Targ} {NewerDeps} -t MPST -c 'MPS ' {PLibs}
```

Including more libraries than you need (hence the -w to suppress warnings) will slow your Link slightly but will simplify the process of adding new programs to your Make rules.

Make also allows you to define your own default rules. For example, instead of assigning a value to COptions, you could instead write a dependency rule

```
.c.o ƒ .c
    C -g {Default}.c
```

where {Default} is automatically replaced by the file name, stripped of its suffix. Then the command

```
Make foo.c.o
```

would generate

```
C -g foo.c
```

Such dependency rules can also be used for target file names that have no suffix. With the dependency rule

```
ƒ .c.o
   Link -o
      {Default} -ot MPST -oc 'MPS ' {Default}.c.o ∂
{CLibs}
```

the command

```
Make foo
```

might generate

```
C -g foo.c
Link -o foo -ot MPST -oc 'MPS ' foo.c.o ∂
HD:MPW:CLibraries:CRuntime.o
HD:MPW:CLibraries:CInterface.o
```

However, you must realize that any time that a target matches the name pattern on the left side of a default rule, Make will search for the components on the right side, *or any rules that might make them*. This means that default rules that specify null suffixes will slow Make considerably.

If you're going to make extensive use of Make, you should probably develop a standard set of rules that will be used for all programs. In particular, if you're going to be building multiple progjects in several folders, you may wish to develop a standard strategy. There are three ways you can define dependency rules:

- In the Makefile in each folder.

- Symbols can be defined globally. Variables such as {COptions} and

{PLibs} can be defined in UserStartup and exported.

- You can change the default rules used by Make.

The default rules used by Make are just standard text dependency rules stored in the data fork of the Make command. If you edit the data fork, you can modify or add to these default rules.

Since Make is an MPW tool, a file of type 'MPST', the **Open** menu command will not normally allow you to edit it. There are two ways around this. One way is to change the file type to 'TEXT', edit the data fork, and then change the file type back to 'MPST'. This will add a shell editing resource to the file, but the resource will be ignored when the tool is run.

A second approach is to copy only the data fork of Make to a text file, make the changes, and then copy the data fork back, as shown in Figure 10–13. With either approach, you should probably first save a copy of the original Make as a precaution.

BUILDING COMMANDS

Version 2.0 of MPW includes a series of commands to make it easier to build programs. These commands generally begin with the word "Build." All are defined by command files, so they can be modified to suit your specific requirements.

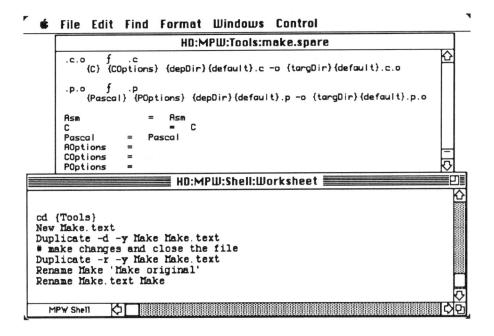

Figure 10–13: Editing Make's data fork

The `BuildCommands` command offers a slight advantage over the `Make` command in that it automatically uses the custom `Make` dependency file created by the `CreateMake` command. It is otherwise similar to `Make`, and, like `Make`, requires a dependency file before it can list the necessary commands to (re)build a program.

BuildCommands

Display commands necessary to build a program

Syntax:

`BuildCommands` *program*	Display commands necessary to rebuild *program*

Options:

`-e`	Rebuild everything, ignoring change dates

Remarks:

`BuildCommands` uses `Make` to analyze dependencies and display the necessary build commands. Any additional parameters to `BuildCommands` will be passed directly to `Make`.

The command

        `BuildCommands` *program*

is equivalent to

        `Make` *program* `-f` *program* `.make`

if [program].make exists, and

        `Make` *program* `-f Makefile`

if it does not exist. Either *program*.make or `Makefile` must contain the dependency rules necessary to build *program*.

Input/Output:

Output	Shell commands to be executed

Examples:

`BuildCommands Normal`	Display commands necessary to build `Normal`

A more significant advantage comes from the `BuildProgram` command, which determines the necessary MPW commands to build a program, then executes them.

BuildProgram

Build a target program

Syntax:

BuildProgram *program*   Perform commands necessary to
                                rebuild *program*

Options:

-e   Rebuild everything, ignoring change
                                dates

Remarks:

BuildProgram is similar to BuildCommands except that it also performs
the necessary commands. It creates a temporary file in the same directory
as the target program to hold those commands.

Any additional parameters to BuildProgram will be passed directly to
Make.

Input/Output:

Output   Progress report on commands as they
                                are executed

Examples:

BuildCommands -e Fourier Build program Fourier from scratch

Once your dependency files are in place, BuildProgram is probably the
most convenient command to use in rebuilding a program that you're
constantly making changes to. The name may be too long to use on a regular
basis, so you might want to define aliases to shorten the typing, as in:

```
Alias Bld 'BuildProgram'
Alias BldAll 'BuildProgram -e'
```

In this case, BldAll would automatically rebuild the program from scratch,
such as when the resource fork contains resources that should be deleted
from the next version of the program.

You can also use custom menu commands to display or execute the build
commands. Such a menu is created by the BuildMenu command, which you
may wish to include in your UserStartup file.

BuildMenu

Create the Build menu

Syntax:

BuildMenu   Perform commands necessary to rebuild
                             [program]

Remarks:

The new menu, entitled **Build**, includes commands to build a program or display the commands necessary to build a program. It also includes "Full Build" options, which rebuilds every intermediate product, without regard to the most recent change date.

Examples:

BuildMenu   Create the Build menu

Chapter 11

MacApp

It certainly is no secret that developing programs for the Macintosh is a complex process, particularly since any program must support Apple's extensive user interface in addition to whatever operations the program might perform on another computer.

To reduce the effort required to develop Macintosh programs, particularly those functions that are common to all programs, Apple's research team spent several years developing a standard application shell that could be used over and over. The result was MacApp, an extensible Macintosh application library, which is available as a separate component of MPW.

MacApp relies on the principles of object-oriented programming to specify standard actions that can be selectively extended or replaced by the developer. If you're not familiar with object-oriented programming, this chapter explains the general concepts as they relate to MacApp.

Release 1.1 of MacApp is a library of standard operations that can be used from a hybrid object-oriented language based on Pascal. This language, known as Object Pascal, is built into the MPW Pascal compiler, and the use of the Object Pascal extensions is described here.

Note that it is possible to use Object Pascal without MacApp. If you are updating a large Macintosh program, this would be a good approach towards developing an extensible library of your own code that could be used with other programs. Because of its design, MacApp cannot be used without an object-oriented language; the MPW Pascal compiler for Object Pascal is the only one that initially supports MacApp, although others are planned.

This chapter provides a brief overview of the MacApp concepts and how to build a MacApp program with MPW. A more detailed tutorial is available in the "Cookbook" chapter of the *MacApp Programmer's Reference*. The

589

definitive MacApp reference sections are provided by other chapters of that manual, as well as the library source code provided with MacApp. The source code can also be purchased separately from APDA.

Compared to most object-oriented languages, Apple uses a different and somewhat simpler terminology in describing concepts in Object Pascal and MacApp. This chapter uses Apple's terminology for consistency with the MPW Pascal and MacApp documentation.

11.1 Object-Oriented Programming

Object-oriented programming is an approach to writing programs popularized by the Smalltalk programming environment. It seems appropriate that MPW include an object-oriented programming language and library as major components, since both the Macintosh and MPW designs were heavily influenced by the early Smalltalk workstations.

As used today, the concept of object-oriented programming depends on two ideas. The first is that programs are defined by a series of active data structures, each with associated code. Secondly, new structures are defined in terms of existing structures, with only a description of the differences necessary to implement the actions of the new structures.

WHAT IS OBJECT-ORIENTED PROGRAMMING?

The phrase "object-oriented programming" has been much used (and abused) in the 1980s, much as "structured programming" was in the 1970s. The phrase has different meanings to different people.

However, some of the languages generally considered to be "object-oriented" are listed in Table 11–1. Most of these languages are hybrid languages based on extensions to an existing language, as Object Pascal is based on Pascal; among those listed, only Smalltalk is a completely new language built entirely around an object-oriented framework.

An important characteristic of object-oriented programming is the use of generic operations with dissimilar data structures. These data structures are referred to as "objects." In a drawing program, these objects might represent individual shapes. In a flight simulator, they might correspond to physical things, such as an airplane or a gauge. The objects can also correspond to more abstract concepts.

The example of shape objects is often used to illustrate such generic operations. A draw operation might be performed on a line object and a circle object but with different results. For the line, the operation would change the color of all the pixels between two points, while for the circle, the color would be changed for all points a given distance from the center point.

Language	Based on
Smalltalk	—
Clascal	Pascal
Object Pascal	Pascal
C++	C
Objective-C	C
Simula	Algol
Flavors	Lisp
Loops	Lisp
CommonLoops	Lisp
Neon	Forth
Object Logo	Logo

Table 11–1: Object-oriented languages

In an algorithmic or procedural language such as Pascal, the decision to treat the two types differently is made by each type of operation. If squares and polygons are added, the drawing code that formerly checked for lines and circles must be modified to check for each of the new types.

In an object-oriented language, each piece of code requests a similar operation, in this case, drawing a shape on the screen. The decision on how to draw a shape is associated with each shape, so if new shapes are added, the only change is to add a procedure for each object to draw the new type. The procedure (or function) associated with an object type is known as a "method" for that object.

Advocates of some procedural languages—notably Ada—argue that such languages provide data abstractions and generic operations and, hence, are object oriented. However, in these strongly typed languages, the type of each data operand is fixed at compile time, thus statically determining the operation that will be performed when the program is run.

By most definitions, an object-oriented language is a language that allows the determination of an action to be deferred until the program is run. This allows dynamic selection at run time of the code corresponding to the actual type used, a process often referred to as dynamic binding.

For example, a redraw routine might be defined for a variety of shapes, such as a circle or a line. Each time the routine is called, the object-oriented language selects the circle or line drawing operation, depending on which shape is used.

To allow structuring of related object types, many object-oriented languages allow defining a new object type in terms of an existing type. By default, the new object will retain all the properties of the existing object, but can selectively replace or extend any of those properties, in addition to adding new properties The definition of a new object type in terms of an existing type is referred to as "inheritance."

It is the combination of both dynamic binding and inheritance that gives the object-oriented approach its power and flexibility.

AN ALTERNATE VIEW

In Object Pascal and MacApp, method calls are conceptually very similar to procedure calls, except that they always operate on an associated data structure, the object. The terminology used in the MacApp documentation is thus very similar to that for standard Pascal.

Other discussions of object-oriented programming adopt different terminology. To read about the subject in professional journals, magazines, other books, and so on, you may first need a brief orientation to the jargon used by the object-oriented programming "jocks."

One common way to describe interactions in object-oriented programs is the "object-message" metaphor, in which an operation in a program is described in terms of a "message" sent to an object. The object, in turn, "decides" what to do in response to the message.

Although this anthropomorphic description makes a compiled program more human than it is, it does help some people understand the object concept better and thus is frequently found. The object-message metaphor emphasizes the active selection made "by" each object, even when the actual implementation is through more prosaic procedural calls.

Another approach toward describing object-oriented programs is the use of a noun-verb syntax, with each program statement mapped onto a simple sentence. In this case, the noun is the object, such as "First circle"; the verb is the operation to be performed, e.g., "draw." We can express the sentences as commands to the program, imperative sentences with the verb before the noun. We might then have the statements:

Draw circle
Draw line
Erase circle

In this case, "draw circle" is not the same statement as "draw line" even though they share the same verb (message), while "draw circle" is different from "erase circle" even though they share the same noun (object).

Within this framework, objects are active data structures that have associated "behaviors" in response to each message. As implemented by most languages, an object is a data structure (usually dynamically allocated) that has one or more associated procedures. What is unusual about these procedures is that they are dynamically selected at run time for each object. Dynamic typing prevents complete resolution of procedures at compile time, although compiled languages (like Object Pascal) perform some compile time analysis to reject obviously incompatible operations.

In most object-oriented languages, each behavior is associated with a specific type of object. Because it is so fundamental to the operation of an object-oriented program, the phrase "type of object" is often given a special name, "class."

When you create an object of a particular type, its future behaviors will be determined by its type: all objects of the same type will have the same behavior. The procedures that implement these behaviors are methods. Methods are different from ordinary procedures in two ways.

First, there can be many procedures named "Draw," as many as one procedure for each type of object. Draw would be the message name, while the behavior for all objects of a given type would be defined by the corresponding method for that type, such as a Draw method for a circle, a Draw for a line, and a Draw for a square.

Second, each method includes an implied parameter referencing the associated data structure or object. A Draw method for a circle would, for example, always reference a circle-type object. This object is referred to by the psuedovariable `self` in most object-oriented languages.

It is certainly possible to force object-oriented languages to be used in a procedural way. One could define only a single object, call it "Global," and define procedures for it. Global's data would, of course, be shared by all the procedures.

But used to its fullest, the object-oriented framework suggests another approach, one structured around operations on a series of different data structures. In Object Pascal and other such languages, you would first determine types of similar objects and then define procedures to perform operations on those types of objects.

BEHAVIOR INHERITANCE

When defining a new type of object, there may be many similarities to an object type already in existence. If the new object type is defined in terms of the old object type, we say the new type "inherits" properties from the older type.

In the Macintosh Toolbox, for example, a dialog box has most of the properties of a window, both in terms of the data retained and its behaviors in response to Toolbox events. A dialog box also has some new properties, such as maintaining a list of dialog items. Thus, you would define a dialog box object type in terms of a window object and then add new methods to handle the dialog items.

Another case in which you use inheritance is when two types have several things in common, and thus it is useful to define a third type that describes those properties shared by both types. There's no reason why the common inheritance is limited to two types, of course. The book *Object-Oriented Programming for the Macintosh* takes this to extremes by building a major example around the quadilateral type, which defines common properties inherited by the square, rectangle, rhombus, and parallelogram object types.

In Object Pascal, the existing type used to define other objects is the "ancestor." A type defined in terms of the ancestor is termed a "descendant." This corresponds to the intuitive meaning of "inherit," although it may be straining the metaphor somewhat.

As with the genealogical usage, ancestry is transitive so that if A is an ancestor of B and B is an ancestor of C, A is an ancestor of C. Instead of the parent-child relationship, Object Pascal refers to the "immediate ancestor" and "immediate descendant," on those rare occasions when it's important to distinguish the depth of the ancestry tree.

However, for most purposes, it doesn't matter how remote the ancestry is. A new type inherits the properties of all its ancestors by default, which are supplemented by its own new properties.

A new type can also define behaviors that are different from those existing for its ancestors. We would say that the descendant type "overrides" the methods of the ancestor.

A descendant type need only override those methods that differ between it and its ancestor. If the behavior of the descendant includes that of the ancestor, the new method need only specify the additional actions. This suggests that a library of object types might be even more powerful than a subroutine library in that small differences for user-defined operations can be specified without duplicating or replacing the library methods. This is, in fact, the fundamental concept behind the MacApp expandable application.

Using MacApp terms, you would "customize" a library type by using it as the ancestor of your own newly defined object that has slightly different properties.

Before proceeding further, it is necessary to note the different terminology used by languages other than Object Pascal. In Smalltalk and many other languages, the ancestor of an object is its "superclass," and the descendant a "subclass." To put it another way, a subclass inherits properties from its superclass. When defining a new class, Smalltalk users refer to "subclassing" an existing class. When used as a verb, the Smalltalk term "subclass" is the same as the MacApp "customize."

The differences in terminology grew out of Apple's attempts to teach object-oriented programming using a Smalltalk-like terminology. In actual practice, the concept of types and ancestry proved easier to teach than classes and superclasses.

Because the simpler Object Pascal terminology is used by MacApp, it will be adopted throughout the remainder of the chapter. If you're using another language with MacApp, you should mentally translate the terms used by the language documentation.

EXAMPLE: A ROAD RACE

To illustrate the object-message and behavior inheritance concepts, let's look at an imaginary problem. For purposes of illustration, we'll use the most illustrative (as opposed to the most efficient) design for the problem solution.

Suppose you were designing an auto racing game in which two or more players compete against each other or against the computer. Each player might control the speed and direction of his or her car up to the limit of a predetermined maximum speed. Each car would have a location on the highway, and the winning car would be the one that reached the destination first.

The problem suggests using a data structure to represent each car in the game, since there might be many cars. In an ordinary Pascal program, Auto might be a record type, with separate records allocated for each car. The Pascal program would also have several routines to do car operations, such as calculating the car's next position, displaying it on the screen, and so on.

In an object-oriented language such as Object Pascal or Smalltalk, there would be a similar data structure for the car. However, the association between the routines and the data structure would be formalized. Instead of several routines that accept a data structure as one of the parameters, you would use routines that are inherently associated with the data structure. As with many other programming abstractions, there's no rule that says you *must* use this approach, but taking advantage of the capability provides a clearer and more coherent design.

So, as with the procedural solution, your object-oriented game would use an Auto data structure. It has variables for location, speed, direction, and a maximum speed. If you're writing your program in Object Pascal, these fields of an object would be declared in much the same way that fields of a record are declared. However, the object would also have associated procedures (or methods).

Once the game is working, you decide to spice it up. Suppose you're going to add off-road driving and give each driver a choice of cars. One would provide speed on the highway, the other would be able to off-road shortcuts. The driving characteristics of the two cars might differ; you might also use different symbols to display the cars on the screen.

Here it might make more sense to have two different types of cars declared as objects, one each for the sports car and the off-road vehicle. Each might have different routines for cornering and drawing the icon on the screen. The off road vehicle might also have a method for driving off-road.

You wouldn't want to have to completely rework your existing code or to duplicate the code between the two types of cars. Instead, you could define the common properties as associated with the Auto type and then customize this type for each car. A diagram suggesting this relationship is given by Figure 11–1. The diagram also shows the variables (fields) and routines (methods) associated with each type.

In this case, the Auto object type has two descendant types, Ferrari and Jeep. Conversely, these two types share a common ancestor, Auto. The two descendant types automatically inherit all the properties of the ancestor, including the speed, direction, and location fields. The two types also share the ancestor's routines for common operations, such as driving down the highway.

Now suppose you want to extend your program to be an all-world racing game, in which the players might switch to a ship at the ocean's edge. Others might choose to use an airplane—in the interest of fairness, a propeller-driven one—for the entire race. All these vehicles share a common property, which is moving across the playing field. Each vehicle, however, implements it differently:

- Autos can drive along a road
- Jeeps can drive on land without a road
- Ships travel in a straight line on the water
- Planes can move in a straight line over any surface.

Although the original design was based on cars, perhaps cars are now an aberration. Ships and planes travel in straight lines, while autos are the only vehicles that must follow roads. So you might want to make moving (rather than driving) be the standard operation, with "normal" vehicles moving from point to point. Ships are confined to water. Autos must drive on roads, but the Jeep knows how to drive off road. The new structure of the object types suggested by these changes is given by Figure 11–2.

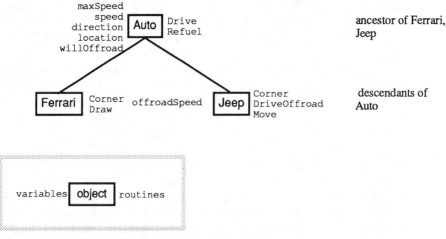

Figure 11–1: Object type hierarchy for driving game

In the new design, the Vehicle type is the ancestor to all types. Instead of being a fundamental object type, Auto is now defined in terms of Vehicle. Normally, you'll want to go in the other direction—define new objects in terms of Auto rather than redefine Auto in terms of a new object—but such changes can be expected as you develop a program's design.

As before, the Ferrari and Jeep have Auto as their immediate ancestor, but they know that Vehicle is a more distance ancestor type. A Ship and a Plane are each immediate descendants of Vehicle.

In addition, we can see the properties of a vehicle are common to the Vehicle and all its descendants. We call this the "domain" of the vehicle type, which includes all types shown in the diagram.

11.2 Object Pascal

An optional component of MPW is the MPW Pascal compiler. In addition to compiling standard Pascal programs, the MPW compiler will also compile programs written in an object-oriented language, Object Pascal, that was used to develop the MacApp libraries.

The Object Pascal language includes all of the features of Pascal, augmented with a limited number of object-oriented features. It has been deliberately kept simple to make it easy for Pascal programmers to learn.

Object Pascal can be used without MacApp, and a simple example of such a program is given in this section. However, since the likely use of Object

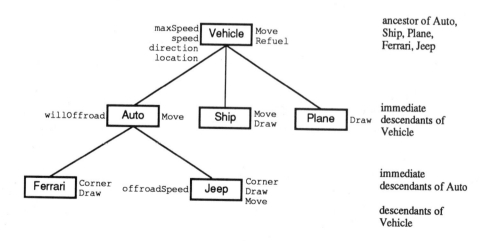

Figure 11–2: Expanded game object type hierarchy

Pascal is to access the MacApp library, the declarations shown here are given in a form consistent with the MacApp naming conventions, the most obvious being the use of the prefix "T" for describing types of objects and "f" for object fields. The complete MacApp conventions are described in the next section.

INTRODUCTION

After 2 years' experience with Clascal, Apple's development group collaborated with Pascal author Niklaus Wirth to refine the design into a new language. The result, Object Pascal, is intended to be a minimal object-oriented extension to Pascal that is easy for existing Pascal programmers to learn. As a consequence, its authors deliberately omitted many features of more complete (and complex) languages.

"Object-oriented programming has been around for a long time, and it's had a hard time obtaining acceptance. Object Pascal is intended to move a large number of programmers in a painless way," explained Larry Tesler, Apple's vice president for Advanced Technology and the mentor of the MacApp development team.

"We sacrificed certain features found in other object-oriented languages because we felt their complexity outweighed the benefits they might have offered," Tesler wrote. Many of those decisions were based on the experiences using and teaching the predecessor language, Clascal.

Object Pascal incorporates Pascal as a proper subset. Programmers using the MPW Pascal compiler may not even be aware that it supports Object Pascal extensions. Those extensions are few in number, as summarized in Table 11–2 and described in the remainder of this section.

DECLARING OBJECTS

The definition of an object in Object Pascal is analogous to the definition of a record in Pascal. As with records, each object declared in the TYPE section of a program includes a declaration of an object's fields. However, the declaration may also include a list of associated procedures.

An object type is a structured type similar to a record in that it includes a list of component fields. Unlike a record type, an object type cannot have variant sections describing different field layouts. A separate mechanism (inheritance) is provided for describing related objects that have both common and dissimilar usages, as will be discussed later.

In addition to component fields, an object type may also include a group of component procedures, which describe standard operations to be performed on the object. The fields and procedures together describe the properties of the object.

Operations on the contents of an object are normally performed through these dedicated procedures. Direct access to the fields allows objects to be used in a way that is similar to records. As a matter of style, any operation that modifies these fields should be through a method for that object.

Declaring object types

```
TYPE
  TSimpleObject = OBJECT   { No ancestor type }
    fData: Handle;
    PROCEDURE SomeProc;
  END;

  TMyObject = OBJECT(TObject)   { Extends TObject }
    fValue: LONGINT;
    FUNCTION AFunc: INTEGER;
  END;
```

Declaring and allocating objects

```
VAR
  oneofmine: TMyObject;
BEGIN
  NEW(oneofmine);
  ...
  oneofmine.Free;
```

Referencing fields and methods

```
Write(oneofmine.fValue);
Write(oneofmine.AFunc);
```

Implementing methods

```
FUNCTION TMyObject.AFunc: INTEGER;
BEGIN
  AFunc := 1;
END;
```

Inheritance

```
TAnotherObject = OBJECT(TMyObject)
  { Replaces TMyObject }
  FUNCTION AFunc: INTEGER; OVERRIDE;
END;

FUNCTION TAnotherObject.AFunc: INTEGER;
BEGIN
  AFunc := 2 + INHERITED AFunc;   { will return 3 }
END;
```

Table 11–2: Object Pascal extensions to Pascal

A simple object type is declared in a manner similar to a Pascal record, as in:

```
TYPE
    THuman = OBJECT
        fAge: INTEGER;
        fWeight: REAL;
        fSex: GenderType;
    END;
```

As with Pascal types, new object types are declared in the TYPE section of a program. Unnamed types (the so-called "anonymous" type of Pascal) used for a single variable or variable list are not allowed for object types.

Most other languages use the term "class" to describe the object type, and this was the term that gave Clascal its name. However, an object type is not much different from any other type in Object Pascal, so this simplified terminology was adopted for ease of learning.

Once declared, the name of the object type defines a new data type, which is called the "reference type." Any variable declared using this type is a "reference variable." Each reference variable may denote a single dynamically allocated object.

Using the prior example, the object type THuman defines a reference type THuman, and in the fragment

```
VAR
    JohnDoe: THuman;

PROCEDURE FairyTail(bard: THuman);
VAR
    butcher, baker, candlemaker: THuman;
BEGIN
    ...
END;
```

the global variable JohnDoe, the parameter bard, and the local variables butcher, baker, and candlemaker are all reference variables for an object of type THuman.

Each object in Object Pascal is dynamically allocated. Objects are allocated using the NEW pseudo-function, similar to the Pascal usage for allocating a record. The function is called with one VAR parameter, a reference variable of the appropriate type, as in:

```
NEW(JohnDoe);
```

The reference variable may also have a value of NIL, which indicates a reference to no object at all. Such a variable should not be used until a subsequent assignment to a non-NIL value.

No guarantees are made as to the actual representation of the reference type, and in particular, it is not assignment compatible with pointer types. In MPW Pascal, an object reference type is represented as a handle to a relocatable block to allow for heap compaction of the relocatable objects. This distinction should be transparent, as reference variables (unlike pointers) are never dereferenced.

Of course, reference types can be used as with any other type. Reference variables will often be used as fields to indicate relationships between various objects.

Once assigned a value, fields of an object can be accessed using the reference variable name and its corresponding field name. However, unlike Pascal pointer types, dereferencing operators are not used.

Using the earlier declarations, the following would reference fields of a THuman object:

```
IF baker.fSex = MaleGender THEN
  Write('The baker weights ',baker.fWeight);
  WriteLn(', and is ',baker.fAge,' years old.')
END;
```

Note that references to the object's field fSex use the notation baker.fSex. This is contrasted with bakerptr^.fSex used for Pascal records and bakerhand^^.fSex for a handle to a Pascal record.

If a series of operations is to be performed on a single object, the Pascal statement WITH can be used to eliminate the need for using the reference variable qualifier and simplify the coding. The previous example becomes:

```
WITH baker DO
BEGIN
  IF fSex = MaleGender THEN
    Write('The baker weights ', fWeight);
    WriteLn(', and is ', fAge,' years old.')
  END
END;
```

METHOD PROCEDURES

An object primarily differs from a record in that it includes component procedures and functions, or methods. Any procedure declared within a declaration of an object type is considered to be a method for that object type, and all methods of an object type must be so declared.

Each object type will usually include a definition of one or more corresponding methods. Methods are defined using the syntax common to other Pascal routine declarations, either as a PROCEDURE or a FUNCTION. This includes typing of the parameters, as well as the type of a function's return value. The parameter list does not include the object itself, since that is supplied as an implied parameter to all methods.

To take the preceding example, a complete description of the THuman object type might be:

```
TYPE
   GenderType = (MaleGender, FemaleGender);
   THuman = OBJECT
      fAge: INTEGER;
      fWeight: REAL;
      fSex: GenderType;
      PROCEDURE GetMarried(spouse: THuman);
      FUNCTION DailyCalories: INTEGER;
   END;
```

In the preceding declaration, both GetMarried and DailyCalories are methods for object type THuman, the former a procedure, the latter a function returning an integer.

Although redundant, the method can optionally be preceded by the type name, as in:

```
THuman = OBJECT
...
   PROCEDURE THuman.GetMarried(spouse: THuman);
   FUNCTION THuman.DailyCalories: INTEGER;
END;
```

This can come in handy, since this is the same syntax required later for the implementation of the method.

For these methods, the corresponding implementation might include procedure bodies of the form:

```
FUNCTION THuman.DailyCalories: INTEGER;
BEGIN
   . . .
END; { DailyCalories }

PROCEDURE THuman.GetMarried(spouse: THuman);
BEGIN
   . . .
END; { GetMarried }
```

Method procedures have one immediate difference from other procedures. They are always called with a reference to a specific object.

Within a method procedure, this object must occasionally be referenced directly, usually when passed as an argument to a method of another object. The psuedovariable SELF is a reference variable for the current object, as in Smalltalk. It can be thought of as the missing (implied) parameter for all method routines and is a reference variable for an object of the corresponding object type.

Within a method, references to fields or methods of the corresponding object do not have to use the prefix SELF. All methods include the implied reference variable as though the statements

```
WITH SELF DO
...
END;
```

surrounded the method. For example, we might write

```
FUNCTION THuman.DailyCalories: INTEGER;
BEGIN              { implied argument SELF: THuman }
   DailyCalories := 1000+10*fWeight;
   { implied SELF.fWeight }
END; { DailyCalories }
```

Methods are referenced in the same way as fields. If a method is being referenced from another object (or a conventional procedure), the method must be qualified by an appropriate reference variable. An extension of the previous example is:

```
VAR
   someone: THuman;
BEGIN
   ...
   Write(someone.DailyCalories);
```

Within a method, other methods can be referenced by just the method name, since the SELF. is implied.

One of the most basic methods is the Free method, which deallocates an object. Unlike the New case, there is an existing object, so the deallocation operation can be a message directed to the corresponding object. This method is provided by the ObjIntf unit of MPW Pascal, and also by unit UObject in MacApp but only for those objects that are defined in terms of type TObject, as will be discussed next.

INHERITANCE

A new object type can be declared in terms of a previously declared object type. This provides the object type with the fields and methods of the earlier object type, or, we would say, the new object type "inherits" the properties of the earlier object type. At the same time, the new type can define its own properties, in addition to any inherited properties.

In fact, the declarative form shown earlier will be rarely used, as most Object Pascal objects will be defined in terms of an existing object, TObject, which is defined by the standard library units of both the MPW Pascal and MacApp. We can redefine object type THuman in terms of TObject by the syntax:

```
THuman = OBJECT(TObject)
   fAge: INTEGER;
   fWeight: REAL;
   fSex: GenderType;
   PROCEDURE GetMarried(spouse: THuman);
   FUNCTION DailyCalories: INTEGER;
END;
```

In Object Pascal terms, TObject is an ancestor of THuman, while THuman is a descendant of TObject. THuman includes all the properties of TObject and also several new fields and methods.

For any property of a type TSomeObj, the domain includes both TSomeObj and any descendants of TSomeObj.

A number of object types can be customized from a single ancestor. New object types can also be customized in terms of other descendant types, with a multilevel hierarchy of types, as shown earlier in the imaginary race game.

An object without ancestors has no standard methods or fields. To provide a few commonly used operations, the object type TObject is defined and implemented in Object Pascal using certain low-level primitives. New user-defined low-level object types will usually be derived from TObject; in the case of MacApp, every object is defined as a descendant of TObject, either directly or indirectly.

The descendant has access to all of the properties of its ancestor, in addition to its own unique properties. The following facetious example illustrates a TProgrammer descendant of the THuman type:

```
Language =
   (fortranLang, basicLang, pascalLang,
    smalltalkLang, objectPascalLang);
TProgrammer = OBJECT(THuman)
   fFavoriteLanguage: Language;
   FUNCTION WillUse(lang: Language): BOOLEAN;
END;

FUNCTION TProgrammer.WillUse(lang: Language): BOOLEAN;
BEGIN
   IF lang = fFavoriteLanguage
     WillUse := TRUE     { no matter what it is }
   ELSE
   BEGIN
     CASE lang OF
     fortranLang:
       WillUse := fAge > 30; { known to old-timers }
```

```
    basicLang:
      WillUse := fAge < 25; { grew up with it }
    objectPascalLang:
      WillUse := TRUE;              { loved by all }
    OTHERWISE
      WillUse := FALSE;       { they hate the unknown }
    END
  END
END;
```

One of the properties of inheritance is that a descendant object may wish to define a different implementation of a method from that defined for the ancestor.

In the earlier game example, the TAuto.Move method would replace the TVehicle.Move, since cars need to be able to follow the path of roads. In Object Pascal, an explicit redeclaration of the method is necessary in the declaration of the descendant type, as in the example:

```
TVehicle = OBJECT(TObject)
  location: Point;
  speed, direction: INTEGER;
  PROCEDURE Move(dest: Point);
END;
TAuto = OBJECT(TVehicle)
  PROCEDURE Move(dest: Point); OVERRIDE;
END;
```

As suggested by the syntax, the Move method of TAuto "overrides" the Move method for TVehicle. The redeclaration must include both the exact parameters (and function mode) of the original method and also the Object Pascal keyword OVERRIDE, as shown. The OVERRIDE is optional in the implementation of the method.

The implementation can completely replace the method from the ancestor type, as in the car example. However, in other cases, it may be desirable to merely modify or extend the inherited behavior.

A reference to an inherited behavior in Object Pascal is through the INHERITED keyword, followed by a method call to either a procedure or function. The method must be defined for one of the object's ancestors.

The following example illustrates this usage:

```
TJeep = OBJECT(TAuto)
  fOffroadSpeed: INTEGER;
  PROCEDURE Move(dest: Point); OVERRIDE;
END;
PROCEDURE TJeep.Move(dest: Point);
BEGIN
  IF OffRoadTerrain(location, direction) THEN
```

```
        speed := fOffroadSpeed;      { slow down }

    INHERITED Move(dest);
END;
```

The method for TJeep changes the speed of the vehicle to that appropriate for off-roading, then calls the method from the ancestor object type, in this case TAuto. If no TAuto.Move method is defined, the call would be handled by TVehicle.Move, if any method was defined for it. If there were none (and presumably none defined for TObject), a compile-time error message is displayed.

When using an object type and its descendants, a one-way assignment and parameter compatibility is provided. A reference variable for a specific object type can always be assigned the reference value for a descendant type, since this is always a safe assumption to make. For example, with the declarations

```
        acar: TAuto;
        avehicle: TVehicle;
```

the assignment

```
        avehicle := acar;
```

is always allowed. This assignment compatibility can also be used with typed parameters, such as a procedure that expects a TAuto parameter.

However, the converse is not true: you cannot write

```
        acar := avehicle;
```

because it won't always be true. The vehicle might instead be a ship or a plane.

The program must explicitly assert that the reference variable for an ancestor type contains a reference to the correct descendant, presumably after some verification of this suitability. Such an assignment is performed using a standard MPW Pascal type coercion function, which is automatically declared for each object type:

```
        acar := TAuto(avehicle);
```

To summarize the use of inheritance in Object Pascal, a new object type will normally include new fields or methods that were not present in the ancestor. It may also redefine (override) the implementation of a method defined in any ancestor. Any method not overriden by the descendant is automatically inherited from the least remote ancestor, and the descendant also inherits all fields of its ancestors.

```
{ Example 11-1: Overriding inheritance in Object Pascal
}


PROGRAM InheritDemo;
{ Demonstrate Object Pascal inheritance }

    USES
  ObjIntf;                          { Required for TObject }

    TYPE
  TCalifornia = OBJECT(TObject)
    { use inherited Free method }
    PROCEDURE PrintName;
    PROCEDURE FetchTimeZone(VAR zone: STRING);
    FUNCTION  FetchZip: LONGINT;
  END; { TCalifornia }

  TCupertino = OBJECT(TCalifornia)
    PROCEDURE PrintName;            OVERRIDE;
    FUNCTION  FetchZip: LONGINT;         OVERRIDE;
  END; { TCupertino }

{ -------------- Methods of TCalifornia --------------
}
  PROCEDURE TCalifornia.PrintName;
    BEGIN
      Write('California');
    END; { PrintName }

  PROCEDURE TCalifornia.FetchTimeZone(VAR zone: STRING);
    BEGIN
      zone := 'PST';
    END; { FetchTimeZone }

  FUNCTION TCalifornia.FetchZip: LONGINT;
    BEGIN
      FetchZip := 90000;
    END; { FetchZip }

{ -------------- Methods of TCupertino ---------------
}
  PROCEDURE TCupertino.PrintName;
    BEGIN
      Write('Cupertino, ');
      INHERITED PrintName;
    END; { PrintName }
```

```
FUNCTION TCupertino.FetchZip: LONGINT;
  BEGIN
    FetchZip := 95014;
  END; { FetchZip }


{ ------------------- Procedures -------------------
}
PROCEDURE PrintEverything(s: STRING; obj: TCalifor-
nia);
    VAR
      azone: STRING;
    BEGIN
      WriteLn('The object referenced by "', s, '"');
      Write('  is located at ');
      obj.PrintName;
      Write('  ');
      WriteLn(obj.FetchZip:5);
      Write('  in the ');
      obj.FetchTimeZone(azone);
      WriteLn(azone, ' time zone.');
      WriteLn;
    END; { PrintEverything }


VAR
    acalif: TCalifornia;
    acuper: TCupertino;


BEGIN
    NEW(acalif);
    NEW(acuper);
    PrintEverything('acalif', acalif);
    PrintEverything('acuper', acuper);
    acalif.Free;
    acuper.Free;
END.
```

Example 11–1: Overiding Inheritance in Object Pascal

EXAMPLE: OVERRIDING INHERITANCE

As indicated earlier, Object Pascal can be used in any program compiled by the MPW Pascal compiler. It is possible to write Object Pascal applications, tools, desk accessories, and so on using the ObjIntf unit supplied with MPW Pascal, without using the MacApp libraries.

To illustrate the use of behavior inheritance in Object Pascal, Example 11–1 is a nonsensical MPW tool that includes one ancestor type and one descendant type. The ancestor type is TCalifornia, and the descendant is TCupertino. The types do not define any fields, but each includes several methods.

Each type knows how to display its name. However, the name of the TCupertino object includes both its name and the name of its ancestor, so the printName method for TCupertino prints a name and then calls its inherited printName. In a realistic program, of course, you would probably define objects like TState and TCity with name and zip fields, but this wouldn't be as clear an example of overriding methods.

When it's time to return a zip code, the TCalifornia object can only manage an approximate guess. The TCupertino has a more precise figure, so it overrides the ancestor's behavior and does not use it. However, TCupertino is in the same time zone as TCalifornia and therefore does not need to define its own behavior for returning the time zone.

If you compile and link the example with

```
Pascal InheritDemo.p
Link -o InheritDemo InheritDemo.p.o -ot MPST -oc "MPS " ∂
  "{Libraries}Interface.o" "{Libraries}RunTime.o" ∂
  "{PLibraries}PasLib.o" "{Libraries}ObjLib.o"
```

then

```
                    InheritDemo
```

should display an output similar to Figure 11–3.

```
    The object referenced by "acalif"
       is located at California   90000
       in the PST time zone.

    The object referenced by "acuper"
       is located at Cupertino, California   95014
       in the PST time zone.
```

Figure 11–3: Output from Example 11–1

11.3 Using MacApp

MacApp is an extensible framework for constructing Macintosh applications. The idea behind MacApp was to implement once the code necessary to implement standard Macintosh operations. The design should automatically handle these standard operations, while at the same time providing the flexibility to allow any one of them to be selectively overridden as the application (or the developer) becomes more ambitious.

As has been described earlier in this chapter, both the automatic inheritance and the selective overriding of behaviors are standard characteristics of object-oriented programming. The approach adopted for MacApp is to build a library of standard behaviors using an object-oriented language.

In release 1.1 of MacApp, this library is built using the Object Pascal language, as implemented by the MPW Pascal compiler. In fact, the MacApp distribution consists of the Object Pascal library sources, as well as commands and examples on using MacApp. Advanced programmers can also write MacApp routines in MPW Assembler. MacApp programs are always applications and must use several MacApp Pascal units, as described later in this chapter.

The remainder of this chapter assumes the use of MacApp with the MPW Pascal compiler. Other object-oriented languages are being evaluated for use with MacApp; for example, a version of the C++ language has been proposed by Apple, with extensions to parallel the Object Pascal world view. With another language, the syntax would be different, but the overall structure of the MacApp library would remain the same.

ADVANTAGES AND DISADVANTAGES

There are a number of significant advantages to using MacApp for Macintosh development. The first and foremost advantage is development speed, particularly in providing all the aspects of an application—multiple windows, printing, error handling—that are normally added last when more conventional approaches are used.

The MacApp libraries provide standard Macintosh behaviors to implement the Macintosh user interface, as well other common actions required by applications.

Unlike source code examples, the libraries do not have to be modified for use; the object-oriented behavior inheritance of Object Pascal allows the code to be used without modifications. That means that the developer can take advantage of extensively debugged libraries, and if new, faster (or more powerful) libraries are released, those benefits are immediately available.

This behavior inheritance also allows more flexible developer-written libraries. As with the Apple-supplied libraries, once code is debugged, the object libraries can be compiled and forgotten.

MacApp allows programmers to bypass learning many of the sections of *Inside Macintosh*. It also provides professional-quality solutions to some of the less straightforward aspects of building an application, such as a failproof memory management strategy.

However, there are some disadvantages and limitations to using MacApp. First and foremost, one must be comfortable with the concepts of object-oriented programming. The interrelationship of various objects and methods is integral to the MacApp design, as is understanding when and how to customize standard MacApp object types into your own types. Needless to say, the MacApp programmer must also master both the overall structure and details of the MacApp library.

It's also still necessary to learn many of the sections of *Inside Macintosh*, such as QuickDraw, the File Manager, and, of course, the user interface. MacApp takes care of events, controls, desk accessories, printing, and memory management for you and simplifies the use of windows and menus. But as your program pushes further and further beyond the supplied examples, it will be impossible to avoid learning more about the implementation of MacApp and the Toolbox. Fortunately, the sources to the MacApp libraries are provided so that you can study and extend them, as necessary.

MacApp is designed for complete applications and does not allow building desk accessories, drivers, or any of the other program types described in Chapter 2. As of this writing, MacApp cannot be used to build MPW Tools, although future changes in MPW and MacApp are certainly possible to support this.

MacApp programs cannot be moved to other computers. While Apple may develop a MacApp library compatible with the Apple IIgs, it has clearly stated that the MacApp library cannot be licensed for non-Apple computers. Also, Object Pascal is not yet available for other systems. Thus, if you're developing a program for several computers, including the Macintosh, you're best advised to use a more portable language, such as C.

As noted already, MPW is a substantial development system, both in the size of problems it can solve and in the speed, memory, and disk space requirements it imposes on your system. This is even more true with MacApp, which will require several megabytes to store the MacApp sources and substantial compilation to build the object libraries. If you don't have a lot of spare space on your hard disk, MacApp is out of the question.

Other points are likely to be outweighed by the advantages of MacApp. There is a certain minimum size for programs developed with MacApp, around 70K. If you're developing a small utility to add to a distribution disk with other software, you may not have enough room left on the disk, no matter how much time MacApp might save you. Apple also imposes additional licensing requirements (beyond those already required for distributing System, Finder, and other system software) for developers who use MacApp, including a small annual license fee.

For some, MacApp will be the only way to complete projects in a reasonable amount of time. For others, one or more of the trade-offs effectively rules out the use of MacApp.

INSTALLING MACAPP

The MacApp distribution must be installed in a hard disk directory. Allowing for object files and sample programs, you should have at least 2 1/2 megabytes free on your hard disk, in addition to room for MPW and MPW Pascal.

The MacApp distribution disks contain:

- Complete sources to the MacApp libraries
- Shell scripts and MPW tools to help build MacApp programs
- Sources for many MacApp sample programs

Normally, the MacApp files are installed in folder {MPW}MacApp:, although this assignment is part of your UserStartup and can easily be changed.

Create a MacApp folder in the {MPW} directory and copy all the folders from the distribution disks to this folder. Next, rearrange the contents of the folders as described the distribution instructions. When the distribution was first copied to floppies, some of the larger folders didn't fit in a single floppy, and the overflow was stored in other folders with names like "More MacApp Sources" and "Still More MacApp Sources."

Finally, you must modify your MPW shell environment to support MacApp. Normally, all this requires is adding the following lines to your {MPW}UserStartup file:

```
Set MacApp "{MPW}MacApp:"; Export MacApp
Execute {MacApp}MacAppStartup
```

If you plan to use MacApp right away, you should execute these commands interactively since they normally would not take effect until the next time you start up MPW.

Once MacApp is installed, the structure of the folders on disk should be similar to Figure 11–4. MacAppStartup defines shell variables for several of the key folders, and those names are shown next to the folders.

For example, the folder 'MacApp Source Files' (defined by the shell variable SrcMacApp) contains the sources to the units that make up MacApp library. These include both the INTERFACE declarations and the IMPLEMENTATION code in Object Pascal and the implementation of a few methods written in MPW Assembler. Binary object code is not included in some distributions; instead, the library routines are compiled as needed when you build a sample program.

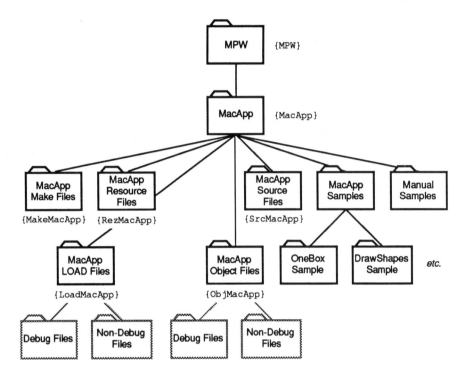

Figure 11–4: MacApp directory hierarchy

MacApp comes with many example programs that illustrate most of the aspects of writing a MacApp program. Assuming you had enough disk space to load MacApp and its sources, these programs are ready to be compiled using MacApp's MABuild command.

BUILDING MACAPP PROGRAMS

With MPW C or Pascal programs, you would use the Make command in conjunction with your own makefile to rebuild the application, as described in Chapter 10. You can also write a simple command file to always compile and link the program.

Because MacApp is designed around a standard application framework, there is also a standard way to build a MacApp program. This building process involves both your source and that of the MacApp library. Each of your modules and your application resources must be compiled, then you must link the program with MacApp's standard library code and resources. Since your program can be built with or without the MacApp debugger (described later), both your source and the library source must be compiled with the appropriate level of debugging.

To manage this complexity, MacApp includes a shell command named MABuild. In earlier MacApp releases, this was formerly called Build, but was changed in MacApp 1.1 to avoid confusion with the BuildMenu, BuildCommands, and BuildProgram commands of MPW 2.0.

The MABuild command file builds any MacApp application using the Make tool, a short makefile written by you, and what it knows about the normal structure of a MacApp program. If you use the standard source file naming convention described in the next section, you should be able to modify a sample makefile and have MABuild do the rest of the work for you.

MABuild is also used to recompile the MacApp library, without building a particular application.

MABuild

Build a MacApp program or the MacApp library

Syntax:

MABuild *program*   Build the application *program* with debugging
MABuild MacApp   Build the MacApp library with debugging

Options:

nodebug   Build the target without debugging
opt   Build the optimized *program* with no debugging
rom128K   Target will run on 128K ROM or later

Unlike standard MPW options, MABuild options must always follow the program name (or the reserved word MacApp).

Remarks:

When building a program, MABuild expects to find in the current directory source file names of the form:

program.make
program.r
M*program*.p
U*program*.p
U*program*.incl.p

MABuild will recompile the library if necessary.

The nodebug parameter disables MacApp debugger code and range checking in the program and the library, making the application much smaller. The opt parameter the application during linking. Opt implies nodebug and has no effect when building object files, such as the MacApp library.

The `rom128K` option builds a program that requires the 128K ROM (Macintosh Plus or 512K enhanced) or later. If you've already decided to target only these machines, this produces more compact MacApp libraries.

Input/Output:

Output   Displayed progress report

Examples:

MABuild OneBox   Build application OneBox with debugging
MABuild MacApp nodebug
                     Build the library without debugging

Normally, you will build programs under development with the debugging code enabled to take advantage of the MacApp debugger. However, when shipping programs to users, you will want to take the debugging code out to protect your design by using `MABuild nodebug`. Shipping the MacApp debugger to unsophisticated users is also considered very user unfriendly.

When building such a "production" application, you will also want to use Object Pascal method call optimization. This is selected by the `opt` parameter, which also implies `nodebug`. Optimization speeds the execution of most method procedure calls and reduces the size of the program. `MABuild` uses the `-opt` option to the `Link` command to remove the unnecessary code.

The biggest speedup provided by optimization is for methods implemented by only one object type. If there's only one method for a given name, it's not necessary to decide at run time which routine to call for these methods, and so the lookup step can be eliminated on any use of that method. It's been estimated that 75 percent of the methods defined in a MacApp program are defined only once.

Most of the remaining methods will be defined for only a few types. Instead of a large method look up table with every possible type and method, much smaller tables can be built with only the necessary entries defined. Other method call optimizations are also performed.

Together, the `nodebug` and `opt` parameters can reduce the size of the application by 100K or more. They're well worth it when you are building a program that will be used by others, even if only for a beta release.

However, building both debugging and nondebugging versions of MacApp programs requires extra time or disk space, depending on which you decide is more readily available.

By default, the approach that requires the least disk space is used. `MABuild` command must recompile the MacApp libraries with the appropriate debugging options if they were different from the previous build. This means that when you build an application without debugging, both the application and the library are completely recompiled. After building the production version of your program, you would then run

```
MABuild MacApp
```

to have a debugging version of the MacApp library ready for use the next time you make changes to your program. This can take 15 minutes or more on a Macintosh Plus.

There's a way to avoid this if you have an extra megabyte of disk space after installing MacApp and building the MacApp object files. You would change MacAppStartup (or insert in your UserStartup after executing MacAppStartup) with the commands:

```
Set SeparateObjects True
Export SeparateObjects
```

With these commands, MABuild will maintain separate object files (and $LOAD Pascal symbol table files) for both the debugging and nondebugging versions of MacApp. Each will be stored in a separate folder, either Debug Files or Non-Debug Files, as shown earlier in Figure 11–4.

TRY A SAMPLE PROGRAM

If you've installed the MacApp sources on your hard disk, you're ready to see one of the sample programs in action. Execute the commands:

```
Directory "{MacApp}MacApp Samples:DrawShapes Sample"
MABuild DrawShapes
```

If the MABuild command is unrecognized by the shell, you need to run the {MacApp}MacAppStartup command file or leave and reenter MPW.

This will compile the simple drawing example. If you haven't yet built the MacApp library, it will also compile it, which means that now is a time to take a coffee break or check your mail.

If your speaker volume is turned up, MABuild will play a little tune to indicate the program is compiled and linked; it plays a funeral march if the build failed for some reason, a more cheery tune for success. These tunes are defined by commands stored in shell variables MacAppFailed and MacAppDone and can be modified by definitions in your UserStartup after the Execute {MacApp}MacAppStartup command. For example, you might instead prefer using the familiar Beethoven melody:

```
Set MacAppDone ∂
    'Beep G,10 G,10 G,10 Eb,85 F,10 F,10 F,10 D,85'
Export MacAppDone
```

as your triumphal motif.

When the build completes, enter

```
DrawShapes
```

to run the program. You should see a display similar to Figure 11–5.

The example allows you to draw simple shapes. Each document window includes a palette (like that of MacPaint or MacDraw) that allows you to choose one of four operations: draw oval, draw rectangle, draw a "heavy" box, or select an existing shape.

Each of the three shapes is a descendant of a common shape ancestor. The "heavy" box is an immediate descendant of the ordinary box, with two customizations. It has a memory-hogging array as one of its fields and is drawn slightly differently, with an extra notation and heavier borders.

If you choose the selection icon, note that the cursor changes appearance over a shape. If you select one of the drawn shapes, the Shades menu is enabled to allow you to change the shade of gray used to fill the interior it. Or a selection can be cut or copied to the clipboard.

The document containing the shapes can be saved, reopened, or printed. The Page menu includes options to show page breaks and to print page numbers on the document.

The MABuild command used earlier compiled DrawShapes with debugging enabled, so this version also includes a Debug menu and a window entitled "Debug Window." Both are supplied by the debugging code included in the MacApp library; use of the debugger is described later.

When you quit the example and return to MPW, you may want to build a production version of the same program to compare the size and speed of the two. Execute the commands:

```
Rename DrawShapes 'DrawShapes with debug'
MABuild DrawShapes opt
```

There will be time for another coffee break while you are waiting for the compilation to complete—unless you are maintaining separate debugging and nondebugging libraries and have already built the nondebugging library.

When the build is done, you will be rewarded with a smaller version of the sample program, about 90K versus 190K for the debugging version. (This is for MacApp 1.1; your mileage may vary). If you run it, it should seem noticeably faster. You will also notice that both the Debug menu and the debugging window are gone.

Other examples included with MacApp demonstrate the use of dialogs, multiple documents types, and text editing. You may wish to build and run some of these as well. To understand the source code, however, you'll have to learn more about the structure of a MacApp program.

11.4 Structure of MacApp Program

By definition, a MacApp program performs all the standard operations of a Macintosh application, conforming to the official Macintosh user interface.

However, because the library provides many of these operations for you, your program must follow the formal structure dictated by the MacApp design. In general, you will use a MacApp-supplied object type to take advantage of certain standard behaviors and then customize that type to describe any behaviors specific to your application or its documents.

NAMING CONVENTIONS

MacApp source files for the libraries and sample programs follow a standard naming convention, as shown in Table 11–3. This also happens to be the convention that the MABuild command and its related Make source files expect, so unless you intend to reimplement MABuild yourself, your programs should also follow this structure.

The major portion of an MacApp program Simple would be in an Object Pascal unit USimple, divided between files USimple.p and USimple.incl.p. The structure of more complex programs may suggest

MacApp source file names

For a MacApp program (named "Simple") written in Object Pascal, the source files used would be:

MSimple.p	main code, with Pascal PROGRAM Simple
USimple.p	INTERFACE for UNIT USimple
USimple.inc1.p	IMPLEMENTATION for UNIT USimple
Simple.r	Rez source code
Simple.make	Make source used by Build command

Optional files

USimple.inc2.p, etc.	Additional source for USimple
Uother.p	INTERFACE for UNIT Uother
Uother.inc1.p	IMPLEMENTATION for UNIT Uother
any.rsrc	Other resources

The files produced by the Build include:

MSimple.p.o, USimple.p.o, etc.	object files
Simple.makeit	shell commands to build application
Simple	the completed application

Table 11–3:   MacApp source file conventions

breaking the program into more than one unit. The program will also include a simple main program and Rez source file. A simplified Make file is required to specify library dependencies and any nonstandard source files, such as a second program unit.

The identifiers used within the source files also follow certain well-defined rules, as suggested by Table 11–4. Again, none of these rules are imposed by MacApp or the Object Pascal compiler, but reflect a consistent programming style adopted by the developers of MacApp. If you use the same style, you'll have just one set of rules to use when reading code that uses both custom and predefined names.

The case of the MacApp identifiers is used to distinguish between different usages. Leading capital letters are used for data types and procedures (including methods), while a leading lowercase letter is used for variables and constants. As the MPW Pascal compiler is case insensitive, these distinctions are actually ignored by the compiler.

MacApp Identifier naming rules

Form	Used for	Sample Name
Case Distinction		
ZName	type or routine	InitToolbox
zName	variable or constant	msgSaveFailed
Prefix		
TName	object type	TDocument
IName	initialize method for TName	IDocument
cName	command constant	cPageSetup
phName	phrase string resource	phRevert
kName	other constant	kWatchDelay
gName	global variable	gAppDone
fName	field of an object	fFileType
theName	field of a record	theCmdKey

Table 11–4:   MacApp Identifier naming rules

Although not required, it's a good idea to avoid using *any* capital letters for local variables in a method or routine. This makes it easier to identify these names when reading the code and reduces the risk of accidental collision with a mixed-case field or global variable. Many local variables begin with a, as in "acommand" or "anobject," to refer to an instance of an object or record.

With the exception of procedures (including Toolbox routines defined by *Inside Macintosh*), most MacApp identifiers begin with a single letter identifying the usage. While it's cryptic at first, once you crack the code, it's easier to see what's going on, without forcing the use of long identifiers.

THE MACAPP WORLD VIEW

A MacApp program is structured around six standard types of objects. Designing a MacApp program requires understanding these six types and where the actions for each type fits into the representation and usage of your program.

A "document" in MacApp corresponds to the customary Macintosh use of the term, what other systems might call a "data file." Most operations in the Macintosh are structured around documents, such as changing the contents of a spreadsheet or printing a memo.

A "view" is a way of looking at a document, and at least one view is maintained by every MacApp program for each open document. Usually there is only one view per document, such as displaying the memo in a What-

You-See-Is-What-You-Get word processor. However, MacProject is a program that looks at a task–scheduling document several ways, one as a crtical path chart, another as a timeline of tasks.

A "frame" is a display of a view. Views are the abstract display of the entire document, while a frame is a snapshot of the view that fits on the screen or a page. A frame is an object that is expected to know how to display itself using QuickDraw, either on the screen or for the Print Manager. It usually defers the actual drawing to the related view.

A "window" corresponds exactly to the Toolbox usage. Most windows contain one or more frames—because the two concepts are separated, it's easy to implement split windows in MacApp. Other than coordinating frames, the standard MacApp actions for a window object take care of resizing, moving, etc. A few windows may be independent of any document, such as the Clipboard window.

Your program will rarely customize windows or frames. Instead, for each document, you would allocate a window and a frame and then associate this with a view. Unless one of the standard views—such as the TextEdit view described later—solves your problem, your program would have to define its own custom view to display and allow editing of your particular view.

A "command" is one of three user actions: a menu selection (or its command-key equivalent), a mouse action, or typing. MacApp creates a new object for each action the user performs, with a single integer (the "command number") used to distinguish the command type. Each such action can be done, undone, or redone again. MacApp 1.0 follows the Macintosh User Interface of only a single undoable operation; so only two command objects are active at one time: the current action and the previous one. The previous action is always made irreversible before the current action is processed.

Finally, everything else not associated with any document, window, or command is part of the "application". Although described as an object, it really covers the overall control structure of a MacApp application. Because there is only ever one application object, MacApp uses an efficiency shortcut of using global variables as a substitute for application field variables.

Following the naming conventions described earlier, these six standard objects are defined as types TDocument, TView, TFrame, TWindow, TCommand, and TApplication. The six types are declared in the main MacApp unit, UMacApp. As will be seen later, several of these types are not used directly but instead are ancestors of custom types for your particular application.

DOCUMENTS AND THEIR VISUAL DISPLAY

Most operations in a MacApp application are structured, either directly or indirectly, around documents. Each open document will have a single TDocument object and one or more each of the TDocument, TView, TFrame, and TWindow objects.

Each of these objects has fields to reference at least some of the other objects. Where there can be a one-to-many relationship—such as more than one window per document—MacApp uses a variable-length list (an object of type TList) to reference all the related objects.

The reference fields relating these four types—documents, views, frames, and windows—are shown in Figure 11–6. These fields are required by MacApp for its own purposes.

Generally, you will customize both the document and the view objects and define your own fields to reference between the two. If there are two types of views, you would (usually) define two reference fields for the document. For example, if you were defining your own MacProject-type document, each document might have one field referencing the critical-path view and another for the timeline view, while the views would reference their corresponding document. The declarations would look like:

```
TProjectDocument = OBJECT(TDocument)
  fCritPathView: TCritPathView
  fTimeLineView: TTimeLineView
...
TCritPathView = OBJECT(TView)
  fProjDocument: TProjDocument;
...
TTimeLineView = OBJECT(TView)
  fProjDocument: TProjDocument;
...
```

Why not, for example, use the fDocument field of a TTimeLineView rather than define a new field fProjDocument? After all, they reference the same object. However, fDocument is typed to the generic ancestor, so you cannot use it with any method or field that is defined for a TProjDocument but not for a TDocument without an extra typecast in each usage.

When you define your own document type, you define methods to read and write the document to and from a disk file. These methods use the File Manager to transfer data between the file and the document object. The contents of the document are referenced by a custom field of the document object but can be stored as a list of objects or records or as a single relocatable block.

When creating an empty document or opening an existing one, document methods are used to create and initialize the views and windows corresponding to the document. The initialization method for a view includes a parameter that references the corresponding document; the normal procedure used to create windows includes parameters for both the document and corresponding view.

How are the contents of a document displayed in a window? Suppose a window has been resized and needs updating:

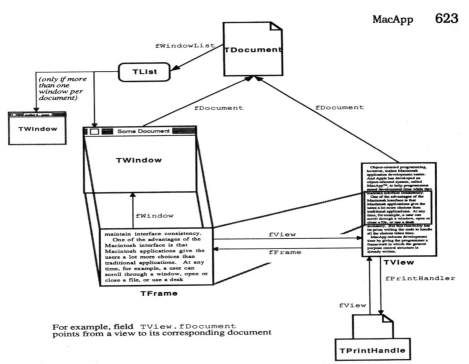

For example, field TView.fDocument
points from a view to its corresponding document

Figure 11–6: Structure of a MacApp document

- The MacApp library traps the update event and starts the operation by calling a method for a window object. The window object will erase the changed content area and then will ask each of its corresponding frame objects to update their display.

- Each frame knows what part of the view it is using, so it knows how to draw the scrolling control within the scroll bars. The frame will, in turn, ask a view object to display itself.

- A view knows how to format the document display but uses a reference to the document to obtain the current contents from the document object.

To handle printing, a fifth type of object is normally allocated for each view. Each view may have an associated print handler, of type TPrintHandler or one of its descendants, usually TStdPrintHandler. When it comes time to print the view, the print handler object supplies the standard printing functionality, such as the job dialog and the calls to the Printing Manager. The view is responsible only for drawing the document, using the same routine as it does when displaying the view within a frame.

Not all views will include a print handler, which is normally installed after the view is allocated and initialized. For example, the window used to Show Clipboard can't be printed and therefore doesn't need a print handler, even if it is the same type of view used to display a document.

Another example in which you may not define a print handler is when you have more than one view per document. In a paint program, the enlarged "FatBits" display might be implemented by a separate view in a separate window. But when you printed the document, you'd want to print the normal view of the window. If the user selects the "Print" operation for a view that does not have a print handler, another view of the same document will be printed.

DESIGNING THE PROGRAM INTERFACE

Many of the software engineering practices originally developed for Pascal remain applicable when using Object Pascal. One such approach is development through stepwise refinement, by which you specify the top-level interfaces and then elaborate with more and more detail until complete.

As mentioned earlier, MacApp programs written in Object Pascal are normally built around one or more Pascal units. Thus, designing the INTERFACE section of the unit(s) corresponds to the top-most design level for a MacApp program.

Suppose you're building a small application called Foo. Associated with the application would be a unit UFoo, which will declare new object types. These custom types include descendants of several of the six standard types.

The reason you must customize the MacApp library-defined types is to provide new methods to either replace or supplement the standard methods. These methods are used to define those actions specific to your program—without them, your program wouldn't do anything!

All applications must customize TApplication, TDocument, and TView to implement those methods. A summary of the most commonly defined methods for each type are shown in Table 11–5.

Custom methods for MacApp programs

TmyApplication customized from TApplication

DoMakeDocument Create a new TmyDocument

TmyDocument customized from TDocument

DoRead	Read document from disk
DoWrite	Write document to disk
DoNeedDiskSpace	Estimate disk space required for DoWrite
DoMakeViews	Create one or more new TmyView
DoMakeWindows	Create new TWindow, e.g. with NewSimpleWindow

TmyView customized from TView

Draw	Display the view
DoMenuCommand	Perform your custom menu commands
DoMouseCommand	Perform mouse commands
DoSetupMenus	Enable custom menu items

Each custom type Ttype will also have an Itype initialization method

Table 11–5: Custom methods required by MacApp programs

Although the corresponding methods have been already declared for the ancestor types, each of these methods must be redeclared for the descendants using the OVERRIDE keyword in the INTERFACE section of your unit. The corresponding descendant methods also must be written in the IMPLEMENTATION section.

The actual structure used by MacApp programs divides each unit into two files, in this case UFoo.p and UFoo.incl.p. UFoo.p can be USEd by the main Pascal program (in file MFoo.p) and inspected to examine the public interface. However, it can also be compiled, in which case it uses an MPW Pascal compiler directive to include the source for the IMPLEMENTATION section, contained in UFoo.incl.p. Example 11–2 shows a simplified version of UFoo.p.

```
{ Example 11-2: MacApp program interface declarations }


(* UFoo.p: Interface for Unit UFoo *)
UNIT UFoo;

INTERFACE

USES
  MemTypes, QuickDraw, OSIntf, ToolIntf, PackIntf,

  UObject, UList, UMacApp, UPrinting; { MacApp units }

  (* any other MacApp units required *)

CONST
  (* custom commands *)

  (* other constants *)
  kFooDocType = 'TEXT';    { file type of readable docs }
  kFooDocCreator = 'FOO!'; { application signature }
  kFooStaggerAmt = 10;     { separation between windows }
  kFooWindRsrcID = 1000;                { 'WIND' resource }

TYPE
  TFooApplication = OBJECT(TApplication)

  FUNCTION TFooApplication.DoMakeDocument]
     (cmdnum: CmdNumber): TDocument; OVERRIDE;
(* redeclare other overridden TApplication methods *)

  PROCEDURE TFooApplication.IFooApplication;
  END; {TFooApplication}


  TFooDocument = OBJECT(TDocument)
    fMsg: Str255;
    fFooView: TFooView;

  PROCEDURE TFooDocument.DoMakeViews
  (forPrinting: BOOLEAN);
     OVERRIDE;

  PROCEDURE TFooDocument.DoMakeWindows; OVERRIDE;
    (* redeclare other overridden TDocument methods here
*)

  PROCEDURE TFooDocument.IFooDocument;
```

```
END; {TFooDocument}


TFooView = OBJECT(TView)
  fFooDocument: TFooDocument;

PROCEDURE TView.Draw; OVERRIDE;
(* redeclare other overridden TView methods here *)

PROCEDURE TView.IFooView(ourdoc: TFooDocument);
END; {TFooView}


IMPLEMENTATION

{$I UFoo.incl.p}    { Source is in a separate file }

END.
```

Example 11-2:   MacApp program interface declarations

The interface declares three new object types—TFooApplication,
TFooDocument, and TFooView. These types override some of the inherited
ancestor methods. You also may need to define new fields or methods for your
object types. A new method usually defined for any new type is the initialization, in this case IFooApplication, IFooDocument, and IFooView.

UFoo.p will normally include certain configuration constants, such as
the document type(s) recognized by the application. However, the only global
variables declared in the INTERFACE section will be those shared between
UFoo and other program units. As will be shown in the next section, the main
program for a MacApp program is very simple, so INTERFACE declared
globals are only necessary when the program is built with more than one
unit, e.g., UFoo and UFooBar.

More substantial applications must also include customized version of
TCommand. Objects descended from TCommand are used for implementing
commands that change the contents of the document so that they can be
undone later on.

For many programs, actions that change the temporary appearance of
the view would not require TCommand objects. For example, a "Show Full
Page" menu item in a painting program would not be a command—you could
implement it directly in the DoMenuCommand of the view. Commands that
change the selection—such as Select All—would be another example, unless
you wish to save the current selection with the document or wish to restore
the selection as part of an Undo of another command.

However, clipboard operations are always implemented as TCommand
objects. Text-based views can use the TTECommand type defined in the

MacApp library, but other views must customize their own TCommand descendant to record the contents of the current selection (e.g., the data to be cut to the clipboard) when the command object is created. The command must also implement the methods to do, undo, and redo the command.

TCommand objects are also used to provide visual feedback when the mouse is down. The DrawShapes example uses this to display the outline of a new shape as it's being drawn.

In general, the sample programs supplied show off most of the capabilities of the MacApp library. If you have a question about how a certain feature is implemented—such as which methods must be defined to support mouse-dragging commands—you can usually find an example in one of the sample programs.

THE MAIN PROGRAM

The main program for a MacApp application is actually very simple. The Pascal compiler and MPW linker expect each complete application to have a PROGRAM section. However, under MacApp, the use of such mundane constructs is limited to a few operations.

A MacApp main program performs the following steps:

- Initialize the Toolbox managers and Printing Manager
- Create an application object (in this case TFooApplication)
- Initialize the application
- Transfer control to the application's Run procedure

The first step is a greatly simplified version of the initialization steps required by any Macintosh applicaton. The second and third are unique to the MacApp object-oriented approach. The fourth step corresponds to calling the MainEventLoop procedure of a conventionally written application. The complete main program for our application Foo is shown in Example 11–3.

Because the main program is so simple, it's virtually the same for every application, with two exceptions. The first is that the names used in the main program must be modified for the particular application. If you were writing a program called Hangman, you could use the MPW shell command

```
replace -c ∞ /Foo/ Hangman
```

to change the names in the example for your application.

The second change necessary is adjusting a single memory management parameter to minimize heap fragmentation. The InitToolbox routine takes a single argument, which is the number of calls to the MoreMasters trap to be performed to allocate master pointer blocks prior to using the heap. As with other applications, this value is normally arrived at through experimentation with the final version of the application.

```
{ Example 11-3: Complete MacApp main program }


(* MFoo.p: Main program for application Foo *)
PROGRAM Foo;
USES
  MemTypes, QuickDraw, OSIntf, ToolIntf, PackIntf,

  UObject, UList, UMacApp, UPrinting; { MacApp units }

  (* any other MacApp units required by UFoo *)

  UFoo;                     { our code to implement Foo }

VAR
  gFooApplication: TFooApplication;

BEGIN
  InitToolbox(8);          { Do MoreMasters 8 times }
  InitPrinting;            { Needed for printing }

  NEW(gFooApplication);    { New application object }
  { Initialize the object }
  gFooApplication.IFooApplication;
  gFooApplication.Run;     { Run until done }
END. { Foo }
```

Example 11–3:   Complete MacApp main program

IMPLEMENTING THE UNIT

MacApp programs are structured around user interactions which are passed to the program in the form of commands, which include a command number. MacApp defines command numbers for the standard interface with names such as cQuit. MacApp normally provides some assistance for each of the standard interface commands, but your program must usually include a small amount of custom code for each of these commands.

In response to most of the standard MacApp menu commands, MacApp will call one or more custom methods for the application, document, or view. The methods that normally must be defined for your customized object are shown in Table 11–6.

Commands and custom methods

Apple Menu

cAboutApp	Draws 'ALRT' resource #201
(Chooser DA)	myview.DoPrinterChanged, myview.DoPagination

File Menu: Documents

cNew	myapp.DoMakeDocument, mydoc.IMyDocument, mydoc.DoInitialState, mydoc.DoMakeViews, mydoc.DoMakeWindows
cOpen	myapp.DoMakeDocument, mydoc.IMyDocument, mydoc.DoRead, mydoc.DoMakeViews, mydoc.DoMakeWindows
cSave, cSaveAs, cSaveCopy, cClose, cQuit	mydoc.DoNeedDiskSpace, mydoc.DoWrite
cRevert	mydoc.DoRead or mydoc.DoInitialState

File Menu: Printing (using TStdPrintHandler)

cPageSetup	myview.DoPagination
cPrint	myview.Draw

Edit Menu

cCut, cCopy	myCutCopyCommand.DoIt†
cPaste	myPasteCommand.DoIt†
cClear, cSelectAll	myCommand.DoIt†

cShowClipboard Standard types handled by TDeskScrapView;
        Others use myapp.MakeViewForAlienClipboard

Application launched from Finder

cFinderNew	Same as cNew by default; override in myapp.OpenNew
cFinderOpen	Same as cOpen
cFinderPrint	Similar to cOpen and cPrint

† myview.DoMenuCommand should allocate appropriate my*xxx*Command
  Handled automatically for TTEView views with TTECommand

Table 11-6:   Commands and custom methods

Most of the File menu operations would be associated with methods of TFooDocument. For example, the various commands that save a document would call the DoNeedDiskSpace and DoWrite methods. If the document is closed or Quit is selected, the user is asked if (s)he wants to save the document, and, if so, the Save operations are performed.

Printing operations generally interact with TFooView methods, including use of the Chooser desk accessory. Support for most printing operations is automatically provided if you use TStdPrintHandler, although you can also write your own print handler as a descendant of TPrintHandler.

If the user launches the application from the Finder (command cFinderNew), MacApp normally starts the program with an implied cNew operation, but you can prevent this by writing a TFooApplication.OpenNew to override the standard one. Opening one or more documents from the Finder is usually handled by the same custom code written to open documents from your application; the same applies to printing documents from the Finder.

Many of the simpler examples use a text-only view to display a document of type 'TEXT'. These programs can take advantage of the TTEView defined in unit UTEView (described later in this chapter). TTEView provides a view that supports all the standard text editing operations, include the entire Edit menu.

Programs that use custom views will have to add a number of custom methods (and probably custom TCommand objects) to support cutting and pasting to the clipboard. MacApp will display the clipboard window using the TDeskScrapView, and it knows how to draw the two standard clipboard types, text ('TEXT') and QuickDraw picture ('PICT'). If your program can cut or paste other types, you should provide a method to generate views for those types.

To support menu and mouse commands, most applications must override the standard DoMenuCommand and DoMouseCommand methods for at least one of the standard objects. Commands are examined by the view, frame, window, and application, with all methods of one object completed before going on to the next. For example, the search order for a DoMenuCommand might be TFooView, TView, TFrame, TWindow, TFooApplication, and TApplication.

Larger applications that perform operations beyond the MacApp standard must define their own command types, each of which will have a corresponding command number and perhaps use a custom TCommand object. Custom commands, of course, require a custom method to interpret them.

Example 11–4 shows a greatly simplified version of the implementation of unit UFoo. A complete MacApp example is given later in this chapter.

```
{ Example 11-4: Sample MacApp program methods }


(* UFoo.incl.p: Implementation for Unit UFoo *)
(* untested *)
CONST
  kStdMsg = 'Foo';

VAR
  { count windows to avoid overlap }
  gFooStaggerCount: INTEGER;


{ ---------------TFooApplication methods---------------
}

  PROCEDURE TFooApplication.IFooApplication;
  BEGIN

     { Use ancestor's initialization, indicating the
       the document file types usable by Foo
     }
     IApplication(kFooDocType);

     gFooStaggerCount := 0;     { to offset each window }
  END; { IFooApplication }


  FUNCTION TFooApplication.DoMakeDocument
     (cmdNum: CmdNumber):
  TDocument;
  VAR
     afoodoc: TFooDocument;
  BEGIN
     NEW(afoodoc);                  { Allocate the document }
     FailNIL(afoodoc);             { Error if it failed }
     afoodoc.IFooDocument; { Initialize document }
     DoMakeDocument := afoodoc;
  END; { DoMakeDocument }


{ ----------------TFooDocument methods----------------
}

  { Initialize this document }
  PROCEDURE TFooDocument.IPictDocument;
  BEGIN
     { Give TDocument method enough info to do all the
```

```
        hard work }
    IDocument
      (kFooDocType, kFooDocCreator, kUsesDataFork,
       NOT kUsesRsrcFork, kDataOpen, NOT kRsrcOpen);

    fMsg := 'Foo';
END; { IFooDocument }


{ Make each view for the document }
FUNCTION TFooDocument.DoMakeViews
    (forPrinting: BOOLEAN);
VAR
    afooview: TFooView;
BEGIN
    NEW(afooview);          { Allocate the document }
    FailNIL(afooview);         { Error if it failed }
    { Set reference to the view }
    fFooView := afooview;
    afooview.IFooView(SELF);  { Initialize view }

END; { DoMakeViews }


{ Make each window for the document }
PROCEDURE TFooDocument.DoMakeWindows;
VAR
    awindow: TWindow;
BEGIN

    { Reference a WIND resource giving the standard
      properties of the window, including its size }
    awindow :=
      NewSimpleWindow
        (kFooWindRsrcID, NOT kDialogWindow,
      kWantHScrollBar, kWantVScrollBar, fFooView);

    { If the boundary rectangle in the WIND resource
      assumes a 342 x 512 screen, this resizes it if
      screen is larger }
    AdaptToScreen(awindow);
    { Each new window is offset toward lower right to
avoid having it completely cover an existing
      window }
    SimpleStagger
      (awindow, kFooStaggerAmt, kFooStaggerAmt,
       kFooStaggerCount); { use & update counter }

END; { DoMakeWindows }
```

```
{ --------------------TFooView methods--------------------
}
{ Initialize a new view }
  PROCEDURE TFooView.IPictView(ourdoc: TFooDocument)
  VAR
     astdprint: TStdPrintHandler;
     aviewrect: Rect;
  BEGIN
     { just a guess }
     SetRect(aviewrect, 0, 0, 1000, 1000);
     IView
        (NIL, ourdoc, aviewrect, sizeFrame, sizeFrame,
        FALSE, hloff);
     fFooDocument := ourdocument;
     fDocument := ourdocument;

     { Do everything you need to support printing of this
        view }
     NEW(stdhand);
     FailNIL(stdhand);
     { initialize }
     stdhand.IStdPrintHandler(SELF, FALSE);
  END; { IFooView }

  PROCEDURE TFooView.Draw;
  VAR
     txth,txtv: INTEGER;
  BEGIN
     { Put a border on it }
     FrameRoundRect(fExtentRect,16,16);

     txth := (fExtentRect.left+fExtentRect.right) DIV 2;
     txtv := (fExtentRect.top+fExtentRect.bottom) DIV 2;
     TextFont(applFont);
     TextSize(24);
     txth := txth - (StringWidth(fFooDocument.fMsg));
     MoveTo(txth, txtv);
     DrawString(fFooDocument.fMsg);
  END; { Draw }
```

Example 11–4:   Sample MacApp program methods

RESOURCES

A completed MacApp program will also require a Rez source file UFoo.r to supply certain required resources. The most common of those resources are summarized in Table 11–7.

MacApp custom resource numbers

Type	Id	Symbolic name	Usage
'ALRT'	201	phAboutApp	About MyApplication alert
'DITL'	201		
'WIND'	≥1000		MyDocument window
'STR#'	256	kIDBuzzString	Used for alternate phrases
'MBAR'	128	kMBarDisplayed	List of menus initially displayed
'MBAR'	129	kMBarNotDisplayed	List of other available menus
'MBAR'	130	kMBarHierarchical	Initial hierarchical menus
'mctb'	128	kMBarDisplayed	Menu color table
'cmnu'	1	mApple	Apple (desk accessory) menu
'cmnu'	2	mFile	File menu
'cmnu'	3	mEdit	Edit menu
'cmnu'	4–63		User-defined menus†
'MENU'	≥ 4		Menus without commands†
'seg!'	any		Name of transient segments
'mem!'	any		Temporary memory reserve sizes
any	≥1000		Application-specific resources

† Each menu item in a 'cmnu' entry has a corresponding MacApp CommandNumber constant. Menus with all items added at run-time (such as a list of fonts) cannot have pre-defined command numbers and thus use the standard 'MENU' resource type.

Table 11–7:   MacApp custom resources

The most important resources for a small MacApp program are the 'cmnu' resources, which associate standard Macintosh menus with MacApp command numbers. Each of the standard menu items has a standard command number defined for it. If you define your own menu items—including those within a hierarchical submenu—you will have to define your own command numbers.

There will be some menus or menu items for which it is not possible to predefine a corresponding command number in the 'cmnu' resources. If you have a menu to select an open window or one of the available fonts on the system, it is not possible to define all the possible values and corresponding command numbers. For such menus, you would define the menu with an ordinary 'MENU' resource. Then, an implementation of a DoMenuCommand (normally for your custom view or document) would use the CmdToMenuItem procedure to convert this to the corresponding menu and item number.

All the resources for a small prototype can probably be adapted from one of the Apple-supplied examples until you better understand the MacApp structure and can write your own resource file.

11.5 Debugging MacApp Programs

The MacApp libraries provide help for debugging a MacApp program, including a MacApp-specific debugger. This allows you to monitor the operations of the libraries and your program through built-in menus and commands, without increasing the size of your finished program. To make effective use of the debugger, you should include in your program additional code to debug your custom operations.

This section summarizes the debugger's capabilities, how it is used, and how you should modify your program to work with the debugger.

THE MACAPP DEBUGGER

MacApp includes an integrated debugger that is linked as part of the MacApp libraries during development. The debugger will always be a part of a MacApp program compiled using MABuild unless you use the nodebug option. The MacApp debugger is designed for use with MacApp programs only and should not be confused with other machine-language or symbolic debuggers, which can also be used with MacApp to a greater or lesser degree.

The MacApp debugger adds its own menu at the end of the menu bar to allow you to set options. It also displays its own window while the program is running, as shown by Figure 11–7 with the OneBox sample program.

The debug window can be resized, moved, made active, and otherwise manipulated using standard Macintosh mouse commands. These window manipulations are handled by the same MacApp library code that supports all window operations.   However, the contents of the window can only be changed by the debugger.

You can transfer control to the debugger by pressing Shift-Option-Command simultaneously. To minimize interactions, the debug window is not automatically brought to the front of the list, which may seem disconcerting at first glance.

When active, the debugger will display its command prompt, which is the greater-than-or-equals sign (≥). From the prompt, you type commands—often single-character codes. A list of the commonly used commands is given by Table 11–8.

Some of the most common commands are to set breakpoints, the trace method routine execution, and the look and the fields of objects. The display

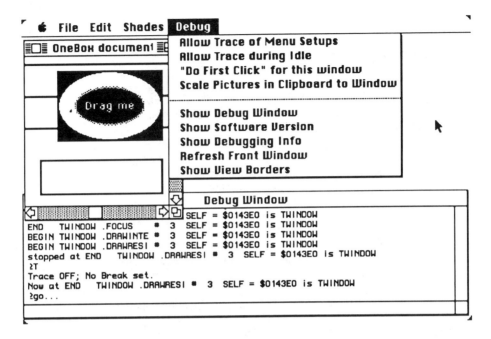

Figure 11–7: MacApp debugger

of these commands is output to the debug window, but can also be directed to a file for more leisurely examination.

Note that to minimize interactions with your application, the debugger does not use the conventional mouse-oriented interface for adjusting the debugger window *while the debugger is waiting for commands.* Instead, two keys are available at the prompt to scroll the window up and down. Three W commands adjust the debug window: one brings it to the front and another sends it to the back. The third resizes the window by allowing you to use the mouse to indicate the top left and bottom right corners of the window, similar to the Smalltalk programming environment.

SAMPLE DEBUGGER SESSION

Before writing your own programs, you should try out the MacApp debugger on one of the sample programs supplied. This will give you an idea of what it is capable of and allow you to make use of the debugger with your application from the beginning.

One of the most useful commands is the breakpoint command, B, which stops the MacApp program at the beginning and end of a particular method. A good place to set a breakpoint in the Draw method of your custom view. Figure 11–8 shows setting a breakpoint in the OneBox sample program.

MacApp debugger commands

Command	Description
Return	Scroll down (only when ≥ prompt shown)
Backspace	Scroll up (only when ≥ prompt shown)
T	Trace method calls (on/off)
R	Display recent method calls
B	Set method breakpoint
C	Cancel breakpoint
I	Display object contents ("Inspect")
S	Display stack frame of active procedure calls
D	Display memory contents
H	Heap display subcommands
S	Stack display subcommands
O	Send copy of debugging output to a file
Q	Send debugging output to a file and don't display it ("Quiet")
WF	Bring debugging window to front
WB	Send debugging window to back
WR	Enable mouse to resize debugging window
X	Toggle debugging flag variables
Z	Performance measurement options
E	Enter MacsBug
G	Leave debugger and resume application ("Go")

Table 11–8:   MacApp debugger commands

When you set a breakpoint, the debugger will ask for a method name. You can specify the particular object type and method for a breakpoint (e.g., TMyView.Box) or just the method itself (Draw). In the latter case, if there is more than one Draw method defined, the breakpoint will stop at any method of that name. This is useful when you don't know the name of the object types.

Now, exit the debugger with the G command. To make sure the Draw method gets called, resize one of the document windows. The debugger will stop at the breakpoint, waiting for a command.

At this point, a useful step is to display the fields of the view object. The inspect command (I) calls a method for the view that displays the fields, as shown in the figure.

When you resume execution, the debugger will run the application until it leaves the Draw method. At this point, you can clear the breakpoint and

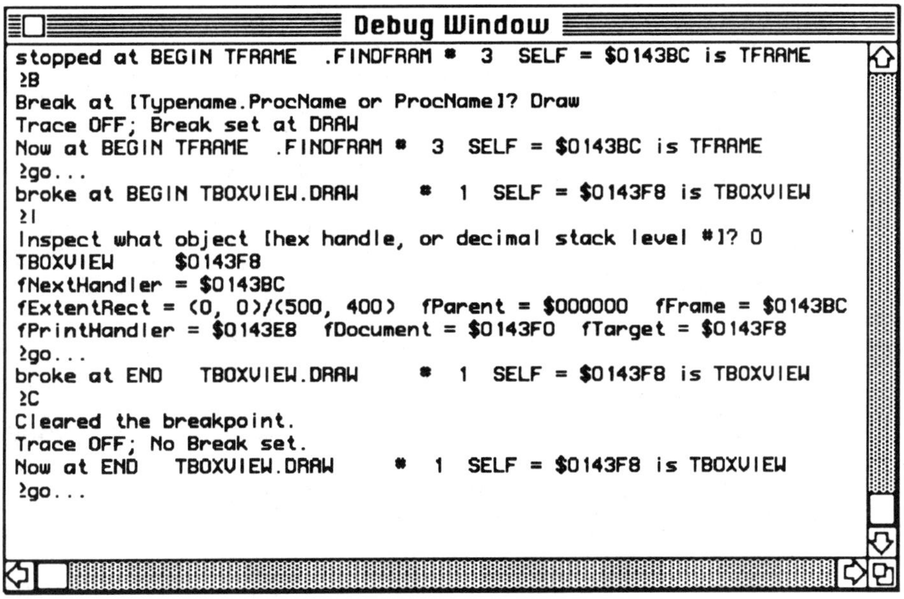

```
▤▭▭▭▭▭▭▭▭▭▭▭ Debug Window ▭▭▭▭▭▭▭▭▭▭▭▭
stopped at BEGIN TFRAME  .FINDFRAM ● 3  SELF = $0143BC is TFRAME    ⬆
?B
Break at [Typename.ProcName or ProcName]? Draw
Trace OFF; Break set at DRAW
Now at BEGIN TFRAME  .FINDFRAM ● 3  SELF = $0143BC is TFRAME
?go...
broke at BEGIN TBOXVIEW.DRAW    ● 1  SELF = $0143F8 is TBOXVIEW
?I
Inspect what object [hex handle, or decimal stack level #]? 0
TBOXVIEW      $0143F8
fNextHandler = $0143BC
fExtentRect = (0, 0)/(500, 400)  fParent = $000000  fFrame = $0143BC
fPrintHandler = $0143E8  fDocument = $0143F0  fTarget = $0143F8
?go...
broke at END    TBOXVIEW.DRAW    ● 1  SELF = $0143F8 is TBOXVIEW
?C
Cleared the breakpoint.
Trace OFF; No Break set.
Now at END    TBOXVIEW.DRAW    ● 1  SELF = $0143F8 is TBOXVIEW
?go...
                                                                   ⬇
◀▭▭▭▭▭▭▭▭▭▭▭▭▭▭▭▭▭▭▭▭▭▭▭▭▭▭▭▭▭▭▭▭▭▭▭▭▭▶◩
```

Figure 11–8: Setting a breakpoint

the application will continue until the next attention signal. Or, if you leave the breakpoint in, it will stop the next time one of the Draw methods is called.

WRITING DEBUGGING CODE

When developing your own MacApp program, you will often want to build your own debugging code into a routine that will be available when you're using the program but won't make the final version bigger or slower.

The options used with the MABuild command set four MPW Pascal conditional compilation flags, which are used by MacApp programs and the MacApp library to selectively include such debugging code. These flags are shown in Table 11–9, along with global variables used to dynamically control debugging.

If you wish to include code in your program that will only be compiled into the development version, you should bracket the code with the Pascal conditional compilation directives:

```
{$IFC qDebug}
  (* debugging code here *)
{$ENDC}
```

Flag†	Conditional compilation Description		
qDebug	Enclosed code is used only for debugging		
qTrace	UObject sets {$D++} for MacApp debugger calls		
qNames	If NOT qTrace, UObject sets {$D+} for MacsBug symbols		
qRangeCheck	UObject sets {$R+} for Pascal range checking		
qNeedsROM128K	Enclosed code is for 128K ROM or later		

Global variables

Variable††	Description	Debugger command
gIntenseDebugging	Use extra debugging code	XI
gExperimenting	Enable experimental features	XX

† Tested with {$IFC *flag*} ... {$ENDC}. Normally MABuild sets all four flags TRUE for debugging, FALSE otherwise

†† Tested with Pascal IF *var* THEN statment. Set to FALSE until enabled by debugger command. Should not be used if qDebug is FALSE.

Table 11–9: Configuration source code flags

This would include any extra validity checks, debugging traces, or error messages that you wouldn't want the user to see. Because any MacApp program built with debugging enabled will include the MacApp debugger, your debugging code can use ordinary Pascal Write and WriteLn calls to write a limited amount of status information to the debugging window if qDebug is true. The flag might more accurately be named qDevelop, since it will usually be true when the developer is testing the program. The display of detailed debugging information is controlled by global variable gIntenseDebugging.

MABuild sets all four flags to TRUE if no options are specified or to FALSE for MABuild ... opt or MABuild ... nodebug. You may want to test one of the other three flags separately. For example, if you have code that must never be range checked, you would bracket it with directives to disable and re-enable range checking, as in:

```
{$R-}
   byte := word;  (* truncate result *)
{$IFC qRangeCheck} {$R+} {$ENDC}
```

However, you would only re-enable range checking if the program was built with range checking enabled. You could also use the MPW Pascal {$PUSH} and {$POP} directives to save the range checking toggle, as in:

```
{$PUSH}
{$R-}
   byte := word;  (* truncate result *)
{$POP}
```

Also shown in the table are two global boolean variables that can be used to dynamically control debugging code while your program is running. These have a default value of FALSE.

One of the variables is normally used to control the level of debugging validation or to display tracing to the debug window. As any experienced programmer knows, large software systems should be permanently "instrumented" with such selective debugging code. Any time you add debugging code during development to find a particular problem, you probably should leave that code in to catch the problem should it reappear; at the same time, you don't want to be drowning in trace output or creeping through validation checks all the time.

Instead, your code checks the value of gIntenseDebugging and performs the extra debugging steps if true. The value of this variable can be toggled from the MacApp debugger with the XI command.

For example, when your program reads a document into memory, it may need to analyze the contents of the document and build a series of data structures corresponding to the document. With qIntenseDebugging enabled, you would write the data structures to the debug window. To avoid excessive output, you would set a breakpoint in your DoRead method, turn debugging on when you reach the breakpoint, and then turn it off again upon exiting the method procedure.

The other variable controls the operation of code you may wish to add to your program but do not consider to be fully reliable. In a single compile, you might typically fix old bugs and add new features, which may introduce new bugs. If you bracket the experimental code with

```
{$IFC qDebug}
IF qExperimenting THEN
BEGIN
   (* new features *)
END;
{$ENDC}
```

the code will not be executed unless the XX debugger command is used to enable experimental features.

References to either variable should always be bracketed by conditional compilation based on the qDebug flag. The variables can only be set to TRUE if the program is compiled with debugging, and there's no need to bloat your production application with unreachable code.

Finally, the qROM128K compilation flag indicates whether the program was built using MABuild with the rom128K option to run only on 128K ROM machines. You might use this if you have code that shouldn't be used or isn't needed with an old ROM machine.

Other information is available through the gConfiguration variable, a record containing a series of fields describing the configuration available to the currently running MacApp program. Information about the hardware (and hardware-related managers) configuration includes the presence of ADB, SCSI, the Macintosh II Sound Manager, a floating point coprocessor, and the particular main Motorola processor—MC68000 or MC68020.

Software configuration information in gConfiguration includes hierarchical menus, the Script Manager, formatted TextEdit, HFS, 128K ROM features, and color QuickDraw. Note that this information is not necessarily determined by the ROM, since the first four are available as RAM-based trap patches in addition to later ROMs.

CUSTOM DEBUGGING METHODS

The final step is to write a debugging method for any object type that you define. The Inspect method for an object is expected to display the fields of the object to the debugging window using WriteLn calls. It will be called whenever the I command is used from the debugger with an object of that type. This is a natural example of the object-oriented approach: Inspect associates an abstract behavior (display debugging output) with several different object types but expects a different interpretation of the behavior for each type.

Your custom Inspect method will always be called to display the contents that type no matter where the object is referenced. For example, if you set a breakpoint in method TView.SetExtent, the I command will call TMyView.Inspect if the SetExtent was performed on a TMyView object.

You must redeclare Inspect as a method of your object with the OVERRIDE keyword. As with the other debugging code, any reference to Inspect should be bracketed by conditional compilation directives, as in:

```
TMyView = OBJECT(TView)
  fNumShapes: INTEGER;
...
{$IFC qDebug}
  PROCEDURE Inspect; OVERRIDE;
{$ENDC}
END;
```

The implementation of the method should begin with a reference to ancestor behavior, which will display the standard fields for the object. The remainder of the method displays any additional fields that you'd like to see when inspecting an object. The entire method should be bracketed by conditional compilation, as in:

```
{$IFC qDebug}
PROCEDURE TMyView.Inspect;
BEGIN
   INHERITED Inspect;  (* show TView fields *)
   WriteLn('fNumShapes=',fNumShapes);
END;
{$ENDC}
```

11.6 MacApp Libraries

The power of MacApp comes in its libraries. These provide all the standard operations necessary to implement the Macintosh user interface, as well as many commonly found problems in building a complete application.

As MacApp evolves, the specifications of the libraries are subject to change. The complete and up-to-date specification of the libraries is provided by the *MacApp Programmer's Reference* and, of course, the MacApp source listings.

This section summarizes the object types defined in each MacApp unit, and the use of each type.

HOW TO USE THE LIBRARIES

As shown in the earlier examples, every unit of a MacApp program will normally include a USES statement for the standard MPW Pascal units:

```
USES
   MemTypes, QuickDraw, OSIntf, ToolIntf, PackIntf
```

As with other Pascal units, a unit used by the interface of one unit must also be included in your program. Most of the MacApp units use these five Pascal units, as well as three standard MacApp units.

The explicit dependencies of the MacApp units are shown by Figure 11–9.

All of the units depend on the definition of a simple object provided by unit UObject. When compiled for debugging, all the units also require three other units—UWriteLnWindow, UMeasure, and UTrace—but these units

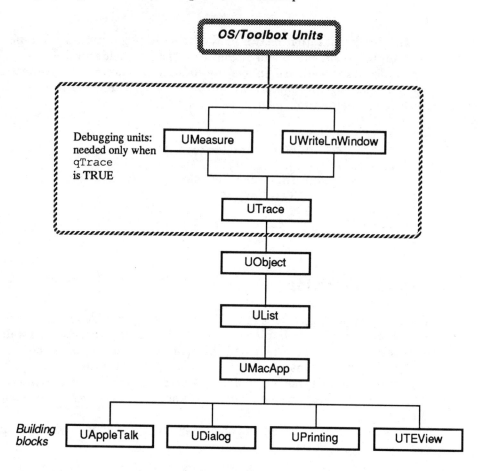

Figure 11–9: MacApp library dependencies

don't need to be included in your declarations unless used directly. All
MacApp programs require UMacApp and thus UList. The remaining units
are "building blocks," optional components designed for specialized requirements.

Your program may need to include additional Pascal units—such as SANE
or AppleTalk—if it makes use of them. Not surprisingly, the MacApp unit
UPrinting requires the Pascal unit MacPrint, which must be included in
your declarations if you use UPrinting.

In the reference material provided for the libraries, each new type is
described in the following three ways:

- **Customize:** Whether you define your own new types in terms of this
  type. "Always" means the type is provided as an ancestor to supply some
  of the behaviors for your own object; "never" means the object is meant
  to use as is.

- **Instantiate:** Whether your code actually allocates an object of this kind. This is closely related to the Customize designation, since types always customized are never instantiated.

- **Call methods:** Whether your program will directly use the methods defined by the library for this type. Methods that are never called are ones used internally by MacApp to provide standard operations. That's not to say you can ignore such methods—if you customize this type, you may have to customize the methods to provide your own operations.

The object types defined by the MacApp library units are summarized in Table 11–10.

UOBJECT

All objects in a MacApp program are defined in terms of `TObject`, which is defined by this unit. `TObject` defines four standard methods used by all objects, in addition to several other methods that are used by the MacApp debugger.

The `Free` method is required to deallocate any object when it is no longer required. As with other methods, it can be overridden by your custom type. If you need to access the standard definition (which calls the Memory Manager to return the relocatable block), your custom `Free` method can use `ShallowFree`, which should never be overridden.

The `Clone` method returns an exact copy of an object. If your custom object includes pointers to records or reference fields for other object, you might override `Clone` to copy these records/objects for the clone. The `ShallowClone` method is always the same as the `TObject.Clone` method and, like `ShallowFree`, should not be overridden.

These four methods are also defined in the `ObjIntf` unit provided by MPW Pascal. If you can get by with only these methods, you don't need to use MacApp at all and can distribute your Object Pascal source code to those who have MPW Pascal but don't have MacApp.

UMEASURE

This unit provides procedures for measuring the performance of a MacApp program and the MacApp libraries during development. It is normally called via MacApp debugger commands, and subdivides the program up into 8-byte buckets and reports the percentage of the time spent in each.

The standard MPW Pascal performance measurement library (unit `Perf`) provides similar capabilities but will also analyze time spent in ROM routines. However, it will not produce accurate results for a MacApp program built using debugging code and thus is suitable for speeding up the final, optimized version of a MacApp program.

Object types defined by MacApp library

Unit UObject

TObject   Standard ancestor object

Unit UList

TList   Used to maintain lists of objects

Unit UMacApp

TCommand   A user command or action
TEvtHandler   Any object that can handle an event
TApplication   This MacApp application
TDocument   A document opened by the application
TView   A view of the document
TFrame   A subset of the view
TWindow   A Toolbox window
TPrintHandler   Used to print a view
TDeskScrapView   A view used by "Show Clipboard"

Unit UAppleTalk

TTalkHandler   A TEvtHandler for network events
TRequester   A TTalkHandler to send ATP packet
TListener   A TTalkHandler to receive ATP packet

Unit UDialog

TDialogWindow   A TWindow used for a modal dialog box
TDialogItem   A view of a dialog item
TKeyHandler   A dialog item with editable text
TRadioCluster   A cluster of radio buttons

Unit UPrinting

TStdPrintHandler   Provides default printing
TPrintStyleChangeCommand   A "Page Setup" command

Unit UTEView

TTEView   A TextEdit view
TTECommand   A command for a TTEView
TTECutCopyCommand   A "Cut" or "Copy" command for a
TTEView
TTEPasteCommand   A "Paste" command for a TTEView
TTETypingCommand   A typing command for a TTEView

Table 11–10: Object types defined by MacApp library

ULIST

When writing MacApp programs, it will often be necessary to keep a variable-length list of other objects. For example, a MacApp application automatically maintains a list of the currently open documents.

The TList object maintains a list of other objects. Objects can be added or deleted from the list, and operations can be performed on each object in a list. TList may be customized if you require additional information about members of the list.

Because TList can be used with any object, the operations are only typed to TObject. When accessing objects already in the list, it will be necessary to explicitly coerce the type to a specific descendant of TObject, i.e., the type of object you originally put in the list.

UMACAPP

This unit is used by every unit that is used by a MacApp program since it includes the definition of the six standard object types TApplication, TCommand, TDocument, TFrame, TView, and TWindow.

Figure 11–10 shows the ancestry of the MacApp object types.

TEvtHandler is the ancestor of all objects that support events. Its immediate descendants include TApplication, TDocument, TView, and TFrame. The type TWindow is a descendant of TFrame.

As noted earlier, the first three types—TApplication, TDocument, and TView—are always customized into your own type to define or override methods specific to your application. TFrame and TWindow are usually used unmodified.

The remaining standard object type, TCommand, is used to communicate user actions to your methods. Many of these commands have corresponding methods provided by UMacApp. For example, the default method to handle cClose will check to see if the document has been modified; if so, a "Save changes..." alert will be displayed automatically by a MacApp library routine.

TCommand must be customized if you want the command to contain additional information specific to your application or documents. For example, the clipboard commands—cCut, cCopy, cPaste, and cClear—would normally require information about what part of your document was selected at the time the command was generated. An example of how to customize TCommand for clipboard operations is provided by the implementation of unit UTEView for text documents.

A special view also provided by UMacApp is TDeskScrapView. The default TApplication uses TDeskScrapView to handle the Show Clipboard menu item.

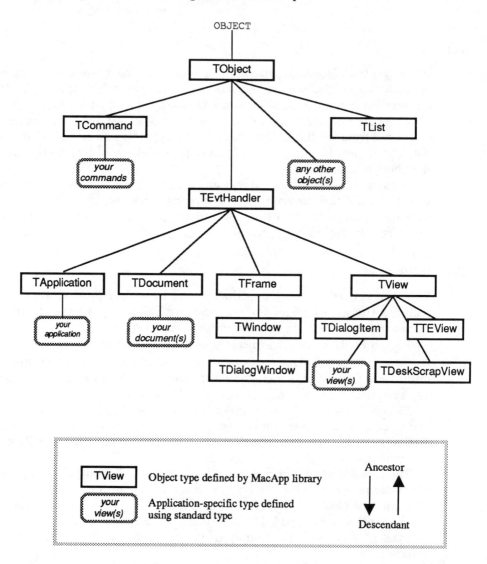

Figure 11–10:   Simplified MacApp object ancestry.

UMacApp also includes a definition of TPrintHandler. This type provides the minimal interface between views and printing. However, the standard methods for TPrintHandler do not actually support printing. Instead, these are defined by a customized version of TPrintHandler, such as described by unit UPrinting.

UPRINTING

TStdPrintHandler is a "stock" solution that provides standard print operations and can be used by many applications. If you allocate a TStdPrintHandler object and assign its reference value to the fPrintHandler field of a view, the view will automatically inherit printing capabilities.

Your program might need to customize TPrintHandler (or TStdPrintHandler) if the stock solution is not adequate. One reason might be to provide a page title that was printed on each page, but not displayed in the screen view.

TPrintStyleChangeCmd is a TCommand descendant that is associated with a specific command operation, the "Page Setup" menu item. Since this affects how a program calculates and displays page break, it is defined as a specific command type.

UTEVIEW

TTEView is a view of a document that supports the standard TextEdit toolbox routines. A MacApp program that uses a TTEView can immediately have a simple unformatted text editor, as the examples supplied by Apple demonstrate. The standard behaviors of the object include handling typing, mouse selection, and drawing the view.

The standard behaviors also support the standard menu commands from the "Edit" menu to move the clipboard to and from the clipboard. These are handled by the TTECommand type and its descendants. A TTECommand is used as is to perform a Clear operation. As the names suggest, the TTECut-Copy and TTEPaste descendants handle Cut, Copy, and Paste. The unit also supports "Select All," which, since it is not undoable, is a handled directly by TTEView rather than by a command object.

Each TTEView object keeps a handle to a standard TextEdit record. If you want to add (or modify) the text from your program, you can use the handle to call TextEdit directly. If you want to disable user modification of the text view by typing or clipboard operations, you can set a boolean field of a TTEView after initialization.

To build a text editor, you could customize TDocument to include a handle to a relocatable memory block contained in the document's text. When you opened a text file, you would read the contents into the block and then create a TTEView that used the same block for its TextEdit operations. When it came time to save the document, you would write the block (which will be updated by TTEView operations) to disk. The TTEView behavior would automatically draw the text for the screen or for printing.

UDIALOG

MacApp doesn't provide any particular advantages for modal dialogs and alerts—ones that typically put up a window and remain until explicitly terminated by an OK or Cancel. These dialogs can operate independently from the MacApp framework, since they do not interact with it. Your MacApp program would build using the same Dialog Manager calls as any other MPW Pascal program.

This unit defines TDialogView and TDialogWindow, which, as their names suggest, are view and window types for dialogs. These types are intended to support modeless dialogs, which are like any other window in that they can be activated and deactivated at will.

The unit also includes a definition of a TDialogItem, which is displayed as part of a TDialogView. Each TDialogItem object will normally correspond to an item in the corresponding 'DITL' dialog item resource. Each dialog item, for example, can be made visible or invisible using the SetVisibility method.

A descendant of TDialogItem is TKeyHandler, which handles editable text boxes; a particular descendant of TKeyHandler, TNumberText accepts only integer values. Another TDialogItem descendant is TRadioCluster, which handles groups of radio buttons. Each group of buttons corresponds to a single TRadioCluster object.

UAPPLETALK

This unit, as its name suggests, defines several new object types for supporting the AppleTalk communications protocols within a MacApp program. The unit is used by the Conference sample program to communicate messages between multiple Macintoshes on an AppleTalk network, which illustrates how it can be used.

The functions of AppleTalk do not correspond to any of the standard six object types—applications, documents, frames, views, windows, and commands. However, the first five represent objects that can handle events, as defined by the OS Event Manager, and thus are implemented through descendants of TEvtHandler. Objects that handle AppleTalk events (event code networkEvt) are also descendants of TEvtHandler and have the common ancestor TTalkHandler.

The Conference sample program is oriented toward sending and receiving messages between two or more AppleTalk nodes. This is well-suited to the AppleTalk Transaction Protocol (ATP), which is designed to reliably transport individual requests (transactions) between two nodes.

The unit defines two descendants of TTalkHandler, the TRequester and TListener types, which handle individual AppleTalk transactions. A TRequester object at one node sends requests across AppleTalk using ATP.

A `TListener` object at another node waits for a request to come in, then executes the code to process that request.

Since each message may be longer than the maximum size of an AppleTalk transaction, the unit also defines two types to handle a series of related transactions or a session. A `TSender` sends a series of related ATP requests, which are received by a `TReceiver`. The `Conference` sample customizes these two types to implement its document-oriented transactions.

Appendix A

Command Summary

This appendix contains a summary of the available commands of MPW 2.0, their parameters and options. This material is copyright matter of Apple Computer, Inc., and is used with its express permission.

In the syntax specifications, [ ] delimit optional parameters, and ... indicates that the parameters may be repeated multiple times.

The following symbols refer to the command's use of the standard input and output streams:

<	input
>	output
≥	diagnostic output

For example, the syntax

```
Quote [-n] [parameter...] > parameters
```

indicates −n may optionally precede a list of one or more parameter values (which are also optional), and the resulting output is a list of parameters.

AddMenu — add menu item

```
AddMenu [menu [item [command...]]]  > menuList
```

Note: item can contain the following metacharacters

(*char* means any character):

/*char*	Assign the keyboard equivalent Command*char*
!*char*	Place *char* to the left of the menu item
^n	Item has an icon, where n is the icon number
(	Item is disabled
<*style*	Item has a special style: *style* can be any of the following:
B	Bold
I	Italic
U	Underline
O	Outline
S	Shadow

Adjust — adjust lines

```
Adjust [-c count] [-l spaces] selection [window]
```

-c count	Repeat the Adjust count times
-l spaces	Shift lines right spaces

Alert — display alert box

```
Alert [message...]
```

Alias — define and write command aliases

```
Alias [name [word...]]  > aliasList
```

Align — align text to left margin

```
Align [-c count] selection [window]
```

-c count   Repeat the Align count times

Asm — 68xxx Macro Assembler

```
Asm [option…] [file…]  < file > listing ≥ progress
```

-addrsize size	Set size of address display
-blksize blocks	Use blocks * 512 byte I/O buffers
-case on	Distinguish between upper and lower case
-case obj[ect]	Preserve case in object file
-case off	Ignore case (default)
-c[heck]	Syntax check only, don't create object file
-d[efine] name	Equivalent to: name EQU 1
-d[efine] name=value	Equivalent to: name EQU value
-d[efine] &name	Equivalent to: &name SET[AC] 1
-d[efine] &name=value	Equivalent to: &name SET[AC] value
-e[rrlog] file	Write errors and warnings to file
-f	Suppress page ejects in listing
-font name[,size]	Set listing font and size
-h	Suppress page headers in listing
-i directory,…	Search for includes in directory,…
-l	Write full listing to output
-o objname	Generate code in file or directory objname
-pagesize l[,w]	Set listing page length and width
-print mode	Equivalent to: PRINT mode
-p	Write progress information to diagnostics
-s	Write short listing to output
-t	Write time and total lines to diagnostics
-w	Suppress warnings
-wb	Suppress warnings on branch instructions

Backup — folder file backup

```
Backup [option...] -from folder -to folder [file...] >
   commands ≥ progress
```

-a	Copy all files in from not in to
-alt	Alternate prompts for disk drives
-c	Create to folders if they don't exist
-check [*checkopt*,]...	Produce reports based on [checkopt]
[*checkopt*]=	
from	From not in to
to	To not in from
allfroms	From not in to even if none
alltos	To not in from even if none
folders	From folders not in to
newer	To's newer than from's
-co filename	Redirect -check reports to filename
-compare [only][,'opts']	Generate compare commands for out-of-date files
-d	Generate delete commands for file in to not in from
-do [only][,'command']	Generate the command string specified by command...
-e	Eject disk when done
-from folder l drive	Specify source folder or drive (1 or 2)
-l	Generate directory listing of from files
-m	Multi-disk—more than one from or to disk
-n	Show folder nesting by indenting commands
-p	Write progress information to diagnostics
-r	Recursively process nested folders
-revert	Revert to files to their from state
-since date [,time] l fname	Process only files since specified time
-sync	Synchronize both source and destination folders
-t type	Process only files of specified type
-to folder l drive	Specify destination folder or drive (1 or 2)
-y	Suppress duplicate -y option

Beep — generate tones

```
Beep [note [,duration [,level]]]...
```

Begin — group commands

```
Begin
  command...
End
```

Break — break from For or Loop

```
Break [If expression]
```

BuildCommands — show build commands

```
BuildCommands program [option...] > commands
```

option...   Make command options

BuildMenu — create the Build menu

```
BuildMenu
```

BuildProgram — build the specified program

```
BuildProgram program [option...] > log
```

option...   Make command options

C — C compiler

```
C [option...] [file] < file > preprocessor ≥ progress
```

-align	Long word align all data
-c	Write comments with preprocessor output
-d name	Equivalent to: #define name 1
-d name=string	Equivalent to: #define name string
-e	Write preprocessor results to output
-elems68881	Generate MC68881 code for trancendental functions
-g	Generate function names in code (implies ga)
-ga	Always generate stack frames (LINK, UNLK)

-i directory	Search for includes in directory
-mc68020	Generate MC68020 code
-mc68881	Generate MC68881 code for floating point operations
-o objname	Generate code in file objname
-p	Write progress information to diagnostics
-q	Optimize for speed at the expense of space
-q2	Optimizer may assume no multitasking
-s segment	Generate code in segment
-u name	Equivalent to: #undef name
-w	Suppress warnings
-x6	Avoid non-stack CLR x instructions
-x12	Generate 68010 code
-x55	Make bitfields signed
-z6	Always allocate 32 bits for enums
-z84	Enable language anachronisms

Canon — canonical spelling tool

```
Canon [option…] dictionary [file…] < file > new
```

-s	Case sensitive replacement
-a	Assembler identifiers (include $, %, @)
-c chars	Consider only the first chars characters

Catenate — concatenate files

```
Catenate [file…]  < file > catenation
```

Clear — clear the selection

```
Clear [-c count] selection [window]
```

-c count	Repeat the Clear count times

Close — close a window

```
Close [-a] [-y | -n] [window…]
```

-a	Close all the windows
-n	Don't save any modified windows (avoids dialog)
-y	Save modified windows before closing (avoids dialog)

Compare — compare text files

```
Compare [option...] file1 [file2]  < file2 > differences ≥
    progress
```

-b	Treat several blanks or tabs as a single blank
-c c1-c2[,c1-c2]	Compare only specified columns
-d depth	Maximum stack depth
-e context	Display specified number of context lines
-g groupingFactor	Grouping factor (matching lines for resync)
-h width	Write differences horizontally
-l	Lower case (i.e. ignore case differences)
-n	Don't write to output if files match
-m	Suppress displays of mismatched lines
-p	Write progress information to diagnostics
-s	Use static grouping factor
-t	Ignore trailing blanks
-v	Suppress line numbers in vertical displays
-x	Don't expand tabs

Confirm — display confirmation dialog

```
Confirm [-t] [message...]
```

-t	Three buttons (Yes, No, Cancel)

Continue —
continue with next iteration of For or Loop

```
Continue [If expression]
```

Copy — copy selection to Clipboard

```
Copy [-c count] selection [window]
```

-c count	Copy the nth selection, where n = count

Count — count lines and characters

```
Count [-l] [-c] [file...]  < file > counts
```

-l	Write only line counts
-c	Write only character counts

CreateMake —create a program makefile

```
CreateMake [-Application | -Tool | -DA] program file...
```

-Application   Create an Application (default)
-Tool   Create a Tool
-DA   Create a Desk Accessory

Cut —
copy selection to Clipboard and delete it

```
Cut [-c count] selection [window]
```

-c count   Cut the next count selections

CvtObj —
convert Lisa object files to MPW object files

```
CvtObj [option...] LisaObjectFile  ≥ progress
```

-n namesFile   Use name substitutions in nameFile
-o objectFile   Create file objectFile
-p   Write progress information to diagnostics

Date — write the date and time

```
Date [-a | -s] [-d | -t]  > date
```

-a   Abbreviated date (e.g. Wed, Jun 18, 1986)
-d   Write date only
-s   Short date (e.g. 6/18/86)
-t   Write time only

Delete — delete files and directories

```
Delete [-y | -n | -c] [-i] [-p] name...  ≥ progress
```

-c   Cancel if a directory is to be deleted (avoids
                        dialog)

-i	Ignore errors (no diagnostics)
-n	Don't delete directory contents (avoids dialog)
-p	Write progress information to diagnostics
-y	Delete directory contents (avoids dialog)

DeleteMenu —
delete user-defined menus and items

```
DeleteMenu [menuName [itemName]]
```

DeRez — resource decompiler

```
DeRez [option…] resourceFile [file…] >      description ≥
progress
```

-c[ompatible]	Generate output compatible with Rez 1.0
-e[scape]	Don't escape chars < $20 or > $D8
-d[efine] name[=value]	Equivalent to #define name [value]
-i[nclude] pathname	Search this path when looking for #include files
-m[axstringsize] n	Write strings n characters per line
-only typeExpr	Process only resources of this type
-p[rogress]	Write progress information to diagnostics
-rd	Suppress warnings for redeclared types
-s[kip] typeExpr	Skip resources of this type
-u[ndef] name	Equivalent to #undef name

Note: A typeExpr may have one of these forms:
  type
  "'type'(id)"
  "'type'(id:id)"
  "'type'(∂"name∂")"

Directory —
set or write the default directory

```
Directory [-q] [directory] > directory
```

-q	Don't quote directories with special characters

DirectoryMenu — create the Directory menu

```
DirectoryMenu [directory...]
```

DumpCode —
write formatted CODE resources

```
DumpCode [option...] resourceFile  > dump ≥ progress
```

-d	Don't dump object code
-h	Don't write headers (offsets, hex, etc.)
-jt	Don't dump jump table
-n	Dump only resource names
-p	Write progress information to diagnostics
-r byte1[,byte2]	Dump code from address byte1 (through byte2)
-rt type[=id]	Dump only resources with this type (and id)
-s name	Dump only resource with this name

DumpObj — write formatted object files

```
DumpObj [option...] objectFile  > dump ≥ progress
```

-d	Don't dump object code
-h	Don't write headers (offsets, hex, etc.)
-i	Use ids, rather than names, in dump
-l	Dump file locations of object records
-m name	Dump only module name, or module with entry name
-n	Dump only the dictionary of names
-p	Write progress information to diagnostics
-r byte1[,byte2]	Dump code from byte1 in file (through byte2)

Duplicate — duplicate files and directories

```
Duplicate [-y | -n | -c] [-p] [-d | -r] name... target  ≥
  progress
```

-c	Cancel if conflict occurs (avoids dialog)
-d	Duplicate data fork only
-n	Don't overwrite target files (avoids dialog)
-p	Write progress information to diagnostics

-r   Duplicate resource fork only
-y   Overwrite target files (avoids dialog)

Echo — echo parameters

```
Echo [-n] [parameter...]  > parameters
```

-n   Don't write return following the parameters

Eject — eject volumes

```
Eject [-m] volume...
```

-m   Leave the volume mounted

Else — alternate conditions

See If

End — end group of statements

See Begin, For, If or Loop

Entab — convert runs of blanks to tabs

```
Entab [option...] [file...]  < file > tabbed ≥ progress
```

-d tabValue   Input tab setting
-l quote...   Left quotes that prevent Entab (default "')
-n   No quote characters, Entab everything
-p   Write progress information to diagnostics
-q quote...   Quotes that prevent Entab (default "')
-r quote...   Right quotes that prevent Entab (default "')
-t tabValue   Output tab setting

Equal — compare files and directories

```
Equal [-d | -r] [-i] [-p] [-q] name... target  >
  differences ≥ progress
```

-d	Compare data forks only
-i	Ignore files in target not in directory name
-r	Compare resource forks only
-p	Write progress information to diagnostics
-q	Quiet - don't write output, just set {Status}

Erase — initialize volumes

```
Erase [-y] [-s] volume...
```

-y	Yes - erase the disk (avoids dialog)
-s	Single-sided - 400K (default 800K)

ErrTool —
create errorfile mapping error numbers to messages

```
ErrTool [option...] [file...]  < file > listing ≥ progress
```

-l	write listing to standard output
-o file/dir	output file or directory
-p	write progress information to diagnostics

Evaluate — evaluate an expression

```
Evaluate [word...]  > value
```

Execute —
execute command file in current scope

```
Execute commandFile
```

Exists — test existence of a file or directory

```
Exists [-d | -f | -w] [-q] name...  > file
```

-d	Check if name is a directory
-f	Check if name is a file
-w	Check if name is a file and writeable
-q	Don't quote file names with special characters

Exit — exit from command file

```
Exit [status] [If expression]
```

Export — make variables available to commands

```
Export [-r | -s] [name...]  > exports
```

-r   Generate Unexport commands for all exported
                            variables
-s   Print the names only

FileDiv—divide file into several smaller files

```
FileDiv [option...] file [prefix]  ≥ progress
```

-f   Split file at formfeed character
-n splitPoint   Split file after splitPoint lines
-p   Write progress information to diagnostics

Files — list files and directories

```
Files [option...] [name...]  > fileList
```

-c creator   List only files with this creator
-d   List only directories
-f   List full pathnames
-i   Treat all arguments as files
-l   Long format (type, creator, size, dates, etc.)
-m columns   n column format, where n = columns
-n   Don't print header in long or extended format
-q   Don't quote filenames with special characters
-r   Recursively list subdirectories
-s   Suppress the listing of directories
-t type   List only files of this type
-x [format]   Extended format with the fields specified by for-
                            mat

Note: The following characters can specify the [format]
  a   Flag attributes
  b   Logical size, in bytes, of the data fork

r	Logical size, in bytes, of the resource fork
c	Creator of File ("Fldr" for folders)
d	Creation date
k	Physical size in kilobytes of both forks
m	Modification date
t	Type
o	Owner (only for folders on a file server)
g	Group (only for folders on a file server)
p	Privileges (only for folders on a file server)

Find — find and select a text pattern

```
Find [-c count] selection [window]
```

-c count   Find the nth selection, where n = count

Font — set font characteristics

```
Font fontname fontsize [window]
```

For — repeat commands once per parameter

```
For name In word...
  command...
End
```

Help — write summary information

```
Help [-f helpfile] [command...] > helpInformation
```

-f helpfile   Alternate helpfile (default MPW.Help)

If — conditional command execution

```
If expression
  command...
[Else If expression
  command... ] ...
[Else
  command... ]
End
```

Lib — combine object files

```
Lib [option...] objectFile...  ≥ progress
```

-b	Big Lib - equivalent to -bf -bs 4
-bf	Open one file at a time, allowing many files
-bs n	Use n * 512 byte input buffer (default n=16)
-d	Suppress duplicate definition warnings
-df deleteFile	Delete modules listed in file deleteFile
-dm name[,name]...	Delete external modules and entry points
-dn name[,name]...	Delete external names, making them local
-mn oldName= newName	Rename module or entry point
-o name	Write object file name (default Lib.Out.o)
-p	Write progress information to diagnostics
-sg newSeg=old[,old]...	Merge old segments into new segment
-sn oldSeg=newSeg	Change segment name oldSeg to newSeg
-w	Suppress warnings

Line — find line in the target window

```
Line n
```

Link — link an application, tool, or resource

```
Link [option...] objectFile...> map ≥ progress
```

-b	Big Link - equivalent to -bf -bs 4
-bf	Open one file at a time, allowing many files
-bs n	Use n * 512 byte input buffer (default 16)
-c creator	Set objectFile creator (default ????)
-d	Suppress duplicate definition warnings
-da	Desk accessory - add NULL to segment names
-l	Write a location map to output
-la	List anonymous symbols in location map
-lf	List file and location of definitions
-m mainEntry	Use mainEntry as main entry point
-ma name=alias	Create an alias for module name
-o resourceFile	Write objectFile (default Link.Out)
-opt	Perform Object Pascal optimizations
-p	Write progress information to diagnostics
-ra [segment]=attr	Set segment resource attributes
-rn	Don't include resource names in objectFile

-rt type=id	Set resource type and lowest id (default CODE=0)
-sg newSeg=old[,old]...	Merge old segments into new segment
-sn oldSeg=newSeg	Change segment name oldSeg to newSeg
-ss size	Maximum segment size (default 32760)
-t type	Set objectFile type (default APPL)
-uf unrefFile	Write list of unreferenced modules to unrefFile
-w	Suppress warnings
-x crossRefFile	Write cross reference to crossRefFile

Loop — repeat commands until Break

```
Loop
   command...
End
```

MABuild — build MacApp program

```
MABuild AppName [options...]
```

Note: the options to MABuild are reserved words (without a - prefix) from the following list:

noexecute   Create the appname.makeit file, but don't execute it.

debug	Include debugging facilities in application.
nodebug	Don't include debugging facilities in application.
opt	No debugging, and optimize method calls.

rom128k	Build an application that can not run on 64K ROMs.
anyrom	Build an application that can run on any ROM.

-...   Options starting with a dash are passed directly to Make.

Defaults are debug and anyrom.

Make — program construction tool

```
Make [option...] target... > commands ≥ progress
```

-d name[=value]   Define variable name as value (overrides makefile)

-e	Rebuild everything regardless of dates
-f makefile	Read dependencies from makefile (default MakeFile)
-p	Write progress information to diagnostics
-r	Write roots of dependency graph to output
-s	Write structure of target dependencies to output
-t	Touch dates of targets and prerequisites
-u	Identify targets in makefile not reached in build
-v	Write verbose explanations to diagnostics
-w	Suppress warnings

Mark — set a marker in a window

```
Mark [-y | -n] selection name [window]
```

-y	Replace existing marker (avoids dialog)
-n	Don't replace existing marker (avoids dialog)

Markers — list markers

```
Markers [window]
```

MDSCvt — convert MDS assembler source

```
MDSCvt [option...] [file...]  < file > output ≥ progress
```

-d	Detab - replace tabs with spaces
-e	Detab input and entab output
-f directivesFile	
	Read case of directives from directivesFile
-g n	Size of Quickdraw global area for main program
-i	Convert include file - don't add PROC and END
-m	Omit BLANKS ON and STRING ASIS from output
-main	Convert main program source
-n	Don't add .a suffix to form output filename
-p	Write progress information to diagnostics
-pre[fix] string	Add prefix to input filename to form output name
-suf[fix] string	Add suffix to input filename to form output

```
        lue                  Output file tab setting
-u c                         Use character c to make macro names unique
-! name                      Name of main program's entry point
```

Mount — mount volumes

```
Mount drive…
```

Move — move files and directories

```
Move [-y | -n | -c] [-p] name… target  ≥ progress
```

```
-c                           Cancel if conflict occurs (avoids dialog)
-n                           Don't overwrite target files (avoids dialog)
-p                           Write progress information to diagnostics
-y                           Overwrite target files (avoids dialog)
```

MoveWindow — move window to h,v

```
MoveWindow  h v [window]
```

New — open new file in window

```
New [name…]
```

Newer — compare modification dates of files

```
Newer [-c] [-e] [-q] file… target > newer
```

```
-c                           Compare creation dates
-e                           Report names that have same (equal) date as
                             target
-q                           Don't quote file names with special characters
```

NewFolder — create folder

```
NewFolder name…
```

Open — open file in window

```
Open  [-n | -r]  [-t]  [name...]
```

-n	Open new file (default name Untitled)
-r	Open file for read-only use
-t	Open file as the target window

Parameters — write parameters

```
Parameters [parameter...]  > parameters
```

Pascal — Pascal compiler

```
Pascal [option...] [file...] < file ≥ progress
```

-align	Long word align all data
-b	Generate A5 references for procedure addresses
-c	Syntax check only, don't create object file
-d name= (TRUE|FALSE)	Set compile time variable name
-e file	Write errors to file
-h	Suppress error messages regarding unsafe handles
-i directory,...	Search for includes in directory,...
-k directory	Create $LOAD files in directory
-mc68020	Generate MC68020 code
-mc68881	Generate MC68881 code for floating point operations
-o objname	Generate code in file or directory objname
-ov	Generate code to test for overflow
-p	Write progress information to diagnostics
-r	Don't generate range checking code
-t	Write compilation time to diagnostics
-u	Initialize all data to $7267 for debugging use
-w	Don't perform peephole optimization
-y directory	Create temporary files in directory

-z—

do not produce debugger specific information PasMat — format Pascal programs

```
PasMat [option...] [input [output]]  < input > output ≥
   progress
```

-a	Set a-	disable CASE label bunching
-b	Set b+	enable IF bunching
-body	Set body+	to disable indenting procedure bodies
-c	Set c+	suppress Return before BEGIN
-d	Set d+	use {...} comment delimiters
-e	Set e+	capitalize identifiers
-entab	Replace multiple blanks with tabs	
-f	Set f-	disable formatting
-g	Set g+	group assignment and call statements
-h	Set h-	disable FOR, WHILE, WITH bunching
-i directory,...	Search for includes in directory,...	
-in	Set in+	process includes
-k	Set k+	indent statements between BEGIN and END
-l	Set l+	literally copy reserved words, identifiers
-list file	Write listings to file	
-n	Set n+	group formal parameters
-o width	Set output line width (default 80)	
-p	Write progress information to diagnostics	
-pattern -old-new-	Modify include names, changing old to new	
-q	Set q+	no special ELSE IF formatting
-r	Set r+	upper case reserved words
-rec	Set rec+	to indent field lists under defined id
-s file	Substitute identifiers based on pairs in file	
-t tab	Set output tab setting (default 2)	
-u	Rename identifiers to match first occurence	
-v	Set v+	put THEN on separate line
-w	Set w+	upper case identifiers
-x	Set x+	suppress space around operators
-y	Set y+	suppress space around :=
-z	Set z+	suppress space after commas
-:	Set :+	align colons in VAR declarations
-@	Set @+	multiple CASE tags on separate lines
-∂	Set #+	smart grouping of assignments and calls
-_	Set _+	delete _ from identifiers

PasRef — cross reference Pascal programs

```
PasRef [option...] [file...]  < file > crossReference ≥
   progress
```

-a	Process includes and units each time encountered
-c	Process includes and units only once
-d	Process each file separately
-i directory,...	Search for includes in directory,...
-l	Write identifiers in lower case
-n	Don't process USES or includes
-ni	-noi[ncludes]	Don't process include files
-nl	-nol[istings]	Don't list the input
-nolex	Don't write lexical information
-nt	-not[otal]	Don't write total line count
-nu	-nou[ses]	Don't process USES declarations
-o	Source written using Object Pascal
-p	Write progress information to diagnostics
-s	Don't write include and USES filenames
-t	Cross reference by total line number
-u	Write identifiers in upper case
-w width	Set output line width (default 110)
-x width	Set maximum identifier width

Paste —
replace selection with Clipboard contents

```
Paste [-c count] selection [window]
```

| -c count | Repeat the Paste count times |

PerformReport—
combine link map and performance data

```
PerformReport [option...]  > reportFile ≥ progress
```

-a	List all procedures, in segment order (default: Produce only partial list, sorted by percentage)
-l linkDataFile	Read link map file (concatenated with ROM.list)
-m measurementsFile	Read performance measurements file (default: "Perform.Out")
-n NN	Show the top NN procedures (default: 50)
-p	Write progress information to diagnostics

Print — print text files

```
Print [option…] [file…]  < file ≥ progress
```

-b	Print a border around the text
-b2	Alternate form of border
-bm n[.n]	Bottom margin in inches (default 0)
-c[opies] n	Print n copies
-ff string	Treat "string" at beginning of line as a formfeed
-f[ont] name	Print using specified font
-from n	Begin printing with page n
-h	Print headers (time, file, page)
-hf[ont] name	Print headers using specified font
-hs[ize] n	Print headers using specified font size
-l[ines] n	Print n lines per page
-lm n[.n]	Left margin in inches (default .2778)
-ls n[.n]	Line spacing (2 means double-space)
-md	Use modification date of file for time in header
-n	Print line numbers to left of text
-nw [-]n	Width of line numbers, - indicates zero padding
-p	Write progress information to diagnostics
-page n	Number pages beginning with n
-r	Print pages in reverse order
-rm n[.n]	Right margin in inches (default 0)
-s[ize] n	Print using specified font size
-t[abs] n	Consider tabs to be n spaces
-title title	Include title in page headers
-tm n[.n]	Top margin in inches (default 0)
-to n	Stop printing after page n
-q quality	Print quality (HIGH, STANDARD, DRAFT)

ProcNames—
display Pascal procedure and function names

```
ProcNames [option…] [file…]  < file ≥ progress
```

-c	Process includes and units only once
-d	Reset total line count to 1 on each new file
-e	Suppress page eject between each procedure listing
-f	PasMat format compatibilty mode

-i pathname,...	Search for includes or USES in directory,...
-n	Suppress line number and level information
-o	Source file is an Object Pascal program
-p	Write progress information to diagnostics
-u	Process USES declarations

Quit — quit MPW

```
Quit [-y | -n | -c]
```

-c	Cancel if a window needs to be saved (avoids dialog)
-n	Do not save any modified windows (avoids dialog)
-y	Save all modified windows (avoids dialog)

Quote—
echo parameters, quoting them if needed

```
Quote [-n] [parameter…] > parameters
```

| -n | Don't write return following the parameters |

Rename — rename files and directories

```
Rename [-y | -n | -c] oldName newName
```

-c	Cancel if conflict occurs (avoids dialog)
-n	Don't overwrite existing file (avoids dialog)
-y	Overwrite existing file (avoids dialog)

Replace — replace the selection

```
Replace [-c count] selection replacement [window]
```

| -c count | Repeat the replace count times |

Request — request text from a dialog

```
Request [-d default] [message…]
```

| -d default | Set default response |

ResEqual—
compares the resources in two files

ResEqual [-p] File1 File2

-p	Write progress information to diagnostics
file1	The name of the first resource file to compare
file2	The name of the second resource file to compare

Revert — revert to saved document

Revert [-y] [window...]

-y	Revert to old version (without dialog)

Rez — resource compiler

Rez [option...] [file...] < file ≥ progress

-a[ppend]	Merge resource into output resource file
-align word I longword	Align resource to word or longword boundaries
-c[reator] creator	Set output file creator
-d[efine] name[=value]	Equivalent to: #define macro [value]
-i[nclude] pathname	Path to search when looking for #include files
-o file	Write output to file (default Rez.Out)
-ov	Ok to overwrite protected resources when appending
-p	Write progress information to diagnostics
-rd	Suppress warnings for redeclared types
-ro	Set the mapReadOnly flag in output
-s[earch] pathname	Path to search when looking for INCLUDE resources
-t[ype] type	Set output file type
-u[ndef] name	Equivalent to: #undef name

RezDet — resource detective

RezDet [option...] file... > dump

-b[ig]	Read resources one at a time, not all at once

-d[ump]	Write -show information, plus headers, lists, etc.
-l[ist]	Write list of resources with minimum information
-q[uiet]	Don't write any output, just set {Status}
-r[awdump]	Write -dump information plus contents
-s[how]	Write information about each resource

Note: Use at most one of -quiet, -list, -show, -dump, and -rawdump.

Save — save contents of window

`Save [-a | window...]`

-a	Save the contents of all windows

Search — search files for pattern

`Search [-s | -i] [-r] [-q] [-f file] pattern [file...] <`
`  file > found`

-f file	Lines not written to output are put in this file
-i	Case insensitive search (overriding {CaseSensitive})
-s	Case sensitive search (overriding {CaseSensitive})
-r	Write non-matching line to standard output
-q	Suppress file name and line number in output

Select — select from a list dialog

`Select [option...] [[item..] | < file]`

-d[efault] item	Item is entered in list and comes up selected
-m[essage] message	Display message in dialog above the list
-q[uote]	Don't quote items in the output
-r[ows] rows	Make the list with this many rows
-w[idth] width	Make the list this many pixels wide

Set — define or write Shell variables

```
Set [name [value]] > variableList
```

SetDirectory — set the default directory

```
SetDirectory directory
```

SetFile — set file attributes
```
SetFile [option...] file...
```

-a [*attributes*]	Attributes (lowercase = 0, uppercase = 1)
-c creator	File creator
-d date	Creation date (mm/dd/yy [hh:mm[:ss] [AM | PM]])
-l h,v	ICON location (horizontal,vertical)
-m date	Modification date (mm/dd/yy [hh:mm[:ss] [AM | PM]])
-t type	File type

Note: Period (.) represents the current date and time.
Note: The following [*attributes*] may be used with the -a option:

L	Locked
V	Invisible
B	Bundle
S	System
I	Inited
D	Desktop
M	Shared (can run multiple times)

A	Always switch launch (if possible)

SetPriv—

set privileges for directories on file servers
```
SetPriv [option...] directory... > information
```

-d [*privileges*]	Set privileges for seeing directories
-f [*privileges*]	Set privileges for seeing files
-g group	Make the directories belong to group
-i	Return information on directories
-m [*privileges*]	Set privileges for makeing changes
-o owner	Make owner the owner of directories

Note: The following [*privileges*] characters may be used with the -d, -f, or -m options (Upper case enables the privilege, lower case disables it):

O   Owner
G   Group

E   Everyone

SetVersion —

version and revision number maintenance

`SetVersion [option...] file  > output ≥ progress`

-csource file	Update the #define Version string in C source
-d	Display (updated) version/revision to standard output
-fmt n*f*.m*f*	Format version/revision according to specification
-i resid	Use specified resource id instead of 0
-p	Write SetVersion's version info to diagnostics
-prefix prefix	Prefix version number with specified prefix
-[p]source file	Update the Version string constant in Pascal source
-r	Increment the revision number by 1
-rezsource file	Update the 'MPST' resource definition in Rez source
-sr revision	Set the revision number to the specified value
-suffix suffix	Suffix the revision number with specified suffix
-sv version	Set the version number to the specified value
-t type	Use specified resource type instead of 'MPST'
-v	Increment the version number by 1
-verid identifier	Use C/Pascal source version id instead of "Version"

Shift —
renumber command file positional parameters

`Shift [number]`

Shutdown —
power down or restart the machine

`Shutdown [-y | -n | -c] [-r]`

-c	Cancel if a window needs to be saved (avoids dialog)
-n	Do not save any modified windows (avoids dialog)
-r	Restart the machine
-y	Save all modified windows (avoids dialog)

SizeWindow — make window be x by y

```
SizeWindow  h v [window]
```

StackWindows —

arrange windows in a stacked fashion

```
StackWindows
```

StdFile — display a Standard File dialog

```
StdFile [[-t TYPE]... | -p | -d] [-q] [-m message]
  [-b buttontitle] [pathname]
```

-b	Specify the default button's title
-d	Select a directory
-m message	Specify a prompt
-p	Select a new filename (SFPutFile)
-q	Suppress quoting of filenames
-t type	Specify file type for SFGetFile dialog

SysErr —
display error messages based on message
number

```
SysErr [-f filename] [-s filename] [-n] [-p]
  errnbr[,insert,...] ...
  SysErr -i idnbr,...
```

-f filename	Explicit error msg file
-i	Report meaning of system id termination codes
-n	Suppress error numbers in displayed messages

-p   Write SysErr's version info to diagnostics
-s filename   Explicit system error msg file (default

                        SysErrs.Err)

Tab — set a window's tab setting

Tab spaces [window]

Target — make window the target window

Target name

TileWindows —

arrange windows in a tile pattern

TileWindows

TLACvt — convert Lisa TLA assembler source

TLACvt [option...] [file...] < file > output ≥ progress

-d   Detab - replace tabs with spaces
-e   Detab input and entab output
-f directivesFile   Read case of directives from directivesFile
-m   Omit BLANKS ON and STRING ASIS from
                        output
-n   Don't add .a suffix to form output filename
-p   Write progress information to diagnostics
-pre[fix] string   Add prefix to input filename to form output
                        name
-suf[fix] string   Add suffix to input filename to form output
                        name
-t value   Output file tab setting
-u c   use character c to make macro names unique

Translate — translate characters

Translate [-p] src [dst] < file > output ≥ progress

-p   Write progress information to diagnostics

-s   Set font, font size, and tab setting of output

Unalias — remove aliases

```
Unalias [name...]
```

Undo — undo last edit in target window

```
Undo [window]
```

Unexport — remove exports

```
Unexport [-r | -s] [name...] > unexports
```

-r   Generate Export commands for all unexported
                                variables

-s   Print the names only

Unmark — delete a marker in a window

```
Unmark name... window
```

Unmount — unmount volumes

```
Unmount volume...
```

Unset — remove Shell variable definitions

```
Unset [name...]
```

Volumes — list mounted volumes

```
Volumes [-l] [volume...] > volumeList
```

-l   Long format (name, drive, size, free, files, dirs)

-q   Don't quote volume names with special characters

Which —

determine what file the shell will execute

```
Which [-a] [-p] [name]  > file ≥ progress
```

-a   Report all commands named "name"

-p   Writes progress information to diagnostics

Windows — list windows

```
Windows [-q]
```


-q   Don't quote window names with special characters

ZoomWindow —

zoom target window to full size

```
ZoomWindow [-b | -s] [window]
```

-b   Zoom to full screen (big)

-s   Zoom back to regular size (small)

Appendix B

MPW Special Characters

Shell special characters

Character	Description
∂c	Treat *c* literally, unless ∂n (Return), ∂t (Tab), ∂f (Form feed)
'string'	treat *string* literally
"string"	treat *string* literally, except for ∂, ', { and `
> file	send standard output to *file*
>> file	append standard output to end of *file*
≥ file	send diagnostic output to *file*
≳ file	append diagnostic output to end of *file*
< file	read standard input from *file*
/string/	Forward pattern-matching scan for *string*
\string\	Forward pattern-matching scan for *string*
{variable}	Replace with value of *variable*
`command`	Replace with output from *command*
cmd1 ; cmd2	Execute *cmd1* and *cmd2*
cmd1 && cmd2	Execute *cmd2* if *cmd1* succeeds
cmd1 || cmd2	Execute *cmd2* if *cmd1* fails
cmd1 | cmd2	Redirect output of *cmd1* to input of *cmd2*

(*commands*)	Group execution of *commands*
# *comment*	Ignore *comment*
...	Provide Commando interactive help

Selection expressions

Selection Range

Expression	Description	Example
§	Current selection	§
¡*n*	Select line *n* lines before §	¡2
!*n*	Select line *n* lines after §	!0
n	Select entire line *n*	22
/*string*/	Search forward for *string*	/END/
string\\	Search backward for *string*	\\#include\\
marker	Select named *marker*	"PROCEDURE Foo"
s1:*s2*	Select from selections *s1* through *s2*, inclusive	\\{\\:/}/
(*selection*)	Group *selection*	(!0):(!10)

Insertion Point

Expression†	Description	Example
•	Beginning of document	•
∞	End of document	∞
Δ*selection*	Beginning of *selection*	Δ/BEGIN/
*selection*Δ	End of *selection*	123Δ
selection¡*n*	*n* characters before *selection*	\\INTEGER;\\¡4
selection!*n*	*n* characters after *selection*	Δ/int Foo()/!4

† The values of *selection* include any valid selection expression
From highest to lowest, the order of precedence is

    / or \\
    ( )
    Δ
    ! or ¡
    :

Simple regular expressions

Character	Description
c	Match *c* as an ordinary character (unless special)†
'string'	treat *string* as ordinary characters
"string"	treat *string* as ordinary characters, except for ', {, ∂
?	match any single character
≈	match as many characters as possible (0 or more), except Return
[*list*]	match a single character in *list* ††
[–*list*]	match a single character not in *list* ††

†	Character	Treated as special...
	∂	except within apostrophes('...')
	? ≈ * + [« ( )	except within range ([...]), or quoted ("...",'...')
	®	only after right parenthesis,)
	•	only as first character
	∞	special as last character
	/ \	special only if used as leading delimiter

††   [list] contains individual characters to be matched, or ranges separated by - signs. For example:

[013]	match 0, 1 or 3
[A-Z]	match uppercase letter
[+*/-]	match arithmetic operator
[]{}[()]	match grouping character

Combining Regular Expressions

Character	Description	Example
*patt**	Match 0 or more of pattern *patt*	[A-Z]*
patt+	Match 1 or more of pattern *patt*	[∂t]+
patt«*n,*»	Match *n* or more of pattern *patt*	[∂t]«2,»
patt«*n*»	Match exactly *n* of pattern *patt*	[∂t]«1»
patt«*n,m*»	Match *n* to *m* of pattern *patt*	[∂t]«0,1»
•*patt*	match *patt* at beginning of line	•[–∂t]+
patt∞	match *patt* at end of line	[–∂t]+∞
(*patt*)	Group *patt* for repeating or tagging	([–:]:)+
(*patt*)®*n*	Tag *patt* as expression number *n*	(≈)®1:(≈)®2

From highest to lowest, the order of precedence is

     ( )
     [ ]   «   »   ?   ≈   *   +   ®
     • ∞

Evaluation expression operators§

Algebraic	Pascal	C	Description (in order of precedence)
	( )	( )	Group expressions
	-	-	Integer negation
¬	NOT	!	Logical NOT
		~	Bitwise NOT
	*	*	Integer multiplication
+	DIV		Integer division§
	MOD	%	Integer remainder
	+	+	Integer addition
	-	-	Integer subtraction
		<<	Bitwise shift left
		>>	Bitwise shift right (sign-extend)
	<	<	Less than†
≤	<=	<=	Less than or equal to†
	>	>	Greater than†
≥	>=	>=	Greater than or equal to†
		==	Equal to†
≠	<>	!=	Not equal to†
		=~	String equal to regular expression
		!~	String not equal to regular expression
		&	Bitwise AND
		^	Bitwise exclusive OR
		|	Bitwise inclusive OR
	AND	&&	Logical AND
	OR	||	Logical OR

Non-integral operands are treated as character strings

† Integer or character string operands
§ As used by the Evaluate, If, Break If commands

Appendix C

Shell Character Options

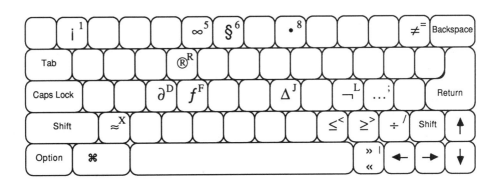

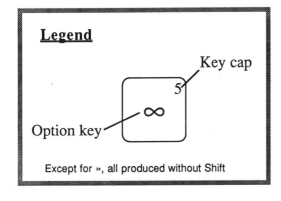

Legend

Key cap

Option key

Except for », all produced without Shift

Description

•	Beginning of line or document
∞	End of line or document
Δ	Beginning or end of selection
¡	Back from selection
§	Current selection
¬	Do NOT match
≈	Match any series of characters
®	Tag regular expression
...	Display parameter dialog
÷	Arithmetic divide
≠	Arithmetic inequality
≤	Less than or equal to
≥	Greater than or equal to
_f_	`Make` rule delimiter

Appendix D

Standard Resource Syntax

```
/* Standard resource syntax */


resource 'ALRT' (129) {
  {50, 50, 250, 250},
  129,                    /* corresponding DITL */
  { OK, visible, 3;
    Cancel, visible, 3;
    Cancel, visible, 3;
    Cancel, visible, 3
  }
};

resource 'BNDL' (128) { /***** Dialog item list *****/
  'MPNT',               /* Signature (creator) type */
  0,                    /* Version */
  {   'ICN#',           /* Desktop icons */
      {0, 128;          /* local id, resource id */
       1, 129           /* local id, resource id */
      };
      'FREF',     /* Files associated with those icons */
      {0, 128;          /* local id, resource id */
       1, 129           /* local id, resource id */
      }
  }
};
```

```
resource 'CNTL' (128) { /***** Dialog item list *****/
  {63, 141, 186, 172},      /* boundary rectangle */
  0,                         /* initial value */
  invisible,                 /* or       visible */
  1,                         /* minimum value */
  0,                         /* maximum value */
  pushButProc,               /* type of control */
/*  Choices are:
  pushButProc             pushbutton (use system font)
  pushButProcUseWFont     pushbutton displayed using window
font
  checkBoxProc            check box (use system font)
  checkBoxProc            check box displayed using window
font
  radioButProc            radio button (use system font)
  radioButProcUseWFont    radio button displayed using
window font
  scrollBarProc           scroll bar
*/
  0,                         /* arbitrary user-defined value
*/
  "Stop"                     /* title */
};

resource 'DITL' (128) { /***** Dialog item list *****/
  { {112, 112, 132, 192}, /* Rectangle for item #1 */
    Button {                 /* A pushbutton control */
      enabled,  /* Are mouse-clicks enabled or disabled?
*/
      "OK"                   /* Name of item */
    };

    {16, 64, 36, 235}, /* Rectangle for item #2 */
    StaticText {             /* Static displayed text */
      disabled, "Please enter your name:"
    };

    {48, 8, 64, 56},         /* Rectangle for item #3 */
    RadioButton {            /* A radio button control */
      enabled, "Mr."
    };

    {64, 8, 80, 56},         /* Rectangle for item #4 */
    RadioButton {            /* A radio button control */
      enabled, "Ms."
    };

    {80, 8, 96, 56},         /* Rectangle for item #5 */
```

```
      CheckBox {              /* A check box control */
        enabled, "Dr."
      };

      {56, 72, 76, 250}, /* Rectangle for item #6 */
      EditText {              /* Editable text */
        enabled, "***Your name here***"
      }
    }
  }
};

resource 'DLOG' (128) { /***** Dialog template *****/
  {100, 100, 254, 380},
  documentProc,            /* window shape: see 'WIND' */
  visible,                 /* or invisible */
  noGoAway,                /* or goAway */
  0,                       /* arbitrary user-defined value
*/
  128,                     /* corresponding DITL */
  "Dialog box"             /* Title */
};



resource 'FREF' (128) { /***** File reference *****/
  'APPL',                  /* file type */
  0,                       /* corresponding ICN# */
  ""                       /* name (not used) */
};

resource 'ICN#' (128) { /***** 32x32 Desktop icon *****/
  {
  /* Data (128 bytes) */
    $"0001 0000 0002 8000 0004 4000 0008 2000"
    $"0010 1000 0020 0800 0040 0400 0080 0200"
    $"0100 0100 0200 0080 0400 0040 0800 0020"
    $"1000 0010 2000 0008 4000 3F04 82A8 4082"
    $"4288 8041 23A9 3022 12A1 C814 0AAE 7F8F"
    $"0402 3007 0201 0007 0100 8007 0080 6007"
    $"0040 1FE7 0020 021F 0010 0407 0008 0800"
    $"0004 1000 0002 2000 0001 4000 0000 8000";
  /* Mask (128 bytes) */
    $"0001 0000 0003 8000 0007 C000 000F E000"
    $"001F F000 003F F800 007F FC00 00FF FE00"
    $"01FF FF00 03FF FF80 07FF FFC0 0FFF FFE0"
    $"1FFF FFF0 3FFF FFF8 7FFF FFFC FFFF FFFE"
    $"7FFF FFFF 3FFF FFFE 1FFF FFFC 0FFF FFFF"
    $"07FF FFFF 03FF FFFF 01FF FFFF 00FF FFFF"
    $"007F FFFF 003F FE1F 001F FC07 000F F800"
```

```
            $"0007 F000 0003 E000 0001 C000 0000 8000"
        }
};

resource 'MBAR' (128) { /***** List of menus *****/
    { 1;                    /* resource id for first menu */
      2;              /* resource id for second menu, etc. */
      3
    }
};

resource 'MENU' (4) {
    4,
    textMenuProc,
    0x7FFFFF7,
    enabled,
    "Style",
    { "Plain",noIcon, "P", noMark, plain;
      "Bold", noIcon, "B", noMark, bold;
      "Italic", noIcon, "I", noMark, italic;
      "-", noIcon, noKey, noMark, plain;
      "Left Justify", noIcon, noKey, check, plain;
      "Center", noIcon, noKey, noMark, plain;
      "Right", noIcon, noKey, noMark, plain
    }
};

resource 'MENU' (3) {    /***** Menu *****/
    3,                     /* Menu ID */
    textMenuProc,          /* definition procedure */
    0x7FFFFFFD,          /* enabling flags for menu items */
    enabled,               /* or   disabled */
    "Edit",                /* Menu title */
    { "Undo", noIcon, "Z", noMark, plain;
      "-", noIcon, noKey, noMark, plain;
      "Cut", noIcon, "X", noMark, plain;
      "Copy", noIcon, "C", noMark, plain;
      "Paste", noIcon, "V", noMark, plain;
      "Clear", noIcon, noKey, noMark, plain
    }
};

resource 'STR ' (128) { /***** Single string *****/
    "This is my string"
};
```

```
resource 'STR#' (128) { /***** List of strings *****/
   { "One";
     "Two";
     "Three";
     "Four"
   }
};

resource 'WIND' (128) { /***** Window template *****/
   {40, 80, 240, 400},
   documentProc,          /* window shape */
   visible,               /* or invisible */
   goAway,                /* or noGoAway */
   0,               /* arbitrary user-defined value */
   "Untitled"             /* Window title */     `
};
```

Appendix E

Operating System Traps

Pascal/C	Assembler	Word	Selector	Compatibility
Apple DeskTop Bus Manager (OS)				
ADBOp	A07C			256K
ADBReInit	A07B			256K
CountADBs	A077			256K
GetADBInfo	A079			256K
GetIndADB	A078			256K
SetADBInfo	A07A			256K
Binary/Decimal Conversion Package (Toolbox)				
CStr2Dec	A9EE	4		Sys3.2
Dec2Str	A9EE	3		Sys3.2
NumToString	A9EE	0		
PStr2Dec	A9EE	2		Sys3.2
StringToNum	A9EE	1		
Color Manager (Toolbox)				
AddComp	AA3B			Color
AddSearch	AA3A			Color
Color2Index	AA33			Color
DelComp	AA4D			Color
DelSearch	AA4C			Color
GetCTSeed	AA28			Color
GetSubTable	AA37			Color
Index2Color	AA34			Color

Pascal/C	Assembler	Word	Selector	Compatibility
InvertColor		AA35		Color
MakeITable		AA39		Color
ProtectEntry		AA3D		Color
QDError		AA40		Color
RealColor		AA36		Color
ReserveEntry		AA3E		Color
RestoreEntries		AA4A		Color
SaveEntries		AA49		Color
SetClientID		AA3C		Color
SetEntries		AA3F		Color

Color Picker Package (Toolbox)

Pascal/C	Assembler	Word	Selector	Compatibility
CMY2RGB		A82E	3	Sys4.1†
Fix2SmallFract		A82E	1	Sys4.1†
GetColor		A82E	9	Sys4.1†
HL2RGB		A82E	5	Sys4.1†
HSV2RGB		A82E	7	Sys4.1†
RGB2CMY		A82E	4	Sys4.1†
RGB2HSL		A82E	6	Sys4.1†
RGB2HSV		A82E	8	Sys4.1†
SmallFract2Fix		A82E	2	Sys4.1†

Compatibility

Pascal/C	Assembler	Word	Selector	Compatibility
SysEnvirons		A090		Sys4.1†

Control Manager (Toolbox)

Pascal/C	Assembler	Word	Selector	Compatibility
DisposeControl	_DisposControl	A955		
DragControl		A967		
Draw1Control		A96D		128K
DrawControls		A969		
FindControl		A96C		
GetAuxCtl		AA44		Color
GetCRefCon		A95A		
GetCTitle		A95E		
GetCtlAction		A96A		
GetCtlMax	_GetMinCtl	A962		
GetCtlMin	_GetMaxCtl	A961		
GetCtlValue		A960		
GetCVariant		A809		Sys4.0†
GetNewControl		A9BE		
HideControl		A958		
HiliteControl		A95D		
KillControls		A956		
MoveControl		A959		
NewControl		A954		

Pascal/C	Assembler	Word	Selector Compatibility
SetCRefCon		A95B	
SetCTitle		A95F	
SetCtlAction		A96B	
SetCtlColor		AA43	Color
SetCtlMin	_SetMaxCtl	A964	
SetCtlMin	_SetMinCtl	A965	
SetCtlValue		A963	
ShowControl		A957	
SizeControl		A95C	
TestControl		A966	
TrackControl		A968	
UpdtControl		A953	128K

Deferred Task Manager (OS)

DTInstall		A082	MacII

Desk Manager (Toolbox)

CloseDeskAcc		A9B7	
OpenDeskAcc		A9B6	
SystemClick		A9B3	
SystemEdit	_SysEdit	A9C2	
SystemEvent		A9B2	
SystemMenu		A9B5	
SystemTask		A9B4	

Device Manager (OS)

DrvrInstall		A03D	
DrvrRemove		A03E	
PBClose#	_Close	A001	
PBControl#	_Control	A004	
PBKillIO#	_KillIO	A006	
PBOpen#	_Open	A000	
PBRead#	_Read	A002	
PBStatus#	_Status	A005	
PBWrite#	_Write	A003	
SIntInstall		A075	MacII
SIntRemove		A076	MacII

Also used by File Manager

Dialog Manager (Toolbox)

Alert		A985	
CautionAlert		A988	
CloseDialog		A982	

Pascal/C	Assembler	Word	Selector	Compatibility
CouldAlert		A989		
CouldDialog		A979		
DialogSelect		A980		
DiposDialog		A983		
DrawDialog		A981		
ErrorSound		A98C		
FindDItem		A984		128K
FreeAlert		A98A		
FreeDialog		A97A		
GetDItem		A98D		
GetIText		A990		
GetNewDialog		A97C		
HideDitem		A827		128K
InitDialogs		A97B		
IsDialogEvent		A97F		
ModalDialog		A991		
NewCDialog		AA4B		Color
NewDialog		A97D		
NoteAlert		A987		
ParamText		A98B		
SelIText		A97E		
SetDItem		A98E		
SetIText		A98F		
ShowDItem		A828		128K
StopAlert		A986		
UpdtDialog		A978		128K

Disk Initialization Package (OS)

Pascal/C	Assembler	Word	Selector	Compatibility
DIBadMount		A9E9	0	
DIFormat		A9E9	6	
DILoad		A9E9	2	
DIUnload		A9E9	4	
DIVerify		A9E9	8	
DIZero		A9E9	10	

File Manager (OS)

Pascal/C	Assembler	Word	Selector	Compatibility
AddDrive		A04E		
FInitQueue	_InitQueue	A016		
HGetVol		A214		HFS
HSetVol		A215		HFS
PBAllocate	_Allocate	A010		
PBAllocContig	_AllocContig	A210		HFS
PBCatMove	_CatMove	A260	5	HFS
PBClose#	_Close	A001		
PBCloseWD	_CloseWD	A260	2	HFS

Pascal/C	Assembler	Word	Selector	Compatibility
PBControl#	_Control	A004		
PBCreate	_Create	A008		
PBDelete	_Delete	A009		
PBDirCreate	_DirCreate	A260	6	HFS
PBEject	_Eject	A017		
PBFlushFile	_FlushFile	A045		
PBFlushVol	_FlushVol	A013		
PBGetCatInfo	_GetCatInfo	A260	9	HFS
PBGetEOF	_GetEOF	A011		
PBGetFCBInfo	_GetFCBInfo	A260	8	HFS
PBGetFInfo	_GetFileInfo	A00C		
PBGetFPos	_GetFPos	A018		
PBGetVInfo	_GetVolInfo	A007		
PBGetVol	_GetVol	A014		
PBGetWDInfo	_GetWDInfo	A260	7	HFS
PBHCopyFile	_CopyFile	A260	54	Share
PBHCreate	_HCreate	A208		HFS
PBHDelete	_HDelete	A209		HFS
PBHGetDirAccess	_GetDirAccess	A260	50	Share
PBHGetFInfo	_HGetFileInfo	A20C		HFS
PBHGetLogInInfo	_GetLogInInfo	A260	49	Share
PBHGetVInfo	_HGetVInfo	A207		HFS
PBHGetVolParms	_GetVolParms	A260	48	Share
PBHMapID	_MapID	A260	52	Share
PBHMapName	_MapName	A260	53	Share
PBHMoveRename	_MoveRename	A260	55	Share
PBHOpen	_HOpen	A200		HFS
PBHOpenDeny	_OpenDeny	A260	56	Share
PBHOpenRF	_HOpenRF	A20A		HFS
PBHOpenRFDeny	_OpenRFDeny	A260	57	Share
PBHRename	_HRename	A20B		HFS
PBHRstFLock	_HRstFLock	A242		HFS
PBHSetDirAccess	_SetDirAccess	A260	51	Share
PBHSetFInfo	_HSetFileInfo	A20D		HFS
PBHSetFLock#	_HSetFLock	A241		HFS
PBKillIO	_KillIO	A006		
PBLockRange	_LockRng	A260	16	HFS
PBMountVol	_MountVol	A00F		
PBOffline	_Offline	A035		
PBOpen#	_Open	A000		
PBOpenRF	_OpenRF	A00A		
PBOpenWD	_OpenWD	A260	1	HFS
PBRead†	_Read	A002		
PBRename	_Rename	A00B		
PBRstFLock	_RstFilLock	A042		
PBSetCatInfo	_SetCatInfo	A260	10	HFS

Pascal/C	Assembler	Word	Selector	Compatibility
PBSetEOF	_SetEOF	A012		
PBSetFInfo	_SetFilInfo	A00D		
PBSetFLock	_SetFilLock	A041		
PBSetFPos	_SetFPos	A044		
PBSetFVers	_SetFilType	A043		
PBSetVInfo	_SetVolInfo	A260	11	HFS
PBSetVol	_SetVol	A015		
PBStatus#	_Status	A005		
PBUnLockRange	_UnlockRng	A260	17	HFS
PBUnmountVol	_UnmountVol	A00E		
PBWrite#	_Write	A003		
	_HFSDispatch##	A260	*	HFS
	_ReadWDCB	A260	15	Share
	_SetUpDef	A260	14	Share
	_SetUpWDCB	A260	13	Share

Also used by Device Manager

16-bit selector in D0

Font Manager (Toolbox)

Pascal/C	Assembler	Word	Selector	Compatibility
FMSwapFont		A901		
FontMetrics		A835		128K
GetFNum		A900		
GetFontName	_GetFName	A8FF		
InitFonts		A8FE		
RealFont		A902		
SetFontLock		A903		
SetFractEnable		A814		Sys4.1†
SetFScaleDisable		A834		128K

International Utilities Package (Toolbox)

Pascal/C	Assembler	Word	Selector	Compatibility
IUDatePString		A9ED	12	
IUDateString		A9ED	0	
IUGetIntl		A9ED	6	
IUMagString		A9ED	10	
IUMetric		A9ED	4	
IUSetIntl		A9ED	8	
IUTimePstring		A9ED	14	
IUTimeString		A9ED	2	

List Manager Package (Toolbox)

Pascal/C	Assembler	Word	Selector	Compatibility
LActivate		A9E7	0	Sys3.0
LAddColumn		A9E7	4	Sys3.0
LAddRow		A9E7	8	Sys3.0

Pascal/C	Assembler	Word	Selector	Compatiblity
LAddToCell		A9E7	12	Sys3.0
LAutoScroll		A9E7	16	Sys3.0
LCellSize		A9E7	20	Sys3.0
LClick		A9E7	24	Sys3.0
LClrCell		A9E7	28	Sys3.0
LDelColumn		A9E7	32	Sys3.0
LDelRow		A9E7	36	Sys3.0
LDispose		A9E7	40	Sys3.0
LDoDraw		A9E7	44	Sys3.0
LDraw		A9E7	48	Sys3.0
LFind		A9E7	52	Sys3.0
LGetCell		A9E7	56	Sys3.0
LGetSelect		A9E7	60	Sys3.0
LLastClick		A9E7	64	Sys3.0
LNew		A9E7	68	Sys3.0
LNextCell		A9E7	72	Sys3.0
LRect		A9E7	76	Sys3.0
LScroll		A9E7	80	Sys3.0
LSearch		A9E7	84	Sys3.0
LSetCell		A9E7	88	Sys3.0
LSetSelect		A9E7	92	Sys3.0
LSize		A9E7	96	Sys3.0
LUpdate		A9E7	100	Sys3.0

MacsBug

	Assembler	Word		
	_Debugger#	A9FF		
	_DebugStr#	ABFF		

Not in ROM

Memory Manager (OS)

Pascal/C	Assembler		Selector	Compatiblity
BlockMove	A02E			
CompactMem	A04C			
DisposHandle	A023			
DisposPtr	A01F			
EmptyHandle	A02B			
FreeMem	A01C			
GetHandleSize	A025			
GetPtrSize	A021			
GetZone	A11A			
HandleZone	A126			
HClrRBit	A068			128K
HGetState	A069			128K
HLock	A029			
HNoPurge	A04A			
HPurge	A049			

Pascal/C	Assembler	Word	Selector	Compatibility
HSetRBit		A067		128K
HSetState		A06A		128K
HUnlock		A02A		
InitApplZone		A02C		
InitZone		A019		
MaxApplZone		A063		128K
MaxBlock		A061		128K
MaxMem		A11D		
MoreMasters		A036		
MoveHHi		A064		128K
NewEmptyHandle		A166		128K
NewHandle		A122		
NewPtr		A11E		
PtrZone		A148		128K
PurgeMem		A04D		
PurgeSpace		A162		128K
ReallocHandle		A027		
RecoverHandle		A128		
ResrvMem		A040		
SetApplBase	_SetAppBase	A057		
SetApplLimit		A02D		
SetGrowZone		A04B		
SetHandleSize		A024		
SetPtrSize		A020		
SetZone		A01B		
StackSpace		A065		128K
StripAddress		A055		Sys4.1†

Menu Manager (Toolbox)

Pascal/C	Assembler	Word	Selector	Compatibility
AddResMenu		A94D		
AppendMenu		A933		
CalcMenuSize		A948		
CheckItem		A945		
ClearMenuBar		A934		
CountMItems		A950		
DeleteMenu		A936		
DelMCEntries		AA60		Color
DelMenuItem		A952		128K
DisableItem		A93A		
DispMCInfo		AA63		Color
DisposeMenu	_DisposMenu	A932		
DrawMenuBar		A937		
EnableItem		A939		
FlashMenuBar		A94C		
GetItem		A946		
GetItemCmd		A84F		Sys4.1†

Pascal/C	Assembler	Word	Selector Compatibility
GetItemIcon	_GetItmIcon	A93F	
GetItemMark	_GetItmMark	A943	
GetItemStyle	_GetItmStyle	A941	
GetMCEntry		AA64	Color
GetMCInfo		AA61	Color
GetMenu	_GetRMenu	A9BF	
GetMenuBar		A93B	
GetMHandle		A949	
GetNewMBar		A9C0	
HiliteMenu		A938	
InitMenus		A930	
InitProcMenu		A808	Sys4.1†
InsertMenu		A935	
InsertResMenu		A951	
InsMenuItem		A826	128K
MenuChoice		AA66	MacII
MenuKey		A93E	
MenuSelect		A93D	
NewMenu		A931	
PlotIcon		A94B	
PopUpMenuSelect		A80B	Sys4.1†
SetItem		A947	
SetItemCmd		A84E	Sys4.1†
SetItemIcon	_SetItmIcon	A940	
SetItemMark	_SetItmMark	A944	
SetItemStyle	_SetItmStyle	A942	
SetMCEntries		AA65	Color
SetMCInfo		AA62	Color
SetMenuBar		A93C	
SetMenuFlash	_SetMFlash	A94A	

Operating System Event Manager

Pascal/C	Assembler	Word	Selector Compatibility
FlushEvents		A032	
GetOSEvent		A031	
OSEventAvail		A030	
PostEvent		A02F	
PPostEvent		A12F	128K

Operating System Utilities

Pascal/C	Assembler	Word	Selector Compatibility
Date2Secs		A9C7	
Delay		A03B	
EqualString	_CmpString	A03C	
GetTrapAddress		A146	
HandAndHand		A9E4	

Pascal/C	Assembler	Word	Selector	Compatibility
HandToHand		A9E1		
InitUtil		A03F		
PtrAndHand		A9EF		
PtrToHand		A9E3		
PtrToXHand		A9E2		
ReadDateTime		A039		
RelString		A050		128K
Secs2Date		A9C6		
SetDateTime		A03A		
SetTrapAddress		A047		
SwapMMUMode		A05D		MacII
SysBeep		A9C8		
WriteParam		A038		

Package Manager (Toolbox)

Pascal/C	Assembler	Word	Selector	Compatibility
InitAllPacks		A9E6		
InitPack		A9E5		
Packages use 16-bit selector on stack#				
	_Pack0	A9E7		
	_Pack1	A9E8		
	_Pack2	A9E9		
	_Pack3	A9EA		
	_Pack4	A9EB		
	_Pack5	A9EC		
	_Pack6	A9ED		
	_Pack7	A9EE		
	_Pack8	A816		128K
	_Pack9	A82B		128K
	_Pack10	A82C		128K
	_Pack11	A82D		128K
	_Pack12	A82E		128K
	_Pack13	A82F		128K
	_Pack14	A830		128K
	_Pack15	A831		128K

_Pack0: List Manager, _Pack2: Disk Initialization Package, _Pack3: Standard File Package, _Pack4: Floating Point Aritmetic Package, _Pack5: Trancendental Functions Package, _Pack6: International Utilities, _Pack7: Binary/Decimal Conversion Package, _Pack12: COlor Picker Package

Palette Manager (Toolbox)

Pascal/C	Assembler	Word	Selector	Compatibility
ActivatePalette		AA94		Color
AnimateEntry		AA99		Color
AnimatePalette		AA9A		Color

Pascal/C	Assembler	Word	Selector	Compatibility
CTab2Palette		AA9F		Color
DisposePalette		AA93		Color
GetEntryColor		AA9B		Color
GetEntryUsage		AA9D		Color
GetNewPalette		AA92		Color
GetPalette		AA96		Color
InitPalettes		AA90		Color
NewPalette		AA91		Color
Palette2CTab		AAA0		Color
PmBackColor		AA98		Color
PmForeColor		AA97		Color
SetEntryColor		AA9C		Color
SetEntryUsage		AA9E		Color
SetPalette		AA95		Color

Printing Manager (OS)

Pascal/C	Assembler	Word	Selector	Compatibility
PrClose		A8FD	$D0000000	Sys 3.3
PrCloseDoc	_PrClosDoc	A8FD	$8000484	Sys 3.3
PrClosePage	_PrClosPage	A8FD	$1800040C	Sys 3.3
PrCtlCall		A8FD	$A0000E00	Sys 3.3
PrDlgMain		A8FD	$4A040894	Sys 3.3
PrDrvrClose		A8FD	$88000000	Sys 3.3
PrDrvrDCE		A8FD	$94000000	Sys 3.3
PrDrvrOpen		A8FD	$80000000	Sys 3.3
PrDrvrVers		A8FD	$9A000000	Sys 3.3
PrError		A8FD	$BA000000	Sys 3.3
PrGeneral		A8FD	$70070480	Sys 3.3
PrintDefault		A8FD	$20040480	Sys 3.3
PrJobDialog		A8FD	$32040488	Sys 3.3
PrJobInit		A8FD	$44040410	Sys 3.3
PrJobMerge		A8FD	$5804089C	Sys 3.3
PrNoPurge		A8FD	$B0000000	Sys 3.3
PrOpen		A8FD	$C8000000	Sys 3.3
PrOpenDoc		A8FD	$04000C00	Sys 3.3
PrOpenPage		A8FD	$10000808	Sys 3.3
PrPicFile		A8FD	$60051480	Sys 3.3
PrPurge		A8FD	$A8000000	Sys 3.3
PrSetError		A8FD	$C0000200	Sys 3.3
PrStlDialog		A8FD	$2A040484	Sys 3.3
PrStlInit		A8FD	$3C04040C	Sys 3.3
PrValidate		A8FD	$52040498	Sys 3.3
	_Printing#	A8FD	*	Sys3.3

32-bit selector on stack

Pascal/C	Assembler	Word	Selector	Compatibility

QuickDraw (Toolbox)

Pascal/C	Assembler	Word	Selector	Compatibility
AddPt		A87E		
AllocCursor		AA1D		Color
AngleFromSlope		A8C4		
BackColor		A863		
BackPat		A87C		
BackPixPat		AA0B		Color
CalcCMask		AA4F		MacII
CalcMask		A838		128K
CharExtra		AA23		Color
CharWidth		A88D		
ClipRect		A87B		
CloseCPort#		A87D		
ClosePicture		A8F4		
ClosePoly	_ClosePgon	A8CC		
ClosePort#		A87D		
CloseRgn		A8DB		
ColorBit		A864		
CopyBits		A8EC		
CopyMask		A817		128K
CopyPixMap		AA05		Color
CopyPixPat		AA09		Color
CopyRgn		A8DC		
DeltaPoint		A94F		
DiffRgn		A8E6		
DisposCCursor		AA26		Color
DisposCIcon		AA25		Color
DisposCTable		AA24		Color
DisposeRgn	_DisposRgn	A8D9		
DisposGDevice		AA30		Color
DisposPixMap		AA04		Color
DisposPixPat		AA08		Color
DrawChar		A883		
DrawPicture		A8F6		
DrawString		A884		
DrawText		A885		
EmptyRect		A8AE		
EmptyRgn		A8E2		
EqualPt		A881		
EqualRect		A8A6		
EqualRgn		A8E3		
EraseArc		A8C0		
EraseOval		A8B9		
ErasePoly		A8C8		
EraseRect		A8A3		
EraseRgn		A8D4		

Pascal/C	Assembler	Word	Selector Compatibility
EraseRoundRect		A8B2	
FillArc		A8C2	
FillCArc		AA11	Color
FillCOval		AA0F	Color
FillCPoly		AA13	Color
FillCRect		AA0E	Color
FillCRgn		AA12	Color
FillCRoundRect		AA10	Color
FillOval		A8BB	
FillPoly		A8CA	
FillRect		A8A5	
FillRgn		A8D6	
FillRoundRect		A8B4	
ForeColor		A862	
FrameArc		A8BE	
FrameOval		A8B7	
FramePoly		A8C6	
FrameRect		A8A1	
FrameRgn		A8D2	
FrameRoundRect		A8B0	
GetBackColor		AA1A	Color
GetCCursor		AA1B	Color
GetCIcon		AA1E	Color
GetClip		A87A	
GetCPixel		AA17	Color
GetCTable		AA18	Color
GetDeviceList		AA29	Color
GetFontInfo		A88B	
GetForeColor		AA19	Color
GetGDevice		AA32	Color
GetMainDevice		AA2A	Color
GetMaskTable		A836	128K
GetMaxDevice		AA27	Color
GetNextDevice		AA2B	Color
GetPen		A89A	
GetPenState		A898	
GetPixel		A865	
GetPixPat		AA0C	Color
GetPort		A874	
GlobalToLocal		A871	
GrafDevice		A872	
HideCursor		A852	
HidePen		A896	
HiliteColor		AA22	Color
InitCPort		AA01	Color
InitCursor		A850	
InitGDevice		AA2E	Color

Pascal/C	Assembler	Word	Selector	Compatibility
InitGraf		A86E		
InitPort		A86D		
InsetRect		A8A9		
InsetRgn		A8E1		
InvertArc		A8C1		
InvertOval		A8BA		
InvertPoly		A8C9		
InvertRect	_InverRect	A8A4		
InvertRgn	_InverRgn	A8D5		
InvertRoundRect	_InverRoundRect	A8B3		
KillPicture		A8F5		
KillPoly		A8CD		
Line		A892		
LineTo		A891		
LocalToGlobal		A870		
MakeRGBPat		AA0D		Color
MapPoly		A8FC		
MapPt		A8F9		
MapRect		A8FA		
MapRgn		A8FB		
MeasureText		A837		128K
Move		A894		
MovePortTo		A877		
MoveTo		A893		
NewGDevice		AA2F		Color
NewPixMap		AA03		Color
NewPixPat		AA07		Color
NewRgn		A8D8		
ObscureCursor		A856		
OffsetPoly		A8CE		
OffsetRect		A8A8		
OffsetRgn	_OfsetRgn	A8E0		
OpColor		AA21		Color
OpenCPort		AA00		Color
OpenPicture		A8F3		
OpenPoly		A8CB		
OpenPort		A86F		
OpenRgn		A8DA		
PackBits		A8CF		
PaintArc		A8BF		
PaintOval		A8B8		
PaintPoly		A8C7		
PaintRect		A8A2		
PaintRgn		A8D3		
PaintRoundRect		A8B1		
PenMode		A89C		

Pascal/C	Assembler	Word	Selector Compatibility
PenNormal		A89E	
PenPat		A89D	
PenPixPat		AA0A	Color
PenSize		A89B	
PicComment		A8F2	
PinRect		A94E	
PlotCIcon		AA1F	Color
PortSize		A876	
Pt2Rect		A8AC	
PtInRect		A8AD	
PtInRgn		A8E8	
PtToAngle		A8C3	
Random		A861	
RectInRgn		A8E9	
RectRgn		A8DF	
RGBBackColor		AA15	Color
RGBForeColor		AA14	Color
ScalePt		A8F8	
ScrollRect		A8EF	
SectRect		A8AA	
SectRgn		A8E4	
SeedCFill		AA50	MacII
SeedFill		A839	128K
SetCCursor		AA1C	Color
SetClip		A879	
SetCPixel		AA16	Color
SetCPortPix		AA06	Color
SetCursor		A851	
SetDeviceAttribute		AA2D	Color
SetEmptyRgn		A8DD	
SetGDevice		AA31	Color
SetOrigin		A878	
SetPenState		A899	
SetPort		A873	
SetPortBits		A875	
SetPt		A880	
SetRecRgn		A8DE	
SetRect		A8A7	
SetStdCProcs		AA4E	Color
SetStdProcs		A8EA	
ShowCursor		A853	
ShowPen		A897	
SlopeFromAngle		A8BC	
SpaceExtra		A88E	
StdArc		A8BD	
StdBits		A8EB	

Pascal/C	Assembler	Word	Selector	Compatibility
StdComment		A8F1		
StdGetPic		A8EE		
StdLine		A890		
StdOval		A8B6		
StdPoly		A8C5		
StdPutPic		A8F0		
StdRect		A8A0		
StdRgn		A8D1		
StdRRect		A8AF		
StdText		A882		
StdTxMeas		A8ED		
StringWidth		A88C		
StuffHex		A866		
SubPt		A87F		
TestDeviceAttribute		AA2C		Color
TextFace		A888		
TextFont		A887		
TextMode		A889		
TextSize		A88A		
TextWidth		A886		
UnionRect		A8AB		
UnionRgn		A8E5		
UnpackBits		A8D0		
XorRgn		A8E7		

Same trap as CloseCPort

Resource Manager (Toolbox)

Pascal/C	Assembler	Word	Selector	Compatibility
AddResource		A9AB		
ChangedResource		A9AA		
CloseResFile		A99A		
Count1Resources		A80D		128K
Count1Types		A81C		128K
CountResources		A99C		
CountTypes		A99E		
CreateResFile		A9B1		
CurResFile		A994		
DetachResource		A992		
Get1IndResource	_Get1IxResource	A80E		128K
Get1IndType	_Get1IxType	A80F		128K
Get1NamedResource		A820		128K
Get1Resource		A81F		128K
GetIndResource		A99D		
GetIndType		A99F		
GetNamedResource		A9A1		
GetResAttrs		A9A6		

Pascal/C	Assembler	Word	Selector	Compatibility
GetResAttrs		A9A6		
GetResFileAttrs		A9F6		
GetResInfo		A9A8		
GetResource		A9A0		
HomeResFile		A9A4		
InitResources		A995		
LoadResource		A9A2		
MaxSizeRsrc		A821		128K
OpenResFile		A997		
OpenRFPerm		A9C4		128K
ReleaseResource		A9A3		
ResError		A9AF		
RGetResource		A80C		Sys4.1†
RmveResource		A9AD		
RsrcMapEntry		A9C5		128K
RsrcZoneInit		A996		
SetResAttrs		A9A7		
SetResFileAttrs		A9F7		
SetResInfo		A9A9		
SetResLoad		A99B		
SetResPurge		A993		
SizeResource	_SizeRsrc	A9A5		
Unique1ID		A810		128K
UniqueID		A9C1		
UpdateResFile		A999		
UseResFile		A998		
WriteResource		A9B0		

Scrap Manager (Toolbox)

Pascal/C	Assembler	Word	Selector	Compatibility
GetScrap		A9FD		
InfoScrap		A9F9		
LoadScrap	_LodeScrap	A9FB		
PutScrap		A9FE		
UnloadScrap	_UnlodeScrap	A9FA		
ZeroScrap		A9FC		

Script Manager (Toolbox)

Pascal/C	Assembler	Word	Selector	Compatibility
Char2Pixel		A8B5	$820C0016	Sys4.1
CharByte		A8B5	$82060010	Sys4.1
CharType		A8B5	$82060012	Sys4.1
DrawJust		A8B5	$8008001E	Sys4.1
FindWord		A8B5	$8012001A	Sys4.1
Font2Script		A8B5	$82020006	Sys4.1
FontScript		A8B5	$82000000	Sys4.1
GetEnvirons		A8B5	$84020008	Sys4.1

Pascal/C	Assembler	Word	Selector	Compatibility
HiliteText		A8B5	$800E001C	Sys4.1
IntlScript		A8B5	$82000002	Sys4.1
KeyScript		A8B5	$80020004	Sys4.1
MeasureJust		A8B5	$800C0020	Sys4.1
ParseTable		A8B5	$82040022	Sys4.1
Pixel2Char		A8B5	$820E0014	Sys4.1
SetEnvirons		A8B5	$8206000A	Sys4.1
SetScript		A8B5	$8208000E	Sys4.1
Transliterate		A8B5	$820E0018	Sys4.1
	_ScriptUtil#	A8B5	*	Sys4.1

32-bit selector on stack

SCSI Manager (OS)

Pascal/C	Assembler	Word	Selector	Compatibility
SCSICmd		A815	3	128K
SCSIComplete		A815	4	128K
SCSIDisconnect		A815	16	MacII
SCSIGet		A815	1	128K
SCSIInstall		A815	7	128K
SCSIMsgIn		A815	12	MacII
SCSIMsgOut		A815	13	MacII
SCSIRBlind		A815	8	128K
SCSIRead		A815	5	128K
SCSIReselAtn		A815	15	MacII
SCSIReselect		A815	14	MacII
SCSIReset		A815	0	128K
SCSISelAtn		A815	11	MacII
SCSISelect		A815	2	128K
SCSIStat		A815	10	128K
SCSIWBlind		A815	9	128K
SCSIWrite		A815	6	128K
	_SCSIDispatch#	A815	*	128K

16-bit selector on stack

Segment Loader (OS)

Pascal/C	Assembler	Word
ExitToShell		A9F4
GetAppParms		A9F5
UnloadSeg		A9F1
	_Chain	A9F3
	_Launch	A9F2
	_LoadSeg	A9F0

Pascal/C	Assembler	Word	Selector	Compatibility

Shutdown Manager (OS)

Pascal/C	Assembler	Word	Selector	Compatibility
ShutDwnInstall		A895	2	Sys4.0
ShutDwnPower		A895	0	Sys4.0
ShutDwnRemove		A895	3	Sys4.0
hutDwnStart		A895	1	Sys4.0
	_Shutdown#	A895	*	Sys4.0

16-bit selector on stack

Slot Manager (OS)

Pascal/C	Assembler	Word	Selector	Compatibility
initSDeclMgr		A06E	32	MacII
sCalcsPointer		A06E	44	MacII
sCalcStep		A06E	40	MacII
sCardChanged		A06E	34	MacII
sCkCardStat		A06E	24	MacII
sDeleteSRTRec		A06E	49	MacII
sExec		A06E	35	MacII
sFindDevBase		A06E	27	MacII
sFindsInfoRecPtr		A06E	47	MacII
sFindsRsrcPtr		A06E	48	MacII
sFindStruct		A06E	6	MacII
sGetBlock		A06E	5	MacII
sGetcString		A06E	3	MacII
sGetDriver		A06E	45	MacII
sInitPRAMRecs		A06E	37	MacII
sInitsRsrcTable		A06E	41	MacII
sNextsRsrc		A06E	20	MacII
sNextTypesRsrc		A06E	21	MacII
sOffsetData		A06E	36	MacII
sPrimaryInit		A06E	33	MacII
sPtrToSlot		A06E	46	MacII
sPutPRAMRec		A06E	18	MacII
sReadByte		A06E	0	MacII
sReadDrvrName		A06E	25	MacII
sReadFHeader		A06E	19	MacII
sReadInfo		A06E	16	MacII
sReadLong		A06E	2	MacII
sReadPBSize		A06E	38	MacII
sReadPRAMRec		A06E	17	MacII
sReadStruct		A06E	7	MacII
sReadWord		A06E	1	MacII
sRsrcInfo		A06E	22	MacII
sSearchSRT		A06E	42	MacII

Pascal/C	Assembler	Word	Selector	Compatibility
sUpdateSRT		A06E	43	MacII
	_SlotManager#	A06E	*	MacII

16-bit selector in D0

Sound Manager (OS)

Pascal/C	Assembler	Word	Selector	Compatibility
SndAddModifier		A802		MacII
SndControl		A806		MacII
SndDisposeChannel		A801		MacII
SndDoCommand		A803		MacII
SndDoImmediate		A804		MacII
SndNewChannel		A807		MacII
SndPlay		A805		MacII

Standard File Package (Toolbox)

Pascal/C	Assembler	Word	Selector	Compatibility
SFGetFile		A9EA	2	
SFPGetFile		A9EA	4	
SFPPutFile		A9EA	3	
SFPutFile		A9EA	1	

Start Manager (OS)

Pascal/C	Assembler	Word	Selector	Compatibility
GetDefaultStartup		A07D		256K
GetOSDefault		A084		MacII
GetVideoDefault		A080		MacII
SetDefaultStartup		A07E		256K
SetOSDefault		A083		MacII
SetVideoDefault		A081		MacII

System Error Handler (OS)

Pascal/C	Assembler	Word	Selector	Compatibility
SysError		A9C9		

TextEdit (Toolbox)

Pascal/C	Assembler	Word	Selector	Compatibility
GetStylHandle		A83D	4	Sys4.1†
GetStylScrap		A83D	6	Sys4.1†
SetStylHandle		A83D	5	Sys4.1†
TEActivate		A9D8		
TEAutoView		A813		128K
TECalText		A9D0		
TEClick		A9D4		
TECopy		A9D5		
TECut		A9D6		
TEDeactivate		A9D9		
TEDelete		A9D7		

Pascal/C	Assembler	Word	Selector	Compatibility
TEDispose		A9CD		
TEGetHeight		A83D	9	Sys4.1†
TEGetOffset		A83C		Sys4.1†
TEGetPoint		A83D	8	Sys4.1†
TEGetStyle		A83D	3	Sys4.1†
TEGetText		A9CB		
TEIdle		A9DA		
TEInit		A9CC		
TEInsert		A9DE		
TEKey		A9DC		
TENew		A9D2		
TEPaste		A9DB		
TEPinScroll		A812		128K
TEReplaceStyle		A83D	2	Sys4.1†
TEScroll		A9DD		
TESelView		A811		128K
TESetJust		A9DF		
TESetSelect		A9D1		
TESetStyle		A83D	1	Sys4.1†
TESetText		A9CF		
TEStyleNew		A83E		Sys4.1†
TEStylInsert		A83D	7	Sys4.1†
TEStylPaste		A83D	0	Sys4.1†
TEUpdate		A9D3		
TextBox		A9CE		
	_TEDispatch#	A83D	*	Sys4.1†

16-bit selector on stack

Time Manager (OS)

InsTime		A058		128K
PrimeTime		A05A		128K
RmvTime		A059		128K

Toolbox Event Manager

Button		A974		
Dequeue		A96E		
Enqueue		A96F		
EventAvail		A971		
GetKeys		A976		
GetMouse		A972		
GetNextEvent		A970		
KeyTrans		A9C3		Sys4.1
StillDown		A973		
TickCount		A975		

Pascal/C	Assembler Word	Selector Compatibility
WaitNextEvent	A860	128K
WaitMouseUp	A977	

Toolbox Utilities

Pascal/C	Assembler Word	Selector Compatibility
BitAnd	A858	
BitClr	A85F	
BitNot	A85A	
BitOr	A85B	
BitSet	A85E	
BitShift	A85C	
BitTst	A85D	
BitXor	A859	
Fix2Frac	A841	128K
Fix2Long	A840	128K
Fix2X	A843	128K
FixAtan2	A818	128K
FixDiv	A84D	128K
FixMul	A868	
FixRatio	A869	
FixRound	A86C	
Frac2Fix	A842	128K
Frac2X	A845	128K
FracCos	A847	128K
FracDiv	A84B	128K
FracMul	A84A	128K
FracSin	A848	128K
FracSqrt	A849	128K
GetCursor	A9B9	
GetIcon	A9BB	
GetPattern	A9B8	
GetPicture	A9BC	
GetString	A9BA	
HiWord	A86A	
Long2Fix	A83F	128K
LongMul	A867	
LoWord	A86B	
Munger	A9E0	
NewString	A906	
SetString	A907	
ShieldCursor	A855	
UprString	A854	
X2Fix	A844	128K
X2Frac	A846	128K

Pascal/C	Assembler	Word	Selector Compatibility

Vertical Retrace Manager (OS)

Pascal/C	Assembler	Word	Selector Compatibility
AttachVBL		A071	MacII
DoVBLTask		A072	MacII
SlotVInstall		A06F	MacII
SlotVRemove		A070	MacII
VInstall		A033	
VRemove		A034	

Window Manager (Toolbox)

Pascal/C	Assembler	Word	Selector Compatibility
BeginUpdate		A922	
BringToFront		A920	
CalcVis		A909	
CalcVisBehind	_CalcVBehind	A90A	
CheckUpdate		A911	
ClipAbove		A90B	
CloseWindow		A92D	
DisposeWindow		A914	
DragGrayRgn		A905	
DragTheRgn		A926	
DragWindow		A925	
DrawGrowIcon		A904	
DrawNew		A90F	
EndUpdate		A923	
FindWindow		A92C	
FrontWindow		A924	
GetAuxWin		AA42	Color
GetCWMgrPort		AA48	Color
GetNewCWindow		AA46	Color
GetNewWindow		A9BD	
GetWindowPic		A92F	
GetWMgrPort		A910	
GetWRefCon		A917	
GetWTitle		A919	
GetWVariant		A80A	Sys4.0†
GrowWindow		A92B	
HideWindow		A916	
HiliteWindow		A91C	
InitWindows		A912	
InvalRect		A928	
InvalRgn		A927	
MoveWindow		A91B	
NewCWindow		AA45	Color
NewWindow		A913	

Pascal/C	Assembler	Word	Selector	Compatibility
PaintBehind		A90D		
PaintOne		A90C		
SaveOld		A90E		
SelectWindow		A91F		
SendBehind		A921		
SetDeskCPat		AA47		Color
SetWinColor		AA41		Color
SetWindowPic		A92E		
SetWRefCon		A918		
SetWTitle		A91A		
ShowHide		A908		
ShowWindow		A915		
SizeWindow		A91D		
TrackBox		A83B		128K
TrackGoAway		A91E		
ValidRect		A92A		
ValidRgn		A929		
ZoomWindow		A83A		128K

LEGEND

Pascal/C	Routine name for higher-level language calls
Assembler	Routine name for assembly calls, if different
Word	16-bit trap word used to call routine
Sel	Selector for trap word, if any (* means selector required)
	For _ScriptUtil, lower 8 bits of selector
Compat	Compatibility requirements:
HFS	Requires "Hard Disk 20" or 128K ROM
Share	Requires shared file environment (e.g., AppleShare)
128K	128K ROM (or later)
256K	256K ROM (or later): Apple Desktop Bus
MacII	Macintosh II: NuBus slots
Color	Color QuickDraw (e.g., Macintosh II)
Sysn.m	Requires System version n.m
Sysn.m†	Requires System version n.m and 128K ROM

Pascal/C   *Assembler*   *Word*   *Selector Compatibility*

Assumes the following System versions:

Model	ROM	System Version (or later)
Macintosh 128	64K	2.0 (later System versions not recommended)
Macintosh 512	64K	3.2
Macintosh Plus, 512Ke	128K	3.2
Macintosh SE	256K	4.1
Macintosh II	256K	4.1

Testing Compatibility

    The glue for routine SysEnvirons will return

Machine type:	128/512, 512Ke, Plus, SE, II
System version:	4.1 or later (otherwise null)
Has color QuickDraw	

Appendix F

MPW for UNIX Users

THERE ARE MANY SIMILARITIES between the MPW development environment and that of the UNIX operating system, in both its AT&T System V and Berkeley (4 BSD) variants.

The MPW shell is written in C and offers a C compiler (at additional cost) with standard libraries that are callable from C programs. A comparsion between the functions available MPW C library and the two major UNIX families is contained in Chapter 8. Generally, those UNIX functions included with MPW C have the same arguments and usage as one (or both) UNIX variants.

The command syntax of the MPW shell is similar to that of the standard UNIX shells, but by no means the same. The following pages outline the use of MPW commands for those already familiar with the standard UNIX shells, to help use MPW interactively to develop programs, or convert existing UNIX command files to run under MPW.

Shells

Two UNIX command shells are widely used to interpret interactive commands and provide access to operating system functions. The Bourne shell (denoted by sh) is the original and standard shell, available on nearly all UNIX implementations or emulations. The C shell (csh) is an enhanced shell with a C-like syntax found only with BSD systems or systems that include BSD features.

Many of the `csh` extensions are found in the MPW shell. However, the actual syntax of `csh` commands is more similar to that of `sh` than the MPW shell, as will be described later.

For the typical minicomputer version of UNIX, editing is performed with an intelligent terminal, using the `vi` command to leave the shell and enter an editor program. The MPW shell includes an integrated full-screen windowing editor, and thus both the shell and editor are available at the same time. Because the two are integrated, any line in any open window can selected and executed as a shell command. MPW also includes editor commands built into its shell that are more related to the editor commands of `vi` (or the `ex` editor) than those of `sh` and `csh`.

As is true for the two UNIX shells, MPW allows you to type line-oriented commands and see the output on your display. Each command can be implemented as a series of shell commands in a text file, or as a compiled program. In the latter case, the MPW command is implemented as a special type of Macintosh program known as an MPW tool, which is different from the customary stand-alone Macintosh program, an application. See Chapter 3 for a discussion of the different program types.

For commands from within the MPW shell, each command has standard input, standard output and standard error (which MPW terms diagnostic) output streams. The MPW shell, like the UNIX shells, allows redirection and piping of each stream. However, the current release of MPW emulates piping by sequential command execution and a temporary file, rather than the concurrent process execution of true UNIX-style piping.

Command Options

As with UNIX, MPW commands designate options by a preceding minus sign ("-"). Also, the relative order in which the options appear generally does not change the meaning of the command.

When you are typing a command with options, MPW relaxes some of the syntax rules that are enforced for UNIX commands. These less restrictive rules include:

- Options may come after positional parameters.
- A single option may be a series of letters, as in

```
Print -size 10 foo.c
```

- Option letters are case-insensitive. Although the o and O options are considered distinct by UNIX commands, MPW commands are expected to treat them as the same.

MPW is also more strict than the UNIX shells in a few areas:

- More than one option cannot be specified after a single minus sign. In the MPW command

DumpCode -rt DRVR System

-rt must be a distinct option, never a combination of the -r and -t options.

- Option parameters must be separated from the option letter by white space. Although some UNIX commands allow the option and parameter to be run together, as in

```
cu -s1200
```

this is not allowed in MPW.

- The -- notation cannot be used to delimit the end of a list of arguments.

- A single - does not indicate that the parameter represents the standard input stream; use Dev:StdIn instead.

If you're writing a command to be used by both UNIX and MPW—or porting an existing command from UNIX to MPW—it's not hard to design a syntax that is compatible with both sets of rules. The most important rule is to make each option a single lower-case letter.

When typing commands (or making a command file), the following rules will allow you to write commands valid for both MPW and UNIX:

- Type the lower-case form;

- Type the options before the positional parameters;

- An option is separated from its parameter by white space;

- Only one option per minus sign.

By these rules, the command

```
cc -o foo -g foo.c
```

would be both a valid UNIX and MPW command syntax.

A standard library function to implement these rules for MPW programs is shown in Example F–1. It returns option letters found, one at a time, from a program-supplied list of valid options. If it detects an invalid option, it displays an MPW-style (rather than UNIX-style) error message indicating the syntax error.

This version of getopt is called using the same parameters as the System V (and 4.3 BSD) function of the same name. As in the UNIX versions, getopt expects a list of valid option letters; if a letter is followed by a colon (" : "), that option requires an option parameter. This allows existing programs that use getopt to be ported without changes.

However, this library version allows the MPW user to enter a command using the more relaxed MPW rules. For example, it automatically converts a typed upper-case option letter to lower-case. More significantly, it will allow options to follow positional parameters (unlike UNIX), so that

```
Delete foo -y
```

is the same as:

```
Delete -y foo
```

```
/* Getopt function for MPW */

/*
   getopt.c: parse command line for option letters

   Designed for MPW commands and MPW C, based on the UNIX
   System V standard function

   Inspired by the public-domain UNIX version by Henry
   Spencer
```

Note:
```
   This function can be used within MPW tools the same
   way as the System V version is used from UNIX pro-
   grams. However, the command syntax rules for the cor-
   responding shells are very different.

   The UNIX command standard assumes all options are
   single-character, and that multiple options can be
   chained after after a single "-".

   MPW allows multi-character options and hence, no
   chaining. Also, upper- and lower-case options are
   treated the same.

   This implements a common subset -- single-letter
   (lowercase) options, no chaining.
```

Key Features
```
* As with the System V Interface Definition, opterr can
  be set
* to zero to suppress automatic display of error
  messages
* Single-character options only (no chaining)
* Map upper case option letters to lower case
* Change order of options and parameters to support MPW
  usage
* Does not recognize "--" or "-" as special
*/

#include <ctype.h>
#include <stdio.h>
#include <string.h>

/* Provide an error message if one is desired */
#define gripe(s1,s2) \
```

```
     if (opterr) \
       fprintf
         (stderr,
          "### %s -  %s%s%s\n",argv[0],s1,optptr,s2); \
     return (BADCH);

#define BADCH (int)'?'

/*
 These variables are defined as extern by any program
 that uses this function
*/
int  opterr = 1,   /* zero if no error message wanted */
  optind = 1,      /* index into parent argv vector */
  optopt;          /* character checked for validity */
char *optarg;      /* argument associated with option */

void shiftto();

/*
  getopt - get option letter from argument vector
*/
int getopt(argc,argv,optlist)
int  argc;         /* from main(argc, */
char *argv[],      /*      argv) */
    *optlist;      /* option pattern desired */
{ char *optptr,*p;
  char *listidx;   /* index into option pattern */
  int argind;

  optarg = NULL;   /* assume no option argument */

/* Unlike UNIX, MPW options can come after positional
parameters, so find the next option anywhere
*/
  for (argind=optind; argind<argc; argind++)
  { if (*(p = optptr = argv[argind]) == '-')
    /* Shuffle arguments around */
    { shiftto(argv, argind);
      optind++;
      optopt = tolower(*++p);
/*Now demand a single-letter option matching the list*/
      if (*++p || optopt == ':' ||
        !(listidx = strchr(optlist,optopt)))
        { gripe("\"","\" is not an option.");
        }
```

```
            if (*++listidx == ':') /*argument should follow*/
              { if (++argind >= argc)      /* none left */
                  { gripe("- The \"",
                      "\" option requires a parameter.")
                  }
                else              /* pass ptr to argument */
                  { shiftto(argv, argind);
                    optarg = argv[optind++];
                  }
              }
          return (optopt);    /* return option letter */
        }
    }
    return(EOF);                /* no option found */
}

/* Re-arrange MPW arguments of arbitrary order to look
like UNIX;
  for example,
    move -p old new -y
  becomes
    move -p -y old new
  In this case, argind = 4 and optind = 2 upon entry
*/
void shiftto(argv, argind)
char *argv[];
int argind;
{ char *lastone;

  if (argind > optind)
    {lastone = argv[argind];
      while (--argind >= optind)
      argv[argind+1] = argv[argind];
      argv[optind] = lastone;
    }
}
```

Example F–1: getopt function for MPW

Since existing programs that use getopt expect only the latter, this MPW version re-arranges the parameter list as necessary to "fool" the program into thinking the command was entered in the UNIX-style order.

A simple program that tests this library function is shown in Example F–2. It allows one option that takes an option parameter, and two that do not. In addition, it expects that there will be a minimum of one positional parameter left after all options and option parameters have been parsed. In this case, the command will not object if the same option is listed more

```
/* Test program for getopt */


#include <stdio.h>

extern int opterr,optind,optopt;
extern char *optarg;
int getopt();

main(argc,argv)
int argc;
char **argv;
{ int c,errflag=0,i=0;

   while ((c = getopt(argc, argv, "yno:")) != EOF)
      switch (c)
      { case 'y':
           printf("-y found\n");
           break;
         case 'n':
           printf("-n found\n");
           break;
         case 'o':
           printf("-o parameter = \"%s\".\n",optarg);
           break;
         case '?':
           errflag++;
      }
   if (optind >= argc)    /* one positional is minimum */
      { fprintf(stderr,
        "### %s -
        Not enough parameters were specified.\n",
        argv[0]);
      errflag++;
      }
   if (errflag)
      { fprintf(stderr,
        "# Usage - %s [-y] [-n] [-o outfile] infile...\n",
        argv[0]);
        exit(1);  /* syntax error */
      }

   for (; optind<argc; optind++)
      printf
         ("Positional arg #%d is \"%s\"\n", ++i,
          argv[optind]);
}
```

Example F–2: Test program for getopt

than once—which is typical for MPW commands but not so for UNIX commands.

Once the command has been compiled and linked with the library routines (see Chapter 8), it can be used to display the results returned by getopt. The output from this command for sample parameters is shown in Figure F–1.

Command names under MPW are generally longer than the their terse UNIX counterparts. MPW commands are often complete words, rather than acronyms or abbreviations. Thus

mv	becomes	Move
wc	becomes	Count

MPW commands are not case-sensitive. Unlike UNIX, print and PRINT refer to same command, but in MPW documentation, including this book, the first letter of each word is normally capitalized (Print). However, you should note that some command parameters are case-sensitive.

A list of corresponding UNIX and MPW commands is shown in Table F–1.

The format of the output of each command, of course, will differ. For example, the UNIX command man will pause at the end of each screen, while the MPW Help command displays all its information at once. The ls and Files commands, while similar in function, take different options and have different long output formats.

There are particularly significant differences in how the compilation

```
Got a b c
Positional arg #1 is "a"
Positional arg #2 is "b"
Positional arg #3 is "c"

Got -y a
-y found
Positional arg #1 is "a"
Got a -y
-y found
Positional arg #1 is "a"

Got a.c -o a
-o parameter = "a".
Positional arg #1 is "a.c"

Got -a
### Got - "-a" is not an option.
### Got - Not enough parameters were specified.
# Usage - Got [-y] [-n] [-o outfile] infile…
```

Figure F–1: Output from Example F–2—Available Commands

UNIX	MPW	Comments on MPW command
aliast	Alias	
ar	Lib	Object files only
as	Asm	
cat	Catenate	
cc	C	Compiler does not Link
cd	Directory	Must specify a directory
chmod -r	SetFile -a L	Make file read-only
chmod	SetPriv	For file server only
chown	SetPriv	For file server only
cmp	Equal	
cp	Duplicate	
date	Date -a	
df	Volumes -l	
diff	Compare	
dis††	DumpObj	
grep	Search	Expressions are different
ld	Link	
lp††	Print	Format options avaiable
lpr†	Print	Format options avaiable
ls	Files	One file per line
ls -l	Files -l	Long output format
ls -r	Files -r	Recursive descent
make	Make	Source format is different
man	Help	
mkdir	NewFolder	
mv	Move	Use Rename if old=new
pc†	Pascal	Compiler does not Link
pr		See lp
print†	Print -h	
pwd	Directory	
rm	Delete -n	
rm -r	Delete -y	
rmdir		See rm -r
split	FileDiv	Default is 2000 lines
touch	SetFile -m .	
tr	Translate	
unexpand†	Entab -t 8	Removes spaces first
vi	Open	
view	Open -r	
wc	Count	Does not include word count
which†	Which	

†   4 BSD
†† System V

Table F–1: Similar UNIX and MPW commands

commands work. First, the result of compiling `sample.c` is `sample.c.o`, not the `sample.o` produced on UNIX.

The MPW `c` command only compiles programs. Unlike the UNIX `cc`, it cannot be used to link programs, which is instead done by the `Link` command. MPW owners will become very familiar with `Link`, since the linking process is considerably more important (and complex) for a typical Macintosh program. Chapter 8 contains a simple `cc` command file that uses both `C` and `Link` commands to compile and linke programs like its UNIX namesake.

Among the comparable commands provided by MPW is the `alias` feature of the `csh`—although without the argument substitution available in `csh`. Example F–3 is a standard list of `alias` command to provide several common UNIX commands in terms of MPW commands. Note again that the correspondence is not exact, but use of these aliases should ease the transition to MPW, not to mention save the time of typing the longer MPW command names.

To make these aliases available each time you start MPW, you might call this file "`.login`". If you stored it in the same directory (folder) as the MPW shell program and its standard command files, you would then modify the `UserStartup` command file to conclude with the command

```
Execute "{ShellDirectory}.login"
```

which would perform the `alias` commands each time you started MPW.

Files

Many operating systems, including UNIX, reference files using a sequence of directory and file names. This sequence is often referred to as a pathname, and for a UNIX file, may take a form such as `/usr/include/stdio.h`, with slashes separating the components of the path.

The internal references to Macintosh files are not stored as a pathname, but such references can be converted to and from textual pathnames. These are often used by programs running within the MPW environment, such as to reference a currently open shell window.

The syntax of a Macintosh pathname is similar to that of UNIX, but with the "`/`" delimiter replaced by a "`:`". The rules under which a leading delimiter is used are also different, in that a Macintosh disk volume reference begins with a name followed by a colon (`Usr:`) instead of a slash (`/usr`). Also, any directory pathname normally ends in a colon, although MPW can often infer the trailing colon if the name is for an existing directory.

A series of corresponding names for the two systems is shown in Table F–2.

```
# Command aliases for UNIX users

Alias cat Catenate
Alias cp Duplicate
Alias date Date -a
Alias df Volumes -l
Alias diff Compare
Alias grep Search
Alias lf Files -m 4
Alias ls Files
Alias mkdir NewFolder
Alias mv Move
Alias pwd Directory
Alias printenv Set
Alias rm Delete
Alias rmdir Delete -y
Alias touch SetFile -m .
Alias vi Open -n
Alias view Open -r
Alias what Search /@(#)/

# Inexact equivalents
Alias cc C          # doesn't link
Alias cd Directory  # null argument displays directory
Alias fgrep Search  # uses wildcards
Alias wc Count      # does not show word count

# TTY driver equivalent
AddMenu Control 'Erase Line/U' 'Clear §:\•\ "{Active}"'
```

Example F–3: Standard UNIX command aliases

UNIX	*MPW*	*Comments*
/local/shar	local:shar	Complete path (file)
/usr/include	usr:include:	Complete path (directory)
sys/foo.h	:sys:foo.h	Partial path
foo.h	foo.h	File
sys	:sys:	Directory
/dev/null	Dev:Null	Reserved pathname
/dev/tty	Dev:Console	Reserved pathname

Table F–2: File and directory pathnames

In addition to the standard Macintosh file names, MPW defines several pseudo-files, each beginning with `Dev:` volume name. Two of these, `Dev:Console` and `Dev:Null`, correspond to standard UNIX `/dev/` special files.

A search for an existing Macintosh file is never case-sensitive; a name of `STDIO.H` or `stdio.h` would match the MPW C header file named `StdIO.h`. However, if you are creating a new file or renaming a file, the capitalization of the name will be used to create the new name.

Other commands involving files are affected by the underlying file system similarities and differences. For example, each file has two dates, a creation date and a modification date. Files may be marked read-only ("Locked", as indicated in the Finder), but most of the remaining UNIX file concepts do not exist in the standard Macintosh file system.

However, such concepts are present with a networked file server such as AppleShare. The AppleTalk Filing Protocol (AFP) provides for owner and group identification, as well as three distinct permissions for each of owner, group and other: read files, read directories, and modify. A file server and the MPW `SetPriv` command provide similar options to those provided by the UNIX `chmod` and `chown` commands.

Macintosh files are different from UNIX files in that there are two parts to a file, the data fork and the resource fork. The data fork is generally used for data files and the resource fork for programs, but this rule is not absolute.

The closest thing to a UNIX magic number is a file type, which is part of neither the data nor the resource fork. The file type distinguishes source files from object files, executable Macintosh programs, MPW tools, device drivers and so on.

A more complete description of Macintosh files is contained in Chapter 2.

Special Characters

As shown in Table F–3, many of the special characters of MPW shell should be familiar to UNIX users. There are a few differences—which may prove annoying to first-time MPW users with a UNIX background—but those differences are intended to reduce the chance that a novice MPW user will unintentionally use a special character, thinking it to be an ordinary character.

The quoting, command combination, evaluation and comment characters are the same as for the two other shells. Basic I/O redirection is the same, but MPW uses the ≥ symbol (part of the Macintosh extended character set) for standard error redirection, and does not support the << (scan input until string) standard input syntax of the UNIX shells. Quoting/escaping special

sh	csh	MPW	Description
${var}	$var	{var}	Variable
"string"	"string"	"string"	Quote with substitution
'string'	'string'	'string'	Quote without substitution
`cmd`	`cmd`	`cmd`	Evaluate cmd
\ line	\	∂	Continue command to next
\"	\"	∂"	Escape quotation character
\n	\n	∂n	New line (return)
\b	\b	∂b	Backspace
\f	\f	∂f	Form feed
\t	\t	∂t	Tab
:	#	#	Line is a comment
;	;	;	Multiple commands per line
(cmd1; cmd2)	(cmd1; cmd2)	(cmd1; cmd2)	Group commands
cmd1 && cmd2	cmd1 && cmd2	cmd1 && cmd2	If cmd1 succeeds, do cmd2
cmd1 || cmd2	cmd1 || cmd2	cmd1 || cmd2	If cmd1 fails, do cmd2
<	<	<	Standard input
>	>	>	Redirect standard output
>>	>>	>>	Append standard output
	>&	≥	Redirect diagnostic output
	>>&	≥≥	Append diagnostic output
|	|	|	Pipe standard output
?	?	?	Match single character
*	*	≈	Match any string
	[A-Z]	[A-Z]	Match character in range

Table F–3: Shell special characters

characters (or line continuation) is performed using the ∂ symbol rather than the more commonplace \.

Like the UNIX shells, the MPW shell expands file name wild cards into actual file names before passing parameters to commands. The rules for constructing such wild card patterns—described in Chapter 6—are generally similar to those of the C shell. However, instead of * as the character to match any series of 0 or more characters in a name, MPW uses the special character ≈, obtained by typing Option-X. See Appendix C for a complete list of extended characters and how to type them.

Shell Programming

The MPW shell supports shell variables and most of the same programming constructs as the UNIX shells. Corresponding commands for writing command files are shown in Table F–4.

sh	csh	MPW	Description
=	set	Set	Set shell variable
break	break	Break	Leave loop
continue	continue	Continue	Continue loop
echo	echo	Echo	Display value
echo \c	echo -n	Echo -n	Display without newline
exec	exec	Execute	Execute command file
exit	exit	Exit	Exit command file
export		Export	Export shell variable
expr	expr	Evaluate	Evaluate expression
for...do ... done	foreach ... end	For ... End	Iterative block
if ... fi	if ... endif	If ... End	Conditional block
set	set	Set	Display or set shell variables
shift	shift	Shift	Shift positional parameters
unset	unset	Unset	Delete variable
	alias	Alias	Define command alias
	setenv	Set, Export	Set & export variable
	unalias	Unaias	Delete command alias
$0	$0	{0}	Name of command file
$1	$1	{1}	Parameter #1, etc.
$#	$#	{#}	Number of parameters
$*	$*	{Parameters}	List of parameters
$@	"$*"	{"Parameters"}	Quoted list of paramters
$?	$status	{Status}	Command status
${HOME}	$home	{MPW}	Home directory
${PATH}	$path	{Commands}	Command directories

Table F–4: Shell programming commands

Shell variables in MPW are always referenced using { } characters to delimit the variable name, and variable names are never case-sensitive. Other than these differences, the standard variables are similar to those provided by the other shells.

In at least one way, MPW is more similar to sh than csh, in that it uses the Export command to define shell variables as global in scope, rather than a special setenv command to define global (or environment) variables. On the other hand, MPW includes the alias and unalias commands of the C shell.

The syntax of the looping constructs is incompatible with either shell, but the capabilities are similar. The same can be said for the evaluation of expressions, using Evaluate and expr, respectively.

As with UNIX, variable definitions go only from the outer to the inner command file, and then only the exported variables. The same rules also apply to command aliases, although Execute (as in the UNIX exec) can be used to redefine either in the current scope.

However, there are two important differences from UNIX in the way MPW limits the scope of data in command files. There is no scoping of Directory (cd) changes, as, unlike UNIX, a new process is not created to execute the new command file. Instead, any changes in the current directory will be reflected when the command file returns.

Also, the Execute command will continue executing the current command file when done, while the UNIX exec command will never return.

Make

MPW includes a Make facility for automating program building. Its goals are similar to those of the UNIX make facility, but, as with other MPW components, the approach is somewhat different.

The most fundamental difference between the two is that the UNIX make command executes the commands as they are displayed, while the MPW Make command only displays the commands to be executed, which are normally selected for execution using the editor. The MPW 2.0 command BuildProgram is, in many ways, more similar to the UNIX make, in that it displays the commands as it executes them; it uses the MPW Make, however, to analyze the dependencies.

As noted earlier, the commands used to compile and link MPW programs are different from their UNIX counterparts, as is the resulting output. Most notably, the compilation of foo.c will produce foo.c.o under MPW, not the foo.o of UNIX.

As with UNIX, the MPW Make command looks for a standard Makefile in the current directory; since the Macintosh file system is case-insensitive, the two files for the UNIX command, makefile and MAKEFILE, would be treated as the same file under MPW. A specific file name can also be specified.

The syntax for the Make input file is substantially different. Table F5 shows a list of special UNIX make characters and their MPW equivalents.

UNIX	MPW	Description
:	ƒ	Separate target, dependency
$@	{Targ}	Target file
$?	{NewerDeps}	Newer dependent files
$*	{Default}	Root name in default rule
#	#	Comment follows
\	∂	Escape line continuation
@		Don't print line
VAR=foo	VAR=foo	Define variable
$(VAR)	{VAR}	Use value of variable
$(CC)	{C}	Pre-defined compiler command
${AS}	{Asm}	Pre-defined assembler command

Table F–5: Corresponding Make syntax

There are several concepts in the UNIX make that do not exist under MPW. A file cannot be designated as .SILENT (nor can a command be preceeded by @), since the MPW command is only displaying commands for later execution, not displaying and executing commands simultaneously, as in the UNIX version.

Some make files specify a target file to be an object file within an archive (object library), as in

```
mylib(func.o):func.o
```

Since the MPW Lib command does not allow selective replacement of modules within an object library, MPW programmer will instead build a series of object files and rebuild the library from those files each time. This also means there is no equivalent to the $% dependency notation for some UNIX systems.

However, the MPW Make does have default rules for mapping files of a given suffix. Rules for compiling C, Pascal and assembler source are predefined, but you can also override these definitions or define your own.

Figure F–2 shows a simple UNIX make file. It provides an inference rule for compiling C source files into object files, and then specifies how to link a program from two object files.

Figure F–3 shows the corresponding input file for MPW's Make command. Note that the delimiter for the rules is different, and that the MPW compliations produce foo.c.o instead of foo.o.

```
OBJ = foo.o foolib.o

.c.o:
  cc -c -g $*.c

foo: $(OBJ)
  cc -o $@ $(OBJ) -lm
```

Figure F–2: UNIX make file

```
OBJ = foo.c.o foolib.c.o
CLIBS = {CLibraries}CRuntime.o {CLibraries}StdCLib.o  ∂
  {CLibraries}CSANELib.o {CLibraries}CInterface.o

.c.o ƒ .c
  C -g {Default}.c

foo    ƒ {OBJ}
  Link -o {Targ} {OBJ} {CLibraries}Math.o {CLIBS}
```

Figure F–3: MPW Make file

Parts of each file do not have a direct counterpart in the other. The UNIX compilation command uses the –c option to suppress linking, while this is unnecessary under MPW, since the compiler never links programs. The UNIX commands go on to link the program using cc; this implies the standard C libraries, with only the optional math library specified using –lm. MPW programs must use the Link command and specify any standard C libraries to be used in the linking, in addition to any optional libraries.

This MPW example also builds a stand-alone Macintosh application, which Link produces by default. Any standard output would be written to the screen, but you when were done with the program, you would be unable to save the output. If you wished to have a line-oriented command run within the MPW environment, and be able to redirect the input and output streams of the command, then you would add additional Link options to build an MPW tool instead of an application.

Bibliography

Books

Most of the books in this section can be purchased from the computer book section of major bookstores, college bookstores, or through the Apple Programmer's and Developer's Association.

Inside Macintosh, Volumes I, II, and III, Apple Computer, Inc. (Reading, Mass.: Addison-Wesley, 1985)

> Describes the original Macintosh, Macintosh 512 and Macintosh XL computers. Required reading.

Inside Macintosh, Volume IV, Apple Computer, Inc. (Reading, Mass.: Addison-Wesley, 1986)

> Describes differences from previous volume for Macintosh Plus, Macintosh 512 enhanced and System release 3.2, dated June 1986. Also essential.

Inside Macintosh, Volume V, Apple Computer, Inc. (Reading, Mass.: Addison-Wesley, 1987)

> Covers new features of the Macintosh SE and Macintosh II. Also describes the RAM-based managers and extensions patched into the Macintosh Plus using System 4.1 (April 1987), including the Script Manager, hierarchical menus, and TextEdit with multiple text styles.

Apple Numerics Manual, Apple Computer, Inc. (Reading, Mass.: Addison-Wesley, 1986)

> Describes details of the Standard Apple Numeric Environment (SANE), used by both Macintosh and Apple II computers. A must for those who intend to make extensive use of floating-point calculations.

Human Interface Guidlines: The Apple Desktop Interface, Apple Computer, Inc. (Cupertino, Calif.: Apple Computer, 1987)

> This book provides guidelines for implementing Apple's standard user interface for both Macintosh and Apple // computers. It also describes the principles underlying the design of that interface.

> The material is considerably expanded and more up-to-date than earlier specifications published in *Inside Macintosh*.

M68000 16 / 32 Bit Microprocessor: Programmer's Reference Manual, Motorola, 4th ed. (Englewood Cliffs, N. J.: Prentice-Hall, 1984)

MC68020 32-Bit Microprocessor User's Manual, Motorola, 2nd ed. (Englewood Cliffs, N. J.: Prentice-Hall, 1985)

> The original Motorola references on the 68000-family chips provide additional information beyond that in the MPW Assembler manual, and are more concise than other books on the subject.

MC68000 / 8 / 10 / 12 Programmer's Pocket Reference Guide Motorola (Austin, Texas: Motorola Seminconductor Products, 1986)

> The reference sections from the above reference manual, shrunk to wallet-sized. A handy 68000 reference to have next to your keyboard, once you've mastered the concepts of the processor and its instruction set. Available from Motorola as document number M68000RG/AD.

MC68881 Floating-Point Coprocessor User's Manual, Motorola (Englewood Cliffs, N. J.: Prentice-Hall, 1985)

MC68851 Paged Memory Management Unit User's Manual, Motorola (Englewood Cliffs, N. J.: Prentice-Hall, 1986)

These manuals describe the standard and optional Macintosh   II coprocessors, respectively. They assume knowledge of the 68000 architecture, and describe programming the specific coprocessors. Although most will not access these processors directly, it's useful to understand what their strengths and limitations are.

You may find that some of the 68000 family publications are not available at your local bookstore, but they can be obtained directly from Motorola. For more information, write to:

> Motorola Semiconductor Products
> Literature Distribution Center
> P.O. Box 20924
> Phoenix, Arizona 85036

How to Write Macintosh Software, Scott Knaster (Hasbrouck Heights, N.J.: Hayden, 1986)

Written by the then-head of Apple's Technical Support group, this book is the definitive book on debugging Macintosh programs. Worth reading after you have read (or attempted to read) *Inside Macintosh.*

Object-Oriented Programming for the Macintosh , Kurt J. Schmucker (Hasbrouck Heights, N.J.: Hayden, 1986)

Describes the use of Object Pascal and MacApp, with additional information on its predecessor, Lisa Clascal, Smalltalk-80, and various existing and planned object-oriented languages.

Using the Macintosh Toolbox with C , Jim Takatsuka, et al (Berkeley, Calif.: Sybex, 1986)

The descriptions in *Inside Macintosh* are oriented towards Pascal and require adaption for use with C. If find yourself having trouble translating between the Pascal description and its C equivalent, this is an early but useful book on the subject.

The C Programming Language, Brian W. Kernighan and Dennis M. Ritchie, (Englewood Cliffs, N. J.: Prentice-Hall, 1978)

This book needs no introduction for those who have already programmed in C. Although a required reference for any C programmer, it is nearly a decade old and by now somewhat obsolete.

C: A Reference Manual, Samuel P. Harbison and Guy L. Steele Jr., 2nd edition, (Englewood Cliffs, N. J.: Prentice-Hall, 1987)

> This book exactly specifies the current *de facto* definition of the C language, including pre-processor semantics and the behavior of standard library routines. It also includes changes that have been made to the C since language since the publication of K&R, including void and enum declarations. The second edition also includes a valuable summary of the draft proposed ANSI C standard, which is expected to dictate future versions of most C compilers, including MPW C.

Pascal User Manual and Report, Kathleen Jensen and Niklaus Wirth, 3rd ed. (New York: Springer-Verlag, 1985)

> A revised edition of the original specification of the Pascal language, updated to include the ISO Pascal Standard. Worth having if you have never used Pascal before. It also helps you to identify the extensions made by UCSD Pascal, Lisa Pascal and MPW Pascal that are not portable to compilers implementing Wirth's original conception of the language.

PostScript Language Tutorial and Cookbook, Adobe Systems, (Reading, Mass.: Addison-Wesley, 1985)

PostScript Language Reference Manual, Adobe Systems, (Reading, Mass.: Addison-Wesley, 1985)

> The standard introductory and reference books for PostScript, the page definition language used by some Apple printers.

Periodicals

Macintosh Technical Notes
Apple Programmer's and Developer's Association
290 SW 43rd Street
Renton, WA 98055
(206) 251-6548

> The official supplement to *Inside Macintosh*, providing official tips and techniques from Apple. Required reading.

MacTutor
P.O. Box 400
Placentia, CA 92670
(714) 630-3730

A monthly technical journal devoted to Macintosh programming. Includes many "unofficial" solutions to topics not adequately discussed by other references, as well as sample programs and information on new products.

Articles

"Design Philosophy Behind Motorola's MC68000," Thomas W. Starnes, *Byte,* April-June 1983

"The Motorola MC68020," Doug MacGregor, et al, *IEEE Micro,* August 1984., pp. 101-118.

"The MC68881 Floating-point Coprocessor," Clayton Huntsman and Duane Cawthron, *IEEE Micro,* December 1983, pp. 44-54.

Good introductions to the 68000 family, if you have access to back issues of these journals at a nearby library. Also available through Motorola (see above) as documents AR208/D, A217/D and AN213/ D, respectively.

"Programming Experiences," Larry Tesler, *Byte,* August 1986, pp. 195-206.

If you're wondering whether object-oriented programming is worth learning or how it can be successfully used, this article describes experiences with several systems, including MacApp.

"Introduction to Object Pascal," Ken Doyle, Mac*Tutor,* December 1986, pp. 49-58.

Describes the implementation of the Object Pascal extensions to MPW Pascal, and optimization techniques used to speed the execution of MacApp programs.

"Sleuthing Trap Compatibility," Joel West, Mac*Tutor,* August 1987.

A comprehensive analysis of the differences in traps available under System 4.1 and earlier releases, particularly for the Macintosh 512 and Macintosh Plus.

Index

The sample programs in this book are available from the author
for a nominal fee. For details please contact:

Joel West
Palomar Software, Inc.
P.O. Box 2635
Vista, CA 92083

Also in the Macintosh Performance Library:

The Complete Hyercard by Danny Goodman

Hard Disk Management for the Macintosh by Nancy Andrews